Nicholson's

GUIDE TO ENGLAND AND WALES

Robert Nicholson Publications
GEOGRAPHIA

A Nicholson Guide

First published 1981

© **Robert Nicholson Publications
Limited 1981**
Original cartography: Fairey Surveys
Limited, Maidenhead to © design by Robert
Nicholson Publications Limited. Maps
revised by Geographia Limited, London.
Maps based upon the Ordnance Survey with
the sanction of Her Majesty's Stationery
Office.
Crown copyright reserved.

Drawings: Dick Reid

Special thanks are extended to all the
national and regional tourist boards and the
numerous organisations who helped with the
preparation of this guide.

Robert Nicholson Publications Limited
17–21 Conway Street
London W1P 5HL

Typeset and printed in England by E. T.
Heron & Co Limited, Essex and London.

ISBN 0 905522 50 8

Contents

Introduction

Each of the regional sections in this guide has been clearly divided into a wide range of topics which will embrace readers' own particular interests: for instance those with a passion for archaeology, bird watching or walking can easily decide where to visit. Our concern has also been to distil the essential flavour of each area—to pinpoint what makes Cornwall different from Norfolk. The sea surrounding this island exercises a powerful magnetism and given the choice many people will head straight for the coast, so we have given it special treatment in each section.

Every place mentioned in the text has a map reference so it can be quickly and exactly located on the grid system imposed on the maps; this puts an end to laborious map reading. Individual maps, to which a Key is given on page 20, accompany each of the 9 regions: these are useful not only as road maps, but also in presenting a vivid picture of the country by dramatic use of colour and hill shading.

Consult the diagram map opposite which shows the way England and Wales have been divided into 9 regions.

The front pages look at a variety of aspects of England and Wales, with a series of maps designed to draw attention to some of the most striking features of these countries: structure and scenery, outstanding beaches, climate (where *is* the wettest place in Britain?), archaeological sites, and other useful information. A brief, illustrated study of architectural styles from the Anglo Saxon period to the present, provides a valuable quick reference for looking at domestic, ecclesiastical, and civic buildings, and is followed by an examination of regional variations of style in rustic buildings.

Enthusiastically researched by a team of authors, the entries reveal both their specialist knowledge and their own preferences: thus you will find the unusual alongside the familiar. The fun begins, however, with your own choice—for, as this book shows, England and Wales provide something for everyone.

Orkney Islands

Shetland Islands

Wick

Hebrides

Fort William

Dundee
Perth
Stirling
Glasgow   Edinburgh

Ayr

Newcastle-upon-Tyne
Carlisle

9

Isle of Man   Middlesbrough

8   York
Leeds   Hull
Manchester
Liverpool
Sheffield

Anglesey

Lincoln

6

Leicester   **7**   Norwich
Aberystwyth   Birmingham
Fishguard   Northampton   Cambridge
5
Gloucester   **3**   Luton
Cardiff
Bristol   London
2   **4**
1
Exeter   Dover
Portsmouth   Brighton
Plymouth   Isle of Wight
zance

Scilly Isles   Channel Islands

The climate

Summer Sunshine
The north and north-west of England often catch the cloud formed by the cool Atlantic airstream, and become overcast. South and south eastern England are often influenced by cyclonic weather from Europe, giving long spells of dry, sunny weather.

hours
over 7
6½ to 7
6 to 6½
5½ to 6
5 to 5½
4½ to 5
4 to 4½
under 4

Summer Temperature
The warm currents of the Gulf Stream keep Britain's winters mild, although in summer the sea has a cooling effect on coastal areas, leaving central Southern England the warmest. The sea here is just warm enough for bathing. The north and upland Britain are cool, although some small parts of western Scotland are sub-tropical.

°Centigrade
over 17
16½ to 17
16 to 16½
15½ to 16
15 to 15½
14½ to 15
14 to 14½
13½ to 14
13 to 13½
under 13

The climate maps were prepared with the kind assistance of the Meteorological Office

Summer Rainfall

The west coast of Britain catches the damp westerly airstreams, which condense on the high ground to make this side of the island much wetter than the east. For example the rainfall at Scathwaite in the Lake District is 131 inches per annum, whereas in Lowestoft in Suffolk it is 23 inches per annum.

inches
under 2
2 to 3
3 to 4
4 to 6
6 to 8
over 8.

Clean Air

15,000 school children collected the information for this map, measuring pollution by assessing its effect on lichens.

For an industrial country, Britain's air is clean; cleaner now than it was 20 years ago, but *pure* air is still distressingly rare, being confined to Devon and Cornwall, the Lake District, the country up against the Roman Wall, and a few isolated pockets elsewhere.

Clean air

Heavily polluted air

The clean air map was prepared with the kind assistance of the Advisory Centre for Education.

Outstanding beaches

A day at the seaside is an institution as British as afternoon tea. Made popular by the Victorians, a trip to the coast is still considered to refresh and revitalise the most weary townsman; the sea air clearing the smoke from his lungs, the salt water washing the grime from his skin. It is only surprising that, with a coastline as rich and varied as Britain's, no one before the Victorians took much notice of it. Now every weekend sees thousands of trippers off to the coast to find a beach where they can sunbathe, swim or simply watch the waves. In addition, piers, promenades, and pavilions in which bands play, characterise many seaside resorts, and invite fishing, strolling, and dancing. Use the descriptions with the map to discover Britain's coast. Bear in mind the beaches indicated are not all sandy; some, like the magnificent shingle Chesil beach, are here simply because they are unusual and beautiful. Refer also to 'The coast' in the following main sections.

The West Country. Catching the full force of the Atlantic, but warmed by the Gulf Stream, the coast is broken and irregular, giving sheltered bays and fine, open sandy surf beaches. It becomes a series of long shingle sweeps in Dorset, backed by cliffs brought to a halt by the superb 18 mile long Chesil beach. Strong currents prevail in most of these places, so swimmers should beware.

The South Coast. More popular for its lively resorts in close proximity to London than for its outstanding beaches which are mostly sand and shingle, sometimes backed by chalk cliffs. This is the retreat of the weekend sailor.

The Kent Coast. Its closeness to Europe has left this coast rich in history. Hastings, Winchelsea, Rye and Deal are all ancient seaside towns, while the most popular resorts are Ramsgate and Margate. The beaches shown are all sandy.

East Anglia. The long sandy beaches at Clacton and Great Yarmouth have made these resorts popular and sometimes crowded. But further north there are miles of unspoilt sand backed by dunes and the low-lying broads and fens.

The Wash to the Humber. Flat sandy beaches backed by low-lying land. Very often unspoilt and deserted.

The North East Coast. Long sandy beaches edging some of England's finest coastal scenery. Generally safe swimming along a breezy seashore. Stand well back when storms roll in off the North Sea.

The North West Coast. Morecambe, Fleetwood and Blackpool have flat sandy beaches, often exposed for miles at low tide. The resorts are all 'kiss-me-quick' and rock candy, but walkers can find solitude on some completely unspoilt sands.

North Wales. Backed often by mountains, ending in cliffs at the sea's edge, the coast is steep and often remote. There are some clean, sandy beaches, Prestatyn and Rhyl being the most well known. Porth Neigwl is a fine remote surf beach.

South Wales. The mountains generally recede here and many of the long, sandy beaches are backed by dunes. So firm and flat are Pendine Sands that they were used in the 1920s for attempts on the land speed record. The beaches are often deserted and the prevailing winds create good surfing conditions in many areas.

9

12°C

13°C

Melness

Dunnet Bay

Sinclair's Bay

Dornoch Sands

Burghead to Fort George

orth Uist,

ula and
h Uist

Big Sand

Peterhead to Fraserburgh

Cruden Bay

Morar

Balmedie

St Cyrus

Lunan Bay

Ganavan

Lower Largo

Kilberry

Rothesay to Innellan

Carradale

Drum Sands

White Sands

Saltcoats to Lendalfoot

Amble to Berwick-upon-Tweed

Druridge Bay

Sandhead

Cresswell

Southerness

Whitley Bay

Redcar

12°C

Duddon Sands

Morecambe Bay

Fleetwood to Blackpool

Prestatyn to Colwyn Bay

Red Wharf Bay

Church Bay to Llanddwyn Bay

Horse Shoe Point (Cleethorpes)

Mablethorpe

berdaron Bay and Porth Neigwl

14°C

Skegness

Barmouth

13°C

14°C

Hunstanton to Wells-next-the-sea

15°C

Winterton to Cromer

Borth

Whitesand Bay

St Brides Bay
to Sandy Haven

Broadhaven to Pendine Sands

Great Yarmouth

Rhossili Bay

Dunwich and Southwold

Morte Bay to Saunton Sands

Porteynon Bay

Margam Sands to Nash Point

Clacton

Mouth to Northcot Mouth

Trebarwith Strand

Minnis Bay

Sandwich Bay

Tregirls Beach

16°C

wquay Beaches

Perranporth

Camber Sands

pel Porth

es Bay

Branscombe Mouth

Chesil Beach

Bournemouth

d

Dawlish

Durdle Door

Studland Bay

Tor Bay to Babbacombe Bay

Whitesand Bay

Slapton Sands

Bigbury

Pendower Beach

Maen Porth

Kennack Sands

Mount's Bay

15°C

17°C

Rivers and canals

England is fortunate still to possess such an extensive network of delightful and under-used waterways. Our principal rivers—the Trent, the Thames, and above all the Severn—have been navigable in an uncontrolled tidal form for many hundreds of years. The canals, on the other hand, nearly all date from the late 18thC. But now the trading boats have nearly all gone from our canal and river network, and we are left with a 2,000-mile linear playground for everyone to enjoy. And there is indeed plenty to enjoy. Inland waterways offer endless opportunities: you can hire a boat from bases all over the network and simply go where you like for a week—or a month if you can afford it.

But the waterways are not just there for people on boats. Most of them have a good towpath which provides an excellent long-distance footpath from one side of the country to the other—and you need never step across a public road. Bird-watchers and lovers of wildlife find the rural canals and rivers like the Thames a haven of peace and a fruitful hunting ground for kingfishers, herons, water rats, ducks, etc—although, of course, the lesser-used waterways are the best for this.

Among the best of the navigable rivers are the Thames and the Nene. The latter is smaller and less well-known than the Thames and flows through some of the finest country in East Anglia. It also features a special kind of 'guillotine' lock gates. Other popular boating rivers are the Trent (good for sailing) and the Yorkshire Ouse, while over in Cheshire is the undiscovered and very delightful river Weaver.

As will be seen from the map, most of the canals radiate from the Midlands, binding the principal towns and centres of industry firmly together. The greatest concentration of waterways in this country is in the Black Country between Wolverhampton and Birmingham, although few inhabitants even know where the canals run. The Black Country canals have fallen on hard times nowadays, but they are fascinating for the insight they provide into the early stages of the Industrial Revolution.

The canals of Northamptonshire, Leicestershire and Warwickshire are the epitome of English rural canals at their most peaceful and pleasant. Further south are the architectural glories of the unnavigable Kennet & Avon Canal.

There are three canals in Wales, all of them traversing superb upland country, and one of them (the Llangollen Canal) sporting the most famous canal aqueduct in Britain. The West Country contains all manner of fascinating derelict canals, many of them with unique engineering features. Up in the north-east is a network of wide waterways which are far removed from the narrow canals further south. The Yorkshire waterways still carry a substantial volume of traffic and convey a type of barge not seen anywhere else in Britain.

So there is an enormous variety of canals in the two countries, each with a slightly different character from its neighbour and completely distinct from canals in other regions. But most of them are worth seeing, whether by boat, by foot or by car. Of course the best way to see any canal is by boat, but this way it takes a long time to cover the waterways (a 6-month trip would just about get round the navigable network) and it cannot include the derelict and forgotten waterways that are strewn about the country.

The sections in the Guide describe the waterways to be found in each area, although some areas naturally have more than their fair share of canal mileage—in which case a selection has been made of the waterways with the most interesting things to see. We hope that with this book and perhaps the relevant one inch Ordnance Survey maps, you should be able to indulge in plenty of rewarding expeditions. For detailed canal navigation, there is a series of Nicholson 'Waterways Guides'.

Rivers
Canals

Dee

Tyne

Ouse

Trent

Witham

Severn

Wye

Avon

Nene

Great Ouse

Thame

Lee

Avon

Wey

Geology

Sedimentary Rocks

These rocks represent deposits which gradually accumulated in horizontal layers on the seashore and at the bottom of rivers, lakes and oceans. Powerful movements of the earth thrust these beds upwards, contorting the layers and thus forming hills.

WEALDEN CLAYS AND SANDSTONES. An oval of land cradled within the downs of Kent and Surrey. The central wooded ridge is surrounded by lowland plains so fertile that they are known as the 'Garden of England'.

YOUNGER CLAYS AND SANDS. These produce excellent soil, hence the gently undulating farmlands found in parts of East Anglia and the London Basin. The rocks are easily eroded: the coastline of Suffolk, for example, is gradually being eaten away by the sea.

CHALK. The rolling hills clothed with springy turf of southern and eastern England are composed of chalk. Their gently rounded slopes contrast strongly with the sheer drop of the cliffs along the coast (e.g. Beachy Head).

JURASSIC LIMESTONE. Limestone gives a slightly bolder and more dramatic version of the scenery produced by chalk. A typical feature of this landscape is that the fields are separated not by hedges but by walls built, like many of the houses in the region, of local stone.

JURASSIC LIMESTONE SCARPLANDS. A broad belt of limestone ridges stretches from the coast of Dorset and Devon to Yorkshire. These ridges include the Cleveland Hills of Yorkshire, Lincoln Edge and the Northampton Uplands and the Cotswolds.

MARLS AND NEW RED SANDSTONE. These were formed between 160 and 190 million years ago when desert conditions existed in Britain. The salt beds of Cheshire almost certainly represent salt lakes which evaporated in the heat. The rocks are of varying resistance; the sandstone tends to stand out as ridges in what is otherwise fairly flat dairyland.

CARBONIFEROUS LIMESTONE AND MILLSTONE GRIT. This limestone owes its name to the fact that it contains measures of coal. It is even more resistant than Jurassic Limestone, thus the "backbone of England"—the Pennine Chain—is underlain by it. Extensive platforms of almost pure limestone are found in the Central Pennines around Malham Tarn. The rock is so porous that despite the heavy rainfall there is no surface water as all the rain immediately soaks through to the subterranean caverns which riddle the area.

MARLS AND OLD RED SANDSTONE. These are rocks of varying resistance. On the coast, they produce steep cliffs separated by deep valleys running inland. These rocks feature mainly in Scotland, where their high iron content accounts for the red soil.

Metamorphic Rocks

These are composed of sedimentary rocks which have been hardened as the result of being subjected to great pressure and heat.

OLD GRITS AND SLATES. These metamorphosed rocks produce the austerely wild scenery which is found in much of Wales, the Lake District and southern Scotland. Intruded volcanic rocks increase the rugged aspect of the landscape.

ANCIENT GNEISS AND SCHISTS. Created up to 2,600 million years ago, these rocks are the oldest found in Great Britain. They form much of the Scottish Highlands and occur also in parts of Wales, Anglesey and the Lake District. The scenery, particularly along the coastline, has a majestic grandeur that becomes positively menacing in parts of the Outer Hebrides.

Igneous Rocks

These rocks are formed of molten material thrust up from the earth's core.

EXTENSIVE LAVA SHEETS. In Skye, Mull and Antrim lava welled out of great cracks in the earth, blanketing the surrounding countryside.

GRANITE MASSES. The scenery of Dartmoor and Bodmin Moor is typical of the bleak landscape produced by granite. The land is unsuited to cultivation and consists of stretches of furze, heather and peat-bog rising to large bare peaks.

Alluvium

Sand, silt and mud deposited by the rivers and tides since the Ice Age. The largest areas of alluvium are the Fens and the Romney Marshes. Both exhibit the same flat, treeless landscape.

Archaeology

Prehistoric

PALAEOLITHIC (Old Stone Age) from 500,000 BC
Britain was barely habitable during this period, because of the southern extension
of the Polar ice-cap and its effect on the climate. Few traces of early man survive.

MESOLITHIC (Middle Stone Age) from 20,000 to 4,000 BC
Until about 6,000 BC Britain was still joined to Europe by a land-bridge. No
permanent dwellings apparently survive, but seasonal camping sites are frequently
indicated by finds of small worked flints and tools.

NEOLITHIC (New Stone Age) from 4,000 to 1,500 BC
Immigration of peoples from Europe introduced agriculture and the domestication
of animals, and the first monuments that are visible today were built during this
period. *Causewayed camps* were probably used as assembly or religious places.
Long barrows were constructed for the burial of the dead. *Long cairns,* barrows
built of stone, were probably used as vaults for a family or social group. *Henges,*
the mysterious circular monuments, sometimes set with stones, which are believed
to have had some religious significance. *Flint-mines,* essential for the manufacture
of tools, were made by digging through chalk and mining out the flint layers
below.

BRONZE AGE from 1800 to 400 BC
The Bronze Age saw the first application of primitive metal technology. The best
known Bronze Age civilisation in Britain was the Wessex Culture, centred on
Wiltshire and Dorset. Some of the finest *henges,* including Avebury and
Stonehenge, belong to this period. *Stone circles, avenues, rows,* and single *standing
stones,* probably usually of religious significance, can frequently be seen in remote
areas. *Round barrows* and *round cairns* replaced the long varieties of the Neolithic,
some cairns having chambers and entrance passages. *Settlements* of round stone
huts with associated *enclosures* are typical of the Bronze and later periods.

IRON AGE from 500 BC to AD 50
The most impressive monuments of this period are the *hill forts,* often having
complex multiple defences and elaborate entrances, occupying hilltops and similar
defensible sites. *Settlements of huts* within enclosures, and their associated *field-
systems,* survive in places, and were often occupied well into the Roman period.
Some of the carved *hill-figures* cut into the chalk downs are Iron Age in date.
Underground structures, called *fogous,* are found in Cornwall and are like the
souterrains found in Scotland and Ireland; their purpose is still unknown.

Roman

AD 43 to the early 5thC
Britain was conquered by the Romans under the emperor Claudius in AD 43.
Military monuments include complex *frontier works,* of which Hadrian's Wall is
the best example; *fortresses* for a legion of 6,000 men, and *forts* for an auxiliary
unit of 500 or 1,000—both built to a standard pattern, with headquarters,
barracks, granaries, workshops, officers' quarters, and a hospital; temporary
marching camps built on campaign; *siege-works* and *camps* built to drill the soldiers
in constructing earthworks; and *signal-stations.* In the civil zone can be seen the
impressive remains of *town walls* and *gates,* often incorporated in later structures;
villas, usually with fine mosaic pavements, architectural detail, and elaborate
central heating; *roads,* frequently followed by modern roads or surviving as
country lanes; *canals; theatres* and *amphitheatres;* and magnificent public *bath-
houses.* More humble monuments also survive: *workshops, potteries,* and the outline
of *field systems.*

Dark Ages

SAXON and CELTIC from the 5th to the 11thC AD
Following the collapse of Roman control and the settlement of Saxon colonists
from the Continent, England and Wales evolved into Saxon and Celtic areas, with
the Saxons dominant in the east and north and the Celts surviving in the west
and south-west. Visible Saxon monuments include massive *linear earthworks,*
which probably marked frontiers rather than served for defence. Defensive
strongholds, known as *burhs,* were built by Alfred and his son against the Danes.
Burial *barrows,* and Christian *churches* and *crosses,* were erected. Celtic monuments
that survive are *defensive* and *monastic* sites, and carved Christian *stones* and
crosses. Iron Age *hillforts* were sometimes reoccupied at this period, both by Celts
and Saxons. Invading Vikings reached many parts of Britain, and their *settlements*
and *forts* have survived in coastal Scotland and on the Isle of Man.

Prehistoric
Dark Age (Saxon & Celtic)
Roman

Skara Brae
Maes Howe
Jarlshov
Dun Telve
Dun Mor Vaul
Finavon
Inchtuthil
Rough Castle
Antonine Wall
Ballochray
Traprain Law
Edin's Hall
Yeavering Bell
Housesteads
Chesterholm
Hadrian's Wall
Chesters
Corbridge
Tynwald Hill
Thornborough Circles
Scarborough
Ribchester
York
Caer Gybi
Aldmondbury
Mam Tor
Pen-y-Corddyn
Bryn Celli Ddu
Arbor Low
Tre'r Ceiri
Caernarvon
Chester
Lincoln
Old Oswestry
Wroxeter
North Elmham
Burgh Castle
Offa's Dyke
Leicester
Grimes Graves
St. David's Head
Midsummer Hill
Devil's Dyke
Nab Head
Chedworth
Parc Cwm
Caerwent
Caerleon
Windmill Hill
St. Alban's
Bath
Avebury
West Kennet
Silbury
London
Old Sarum
Stonehenge
Lullingstone
Richborough
South Cadbury
Hod Hill
Bignor
Tintagel
Portchester
Fishbourne
Pevensey
Lydford
Dartmoor
Maiden Castle
Cissbury
Chysauster

16

Architectural styles

Anglo-Saxon (410–1066)

Buildings composed of fragments or of rough copies of Roman architectural details. Arches were semicircular, whilst windows had either round or triangular heads. Vaulting was plain and simple. Decoration limited. Wall angles in 'long and short' courses. Typical examples—the churches at Greenstead, Earls Barton and Bradford-on-Avon.

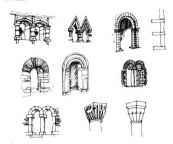

Norman (1066–1189)

Norman architecture is bold and massive with semicircular arches, ponderous cylindrical piers and flat buttresses. Windows are small and deeply splayed. Rib and panel vaulting introduced. Elaborately carved mouldings are important features of the style.
Typical examples—the keep and chapel of the Tower of London; the crypt of St Mary-le-Bow, Cheapside; Durham Cathedral; Barfreston Church, Kent.

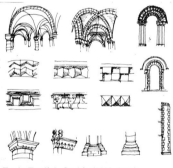

Early English Gothic (1189–1307)

Use is made of the pointed arch. Tall and narrow lancet windows give height to the buildings whilst projecting buttresses and pinnacles are developed. Massive Norman pillars are replaced by groups of slender shafts. Introduction of dog-tooth ornament. Typical examples—Salisbury Cathedral; the Galilee Porch, Ely; Stokesay Castle, Shropshire; Little Wenham Hall, Suffolk.

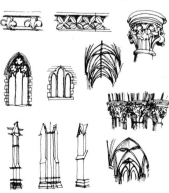

Decorated Gothic (1307–77)

Windows increased in size, and angle buttresses, set diagonally, were introduced. Window tracery consisted of geometric forms, later curvilinear or flowing lines were introduced. Battlemented parapets were used. An increased number of intermediate ribs were used in vaulting. Carving was generally more naturalistic.
Typical examples—the Angel Choir, Lincoln Cathedral; the Eleanor Crosses; Penshurst Place, Kent; Ightham Mote, Kent; Ludlow Castle, Shropshire.

Perpendicular Gothic (1377–1485)

Window tracery and panelling have vertical lines. Windows are enlarged whilst fan vaults, with their numerous ribs and panels, are typical. Hammer-beam roofs are numerous; piers more slender, whilst the Tudor rose, the portcullis and the fleur-de-lys are all characteristic ornaments. Typical examples—Westminster Hall, London; Haddon Hall, Derbyshire; Hever Castle, Kent.

Tudor (1485–1558)

Houses were usually timber-framed with lath and plaster panels. Brick became a fashionable material, whilst moats and elaborate gatehouses were retained as architectural features. Chimney stacks became very prominent. Typical examples—Compton Wynyates, Warwickshire; Bramhall Hall, Cheshire; Tattershall Castle, Lincolnshire; Hampton Court Palace, London.

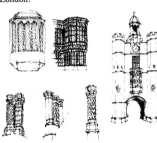

Early Renaissance (1558–1625)
Elizabethan Architecture (1558–1603)

The age of great mansions. It was a transition style with Gothic features and Renaissance details.
Typical examples—Little Moreton Hall, Cheshire; Hardwick Hall, Derbyshire; Montacute House, Somerset.

Jacobean Architecture (1603–1625)

The great houses were large, imposing and in the grand manner. Classic columns and entablatures replaced the quaint irregularity of Elizabethan architecture. Decoration,

particularly carving, was lavish.
Typical examples—Keevil Manor House,
Wiltshire; Hatfield House, Hertfordshire;
Knole House, Sevenoaks, Kent.

Late Renaissance (1625–1837)
Stuart Architecture (1625–1702)

For the first time in England architecture
was determined by individual architects. The
two most influential architects were Inigo
Jones and Wren. Inigo Jones (1573–1652)
was an ardent disciple of Italian Renaissance
architecture following prolonged studies in
Italy. Sir Christopher Wren (1631–1723) was
strongly influenced by the French
Renaissance.
The verticality of the Elizabethan gable was
replaced by the straight wall crowned by the
strong horizontal line of the cornice. Roofs
were hipped and sometimes hidden by
parapets. The large built-up window was
abandoned for small rectangular ones set in a
large wall space. Under Wren, classic
features such as domes and columns were
used for architectural emphasis. Typical
examples—Banqueting House, Whitehall,
London; Queen's House, Greenwich; St
Paul's, Covent Garden, London; Sheldonian
Theatre, Oxford; Pembroke College Chapel,
Cambridge.

Victorian (1837–1901)

Tradition ceased to maintain its former
power. Architects grouped themselves under
the banners of the 'Greek Revival' and the
'Gothic Revival' and the battle of the styles
began in earnest. In the late Victorian period
the characteristic elements were the use of
iron and glass for railway stations, exhibition
halls, warehouses and bridges. Typical
examples—Birmingham Town Hall;
Westminster Palace, London; St George's
Hall, Liverpool; the Palm House, Kew.

Georgian Architecture (1702–1837)

The Baroque style strove for greater freedom
in design and novelty of treatment whilst the
influence of the work of Italian architects
like Palladio was profound. The smaller
Georgian houses were simple rectangles with
handsome entrance doors. The last 30 years
of the period saw the development of the
Regency style with fine town planning
schemes and the profusion of wrought iron
work in canopied windows and balconies.
Typical examples—Royal Crescent, Bath;
Blenheim Palace, Oxfordshire; Chiswick
House, London; Mereworth Castle, Kent;
Portland Place and Regent's Park, London;
Brighton Pavilion.

Twentieth Century

In the early part of this century the Classic
and Renaissance styles were reserved for
civic architecture, the Gothic style for
churches and educational buildings.
Domestic architecture ran amuck amongst
the Georgian, Tudor and Jacobean styles,
and the suburban ideal proliferated. Steel-
framed construction produced fresh
alternatives. But with the profusion of new
materials and the development of more
sophisticated mechanical servicing almost
anything could be done, and nearly
everything was done. Look around you to see
the result.
Typical examples—Liverpool Cathedral;
Arnos Grove Underground Station, London;
Boots Factory, Nottingham; Alton Housing
Estate, Roehampton, London; Liberty's,
London.

Rustic buildings

West

Cornish buildings often have slate roofs and granite walls, sometimes hung with tiles. In Devon and Dorset thatched cottages are typical, complete with rubble walls, plastered and whitewashed or built of granite blocks. Some houses in Dorset have limestone roofs. In Wiltshire numerous houses were built of porous chalk block, with a thatched roof, whilst in the Cotswolds you have fine limestone buildings.

East

Flint work has been the signature of East Anglia since Saxon times. Sometimes a complete wall was faced in pebbles, while doors and windows were squared off with brickwork.

Thatching, often used for roofs, is seen at its best in Norfolk. Here distinctive surface patterns are created by the laying and cutting of reeds. In Suffolk many half-timbered houses have ornamental plasterwork known as pargetting. First used in the Elizabethan age, it developed in the 17thC, but was out of fashion by the middle of the 18thC. Pantiled roofs are typical. Imported from Holland by the end of the 17thC, they are virtually unknown in the western half of the country. In Lincolnshire red brick houses were gabled in the Dutch style.

South

Sussex is rich in tile-hung houses. A feature of south-east England since the 17thC, tiles were hung on wood-and-plaster walls of houses to protect them from the weather. Weather-boarding, used for farm building since the late 16thC, was adopted for cottages and smaller houses in south-east England by the end of the 18thC. It was usually oak or elm pegged to timber-framing. Mathematical tiles were introduced in the south-eastern counties in the middle of the 18thC and used well into the 19thC. They provided a cheap means of giving a fashionable appearance to timber-framed buildings while avoiding the brick taxes.

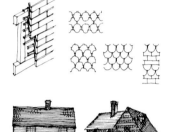

Midlands and the North

Box-framed houses with darkened timbers and white painted walls are typical of Cheshire. The houses of Derbyshire are of mellow stone with slate roofs, and simple ornamentation. In the Lake District slate roofs are common. Walls are usually rubble, set on a base of hewn stone, often plastered over and whitewashed. In Shropshire timber-framed houses were built on a base of local red sandstone. Slate instead of thatch was used for the roofs resulting in sturdy beams.

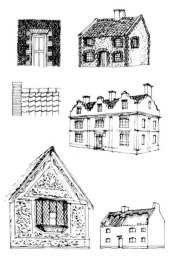

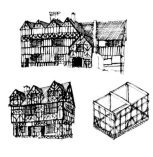

Maltings

Mostly 19thC, these buildings lack the rural charm of their country cousin, the oast. They are used for preparing and storing malt, barley or other grain which is steeped in water until it germinates, and then dried in a kiln for use in brewing or distilling. These kilns have high pyramid roofs of slate and louvered cupolas for ventilation.

Wales

Buildings were usually constructed of slate and stone.

In the 15thC timber-framed buildings were sometimes built on cruck trusses, and roofed in straw. There was no smoke hole in the roof; the smoke escaped through the windows and doors.

Some sturdy stone-built houses in Pembrokeshire (now part of Dyfed) have massive side chimneys which are rounded in the top stage. In Montgomeryshire (now part of Powys) houses sometimes have a rush thatch roof with a turf-ridge, whilst in Cardiganshire (now part of Dyfed) thatched roofs are often laid in decorative patterns.

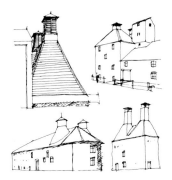

Windmills

Windmills, like watermills, were in use from the 12thC and not superseded until after the advent of steam power in the 18thC. They were mainly used for milling wheat into flour.

Most windmills were either post mills or smock mills. In the former the whole chamber, built of a light timber-framed construction and containing the gears and millstones, could be rotated according to the direction of the wind. In the latter only the 'cap' could be turned, whilst the machinery was contained within a brick or weatherboarded tower.

Map key

○—17 Motorway and junction number

A road primary route

A road

B road

Other roads

Main railway

Private railway

Canal

River

Height above sea level in feet

3,000 and above

1,000–3,000

200–1,000

0–200

·1334 Spot height

Built up area

County boundaries

Boundary of Nicholson's guide areas

Touring maps in each section are at a scale of 1:1,050,000

The West Country I

Moors, tight coombes and the sea are the essential elements of Britain's most westerly counties. At the farthest western point are the Isles of Scilly – they are the tops of long submerged granite hills that were once linked to Cornwall as part of the long lost kingdom of Lyonesse. Cornwall has more sea coast than anywhere else in England, and all of it is spectacular. Don't ignore inland Cornwall, the wooded valleys of the Camel and the Fowey are remote and rich with fuchsias and veronica in high summer.

Devon is rich and varied. You can lose yourself in the steeply banked lanes full of ferns and foxgloves and the cosy cob and thatch villages aren't far removed from their counterparts on chocolate boxes. But tear yourself away from the Devonshire cream and rough cider to see craggy Dartmoor or the gorselands of Exmoor, and slip quietly down one evening to the peaceful ports still redolent with the memories of the great sailing days when Devon men scuttled the galleons of Spain.

Somerset and the new county of Avon has a quieter inland beauty with stone building that reaches its apotheosis in Bath – a masterpiece of town planning. Don't avoid busy Bristol, it is the hub of the region and a good cultural centre.

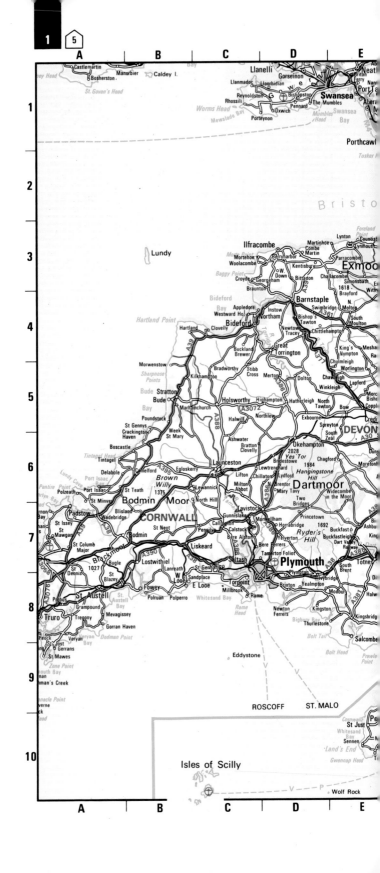

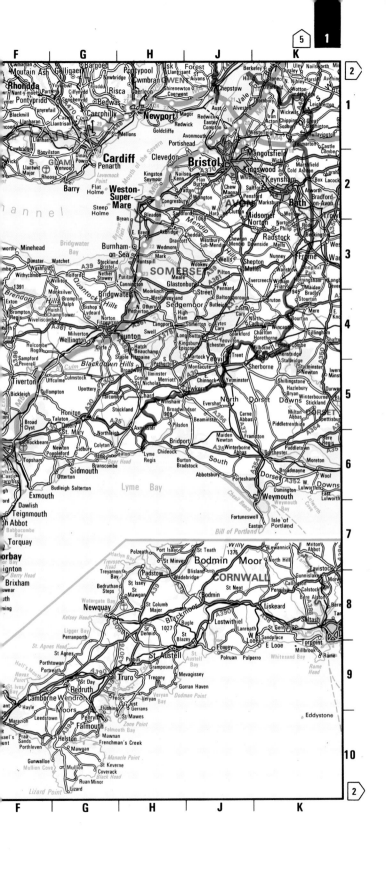

The coast

Appledore and Instow   C4
Devon. Pop 800. EC Wed. The two towns stand on either side of the Torridge Estuary. Appledore has an elegant strand of quayside houses and the largest covered shipyard in Britain. Instow is a good spot for light dinghy sailing and children's games on the sandy beaches. Winkle, cockle and scallop gathering on the mud flats.

Bedruthan Steps   A8
Cornwall. Towering cliffs owned by the National Trust and great rocks that are a magnificent sight when the surf is rushing over them. Caverns and tiny inaccessible beaches. Look out for Queen Bess, a rock in the profile likeness of Queen Elizabeth I. Here is some of the finest coastal scenery in the area.

Beer   G6
Devon. Pop 1,500. EC Thur. Snug and sheltered fishing village that lies below the dazzling chalk cliffs. Lacemakers and smugglers have made Beer famous, although no one knows how it got its name. Always warm and cosy—you can hear the heavy droning of contented honey bees among the fuchsias by the sea.

Boscastle   B6
Cornwall. A landlocked, natural harbour which has an incredibly narrow entrance. The tiny village is surrounded by steep hills and the Normans built their castle on rising ground ½-mile up from the harbour. Small, pleasant cottages scramble up the hillside. Watch out for the dramatic 'blowhole' when rough seas blow spray right across the harbour about an hour before low tide. Visit the macabre museum of witchcraft. The Floral Dance is performed once a week in the summer.

Branscombe   G6
Devon. Pop 500. EC Thur. Branscombe is a tiny inland village. Come here for the long stretch of unspoilt pebble beach. Owned by the National Trust, it has never been developed. Shore fishing and swimming. A marvellous cliff walk from Branscombe to Beer offers sweeping views of the bay.

Brixham   F8
Devon. Pop 10,700. EC Wed. Once the country's leading fishing port, now only a few trawlers work regularly. But the harbour with its replica of Drake's Golden Hind and lobster pots has the full nautical air. You can take a cruise around Tor Bay and visit Brixham Cavern, rumoured to have been inhabited in the Stone Age. The old village, climbing the hill behind the harbour, is mostly Victorian. Pebble beach at Shoalstone and swimming pool.

Brixham

Bude   B5
Cornwall. Pop 4,000. EC Thur. Cornwall's quiet and modern resort is gradually expanding and is now one of the best surfing areas (Crooklets beach to the north is best). Bude started as a seaport for the Bude Canal (1819–26), which went 30 miles inland to Launceston and was used mainly for sand. Now only part of the canal is navigable. The spacious plain-looking town centre has a modest castle. Away from the river mouth, swimming is excellent from firm, sandy beaches. All the amenities of a good holiday resort.

Budleigh Salterton   F6
Devon. Pop 4,200. EC Thur. A quiet small town, in the green valley of the River Otter, that has remained peaceful. The beach has smooth round pebbles, the clear sea water has made snorkelling popular. The walk on the 500-foot-high red cliffs gives amazing views of the whole of Lyme Bay. Visit the Arts Centre in an 18thC thatched house.

Burnham-on-Sea   H3
Somerset. Pop 12,300. EC Wed. The tide goes out for miles here and the miles of firm sands have made this a modest but popular resort. There's a lighthouse, and on Stert Island oyster-catchers have their nests. Go into the church of St Andrew, not for its architecture, but for the carved angels by Inigo Jones and Grinling Gibbons from the altar of Whitehall Palace Chapel.

Cape Cornwall   E10
Cornwall. Stone-walled fields wander down to the sea in this totally remote village. Worth a visit to feel the essence of Cornwall which is summed up here among the silent cliffs and the rugged capes.

Clevedon   H2
Avon. Pop 15,100. EC Wed. A tree-shaded, attractive town with some good early 19thC seafront houses. It's a mecca for bowls enthusiasts, there are tournaments on the smooth greens throughout the summer. Beaches are mostly pebbles. Visit nearby Clevedon Court. Lovely walking country.

Clovelly   C4
Devon. Pop 400. EC Wed. The steep cobbled main street of Clovelly is incredibly picturesque. Cottages are bright with flowers and you have to leave your car and walk down to the tiny harbour. The old or tired can be driven up the hill by Land-Rover. Don't miss the lovely drive through the woods above the village. Nearby is the Iron Age hill fort of Clovelly Dykes.

Coverack   G10
Cornwall. EC Sat. Fishing village in a small cove on the east side of the Lizard, which has succumbed only slightly to the tourist invasion. Clear sea waters reminiscent of more southerly regions. Tiny and friendly, but swimming is sometimes dangerous. Good fishing.

Crackington Haven   B5
Cornwall. For sheer dramatic beauty this is a place not to be missed. Enormous black cliffs rise up to more than 400 feet. To the west are the Strangles, the rocky resting place for many ships—above the rocks High Cliff soars to 730 feet, the highest in Cornwall. The rocky beach is sandy at low tide. Surfing.

Dartmouth   F8
Devon. Pop 6,700. EC Wed. MD Fri. The mouth of the River Dart, a mile away, is still guarded by two romantic castles, and this small town retains its naval and defence connections. The College trains future officers for the Royal Navy and there are moorings for training ships and minesweepers. The long quay is the boarding point for boat trips up the peaceful River Dart. Don't miss The Butterwalk, a row of 17thC houses supported on granite pillars; Agincourt House and the old Customs House.

Dawlish   F7
Devon. Pop 10,000. EC Thur, Sat. The place to come to for the red Devon sand; the beach at Dawlish positively glows, and the famous black swans at the landscaped garden known as the Lawn. An attractive Victorian seaside town only slightly marred by the railway going along the sea front. Southern beaches provide sheltered bathing. Between Dawlish and Exmouth is Dawlish Warren, miles of sand dunes with chalets and caravan sites.

Exmouth   F6
Devon. Pop 26,800. EC Wed. The fashion for sea bathing in the 18thC has left Exmouth a

legacy of fine villas, especially in the Beacon. The town overlooks the mouth of the wide Exe River and there is plenty of sailing activity. The town is busy and well equipped for the holiday trade; good beaches at Sandy Bay. See the picturesque Point of View, a group of almshouses with a chapel.

Falmouth G10
Cornwall. Pop 17,000. EC Wed. Harbour, seaside resort and dockyard are the three faces of Falmouth. It is superbly sited at the estuary of seven rivers and guarded by two of Henry VIII's forts. Take the scenic journey along Castle Drive to Pendennis Point where the views are magnificent. Note also the amazing tropical gardens at Kimberly Park. Falmouth Docks are still flourishing, maintaining and repairing tankers and salvage ships. Some bathing at low tide. Maritime museum.

Flushing G9
Cornwall. A long waterfront of elegant 18thC houses that look across to Falmouth. Because of its sheltered position it has the warmest winter climate in the British Isles. Sailing centre.

Fowey B8
Cornwall. Pop 2,300. EC Wed. Pronounced 'Foy'—a town for sailors and ship watchers, Fowey is full of marine activity with large ships turned by tugs in the deep harbour to load up with Cornish china clay. Take a boat trip to get the full flavour of the 6 miles of navigable tidal Fowey River. Safe, sandy beach at Readymoney Cove. A big sailing centre.

Frenchman's Creek G10
Cornwall. Scene of Daphne du Maurier's romantic pirate novel, it is still a beautiful tree-hung tidal waterway. Best seen from a boat if you drift lazily from the Helford River under the overhanging trees.

Hartland Point B4
Devon. Headland in north-west Devon where the coast turns abruptly from a north to an eastward direction. The 700-foot moors of Hartland's plateau, with its little market town, end abruptly here in storm-swept cliffs, breached by hidden combes. Jagged boulders reach out to where the coast used to be, showing how the land has receded under the relentless pounding of the Atlantic waves.

Hell's Mouth F9
Cornwall. Can seem a fearful place in rough weather; spectacular views of the sea and sea birds. Caves and tunnels lead for miles under the cliffs. Clifftops, many owned by the National Trust, are unspoilt and you can walk on the springy turf from Portreath to Godrevy Point.

Ilfracombe D3
Devon. Pop 9,800. EC Thur. North Devon's largest resort that has many beautiful beaches, two of which are reached by tunnels through the rock. You can walk or drive the short distance to Woolacombe where there are 2 miles of surfing beach below the sand hills. An ideal centre for visiting Exmoor and the Doone Valley. All the amenities of a big resort.

Land's End E10
Cornwall. Beyond the little seaport of Penzance, surrounded by fields of broccoli and daffodils, a hammerhead of granite rock divides the Atlantic Ocean from the English Channel. This bare, treeless, stone-walled plateau, up to 800 feet high, culminates dramatically in the cliffs of Land's End, England's westernmost point. Here the tides and storm-pressed swells of the wide Atlantic surge ceaselessly round the Longships Lighthouse, 1¼ miles out. marking a dangerous off-shore reef.
Wolf Rock Lighthouse is 8 miles out to sea, and further out still is the infamous Seven Stones Reef where the oil tanker, Torrey Canyon, was wrecked in 1967.

Lizard Point G10
Cornwall. The main road south, A3083, from Helston to the Lizard crosses the wild Goonhilly Downs, common land ablaze with Cornish heather in August, famous for its satellite comunications station. Lizard Point, England's southernmost bastion, has a lighthouse, hidden coves below steep cliffs, and a remarkable red-and-green veined igneous rock called serpentine. Craftsmen shape this into souvenir ashtrays and ornaments.

Looe B8
Cornwall. Pop 4,100. EC Thur. The approaches to Looe are more beautiful than the town itself. Steep wooded valleys and abandoned wooden hulks on the mud flats lead you to expect a romantic village. But now Looe is a rather commercialised holiday town, though in pleasant surrounding countryside. Good walks at low tide across the narrow estuary. All the amusements are here, speed boats, slot machines and good bathing. Looe Island is now a bird sanctuary.

Looe, Cornwall

Lundy Cove A6
Cornwall. Between Port Isaac and Polzeath, this sheltered sandy beach is an ideal spot for secluded picnics. Safe swimming in calm weather, and lovely walks along coastal paths with extensive views.

Lundy Island B3
Devon. A 23-mile sea trip from Ilfracombe to this tiny island in the Bristol Channel, takes 2 hours. Mostly inhabited by puffins, seals, and wild ponies, although there are about 20 people. The island is owned by the National Trust.

Marisco Tavern, Lundy

Lynton and Lynmouth E3
Devon. Pop 2,000. EC Thur. Lynton stands 600 feet above Lynmouth but the two places are connected by road and a cliff railway. Shelley, Wordsworth and Southey were all entranced by the romantic beauty of this spot. Heavily wooded with rushing streams running down from Exmoor, Lynmouth's picturesque harbour is backed by thatched houses. Walks behind Lynmouth to Watersmeet, Valley of the Rocks and beautiful Exmoor. Coastal walks to Lee Bay and Woody Bay.

Marazion F10
Cornwall. Pop 1,400. EC Wed. A jumble of cottages and winding streets on the edge of Mounts Bay; at low tide a causeway gives access to St Michael's Mount. Best view of the Mount is from the west side of the town. Safe, shallow bathing.

Mevagissey A8
Cornwall. Pop 2,100. EC Thur. One of Cornwall's most famous resorts and almost traffic free, a steep, slate-hung fishing village that remains relatively unscathed by over-

development. Now a shark fishing centre. Has a good 1842 Methodist chapel and a small inland church with a Norman font. It is a holiday town but still has a native Cornish air. Good bathing at Polstreath and Portmellen.

mevagissey

Minehead **F3**
Somerset. Pop 8,100. EC Wed. Daniel Defoe called Minehead the best port and safest harbour in Somerset, and it still has a village air. The scene of the church, cottages and harbour belie the existence of the neighbouring holiday camps. At the other end of Blue Anchor Bay is the small village of Watchet with an interesting 15thC church. Here Coleridge was inspired to write 'The Ancient Mariner' in 1797. Boat trips from the 17thC Quay Town harbour. Sailing, swimming and water skiing in Blue Anchor Bay.

Morwenstow **B5**
Cornwall. Pop 600. An inn, a few cottages, a church and a bosky combe of windswept trees make up this tiny village overlooking the Atlantic. Rising above the trees are the vicarage chimney stacks in the shape of miniature Gothic towers. All part of the Gothic fantasy of the builder, the Rev. Robert Hawker Celtic poet and Tractarian priest of the village from 1834–75.
The church of St Morwenna has a dim, religious atmosphere, and was the scene of the first Harvest Festival service. Look out for the driftwood hut on the splendid cliff where Hawker went to meditate. See also Tonacombe to the south of the valley, a fine 16thC manor house.

Mousehole **F10**
Cornwall. Pop 2,000. EC Wed. Pronounced 'Mowsal', once the centre of the pilchard fishing industry and now an attractive port—so filled with summer visitors. Up the hill at Paul Church is Dolly Pentreath's tomb—she was the last speaker of the Cornish language and died in 1777.

Newquay **G8**
Cornwall. Pop 15,000. EC Wed. Cornwall's largest holiday resort, rightly famous for its beaches, rocks and magnificent surf. Here are some of the finest beaches in Britain, all sandy and safe. Great breakers roll into Fistral Bay where the surfing is excellent. Lusty Glaze and Tolcarne are the more sheltered family beaches. There are 2 miles of surf at Watergate Bay, a short car ride to the east. It's worth a walk to the Gannel Estuary and the unspoilt St Columb Minor, where you can get some idea of what the area was like before the developers moved in. The town is almost one large hotel, always full in the season. Bring your Malibu board.

Newquay

Padstow **A7**
Cornwall. Pop 2,700. EC Wed. Began life as one of the largest mediaeval towns in Cornwall and still retains its unspoilt narrow streets and stone buildings. The old town is full of small cottagey houses with gardens overflowing with fuchsias and a maze of crooked streets sloping down to the harbour. From Padstow there are lots of good walks—take the public path to Chapel Stile above Brabyn's Yard and on to St George's Cove. On May Day the town holds the Hobby Horse Dance Festival.

Paignton **F7**
Devon. Pop 30,300. EC Wed. Devon's family holiday resort, a bustling town overlooking Tor Bay. The beach slopes so gradually that it's ideal for children. There is a pier, a Festival Hall, a fine zoo, and lovely public gardens.

Penzance **F10**
Cornwall. Pop 19,400. EC Wed. MD Thur. A beautiful town wrapped around by Mounts Bay, it expanded in Regency times to become the Brighton of the west. Full of pleasing houses in luxuriant gardens, Penzance remains a fashionable town to stay in and enjoy the winter sunshine. The climate is mild and sub-tropical plants thrive. Boats to the Scilly Isles, and shark and mackerel fishing trips. Safe, sheltered beaches.

Perranporth **G9**
Cornwall. Pop 3,600. EC Wed. The heart of surfing country, long stretches of golden sand and constantly thundering surf. The dunes and rough tufty grass are disturbed only by the craggy Gull Rocks. Just off the sandy tracks among the caravans are the few remaining walls of St Piran's, among the earliest Christian buildings in England (6th or 7thC), uncovered from the sand dunes in 1835.

Plymouth **D8**
Devon. Pop 250,000. EC Wed. MD Mon. It was to Plymouth's natural harbour that Sir Francis Drake returned after sailing round the world in 1580. On the Hoe is where he finished his game of bowls before tackling the Spanish Armada in 1588. In 1620 the Pilgrim Fathers set sail in the Mayflower from the point now called Mayflower Steps. The historic city was the target for German bombers during World War II and much of it was flattened. Now most of the central area is new, the planning is spacious but unsympathetic. The naval dockyard at Devonport is still an important strategic base and the fleet can frequently be seen in Plymouth Sound. Of interest: The Hoe; the Citadel; Smeaton's Tower (the lighthouse on the Hoe which once stood on the Eddystone rocks); the view from the roof of the Civic Centre; the Barbican area; and to the west the two Tamar Bridges. Sailing but little bathing.

Plymouth

Polzeath **A6**
Cornwall. EC Wed. Very popular seaside town with a superb setting; a long, sandy bay protected on the north by Pentire Point and the rocky island of Newland; to the south the distant view of Stepper Point. Rather too many shacks and bungalows—but superb sandy beaches overlooked by low hills and cliffs; the surfing is good.

Porlock Weir **F3**
Somerset. Pop 1,300. EC Wed. Tiny, hidden little quay which is surrounded by a group of attractive whitewashed cottages. Some sailing and a good starting point for walking through steep bluebell woods. Porlock village lies on the hillside where the A39 road climbs dramatically at a gradient of 1 in 4.

Port Isaac   A6
Cornwall. Pop 1,000. EC Wed. Still an active fishing port—steep, sheltered and severe. It is full of little slate-hung houses with tiny gardens crammed with shells brought home from exotic voyages. The harbour is full of lobster pots, and you can take a trip out to sea for some mackerel fishing. Cars have to be left on the hill above the village.

Praa Sands   F10
Cornwall. Good beach, 1 mile of sands edged with holiday houses and camping sites. The western end is sheltered and the surf comes in with a beautiful calm sweep.

St Agnes   G9
Cornwall. Gorse and bracken cliff tops command a view from Land's End to Newquay from St Agnes Head. There are gaunt remains of engine houses once used for the tin mines. The tiny cottages are fast being out-numbered by the tourist bungalows. Handsome Georgian Methodist chapel. Rocky coves and sandy beaches.

St Ives   F9
Cornwall. Pop 9,700. EC Thur. Artists were attracted to this town in the 19thC because of the quality of the light, and it remains a town full of sculptors, painters and potters. Granite, cobbles and silver blue slates catch the almost mediterranean light. Visit the Penwith Art Gallery; Bernard Leach potteries; and the church for Barbara Hepworth's huge 'Mother and Child'. Surfing from Porthmear Beach, sheltered swimming in the harbour, and from the sands of Carbis Bay.

St Mawes   A9
Cornwall. Pop 700. EC Thur. Serenely contemplating its incomparable marine views, St Mawes has the air of rich retirement. Sun-tanned mature sailors ease their expensive yachts into the Carrick Roads, and return for gin slings in the bars of the quietly opulent hotels. You can smell the lobsters and mayonnaise around supper time. The perfect Tudor castle remains glowering at France.

Seaton   G6
Devon. Pop 4,500. EC Thur. Small resort with pebble beach that shelves steeply. Close by, the tiny village of Axmouth, with its harbour and golf course, remains unspoilt. The wide valley of the Axe River behind the town is often full of cormorants and other sea birds.

Sidmouth   G6
Devon. Pop 12,000. EC Thur, Sat. Old fashioned seaside at its best. Queen Victoria stayed here as a young girl, and the place still has the hallmarks of gentility. Elegant Fortfield Terrace crowned by imperial eagles holds sway over the smooth cricket pitch. Peak Hill and Salcombe Hill guard the town on each side, but the best spot for sea views is up Jacob's Ladder, a lookout tower in the Connaught Gardens. West beach, sandy and safe.

Slapton Sands   E8
Devon. An excellent 3-mile stretch of beach, bordered on the landward side by low-lying farmland and freshwater lakes, now a nature reserve with many rare marsh birds. Excellent bathing, ideal for children.

Tintagel   A6
Cornwall. Pop 1,300. EC Wed. Legend and landscape combine to produce an air of romance that is still strongly felt in King Arthur's mythical birthplace. The castle, built in 1145 for the Earl of Cornwall, has been split by the sea's erosive action. The gateways and outer courts are on the mainland while the great hall and inner courts are isolated on an island. Below is a tiny shingle beach and Merlin's Cave. The remains of a great Celtic monastery can be seen on the highest point of the island. Go on a stormy, wet day and the full force of the Atlantic greyness and powerful scenery will convince you that legendary knights and kings walked these incredible cliffs. The village has teashops, an old post office, and a museum of sorcery.

Torquay   F7
Devon. Pop 54,000. EC Wed, Sat. Smart, warm and amusing—Torquay is Devon's nearest thing to Cannes. Its palm trees, illuminated promenades, modern theatres and superb harbour have made Torquay a beautiful and successful resort. Spend a few days here to enjoy exotic sub-tropical gardens, the marine drive and the good beaches and sailing all round the bay. About 1 mile east of the harbour is Kent's Cavern, one of the oldest human dwelling places in Britain. Torquay is that rare thing 'an ideal centre' in the middle of 20 miles of varied coastline, with the hinterland of beautiful countryside. Best beaches in Torquay: Livermead Sands, Corbyn Sands, Beacon Cove.

Trevose Head   H7
Cornwall. Great spot for a real taste of Cornwall's rocky coast. Go up to the little grass hills along the shore and look towards Dinas Head. On the south side of the headland Constantine Bay offers good, sandy swimming beaches. Visit the lighthouse.

Treyarnon Bay   H7
Cornwall. A beautiful sweep of beach, quiet, relaxed and not over-developed. Unsafe to swim at low tide or near rocks on the south of the beach—but there is a natural pool among the rocks on the north. Surfing.

Weston-super-Mare   H2
Avon. Pop 50,800. EC Thur. Perfect for travel agents' brochures, because there really are acres of golden sands in Weston Bay. Donkey rides and pony carriages, and now a popular sport is sandyacht racing. There is everything you need here, even 2 indoor pools if it's too cold to bathe outside.

Westward Ho!   C4
Devon. Pop 2,200. EC Tue. Named by Victorian developers after Charles Kingsley's novel about sturdy Elizabethan sailors, the town has grown into a popular resort. The beach is good for surfing and the 650-acre common is perfect for seaside family picnics. Fine golf course and good bathing beaches.

Zennor   F9
Cornwall. Pop 300. Treeless heather-strewn tors slope down to the valley where the little granite village stands. Awe-inspiring granite cliffs sweep into a sea that constantly changes colour with the sky.

Isles of Scilly   C10
An archipelago of some 150 islands and rocks that lies 25 miles to the south-west of Land's End, reached by sea or air from Penzance. There are 5 main inhabited islands. The sea between is very shallow, at one time the islands were probably linked. So mild it is said they have only two seasons—spring and summer. Spring flowers bloom in profusion, bird life abounds and dolphins, porpoises and seals are common. The first sight of the islands from the sea can be disappointing: they are small, bare and close together, and lack the majestic cliffs of Cornwall. But they have a variety of their own, there are good sandy beaches which are seldom crowded. The islanders are friendly, and they have arranged things well; they

Hugh Town, St. Marys, Scilly Isles

pick flowers for export between November and April so they can take visitors during the whole summer. Fairly accessible but seldom overwhelmed with visitors, they keep their distinctive local administration, and a sense of separate identity from the rest of Britain. In ancient times the islands were regarded as an ideal burial place for Bronze Age heroes who named the Scillies 'Isles of the Blest'. Their more recent history has been dominated by the local feudal landlords on Tresco, the Dorrien-Smiths. This family leased the islands 1834–72 and they introduced not just flower farming but compulsory education.
Bryher. The island has about 80 inhabitants. On the west the seas are seldom calm—Shipman's Head is the place for watching the breakers.
St Agnes is the most westerly, craggy and remote with about 70 inhabitants and a sturdy lighthouse. To the east lies the island called The Gugh, full of ancient tombs.
St Martin's. About 140 people. Once very insular with lots of inter-marriage. The south-west side is sheltered and cultivated, and the north-east is open downland that rolls down steep cliffs into the sea. There is one shop and five good beaches.
St Mary's is the largest island with the Scillies' only town, Hugh Town, on the harbour where the 'Scillonian' arrives every day from Penzance and the launches leave every morning for the off islands. Along the main street are good examples of the low-built granite houses that suit these exposed places. The New Church was simply built in 1835 and it has above the door the large wooden lion, rescued from Sir Cloudesley Shovel's wrecked flagship in 1707. Go to see the Star Castle built in the shape of an eight-pointed star, 1593–94. The main Bronze Age tombs on St Mary's are at Porth Mellan, Bant's Carn and Innisidgen.
Tresco. The second largest island is still the home base of the Dorrien-Smith family, and their Victorian home, Tresco Abbey is surrounded by verdant sub-tropical gardens is open to the public. Look out for the Valhalla Maritime Museum in the gardens, with a collection of ships' figureheads. On the northern, bleaker end of Tresco are Cromwell's Castle and the church of St Edula. Beaches are sandy.
The other tiny islands are uninhabited and easy to visit by sea. There are special trips arranged to watch the sea birds on Annet and the black rabbits on Samson.

Inland towns & villages

Barnstaple   **D4**
Devon. Pop 17,300. EC Wed. MD Tue, Fri. An ancient town that was a borough as early as the 10thC. It was also an important harbour until the mouth of the River Taw silted up but it is still the commercial centre of North Devon. See the 13thC 16-arch bridge, St Anne's Chapel (now a museum) where John Gay, who wrote 'The Beggar's Opera', was a pupil when it was still a grammer school, and the colourful Pannier Market.

Bath   **K2**
Avon. Pop 84,500. EC Mon, Thur. MD Wed. This is one of the finest 18thC cities in Europe, although it was already resort in Roman times. Planned for pleasure and spurred on by the spa's health-giving qualities, the city is a masterpiece of Georgian architecture, designed by John Wood and made fashionable by Beau Nash. Visit the Pump Room for coffee, accompanied by a string orchestra; take the waters (warm and rather nasty), and see the Roman baths.
Don't miss the Royal Crescent, the Circus, Robert Adam's Pulteney Bridge, the restored Assembly Rooms which house the Museum of Costume, and Sally Lunn's house, one of the oldest in the city.

Bideford   **C4**
Devon. Pop 12,600. EC Wed. MD Tue, Sat. The Kingsley novel 'Westward Ho!' was set in this famous seaport. There are many mediaeval streets and the lovely 24-arch bridge part of which was built in the 15thC.

Blisland   **B7**
Cornwall. Pop 500. On the moors around the town are vestiges of pre-Christian stone circles and monoliths. On the sloping valley within is this little granite village, of Georgian and earlier houses clustered around a green lawn.
Don't miss the marvellous church dedicated to St Probus and St Hyacinth with its colourful carved screen.

Bodmin   **B7**
Cornwall. Pop 10,400. EC Wed. MD Sat. Cornwall's county town with a long history that goes back to the Iron Age, when the hills around were thickly populated. In the middle ages it was the centre of a cult surrounding the relics of St Petroc, and the town then had 12 churches and a monastery. The only surviving church is St Petroc, the largest in Cornwall. The misty Bodmin Moor surrounds the town and gives it an air of Celtic mystery—once you leave the busy main road.

Bristol   **J2**
Avon. Pop 421,800. EC Wed, Sat. MD Fri, Sat. The business and communications centre of the west, Bristol's history goes back to the 10thC. The port's business has moved down to Avonmouth with the arrival of container traffic, and the port where John Cabot set sail for America in 1497 is now a quieter place. Trade in sugar, tobacco, and rum made Bristol rich and the great churches are evidence of the town's mediaeval prosperity. Be sure to visit St Mary Redcliffe church, which dates from the 13thC, and is widely regarded as the finest parish church in England.
An evening can be spent at the Theatre Royal, England's oldest theatre, restored and linked to the Palladian Cooper's Hall which now serves as the theatre's entrance foyer. The city has an excellent university and art gallery, both endowed by the Wills family, whose fortune was made from tobacco in Bristol. Go up to Clifton where the Georgian squares and terraces are equal to those in Bath. High above the Avon gorge is Brunel's famous suspension bridge, designed in 1830, that looks as though it was just lightly thrown across the chasm, and don't miss his great iron ship the 'Great Britain' in the City Docks.
Also of interest: the cathedral; Lord Mayor's Chapel; and the Arnolfini Gallery for modern paintings.

Clifton Suspension Bridge, Bristol

Camelford   **B6**
Cornwall. Pop 1,544. EC Wed. A small busy town situated between the coast and Bodmin Moor. According to legend, Arthur's Camelot was situated here and he fought his last battle at Slaughter Bridge one mile north. Of interest: the moor—a path leads on to it south of the town; Delabole Slate

Bath, Royal Crescent

Quarry which is the largest in England and has been worked continuously since Elizabethan times—look down into the enormous crater from the viewing platform; North Cornwall Museum and Gallery.

Cheddar J3
Somerset. MD Wed. A picturesque village famous for its cheese and its gorge. The 450-foot limestone cliffs of the gorge are best seen when approaching from the north. There are several caves open all year; some have 'touristy' set pieces but there are marvellous stalactites and stalagmites in rich colours. Stone Age tools and weapons can be seen and there is a 12,000-year-old skeleton. Visit the Motor and Transport Museum.

Dunster F3
Somerset. Pop 1,000. EC Wed. One of Somerset's most beautiful towns with its octagonal Yarn Market and romantically perched castle. The castle has belonged to the Luttrell family since 1376, and is open to the public. Look out for the mainly 17thC Luttrell Arms Hotel, and the round mediaeval dovecote in the garden of the splendid St George's Church

Dunster

Exeter F6
Devon. Pop 95,600. EC Wed, Sat. MD Fri. Devon's capital city is still dominated by William the Conqueror's Rougemont Castle and the great cathedral in its own quiet close. Large areas of the city were rebuilt after the war and it has lost much of its character. The university is worth visiting for its fine site. Visit the Guildhall, the unique Maritime Museum and the old building known as Mol's Coffee House.

Honiton G5
Devon. Pop 5,100. EC Thur. MD Tue. Once famous for its wool, Honiton is now famous for its lace, produced since Elizabethan times and its potteries and ancient glove industry. An annual fair has been held here every July since 1257.

Langport H4
Somerset. Pop 800. EC Wed. One of the lesser known attractive inland towns in Somerset, it is tightly built around a square with a fine church and good early Georgian houses. Look at the Ham stone, round-arched Guildhall (1733), All Saints Church for its good glass and the Hanging Chapel over Eastern Gate.

Launceston C6
Cornwall. Pop 5,300. EC Thur. MD Tue. The first town you come to in Cornwall if you are travelling from Devon—once over the Tamar and you are in the Duchy. It has a good skyline, the Norman castle on its steep hill with the huddle of houses around. The great church of St Mary Magdalene is a triumph of 16thC Cornish craftsmanship. Look out for beautifully carved granite, particularly the Mary Magdalene surrounded by minstrels. Visit also the market square, the castle remains and the elegant Georgian Castle Street.

Lostwithiel B7
Cornwall. Pop 1,900. EC Wed. The capital of Cornwall in the 18thC, this town has a lot to offer. Small and neatly planned, the main street shows off the whole range of English domestic architecture from the mediaeval Duchy Palace to the Guildhall of 1740. The church of St Bartholomew has a spire like those seen in Brittany, giving the whole town a French air. One mile north west are the ruins of the 12thC Restormel Castle.

Mells K3
Somerset. Pop 700. Feudal dignity is the quality of this stone village. The great church of St Andrew has a majestic tower 104 feet high, and it seems to rise out of the trimmed yew hedges of the Manor House gardens. The grave of Ronald Knox, Roman Catholic priest and scholar, is near the east wall of the graveyard.

Redruth G9
Cornwall. Pop 10,800. EC Thur. MD Fri. Like so many of Cornwall's inland towns, Redruth at first sight seems dull, but its interest lies in its history. With Camborne, it was at the heart of the Cornish tin and copper mining district. The viaduct of the West Cornwall Railway and the ruined mine workings still dominate the town.
A house at the back of Druid's Hall was the home of William Murdock, the inventor of gas lighting, who lit his own house by gas as early as 1792. Look at the unusual church, a strange combination of a 15thC granite tower with 1756 classicism.

St Just-in-Roseland H9
Cornwall. Pop 3,600. EC Thur. The visitor comes here not so much for the charming village as for the country's most beautiful churchyard. At the lychgate you look down on the top of the church tower, and the richly planted hillside studded with tombs, to the calm waters of the creek.

Selworthy F3
Somerset. Pop 600. A superb approach to this Exmoor village from the west, as the road tunnels under overhanging trees. The white-washed cottages, church and tithe barn make a traditional English rural scene at this gateway to Exmoor. Good riding centre.

Somerton J4
Somerset. Pop 3,200. EC Wed. A warm stone-built town that comes to life in the market place. Here the full quality of the grouping of the church, cross, market hall and 16th and 18thC houses becomes apparent. Look out for the almshouses, built in 1626.

Taunton G4
Somerset. Pop 37,400. EC Thur. MD Sat. For generations farmers from the surrounding Blackdown, Brendon and Quantock hills have brought their produce to Taunton market. It's still a thriving trading centre and worth a visit, not just for its fine churches and houses, but also for its importance as an historic centre of revolution. Look at the castle and its museum, St Mary's Church and the Market Hall.

Tavistock D7
Devon. Pop 7,600. EC Wed. Birthplace of Sir Francis Drake, and site of a fine ruined Benedictine abbey. The area was a thriving base for copper mining in the early 19thC. At its height the great Consols copper mine was one of the richest in the world. Visit Morwellham (3½ miles south west) once a thriving port of the mining trade—now a museum of industrial archaeology.

Totnes E7
Devon. Pop 5,800. EC Thur. MD Tue. A charming old town above the River Dart. Steeply raked Fore Street and High Street have some fine old buildings including a rare survival, the East Gate. Totnes is still a centre for the livestock industry and now also for antiques and craft shops especially in the Butterwalk. Visit the church of St Mary, a good example of 15thC architecture.

Truro A8
Cornwall. Pop 15,700. EC Thur. MD Wed. Lying in a bowl of hills, Truro is a pleasant well kept town that has taken care of itself. It is unofficially the capital of Cornwall, and it does have the county's only cathedral. It's the cathedral you first notice, its three graceful towers rising above the rooftops. From its mediaeval origins Truro has grown into a well planned city with some notable 18thC streets, particularly Lemon Street and Boscawen Street.

Look out for the elegant Walsingham Crescent, the Victorian park of semi-tropical plants, and the superb viaduct (built in 1908) that carries the railway into Truro over 28 granite arches.

Wells J3
Somerset. Pop 8,600. EC Wed. MD Wed, Sat.
Dominated by the massive carved stone cliff of the cathedral's west front, Wells seems like a tiny town dedicated to serving the cathedral. The Vicar's Close is a range of early houses, some definitely of mediaeval origin. Look out for the Bishop's Palace (begun in 1206) and fine Cathedral School.

Widecombe-in-the-Moor E6
Devon. Pop 600. A Dartmoor village associated with the folk song 'Widecombe Fair'. There is the interesting 14thC church of St Pancras with a 120-foot-high tower, and the 15thC Church House. The fair is held on the second Tuesday in September.

Regional features

Celtic Crosses
The cross on a circle is an ancient relic of Celtic Christianity, often elaborately carved from granite. Good examples at St Buryan, Lanherne, St Mawgan, St Michael's Mount, Chapel Amble, St Kew, Minions and St Cleer, all in Cornwall.

China Clay Tips
Like a moonscape the grey white cones of the china clay workings dominate parts of the Cornish scene. Often surrounded by milky greenish lakes, you'll see them north of Newquay and at Nanpean – spectacular ones at St Stephen in Branell, and St Austell.

Cob Cottages
Can be found throughout Devon but the best examples are at Dunsford. The cob is a mixture of clay and straw. An old Devon saying runs: 'All cob needs is a good hat and good pair of shoes', ie roof and plinth, because damp is the main enemy.

Cornish Tin Mines
Throughout Cornwall you will see the tall chimneys of the disused tin mines. Vast pumping engines were built at the end of the 18thC, which pumped out the water which the miners always battled against. In the 1930s Cornish tin became too expensive compared with tin from Malaya, but there's plenty left and the industry is starting to revive. Good workings to be seen at St Agnes, Carn Brea, Camborne and Morvah.

workings, deserted tin mine

Lighthouses
On the hazardous coasts of Devon and Cornwall you see many stalwart lighthouses. The most southerly in Britain is the Longships Lighthouse 1½ miles off Lands End.
Good lighthouses to visit—*Cornwall:* St Agnes, St Anthony, Trevose, Pendeen, Scilly Isles; *Devon:* Bull Point, Hartland Point, Lynmouth, Plymouth, Start Point.

Famous people

King Arthur (died c538) J4
Cadbury Castle, Cadbury, Somerset.
Thought to be the site of Camelot and King Arthur's Court, where Lancelot, Guinevere, Sir Tristram, Kay, Bedevere, Merlin, Gawain and all gathered. It is said that on St John's Eve, midsummer, you can hear the horses' hoofbeats as Arthur and his knights ride down from Camelot to drink at the spring near Sutton Morris church.
Tintagel and Glastonbury also have strong associations with Arthur. Legend persists

that the king was born in Tintagel Castle, Trevena, Cornwall. The ruins of that ancient stronghold still glower over the wild Cornish coast. At Glastonbury Abbey, King Arthur and Guinevere are said to be buried in front of the high altar. But Arthurian relics are everywhere: Winchester claims the Round Table, and Dover Castle, Gawain's skull.

S. T. Coleridge G3
Coleridge Cottage, Nether Stowey, nr Bridgwater, Somerset. The poet lived in this small house 1797-1800 for the sum of £7 per year. During his stay 'The Ancient Mariner' was written (it was planned during a walk across the Quantocks in November 1797), and 'Christabel'.

Lorna Doone F5
Old Blundell's School, Station Rd, Tiverton, Devon. R. D. Blackmore's famous historical novel, 'Lorna Doone,' haunts Exmoor, from Pinkery Pond to Minehead, to the Bristol Channel. Doone Valley itself is not nearly so dark and romantic as Blackmore's tantalising description, but close your eyes and you can hear that rowdy band of highwaymen and murderers returning to their lair in the valley. There are traces of the foundations of huts from the real Doones' settlement dating from the 17thC.
Blundell's is where Blackmore, like his hero, John Ridd, went to school in 1836 at the age of 11. The north-east façade of the building has hardly changed since then.

Sir Francis Drake (1540-96) D7
Buckland Abbey, Yelverton, Devon. Drake bought this 13thC Cistercian monastery from the Grenville family in 1581.
There are reminders of Drake in many parts of Devon: he was born in Crowndale, near Tavistock (a tablet on a nearby farmhouse bears witness to the demolished house), and married in St Budeaux, Bossiney. The abbey is now a museum devoted to Drake.

Dame Daphne du Maurier (1907- B8
Menabilly, Fowey, Cornwall. This was the house of the famous authoress and on which 'Frenchman's Creek' and Mandalay in 'Rebecca' were based. *Private.*

Sir Arthur Quiller-Couch
(1863-1944) B8
The Haven, Fowey, Cornwall. This waterside house was the home of the author of some of the best stories about Cornwall. He was born here and in 1937 became mayor of the town, which is the setting for his novel 'The Astonishing History of Troy Town'.

Cathedrals, abbeys & churches

Culbone church

St Clement, Cornwall   *St Mary, Taunton*

Bath Abbey K2
Bath, Avon. The amazing west front carved with ascending and descending angels on Jacob's Ladder is only a foretaste of the delights inside the abbey. Simple fine fan vaulting extends throughout the chancel, aisles and nave. Look out for Prior Bird's Chantry, an elegant carved corner. The abbey is full of memorials, 614 tablets commemorate those who lived and died in Bath during its heyday as a spa. In AD972 in a Saxon abbey on the site of the present building, Edgar was crowned King.

Buckfast Abbey   E7
Buckfast Abbey, Devon. This abbey church of the Benedictine monks is an amazing example of faith and skill; the monks themselves built the abbey in 30 years from 1908. It is an impressive, rather than beautiful, building. You can buy Buckfast honey, pottery, images, pictures and, to revive you, Buckfast tonic wine.

Culbone Church   E3
Culbone, Somerset. Everything in Culbone is tiny, including the church which is the smallest in regular use in England, at just 12 feet wide. It stands in the woods on the site of a mediaeval leper colony. There are no lepers there today but the village can still only be reached by footpath from Porlock Weir 2 miles away.

Downside Abbey   J3
Downside, Somerset. A mainly Victorian range of monastic buildings, and now a school run by the Benedictine community. The church is a memorable mixture of Victorian and 20thC work, chiefly by Thomas Garner and Sir Giles Gilbert Scott, architect of Liverpool's Anglican Cathedral. The tower is 166 feet high and the length of the church 328 feet, making the whole into a cathedral-sized building. A scene of great harmony—there is a spiritual atmosphere here.

Exeter Cathedral   F6
Exeter, Devon. If you visited Exeter Cathedral 600 years ago it would have appeared much as it does now, although its origins go back at least 900 years. On the west front an amazing array of 14thC sculpture survives, while the elaborate mouldings and vaults give the interior a unique richness. The two transept towers are the main Norman survivors. Look out for the clock in the North Tower, the minstrels' gallery over the north porch, and the 59-foot-high Bishop's Throne. There is a peal of 13 bells, and the curfew is still rung each evening.

Holy Cross   E5
Crediton, Devon. More like a collegiate church than a parish one, it seems almost too splendid for the peaceful little town. Of red sandstone, it was begun as a cruciform church in the 12thC with a noble central tower. Worth a visit for its dignified splendour.

St Catherine   H4
Swell, Somerset. A rare survivor, this church is of 12thC origin, with some later additions. Tucked away off the Taunton-Langport road, it has to be reached through a farmyard. Inside it is small, white, simple—and very moving.

St Mary   H5
Ilminster, Somerset. A great church with a soaring central tower that has dominated this little town since the 15thC. Clear glass lets in the sun on to the amazing monuments. Note especially those to the Wadham family, who are commemorated by exceptional brasses. Good 18thC brass chandelier.

St Mary   G6
Ottery St Mary, Devon. Largely built in the 1340s by Bishop Grandisson who modelled it on Exeter Cathedral. It does look like a rather squat version of Exeter from the outside; within it is very grand with a fine fan-vaulted aisle. Full of interesting tombs.

St Michael   J4
North Cadbury, Somerset. Classic example of Somerset Perpendicular style, this church makes a good village group alongside the manor house. Glorious chancel that might have been built for a college to use. Note the rare 15thC painted glass in the west window.

SS Probus and Gren   A8
Probus, Cornwall. This early 16thC tower is the tallest in Cornwall. Carved granite and light loftiness are its two characteristics. Note the three great eastern windows.

SS Probus and Hyacinth   B7
Blisland, Cornwall. Solidly made of blocks of moorland granite, this church gazes over a steep, wooded valley. Inside slate floors, white walls and wagon roofs quietly set off the flamboyant carved screen that gives the rich chancel its air of festal mystery. There is an early 15thC brass commemorating one of its rectors.

St Winwalloe   G10
Church Cove, Gunwalloe, Cornwall. Imposingly sited in total isolation by the sea, its tower stands alone built into the rock. The grey-green pillars of the arcade look as though they have been under water for years. Worth seeing for a taste of ancient Cornwall.

Truro Cathedral   A8
Truro, Cornwall. Built from 1880 to 1909 to designs by J. L. Pearson, the cathedral rises out of the centre of the town. The style is a late Victorian interpretation of Early English and Normandy Gothic. Inside is a constantly changing series of vaults and vistas. The colouring is cool, the granite Doulting and Bath stone being untouched, so that the glass and embroideries provide the colour. As an example of the Victorian Gothic revival Truro Cathedral is masterly.

Truro Cathedral

Wells Cathedral   J3
Wells, Somerset. It was in AD909 that Wells became the see of a bishop, and the present cathedral dates from two main periods 1180–1240 and 1290–1340. On the west front is the most extensive array of mediaeval sculpture to survive in Britain—12th and 13thC. The three towers were not built until the late 14th and 15thC. The most exciting features of the interior are the inverted arches that support the columns, which in turn support the massive weight of the central tower. Of interest: the 14thC astronomical clock with knights that joust every hour; the glass in the Lady Chapel; the green and gold Jesse window in the choir; and the stair to the marvellously vaulted Chapter House.

Castles & ruins

Compton Castle   F7
Devon. 1 mile N of Marldon. One of the many fortified manor houses of the West Country, strengthened as a defence against the French. The castle lies low against a backdrop of Devonshire countryside. It is built around a courtyard and retains its chapel, great hall and kitchen. Still the home of the Gilbert family whose ancestors include Sir Humphrey Gilbert, who colonised Newfoundland in 1583. A romantic and beautiful place. *Closed winter.*

Dartmouth Castle   F8
Dartmouth, Devon. One of a pair of castles built for the defence of the entrance to the River Dart in the 15thC. Now cared for by the Department of the Environment, it remains in superb condition and should be visited as a lesson in coastal defence.

Dunster Castle   F3
Dunster, Somerset. Owned by the same family since 1376, this castle stands high on a hill overlooking the little market town. Parts of the structure go back to 1070, most of the form you see today was built between the 13th and 19thC. In the late 17thC the dining room was panelled, the gorgeous rich

plaster ceiling installed, and the carved staircase added. In the banqueting hall are 6 magnificent coloured leather panels from Spain showing the story of Antony and Cleopatra. Dunster Castle has kept a very 'lived in' feel and is a warm, welcoming castle to visit. *Open mid week summer.*

Glastonbury Abbey J3
Glastonbury, Somerset. The remains of a great abbey. The most substantial part left standing is the Lady Chapel with its sculptured doorways and late Norman decoration. The Abbot's kitchen, the main survivor of the monastic buildings, is one of the most complete and best preserved mediaeval kitchens in Europe, with fireplaces fitting into the four corners to create an octagon. It must have been a very warm place to cook in!
The monastery gatehouse with its two entrances, one for vehicles and one for pedestrians, survives. The abbey at Glastonbury was founded about the year AD700, but legend persists that it was founded by Joseph of Arimathea who travelled to Britain with the Holy Grail and began evangelizing from an oratory on the marshes. It is King Arthur's legendary burial place of Avalon.

Glastonbury

The kitchens, Glastonbury

Pendennis Castle G10
Nr Falmouth, Cornwall. One of the chain of castles which Henry VIII erected from 1538 onwards in the face of a French invasion threat, Pendennis was started in 1544 and built quickly. Its final form is a circular keep in the centre of two rings of fortified walls. The battlements would still have to be stormed, as the complete portcullis and drawbridge are preserved. The main octagonal room in the castle has walls 16 feet thick.

Powderham Castle F6
Kenton, Devon, 8 miles SE of Exeter on A379. In the middle of a great park stocked with deer stands the ancestral home of the Earls of Devon. Built in 1390, damaged in Civil War skirmishes, and restored in the 18th and 19thC, it has the air of a formidable castle that has been domesticated. Displays of falconry. *Closed winter.*

Restormel Castle B7
Cornwall. 1 mile N of Lostwithiel. The first castle was built here in 1100 and the circular walls were added later. The ruins stand inside a 60-foot-wide moat on an artificially steepened hill. The remains include the gate, keep, great hall, kitchens and guest chamber. The castle's defences are perfect though they saw very little action. Nearby stands the 18thC Restormel House with its Gothic battlements.

St Mawes Castle A9
St Mawes, Cornwall. Henry VIII's great fortress, built to protect these tidal waters from the French, and sister castle to Pendennis. It was finished in 1540 and has the form of a clover leaf with its stalk marking the entrance. Rumour has it that the castle represented a Tudor rose in plan, as a compliment to Henry. The decorative carvings indicate the early flowering of the Renaissance in England.

St Michael's Mount F10
Penzance, Cornwall, ½ mile from shore at Marazion. A totally romantic pile of masonry that crowns the rock of St Michael off the coast of Penzance. Once the home of Celtic saints, it was visited by St Michael the archangel and became a shrine. Secularised after the Reformation in 1660, it was sold to the St Aubyn family who modified the monastic buildings into a mansion. Now visited for its tropical gardens and the magnificent prospects of Land's End and the Lizard. At high tide it is an island, but a causeway from Marazion links the Mount to the mainland at low tide.

St. Michael's Mount

Unusual buildings

A la Ronde F6
Exmouth, Devon. A unique house built in 1798 by the two Misses Parminter. The rooms radiate from the central octagonal hall 45 feet high. Above this is the Shell Gallery where those indefatigable ladies gallantly stuck all the shells on in intricate patterns during long winter evenings. The design of the house was based upon that of San Vitale at Ravenna; the inspiration for the seaweed and feather pictures came from the devoted sisters themselves.

Gwennap Pit G9
Gwennap, Cornwall. On A393 between Falmouth and Redruth. Gwennap Pit sometimes called the Methodist Cathedral, is a natural amphitheatre caused by the subsidence of a mine. John Wesley, when preaching at Gwennap in 1762, discovered the pit when he and his congregation were forced to find shelter from a wild gale. The pit was remodelled in 1806 with seating for 20,000 people, and now looks rather like a classical Greek theatre. Services are still held in it.

Haldon Belvedere E6
Doddiscombsleigh, Devon. Built by a one-time Governor of Madras to remind him of the delights of the Orient in this bleak setting on the moors near Exeter. The floor of the hall and the spiral staircase in the south-east tower are made of rare marble, the gift of the Nizam of Hyderabad. Now lived in by a farmer, it opens occasionally.

Huer's House G8
Towan Head, nr Newquay, Cornwall. In the days when the town's wealth came from pilchard-fishing, men called huers kept watch from cliff-top stations. As soon as the sea turned red, which heralded that the pilchard shoals were in the bay, the huer cried 'Heva! Heva!' and the fishermen came running. This watchtower was in use until the late 19thC.

Knill Monument F9
St Ives, Cornwall. Just south of St Ives, John Knill, mayor of the town in 1782, erected this stone pyramid. Showing a rare determination to ensure that his name lived forever, Knill provided in his will for a group of 10 young virgins and two elderly ladies to dance around the pyramid on the 25th July each year singing Psalm 100. Clearly that is the only day in the year to visit this spot.

Lantern Hill D3
Ilfracombe, Devon. High on a steep hill the tiny chapel of St Nicholas, patron saint of sailors, has shone a light to guide boats into the harbour since the Middle Ages.

Saltash Bridges K8
Saltash, Cornwall. Isambard Kingdom Brunel's Royal Albert Bridge was an engineering feat in 1859—a mighty iron bridge that is a combined suspension and arched bridge on giant granite piers. It took the Great Western Railway into Cornwall from Devon. Now there is a modern (1963)

road bridge alongside, that is a simple steel and concrete suspension structure.

Wadebridge Bridge H8
Wadebridge, Cornwall. A magnificent mediaeval bridge, it has 17 arches, is 320 feet long, and still stands, although it was finished in 1468. The piers are said to have been sunk on a foundation of packs of wool.

Houses & gardens

Antony House C7
Torpoint, Cornwall. 5 miles W of Plymouth via Torpoint car ferry. A disciplined stone centre block is joined to brick-built wings by colonnades—a perfect design that has hardly been altered since 1721. The same family has lived on the site since 1492, among them Sir Richard Carew, the Elizabethan author of 'The Survey of Cornwall', which gives an unforgettable picture of England at the time of the Armada. The present house is a rare example of classical perfection in Cornwall, crisp and severe in silver granite. Panelled rooms and portraits are some of the attractions for visitors today.
Sweeping lawns, fine trees and clipped yew hedging form the basis of the garden, which runs down to the River Lynher. There is a certain amount of topiary including an enormous cone, some giant ilex trees planted in 1760, and a maidenhair tree. *Closed winter.*

Clevedon Court H2
Clevedon, Avon. A well preserved mediaeval manor house dating from the early 14thC. Look at the upstairs chapel with its fine windows, and take a wander along the terraced gardens laid out in the 18thC. Thackeray stayed here and wrote part of 'Vanity Fair'; the house is renamed 'Castlewood' in his 'Henry Esmond'.

Cotehele House C7
Cornwall. 2 miles W of Calstock. The least changed mediaeval house in Britain; to visit Cotehele is to absorb deeply the atmosphere of the past. Built 1485–1539, its two granite quadrangles give it the air of an Oxford college set down in a beautiful Cornish garden, and encircled by a large well-wooded park. The great hall has all the armour, banners and plain furniture of the time when the house was new. In the chapel is a clock that was there in 1489.
The informal part of the garden around the charming mediaeval dovecot retains a Cornish wildness. Set around the water garden with its ferns, primulas and irises are some lovely rhododendrons, azaleas and white wistarias, palms, bamboos and maples. *Open summer; gardens all year.*

Dyrham Park K1
Dyrham, Avon. Off A46 S of junction 18 M4. 250 acres of parkland and gardens and a splendid 17thC house with fine tapestries. There's a fascinating orangery where lemons, grapefruit and mimosa grow. The park has two lakes and a herd of fallow deer.

East Lambrook Manor H4
Somerset. 2 miles N of South Petherton. A sophisticated cottage garden, created by the late Margery Fish, author of many gardening books, where old favourites and rare species thrive together in gay but controlled abandon. The mellow stone walls of the 15thC house shelter eucalyptus, clematis, fuschias and euphorbias. There is also a little silver garden, and a woodland ditch garden with hellebores, hardy geraniums, violets and primroses beneath the willows. The house is noted for its fine minstrel gallery.

Glendurgan Garden G10
Cornwall. 4 miles SW of Falmouth, 12 miles SW of Mawnan Smith. A wooded valley garden sloping gently down to the estuary and containing many exotic species. Near the house can be found a Mexican agave and in the walled garden many interesting climbing shrubs. There are also large groups of the South American evergreen *drimys winteri*, and down by the water garden, Asiatic primulas and gunneras. Also see the maze. *Closed winter.*

Knightshayes Court F5
Devon. 2 miles N of Tiverton. A garden thoughtfully planned to embrace a wide variety of plants and moods. In a series of small individual areas enclosed by castellated hedges, groups of gentians and alpines can be found, and a circular unadorned pool. The woodland garden, at its best in spring, provides meandering walks. *Closed winter.*

Montacute House J4
Montacute, Somerset. Perhaps the finest Elizabethan house in England. Very few changes having been made since it was built. Tall, symmetrical, with large windows, it is undeniably handsome and the Ham stone glows in the sun. On the garden side the little walls and summer-houses present a picture of a complete Elizabethan garden. The interior has good panelled rooms with elaborate fireplaces, and the furnishings are enriched by the addition of a collection of Tudor and Jacobean portraits and heraldic glass. *Closed winter.*

No. 1 Royal Crescent K2
Bath, Avon. The Royal Crescent is a magnificent semi-elliptical terrace of 30 houses and is the epitome of Bath's famous Georgian architecture. This house has been completely restored and furnished in the style of the period, when the fashionable flocked to Bath for the season and to take the waters.

Saltram House D8
Plymouth, Devon. 2 miles W of Plympton. The plain, orderly entrance front gives no clue to the richness of the inside—for Saltram has some of the finest 18thC neo-Classical decoration in the country. The salon and dining room were decorated by Robert Adam down to the fittings and carpets. Note how he skilfully echoed the patterns of the ceilings in his carpets. All the contents are of enormous interest, furniture, pictures, pottery and porcelain. Sir Joshua Reynolds' portrait of the two Parker children remains where it was first positioned, over the fireplace in the morning room. The park is well landscaped. *Open summer. Gardens all year.*

Tintinhull House J4
Somerset. 5 miles NW of Yeovil. A beautiful 4-acre garden largely created by Mrs P.E. Reiss who gave the property to the National Trust in 1953. Symmetrical layout, immaculate lawns, flagstone paths, and neatly clipped cone-shaped box hedges provide good contrast to the loosely planted borders where red roses, regalia, day lilies, and blue agapanthus mingle happily. *Closed winter.*

Trelissick Gardens G9
Devoran, Cornwall. 8 miles S of Truro. Marvellous early flowering trees and bulbs brought out by the warmth of the Gulf Stream. Especially magnolias, camellias and rhododendrons. Lovely views of the River Fal estuary and a fascinating smell of pine on a damp windy day. Nature trail.

Trengwainton Gardens F10
Cornwall. 2 miles NW of Penzance on B3312. Tender plants from all over the world, especially New Zealand, Chile, Australia, the Himalayas and Burma, are assembled here in the shelter of the walled garden. The collection was built up over 40 years by Lt-Col Sir Edward Bolitho who presented it to the National Trust in 1961. There are many half-hardy shrubs as well as magnolias and rhododendrons. At its best in the spring. *Closed winter.*

Tresco Abbey C10
Tresco. Isles of Scilly. A sub-tropical garden created by Augustus Smith, Lord Proprietor of the Scilly Isles in 1834, it is well worth the travelling necessary to reach it. Pink and

white lampranthus are good examples of the many mesembryanthemums; ixias, sparaxis, hebes, acacias and pelargoniums grow prolifically amongst the yuccas and succulents of the rock garden. Also bananas and cacti; with budgerigars nesting in the palms. There are many palms including the New Zealand Cabbage Tree. Daffodils, of course, are also, here, particularly the 'Scilly White' and 'Soleil d'or' believed to have first been planted by mediaeval monks.

Museums & galleries

Allhallows Museum G5
High St, Honiton, Devon. Fine displays of Honiton lace, relics of the world wars, a reconstructed Devon kitchen, and the bones of a 100,000-year-old straight-tusked elephant, hippo and ox, all unearthed from the Honiton by-pass.

American Museum K2
Claverton Manor, Avon. 3¼ miles SE of Bath. The New World re-created above the valley of the Avon. 18 period rooms with original furniture dating 1680–1860 depict American life from the elegance of Washington's Mount Vernon to the New England country store with cracker barrel and stove.

Bath Museum of Costume K2
Assembly Rooms, Bennett St, Bath, Avon. The world's largest collection of costumes from the 17thC to the present, including Byron's Albanian dress.

Bath Roman Museum K2
Abbey Churchyard, Bath, Avon. Adjoining the fabulous Roman baths of 'Aquae Sulis', the museum holds relics from the baths and other Roman sites: altar stones, pewter, utensils, lead plumbing and pottery.

Bristol City Museum & Art Gallery J2
Queen's Rd, Bristol, Avon. The gallery holds the great altarpiece by Hogarth, works by Constable, Gainsborough, Reynolds, collections of Bristol glass, Chinese ceramics and ivories. The museum has fine collections of archaeological, geological and natural history specimens as well as science and transport exhibits.

The Cornish Museum B8
Lower St, East Looe, Cornwall. A folklore and crafts museum with a special collection related to magic and witchcraft. Also local history; fishing, tin mining and travel. *Closed winter.*

Exeter Maritime Museum F6
The Quay, Exeter, Devon. In a group of warehouses on the quay, and in the water, is a unique collection of working craft from all over the world, including an Arab pearling dhow, a 320-ton Danish steam tug and a collection featuring boats that have been rowed across the Atlantic. Boating and launch trips are also available.

Fleet Air Arm Museum J4
Royal Naval Air Station, Yeovilton, Somerset. A fine display of aircraft, model aircraft and ships illustrating the development of naval aviation from 1910 to the present. Medals, uniforms and pictures.

The Holburne of Menstrie Museum K2
Great Pulteney St, Bath, Avon. This elegant Palladian building houses one of the finest collections of silver in the country. Porcelain, important paintings and miniatures, including the work of Gainsborough, Reynolds and Stubbs. Craft study centre and various exhibitions.

Morwellham Quay D7
Morwellham, nr Tavistock, Devon. The Museum in this historic river port on the Tamar is devoted to industrial archaeology. Fine views of the Tamar Valley.

Museum of Witchcraft B6
Boscastle, Cornwall. 5 miles N of Camelford. Claimed to be one of the most extensive and least-known museums of witchcraft and black

magic in Europe, the collection includes paintings by diabolist Aleister Crowley, the skeleton of witch Ursula Kemp, executed in 1589, and the thigh bone of a Tibetan sorcerer-priest. There are also samples of witches' flying ointment and powder used for wasting-away magic.

Plymouth City Museum and Art Gallery D8
Drake Circus, Plymouth, Devon. Reynolds family portraits, Joshua Reynolds's diaries, the Cottonian Collection of paintings, a small but superb collection of silver including the Drake Cup, and the Eddystone salt are all here. Also local and natural history and model ships.

Somerset County Museum G4
Taunton Castle, Taunton, Somerset. This partly 12thC castle was the scene of Judge Jeffreys' 'Bloody Assize' in 1685. The museum now contains local antiquities, costume, dolls, ceramics and glass. Also natural history and geology.

Street Shoe Museum J4
Clark's Factory, Street, Somerset. A collection of shoes from Roman times to 1950. Including shoe buckles, shoe-making machinery, fashion plates and showcards, and an illustrated history of shoe-making by the firm since its founding in 1825 by Cyrus Clark.

Valhalla Maritime Museum C10
Tresco Abbey, Tresco, Scilly Isles. Housed in a 19thC building of rough sea-boulders and timber from wrecked ships, the museum offers a fascinating collection of wood-carvings dating from the 17thC—many figureheads and ships' ornaments. *Closed winter.*

Wheal Martyn Museum H8
Carthew, Cornwall. 2 miles N of St Austell on A391. This is the very heart of 'clay country' and the open-air museum illustrates Cornwall's most important industry. Completely restored 19thC clay works with working water-wheels, tools, machinery and wagons. Working pottery.

Botanical gardens

Bicton Gardens F6
Devon. 3½ miles N of Budleigh Salterton on A376. There are three quite distinct gardens: the Italian, a classical sweep of lawns and water dotted with statuary and fountains; the American, with species from that continent including the scarce Montezuma pine; and the Pinetum, with an outstanding collection of conifers. All can be viewed from a narrow-gauge railway. Also countryside museum. *Closed winter.*

Killerton F6
Broadclyst, Devon. 5 miles NE of Exeter. Tender and rare shrubs and trees flourish here, due to both the mild climate and the acid volcanic soil. There are some beautiful magnolias, eucalyptus, enormous tulip trees, the vibrant South American embothrium and some old cork oaks with their grey textured bark.

Probus County Demonstration Garden H9
Probus, Cornwall. 5 miles NE of Truro off A390. Display plots showing every aspect of cultivation—which provide guidance in looking after and improving your own garden. Demonstrations frequently arranged, with experts on hand once a week. There's a collection of herbs, bamboos, a children's garden and demonstration plots for the retired and the disabled.

Rosemoor Garden Charitable Trust D4
Nr Great Torrington, Devon. Off B3220. An all-year-round garden in a woodland setting. Just about everything grows here, but look for the old-fashioned roses, the raised beds of alpines, the conifers and rhododendrons. It covers about 7 acres.

Zoos, aquaria & aviaries

Bristol Zoo **J2**
Clifton, Bristol, Avon. Many difficult and rare species have been bred here: okapi, white tigers, polar bears and black rhinoceros. Animal houses include the monkey temple and several aviaries exhibiting tropical birds from all over the world.

Cricket Wildlife Park **H5**
Somerset. 3 miles E of Chard on A30. In a beautiful unspoilt setting with ponds and a stream is this 80-acre park with animals from all over the world. Penguin pool, walk-through aviary and pet's corner. Many birds live wild on the water. Lovely gardens and children's play area.

Newquay Zoo **G8**
Trenance Park, Newquay, Cornwall. A fairly new zoo in over 8 acres of landscaped gardens. Good selection of wild animals, walk-through tropical aviary, penguins, reptiles, and a pet's corner.

Paignton Zoological & Botanical Gardens **F7**
Tweenaway Cross, Paignton, Devon. 100 acres of zoo and gardens in the beautiful Clennon Valley, with a reputation for breeding animals. Fine collection of monkeys and parrots. Don't miss the red-faced spider monkeys, pigmy hippo, kookaburras, electric eel and piranha. Also reptile house and miniature railway.

Plymouth Aquarium **D8**
The Hoe, Plymouth, Devon. One of the finest aquaria in Europe, with many rare and interesting examples of marine life.

The Tropical Bird Gardens **K3**
Rode, nr Bath, Avon. A small zoo set in the beautiful gardens of Rode Manor. The population includes macaws, flamingos, penguins, vultures, owls, and many exotic birds. 17 acres of woodlands, gardens and a lake.

Woolly Monkey Sanctuary **C7**
Murrayton, Cornwall. Off the B3253. 4 miles E of Looe. This is the special home of the rare Amazon Humboldt's woolly monkeys. They live in a huge cage on the lawn, but can swing across from tree to tree with the help of handy ladders and ropes, or roam freely among the visitors. Don't touch—they bite. *Closed winter.*

Nature trails & reserves

Braunton Burrows National Nature Reserve Trail **D4**
Nr Braunton, Devon. Dunes and seashore. There are two trails—1¼ miles through the dunes (start at the American Road Car Park) and 1½ miles along the shore (start at the south end of American Road). Booklets from the Nature Conservancy Warden, Pounds Mead, Hills View, Braunton.

Bridgwater Bay National Nature Reserve **G3**
Somerset. Excellent for waders, winter wildfowl, including regular large numbers of white-fronted geese, and unique late summer/autumn moulting shelduck flock. Best observed from Start Point area, reached via A39 west from Bridgwater to Cannington, Combwick and Steart; or via A38 north from Bridgwater to West Huntspill, thence along Huntspill River and northwards.

Ebbor Gorge National Nature Reserve Trail **J3**
Nr Wells, Somerset. Mainly woodland birds in a superb scenic area. Start at the car park. Guide available at the nearby display centre at Ebbor Gorge National Nature Reserve, and further details from the Nature Conservancy Council Warden, East House, Wookey Hole, Wells.

Lundy Nature Reserve **B3**
Lundy, Devon. Boat from Ilfracombe. Breeding seabirds, raven, buzzard, and a wide variety of migrants. Field Station and Bird Observatory are in the Bristol Channel. Full details from The Agent, Lundy, Bristol Channel, via Ilfracombe, Devon.

Quantock Forest Trail **G4**
Quantock Forest, Somerset. Birds and other wildlife including buzzard and red deer of a commercially managed forest. 1–3 miles. Start at Seven Walls Bridge. Forestry Commission guide available at the site.

Slapton Ley Nature Reserve **F8**
Slapton, Devon. Open water and reedbed birds. Migrant waders, terns and passerines. Field Studies Centre and Bird Observatory. Full details from Field Studies Council, 9 Devereux Court, Strand, London WC2.

Slapton Ley Nature Trail **F8**
Slapton, Devon. Birds of open water, reed and lake margins. 1½ miles, starting at Slapton Bridge. Leaflets available.

Yarner Wood National Nature Reserve Trail **E6**
Nr Bovey Tracey, Devon. Woodland birds and woodland conservation. 3 miles. Free guide from the Nature Conservancy Council Warden, Yarrow Lodge, Yarner Wood, Bovey Tracey.

Birdwatching

Chew Valley Reservoir **J2**
Avon. 8 miles S of Bristol. This reservoir is among the most important wildfowl waters in the country, with a wide selection of duck in winter. Gadwall and the feral ruddy duck are among the breeding birds. In both spring and autumn the area is noted for its passage waders and black terns. Kingfishers are readily seen. There are good public viewpoints at the dam, Herriott's Bridge, Heron Green and Villice Bay. Permits from the Fisheries Officer, Bristol Waterworks, Woodford Lodge, Chew Stoke, Bristol.

Dartmoor **D6**
Devon. A vast area, but much can be seen from the roads and there is ample scope for exploration on foot. Breeding birds include red grouse, buzzard, curlew, raven, dipper, wheatear, ring ouzel, whinchat, stonechat, redstart, wood warbler and grey wagtail. In addition, Burrator and Fenworthy reservoirs have small numbers of winter wildfowl. Recommended areas are: Black Tor—Yes Tor (upland birds); the moors and heaths of the central area; and the oak woodland from Dartmeet (A384) towards Buckfastleigh.

Exe Estuary **F6**
Devon. Between Exeter and Exmouth, best observed from Powderham, Starcross and Dawlish Warren on the west side, and Lympstone on the east. Excellent for waders at all seasons, with interesting greenshank, spotted redshank, godwits, purple sandpipers at Exmouth, and especially good for duck in winter, brent geese and both Slavonian and black-necked grebes. Dawlish Warren adds seaward views and sanderling in winter.

Exmoor **E3**
Somerset. Moors, combes and deep-wooded valleys with many birds including red grouse, merlin, buzzard, dipper, pied flycatcher, nightjar, warblers.

Hayle Estuary **F9**
Cornwall. Best observed from A30. A good selection of winter and autumn waders occurs, the latter including spotted redshank, godwits, curlew, sandpiper and little stint. Winter wildfowl include wigeon and pintail, and Slavonian grebes are regulars.

Lye Rock **B6**
Nr Bossiney, Cornwall. N of Tintagel. A superb piece of coastal cliff. The largest puffin colony in Cornwall and a good breeding ground for auk. Also buzzard, razorbill and guillemot.

Isles of Scilly   **C10**
Seabirds and migration: Western Rocks and Gorregan for breeding auks and kittiwakes. Annet is outstanding with manx shearwaters, storm petrels, puffins and terns. St Mary's, Tresco and St Agnes are excellent for migration, and Horse Point, St Agnes for sea-watching. The islands are famous for rare migrants and vagrants. Regular sailing and, in summer, BEA helicopter service from Penzance.

Tamar Estuary   **K8**
Devon. An estuary complex with good numbers and a variety of autumn and winter waders, and winter wildfowl including occasional white-fronted geese. Of particular interest are wintering avocets and black-tailed godwits. In the north of the area, Weirquay and Bere Ferrers offer good views of the Tamar and Tavy respectively, the former being good for seeing the avocets, while the Torpoint area is recommended at the southern end

Brass rubbing

The following is a short list of churches that have brasses for rubbing. Permission is almost invariably required.
Cornwall. Callington, St Mellion, Fowey, Mawgan in Pyder, St Columb Major and St Michael Penkivel.
Devonshire. Dartmouth (St Saviour), Exeter Cathedral, Stoke Fleming, St Giles-in-the-Wood.
Somerset. Ilminster, South Petherton, Wells Cathedral, Yeovil.

Fossil hunting

Visit the local museum. Its fossil collection usually states where individual fossils have been found. When visiting quarries always seek permission to enter if they look privately owned or worked. Be careful of falls of rock.

Bath Avon
Plant remains can be found in the spoil heaps of the old coal mines in the Radstock, Camerton and Midsomer Norton areas.

Bleadon Somerset
Gravel pits in this area have yielded Pleistocene bones and antlers.

Bridgwater Bay Somerset
Search the lower Jurassic of the cliffs and foreshore west of Bridgwater, i.e. Watchet, Kilve and Hinkley Point.

Bude Cornwall
Look for arthropods and fish fossils in the cliffs.

Cheddar Somerset
Many exposures of fossils in the limestone of the Mendips around Cheddar, Burrington Combe, etc.

Crackington Haven Cornwall
The coastal parts of the culm yield lamellibranchs and goniatites.

East Somerset Quarries
Jurassic fossils in exposures in quarries at Chesterblade, Corton Denham, Dundry, Dunkerton, Keynsham, Maperton, Marston Magna, Midford, Shepton, Beauchamp and Welton.

Haldon Hills Devon
Look for fossil coral particularly in exposures of the limestone.

Quarries Somerset and Avon
Numerous quarries of carboniferous limestone give corals and brachiopods, notably, Backwell, Binegar, Burrington, Cleeve, Dulcote, Failand, Long Ashton, Portishead, Waterlip and Wrington.

River Taw Devon
Along the coast and in quarries. Lower carboniferous plants, corals, brachiopods and fish remains near Bishops Tawton, Bideford, Fremington and Westleigh.

Seaton Devon
Plentiful Cretaceous and Jurassic fossils along this coast at Seaton, Beer, Branscombe and east of Seaton in and below the cliffs.

Winford Somerset
Quarries here yield milstone grit goniatites.

Moors

Bodmin Moor
Cornwall. Open moorland 12 miles wide, owned by the Royal Duchy of Cornwall and grazed by cattle and ponies belonging to the 'commoners' of neighbouring farms. Rocky outcrops of granite, reaching 1,375 feet on Brown Willy and 1,311 feet on Rough Tor, give wide views. Great walking and riding country, easily reached from Bodmin, Camelford, Launceston and Liskeard.

Dartmoor
Devon. In the heart of Devon this magnificent 365-square-mile expanse of granite moorland, the Dartmoor National Park, rises steeply from surrounding farmlands to heights of around 2,000 feet. Grazed since Saxon times by herds of half-wild ponies and hardy cattle owned by local farmers. Grand riding and walking country, but caution is needed in the north where the highest point, High Willhays, 2,039 feet, lies on a military firing range (check at the local post offices for firing days). Rocky outcrops called 'tors' make good landmarks and viewpoints, but beware of sudden mists. Picturesque reservoirs lie in the valleys, or combes, especially Burrator in the south, as the rainfall is very heavy—80–100 inches annually. Wistman's Wood, 1 mile north of Two Bridges, is a nature reserve of fantastic oaks, dwarfed by exposure. Stately spruce woods at Bellever and Fernworthy. Enormous open-cast china clay workings north of Ivybridge. Grim prison at Princetown. Many prehistoric remains, including hill forts, standing stones and barrows.
Charming unspoilt towns ring Dartmoor and offer homely accommodation, notably Okehampton, Chagford, Moretonhampstead, Buckfastleigh, Totnes, Yelverton and Tavistock.

Exmoor
Somerset and Devon. National Park on 265 square miles of high, breezy moorlands facing the Bristol Channel, with views north to the South Wales mountains. It's ideal walking and riding country. Source of the River Exe, home of hardy half-wild ponies, red deer and scene of R. D. Blackmore's romantic historical novel 'Lorna Doone'. Reached from the coastal resorts of Ilfracombe, Lynmouth and Minehead by tortuous roads with fierce gradients. Finest scenery at Heddon's Mouth Valley, where oak woods run down to the cragbound shore. Highest poin is the 1,705-foot Dunkery Beacon.

Sedgemoor
Somerset. Aptly named, this dead-flat plain, 25 miles across in each direction, was for long a wilderness of sedges, reeds and rushes. Here, on the Isle of Athelney, around AD878, King Alfred burnt the cakes while planning campaigns against the invading Danes. Here too, in 1685, the rebel Duke of Monmouth was defeated by King James II. Nowadays the moor is all well drained farmland, with fascinating basket willow beds around Langport. These are pollarded willow trees which grow in ditches. They are called 'withies' and go to make wicker work.

Hills & combes

Blackdown Hills
This broken upland plateau between Honiton in Devon, and Taunton in Somerset, is a maze of valleys winding every way. Highest point, on the north face, is Staple Hill, 1,035 feet.

Brendon Hills
Somerset. Inland from Minehead, near Dunster with its castle and quaint market square, the Brendons form an eastern extension of Exmoor. More rugged and open, with huge woods of spruce and Douglas fir, they reach 1,390 feet on Lype Hill. Explore the scenic upper Exe along the A396, winding south towards Tiverton.

Combes and woods
Magnificent forests of Douglas fir, Corsican pine, and other tall conifers have been established locally by the Forestry Commission and private landowners, notably in the Glynn Valley east of Bodmin (Bodmin Forest) and over Haldon Hill, east of Exeter (Exeter Forest). The Cornish elm, a stately hedgerow tree with a slender crown, originates here and is now widely planted elsewhere in England, though its numbers were decimated by Dutch Elm disease in the early 1970s.
Outstanding natural woods, owned by the National Trust, at Arlington Court, near Barnstaple, Holne Woods, 10 miles west of Newton Abbot, Lydford Gorge near Tavistock, Lynmouth, and Goodmeavy near Yelverton. Fine arboreta, or collections of specimen trees, open to the public at Killerton, north-east of Exeter, and Bicton, near Budleigh Salterton.

Mendip Hills
Somerset. Ridge of limestone hills, 25 miles long, wending south east from Weston-super-Mare on the coast south west of Bristol to Shepton Mallet. The area is waterless except for Chew Valley Lake on the north, and there are many old lead mines, now exhausted. Precipitous winding gorges of white rocks run down to Cheddar and Wookey on the south where huge underground caverns are open to the public.

Quantock Hills
Somerset. Between Taunton and Minehead on the coast, this 12-mile range affords gently rounded scenery, nowhere over 1,260 feet. Tall woods of Douglas firs, introduced from Oregon, shelter a native herd of red deer which range across breezy commons that give expansive views over the Bristol Channel.

Rivers

River Dart
Devon. The River Dart begins as 2 moorland streams close to the highest point of Dartmoor. The East Dart runs through Postbridge and the West Dart through Two Bridges, to join at Dartmeet, an exceptionally beautiful spot where you will find an ancient stone 'clapper' bridge for packhorses, an old arch bridge for cars, and a restaurant. The River Dart then cuts through a deep valley wooded all the way to Totnes, where it becomes navigable by small craft.

River Exe
Devon. The River Exe rises in Somerset on a high moorland ridge of Exmoor, within a few miles of the Bristol Channel. Flowing first east, then south, right across Devon, it follows a deep, winding and narrow valley fringed with oak woods, past Tiverton to the cathedral city of Exeter. Aided by a canal, coastal craft can ascend this far. Below Topsham the River Exe flows through a broad sandy estuary to its narrow outlet, checked by sandbanks, at Exmouth.

Rivers Fowey and Fal
Cornwall. Typical Cornish rivers, these 2 streams rise on high hills, cut through very narrow and deep valleys, and end in harbours that once sheltered the sailing ships of merchant venturers in the Elizabethan age. Magnificent Douglas fir forests fringe the Fowey south of Bodmin. At Falmouth, south of Truro, the Fal ends in a great estuary, deep enough for the world's largest ocean-going ships to anchor safely.

River Parrett
Somerset. Central Somerset forms a broad, flat plain, broken by little hills and artificially drained low marshes, which is the basin of the big River Parrett. This draws together the waters of lesser streams from encircling hills on the south, including the Yeo from Yeovil, and the Tone from Taunton. At aptly-named Bridgwater, the lowest road crossing, the River Parrett becomes tidal and navigable, flowing forth towards broad mud-flats at Burnham-on-Sea.

River Tamar
Famous as the boundary between Saxon Devon and the ancient Celtic kingdom of Cornwall, the River Tamar rises on the Morwenstow Hills, near Hartland, only 4 miles from the peninsula's north coast. Flowing due south past Launceston with its castle, it cuts a deep, well wooded valley between Tavistock in Devon and Callington in Cornwall. At Saltash, just west of Plymouth's port and naval base, it has become a broad tidal estuary, crossed by a high railway viaduct and a modern road bridge.

Rivers Taw and Torridge
Devon. These 2 North Devon rivers share a common estuary, close to the little seaport and shipbuilding town of Appledore, on what the geographers confusingly call Barnstaple or Bideford Bay. The Taw flows in north westwards from mid-Devon, past the old port and bridgehead town of Barnstaple. The Torridge comes from the Cornish border, flowing north-east past Great Torrington, and the 'twin' seaport and bridgehead town of Bideford. Both harboured sea-dogs and men-of-war in Elizabethan days, and are thronged with holiday craft and fisherman today.

Canals

The Chard Canal
Somerset. Historically, this canal is remarkable for its very short life. A late starter, it opened for traffic in 1835 and was closed after a mere 25 years of profitless existence. However there is luckily quite a lot to see of the navigation, which contained 3 tunnels and 4 'inclined planes'. The best things to see, but don't expect to find too much water, are the aqueduct and embankment across the Tone Valley outside Taunton and the inclined plane and the entrance to the mile-long tunnel at the village of Wrantage (the old canal pub on the A378 road is still open). At Ilminster there is, again, a tunnel and an inclined plane close together. The boats used to travel down the inclined planes in water-filled tanks running on rails, and at Ilminster a change in height of over 80 feet is accounted for in this way. In Chard itself the final inclined plane can be traced, but little else remains.

The Exeter Ship Canal
Devon. This is one of the oldest canals in Britain, built in the 16thC well before the canal system as we know it today had even been thought of. The canal starts in Exeter and, fed by the River Exe, pursues its own course for just 5½ miles down to rejoin the Exe Estuary near Topsham. The canal is still occasionally used by small ships, which bring petrol to a wharf just outside Exeter. There are several locks, with circular balance beams, and all the bridges either lift or swing, in order to accommodate the considerable headroom of sea-going craft. The towpath provides an unusual circular walk along the canal from Exeter down to within a mile of the last lock into the estuary. At this point there is a small ferry across to Topsham. Visit the remarkable Maritime Museum in the terminal basin at Exeter.

The Grand Western Canal
Devon & Somerset. An intriguing little waterway, formerly envisaged as part of a

canal connecting the Bristol Channel with the English Channel. Only the north end of the canal was built, and an 11-mile branch to Tiverton. But there is a lot to see, although most of the canal is today without water.

Archaeological sites

Cadbury Castle   **J4**
South Cadbury, Somerset. For several centuries Cadbury Castle has been popularly regarded as the site of King Arthur's Camelot, and recent excavations have shown evidence of fortifications and buildings of the Arthurian period. The basic rampart system is Iron Age, with phases of building dating from an earth bank of the 5thC BC through to a dry-stone wall destroyed by the Romans. During the Roman period the hilltop was apparently cultivated, and remains of a Romano–British temple have been found. In the late 5th–6thC, the Arthurian period, the defences were refurbished and a hall built inside. Later structures on the site date mostly from the early 11thC, when Aethelred the Unready built a defensive wall against the Danes. There are also traces of mediaeval walls.

Charterhouse-on-Mendip   **J2**
Nr Blagdon, Somerset. Charterhouse was an important lead-mining centre during the Roman period, and traces of their workings can be seen on the surface as shallow depressions marking the filled-in pits and trenches cut to extract the ore. The settlement associated with the mines lay in Town Field, and an earthwork to the west of this may have been an amphitheatre.

Chysauster Ancient Village   **F9**
Gulval, Nr Penzance, Cornwall. Chysauster is a classic example of a peculiarly Cornish type of Iron Age settlement and one of the earliest mining communities in Britain. The number of huts suggests a village settlement, although there are no defences. The basic hut type is roughly circular, enclosed in massive walls, with rooms for living and storage opening on to a central unroofed courtyard. The site dates from the 1stC BC, and though there is evidence for its continuing into the Roman period, its character is native rather than Romano–British.

Dartmoor   **D6**
Devon. Dartmoor has several groups of visible antiquities, probably dating from the early Bronze Age. Circular stone enclosures containing stone hut-circles, their walls supported by banks of earth, can be seen at Grimspound, and at Legis Tor. Stone avenues and rows survive at Merrivale and Trowlesworthy Warren; groups of similar monuments can be seen at Ditsworthy Warren, Erme Valley and Shovel Down.

Halligey   **G10**
Trelowarren, Cornwall. One of the best-preserved of the Cornish fogous, a type of subterranean structure which has parallels in Scotland, Ireland and Brittany. They were probably constructed during the 1stC BC, and were built by excavating a trench, lining and roofing it with stone, and replacing the soil on top. Their purpose is unknown: defensively they would be deathtraps, and they are rather oddly constructed for storage.

Ham Hill Camp   **J5**
Nr Montacute, Somerset. Covering nearly 200 acres this Iron Age and Roman hill fort is one of the largest in Britain. It is L-shaped and unique in having an inn within the boundary.

Hembury Fort   **G5**
Nr Honiton, Devon. Commanding a marvellous view of the surrounding countryside, this Iron Age hill fort is the finest in Devon. It is built on the site of an earlier Neolithic causewayed camp, the most westerly of this sort in Britain, which appears to link its builders with the tribes of Salisbury Plain.

Lydford Castle   **D6**
Lydford, Devon. One of the most westerly of the fortified strongholds (*burhs*) established across southern England by Alfred and Edward the Elder as defences against the Danes in the late 9th and early 10thC. In the case of Lydford, an earthwork bank was constructed across the neck of a river promontory to create a defensible position. A Norman keep was built on the site during the 12thC to house offenders.

Roman Baths   **K2**
Bath, Avon. The small Roman town of Aquae Sulis grew up around its curative hot springs, and the baths built there form one of the best-preserved Roman monuments in western Europe; until recently they were still in use. The Great Bath was surrounded by a colonnade, of which the piers survive, and was probably open to the sky; the oblong Lucas Bath and small circular bath were contained in rectangular halls. Details of the Roman plumbing, the heavy lead linings to the baths, and fragments of mosaic floors are visible. The Roman Baths Museum displays finds from the site, including a bronze head of Minerva and, one of the finest pieces of Romano–British art, a carved Gorgon head from the façade of the Temple of Sulis Minerva, the presiding goddess of the springs.

Stony Littleton Long Barrow   **K2**
Wellow, Somerset. These characteristically Neolithic tombs were probably designed as vaults for families or groups rather than as burials for one individual. Stony Littleton barrow consists of a stone-built chamber and access passage, covered with a long earth-barrow—the finest English example of this is at West Kennet in Wiltshire. *Access from the farm.*

Tintagel   **A6**
Cornwall. The ruined monastery at Tintagel is without parallel in Celtic Britain for the sophistication of its rectangular buildings. The site occupies a dramatic headland, and may have been chosen initially for a solitary hermitage; the monastery was defined by a broad bank and ditch across the neck of the promontory. The buildings are arranged in groups, and include a library, guest-house, and cells for the monks. Despite legend there is no evidence of any connection with King Arthur. A 12thC castle now dominates the promontory.

Footpaths & ancient ways

South-West Peninsula Coast Path
The longest unbroken path in Britain, covering 515 miles from Minehead, Somerset, along the coast via Ilfracombe, Devon; Newquay, St Ives and Penzance, Cornwall; Plymouth, Torquay and Seaton, Devon to Poole Harbour in Dorset. In Somerset the path crosses the wild and desolate moorlands of Exmoor, with Dunkery Beacon rising over 1,700 feet above sea level. North-west of Lynton, Devon, the path leads through the magnificent Valley of Rocks, to Woody Bay, a tiny seaside resort surrounded by steep, wooded cliffs. From there the old coach road, now a green track, leads to Hunter's Inn.
There are 268 miles of pathway along the north and south coast of Cornwall, hugging the cliff tops with spectacular views of headlands, beaches, and quaint harbours and fishing villages.
From Newquay to Perranporth the path goes through sand-dune country. The inland way from Holywell, 3 miles from Newquay, to Penhale Sands, leads to the famous lost church of St Piran, once buried in the drifting sands.
Past Land's End, marked by a few tourist features inevitable in so famous a spot, the footpath follows some of the finest stretches of rugged coastline. Walking along the path

from Sennen Cove, 2½ miles away, all the commercial paraphernalia of modern life is happily out of sight.

Between Polkerris and Fowey, 4 miles away, there are spectacular views of Gribbin Head looking westward across the Fowey Estuary to the surrounding steep cliffs and wooded slopes. Fowey itself (pronounced 'Foy') is a picturesque Cornish town of labyrinthine cobbled streets.

Eastwards the path covers 93 miles of south Devon. The section across Bolberry Down from Bolt Tail to Bolt Head and The Warren are both protected by the National Trust and cross magnificent cliff tops, with wooded slopes descending to Salcombe with its waterside houses and ruined castle. The 72 miles of Dorset path offers cliffs, downland, shingle and sand-dunes. Above Old Harry Rocks at Handfast Point the last stretch of the Peninsula Coast Path passes through Studland hamlet, along the shore of Studland Bay to the ferry at South Haven Point, with Sandbanks, Poole and Bournemouth within sight across the water.

Regional sport

Angling
Salmon can be taken on the Rivers Camel, Fowey, Plym and Tamar. The West Somerset 'fens' present a vast area of good coarse fishing possibilities. What makes West Somerset particularly good is the large number of rhines, or drainage dykes, which provide nurseries for small fish. North and south Devon offer splendid game fishing on most rivers. Devon is particularly worried about the spread of the salmon disease UDN, and the authority handbook contains the appropriate rules.

Fishing licences and guides from the three River Authorities of Somerset, Devon and Cornwall.

Canoeing
River Exe, Devon. One of the most spectacular spectator sports ever. Competing in the Exe Descent over 100 canoeists race the 18 miles down the turbulent River Exe to Exeter, with breathtaking descents down 15-foot weirs and rock-filled rapids.
At Cowley 'Steps' skin divers fish out broken canoes and half-drowned canoeists who plunge down this turmoil of savage water. *Mid-Nov.*

Rugby
Rugby Union is played in Cornwall with the same fierce Celtic enthusiasm that keeps the game so much alive in the Welsh valleys. The two best teams are Camborne and Redruth. Such is the strength of Cornish Rugby that most international touring teams come down to play.

Sailing
The deeply incised south coasts of Devon and Cornwall are a sailing paradise to rival the more crowded Solent. The area contains the two finest deep water harbours on the south coast, Falmouth, with the Carrick Roads, and Plymouth. The following sailing clubs, and many others, offer temporary membership:
Salcombe Yacht Club. Salcombe, Devon. Estuary sailing. Classes of dinghy sailed: Hornet, Solo, Salcombe Yawl, Mirror, and Handicap. Racing season Mar–Dec. Launching off beach and slipways all times except last hour of tide. Dinghy parking space available.
Mayflower Sailing Club. Plymouth, Devon. Plymouth Sound and open sea sailing. Classes of dinghy sailed unrestricted. Racing season Apr–Sep. Launching from slip at all states of the tide. Dinghy parking space—permit required.
For further details the Devon County Tourist Office, County Hall, Exeter, Devon, publish an excellent booklet, or for the rest of the area contact the West Country Tourist Board, Trinity Court, 37 Southernhay East, Exeter, Devon.

Shark fishing
Centred in Looe and Falmouth on the south Cornwall coast, where the holidaymaker as well as the serious fisherman can hire the tackle, book on a boat and cruise 20 miles offshore fishing for blue shark, makos and porbeagles that can weigh well over 100 lbs! Late afternoon sees the day's catch being weighed on the quayside, and the size of the fish will amaze you.
All the sea angling is good around this coast, 'wreck' fishing yielding superb specimens. Virtually every harbour has boatmen operating trips.

Skittles
The traditional game for the dedicated indoor sportsman and drinker of southern Somerset, and not to be confused with its expensive modern American counterpart 'ten pin bowling'. One pub in two has its wooden skittle alley, and local competition is fierce.

Sub-aqua
The clear waters and rocky foreshore of the Isles of Scilly, south Cornwall and south Devon, warmed by the Gulf Stream, make for excellent diving conditions—and wrecks are more concentrated here than in any other offshore area.
The local boatmen will either hate you (divers have a bad reputation in some areas here) or hire out their boat and crew and take you to some superb sites like the Manacles and the Lizard. Diving centre at Fort Bovisand, Plymouth.

Surfing
This sport is a way of life along the north Cornwall and Devon coasts. When a good swell comes in, uninterrupted, off 3,000 miles of Atlantic it meets the gently sloping sandy beaches between Polzeath and Porthmeor. Then 'surfs up' and out come the malibu boards and their tanned and salt encrusted riders. Spectacular to watch, exhilarating to participate. Newquay is the centre of activity. Boards can be hired at various points along this coast. You can surf elsewhere in Britain, but this is where it 'happens'!

Festivals, events & customs

There are a number of local festivals and events—contact the local Information Centre for details.

Bath Festival
Bath, Avon. This famous international music festival was started by Yehudi Menuhin, who trained the festival orchestra and has played an active part from the first Bath Festival in 1959. Modern British music is now prominent. Performances are in the Assembly Rooms, Guildhall, the Abbey and Wells Cathedral. *10 days in June.*

Carnivals & fairs
It would seem almost unfair that the West Country should have such a seemingly endless supply of merry-making throughout the year. From May to the Guy Fawkes Carnivals in November it would almost be possible to see a fair or carnival in one town or another every week.

Dawlish Arts Festival
Dawlish, Devon. Started as a local festival, it now attracts performers and enthusiasts from all over the country. Concerts are held in the parish church, and the repertory company puts on a new production each year. *Mid June.*

Hobby Horse Dances
A custom probably surviving from ancient fertility rites celebrating the coming of spring is still retained in processions through the streets of Padstow and Minehead. *May Day.*

Minehead & Exmoor Festival
Minehead, Somerset. Begun as a small festival run almost entirely by the pupils of

Minehead Grammar School, the festival has expanded to include neighbouring Dulverton, Taunton and Exeter, and events include music, folk dancing, drama, pottery exhibitions and painting. Every year the Festival Society commissions a special work. *2 weeks in July.*

Thornbury Arts Festival
Thornbury, Bristol, Avon. Now boasting a new Armstrong Hall, the festival has expanded to include performances by distinguished visiting companies such as the London Opera Group. But the tone of the Thornbury Festival is still set by the blend of amateur and professional talent. *1 week in early May.*

Special attractions

Babbacombe Model Village   F7
Torquay, Devon. An excellent model village, which features a model farm, churches and even an illuminated football match, in an attractive woodland setting. Fascinating for the children.

Burgh Island Ferry   E8
Off the Kingsbridge–Plymouth Rd (A379) at Aveton Gifford. Burgh Island can be reached at low water by a causeway but when the sands are covered there is a most unusual ferry with a high platform on four stilts, and at the foot of each stilt is a motorised caterpillar track. The ferry literally walks across to its destination.

Butlin's Holiday Camp Amusement Park   F3
Minehead, Somerset. For boating, swimming, miniature railway and monorail. The park is open to day visitors for a fee. Very good value as once you are in all the rides are free.

Dart Valley Railway
Buckfastleigh, Devon. **(E7)** Running 7 miles along the River Dart from Buckfastleigh to Totnes-Riverside, the railway gives the traveller breathtaking and beautiful views of the River Dart which are denied to the motorist. All trains are hauled by steam engines of the Old Great Western Railway. *Kingswear, Devon.* **(F8)** This line runs from Paignton to Kingswear, with unusual views of Tor Bay and the lower reaches of the River Dart.

Donkey Rides   H2
Weston-super-Mare, Somerset. Donkeys and Punch and Judy on the beach are part of the traditional, but disappearing, English beach scene. Weston has both. The donkey rides are still great favourites with the children and have been here since the mid-19thC. The animals are bred locally, take their first rider at the age of 2 and are retired after 14 or 15 years' work.

East Pool Winding and Pumping Engine   G9
East Pool, Cornwall. Beside the A30 road between Redruth and Camborne is a reminder of Cornwall's once great industry, tin mining. Above the deserted mine at East Pool stands an old stone engine house and stack complete with preserved Victorian machinery. Open to the public. *Closed winter.*

Forest Railway   B7
Dobwalls, Cornwall. On the A38 road between Liskeard and Bodmin. On entering Dobwalls going westward, turn right on the road to St Cleer. Half a mile up the road you will come to the Forest Railway, a 7¼-inch gauge line. There is a car park, picnic area, swings and slides. The line has an interesting selection of model American steam locomotives, and a comprehensive signalling system. Railway museum.

Goonhilly Down Radio Station   G10
Helston, Cornwall. Two gigantic reflectors for receiving radio signals from space satellites. *Viewing area open daily.*

SS Great Britain   J2
Bristol, Avon. An early steamship designed by that erratic genius, the great Isambard Kingdom Brunel. The Great Britain was large for her time (1843) at 3,618 tons, and the first ship of any size to rely solely on screw propulsion. In 1866 she was driven ashore in the Falkland Islands and used as a coaling hulk. In 1970 she was towed home to Bristol, and appropriately enough the tow was also a great feat of engineering and seamanship. Now in dry dock at Bristol, there are well-signposted routes to reach her.

Kent's Cavern   F7
Ipsham Rd, Wellswood, nr Torquay, Devon. Once occupied by prehistoric man. Stalactites and stalagmites. The skull of a sabre-toothed tiger was found here and is now in the Torquay Museum, with other finds. *Open daily.*

Wookey Hole Cave Museum   J3
Wookey Hole, Somerset. This is the earliest known home of man in Britain. The museum displays a fine selection of Celtic and Roman relics, as well as the earlier remains of animal and human bones, cooking utensils and jewellery. Visit the Witch of Wookey in the Great Cave—a massive stalagmite said to be a petrified old woman. Also fairground collection and Madame Tussaud's Store Room.

Regional food & drink

Bath
The city has given its name to many sorts of food; Bath Buns, a yeast bun filled with candied peel and sultanas, originated there; Bath Chaps are pigs' cheeks smoked and salted (Bath had the reputation of making the finest); and the Bath Oliver is a famous type of dry biscuit.

Cider
From the Somerset and Devon apple orchards, draught cider is made and is available in most pubs. Known locally as 'scrumpy', it is deceptively alcoholic and more bitter than Kentish cider. The making of 'scrumpy' can be seen at Sheppy's Farm, near Wellington; also Lancaster's Farm at Felldown Head, near Tavistock.

Cheese
Just about the most famous cheese in the world, Cheddar, originated in the Somerset village of that name. It is now made in many countries. Dorset Blue Vinny (or veiny) is a much rarer cheese, has a Stilton-like blue veining and is made from hand-skimmed milk.

Clotted Cream
Cream teas are a speciality in Devon and Cornwall, served with scones and strawberry jam but without butter. The cream (and good butter) is produced from the South Devon breed of cattle, rarely seen outside the West Country. Clotted cream is at its best bought loose by the pound, but most shops and some farms provide a postal service too. Devon cream is very slightly whiter and runnier than Cornish, which is very solid.

Cornish Mead
A fermented drink of honey and water with wild flowers or spices for flavour. The word 'honeymoon' is derived from the old custom of drinking mead for 30 days after the wedding feast. Still made in Cornwall.

Cornish Pasty
Traditionally the tin-miners' portable lunch, which was shaped like a torpedo to fit in his pocket. Various meats are used, but mutton is usually mixed with potatoes and onions and always swedes, enclosed in a pastry which is pinched high along its entire length. Known locally as 'tiddy-oggies'.

Sally Lunn
A sweet light cake of flour, eggs, yeast and cream baked in a muffin hoop. Available in and around Bath.

The Southern Counties 2
and Channel Isles

Six counties and the Isle of Wight and the Channel Islands, all part of the tightly woven historical fabric of southern England. Dorset, still haunted by the spirit of Thomas Hardy, must be one of the loveliest counties. It has a long intriguing coastline and the mysterious Isle of Purbeck, while inland it is rich in stone manor houses sitting serenely on their richly farmed acres.

Hampshire seems less lush especially around the pine and heather lands near Aldershot where the army trains the recruits. But the main part of Hampshire is chalky downland with swift flowing rivers full of trout, and the microcosm of England's countryside is to be found at Selbourne where Gilbert White examined nature in his inimitable way. Gloucestershire and Oxfordshire are all full of towns and villages that grew out of the local stone. Oxfordshire and Berkshire are thick with history – they have grown up around the royal Thames linking learning and majesty to the nations capital. The Channel Islands each have their own style but they are still little bits of England despite their French connections.

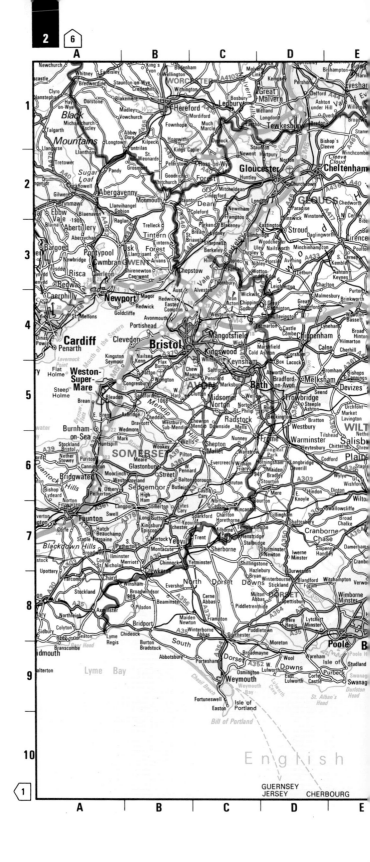

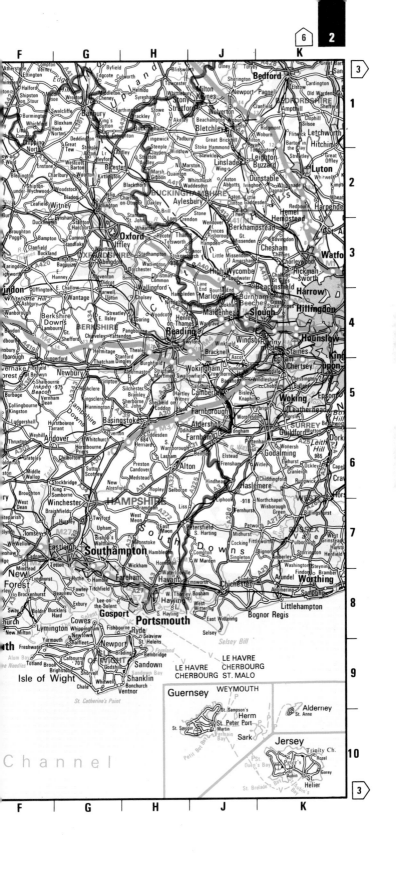

The coast

Abbotsbury C9
Dorset. Pop 500. A large village of orange-stone, which inherited 2 fine Benedictine legacies: the stone-buttressed Great Tithe Barn built by the monks in the 15thC and the famous Swannery which once housed thousands of swans; today there are about 300. Camellias and hydrangeas flourish in the Sub-Tropical Gardens, one of the most important and varied collections in the country. Splendid panoramic view of the coast from White Hill.

Alum Bay F9
IOW. From this considerably commercialised bay comes one of the most popular souvenirs of a holiday on the island—the coloured Bagshot sands from the cliffs that surround the bay. But do not be tempted to collect your own as the cliffs are very dangerous. Here Marconi made his first radio transmission, a fact commemorated by a memorial stone on the cliff top. Good bathing from sandy beach.

Bembridge H8
IOW. Pop 3,200. Unexploited by commercial tourism, Bembridge remains reasonably free from invasion. Its prominence as a sailing centre derives from its wide natural harbour, from whence its famous lifeboat is frequently launched. The only windmill on the island is found here. Good bathing.

Bonchurch H9
IOW. Famous for its natural beauty this old village, with H. de Vere Stacpoole's tree-framed pond and a tiny Norman church, has been host to Tennyson, Dickens, Macaulay and Anna Sewell (author of 'Black Beauty').

Bournemouth E8
Dorset. Pop 153,000. MD (at Winton) Tues, Fri & Sat. Bournemouth started as a holiday resort nearly 200 years ago. Its character derives from its hilliness, the chines, once an infamous smugglers' route, running down to the sea and the ubiquitous pine trees. The extensive pleasure gardens, superb sandy beaches and excellent entertainment facilities prove most attractive to the holiday maker. Very good bathing.

Bridport B8
Dorset. Pop 6,400. EC Thur. MD Sat. This straggling brick town is one of the best in Dorset, a beautiful townscape. The wide streets and broad pavements are a relic of the time when this was the main rope and net producing town in the country – the ropes were hung along the streets to dry after spinning. It retains its Georgian ambience. The town hall, designed by William Tyler, and the 15thC church are particularly worth visiting. About a mile south lies West Bay, offering 2 good bathing beaches. Fishing and sailing.

West Bay : Bridport, Dorset

Chesil Beach C9
Dorset. This 15-mile-long blue clay reef connects Abbotsbury and Portland. A huge sea wall of shingle constantly cast up by stormy seas and south-westerly gales encloses a stretch of water known as the Fleet (where Barnes Wallis tested his 'bouncing bomb' in WW II). Plentiful mackerel close to the shore. Treacherous currents make swimming dangerous.

Christchurch E8
Dorset. Pop 31,000. EC Wed. MD Mon. This old monastic town between the estuaries of the rivers Avon and Stour has a splendid priory, situated behind Christchurch Quay, built by the Saxons, with later additions up to Renaissance times. Nearby is the Red House Museum, housing examples of the wild life of the area. Golden sand and safe swimming at Avon Beach and Friars Cliff, with panoramic views of the Isle of Wight.

Cowes G8
IOW. Pop 19,000. EC Wed. Today the internationally-famous hub of the yachting world, Cowes has been strongly connected with the Royal Navy since the great ships were built and fitted here in the 18thC. The Royal Yacht Squadron on Victoria Parade retains the circular gun platform which is all that remains of Cowes Castle, built by Henry VIII. Cowes Week at the beginning of August is the peak of the May to September yacht-racing season. East Cowes is the centre of the hovercraft industry.
For those inclining towards Victoriana rather than yachts, Osborne House is only a mile away. Prince Albert conceived the design as an Italian villa, in close collaboration with Thomas Cubitt. After Queen Victoria's death here in 1901, the house was given to the nation. Visit the state and private apartments, the gardens, and the Royal playhouse, or Rumpus Room, known as the Swiss Cottage, which houses in miniature everything from portraits and royal garden tools to stuffed peacocks and crocodiles. Shingle beaches, some swimming.

Hamble G7
Hants. Pop 3,000. Although it has been a popular yachting centre for decades, this village is still appealingly unpretentious. The old village centre can be approached by the waterside walk. Try some of the local crab and lobster. Marshy foreshore.

Hayling Island H8
Hants. Pop 13,200. EC Wed. This 4-mile-square island of flat fields and straggling hamlets is between the waters of Langstone and Chichester harbours. The object of intensive seaside development in the early 1930s, it is a popular holiday centre. Excellent beach. Sailing, sea fishing.

Lulworth Cove D9
Dorset. Pop 1,300. EC Wed. This famous beauty spot in West Lulworth is much frequented by tourists. It even has its own butterfly, the Lulworth Skipper. The 3-mile-long bay, almost enclosed by the surrounding cliffs, offers splendid bathing facilities. Nearby is Durdle Door, a natural limestone arch jutting right out to sea. Do observe warning signs on cliffs; stay away from the edges and don't go too close to the bases, as rocks are likely to crumble.

Lyme Regis A8
Dorset. Pop 3,400. EC Thur. This one-time port lies sheltered by The Cobb, an ancient, curved stone jetty, immortalised by Jane Austen, which creates a small artificial harbour. It has existed since the reign of Edward I when Lyme was granted its royal title. The museum houses many relics of the attempted rebellion by the Duke of Monmouth in 1685. Fine views from the Golden Cap (617 feet), the highest cliff in southern England. Sailing and water-skiing from Lyme Bay. Some sandy beaches at low tide.

Lyme Regis, Dorset.

Newtown   **G8**

IOW. A romantic, pretty village, the most ancient borough of the island, and formerly a thriving port. Only a small 17thC Town Hall and a few cottages remain. Oyster-fishing. Sandy beaches at Newtown Bay.

Poole   **E8**

Dorset. Pop 111,000. EC Wed. Poole is by far Dorset's largest town with residential and industrial suburbs surrounding the huge 60-mile-round natural harbour which is said to be the second largest natural harbour in the world. The quayside is an attractive setting for the busy trading vessels, shipbuilding yards and the manufacture of famous Poole Pottery. The harbour forms the recreational centre, offering facilities for boating, shark fishing and trips round the harbour islands. Take a boat to Brownsea Island, a naturalist's haven protected by the National Trust, offering splendid views of the Dorset coast – open in summer only. Poole Bay has long beaches of firm white sand.

Portland Bill   **C9**

Dorset. Pop 12,000. The Bill projects from the narrow, rugged length of limestone known as the Isle of Portland. The inhabitants of this dramatic land, which is devoid of almost all vegetation, are a race unto themselves. An impressive old lighthouse on the Bill is a popular birdwatching station. Famous Portland Stone was quarried here for St Paul's Cathedral. Good bathing from Church Ope Cove for careful swimmers.

Portsmouth   **H8**

Hants. Pop 200,000. EC Mon, Wed, Thur. MD Thur, Fri & Sat. The visitor should first drive to Portsdown Hill to view a vast panorama of dockyards and military bases. Resolute penetration through tedious miles of 19thC terraced cottages toward the Guildhall and Old Portsmouth will be much rewarded. Nelson's perfectly preserved 18thC oaken flagship 'HMS Victory' is essential viewing. The residential district of Southsea still retains an Edwardian seaside charm. Sand and shingle beaches. Hovercraft to and from the Isle of Wight operate from here.

Ryde   **H8**

IOW. Pop 23,200. EC Thur. Overlooking the Solent, Ryde is the principal point of entry to the island. A thoroughly modern resort whose streets climb up Ashley Down. Unremarkable architecturally, the town is popular with holidaymakers, with its good entertainment facilities for all the family. Five miles of sandy beaches.

Sandown   **H9**

IOW. Pop 16,000. EC Wed. A flourishing holiday resort, commanding golden miles of sand between Culver Cliff and Luccombe Chine. It owes much of its popularity to the excellent sandy beaches, the amusement parks and the mile-long Esplanade, well furnished with every kind of traditional seaside entertainment.

Seaview   **H8**

IOW. Pop 1,300. EC Thur. Situated on a small promontory at the north-eastern corner of the island, Seaview is noted for its prawns and lobsters. There is also a flamingo park. A favourite resort for a spot of peace. Good bathing, from sandy beaches.

Shanklin   **H9**

IOW. Pop 16,000. EC Wed. Cliff-top hotels overlook this elegant town. Here Keats wrote part of 'Endymion'. Shanklin Chine and the Crab Hotel in the Old Village are particular tourist attractions. Sheltered sandy beaches. Golf and sea-fishing.

Southampton   **G7**

Hants. Pop 212,000. EC Mon, Wed, Thur. MD Sat. Despite extensive devastation during the Second World War, Southampton is rapidly establishing itself as a regional capital of an important part of England. Maintaining its pre-eminence as a passenger port, it is also a commercial and industrial centre with a modern university and an impressive Civic Centre. There is an historically interesting walk along the ancient city walls, towers and survivors of the original seven gateways, and many riverside walks. Sand and shingle beach at nearby Lepe.

Ventnor   **H9**

IOW. Pop 7,000. EC Wed. The only major town on the southern side of the island it is older yet more discreet than its later rivals and is noted for its climate and continental appearance. The esplanade is not long but holiday visitors are well catered for. Ventnor is sheltered by St Boniface Down, the highest point on the Island (785 feet). Fine sheltered walks can be taken along the 6 miles of the Undercliff, westwards towards the lighthouse at St Catherine's Point. The Botanic Gardens are well worth a visit to see the magnificent central rose gardens and rare plants and palm trees growing out of doors. Sandy beaches.

Weymouth   **C9**

Dorset. Pop 42,000. EC Wed. MD Thur. A jolly seaside town which became fashionable in the 18thC among the rich and royal sea-bathers. An elegant promenade of Georgian and early Victorian houses with a statue of George III in the centre. Safe bathing and sandy beaches.

Yarmouth   **F8**

IOW. Pop 1,000. EC Wed. This cheery small harbour with an attractive central square, ever busy with island visitors arriving by ferry, has a continental atmosphere. A 16thC castle is a focal point of historical and architectural interest. Steep sand and shingle beach.

Yarmouth, Isle of Wight

The Channel Islands

Five very different islands all trying to keep their individual qualities and all engrossed in keeping up appearances for the tourist. Although the Channel Islands are closer to France, they are deeply English with a slight continental veneer.

There are plenty of air services from London and other airports to Jersey and Guernsey, and the Sealink ferries carry cars and passengers from Weymouth and Portsmouth. The climate is sunny and frosts are rare. Cigarettes, perfume and spirits are free of VAT and have low duty.

Jersey   **K10**

The largest of the Channel Islands with a stunning coastline, superb sands and a rich assortment of places to stay.

All along the north coast the cliff scenery is splendid; a good inland route makes a change along the Route du Nord leading to St John. Don't miss Bouley Bay among the wooded hills, and, inland, Gerald Durrell's delightful zoo for endangered species. On the east coast Gorey is a bright little fishing village dominated by the mighty Mont Orgueil Castle. Visit the pottery. St Aubin's Bay on the south coast has over 3 miles of sands with safe bathing linked by the coast road to St Helier. Superb walk to the rocks at Corbière from St Aubin's along the old rail track. Shingle beaches at Belcroute Bay, overhung by trees and deep cut out of the red rock; a good beach at Portelet Bay.

St Brelade's Bay. If you had to choose the best beach in Jersey, this would be it. A fine 2-mile sweep of sand—with small hotels among the pines. Good bathing, boating, water skiing.

St Helier is the main town and port, with some modern development. The old quarter round the harbour is the best part to wander around, and at night there is dancing, cabaret and night clubs. The Napoleonic fortifications at Fort Regent are now converted into an entertainment and sports centre with swimming pools, squash courts and a solarium. Another attraction is the old covered market with its colourful display of fruit, vegetables and flowers.

St Ouen's Bay is on the west and full of bouncing breakers ideal for surfing—there are 5 miles of sand backed by grass and duneland.

Guernsey J9

You fly in over acres of greenhouses where Guernsey tomatoes are grown in the north of the island, and to the south-west the green hills with their cliffs drop down to magnificent beaches.

The best surfing is at Vazon Bay with its vast stretches of sand. Rock pools are fun for the children at Cobo and in the north the silver sands at L'Ancress make an ideal sheltered family beach.

In Guernsey the hotels tend not to be right on the beaches and the local buses are the most efficient local transport to the sea. A picnic lunch and a whole day by the sea is very much the Guernsey pattern.

Fermain Bay, lying south of St Peter Port, has a fine Martello Tower and wooded cliffs. Petit Bôt is a popular southern bay reached down a winding lane; at low tide there's plenty of fine sand.

St Peter Port, the capital, tumbles down the hillside, all grey and white until the town stops on the waterfront, at the spectacular harbour full of yachts and inter-island boats. Beaches are good and on a rare dull day you can spend hours in the covered French-style market.

Alderney K9

A mere quarter of an hour from Guernsey in one of Aurigny's tiny butterfly planes, and you can be on this simple and unspoilt island. Only 3½ miles long and a mile or so wide, it's a peaceful paradise if you like the sea, cliffs and sea birds.

Miles of cliff and beach walks; on the eastern and northern side of the island are several good safe beaches of rock and fine sand: Longy Bay, Corblets Bay, Saye Bay and Braye Bay.

St Anne is the only town—cobbled streets, an attractive church and some 15thC buildings around Marais Square. Lots of the houses in St Anne have been discreetly converted by exiles from England.

Sark J10

Small, secret and supervised by Le Seigneur from the Seigneurie. This small island is reached by the sturdy steamer and fast passenger launches. No motor traffic is allowed. Perfect escape if you like stiff walks and exploring coves and caves. A haven that really does offer the visitor complete refuge from the 20thC.

Herm J9

Take a 20-minute ride by motor launch from St Peter Port, Guernsey, to this tiny, enchanted island. Within its 1½-mile length the scenery changes from steep cliffs and bracken-covered hills in the south, to duneland and long sandy beaches towards the north. Shell Beach and Belvoir Bay are the popular beaches, leaving the rest of the island to more intrepid explorers.

Inland towns & villages

Banbury G1
Oxon. Pop 31,000. EC Tue. MD Tue, Sat. Immortalised in nursery rhyme and famous for its original spiced cakes, this quaint town is now a thriving industrial centre. Much of the original Banbury including the cross itself has disappeared; the present cross dates from only 1859.

Bibury E3
Glos. Pop 700. In the Coln Valley the road runs into the pretty village of Bibury. At right angles to the river stands a row of stone-built weavers' cottages, Arlington Row, now the property of the National Trust. A partly Saxon church stands next to 17thC Bibury Court.

Blandford Forum D8
Dorset. Pop 3,700. EC Wed. MD Thur. Set on the River Stour, this town is now mainly Georgian, older buildings having been almost entirely destroyed by fire in the 18thC. The church of SS Peter and Paul, with its cupola-topped tower, and the Town Hall are particularly fine period buildings.

Bourton-on-the-Water E2
Glos. Pop 2,250. EC Sat. Literally 'on-the-water'—the Windrush flows right through the centre of this beautiful village. The picturesque low-arched bridges only just clear the water. The broad village green lying parallel to the river extends to the south where it is flanked by Cotswold stone houses. Now nearly spoilt by tourism. It features an inland marine aquarium, a collection of tropical birds and the famous model village.

Bradford-on-Avon D5
Wilts. Pop 8,000. EC Wed, Sat. This pleasant and ancient town has the fine Saxon church of St Lawrence. The 12thC parish church houses the earliest English Bible used in a church—a reprint in 1572 of the 1568 Bishop's Bible. The Tithe Barn now houses a museum of Wiltshire agricultural implements. The Town Bridge, which originated in the 14thC, is notable for its lock-up, built into the parapet.

Burford F2
Oxon. Pop 1,400. EC Wed. A Cotswold stone village that has retained its quiet beauty. Visit the unusual Norman church which now has a spire and is decorated with good carvings. In the Tolsey (old toll house) there is a museum which illustrates the history of England as it affected a small country town. The quietly flowing Windrush River is crossed by a narrow, three-arched stone bridge.

Burford, Oxfordshire

Castle Combe D4
Wilts. Pop 500. EC Tue, Sat. A splendid village with a 15thC market cross at its centre. The Manor House dates from 1664. Voted England's prettiest village.

Castle Combe, Wiltshire

Cheltenham D2
Glos. Pop 76,000. EC Wed. MD Thur. An air of refined graciousness pervades this quiet

residential Regency town. Cheltenham's former popularity as a spa was established by George III. Today, it is a prosperous commercial and educational centre, long associated with sport and the arts, though the waters can still be taken at the Pump Room in Pittville Park, an elegant building ideally situated amidst flower displays and specimen trees. The broad, tree-lined Promenade is an excellent shopping centre. The theatre has a long history in Cheltenham, though the theatre that stands today was only built in 1891.

The Promenade Cheltenham

Chipping Campden   E1
Glos. Pop 2,000. EC Thur, Sat. The most northerly of the Cotswold towns and probably the most beautiful architecturally. Its early prosperity owed much to the patronage of a wealthy wool merchant at whose expense the striking parish church was built, with a fine 120-foot high tower. The finest building though is the 17thC Market Hall.

Chipping Norton   F1
Oxon, Pop 4,800. EC Thur. MD Wed. An abundance of old Cotswold houses adorns the highest town in the county (700 feet). It is a very old town, mentioned in the Domesday Book. Hospitable coaching inns, for example the Crown and the White Hart, still offer rest and refreshment to the visitor.

Cirencester   E3
Glos. Pop 14,500. EC Thur. MD Fri. In Roman times, as Corinium, this was Britain's second largest town, and a major strategic and trading centre. Hence the wealth of Roman remains—a never-ending source of joy to all itinerant archaeologists. A unique attraction is the direct access from the town to Earl Bathurst's vast 18thC landscaped park, with its central broad avenue, bordered by chestnuts. The 15thC 'wool' church is well worth a visit.

Cookham   J4
Berks. Pop 5,500. EC Wed, Thur. Immortalised by Sir Stanley Spencer, whose paintings may be seen in the old village hall and the Tate Gallery. Cookham represents all that is best in Thames-side villages. The office of the Keeper of the Royal Swans is located here.

Corsham   D4
Wilts. Pop 10,000. EC Wed. A pleasing village with an interesting restored church—St Bartholomew's—and many attractive houses. Of interest—Corsham Court, an Elizabethan mansion with Georgian embellishments, and parkland laid out by Capability Brown.

Dorchester   C8
Dorset. Pop 13,800. EC Thur. MD Wed, Sat. A truly historic town with antecedents in the Stone, Bronze and Iron Ages. King John used it as a hunting centre and in 1685, Judge Jeffreys held his 'Bloody Assizes' here. Much loved and written of by Thomas Hardy, Dorchester has a county museum, a military museum, an interesting old Shire Hall and the only complete layout of a Roman town house in Britain.

Dorchester   H3
Oxon. A beautiful town on the River Thames that still has the air of distinction appropriate to one of the oldest English cities. The large abbey church is worth seeing for its Decorated architecture; in the Jesse window behind the altar the stonework and glass reach new heights of splendour. The recumbent figure of a knight, probably carved in 1300, has a very modern feel. Good antique shops in the main street.

Gloucester   D2
Glos. Pop 90,100. EC Thur. MD Mon, Sat. Now a busy manufacturing centre, its earlier pre-eminence as an inland port was created by the construction of the canal between Gloucester and Sharpness in 1827. The city is cruciform in design, with four main 'gate' streets, preserving an abundance of historical features.

Godshill   G9
IOW. Pop 1,400. EC Sat. High on their hill the church of the Lily Cross and its surrounding cottages are a sharp contrast to the sprawling commercialisation below it. The early 14thC church has great charm and fine detail. Nearby is Appuldurcombe House, now a preserved Palladian shell set in gardens laid out by Capability Brown.

Goring   H4
Oxon. Pop 2,100. This village lies in the gap cut through the Chilterns by the Thames; the deep valley of hanging woods gives the river a dramatic setting. It was once a ford where the ancient Ridge Way and Icknield Way joined. The church at Goring is worth a special visit for its Norman tower, old bell (1290), and good brasses.

Henley-on-Thames   H4
Oxon. Pop 11,400. EC Wed. MD Thur. This market town really comes to life in the first week of July when the famous regatta is held on the river. Henley has an air of slightly pompous prosperity in the centre; the superbly elegant 18thC bridge has a carved head of Father Thames looking downstream, and a similar head of Isis looking upstream. Fishing and boating.

Hurley   J4
Berks. Pop 2,000. EC Wed. A pleasant riverside village complete with half-timbered houses and Norman church. A good spot to picnic or hire a punt and drift down the Thames. Full of calm riverside beauty.

Lacock   D4
Wilts. Pop 1,400. EC Mon. A preserved piece of old England with many fine buildings and inns. The church of St Cyriac has 14thC origins, and Lacock Abbey was founded in 1229 for Augustinian canonesses. It later became the centre where William Talbot laid the foundations of modern photography.

Maidenhead   J4
Berks. Pop 48,300. EC Thur. MD Fri. Now a commuters' town, but in an unrivalled setting on this beautiful stretch of the Thames and a good centre for exploring the surrounding country. Close by are the beechwoods of Cliveden, the famous Boulter's Lock, and the village of Taplow. Maidenhead looks best from the river and it is a good place to shop. Note the unusual modern library.

Marlborough   F4
Wilts. Pop 6,000. EC Wed. MD Wed, Sat. Renowned for its long and wide High Street, along both sides of which the London–Bath coaches passed whilst a market was held in the centre. Many hotels and inns in the town were established during the 18thC. A good centre for visiting the Savernake Forest.

Marlborough, Wiltshire

Milton Abbas   D8
Dorset. Pop 600. EC Wed. A very pretty, mostly thatched village built in the 17thC, to a plan by Capability Brown, by the first Earl of Dorchester to replace the market town of

Milton Abbas which was demolished as it spoilt his Lordship's view! The abbey was founded in AD935, but the present building dates from the 15thC.

Milton Abbas. Dorset

Moreton-in-Marsh F1
Glos. Pop 2,500. EC Wed. The Roman Fosse Way runs straight through the centre of this cosy, small, wool town, which is now the administrative centre of the North Cotswolds. Nearby is the Four Shires Stone, which until 1931 marked the intersection of the boundaries of Gloucestershire, Warwickshire, Oxfordshire and Worcestershire.

Newport G8
IOW. Pop 22,300. EC Thur. MD Tue. The island's 'capital' and main harbour, at the head of the tidal estuary of the River Medina. The town's charter dates from the 12thC and it retains much of its former character. Charles I was held in exile here. The Guildhall, erected in 1816, was designed by John Nash. To the north of Newport lies Parkhurst Forest, the island's only significant belt of woods, near the prison.

Oxford G3
Oxon. Pop 114,000. A beautiful city and university. The main cross road in the city centre is known as Carfax; in the centre is the tower that was once part of St Martin's Church. Climb up to the top, and amongst the spires of Oxford you get a good idea of the layout of the town.
Just past St Aldates Street is the main gate (Tom Tower) of Christ Church, with Oxford's largest college quadrangle. Christ Church Hall (1529) is one of the loveliest in the University, lined with solemn portraits of distinguished alumni. Don't miss the art gallery at Christ Church. Close by the hall is the entrance to the cathedral which is also the college chapel. Along Merton Street is Corpus Christi College (1517), with its amazing sun-dial in the quad. A tiny street between Corpus and Merton colleges takes you to Christ Church Meadow, a glorious green space that lies between the River Thames, the colleges, and the busy High Street. Merton College's statutes go back to 1264 and the college has the oldest library in England. It still keeps some of its books chained. Near the end of Merton Street is the Botanic Garden, and a rose garden commemorating the research workers who discovered the importance of penicillin. Opposite is Magdalen College with its glorious tower where Oxford choristers greet May Day from the roof. Magdalen must be the only college in the world to have its own deer park. Along the High Street you pass Queen's, All Souls, and University colleges. Take a special look at Brasenose College which has a subtle modern court blending perfectly with the ancient fabric. New College was founded in 1379 and has a

River Isis at Oxford

Radcliffe Camera : Oxford

S. Mary, Oxford

particularly fine chapel. Through a gateway at the end of New College Lane is the Sheldonian Theatre built in 1669 by Sir Christopher Wren and surrounded by giant sculpted heads of Roman emperors. It is used for university ceremonies and concerts. Behind the Sheldonian is the Divinity School (c1427–90), a rare, perfect example of 15thC Perpendicular architecture.

Sedilia. Merton College, Oxford

Sedilia : S. Mary, Oxford

Along Broad Street is Blackwell's world renowned bookshop; next to it is Trinity, a college with some unusual modern buildings. Balliol, Jesus (where Lawrence of Arabia was an undergraduate), Exeter and Lincoln colleges are all worth visiting.
There are so many treasures in Oxford that you will have to return; don't miss the Victorian red-brick splendours of Keble, or the cool modern academicism of St Catherine's College, designed by the Danish architect Arne Jacobsen. Oxford is more than just its buildings, it is a city with a unique atmosphere of learning and pleasure. Glide slowly down the Thames, or Isis, in a punt on a lazy summer afternoon and you could be in a beautiful dream.

Oxford

Paradise D2
Glos. Just north of Painswick on the Cheltenham Road lies this charming hamlet, named by Charles I. Complete with the Adam and Eve Inn, it lies parallel with the beautiful Slad Valley.

Romsey F7
Hants. Pop 10,000. EC Wed. Set on the edge of the New Forest, this market town has a fine Abbey church founded as a nunnery in the 10thC. Also of interest is King John's House, a 13thC hunting lodge with good carving. Nearby is Broadlands, home of the late Earl Mountbatten.

Salisbury E6
Wilts. Pop 36,400. EC Wed. MD Tue, Sat. A truly splendid cathedral town, with numerous fine buildings, especially in the Cathedral Close. The Salisbury and South

Wiltshire Museum houses most of the objects found during excavations of nearby Stonehenge.

Selborne H6
Hants. Pop 1,000. EC Wed. The home of Gilbert White, the naturalist, this pleasant place houses his museum and the Oates Memorial Museum. The church of St Mary was restored by White's great-nephew in the 19thC. By its south door stands the yew tree which, when Gilbert White measured it over 200 years ago, had a girth of 23 feet!

Sherborne C7
Dorset. Pop 9,300. EC Wed. MD Thur. A fine country town housing an abbey, a school founded by Edward VI, two castles and a thriving dairy industry. Sherborne Castle was built by Sir Walter Raleigh, and in 1688 William of Orange made his Proclamation from it.

Stow-on-the-Wold F2
Glos. Pop 1,800. EC Wed. Delightfully rural, this one-time centre of the wool industry grew in geographical significance in the middle ages. Several features of historical interest remain—the old market cross and stocks stand in the market square, just east of Fosse Way. The Stow Fair, once a livestock market though now mainly a show and horse sale, is still held in May and October annually. Good antique shops.

Streatley H4
Berks, Pop 800. Intact and unspoilt, discreetly Georgian, possessing a unique village hall converted from a 19thC malthouse. Ascent of Streatley Hill will afford a fine vista towards the Thames.

Stroud D3
Glos. Pop 19,100. EC Thur. MD Sat. The largest town in this Southern Cotswold region, Stroud is an important business centre. Situated in the main valley of the River Frome, it has since Tudor times been noted for its fine quality cloth. The characteristically steep, narrow streets are disappearing in the course of urban redevelopment.

Tewkesbury D1
Glos. Pop 9,000. EC Thur. MD Wed, Sat. The construction of the M5 motorway has relieved this ancient town of much congestion and noise. Strategically sited at the confluence of the rivers Avon and Severn, it was the scene of a Yorkist victory in 1471, when many Lancastrians were massacred in a field known to this day as 'Bloody Field'. Narrow alleyways. Elizabethan timber-framed houses and ancient inns are all dominated by the massive 12thC abbey church.

Tewkesbury

Wantage G3
Berks. Pop 8,000. EC Thur. MD Wed, Sat. Once notorious for dubious bloodsports and nefarious activities, Wantage has now become respectable. The birthplace of Alfred the Great, commemorated by a noble statue in the market square. Once a sheep-trading centre. The entrances to the almshouses have been paved with sheep's knuckle-bones. More bones (human) and tombs to be found in the 13thC church of SS Peter and Paul.

Whippingham G8
IOW. Closely associated with Queen Victoria and Prince Albert. The church, which Albert helped to design, was attended by the Royal Family during their stays at Osborne.

Winchester G6
Hants. Pop 31,000. EC Thur. MD Wed, Fri & Sat. This was King Alfred's capital, but it dates from pre-Roman times. Set at the beginning of the Pilgrim's Way, the town is full of interest, including its castle, cathedral, the Royal Green Jackets Museum, the West Gate Museum, and Winchester College. A good view over the city and surrounding Itchen valley can be had from St Catherine's Hill.

Windsor J4
Berks. Pop 30,000. EC Wed. MD Sat. Although overshadowed by the great royal castle, the town of Windsor asserts an individual dignity. Wren's Guildhall exhibits rare paintings and a history of Windsor. Across the Thames lie the playing fields of Eton College which was founded in 1440. Four miles north is Stoke Poges where Thomas Gray is buried in the churchyard he made famous in his 'Elegy'.

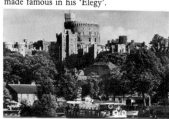

Windsor Castle

Witney F2
Oxon. Pop 14,000. EC Tue. World-famous blanket-making town on the River Windrush. It has an unusual Butter Cross whose gabled roof has a clock tower and a sun-dial. The old Blanket Hall has an eccentric one-handed clock. At nearby Cogges there is a recreated Edwardian farm and a museum of the countryside.

Hill figures

You get a strong feeling of the presence of early man in this region, not just earthworks but huge men and creatures formed in the chalk. Scouring, to keep the figures clear, takes place at regular intervals.

Alton Barnes Horse E5
Wilts. 1 mile N of Alton Barnes. A sleek chalk-white creature with slim legs and head, poised for a quick canter 250 feet above the Vale of Pewsey. 162 ft long.

Cerne Giant C8
Giant Hill, Dorset. ¼ mile NW of Cerne Abbas. This naked figure wielding a mighty caveman's club is thought to be a fertility symbol. 180 feet high and 45 feet across the shoulders. The club is 120 feet long. Above on the hilltop is the enclosure where the rites of spring were performed on May Day.

Cherhill Horse E4
Wilts. 4 miles E of Calne, nr Cherhill. A fine figure of a white horse with a noble eye four feet in diameter, once inlaid with upturned bottles. Souvenir-hunters had carried away the bottles by 1872. 140 feet across.

Laverstock Panda E6
Wilts. 1 mile N of Salisbury off A30. In honour of the union (unsuccessful) between Chi-Chi and An-An at the London Zoo this cuddly panda head mysteriously made its appearance at Laverstock in 1969. 55 feet by 40 feet.

Pewsey New Horse E5
Wilts. 1½ miles S of Pewsey. Last of the Wiltshire horses, cut in 1937 by the Pewsey Fire Brigade in honour of the Coronation of George VI. It lies close to the supposed position of the Pewsey Old Horse which is no longer visible. 65 feet across.

Uffington White Horse　　　　F3
Berks. 2 miles S of Uffington. Popular legend has it that the white horse is associated with King Alfred's victory over the Danes in AD871. Probably dates from 100BC; 360 feet long. Some say it's not a horse but a dragon due to its rather disjointed body and beaked head.

Westbury Horse　　　　D5
Wilts. 1 mile SW of Bratton. Soft-eyed creature with a long tail. The first Westbury Horse probably dated from the Iron Age. The present one is thought to have been made in the early 18thC but was transformed by a Mr Gee in 1778, which act earned him the title of 'vandal'. 182 feet long.

Woolbury Horse　　　　G6
Hants. 2 miles E of Stockbridge. A small, frail figure believed to represent the mount of a local 18thC highwayman who waylaid the Winchester-Salisbury coaches. 27 feet long; outlined with rough flints.

Famous people

Jane Austen (1775–1817)　　　　H6
Chawton Cottage, Chawton, Hants. The author lived here 1809–17, and most of her novels, including 'Emma' and 'Persuasion', were written or rewritten in the general sitting room. The red-brick house is now a museum of personal relics. Her tomb can be seen in Winchester Cathedral.

Winston Churchill (1874–1964)　　　　G2
Blenheim Palace, Woodstock, Oxon. The statesman and author was born here in a small unpretentious bedroom, which now contains his personal belongings. He is buried at the nearby village of Bladon.

Charles Dickens (1812–70)　　　　H8
393 Commercial Rd, Mile End, Portsmouth, Hants. Dickens was born in this house. Now restored and furnished in the style of period.

Thomas Hardy (1840–1927)　　　　C8
Hardy's Cottage, Higher Bockhampton, Dorset. 3 miles NE of Dorchester. Wherever you turn in Wessex it is certain that Hardy was there, and has written about it. Waterston Manor, west of Puddletown, was Bathsheba's home in 'Far from the Madding Crowd'. Bere Regis is the Kingsbere of 'Tess of the d'Urbervilles', Bournemouth is Sandbourne, and Salisbury is Melchester. The small thatched cottage smothered in greenery and set in an acre of gardens at Higher Bockhampton is where Hardy was born. The study from his house at Max Gate has been reconstructed in the Dorset County Museum, Dorchester.

Victor Hugo (1802–85)　　　　J9
Hauteville House, 38 Hauteville, St Peter Port, Guernsey, C.I. Victor Hugo lived here. Now a museum devoted to his relics, furniture, tapestries and china.

Richard Jefferies (1848–87)　　　　E4
Coate Farm, Swindon, Wilts. The son of a Wiltshire farmer, the naturalist and novelist was born in this house, not far from the ancient Ridgeway path which Jefferies featured in so many of his writings. The house is now a museum and contains manuscripts, first editions and personal items. *Closed winter.*

T. E. Lawrence (1888–1935)　　　　D8
Clouds Hill, nr Wareham, Dorset. About the time Lawrence of Arabia enlisted in the Royal Tank Corps in 1923, he leased a derelict cottage, Clouds Hill, which he rebuilt and later described as being 'alone in a dip in the moor, very quiet, very lonely, very bare . . . I don't sleep here, but come out 16.30 till 21.00 nearly every evening, and dream, or write or read by the fire, or play Beethoven and Mozart to myself on the box'. There is a sculpture of him in Arab dress in the Saxon church of St Martin.

Earl Mountbatten of Burma
(1900–1979)　　　　F7
Broadlands, Romsey, Hants. During his distinguished career, Lord Louis Mountbatten held many high offices, including that of last Viceroy of India. Special exhibition tracing his eventful life overshadowed by his tragic death.

Catherine Parr (1512–48)　　　　E1
Sudeley Castle, Glos. ½ mile S of Winchcombe off A46. This was the home of Henry VIII's sixth wife after his death and her marriage to Thomas Seymour. The castle was given to Seymour by a grant of the council. Catherine died there after giving birth to her first child. A picturesque window in the old building belongs to the room still called 'Queen Catherine's nursery'.

Stanley Spencer (1891–1959)　　　　J4
King's Hall, Cookham-on-Thames, Berks. Collection devoted to the paintings, drawings and personal effects of Spencer, who was born in Cookham. His painting of 'The Last Supper' hangs in the local church.

Alfred, Lord Tennyson (1809–92)　　　　F9
Farringford, Freshwater, IOW. The home of the Poet Laureate from 1853 (now a hotel) where he wrote much of his best work. Tennyson Down, near the Needles, where the poet walked every day, has a monument to him. In 1867 he was forced to leave the island because of over-enthusiastic sightseers and souvenir hunters.

Gilbert White (1720–93)　　　　H6
The Wakes, Selborne, Hants. The home of naturalist and author of 'The Natural History of Selborne', Gilbert White. White was born in The Wakes, and died there. The 17thC house set in 29 acres is now a museum with 40,000 volumes on natural history and polar explorations in the library, and personal relics of White and Antarctic explorer Captain Oates.

Cathedrals, abbeys & churches

Christchurch Priory　　　　E8
Christchurch, Hants. The Priory was founded in 1150 in what was then called Twineham. Reputed to be the longest parish church in England, measuring 312 feet, the choir and towers date from the 15thC, the nave is Norman. It contains a memorial to the poet Shelley and is surrounded by peaceful gardens.

Gloucester Cathedral　　　　D2
Gloucester, Glos. Approaching the city from the west or from the dock you always see the Perpendicular tower of the cathedral. This tower was built around 1450, the last major addition to the cathedral founded in 1089 apart from the Lady Chapel which completed the rebuilding in 1499. Inside note the giant round piers in the nave, and the great stone vault at the east end that frames the curtain wall of mediaeval stained glass.

Oxford Cathedral　　　　G3
Oxford, Oxon. Now a part of Christ Church College, but still the city's cathedral, it is a great Norman church topped by the 13thC spire. It has a solid air which has survived the rigorous Victorian improvements. Sir Gilbert Scott was responsible in the 1870s for the new east rose window and the arcade. There is glass from the 14th and 17thC and a fine 17thC organ.

St George's Chapel　　　　J4
Windsor, Berks. The chapel of the Order of the Garter, decorated with feudal banners, dates from the 15thC and is vaulted and elaborately decorated, with a 19thC sculpture of a bare-breasted Princess of Wales by M. C. Wyatt. The finest example of Perpendicular architecture in England. It is now the burial place of Royalty.

St John the Baptist   E3
Cirencester, Glos. A 15thC 'wool' church,
built when Cirencester was the greatest wool
market in England, with a 3-storey porch
which was at one time the Town Hall. The
nave is of great height, and the wine-glass
pulpit dates from 1450.

St Lawrence   D5
Bradford-on-Avon, Wilts. This tiny church
dates from before the Norman invasion of
England, possibly late 7thC. Its height is
only slightly greater than its length. By the
19thC it was used as both a cottage and a
school, but it is now restored to a chapel
again.

Bradford-on-Avon, Wiltshire.

St Mary the Virgin   E3
Fairford, Glos. A church which is renowned
for its 15thC stained glass windows, made by
Henry VIII's master glass painter, Barnard
Flower. The complete series of 28
illustrations represents the Christian story
from Creation to Last Judgement.

St Mary the Virgin   G3
Iffley, Oxon. A famous 12thC church with
two Norman arches and an early English
sanctuary. Altogether a very fine building.

St Michael and All Angels   H3
Rycote, Oxon. A 15thC chapel frequented by
Charles I and Queen Elizabeth when they
visited the area. The interior has 15thC
benches and 17thC family and Royal pews.
The altar piece and communion plate are
also 17thC.

Salisbury Cathedral   E6
Salisbury, Wilts. Unique in Britain because
this cathedral is the only one built as a single
conception. Foundation stones were laid in
1220 and 60 years later the cathedral was
complete; the only addition, in 1334, being
the great 404-foot spire, the interior wooden
framework of which can be viewed.
The building is in complete harmony with
its site, partly because it is built of Chilmark
stone which was quarried only 12 miles
away. Inside, total perfection and a certain
austerity comes from the regular consistency
of dark Purbeck marble shafts and lancet
windows. The Lady Chapel is where the
Purbeck shafts are at their most
attenuated—here the cathedral has an
abstract, modern feel. The library holds one
of the remaining original copies of the
Magna Carta and some beautifully
illuminated works collected in the 11thC.

Salisbury Cathedral

Sherborne Abbey Church   C7
Sherborne, Dorset. A former Benedictine
foundation, now a parish church, with a
Saxon doorway and Great Tom—a tower bell
presented by Cardinal Wolsey. The fan
vaulting is very fine; monuments include
those of the 13thC abbots and the coffins of
the Saxon kings Ethelbald and Ethelbert.

SS Peter and Paul   D8
Blandford Forum, Dorset. John Bastard
designed and built this fine church following
the 1731 fire which destroyed much of the
town. It is Georgian in style, in ashlar with a
cupola-topped square tower—an interesting
period church.

Wimborne Minster   E8
Wimborne, Dorset. A twin-towered church
which dates from Norman times. The choir
stalls are Jacobean and there is a 15thC
Flemish glass window. The astronomical
clock in the west tower dates from 1320 and
shows the sun and moon rotating around the
earth. There is also a fine chained library.

Winchester Cathedral   G6
Winchester, Hants. The longest cathedral in
Europe, started in 1079 when Winchester
was capital of England. It was one of the
richest sees in England during the middle
ages and the powerful Bishop William of
Wykeham enriched his cathedral by adding a
veneer of the Perpendicular style on the
Norman base (1371–1400). Apart from
having the longest nave in Europe (560 feet),
Winchester has the largest Early English
retro-choir in the country and no less than 7
elaborately carved chantry chapels.

Castles & ruins

Basing House   H5
Basingstoke, Hants. The ruins of a house that
was destroyed in the Civil War. The Tudor
garden walls and the remains of the
gatehouse can be seen, together with an
exhibition of the history of Basing. Guided
walks available.

Berkeley Castle   C3
Avon. Off A38 between Bristol and Gloucester.
A long range of mostly 14thC buildings that
date from a remodelling of the castle in 1350
on the 12thC foundations. This is one of the
oldest inhabited castles in England, still lived
in by genuine Berkeleys. Don't miss the
dungeon cells where King Edward II was
murdered, nor the ancient bowling alley.

Broughton Castle   G1
Oxon. 2 miles W of Banbury Cross. Home of
the Lord Saye and Sele for 600 years. Much
of the 13thC house remains but it was
greatly enlarged in the 16thC. Fine
panelling, fireplaces and plaster ceilings and
good period furniture. The house sits on an
island in the middle of its moat. See the
display of arms and armour.

Carisbrooke Castle   G8
IOW. 1¼ miles SW of Newport. Well known
and well worth the climb, this 20-acre castle
stands proudly above the village. Standing
on the site of a Roman fort, the keep was
built by the Normans. The gatehouse was
finished in 1470, and the outer walls were
run up as an emergency measure in 1588 by
local labour when the Armada was on its
way. There is a 161-foot-deep well with a
16thC water-wheel once worked by prisoners
but today by a donkey.

Corfe Castle   D9
Isle of Purbeck, Dorset. There is something of
a picture book quality about the gaunt ruins
of the castle and the picturesque village. But
a sinister sensation still comes from these
great stones. Built on a conical hill, it has a
history of mediaeval cruelty, treachery and
revenge. It was destroyed after Cromwell had
besieged it during the Civil War.

Corfe Castle, Dorset

Lulworth Castle   D9
East Lulworth, Dorset. This westerly corner
of Purbeck is full of interest and Lulworth
Castle is still a romantic spot. Set on rising
ground in an opening between Flowers
Barrow and Binden Down, the castle stands
four-square among clumps of beeches. A
square, lofty, battlemented block, Lulworth
appears to be the essence of all castles, but it
was built in the 17thC as a second home by
the third Lord Howard of Binden and was
gutted by fire in 1929. *Admission only on
application.*

Portland Castle   C9
Castletown, Dorset. Like an open fan the
castle presents its curved face towards
Weymouth Bay. It was built in 1540 by
Henry VIII as one of the many castles in a
line of defence that ran from Kent to
Cornwall. Henry had an obsessive fear of
French invaders, and this line of sturdy
castles certainly made him feel prepared for
anything.
Portland is one of the best preserved of these
castles. Its Portland stone ashlar has
remained clean cut and sharp. Look inside at
the complete range of garrison quarters and
feel the presence of those tough Tudors.
Closed winter.

Sandsfoot Castle   C9
Nr Weymouth, Dorset. Built to protect
Weymouth Bay as a companion to Portland
Castle only 2 miles away. Its heavy cannon
were designed to cross fire with Portland's.
Sandsfoot now looks sad and worn.
Constructed in 1541, the garrison quarters
still remain, although the octagonal gun
room has now slipped into the sea. The
walls and gate tower remain intact.

Windsor Castle   J4
Windsor, Berks. The largest inhabited castle
in the world covering 13 acres, and a
favourite home of the Queen. It is the size of
a small town with its own chapel, barracks
and state apartments all still functioning. Its
silhouette as seen from the long walk in the
Great Park is mostly a 19thC creation,
although the origins of the castle go right
back to William the Conqueror. When the
Queen is not in residence the inside of the
castle can be visited. It is full of treasure.
The Castle is surrounded by the 4,800-acre
Great Park.

Unusual buildings

Alfred's Tower   C6
Stourton, Wilts. Not content with the
creation of the amazing Stourhead Gardens
nearby, Henry Hoare built splendid follies
around the edge of his park in 1768. The
most noticeable is this tower, on the
790-foot-high Kingskettle Hill which rises to
a height of 160 feet above the spot where
King Alfred raised his standard against the
Danes in AD878. Triangular in shape with
turrets on each corner, the structure is
completely hollow. A statue of King Alfred
stands over the entry in a little niche.

Arlington Mill   E3
*Bibury, Glos. 7 miles NE of Cirencester on
A433.* In one of the loveliest of Cotswold
villages, this mill was both a cloth mill and a
corn mill, and the pretty cottages, Arlington
Row, were the homes of the weavers. It
stands where it has stood since it was
recorded in the Domesday Book, alongside
the River Coln. The existing building is
mostly 17thC. It has working machinery, and
a museum of arts, crafts and Victoriana.

The Great Barn   F3
Great Coxwell, Berks. SW of Faringdon. This
must be the most beautiful barn in the
country. Built by monks in the 13thC as a
tithe barn, its sheer size suggests that the
monks did pretty well. Built of ornate
brickwork and roofed with stone tiles, its
size, 152 feet long by 51 feet high, explains
why William Morris said it was 'as noble as
a cathedral'.

Houses & gardens

Ashdown House   F4
Nr Lambourn, Berks. 2¼ miles S of Ashbury.
A very tall house that is unusual in being
made of chalk blocks. Built by an unknown
architect in 1665 for the first Earl of Craven,
who dedicated it to Elizabeth, Queen of
Bohemia. The house is topped by a little
viewing room under a dome. There must
have been a great deal of running up and
down stairs as the stairway occupies about a
quarter of the house. Fine gardens.

Ashdown Park : Berkshire

Athelhampton Hall   C8
*Nr Dorchester, Dorset. ½ mile E of Puddletown
on A35.* A very fine house that remains
essentially mediaeval, surrounded by walls
and courts and almost encircled by the river.
Inside the house the great hall is one of the
finest examples of 15thC domestic
architecture in England. Thatched stables
and dovecot.

Beaulieu Palace House & Abbey   G8
Beaulieu, Hants. Once the Great Gatehouse
of the 13thC Abbey, the house has been
owned by the same family since 1538. The
Abbey, in ruins since it was destroyed in the
Dissolution, was founded by the Cistercians
in 1204. There is an exhibition of monastic
life on display. In the grounds there is a
high-level Monorail. The home of the
National Motor Museum.

Blenheim Palace   G2
Woodstock, nr Oxford, Oxon. A handsome
gift from Queen Anne to her favourite
soldier, the Duke of Marlborough, to
celebrate the victory at Blenheim. It has a
certain martial splendour as you will see
from the heaps of trophies the architect
Vanbrugh has displayed along the roof line.
Inside, it must be the most palatial of all the
stately homes. The greatest artists and
craftsmen of the day worked on the interior.
The garden and lake are by Capability
Brown. The formal parterre gardens with
ponds and fountains were created at the
beginning of this century.

Blenheim Palace, Oxfordshire.

Buscot Park   F3
Berks. 3 miles NW of Faringdon. Water plays
the main part in this skilfully designed
garden by Harold Peto. A long grassy walk
with a narrow central canal, planted with
water lilies, drops in stages to the 20-acre
lake created by Capability Brown. The
various levels are marked with fountains,
bridges, statuary and vistas. The house is
charming – 18thC in the Adam style with
superb painted panels by the pre-Raphaelite,
Burne Jones. *Limited opening.*

Compton Acres   E8
*Dorset. Between Bournemouth & Poole in
Canford Cliffs Road.* Originally expensively
converted from moorland, this estate is
famous for its 7 separate and quite distinct
gardens. One, designed, planted and
decorated in the Japanese manner includes
pagodas, figures and lanterns reflected in a
pool crossed by stepping stones. Another, the
Italian garden, features a long Roman-style
pool with formal urns and statues. The semi-
tropical glen contains jacarandas, eucalyptus,
palms, mimosa and Himalayan
rhododendrons. There are also rock and
winter gardens, a heather dell, and Palm
Court with its valuable marble and bronze
sculpture. *Closed winter.*

Forde Abbey   A8
Dorset. 4 miles SE of Chard. Originally a 12thC Cistercian monastery and now a private house. The gardens cover 25 acres and are full of lovely lakes. Inside the house much 12thC work remains, and don't miss the superb collection of Mortlake tapestries. *Closed winter.*

Furzey Gardens   F7
Minstead, Hants. 2½ miles N of Lyndhurst. Set in the heart of the New Forest in an ancient village with an interesting 13thC church. The 8 acres of gardens were laid out in the 1920s. Particularly attractive in spring when the azaleas and rhododendrons are in bloom, and in autumn when there is a blaze of dazzling colour.

Hidcote Manor Gardens   E2
Hidcote Bartrim, Glos. 4 miles NE of Chipping Campden. Definitely not to be missed, being one of England's most beautiful 20thC gardens with views over the Vale of Evesham. Laid out by Major Lawrence Johnston, over 40 years, in a series of small hedged compartments, each devoted to particular colourings or species. *Closed winter.*

Kiftsgate Court   E1
Mickleton, Glos. 3 miles NE of Chipping Campden. Adjacent to Hidcote, a charming garden with an exceptional collection of species and old fashioned roses. Cuttings and plants can be purchased. *Closed winter.*

Milton Manor   G3
Nr Abingdon, Berks. Wander down the pretty village street at Milton to the gates of this lovely house which is well hidden. Largely 17thC with Georgian wings, the house contains two great surprises, a chapel and a library in the elaborate Gothic taste. All the rooms are handsome and the grounds well matured within mellow walls. *Closed winter.*

Pussey House Gardens   F3
Berks. 5 miles E of Faringdon. Offering a wide variety of interest, from the lovely terrace dotted with dianthus, sysirinchium and blue flax, to the elegant chinoiserie bridge spanning the lake, whose banks are planted with waterside species. *Closed winter.*

Rousham House   G2
Steeple Aston, Oxon. 12 miles N of Oxford. William Kent's only surviving landscape design to remain unaltered. Starting from the old bowling green, complete with original seats and Scheemakers sculpture, bear left to find the Praenoste arcade which illustrates Kent's great passion for Roman antiquity in a sylvan setting. Such is the Venus' Vale, an upper and lower cascade between which is the great pond decorated with lead figures dated 1701. Further on from the little Doric Temple note the distant Temple of the Mill and an artificial ruin, both used by Kent purely to please the eye. *Closed winter.*

Savill Garden   J4
Windsor Great Park, Berks. Off A30 via Englefield Green. Started in 1932 in Windsor Great Park by Sir Eric Savill as a small water garden. It has since been enlarged to cover over 20 acres of woodland, water and bog gardens. The heather garden makes a colourful use of a natural valley and the Punchbowl is a perfect example of bank planting with shrubs and trees. The azaleas and Japanese maples are particularly fine. *Closed winter.*

Stonor   H3
Stonor, Bucks. 4 miles N of Henley-on-Thames off A480. Set in a wooded fold of the Chiltern Hills, it has a most beautiful position. The house shows some very early domestic architecture having been started in 1190. St Edmund Campion set up his secret printing press here in 1581 which led to his execution in the Tower of London. It has always been a centre of Catholicism, even through the period of conflict with the Church of England, and Mass is still celebrated each day in the chapel. Fine

rooms with beautiful painted and stained glass windows, as well as furniture, tapestry, sculpture and drawings.

Stourhead   C6
Wilts. 3 miles NW of Mere in Stourton village. Designed to be walked round in an anticlockwise direction, this garden, created in 1741–50 by the architect Flitcroft for Henry Hoare in the romantic Italian style, features magnificent conifers and a huge tulip tree. Glimpsed from the grotto with its sculpture by Rysbrack is the great lake, home of swans, ducks and crested grebe.

The Pantheon, Stourhead, Wiltshire.

Sudeley Castle   E1
Winchcombe, Glos. The present house was greatly renovated in the 19thC, though its history goes back to Tudor times and beyond. Famous as the home of Catherine Parr. Fine furniture, paintings, gardens and chapel.

Museums & galleries

Abingdon Borough Museum   G3
The County Hall, Abingdon, Berks. Relics from the mediaeval abbey, pewter plate, uniforms and arms from the 16th–19thC, toys, fossils, ornaments and tools from local Saxon graves, all housed in the 17thC County Hall.

Ashmolean Museum of Art and Archaeology   G3
Beaumont St, Oxford, Oxon. The oldest public museum in Britain, first opened in 1683, it is rich in Egyptian relics. Drawings by Michelangelo and Raphael, 16th and 17thC silver, bronzes, snuff-boxes, and the Hill collection of musical instruments.

Buckler's Hard Village and Maritime Museum   G8
Buckler's Hard, Hants. 5 miles NE of Lymington. A tiny 18thC hamlet on the lower reaches of the River Beaulieu which was a ship-building centre, due to the plentiful supplies of oak from the nearby New Forest. Much of Nelson's fleet, including his favourite ship the 'Agamemnon', was built here. The Maritime Museum traces the history of the village and the ships that were built here. Also trips on the river.

Corinium Museum   E3
Park St, Circencester, Glos. Roman antiquities from the site of Corinium Dubunnorum. Fine mosaic pavements, provincial Roman sculpture.

Devizes Museum   E5
Long St, Devizes, Wilts. Important Stourhead collection of Bronze Age urns, beakers, grave goods and ornaments excavated from barrows on Salisbury Plain in the early 19thC.

Dorset County Museum   C8
Dorchester, Dorset. Finds from the Iron Age fort at Maiden Castle. The Thomas Hardy Memorial collection includes manuscripts, notebooks, drawings and the reconstructed study from Hardy's house, Max Gate (Dorchester).

National Motor Museum G8
Palace House, Beaulieu, Hants. One of the finest collections of vintage cars, commercial vehicles, motorcycles and bicycles in the world. 1895 Knight, 1896 Pennington and the 1865 English Bone Shaker.

Old Town House E8
High St, Poole, Dorset. This 14thC building is now a small museum. Exhibits devoted to local history, pottery, industrial archaeology and a Bronze Age dug-out canoe dredged up from Poole Harbour in 1964. *Closed winter.*

Russell-Cotes Art Gallery and Museum E8
East Cliff, Bournemouth, Dorset. Items associated with Napoleon and Sir Henry Irving. Fine collection of Victorian painting, watercolours and drawings.

St Peter's Bunker Museum K10
St Peter's Parish, Jersey, C.I. Grisly collection of Nazi German equipment and war relics. *Closed winter.*

Salisbury and South Wiltshire Museum E6
St Ann St, Salisbury, Wilts. Most of the finds from Stonehenge are here. A wide selection of mediaeval pottery, a Roman mosaic pavement from Downton and the celebrated giant figure carried in the midsummer Guild Pageants.

HMS Victory and the Portsmouth Royal Naval Museum H8
H.M. Naval Base, Portsmouth, Hants. Relics of Lord Nelson and the Victory are housed in the oldest part of Portsmouth dockyard, directly opposite HMS Victory. Centrepiece of the museum is a panorama of the battle of Trafalgar by W. L. Wyllie.

Botanical gardens

Exbury G8
Hants. 4 miles SE of Beaulieu. A world-renowned 200-acre garden planted by the late Lionel de Rothschild in 1918. Noted for the Exbury strain of hybrid azaleas and rhododendrons. The breeding of this strain was started by Anthony Waterer some 40 years ago at Knaphill nursery and forms the basis of the comprehensive collection seen today. *Closed winter.*

University Botanic Garden G3
High St, Oxford. The oldest botanic garden in Britain, founded by Henry, Lord Danvers, in 1621. Six acres pleasantly situated by the river. Fine species collections of rare plants. Entrance arch by Inigo Jones.

Westonbirt Arboretum D3
Glos. 3 miles SW of Tetbury. Here, in one of the world's oldest arboreta, we find the greatest variety of trees and shrubs in the British Isles, shown to their best advantage by the skilful planting and foresight of Robert Stainer Holford who began the garden in 1829 on rough pastureland.

Zoos, aquaria & aviaries

The Birdland Zoo Gardens E2
Bourton-on-the-Water, Glos. One of the major bird collections in Britain, gathered in the Cotswolds. Among the 600 birds many are rare and seldom seen in captivity. Leadbeater's cockatoos, great black cockatoos, purple-crowned turacos. Tropical house and penguin pool. Shell exhibition and art gallery.

Cotswold Wildlife Park F2
Oxon, 3¼ miles S of Burford off A361. A large walk-through aviary in the garden; the animals are kept in natural surroundings. Look out for the red pandas from the eastern Himalayas. Animal brass rubbing centre.

Jersey Zoological Park K10
Les Augres Manor, Trinity, Jersey, C.I. A zoo specializing in threatened species and founded by Gerald Durrell, author and animal-lover. The collection includes reptiles, gorillas, orang-utans, a colony of black and white colobus monkeys, spectacled bears and flying foxes from Rodriques. Look out for the lovely lizard native to this island.

The Lions of Longleat D6
Longleat Park, Warminster, Wilts. This famous lion reserve also includes herds of giraffe, zebra and antelope as well as monkeys and a group of Bengal tigers in the 200-acre Longleat park. Admission by private car or coach. Take a trip on the Safari Boat—you can buy buckets of fish to feed the sea lions while you float around the lake.

Marwell Zoological Park G7
Colden Common, nr Winchester, Hants. 7 miles SE of Winchester on the A333. One of Britain's largest zoos with nearly 1,000 animals in a huge parkland setting. Lots of favourite animals as well as some rare breeds like the Asiatic lion, Sumatran tigers, many kinds of deer, antelopes and zebras. Also flamingoes and other birds, a children's zoo and playground.

Slimbridge Wild Fowl Trust C3
Slimbridge, Glos. 2 miles N of Berkeley Rd. Finest collection of wild fowl in the world, founded by Peter Scott in 1946. Rare species include Aleutian Canada geese, king and spectacled eiders, harlequin, Hawaiian geese. There are 6 observation towers and 15 hides in the sea wall for visitors.

Windsor Safari Park J4
Winkfield Rd, Windsor, Berks. 150-acre safari park with 7 drive-through reserves, first opened in 1969. Lots of things to see and do. Children's farmyard, Tropical House and Parrot show, Nature walk and Whale and Dolphin show.

Nature trails & reserves

Aston Rowant National Nature Reserve Trail H3
Aston Rowant, Oxon. Start at car park at the reserve. Mainly of botanical interest, but a good selection of commoner species may be seen along this beechwood and chalk grassland trail, 1½ miles. A guide is available.

Brownsea Island Nature Reserve E8
Brownsea Island, Dorset. Heath, woodland, marsh, lake and shore birds at all seasons; breeding species include heron, terns and nightjar. Access via boats from Sandbanks or Poole Quay; restricted private landing. Guided tours on certain days. There is also a nature trail (1¼ miles), starting from Brownsea Island Quay. Dogs not allowed. *Summer only.*

Farlington Marshes Nature Reserve H8
Hants. Part of Langstone Harbour and a splendid area for waders and winter wildfowl, especially brent geese. Access near junction of A27 with A2030; no permit required.

Forest of Dean Nature Trails C2
Glos. As many as 9 trails may be available in any year. 2 of these are: Speech House Forest Trail (2¼ or 1¼ miles), beginning either at Speech House or the Beechenhurst Picnic Place; and Edge End Forest Trail (3¼ or 2¼ miles), which starts at the Edge End picnic place. Both provide a good cross-selection of typical forest birds.

Hengistbury Head Nature Trail F8
Hants. Start at Ranger's Cottage at Hengistbury Head. Birds of heathland, oak woodland, saltmarsh and shore. Also of geological interest. 2 miles. Guide available at the start of trail.

Isle of Wight Nature Trails G9
IOW. There are 6 different well marked nature trails in the island, including that at

the River Medina, near Newport, where shore birds, cormorant, kingfishers, etc can be seen. All details from the Isle of Wight Tourist Board, 21 High St, Newport, Isle of Wight.

New Grounds Nature Reserve   C3
Slimbridge, Glos. Follow sign off A38 S of Cambridge. Not only one of the world's best waterfowl collections but headquarters of the Wildfowl Trust and its research branch. Captive birds augmented by large numbers of Bewick's swans and duck, including pintail in winter, with spectacular flocks of white-fronted geese on adjoining Dumbles. Migrant waders. Peregrine and water rail regular in winter. Full details from the Wildfowl Trust, Slimbridge, Glos.

Radipole Lake Reserve   C9
Weymouth, Dorset. Fine area of lake and reed-bed with breeding reed warblers and bearded tits and a wide selection of passage migrants and winter wildfowl. Public access at southern end allows good views of much of the area, and there is a nature trail starting at the south end of the lake. Details of restricted reserve area from RSPB, The Lodge, Sandy, Beds.

RSPB Reserve   E8
Arne, nr Wareham, Dorset. Dorset heathland with breeding nightjar, stonechat and Dartford warbler; good selection of wildfowl and waders in autumn and winter. Access strictly by permit only (except at Shipstal). Details from RSPB, The Lodge, Sandy, Beds.

Thorncombe Wood Nature Trail   C8
Higher Bockhampton, Dorset.E of Dorchester, off A35. Typical birds of mixed woodland, 2½ miles. Leaflet available at the start of trail.

Birdwatching

Forest of Dean   C2
Glos. An outstanding forest area of the region, also well served by roads and free of access in many areas. Full details of nature trails are available from The Forestry Commission, Crown Offices, Coleford, Glos. As well as most of the typical woodland birds, the forest has kestrels, sparrowhawk, nightjar, raven, wood warbler, owls, ringdoves, heron, snipe, redstart and pied flycatcher, with dipper and grey wagtail on its streams.

Langstone Harbour   H8
Hants. A large area of intertidal mud and salt marsh between Portsmouth and Hayling Island, which can be examined from various points around its boundary. Excellent for waders at all seasons, but especially autumn and winter, and notable for its winter wildfowl which include duck, large numbers of brent geese, divers and grebes.

New Forest   F7
Hants. One of Britain's most outstanding woodland areas, with added heathland, has a rich variety of typical species and breeding specialities such as wood warbler, hawfinch, hobby, sparrowhawk, buzzard, honey buzzard, stonechat, warblers, nightjar, red-backed shrike and woodlark. The forest is crossed by various roads and access is unrestricted at many places. In addition there are forest nature reserves and nature trails. The Forestry Commission or the Nature Conservancy Council at Red Lodge, Lyndhurst, for full details.

Poole Harbour   E8
Dorset. This vast area lies west of Bournemouth and Poole and, in spite of various developments, is very good for birds—grebes, duck and waders in winter and autumn being the main attractions. Studland, Arne and Brownsea overlook the area, but additional vantage points include South Haven Point, the caravan site at Rockley Sands and the Shore Road north of the ferry.

Portland Bill   C9
Dorset. Easily reached and well signposted from Weymouth, this is a fine birdwatching area. Here seabirds include auks, shag, kittiwake, and fulmar in summer. Spring and autumn migration produces a wide variety of passerines, often including rarities. Portland Bird Observatory and Field Centre makes an ideal base for the serious birdwatcher: details from The Warden, Old Lower Light, Portland, Dorset.

Salisbury Plain   E6
Wilts. An area of chalk downland and associated belts of trees. The A360 between West Lavington and Shrewton, plus the minor road to the east, are good viewpoints. Notable breeding birds include hobby, buzzard, stone curlew, wheatear, and quail.

Virginia Water   J4
Berks. This area is within easy reach of London, lying south-west of Egham and north of the A30. The large lake is good for waterfowl and is well known as a favourite site for the feral Mandarin duck. The surrounding woodland has a good variety of birds, including woodcock, woodpeckers and hawfinch.

Brass rubbing

The following is a short list of churches that have brasses for rubbing. Permission is almost invariably required.
Berkshire. Childrey, Shottesbrooke, Sparsholt, Windsor (St George's Chapel and Parish Church).
Dorset. Thornocombe, Puddletown, Shapwick.
Gloucestershire. Chipping Campden, Cirencester, Deerhurst, Northleach, Wotton-under-Edge ('Woolmen' figure brasses at Cirencester and Northleach), Minchinhampton, Fairford.
Hampshire and the Isle of Wight. Crondall, Freshwater, Havant, Headbourne Worthy, King's Somborne, Ringwood, Thruxton, Winchester (St Cross).
Oxfordshire. Brightwell Baldwin, Burford, Chinnor, Dorchester, Great Tew, Mapledurham, Oddington, Oxford (Merton College Chapel, New College Chapel and University Church), Thame.
Wiltshire. Clyffe Pypard, Dauntsey, Mere, Salisbury Cathedral.

Fossil hunting

Visit the local museum. Its fossil collection usually states where individual fossils have been found. When visiting quarries always seek permission to enter if they look privately owned or worked. Be careful of falls of rock.

Aust
Glos. The cliffs immediately under the eastern side of the Severn Bridge are full of Rhaetic fish bones and remains, small oyster and mussel shells.

Barton-on-Sea
Hants. Cliff sections crowded with Eocene fossils.

Cheltenham
Glos. Crickley and Leckhampton Hills for oolite fossils in quarries wherever you can find them.

Cotswolds
Glos. Many rich fossil-bearing exposures. Try around Cirencester, Halmore, Mobley, Purton, Woodford and Whitfield.

Dorset Coast
The whole succession of Jurassic rocks and fossils is splendidly displayed in the foreshore and cliffs from the Devon border to Swanage.

Durlston Bay nr Swanage, Dorset. Masses of freshwater shells and small crustacea. A rare possibility here in a thin bed is to find fossils of primitive mammals, dwarf crocodiles and fishes, and occasionally insects.

Faringdon F3
Berks. Pits of highly fossiliferous sponge gravels in this district are abundant with sponges, bryozoa, brachiopods and echinoids.

Isle of Wight F9
The cliffs of Alum Bay, Whitecliff Bay, Headon Hill and Colwell Bay yield many fossils of the Caenozoic period. The coast near Atherfield Point, of greensand, is full of large bivalves. At Brook Point is a mass of prostrate fossil tree trunks much broken up by wave action.

Kirtlington G2
Oxon. Quarries have thick beds largely of brachiopods.

Langton Herring C9
Dorset. Exposed at Herbury, the great oolite clays provide a bed full of brachiopods and oysters.

Lyme Regis and Charmouth A8
Dorset. The fossil collector's paradise. Ammonites of all sizes abound in the lias; some on the foreshore are incredibly 2 or 3 feet in size. Belemnites, crinoids and molluscs, and the occasional tooth or vertebra of the large marine reptiles can also be found. Visit Lyme Regis Museum. This town is famous for fossil collector Mary Anning, who in the late 19thC extracted fabulous large skeletons from its cliffs.

Minchinhampton Common D3
Glos. The quarries here have yielded well preserved shells in a matrix of white oolite limestone which are to be found in many museums.

Oxford Area G3
Oxon. Quarries in the Oxford area yield large upper Jurassic fauna of ammonites, oysters, brachiopods, corals, gastropods and occasional bones. Beckley Headington, Kidlington, Kirtlington and Littlemore.

Wiltshire F4
Most of Wiltshire is chalk and many fossils can be found in quarries and road cuttings in Alderbury, Downton, Fyfield, Marlborough, Oare and Pitton.

Forests

Forest of Dean C2
Glos. In west Gloucestershire, between the rivers Severn and Wye, the Royal Forest of Dean stands on a high plateau, surrounded by splendid views, especially at Symonds Yat Rock. Here are mighty oaks, planted by Nelson for warship timbers, tall beeches and ash trees, and a full range of coniferous trees from Europe and North America. Mines and quarries for coal, iron ore, lime and sandstone, scarcely used today, date from Roman times. Herds of half-wild sheep graze the roadsides.

New Forest F7
Hants. In 1079 William the Conqueror created this Royal Forest, now occupying 145 square miles of south-west Hampshire between Southampton and Bournemouth, as hunting country for red deer, still present today. Three-fifths is open heath, providing pastures for herds of half-wild ponies, young cattle and pigs owned by the Commoners, who are peasant farmers holding historic rights. Two-fifths is woodland with veteran picturesque oaks and beeches, giant hollies and well-tended plantations of Scots pine and Oregon Douglas fir. Many Forestry Commission camp sites, car parks, picnic points, and way-marked trails. Riding.

Savernake Forest F4
Wilts. Set high on the Wiltshire Downs east and south of Marlborough, Savernake was once a Royal Forest, and later a nobleman's chase for hunting spotted fallow deer. Today the Forestry Commission tends its magnificent groves of oaks and beeches, and provides access to woodland walks from car parks with picnic places.

Hills

Berkshire Downs G4
Berks. An expanse of lonely chalk uplands, up to 1,000 feet high, between Abingdon in the Thames Valley and Newbury on the River Kennet. Traversed by the wide Ridgeway, an ancient drovers track for bringing cattle to London from the west. On the north face is the famous White Horse of Uffington, a figure first carved in chalk by Celtic tribesmen, and renewed by King Alfred. Today strings of racehorses are exercised across the spring turf of the downs.

Christmas Common H3
Oxon. Nearly 800 feet above sea level, this hilltop village stands on the Chiltern ridge above Watlington in south-east Oxfordshire. From the steep chalk escarpment at Watlington Hill, a National Trust property nearby, views extend north and west over the broad Thames Valley. Slopes on either side are clad in tall beechwoods, some privately owned, others part of the national Chilterns Forest. Quaint thatched cottages, walled with flint or 'cob', abound.

Cleeve Hill E1
Glos. 5 miles north-east of Cheltenham, Cleeve Hill is the highest of the Cotswolds. Its windy summit commands magnificent views west over the Vales of Gloucester and Worcester to the Malvern Hills and the Forest of Dean. Eastwards the Midlands open out, with nothing to challenge Cleeve's 1,083 feet anywhere across England.

Cotswolds D3
Magnificent range of limestone hills running for 70 miles north-east from Bristol past Gloucester to Banbury in Oxfordshire, with a general height of 800 feet. Their steep scarp slopes, facing the Severn Vale to the north west, are threaded by winding valleys clothed in tall beechwoods.

Dorset Downs C8
Dorset. Range of chalk hills, 600 feet in general height, running north east for 40 miles from Dorchester towards Salisbury, Wiltshire. Green pastoral country, grazed by countless sheep and cattle, and broken by the deep valleys of 'winter bournes', streams that flow only after heavy winter rains. Includes the well-wooded Cranborne Chase, featured in Thomas Hardy's novel 'Tess of the D'Urbervilles'.

Hampshire Downs G6
Hants. Surrounding the county town of Winchester, the Hampshire Downs form rolling uplands with a dry chalk soil. Old drove roads, now modernised, run through green pastures and fertile arable fields, broken by straight shelter belts of beech. The few market towns, Andover, Basingstoke, Alton and Petersfield, stand in river valleys.

Inkpen Beacon F5
Berks. Relics of past and present jostle each other on this 974-foot chalk summit, set near the meeting point of Berkshire, Hampshire and Wiltshire, 10 miles south west of Newbury. Has an Iron Age fort, prehistoric and modern trackways, Celtic fields, a mediaeval gibbet, and tractor ploughing for wheat on the downland summit. Wide views over the Thames and Kennet valleys; tricky road up.

Liddington Castle F4
Wilts. Highest of the Wiltshire Downs, this prominent sheep-grazed summit rises to 910 feet, standing sentinel over the bustling 'new town' of Swindon 5 miles north. Close by, at Coate Farm, is Richard Jefferies country, where the famous 19thC naturalist wrote his inspired prose-poems, based on intimate first-hand observation of the countryside.

Marlborough Downs E4
Wilts. Between the old towns of Marlborough and Calne, on the London to Bristol highway, A4, these high chalk hills

rise to nearly 900 feet and provide grand country for riding, or training racehorses. Their unique concentration of ancient monuments includes the Avebury stone circle, Silbury Hill and the Wansdyke, a prehistoric boundary ditch, 15 miles long.

Pilsdon Pen   **B8**
Dorset. At 908 feet Pilsdon Pen is the highest of the dramatic range of sandstone and limestone hills that give a mountainous aspect to west Dorset. Standing close to the B3164 road from Axminster to Beaminster, it commands the fertile Marshwood Vale, where higgledy-piggledy hillside fields are flanked by odd-shaped woods of pine, oak and larch.

Queen Elizabeth Country Park   **H7**
Gravel Hill, Horndean, Nr Portsmouth, Hants. Jointly managed by Hampshire County Council and the Forestry Commission the park is half open downland and half beach and conifer forest. Miles of footpaths and horse-riding tracks as well as a grass-skiing and hang-gliding centre. The quieter parts of the park are rich in wildlife. There are also demonstration areas on forestry, sheep management and the Butser Ancient Farm project.

Meadows & marshes

Avon Water Meadows   **E6**
From Salisbury in Wiltshire, south to its mouth at Christchurch in Hampshire, the River Avon is bordered by unique water meadows. Artificially drained, these meadows were formerly artificially flooded, too.

Cricklade Meadows   **E3**
Wilts. Though the land around Cricklade, on the old Roman road (A419) lies high in the Thames Valley, it is level and must be artificially drained to provide pasturage. Towards Fairford, Gloucestershire, on A417 to the north, large gravel pits now filled with surface water are being landscaped as boating lakes. Lechlade, an old stone village, marks the limit of Thames navigation. 'Lade', an Anglo-Saxon word, signifies 'ditch'.

Lymington Saltings and Beaulieu River   **F8**
Hants. At the mouth of the Lymington River, in Hampshire's New Forest, flat salt marshes were formerly enclosed at high tide, so that brine evaporated, leaving dry salt. Best seen from the ferry to Yarmouth, Isle of Wight. Beaulieu, 6 miles east, has an old tide-mill on the Beaulieu River; also the famous Bucklers' Hard, a steep gravel beach on which wooden warships were built, then slid downhill into the water. Good inland yacht anchorage.

Salisbury Plain   **E6**
Wilts. A broad expanse of grassland on a chalk subsoil, occupying some 250 square miles of uplands north of Salisbury. Used today mainly for military training. The Plain is dominated by Stonehenge, Britain's finest prehistoric stone circle.

Thames Valley   **G3**
From its well-head source high on the Cotswolds near Tetbury, Gloucestershire, the stripling Thames winds gradually down past Oxford to cross the Chiltern Hills through the Goring Gap, close to Reading, Berkshire. Its upper vale is a broad grassy plain, studded with tall elms and quaint lopped willow trees.

Vale of Berkeley   **C3**
Glos. A level lowland plain running north west from Bristol along the course of the River Severn. It extends beyond Gloucester, to Tewkesbury. 50 miles long, though never more than 10 miles wide, it is framed by the steep Cotswolds on the east, and the Forest of Dean and the Malvern Hills to the west.

Rivers

The Bristol Avon   **D4**
Rising near Malmesbury, the 'Bristol' Avon follows a broad vale past Chippenham and Melksham to Bradford-on-Avon, where it enters its remarkable deep narrow valley cutting through the Cotswolds to join the Severn and out to sea at Avonmouth. Small craft can sail up it as far as Bath, and below Bristol ocean steamers cruise up through the Avon Gorge on its tidal flow. A splendid suspension bridge crosses from one limestone bluff to another at Clifton, west of Bristol.

The Hampshire Avon   **E6**
Despite its name, this river rises near Devizes in Wiltshire, flows through the fertile Vale of Pewsey, and then crosses Salisbury Plain southwards in a long narrow hollow to Amesbury, just below Stonehenge. Below Salisbury, where its water meadows form a fitting flat setting to the tall cathedral spire, it meanders down a narrow valley of drained pastures, just west of the New Forest heights, reaching the English Channel at Christchurch.

River Severn   **B3**
Glos. The Severn, Britain's longest river, comes down from Shropshire and the far Welsh hills past Worcester. It is navigable by barges and pleasure craft throughout Gloucestershire, and below Gloucester, the ancient bridgehead, it becomes tidal, broadening out to its great estuary. This is crossed, near Chepstow, by a 4-mile railway tunnel and the magnificent modern suspension bridge, 1½ miles long overall.

River Stour   **D8**
Dorset. Rising from a beautifully landscaped lake in the National Trust's property of Stourhead, south west of Mere in Wiltshire, the Stour meanders south across the fertile flat clays of Blackmoor Vale to Sturminster Newton in Dorset. Then it cuts right through the high range of the white chalk Dorset Downs at Blandford Forum, emerging at Wimborne Minster to wind behind Bournemouth to Christchurch harbour on the Hampshire coast. A fine trout stream, with some salmon.

Rivers Test and Itchen   **G7**
Hants. Small rivers these, flowing down narrow valleys in the Hampshire chalk downs, the Test from Whitchurch and Romsey, and the Itchen through Winchester. Flowing on either side of Southampton, they unite there as Southampton Water, a broad tidal estuary that can safely carry the world's largest passenger ships up to the busy docks and landing stages.

River Thames headwaters   **G3**
Oxfordshire, Berkshire, east Gloucestershire and north Wiltshire are all drained by the great River Thames or its tributaries, flowing slowly south east past Reading towards London and the North Sea. Near Oxford the main river, or Isis, stream is joined by the Windrush, Evenlode and Cherwell rivers from the north, and at Reading the Kennet comes in from the west. In past centuries the Thames was a major trade route; its flow was controlled by locks, and sturdy horses trod its towpaths, pulling barges. Today it is thronged with pleasure craft, which penetrate upstream as far as Lechlade in Gloucestershire, 350 feet above sea level. The Thames' source is a well beside the Cotswold highway, A473, 4 miles south west of Cirencester.

Canals

The Gloucester and Sharpness Canal
A 16-mile ship canal from Sharpness to Gloucester, this was the world's biggest canal (in cross-sectional dimensions) when built by Thomas Telford in the 19thC. It was

constructed to avoid the dangerously shallow and twisting course of the tidal River Severn, and still carries plenty of tankers and coastal barges. There are only two locks (one at each end) but plenty of swingbridges.

The Kennet and Avon Canal
This superb waterway linking London with Bristol is not at the moment fully navigable, and is the subject of a massive restoration effort by volunteers and BWB, who are steadily reopening more locks and more miles of navigable waters every year. It runs through delightful countryside, passing handsome towns like Hungerford, Devizes and Bath, and is ideal for walking. Things to see: outside Bath the elegant Dundas Aqueduct, carrying the canal over the River Avon. At Devizes the steam-operated Crofton Pumping Station and a flight of 29 locks on a single hillside; the bridges in the town are architectural gems. Horse-drawn barge trips from Newbury and narrow boat trips from Reading.

The Oxford Canal
A very pretty narrow canal running north from Oxford to Banbury, Rugby and Coventry, it opened up in 1790 a continuous transport link from Birmingham to London via the Thames. It thus had the same effect as the opening of the London to Birmingham railway in the 1840s and the M1 motorway in 1959. Engineered by James Brindley, the most famous of the early canal engineers, it winds about the countryside in a way that only Brindley's canals do. It is navigable throughout, and very popular among pleasure boaters.

The Thames and Severn Canal
Disused since 1927, this used to run from Lechlade on the River Thames to Cirencester, Stroud and the Severn Valley, piercing the Cotswold escarpment with a mighty tunnel. 2¼ miles long, the Sapperton Tunnel excited comment around the country in its day—it was even visited by the inquisitive King George III—and it remains the second longest canal tunnel ever built in Britain. The tunnel is easy to find just off the Fosse Way south of Cirencester close to the source of the River Thames. There are fine portals at either end, and a canal pub still stands by the eastern entrance.

The Oxford Canal at Chalgrove

Archaeological sites

Avebury   E4
Wilts. The largest of the great Neolithic henge monuments, of which Stonehenge is the best known. Avebury, which includes stone circles and earthworks, has been restored to give a clear picture of the original monument. From it the West Kennet Stone Avenue runs south eastwards, linking it with a second henge at The Sanctuary.

Chedworth Villa   E2
Chedworth, Glos. Chedworth is a classic example of a Romano-British country villa, and is one of the best preserved in the country. Two suites of baths survive, showing the usual method of Roman heating through piles laid between the short tile columns that supported the floor. There are

several mosaic floors; the finest has figures of nymphs and satyrs, with the four seasons in the corners. The north east corner of the site contains a 'nymphaeum', an ornamental fountain structure built over a spring. Finds from the excavations are displayed in the site museum.

Cirencester   E3
Glos. After London, Corinium Dubunnorum was the largest city in Roman Britain. The site of the old town has been excavated, and there are many finds in the museum. Sections of the city wall have been preserved in the abbey gardens; the amphitheatre is visible on waste land in the south west of the town. The Corinium Museum has a fine collection of mosaics, stone architectural decoration, and small objects.

Dorchester   C8
Dorset. Roman Durnovaria. Fragments of the town walls and ditches are visible; the Roman amphitheatre, capable of seating 10,000 people, was adapted from a late Neolithic or Bronze Age henge monument, the Maumbury Rings, and survives on the outskirts of the town. The Dorset County Museum houses local prehistoric and Roman finds.

Hod Hill   D7
Nr Blandford Forum, Dorset. Like Maiden Castle, Hod Hill belonged to the series of Iron Age hill forts taken by Roman forces (led by the future Emperor Vespasian) during the conquest period. At Hod Hill, a Roman garrison was installed in a small fort built into the north west corner of the hill fort; the outlines of this are still visible.

Maiden Castle   C8
Nr Dorchester, Dorset. One of the most impressive of the great hill forts constructed during the Iron Age. The complex system of earth ramparts and ditches, and the elaborate entrance defences, are still clearly visible. Excavation has provided dramatic evidence of the Roman siege in AD43, including a skeleton with a catapult bolt lodged in the spine. The defended circuit also contains an earlier Neolithic camp, marked by ditches with causeways across, and traces of a late Roman temple of the 4thC. Finds from the site are now in Dorchester Museum.

Old Sarum   E6
Nr Salisbury, Wilts. Old Sarum was abandoned as a cathedral city and the See moved to Salisbury (New Sarum) in 1217, after which the former site slowly decayed. The earliest visible remains are the outer earth ramparts of an Iron Age hill fort; there is some evidence of Roman occupation, but Roman Sorviodunum may lie on lower ground to the west, since Roman policy was to move local peoples away from defensible sites. Later a Saxon town was established on the hill, followed by a Norman town with cathedral and castle; it is these Norman remains which dominate today.

Portchester Castle   H8
Portchester, Hants. Portchester is the most westerly in the series of Saxon Shore forts built by the Romans in the later 3rdC, and the only one to retain its former commanding position over the sea. The entire wall-circuit survives, with much mediaeval retouching, and most of the massive semi-circular bastions and gate-towers. The site was adapted as a castle by the Normans, and a keep constructed in the north west corner.

Silbury Hill   E4
Silbury, Wilts. The highest man-made hill in Europe, this large mound at Silbury dates from the late Neolithic or early Bronze Age. Its purpose is unknown, even after many excavation attempts, but it may form part of the contemporary Avebury religious complex.

Stonehenge   E6
Nr Amesbury, Wilts. The most famous of Britain's prehistoric monuments. Stonehenge

has given rise to innumerable theories as to its use. The henge was constructed in several phases during and before the early Bronze Age; the circle and horseshoe now standing date from c1550BC. The massive blue-stones and sarsen stones that make up the circles are not native to the area and may have been carried by earlier glacial action rather than by any feat of ancient engineering. Contrary to popular belief, the Druids, who did not reach Britain till the 3rdC BC, had no connection with the henge; however, some religious explanation for the site is likely. Some of the vertical and cross stones still show the mortice and tenon shapings by which they were held in place.

Stonehenge

Wallingford H3
Berks. During the latter part of King Alfred's reign and that of his son Edward the Elder (late 9th–early 10thC), a system of fortified strongpoints (*burhs*) was established in southern England against the Danes. Wallingford was one of the largest of these, intended to protect a Thames crossing of great strategic importance. The town was defended within a rectangular enclosure of earth bank and ditch; the remains of these can be seen in the public park.

West Kennet Long Barrow E4
West Kennet, Wilts. The long barrow is a characteristic tomb used during the Neolithic period, consisting of a stone-built chamber and entrance passage covered with a long earth mound. West Kennet is one of the best-preserved of these, its chamber surviving intact and much of the walling still standing—despite the massive size of the blocks and the absence of any mortaring.

Footpaths & ancient ways

Harrow Way
The Harrow, or Hoar, Way was once the main route from Dover to the Devon coast. In mediaeval times the Pilgrims' Way took over the eastern section of the route, but in the west the ghosts of Celtic commercial travellers are still said to haunt the way. From Dover to near Basingstoke, Hampshire, the Way passes over the Downs to Weyhill and the site of the sheep fair where the Mayor of Casterbridge sold his wife in Hardy's novel. On to Salisbury Plain, close by Stonehenge, to Steeple Langford, Wiltshire, and Alfred's Tower (800 feet) overlooking Stourton and Kilmington. In Dorset, within 3 miles of Cerne Abbas, the Way joins the Ridgeway en route for

Icknield Way
Reputed to be the oldest trade route in England, the Icknield Way once stretched from the Wash to the Channel. Today it can be traced from Thetford in Norfolk to Cambridge, then to Letchworth and Tring in Hertfordshire, over the Thames near Streatley and along the line of the Berkshire Downs to the source of the Kennet in Wiltshire.
Most of the road has been Romanised, and the eastern section of the Way has either disappeared altogether or become a metal road, but there are still miles upon miles of beautiful walking country to explore. One of the finest sections for walking is along the green road from Upton to Wantage. On the Berkshire Downs the Way passes Blewbury, where Kenneth Grahame used to live.

The Ridgeway Path
This is one of the long-distance paths designated by the Countryside Commission. The path runs for 85 miles from near Avebury, in Wiltshire, by Barbury, Liddington, Uffington, Segsbury, Streatley, Princes Risborough to Ivinghoe Beacon in Buckinghamshire. It follows in part the prehistoric trackways that were the trade routes of ancient Britons and ancient drovers tracks. There are a number of burial mounds, long barrows, round barrows and Iron Age hill forts to explore along the way. There are fine views across the North Wessex Downs and the Chilterns. At Hackpen Hill the path reaches a height of 900 feet before it slips down to Barbury Castle below. Near Goring the downlands rise to over 700 feet with spectacular views over the Vale of the White Horse to the north. At Britwell the path joins the Icknield Way for 10 miles across Oxfordshire to the borders of Buckinghamshire, and then on to Ivinghoe Beacon.

Regional sport

Cricket
Broadhalfpenny Down, 2 miles north-east of Hambledon on the B2150 from Havant, is widely regarded as the birthplace of cricket as it is known today. The Hambledon Cricket Club was founded in 1760 and there is a monument to the club opposite the Bat and Ball inn. The Hampshire County Cricket Club continues the tradition and is one of the country's leading cricket teams. The county ground is at Banister Park, Northlands Road, Southampton, but they do use other pitches in the county for big matches. Details from the Secretary at Banister Park or Tel 23286.

Fishing
England's most famous trout stream, the River Test, flows through some of Hampshire's least spoilt countryside. Not surprisingly fishing here is expensive and mostly privately owned. Day tickets can, however, be obtained from the Greyhound Hotel, Stockbridge, 9 miles north-west of Winchester.

Sailing
Dorset and Hampshire is one of the finest maritime playgrounds in the world.

Poole Harbour, Dorset. This is the second biggest natural harbour in the world (Sydney, Australia, being the biggest). Superb dinghy sailing with good breezes uncluttered by trees and buildings. Parkstone Yacht Club races a wide variety of dinghies and will accept temporary members for a small monthly subscription. Contact the Secretary.
The Solent is the area of water bounded by the Hampshire and Dorset coast, and the northern coast of the Isle of Wight. There are yacht clubs dotted along every inlet from Lymington in the west to Chichester and Langstone Harbours in the east. Moorings for yachts and cruisers are expensive and the waiting lists are long.
Many clubs have temporary membership schemes, but the visitor is advised to obtain a list of clubs' secretaries from the Secretary, Royal Yachting Association, Victoria Way,

Sailing near Cowes

Woking, Surrey. Tel Woking 5022.
Cowes Week. This gigantic international festival of sail takes place at the beginning of August. Races are staged by individual Solent yacht clubs, but the whole thing is organised by a central committee. By tradition all the big classes of yachts are started from a line extending to seaward from the Royal Yacht Squadron Club House at Cowes.

Surfing
The Severn Bore, Glos. The Bore is an occasional tidal wave which races up the River Severn at speeds around 10 to 12 miles per hour and at a height varying from 6 to 10 feet. In recent years it has become a great challenge to surfers who have a wave they can ride (in theory!) for 6 or 7 miles.
A favourite starting point is the Bird in Hand Pub near Minsterworth where the A48 Gloucester/Chepstow road runs along the river bank for about 1½ miles.

Skin Diving
Swanage, Dorset. There is a diving school on the pier where you can take instruction and hire all the gear. Good safe diving.
Chesil Cove, Portland, Dorset. Exciting diving, deep and interesting. Wrecks and lots of life. Good facilities at Ron Parry's dive shop.

Festivals & events

There are a number of local festivals and events—contact the local Information Centre for details.

Canal race: Devizes to Westminster   E5
Devizes, Wilts. The Kennet and Avon Canal, built to link London to Bristol, is the route of an exciting and arduous canoe race from Devizes to Westminster. The toughest canoe race in the world; 125 miles non-stop in under 19 hours. The record is held by the Services. Because of the state of the canal in many places the first man home has to be as good on his feet as with a paddle. Parts are dry and the canoe has to be carried for as much as 1 mile. *Easter.*

The Cheltenham Festival   D2
Cheltenham, Glos. One of the most important festivals in Britain with many first-performance successes. The theme is new works by British composers, though equal time is given to established works. *Early Jul.*

Jersey Good Food Festival   K10
Jersey, C.I. Restaurants entering the competition are visited by a panel of French and English gourmets during a 2-week period and are awarded gold, silver or bronze plaques in the shape of a toque (chef's hat); the greater the number of toques the higher the commendation. *May.*

Purbeck Festival of Music   E9
Isle of Purbeck, Dorset. A free and easy miniature Glyndebourne in the Isle of Purbeck, with concerts given in the local village churches and country houses by amateurs and professionals. Wine and cheese and evening dress. *Early Aug.*

Southern Cathedrals Festival   G6
Festival of music presented by the combined choirs of Chichester, Salisbury and Winchester Cathedrals, and held each year consecutively in each cathedral. *Late Jul.*

Stroud Festival   D3
Stroud, Glos. Festival of religious drama and the arts, with a tradition of mixing professional and amateur performances. There are exhibitions of local arts and crafts and poetry readings. *Late Oct.*

Windsor Festival   J4
Windsor, Berks. Festivals at Windsor date from the 14thC jousting contests. Now the entertainment is strictly musical—with concerts and recitals by some of the world's leading musicians and singers. *Late Sep.*

Special attractions

Bourton-on-the-Water Model Village   E2
Bourton-on-the-Water, Glos. A delightful model of an equally attractive village. Both model and subject are built from the warm Cotswold stone, and the similarity between the two is quite staggering.

The Falconry Centre   C2
Newent, Glos. A magnificent collection of about 32 species of birds of prey. Fine museum, and courses given in falconry.

Frontier City   F4
Littlecote House, Hungerford, Berks. A real wild west town with all the expected buildings; sheriff's office and jail, saloon, livery stables with horses, gunsmiths and rifle range where you can try your hand. Also a museum, an Indian reservation with the occasional Indian, stage coach and covered wagon. Watch out for the cowboys who mosey into town from wild west clubs.

Great Western Railway Museum   F3
Faringdon Rd, Swindon, Wilts. Brunel, the great engineer, pioneered the GWR in the early days of steam. Historic locomotives of the time are shown with an interesting collection of Brunel mementoes.

Worldwide Butterflies   B7
Compton House, Sherborne, Dorset. Off A30. An historic house which has a palm house with a tropical indoor jungle and breeding hall full of butterflies from around the world living amongst the foliage. You can see the butterflies through all stages of their development. Also Britain's only silk farm next door at Lullingstone, where the silk for the robes of the last two coronations and many other Royal occasions was made.

Regional food & drink

Cakes
The English fascination with wrapping food in pastry is not confined to Cornwall. Banbury Cakes and Clifton Puffs are examples of mixed dried fruit pastries which are prepared in this way. Lardy Cakes abound in Wiltshire towns, lard traditionally coming from the local Wiltshire pigs.

Channel Islands food
The milk from the famous Jersey and Guernsey breeds of cow is delicious, with thick yellow cream. The islands are also famous for seafood particularly lobsters, crabs and mussels. There is a soup made from conger eels which are landed here. Because of the mild climate early new potatoes, tomatoes and fresh vegetables are produced in abundance.

Cheeses
Caerphilly. Although originating from Glamorgan, it is now made in the west country, and is a very mild-flavoured small, white cheese.
Cheddar. One of the most famous British cheeses which, although produced all over the world, is still made in this area, of which Shepton Mallett is the centre of the cheese industry. A pale yellow cheese of firm texture.
Double Gloucester. A smooth-textured honey-coloured or light red cheese with a somewhat fuller flavour than cheddar.
Dorset Blue Vinny. A strong tasting, deep blue veined cheese with a stiff crumbly texture. It is made from partly skimmed milk which is unusual in this country. Eat it with a local crispbread roll called 'Dorset knobs'.

Meat
Wiltshire is traditionally a 'pig' county. Bacon and hams were cured not only from the local Wessex saddlebacks, but also from overseas pigs who rested on the Downs en route for London from Bristol. A sausage industry has now been built up on this historical base. Venison from the deer of the New Forest is a speciality of Hampshire.

London's Country and Coast

3

This part of England depends largely on London but that doesn't mean it has been totally urbanised. Kent, Surrey and Sussex have some of the country's loveliest countryside; you can feel that men have cultivated it for centuries and that it has been inhabited for a very long time. The Romans lived here, St Augustine landed in Kent, the Saxons and the Normans made their presence felt. Arriving by sea from Europe, you will see all the basic Englishness of this part of the world; from the white cliffs at Dover to the trim hedges, rolling downland and cosy cottages. Now Britain is part of the European Community this is, more than ever, England's doorstep to the continent. Vulnerable and lovely countryside needs constant watching and the ancient towns and villages need vigilant care to save them from the advance of the metropolis, the motorways, and the juggernauts.

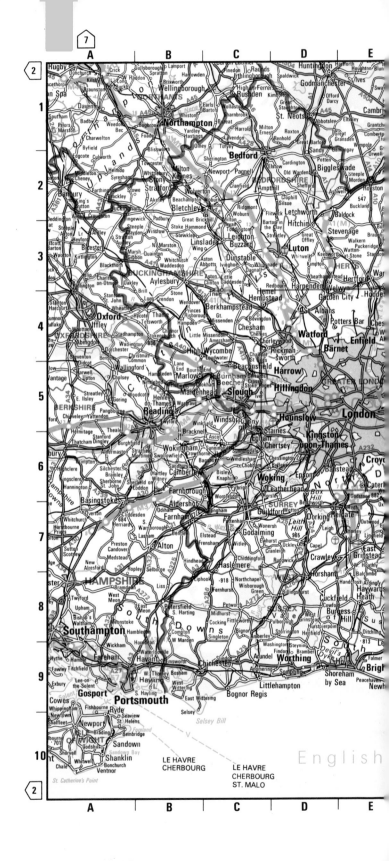

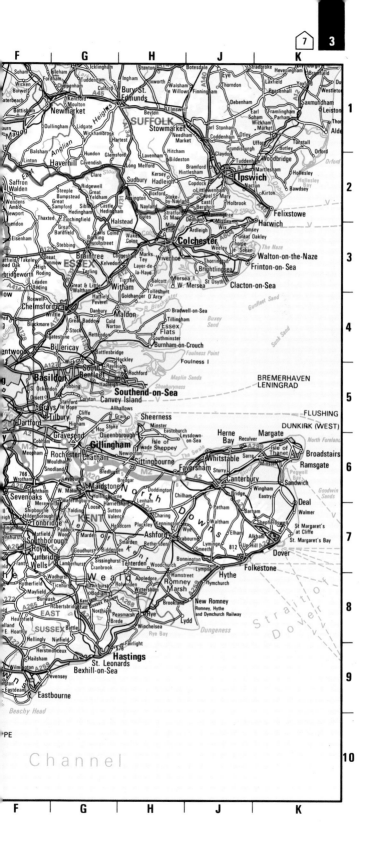

The coast

Allhallows G5
Kent. Pop 600. A weird and wonderful Thames estuary spot, once destined to be a Londoner's holiday resort: it never quite made it. Now it's the hinterland of industry and oil refineries—when the tide goes out there are miles of mud and vast numbers of sea birds. Beach: shingle and mud.

Beachy Head F9
E. Sussex. 500-foot-high chalk cliffs topped with smooth turf. Dizzy views from up here, but keep well away from edges—erosion makes them extremely dangerous.

Bognor Regis C9
W. Sussex. Pop 34,400. EC Wed. Oddly disconnected, Queen Victoria's 'dear little Bognor' was developed on a quiet scale in the 1820s a mile away from the original village of Bersted. A modest imitation of the bigger resorts. Probably the original of Jane Austen's 'Sanditon'. Unselfconsciously developed for the well-to-do, it didn't really fill up until the 20thC. There is a brand new leisure/entertainment centre on the seafront. Sandy beach with safe bathing except near the rocks at the western end.

Bosham B9
W. Sussex. Pop 3,200. EC Thur. Pron. 'Bozzam'. A full stop between two inlets of sea; flint, brick and tile-hung cottages huddled delightfully round the water's edge in Chichester harbour. The road on the south side of the village is flooded at high tide. From the tarred buildings on the quay there are fine views to the estuary with Turneresque sunsets. The Bayeux Tapestry depicts Harold setting sail from here to Normandy. Swimming is dangerous near the harbour.

Bosham

Brighton E9
E. Sussex. Pop 160,000. EC Wed, Thur. Like its more sedate neighbour, Hove, Brighton is a brilliant, beautiful town: the essence of the English seaside. The three miles of promenade by the sea have everything: indoor and outdoor pools, two piers (only one is still open), the world's first electric railway, waxworks and an aquarium. The latest developments are turning Brighton into an international centre with a commercial air—the new conference and entertainment centre and the huge yachting marina with its hydrofoil service to France. The town was built for relaxation and the Royal Pavilion was the Prince Regent's pleasure dome. A visit is a must; nowhere else in the West are there such sumptuous oriental rooms. The town is full of marvellous shops, antiques, Victorian churches, cinemas, parks and gardens. Brighton is only an hour from London on fast trains. Visit the Lanes, the Theatre Royal, Churchill Square, the museum and Preston Park.
Beaches: pebble with some shingle at low tide; life guards.

Brighton: Regency Square

Broadstairs K6
Kent. Pop 20,000. EC Wed. Uneven 19thC terraces, cottages and pubs focus on a pint-sized harbour hugged by a horseshoe of squat chalk cliffs. Here, in Bleak House, Dickens wrote 'David Copperfield'. More cottagey than the rest is Harbour Street, twisting its way through York Gate to a sandy foreshore.
The North Foreland Lighthouse, built in the late 17thC, is worth a look.

Clacton-on-Sea J3
Essex. Pop 38,000. EC Wed. MD Tue. Since the Victorians popularised the English seaside, Clacton has grown from a collection of villages into a thriving resort. The 1870s produced the Royal and Grand Hotels and the obligatory Marine Parade. Cheerful and busy, the pier has a switchback and all the amusements you need; there are band concerts and crazy golf.
Beach: long, sandy with diving boards and platforms.

Cuckmere Haven F9
E. Sussex. Beautiful estuary between white cliffs with an unspoilt shingle beach where bathing is safe away from the river. The valley of flat meadows is a real haven of peace, now part of the Seven Sisters Country Park.

Deal K6
Kent. Pop 25,500. EC Thur. A Tudor castle in the shape of a clover leaf, a steep pebble beach, the beat of military marches from the Royal Marines School of Music, and one of Britain's most modern piers. Once a Channel port, it was planned as two parallel roads front and rear, with a mesh of alleys criss-crossing the gap, and Middle Street snaking between the lot. It is claimed as the landing place for Julius Caesar's invasions. Of interest: the church of St Leonard, with distinctive cupola and splendid Pilot's Gallery (1685).
The steep beach, ideal for fishing, is safe only if swimmers stay close in.

Dover K7
Kent. Pop 34,000. EC Wed. MD Thur, Sat. One of the original Cinque Ports it is now the front door to Europe, breezy and businesslike. It spills inland from the harbour up a valley between chalk headlands. To the left are the famous white cliffs, whilst to the right is the mighty castle, dominating both town and harbour. The 13thC hostel for pilgrims, the Maison Dieu Hall, the Roman lighthouse and newly discovered Painted Villa are fascinating. Safe bathing with sand and shingle beach.

Dungeness J8
Kent. A windy promontory pointing into the English Channel; Dungeness is a ledge of gravel that is still growing. A quiet and lonely spot, although it has a bird sanctuary, two lighthouses and a mammoth nuclear power station.
Beaches: shingle, fishing safer than bathing. Strong currents.

Eastbourne F9
E. Sussex. Pop 70,500. EC Wed. An elegant resort of Georgian and Victorian character. Congress, Winter Gardens and Devonshire Park theatres present star-studded entertainment. Major international tennis tournaments are held here each year. Wooden groynes split the shingle beach into compartments; safe bathing.

Faversham H6
Kent. Pop 15,000. EC Thur. MD Wed, Fri, Sat. A market town, formerly a flourishing port, hung round a navigable creek of the Swale estuary. Dignified Georgian fronts to the houses hide fine 16thC details. The best are in Abbey Street and Court Street.
Shingle beach at Graveney Marshes to the north-east.
Look out for the interesting restoration of the gunpowder mill and the Fleur de Lys Heritage Centre.

Folkestone J7

Kent. Pop 44,000. EC Wed. MD Mon, Tue, Fri & Sat. An important cross-Channel port of unassuming terraces and gardens carved from the wooded chalk cliffs, it was developed in the middle of the last century as a popular seaside resort. Narrow old streets wind down to the original fishermen's quarters near the harbour. On the cliffs is one of the 74 Martello towers, part of a chain of small forts built to defend England from invasion by Napoleon. The 1¼-mile long promenade, the Leas, is complete with bandstand, pavilion and gardens.
Good sandy beach, safe and clean.

Folkestone

Harwich J2

Essex. Pop 15,000. EC Wed. A port for more than 10 centuries, the kind of place you usually pass through on the way to board a ship. A mediaeval street pattern with some Georgian houses and weather-boarded inns. Ships provide constantly moving scenery, the largest car ferries from Holland docking at Parkeston Quay. Lighthouses and a late 17thC treadmill crane are reminders of harsher seafaring days. Dovercourt is the seaside area.
Bathing on sandy beaches.

Hastings and St Leonards G9

E. Sussex. Pop 74,000. EC Wed. The old town of Hastings is one of the Cinque Ports. It is an intriguing collection of bent-backed houses and narrow twisting streets. On a sweep of the beach beneath the rugged cliffs are gangling timber-framed huts for drying nets—as elegant as the giants of La Mancha. Modern Hastings has good hotels, shops, entertainments, concerts, and Pelham Crescent, one of the most elegant crescents on the south coast. On the cliffs are the ruins of the Norman castle. Six miles to the north-west is Battle, the spot where William the Conqueror defeated Harold in 1066. St Leonards adjoins Hastings and is a unique example of a Regency new town planned and developed in the 1830s by James and Decimus Burton. Fashionable in the 19thC, its heart is the Royal Victoria Hotel on the sea front. A long valley of landscaped gardens climbs up from the sea front dotted with stately houses.
Look out for North Lodge, once the home of writer Rider Haggard, and the fairy-tale Gothic Clock House.
Beach: long—sand and shingle; safe bathing.

Pelham Crescent, Hastings

Hythe J7

Kent. Pop 12,000. EC Wed. Hythe is another of the original Cinque Ports. It lies half a mile inland in a commanding position riding a steep hill. A leafy place of narrow streets, with mellow 18thC buildings dominated by a large church with a celebrated 13thC chancel. Near the foreshore the mood changes from the homespun grid of streets on the hill to seaside-suburban. The home of the Romney, Hythe and Dymchurch Railway, the world's smallest public steam railway. Boating on the Royal Military Canal.
Beach: shingle and sand.

Littlehampton C9

W. Sussex. Pop 19,000. EC Wed. Little Victorian resort, once an important port, at the mouth of the fast flowing River Arun with excellent boatyards. Miles of safe, sandy beaches, particularly good across the river. Good fishing and boating.

Maldon G4

Essex. Pop 14,000. EC Wed. MD Thur, Sat. A compact little town on one of the few hills in Essex. The liveliest part of the town is by the River Blackwater where fishing and sailing boats cluster round the Hythe. Of interest are good 15thC buildings in the High Street, and the triangular tower of All Saints' Church—the only one in England. A very nautical air pervades, although the town is 12 miles from the open sea.

Margate K5

Kent. Pop 50,000. EC Thur. MD Tue (summer only), Thur, Fri. A bit of a dog's dinner now, but once popular with wealthy Victorians. The arrival of the Saturday Boat, which brought Londoners down for the weekend, was a great social event. This was the first of the villages on the Isle of Thanet to develop as a seaside resort. It was a local Quaker who invented the bathing machine in 1753. Development began in earnest in 1769 when Cecil Square was laid out. It soon became a resort for the 'nobility and persons of fashion'. In humbler streets behind the front there is a fantastic 19thC folly on Grotto Hill. On the front is Dreamland, a razzmatazz Disney-style amusement park. Wide sandy beach in front of a lively promenade with safe bathing.

Ramsgate K6

Kent. Pop 40,000. EC Thur. MD Thur, Fri. An old seafaring town, it is now a miniature Monte Carlo sprawled over two chalk cliffs with an artificial harbour for small boats. It figured prominently in the evacuation of Dunkirk in 1940 when 80,000 soldiers were landed at the port. West of the harbour are white cliffs capped by promenades and lawns. It has one of the finest Victorian churches in England, designed by Pugin. At nearby Pegwell Bay the hovercraft operates to and from France. Long sandy beach to the east of the harbour. Safe bathing.

Ramsgate

Rochester G6

Kent. Pop 56,000. EC Wed. MD Fri. An endearing old town, once a Roman settlement by a ford across the River Medway. The town grew in importance when it was made a bishopric by St Augustine in 604. The present cathedral was begun in 1077 on the site of his church. Also a busy thriving port.
Rochester is dominated by the Norman castle, set on a low cliff above the river, with one of the finest and best preserved keeps in England. It was at Gad's Hill, on the north west outskirts of the town, that Charles Dickens made his home. Note the Tudor building in King's School; and Restoration House, built 1587, where Charles II stayed on his way to London to claim his throne. See the brand new Dickens Centre in the old Eastgate House Museum.

Rye H8

E. Sussex. Pop 4,500. EC Tue. MD Thur. Set above a hill of sandstone rock, the Rye roofscapes leap-frog over each other in an ever-ascending scale to the apex of a church spire. A hill fort and an important port once washed by the sea, the town is now marooned in the flatness of the Sussex landscape, with the sea a thin line on the

horizon. There is still some of the smugglers' swagger left in the courtyards and cobbled streets. Of interest—18thC Water House, Town Hall, Ypres Tower, Lamb House, Mermaid Inn and 12thC church.
Safe bathing in calm weather from the shingle beach between Rye Harbour and Winchelsea Beach.

St Margaret's Bay   K7
Kent. The place to start if you want to swim across the Channel, as this bay is the nearest point to France. High crumbling chalk cliffs all round; shingle beach.

Sandwich   K6
Kent. Pop 4,500. EC Wed. MD Thur. A picturesque town, one of the original Cinque Ports and the chief harbour for the export of wool in the 13thC. It was nearly ruined by the silting up of the River Wansum in the 15thC and 16thC. Later prosperity was based on the Protestant clothworkers who arrived from France and Holland in 1560. Look at the quaint mid-16thC gatehouse with drawbridge.
Safe swimming at Sandwich Bay to the east. A sandy beach, one mile wide at low tide.

Selsey Bill   C9
W. Sussex. Fast eroding Channel headland with good fishing from a shingle beach. Once an island in ancient times. There is a tiny village almost engulfed by holiday camps. Since the discovery of a Greek amphora offshore, skin diving has become popular. The Saxons landed here in 477; so did St Wilfred when he aimed to convert the Saxons to Christianity.

Southend   H5
Essex. Pop 200,000. EC Wed. MD Tue, Thur. It is London's nearest seaside and everything is on a big scale. The pier is the longest in the world but the end burnt down and its future is in question.
The domed Kursaal is an amusement centre. At night the Golden Mile is less bright now but is still England's answer to Sunset Strip. As the town has grown is has consumed surrounding villages which remain, like Leigh-on-Sea, as quiet oases. When the town is full of day visitors it's a roaring bawdy place not suitable for the sensitive, but great if you like cockles. Beach: sand and shingle, muddy in places.

Whitstable   J6
Kent. Pop 25,000. EC Wed. MD Thur. Famous since Roman times for its oysters and as the harbour of Canterbury, it stands unselfconsciously on the southern side of the wide Thames Estuary. Developed first inland around its parish church, it spread out along the High Street to the shore itself. The transition from bay windows and brickwork to shipyards and sail lofts round old inns and narrow streets is sharp and hearty. And finally there is the sea, framed in weather-boarding or rigging and just about as exhilarating as ever in this quiet and sleepy town.
Stroll along the Sea Wall and Island Wall and the Street, a unique finger of land jutting out to sea. Safest place along the Kent coast for bathing. Shingle and sand beach.

Winchelsea   H8
E. Sussex. Pop 600. EC Wed. Late 13thC town replacing the original town swallowed by the sea in a series of violent storms. Only half built, it stands on a hill, an affluent backwater of green grass verges and neat Georgian houses. Defoe described it as the skeleton of an ancient city rather than a real town. The sea is now two miles away and kept in check by a sea wall.
Among notable features are three gates surviving from 13thC defences; the much restored Court Hall; the 14thC decorated parish church with some fine canopied tombs; a ruined Franciscan priory chapel. Long shingle beach to the south. Submerged obstacles and mud holes on the beach, but otherwise safe.

Worthing   D9
W. Sussex. Pop 88,000. EC Wed. MD Thur, Sat. In this residential holiday town, Georgian and Victorian terraces mingle with pleasant pedestrianed roads, but clash with a disastrous shopping centre.
Of interest: the museum, the theatre, fishermens' cottages in the east of the town. There is a 960-foot-long pier.
Beach: shingle and sand, safe for bathing.

Inland towns & villages

Alfriston   F9
E. Sussex. Pop 700. EC Wed. A muddle of half-timbered houses by the River Cuckmere under the shadow of the South Downs. The great church, its heart, sits astride an ancient Anglo-Saxon mound. Pre-heyday of the smugglers is the 14thC wattle-and-daub Church House, whilst the 15thC Star Inn is one of the oldest in England.
Of interest: a Saxon cemetery, long barrow and round barrow behind the little town.

Ampthill   C2
Beds. Pop 5,500. EC Tue. MD Thur. One of the best towns in Bedfordshire with some splendid 18thC houses. The castle where Henry VIII sent Katherine of Aragon to await her divorce has gone, but you can still walk beneath the 300-year-old oaks in Ampthill Park.
Look out for Avenue House in Church Street, a fine 1780 house with a magnificent garden.

Arundel   C9
W. Sussex. Pop 2,500. EC Wed. An important town before the Conquest, it's now pre-eminently Victorian. The mighty Norman castle is complete with crenellated keeps, embattled barbican towers and intact wooden drawbridge. Overlooking the valley of the River Arun with the town at its feet and backed by beech woods, it was painted by Turner and Constable.
The grandiose French Gothic of the Victorian cathedral adds light relief.
Of interest—14thC church of St Nicholas and remains of the 12thC priory.

Aylesbury   B3
Bucks. Pop 41,000. EC Thur. MD Wed, Sat. County town of Buckinghamshire; home of the plump white ducks and centre of the broad fertile Vale of Aylesbury. It is gaining in importance as a cruising centre for the Aylesbury arm of the Grand Union Canal. Now ringed with modern roads, an enormous new county office rears its vacuous head over the town centre. The 14thC King's Head is a marvellous inn: you can even take a drink sitting in Cromwell's chair.
Of interest: Roman exhibits at the Bucks County Museum, and the church of St Mary.

Bedford   C2
Beds. Pop 73,000. EC Thur. MD Wed, Sat. An unassuming town happily related to the River Ouse, which, flanked by gardens, wanders through the town. The nearby village of Elstow is where John Bunyan was born in 1628, and the Moot Hall houses a good Bunyan exhibition. In the library at Bedford manuscripts relating to Bunyan and 'Pilgrim's Progress' can be seen. The town has 4 old churches and 4 public schools.

Of interest: the Bedford Museum and the
Cecil Higgins Art Gallery.

Biddenden G7

Kent. Pop 2,000. EC Wed. An essay in half-
timbering with ancient weavers' cottages and
the mediaeval Cloth Hall, set in the Weald
of Kent along a homely village street, short
and perfect.
Of interest: 15thC Vane Court and 16thC
Castwisell Manor.

Bishop's Stortford F3

Herts. Pop 22,000. EC Wed. MD Thur.
Worth a visit for its maltings (where barley
was prepared and stored for beer making)
red brick and white weather-boarding with
fine towers.
Of interest: the 15thC church of St Michael
and the Old Vicarage where Cecil Rhodes
was born.

Canterbury J6

Kent. Pop 36,000. EC Thur. MD Mon, Wed.
Originally a large Roman town sited on
sloping ground where Watling Street forded
the River Stour. A centre for pilgrims from
all over Europe following Becket's death in
1170 until the destruction of the martyr's
shrine by Henry VIII. It was also a refuge
for many Flemish and Huguenot immigrants
in the late 16thC. The town and cathedral
suffered both during the Civil War and the
Second World War.
Of interest: Mercury Lane down which the
cathedral peeps; Christ Church gate sculpted
in ceremonial gear, adding a touch of dignity
to the small market
place. Through the gate
of the precinct, the
sudden splendour of the
Cathedral needs to be
seen to be believed.
And all around are
memories of Chaucer,
Falstaff and Cobbett.
Telling remains of
14thC and 15thC city
walls and the 14thC
Westgate, intact; ruins
of a Norman castle;
excavations of a Roman
town house; 16thC
Weavers' House; and
17thC Falstaff Hotel.
Associations with
Chaucer's Canterbury
Tales (c1387).

Chalfont St Giles C4

Bucks. Pop 7,000. EC Thur. John Milton
moved here in 1665 to escape the London
plague. Worth a visit to see his tiny cottage,
now a museum, where he wrote his epic
poems, 'Paradise Lost' and 'Paradise
Regained'. The village green looks
prosperous and there are good shops. The
church of St Giles has some wall paintings
from the middle ages.

Chelmsford G4

*Essex. Pop 58,000. EC Wed. MD Tue, Fri,
Sat.* The county town; not as steeped in
history as neighbouring Colchester but a
busy modern centre. The late mediaeval
parish church is now the cathedral and has
been restored and extended. The nearby
village of Writtle is worth a side trip for its
lovely pond and green. Visit the Chelmsford
and Essex museum and the Shire Hall.

Chichester C9

W. Sussex. Pop 21,000. EC Thur. MD Wed.
A Roman, mediaeval and Georgian city
dominated by the remains of the Roman
plan—two long, straight main streets crossing
at right angles. At their junction stands the
fine 16thC Market Cross, originally the
focus of a market place. An unspoilt town of
stately buildings, its cathedral stands to one
side of West Street and its 277-foot spire is a
focal point of the West Sussex coastal plain.
In the Bishop's Palace, the chapel and walls
of the great kitchen are 13thC and the
gateway 14thC. The 18thC Pallant House
and the Council House are stimulating.
Nearby is the Roman palace of Fishbourne.
Good Festival Theatre at Oaklands Park.

Chiddingfold C7

Surrey. Pop 2,700. EC Wed. Once one of the
centres of the mediaeval glass-making
industry set in the Weald near the Sussex
border, it's a large handsome village with a
row of bulky tile-hung Georgian cottages
facing a triangular green with a pond and a
14thC church.
Of interest: the 14thC Crown Inn in half-
timbering and the Manor House of 1762.

Chiddingstone F7

Kent. Pop 900. This almost intact
Elizabethan village is preserved by the
National Trust. It has timber-framed
buildings with barge-boarded gables and
pendants, brick nogging and all the niceties
of Tudor England. Interesting 18thC
rectory; also Chiddingstone Castle, a 19thC
restoration with Stuart and Jacobite pictures
and an Ancient Egypt collection.

Chilham J6

Kent. Pop 1,500. EC Thur. Reached by
narrow lanes, a handful of buildings grouped
casually around a small square on a narrow
plateau of land between church and castle.
Fine views through limes to the rolling
country around the River Stour.
Chilham Castle was built in 1616 by Inigo
Jones around a 12thC Norman keep.
Neolithic long barrow and, at Dane Street,
several handsomely-grouped farms with oasts
and half-timbered farmhouses.

Colchester H3

Essex. Pop 80,000. EC Thur. MD Sat. One
of the oldest towns in Britain. Colonised by
the Romans under Claudius in AD49, it was
here that Queen Boadicea, in AD61, led the
local tribes in a major revolt against the
Romans. The city walls are the chief visible
reminder of Colchester's Roman past,
particularly the massive Balkerne Gate. The
museum has a fine collection of Roman
relics including a rare gravestone of a
centurion. The keep of the Norman castle is
the largest in Europe, massive and splendid.
The town hugs the hill, its outline
punctuated by the tower of the Italianate
Edwardian town hall and the huge Victorian
water tower. Fine streets of 17thC and
18thC houses have been progressively sacked
by developers. Visit Bourne Hill, the 16thC
mill, Holy Trinity church with its Saxon
tower, and the Minories Art Gallery for
Constable drawings.

Dedham H2

Essex. Pop 1,700. EC Wed. The best little
town in Essex. Wander among the ancient
houses along the High Street and Mill Lane
towards the River Stour. St Mary's church
(1500) was often painted by John Constable.

Farnham B7

Surrey. Pop 31,500. EC Wed. A good
Georgian base topped by the domestic brick
buildings and Wayneflete Tower of Farnham
Castle. Two Georgian streets, West and
Castle, are full of fine houses; note especially
Willmer House, now a museum and a
vigorous example of Farnham Baroque.
Birthplace of that jolly radical William

Cobbett. Fine views of the Surrey countryside from the 500-foot-high Hogs Back on the road to Guildford.

Finchingfield G2
Essex. Pop 800. EC Wed. This is it, a perfect English village, with a church on the hill, duckpond, village green, haphazard lanes and gabled Guildhall—even a windmill to the north.

Godstone E6
Surrey. Pop 5,500. EC Wed. An unspoilt village green, only 19 miles from London. A little church, with a pretty shingled spire, among the trees. Almshouses by the church have a domestic chapel with a cosy fireplace in the nave to warm the inmates.

Goudhurst G7
Kent. Pop 3,000. EC Wed. A very pretty village surrounded by orchards and hop gardens, it climbs a hill with the village pond at the bottom and the solid sandstone church, a mixture of Classical and Gothic, at the top. The whole place is an encyclopaedia of Wealden building. Explore the 16thC Church House and discreetly handsome inn.

Goudhurst

Great Bardfield G2
Essex. Pop 1,000. There are three Bardfields; Great, Little and Bardfield Saling, all along the River Pant. Great Bardfield has a broad, sloping High Street, with a nice variety of mediaeval and Georgian houses. The 16thC museum has a good show of local crafts. A popular place for artists, it retains a bohemian air. Visit the 14thC church, Cottage Museum and the restored windmill.

Haddenham B4
Bucks. Pop 2,300. EC Wed. Unusual combination of good modern houses and fine old ones, built with the traditional local material, wichert (a chalky marl mixed with straw and water). Church and village pond on the edge of the green.

Hambleden B5
Bucks. Pop 1,600. The full feudal scene, from manor house to village pump. Look into the museum for Roman farm implements found nearby. Don't miss the great weather-boarded water mill, one of the few left along the Thames, and the huge church.

Harlow (New town) F3
Essex. Pop 80,000. EC Wed. MD Tue, Fri, Sat. One of the first of Britain's new towns started in 1947 to provide homes and jobs for Londoners. Planned by Sir Frederick Gibberd it pioneered pedestrian shopping areas, landscaping schemes for a whole town, and the first tower block of flats in Britain. Good modern sculpture by Moore, Rodin and Hepworth.

Hatfield D4
Herts. Pop 25,000. EC Mon, Thur, MD Wed, Sat. Hatfield new town has grown up only since 1947, but across the railway in old Hatfield small, plain Georgian houses mount the hill crowned by the Jacobean home of the Cecils. Inside the gates of Hatfield House a heady feeling of Elizabethan splendour survives, keeping the 20thC firmly at bay. Visit the 13thC church of St Etheldreda too.

Lewes E9
E. Sussex. Pop 14,000. EC Wed. MD Mon, Tue. Half in a hollow and half up a hill, dominated by the Norman keep of the castle, with the Downs rising all about it and the Channel beyond, it's very much the county

town. Important already in Saxon times, it was the site of the first Clunaic priory in England. The curious 16thC house at Southover was given to Anne of Cleves by Henry VIII after their divorce in 1540. It houses a collection of furniture, costumes and household equipment. The Bull House Restaurant was once the home of Tom Paine, the 18thC pamphleteer. Also see the Sussex Archaeological Trust's collection at Barbican House.

Little Gaddesden C3
Herts. Pop 1,200. A manor house of 1576 with trimmed yew trees; magnificent sweeps of beechwoods; and a 19thC Gothic extravaganza; all are found around this village. Ashridge House was rebuilt in 1809 by James Wyatt, and inside the chapel and dizzily high tower are superb examples of Wyatt's romantic Gothic work.

The Mardens B8
W. Sussex. Four tiny hamlets—hardly anything to them, but they have that indefinable something. East Marden, a handful of flint cottages and church in a cup-shaped hollow; North and Up Marden, church, farms and trees, whilst West Marden is larger with no church, but an armful of delightful flint cottages straggling up a hill. Lovely 13thC church at Up Marden, simple and dignified.

Marlow B5
Bucks. Pop 12,000. EC Wed. Walk straight on to the suspension bridge to catch the essence of Marlow. Here the Thames is at its best, crowded with weekend boatmen and swans. At the elegant inn, the Compleat Angler (named after the book of the same title written in 1653 by Izaak Walton) you can enjoy a riverside meal and then a stroll along the towpath or through the little Georgian and gabled town for tea. Makes a perfect English afternoon. A favourite haunt for anglers.

Mistley J2
Essex. Pop 2,100. EC Wed. An Essex town with strong leanings towards Suffolk. It stands on the River Stour, where at high tide the river is over a mile wide, and in autumn is graced by gatherings of hundreds of mute swans. Attempts to turn the town into an 18thC spa failed; only two elegant Adam church towers remain looking incongruous among the sturdy Victorian maltings. A tree-lined walk takes you into Manningtree, a neat Georgian neighbour famous for its sailing barges.

Mistley, Essex: The Adam Towers

Much Hadham E3
Herts. Pop 2,100. EC Wed. Essence of English country life as it is lived—by some. A street of sustained quality, full of well-maintained 18thC houses and 16thC and 17thC cottages. A country gentleman's house (1740) has the best name in the village, The Lordship, and lives up to it. This showpiece village was once the seat of the Bishops of London and their palace can still be seen.

Old Warden D2
Beds. Pop 500. A model village full of pretty thatched cottages, built for his tenants by the Victorian Lord Ongley. But the real reason for a visit here is the Shuttleworth Collection of old aeroplanes on the airfield 1¼ miles north-east of the village. On an exhibition day you might well see a genuine 1909 Bleriot actually flying.

Saffron Walden   **F2**
Essex. Pop 10,000. EC Thur. MD Tue, Sat.
Once a very prosperous town, its wealth
coming from the wool trade in the middle
ages and the growing of saffron for medicine
as well as a dye. Three splendid pubs, the
Sun Inn, the Cross Keys and the Rose and
Crown. The nature reserve at Hales Wood is
3 miles to the north-east. The great Jacobean
mansion of Audley End lies a mile to the
west in a beautiful landscaped park. Its
Great Hall and good picture collection are
well worth a visit.

St Albans   **D4**
Herts. Pop 52,000. EC Thur. MD Sat. Now a
busy centre of commuter territory, but you
don't have to look far to find over 2,000
years of history. Start with Verulamium, the
Roman city, now almost completely
excavated: the hypocaust (Roman underfloor
heating), mosaic floors, semi-circular theatre
and fine Roman walls make you wonder how
far the modern city really has advanced. The
dominant feature of St Albans is the great
abbey, with its long nave and short tower.
Some rare, recently uncovered, mediaeval
wall paintings cheer the solemn atmosphere
of the Norman nave; these were whitewashed
over by the Puritans. The town's modern
growth has emasculated much of the city.
Visit St Michael's Saxon church, Romeland
and Fishpool Streets and Gorhambury
House.

Shoreham   **F6**
Kent. Pop 1,900. EC Wed. Snug in the
saddle of land between long and high chalk
ridges thickly wooded with beech and oak.
By the old ford across the River Darent, half
a mile from the main road, stands the house
where Samuel Palmer, the painter, lived,
during his most creative period in the 1830s.
Of interest—the Old George Inn and Filston
Hall, a delightful and unusual 17thC moated
house.

Smarden   **H7**
Kent. Pop 1,000. Hospitable-looking half-
timbered cottages, terrace the street. The
14thC stone church at the west end has a
charming lych gate. Fine examples of half-
timbering in the Dragon House and
Chessenden. Interesting farmhouses in
Hamden (1¼ miles south-east), and Watch
House (1½ miles north-west).

Stoke Poges   **C5**
Bucks. Pop 4,000. EC Wed. Here is the
churchyard which inspired Thomas Gray's
'Elegy'. The monument to Gray is in a
meadow by the church; 18thC Stoke Park
with landscaped park is now a golf club.

Tenterden   **H7**
Kent. Pop 6,000. EC Wed. MD Fri. The
finest example of a traditional weather-
boarded and tile-hung Kentish town. A tiny
settlement in Roman times, it wasn't until
Edward III encouraged the Flemish weavers
to settle in England in the 14thC that the
town prospered. A small market town
situated on a ridge of high ground, it is one
very long High Street, with a mixture of
trees, pavements and wide grass verges. The
church stands about half way up. Basic
character remarkably well preserved. 14thC
Pittlesden Gatehouse is impressive. Also
18thC Westfield House and 19thC Town
Hall. Some fine 18thC headstones in the

churchyard. See the new local history
museum and the station for the Kent and E.
Sussex Steam Railway.

Thaxted   **F2**
Essex. Pop 2,000. EC Wed. A modest,
harmonious town of white plastered and
overhanging timber-framed houses and a
beautiful church that must be seen. The
Guildhall is a confident expression of 15thC
merchant competence. Also see Clarence
House opposite the church.

Thaxted. The Guildhall

Tunbridge Wells   **F7**
Kent. Pop 44,500. EC Wed. A rural hamlet at
the turn of the 19/18thC when people first
took the waters from its chalybeate spring, it
was rapidly developed into a fine Regency
spa. Almost unchanged today, the Pantiles, a
colonnaded promenade with raised music
gallery and lime trees, first laid out in
1638—the perfect pedestrian precinct.
See Calverley Crescent, built in the 1830s by
Decimus Burton, and the 17thC church of
King Charles the Martyr with fine plaster
ceiling, wooden cupola and clock of 1759.
Walk across the common to High Rocks, a
picnic area since the 17thC.

Ware   **E3**
Herts. Pop 14,700. EC Thur. MD Tue. John
Gilpin's horse brought him down this long
High Street following the River Lea. It is a
good gabled street which widens at the
Regency Old Town Hall. Here Lady Jane
Grey was declared Queen in 1553. The
church and nearby Fanhams Hall are worth
visiting. The Great Bed of Ware, 10 foot
wide and 11 foot long, now in the Victoria
and Albert Museum, originated here.

Welwyn Garden City   **D3**
Herts. Pop 40,000. EC Wed. The spirit of
reformer Ebenezer Howard lives on at
Welwyn. He wanted to build clusters of
towns that combined the virtues of town and
country. The town centre is worth a look.
Generously planned and planted, it's now
more garden than city.

Westerham   **.** **E6**
Kent. Pop 4,200. EC Wed. A small country
market town on a hill at the end of the
Darent Valley. Houses huddle round the
tapering green with the church as focal
point. General Wolfe was born here at
Quebec House in 1727, and nearby Winston
Churchill's house, Chartwell, was his home
until his death.

Regional features

Cinque Ports
The principal bastions of England during
the mediaeval wars with France, these five
ports were Hastings, New Romney, Hythe,
Dover and Sandwich. Rye and Winchelsea
were made Cinque Ports in the 14thC. As
their harbours silted up they lost their
power.

Hill Figures
Ditchling Cross. E. Sussex. 5 miles NW of
Lewes. Dating from the Battle of Lewes in
1264, when Simon de Montfort defeated
Henry III, it is a Greek type of cross 100
feet wide.
Litlington Horse. E. Sussex. Hindover Hill,
nr Litlington. The present white horse,
carved in the chalk hill, dates from about
1925. An earlier figure was cut for the
coronation of Queen Victoria, but no trace
remains.
Whipsnade White Lion. Beds. 1 mile N of
Dagnall. Cut into the chalk face of
Dunstable Downs, it is 500 feet long and

edged in cement. Modern.

Wilmington Long Man. Wilmington, E. Sussex. Carved into the chalk north face of Windover Hill overlooking the village, the gigantic threatening figure 231 feet high holds a staff in each hand. Origin unknown, but probably Saxon.

Wye Crown. Kent. 1 mile SE of Wye. Cut to celebrate the coronation of Edward VII in 1902, it is 240 feet wide.

Martello Towers
Kent and Sussex. A chain of 74 small forts built by the Royal Engineers between 1810 and 1812 as a defensive line between Seaford and Folkestone against invasion by Napoleon. Two-storeyed brick-built towers with a gun mounted on a revolving platform, they were about 30 feet high, 25 feet in diameter and 6 feet thick.

The design was based on the *Torre della Mortella* on the island of Corsica which impressed the English in the campaign of 1794. Each tower housed a garrison of 25 men in the upper part, with stores and ammunition below.

Oast Houses
Commonly found in Kent and Sussex they date back to the 16thC when brewing with hops was first practised in England. Formerly picked by hand, the hops ripen in late August or September. The green cones are dried to a 10 per cent moisture content by hot air for 8 to 10 hours in a special kiln, the oast house. This is usually circular, with a cowl on top which turns with the wind whilst a vent controls the ventilation. After drying, the hops are taken from the kiln, cooled, and pressed into sacks.

Hops are grown in the south-east chiefly in the Medway valley from Tonbridge through to Staplehurst, and in a belt from Faversham to Canterbury. Some of the best examples of the many thousands of oast houses are at Belting, Hadlow, Cobham and Boughton, Kent.

Chiddingstone, Kent.   *Boughton, Kent.*

Windmills
Good examples of post mills are at Chillenden, Kent; Clayton, E. Sussex; and at Pitstone Green, Bedfordshire which is the oldest dated mill in England. At Outwood, 5 miles south-east of Redhill, Surrey, is the oldest working windmill in Britain, which was built in 1665. Examples of smock mills are at Cranbrook, Kent; Shipley, W. Sussex; and Stansted Mountfitchet, Essex. Fine 55-foot-high tower-windmill in working order at Polegate, 4 miles north of Eastbourne, E. Sussex.

The Yeoman Farmer's House
Kent. Due to an abundance of oak in mediaeval times in Kent, and the simplicity of the technique of timber framing this type of house became a standard design for the prosperous farmer. The house often included a central hall with a tall window under jutting eaves. These eaves were supported by diagonal bracing from the inner sides of the projecting upper storeys. Typical examples are Hawkenbury Farm, near Staplehurst, Stoneacre, Otham, and Old Bell Farm, Harrietsham. But you can see others in most villages in the country.

Yeoman's House

Famous people

Anne Boleyn (1507–36)   **E7**
Hever Castle, Hever, Kent. A warm brick Tudor castle where Anne was born, still moated and wearing well. Now extended and improved by the Astor family, it is surrounded by beautiful gardens and a collection of Italian sculpture. Anne Boleyn was a lady of Henry VIII's court and she became his second wife. She only enjoyed Henry's company for three years. He tired of her, and she was beheaded. Hever has all the atmosphere of those dangerously elegant days. *Closed winter.*

Winston Churchill (1874–1965)   **E7**
Chartwell, nr Westerham, Kent. This house is where Churchill recharged his batteries during his wartime leadership, and it is the place he loved above all others. The house is not particularly distinguished, but it has long views over the Kentish Weald and is full of associations. The National Trust is careful to keep the house as it was when Churchill lived there. You can see the study where he wrote (usually writing standing up at a special desk), and rooms full of his own oil paintings. In the gardens is the fishpond where the elder statesman fed his carp, and you can examine the long wall which he built with his own hands, as a relaxing therapy after troubled wartime days. *Closed winter.*

Charles Darwin (1809–82)   **E6**
Downe House, Downe, Kent. Where Darwin lived from 1842 onwards, worked and wrote his controversial 'Origin of Species'. The 18thC house now contains relics and mementoes of Darwin and other scientists.

Benjamin Disraeli (1804–81)   **C4**
Hughenden Manor, High Wycombe, Bucks. Disraeli lived here from 1847 until his death in 1881. Contains much of his furniture, pictures, books and relics. Though he has a monument in Westminster Abbey, he is buried here.

Henry James (1846–1916)   **H8**
Lamb House, Rye, E. Sussex. Henry James felt that England fulfilled all his dreams of European civilisation, and Rye is very near perfection as an English town. After a spell in London, James moved to Rye where he bought the elegant simple 18thC Lamb House. *Closed winter.*

Rudyard Kipling (1865–1936)   **G8**
Bateman's, Burwash, E. Sussex. Built in 1634, the house contains furniture and relics of the writer. The surroundings are described in 'Puck of Pook's Hill'. There is also a working watermill.

Florence Nightingale (1820–1910)   **B3**
Claydon House, Winslow, Bucks. Florence would visit her sister Lady Verney at this house, owned by the Verney family since 1471. Her bedroom and belongings are on view, together with paintings of the Crimean War. The house itself is worth a visit.

Samuel Palmer (1805–81)   **F6**
Shoreham, Kent. The Water House, Shoreham, is where Palmer lived from the 1830s. One of England's finest pastoral painters, he was inspired by the peace and beauty of the countryside around Shoreham. His Shoreham Period was the most productive and creative of his life and the atmosphere of his Valley of Vision can still be sensed in this Kent village. Although his house is not open to the public a visit to this village gives all the background you need.

Cecil Rhodes (1853–1902)   **F3**
Rhodes Memorial Museum, Old Vicarage, Bishop's Stortford, Herts. The house where he was born now contains his possessions and collections illustrating his life and works and his effect on the history of South Africa and of Rhodesia, named after him.

George Bernard Shaw (1856–1950)   **D3**
Shaw's Corner, Ayot St Lawrence, Herts. This brilliant, witty playwright moved to Ayot St

Lawrence in 1906. The house is a simple late Victorian one in this quiet corner of Hertfordshire. Shaw's rooms are exactly as he left them, and his study and desk still keep the dry Fabian air of learning coupled with hard work. The village has a good inn and the beautiful Brocket Park is nearby.

General James Wolfe (1727–59) **E7**
Quebec House, Westerham, Kent. A mainly 17thC house where Wolfe spent his early years. Contains a collection of his possessions. *Closed winter.*

neckman, Quebec House

Cathedrals, abbeys & churches

Canterbury Cathedral **J6**
Canterbury, Kent. Mecca for pilgrims in the middle ages who visited the shrine of St Thomas à Becket. The place of Becket's martyrdom is marked by a plaque on the floor.
The cathedral was founded in 597, but nothing built before the Conquest survives. William of Sens, the great master-mason of the early Gothic style, was the architect of the choir and apse. A man of great ability and an ingenious workman in wood and stone, his design was as revolutionary in England as that of St Denis in France. Henry Yevele designed the nave in 1374. Externally the cathedral is dominated by the Bell Harry Tower designed by John Wastell in the late 15thC. In the Trinity Chapel on the south side is the magnificent tomb of Edward the Black Prince, Edward III's son who died in 1376. Canterbury is a treasure house of 13thC stained glass; the chapter house has a fine wooden ceiling; and the Perpendicular cloisters on the north have a solitary beauty.

Chichester Cathedral **C9**
Chichester, W. Sussex. Founded in 1080 it was much altered after the great fire of 1187 although the leisurely bay-to-bay rhythm of the original 12thC building has been preserved. Romanesque from end to end, it's an imposing feature in the flat landscape around, with the Downs a gently rising backcloth. Note the double aisles, resulting from former lateral chapels, fine central spire, Norman nave and Transitional retrochoir. The detached bell-tower is the only example in an English cathedral. Look out for the modern tapestry by John Piper and painting by Graham Sutherland.

Greenstead-juxta-Ongar **F4**
Essex. Famous as the only surviving log church in England, dated 1013. The nave is built of oak trees split vertically and set in an oak sill. The tower is timber too, weather-boarded outside with a sturdy spire.

Rochester Cathedral **G6**
Rochester, Kent. Unassuming cathedral on the edge of the old city, facing eastward across the Medway to the low line of the Kentish hills. Modest in appearance and dimension, its nave is plain Norman. Gradually developed from 1179 to 1240, whilst the central tower was built in 1904. Externally it has little distinctive craftmanship with the exception of a fine Norman doorway on the west. Inside, note the walled choir and several good tombs.

west doorway, Rochester   *Battle Abbey*

St Albans Abbey **D4**
St Albans, Herts. 11thC at its heart, the abbey has grown irregularly, resulting in the second longest nave in England. Built around the shrine of St Alban, the first English martyr, the central tower used red Roman bricks taken from Roman sites nearby. On the Norman nave piers are a rare series of mediaeval wall paintings that were covered with whitewash for centuries.

St Bartholomew **E9**
Brighton, E. Sussex. This is the kind of church that brings you to your knees. A great Noah's Ark of brick, rising to 135 feet, out-topping even Westminster Abbey. Inside, the local architect Edmund Scott built a completely plain brick church, unusual particularly for the 1870s, in that it depends only on size and proportion for its effect. The scale is Byzantine around the high altar with sumptuous plain slabs of marble and a dauntingly simple baldachino. Perfect 'arts and crafts' candlesticks and metalwork—the silver altar in the Lady Chapel is refined late Victorian work at its richest. This is a church that overwhelms with its own terrifying but simple grandeur.

St Lawrence Church **F4**
Blackmore, Essex. A carpenter's paradise—one of the most impressive timber towers in England. Go inside and look up the tower: a mass of great beams lead up to the belfry.

St Mary the Virgin **D8**
Sompting, W. Sussex. A famous 11thC church with a Saxon tower on the south slope of the Sussex Downs. The tower is topped by a Rhenish Helm spire which is unique in England. The rest of the church is late 12thC with good stone vaults and the whole place still has an untouched air of peaceful holiness.

Waltham Abbey **E4**
Waltham Abbey, Essex. King Harold was buried here after his defeat at the Battle of Hastings in 1066. The Norman nave remains but is a mere fragment of the great abbey that Henry II built to expiate the murder of Thomas à Becket. There is a massive majesty about the great stone piers and this has been enhanced by some good Victorian glass. The Burne-Jones east window is worth a special look.

Castles & ruins

Battle Abbey **G8**
Battle, E. Sussex. It was before the Battle of Hastings that William of Normandy vowed he would build an abbey should victory be his. The large abbey was consecrated in 1094 in the presence of William Rufus. Now only a few ruins remain, but it is very impressive. The high altar stands on the actual spot where King Harold fell in 1066. Note the Decorated style gatehouse, it is one of the finest in England.

Berkhamsted Castle C4
Berkhamsted, Herts. A favourite royal
residence up to the reign of Elizabeth I, only
the moat and earthworks now remain. The
11thC Norman castle was once host to
Thomas à Becket, Chaucer and the court of
Henry VIII.

Bodiam Castle G8
Bodiam, E. Sussex. Ten miles NW of
Winchelsea, it stands in a moat of water
lilies. Built in 1385 under the licence of
Richard II in case of possible invasion by
France. Octagonal in plan, it is approached
over an oak bridge which spans the moat. An
intruder would then be under fire from the
towers and have to pass the barbican and
cross a 10-foot moat, in order to storm the
main gatehouse. It looks intact but is only a
shell—a roofless but well preserved ruin. The
original iron-plated oak portcullis remains.
Owned by the National Trust. *Closed winter.*

Bodiam Castle

Deal Castle K6
Deal, Kent. A squat castle within thick walls,
it was the middle one of three castles, built
by Henry VIII, as part of a package deal of
20 forts built in 1540 as a defensive system
in case of invasion (prompted by the Pope's
call for a crusade against England following
Henry's break with the Church of Rome). It
was the largest and most elaborate of all his
forts; planned like a Tudor rose, and sunk
within a dry moat, it had 145 gun openings.

Dover Castle K7
Dover, Kent. The castle commands this
important harbour at the start of the shortest
sea route to the Continent. For centuries
Dover was the key to England, and vast
sums were spent on its fortifications. The
main fortifications of the castle belong to the
late 12th–13thC; the fine rectangular keep
was built in the 1180s—the first time that
concentrically arranged fortifications had
been used in England. The circuit of
enclosing walls was altered during the
Napoleonic period when the tops of the
towers were cut and the stumps strengthened
for gun emplacements. High up on the white
cliffs it stands frowning like a clap of
thunder. Don't fall off.

The keep, Dover Castle

Castle Hedingham G2
Essex. One of the mightiest castles of East
Anglia and still standing high above the old
trees as a reminder of Norman power. Built
by the powerful de Vere family in 1140, the
keep is one of the best preserved examples in
England. Very little could penetrate walls
11-foot thick, whilst 100-foot-high towers
would repel any invader. Over the moat a
15thC bridge leads into a Norman interior
with original zigzag decoration.

Herstmonceux Castle F8
Herstmonceux, E. Sussex. With imposing
towers and battlemented façade of
magnificent brickwork surrounded by a
moat, its external regularity is reminiscent of
the earlier Bodiam. Built in 1440 by Sir
Roger Fiennes, a civil servant under Henry
VI, it is richly evocative of Tudor England.
Main feature, a massive gateway. Dismantled
in 1777, it remained a ruin until extensively

restored in 1933. Now the home of the
Royal Observatory. The grounds are open to
the public in summer.

Unusual buildings

De La Warr Pavilion G9
Bexhill-on-Sea, E. Sussex. Built in 1933-6
and designed by Eric Mendelsohn, a leading
German architect, and Chermayeff. Amply
glazed, this is a pioneering product of
modernist design, with clean long lines
extending towards the sea.

Eton College

Eton College C5
Eton, Bucks. England's most exclusive and
best known school. Founded by Henry VI in
1440 it is a bastion of tradition and has
turned out many famous men. Worth a visit
for its range of courts and lovely chapel
which retains some rare wall paintings dating
from 1479. The college and its neighbour
Windsor Castle across the river are the last
remnants of the feudal past, and they're both
still thriving.

Gothic Temple B2
Stowe Park, Stowe, Bucks. Designed by
Gibbs in 1713, it is triangular in plan with
hexagonal turrets at the corners, the walls
between having castellated gables. The first
floor has a gallery with tall Gothic windows
looking out on to Stowe Park. Now in the
grounds of a school, but often open.

Lancing College D9
Lancing, W. Sussex. Founded by Nathaniel
Woodward, it was built high up on a
beautiful exposed site in 1848. Designed by
R.C. Carpenter in the Gothic tradition with
the right mixture of competence, sincerity
and common sense. The triumph is the
chapel, a massive monument in the French
style.

Lancing College Chapel

The Piers E9
Brighton, E. Sussex. The one original English
contribution to the seaside, beach and sea
apart, were these elegant cast-iron insects
striding out to sea. No seaside resort is a
proper one without a pier. Like the best of
Mississippi paddle steamers, but
permanently tethered to the land, they were
for landlubbers and sailors alike. Brighton,
not to be outdone, has two piers. West Pier
was built in 1868 and Palace Pier in 1891.
Now closed, the West Pier is sedately
classical in style. The Palace Pier, more
delightfully vulgar, swells out into a spacious
platform of sun decks, an amusement hall,
peep shows and a shopping arcade.
Unashamedly grand with elaborate façades,
white columns and golden-domed towers.

Royal Holloway College C5
Surrey. S of Egham on A30. This is the
largest Victorian building in the Home
Counties—built as one of the first Ladies'
colleges, in 1879, by a rich industrialist, it is
modelled on Chambord in the Loire Valley
and is made of red brick and stone. Its sheer
size is staggering—every young lady had two
rooms. Now they admit men and it's not
quite the same.

Royal Pavilion E9
Brighton, E. Sussex. Originally a house leased
by the Prince of Wales in 1786 and

redesigned by Henry Holland in an attractive Classical design with central rotunda and dome. In the early 19thC tastes changed. There was a diversion from the Neo-Classical to the architecture of India, China and Egypt as well as dabbling in castellated houses, rustic cottages and Italianate villas. Nash, commissioned to redesign the house, began in 1816 by throwing over the outline of Holland's building a richly oriental fancy dress with pinnacles, minarets and imposing onion-shaped domes. He mixed his motifs lavishly, especially inside, where the interiors are both Chinese and Gothic. Externally, it's more sedately Indian with the delicate pierced stonework and well-fed domes, an apparition in lime-green and cream (colours you always seem to come face to face with wherever you walk in Brighton). The inside is brilliant and ornate with sumptuous furnishings, and the mighty kitchens have been reconstructed.

Sham Church Folly C7
Peper Harrow, Surrey. A beautiful sham church ruin built by Lord Middleton in the mid-19thC in the form of a ruined east wall incorporating a genuine Decorated window in grey stone.

Shell Room and Grotto C2
Woburn Abbey, Woburn, Beds. Like a large stone igloo, with unglazed windows, star patterned floor and walls richly decorated with thousands of ormer shells. In the North garden, near the Chinese Dairy. Built in the 18thC.

Telegraph Hill D7
Chatley Heath, Cobham, Surrey. Before the days of the electric telegraph this signal post was one of 13 semaphore stations built to send messages from the Admiralty in London to the fleet at Portsmouth dockyards. The 75-foot-high hexagonal tower once had wooden arms on top which were worked by pulleys to spell out the messages.

University of Sussex E9
nr Brighton, E. Sussex. Opened in the 1960s, it was built by Sir Basil Spence in the 200-acre Stanmer Park. The best of the Oxbridge collegiate trappings (quadrangles and water) are gathered together in superb rolling downland with a backcloth of Rowland Hilder beeches. Has a round chapel based on the beehive tombs at Mycenae.

Houses & gardens

Ascott House C3
Wing, Bucks. A former hunting lodge set in charming grounds planted with unusual trees, thousands of naturalised bulbs and with a French formal garden. The house contains a treasure of French and Chippendale furniture, ancient Chinese porcelain, and paintings by Hogarth, Rubens and Gainsborough; all given to the National Trust by the Rothschilds. *Closed winter.*

Audley End F2
Saffron Walden, Essex. Thomas Howard, Earl of Suffolk, began the house in 1603. In 1720 Vanbrugh demolished the original house and remodelled the great hall. Later additions and decoration by Robert Adam.

Crittenden House G7
Matfield, Kent. A charming Kentish farmhouse garden surrounded by orchards. A cornucopia of ideas; a particularly interesting one being the conversion of 3 old pits into water gardens. *Irregular opening, summer.*

Great Dixter G8
Northiam, E. Sussex. 15thC half-timbered manor house. The gardens, designed by Sir Edwin Lutyens, are a connoisseur's delight full of fascinating plants, colour and fragrance—yew hedges, topiary and flower borders; naturalised daffodils and fritillaries; peonies, fuchsias, rose garden. *Closed winter.*

Hatfield House D4
Hatfield, Herts. One of the 4 or 5 major Jacobean houses in the country. E-shaped plan, with a plain front and lavish carving and stonework on the garden side. Traditional Great Hall with minstrels' gallery; the great staircase is superbly carved and covered with figures of cherubs and trophies. Full of tapestries and fine furniture as well as a collection of Queen Elizabeth I's belongings, including her silk stockings and gardening hat. *Closed winter.*

Hever Castle E7
Kent. 3 miles SE of Edenbridge off B2026. Small quadrangled castellated house with a surrounding moat, rebuilt 1462. Many recent additions and alterations but the exterior is unchanged. Home of Henry VIII's second wife, Anne Boleyn, it has a fine gateway and drawbridge and magnificent gardens with a 35-acre lake and fine collection of classical sculpture in the Italian garden. *Closed winter.*

Ightham Mote F6
Ivy Hatch, Kent. Set among trees and meadows, with peacocks in the gardens, a well preserved manor house of varied domestic styles blended ingeniously into a mediaeval and Tudor whole, with moat still encircling the house. The mediaeval part includes the 14thC Great Hall, in the east wing, entered from a courtyard, and the chapel and kitchen. *Open Fridays only.*

Knebworth House D3
Knebworth, Herts. The house is still lived in by the descendants of Sir Robert Lytton who started building it in 1492. The present outline of the house is Victorian and the elaborate exterior decorations, gargoyles and copper domes, have transformed the simplicity of the original red-brick Tudor building. Inside: 5 centuries of furniture, paintings, books and manuscripts. One of the finest examples of Jacobean panelling exists in the Banqueting Hall. The gardens and park contain a lot of the 'usual' stately home attractions.

Knole House F6
Sevenoaks, Kent. Half a mile from Sevenoaks and set on a flat plateau of land in the undulating blanket of a large park of deer, old oaks and beeches. This imposing large house, richly decorated and furnished, has one of the finest of Jacobean staircases. Built around 3 main courtyards with an entrance gate tower, it is one of a number of Jacobean great houses built, or extensively remodelled, during the early part of the 17thC. Originally an old manor house patched up by the Archbishop of Canterbury in 1456. The Archbishop then built himself a great new palace. Seized by Henry VIII in 1532 and substantially extended. The estate was granted to Sir Thomas Sackville in 1566 by Elizabeth I, and in 1604 he undertook the major remodelling of the whole estate. Virginia Woolf used it as a model for the house in her novel 'Orlando', the manuscript of which can be seen in the main entrance hall. Paintings by Van Dyck and Reynolds are among the collection.

Layer Marney Tower H3
nr Colchester, Essex. 1 mile S of B1022. The tallest Tudor gatehouse in England stands 8 storeys high in brick with unique terracotta trimmings. The house was never completed on its original scale and a range of smaller extensions was tacked onto the gatehouse. Surrounded by yew hedges and rose gardens. *Closed winter.*

Luton Hoo D3
Luton, Beds. Stands in a great park landscaped by Capability Brown. The view of the lakes from the house is a triumph of 18thC landscape art. The house was originally designed by Robert Adam but a series of fires and alterations make his work hard to find. The body of the main house is

now the creation of Mewes and Davis, architects of the London Ritz Hotel. The house stands today as a daunting display of Edwardian wealth, and houses a collection of treasures from mediaeval religious art to Fabergé's fabulous more worldly trinkets. *Closed winter.*

Mentmore Towers C3
Cheddington, Bucks. 8 miles N of Tring. The famous home of the Victorian Prime Minister, the Fifth Earl of Rosebery, which sprang into the news with the enormous auction of one of the world's largest collections of art treasures. Built in 1855 by Sir Joseph Paxton, architect of the Crystal Palace, it is now the home of the World Government of the Age of Enlightenment, an exhibition of whose work is on display.

Nymans Gardens E8
W. Sussex. S of Handcross 1 mile along B2114. A garden famous for its rhododendrons, magnolias and camellias. Especially noted for the shrub *eucryphia nymansay*, first raised here in 1915. Of interest to homesick Antipodians is the Tasmanian garden. National Trust. Pick up a leaflet on entering, to help you identify the plants.

Parham House C8
Amberley, W. Sussex. An Elizabethan mansion begun in 1577 by Sir Thomas Parham who sailed with Drake to Cadiz. A Tudor house in a Tudor landscape of big trees, bracken and deer, facing the bare Downs with a church on the lawn. There is a Great Hall with unusually tall mullioned windows and plastered ceiling; straightforward, but welcoming. Elizabethan, Jacobean and Georgian portraits. Fine walled gardens. *Closed winter.*

Paycocke's G3
Coggeshall, Essex. One of the best examples in England of a merchant's house of 1500. Impressive timbers and carving, and the inside glows with a collection of 16thC and 17thC furniture. National Trust. *Closed winter.*

Penshurst Place F7
Penshurst, Kent. The birthplace of Sir Philip Sidney (1554-86), soldier, poet and statesman. A typical, well preserved mediaeval manor house enlarged and added to in the Elizabethan period. A fine 14thC hall intact with screen at one end and dais at the other. Furniture, portraits and armour from the 15thC onwards. Terraced formal gardens, begun in 1560. *Closed winter.*

Penshurst Place

Polesden Lacey D6
Surrey. 3 miles NW of Dorking via A246. One of the loveliest gardens near London, with herbaceous borders, terraces and beech walks. Stroll along the terrace to see the superb view of Ranmore woods—English landscape at its best. The playwright Sheridan lived in a house on the site and his wife laid out part of the gardens. *Closed winter.*

St Osyth Priory J3
Essex. 4 miles W of Clacton on B1027. Glorious collection of monastic buildings around smooth lawns and gravel paths. No monks tread the cloister here, only peacocks; and inside, the present owner's sophisticated collection of jade is a far cry from monastic simplicity. Go for the great gatehouse, alive with sparkling flint patterns. *Closed winter.*

Scotney Castle G7
Lamberhurst, Kent. Off A21. A very romantic place like a scene from 'The Lady of Shalott'. A beautiful ruined castle surrounded by a moat filled with water lilies and fringed with ferns, set all around with acres of lovely gardens. Take a look at the

heather-thatched ice house used before the days of fridges and freezers. *Closed winter.*

Sissinghurst Castle G7
Kent. Off A202 E of Sissinghurst. The creation of Victoria Sackville-West and Harold Nicolson, it is one of England's loveliest sights incorporating small, highly individual walled gardens within a formal plan. Worth noting are the White Garden, herb garden and old fashioned cottage garden as well as the little nut grove. National Trust. *Closed winter.*

Stowe Park B2
Stowe, Bucks. England's genius for landscape gardening can be seen in all its splendour at Stowe. A verdant landscape full of elegant temples and monuments. Don't miss the Temple of Worthies where even King William III acquires a Greco-Roman look. All the best geniuses of the 17th and 18thC worked on the house: Vanbrugh, Robert Adam, William Kent and Grinling Gibbons. *Irregular opening.*

Uppark House B8
South Harting, nr Petersfield, W. Sussex. A red brick house with stone dressings built between 1685 and 1690 at the top of a valley within a mile of the crest of the North Downs. A Wren styled country house, comfortable to look at with landscaped grounds designed by Humphrey Repton in the 18thC, with pastures in one long sweep to the house walls like fitted carpets. Inside an unusually complete preservation of an 18thC interior. *Closed winter.*

Waddesdon Manor B3
Aylesbury, Bucks. Off A41. A country mansion built like a French château and surrounded by 160 acres of parkland. Built for Baron Ferdinand de Rothschild in 1880, its contents include paintings by Great Masters of the English, Italian and Dutch schools as well as Sèvres porcelain, furniture and carpets. Japanese Sika deer roam in the park and tropical birds fly in the aviary.

West Wycombe B4
West Wycombe, Bucks. N of High Wycombe on A40. A fine village of 17th and 18thC houses next to the house and park of the same name. The Dashwood family came into possession of the land in 1698 when the three storey Palladian house was built. The grounds were landscaped by Repton and contain a swan-shaped lake and temples. On a hill in the park the parish church stands next to a Mausoleum styled after Constantine's Arch in Rome. The infamous Hell Fire Club would meet in the golden ball on top of the church as well as in the caves in the grounds to practise satanic rites.

Woburn Abbey C2
Woburn, Beds. One of the stateliest stately homes of England, and even the incredible commercialisation cannot detract from the gracious view of the west front when you first see it across the landscaped park. Part of the house was demolished in 1950 but more than enough remains, including the richly decorated state rooms with Rococo ceilings. In the park is an amazing collection of buildings—standard trimmings for a stately home, including a Chinese dairy, shell grotto, ice house, sculpture gallery and of course a maze.

Wrest Park D2
Silsoe, Beds. For England this is an unusually formal canal garden; from 1706 it was laid out in radiating beds and canals, with long vistas leading to a series of garden ornaments. *Grounds only. Closed winter.*

Museums & galleries

Anne of Cleves House E9
High St, Southover, Lewes, E. Sussex. Picturesque half-timbered 16thC house holds an interesting collection of furniture, costumes, household equipment, ironwork and the Potter collection of chalk fossils.

Brighton Museum and Art Gallery E8
Brighton, E. Sussex. A fine collection illustrating Sussex archaeology and history; the Willett Collection of English pottery; 18thC furniture; British paintings of 19thC–early 20thC; watercolours and drawings.

Chelmsford and Essex Museum G4
Oaklands Park, Chelmsford, Essex. A mixed bag of a museum. Tunstill Collection of English drinking glasses; collection of eggs; 300-odd specimens of British birds; and a good collection of Roman Essex finds.

Colchester and Essex Museum H3
Colchester, Essex. The Castle, a mighty Norman keep built on the foundations of a Roman temple, houses an impressive archaeological collection from Essex and Roman Colchester dating from the Stone Age to the 17thC.

Elstow Moot Hall C2
Elstow, nr Bedford, Beds. Once used as a meeting-place and Sunday School of the Bunyan congregation, it now contains a fine 17thC collection associated with John Bunyan.

Potter's Museum D8
Bramber, W. Sussex. Macabre but enchanting taxidermy collection, first opened in 1861. It includes a series of tableaux of stuffed kittens, red squirrels, rabbits and rats in such settings as 'The Cock Robin Story'.

Royal Tunbridge Wells Museum and Art Gallery F7
Civic Centre, Tunbridge Wells, Kent. Delightful Victoriana—a permanent collection of paintings, garments worn by Queen Victoria, dolls, large dolls' house, bygones, prints of old Tunbridge Wells.

Smallhythe Place H7
Kent. 2 miles S of Tenterden on E side of B2082. Cosy half-timbered house of 1480, once owned by Dame Ellen Terry and now a memorial to her. The museum also includes relics of Irving, Mrs Siddons, David Garrick, other actors and actresses. *Closed winter.*

The Towner Art Gallery F9
Borough Lane, Eastbourne, E. Sussex. Good collection of paintings depicting Sussex scenes; delightful Georgian caricatures and the Bell collection of British butterflies.

Weald and Downland Open Air Museum C9
Singleton, W. Sussex. 5 miles N of Chichester on A286. A fantastic collection of historic 14thC–19thC buildings saved from destruction and re-erected at the foot of St Roche's Hill in 37 acres of meadows and woodlands. Includes two mediaeval farmhouses and a 16thC treadwheel. Nature trail and attractive picnic sites.

Botanical gardens

Bedgebury National Pinetum G7
Goudhurst, Kent. First planted in 1924, the forest consists of over 200 species of temperate zone cone-bearing trees laid out in genera. Of great use to foresters and botanists, it is sited in the lovely undulating countryside of the Weald of Kent.

Sheffield Park Garden F8
E. Sussex. 5 miles NW of Uckfield. A perfect English country environment. 142 acres of woods, parkland, gardens and 5 lakes, on different levels, originally laid out in the 18thC. There are colourful rhododendrons and azaleas, rare specimen conifers and eucalyptus; water-lilies, daffodils, bluebells, autumn flowers, and reputedly the ghost of a headless lady! *Closed winter.*

Wakehurst Place Garden E8
E. Sussex, 1½ miles NW of Ardingly on B2028. Owned by the National Trust and used as an extension of the Botanical Gardens at Kew, Wakehurst offers 476 acres of woodlands and gardens. A haven of exotic plants, trees and shrubs; ponds and lakes are linked by a watercourse.

Wisley Garden C6
Wisley, Ripley, Surrey. This is the garden of the Royal Horticultural Society where every possible form of gardening is indulged; there are experimental laboratories and gardens, and perfect examples of planting to delight and encourage all gardeners, from allotment holder to expert. Greenhouses and pinetum, rock garden and dazzling masses of azaleas, camellias, roses and rhododendrons. Also fruit and vegetable trials.

Zoos, aquaria & aviaries

Birdworld Zoological Gardens B7
Holt Pound, nr Farnham, Surrey. An attractive setting for a fine collection of birds from all over the world. There is also an aquarium of very varied fish.

Brighton Aquarium & Dolphinarium E9
Marine Parade, Brighton, E. Sussex. Over 80 tanks illustrating marine life, also very agile and intelligent dolphins and sea-lions.

Chessington Zoo D6
Chessington, Surrey. This constantly expanding zoo is always good for children. There are plenty of gardens, a miniature railway and the best thing is a splashy hippo wallow. Landscaped enclosures for tigers, leopards, pumas, penguin pool and a fine ape house.

Colchester Zoo H3
Stanway Hall, Colchester, Essex. Worldwide collection of animals and birds including orang-utans and giant tortoises, but especially good for big cats: lions, tigers and leopards. Also black panthers and cheetahs.

Flamingo Gardens and Zoological Park C1
Weston Underwood, Olney, Bucks. The largest collection of flamingos, waterfowl and cranes in the world. Rare animals on show include the Tibetan yak and Bactrian camel.

Mole Hall Wildlife Park F2
Widdington, Newport, Essex. In this small mixed collection, around a moated Elizabethan house, are some very rare woolly monkeys, snowy owls and several cat species.

Whipsnade Park Zoo C3
Whipsnade, nr Dunstable, Beds. 500 acres of animal park, good for wild horses, white rhinos, deer and gazelle. It is run by the London Zoo. Travel through the enclosures on the Umfolozi railway.

Woburn Wild Animal Kingdom C2
Woburn Park, Woburn, Beds. The largest game reserve outside Africa, covering 3,000 acres with animals roaming in enclosures. There's a lake full of hippos and sea-lions and chimpanzees living on an island.

Nature trails & reserves

Blackdown Nature Trail C8
W. Sussex. 1 mile SE of Haslemere, off Tennyson's Lane. Highest spot in the county with superb views to the South Downs; there are Scots pine, and oak woods, deer; meadow pipits, and yellowhammers.

Coombe Hill B4
Aston Clinton, Bucks. 17 miles W of Wendover S of B4010, leading from Chequers Court. This is a nature trail with the highest viewpoint of the Chilterns. There are spectacular views of Aylesbury and the woods surrounding Chequers.

The Devil's Punch Bowl Nature Trail C7
Nr Hindhead, Surrey. 150 yards N of traffic light on A3. In the magnificent open countryside of sandy soil, heath and gorse,

with pines on the higher ground and oaks on the lower ground, the trail starts at the National Trust car park.

East Head Nature Walk   **B9**
West Wittering, W. Sussex. There is a circular walk round the beach and sand dunes of this spit of land east of Chichester harbour. Dune reclamation work, mud flats and a fine assortment of wildlife can be seen along this coast. Start behind the beach west of West Wittering.

Hatfield Forest   **E3**
Nr Bishop's Stortford, Essex. Forest and lakes rich in wildlife. Fallow deer, badgers, tufted duck and teal. The trail starts at the Shell House by the lake. *Turn off B183 ½ mile W of Hatfield Broad Oak—entrance 2 miles.*

**Kingley Vale National
Nature Reserve**   **C9**
West Stoke, Chichester, W. Sussex. Largely chalk downland, it has possibly the finest yew wood in Europe. The trees are so large and cast such deep shadows that only very special flora grow there.

Maulden Wood   **C2**
Ampthill, Beds. A mixed coniferous and lush broad-leaved forest. The trail begins *1 mile N of Clophill on the A6, the main London–Bedford road.*

Birdwatching

Abberton Reservoir   **H3**
Essex. 4 miles S of Colchester on the B1025. Has the largest population of wildfowl in Britain: widgeon, Bewick's swan, smew, black tern, red-crested pochard. Access to the reservoir is restricted, but there are excellent views of the area from the nearby roads.

Beachy Head   **F9**
E. Sussex. S of Eastdean off A259. This chalk headland (575 feet high) is a magnificent spot from which to observe offshore sea birds: divers, terns, gulls; also warblers, flycatchers. The centre for migration studies in Sussex.

Blackwater Estuary   **H4**
Essex. Off the B1026 nr Goldhanger. A good spot for wildfowl, it has Brent geese, widgeon, shelduck, redshank and godwits. The best place to start is from the Bradwell Bird Observatory on the southern shore near Dengie Flats.

Dungeness   **J8**
Kent. S of Lydd on the ring road. A bleak promontory of shingle, gorse and brambles which juts into the Channel. A good spot to study bird migration; more than 6,000 birds are ringed here every year. Divers, common and herring gulls, Arctic and roseate terns, waders.

Sandy   **D1**
Beds. 9 miles E of Bedford near A603 1 mile from Sandy. The Lodge Reserve is the headquarters of the Royal Society for the Protection of Birds. It covers 104 acres of mixed woodland, parkland, heathland and valleys. Walk the mile-long nature trail and see the birds, including woodpeckers, nuthatch, redstart, chiffchaff, willow warbler, tree pipit and dunnock.

Swale Estuary, Isle of Sheppey   **J6**
Kent. This huge area of mudflats, salt and freshwater marsh, is marvellous for wildfowl along the sea walls, and freshwater waders on Windmill Creek. Sea duck off Shell Ness.

Tring Reservoirs   **C3**
Herts. 2 miles N of Tring. Once a marshland, it lies at the foot of the Chilterns. Famous for the breeding of the little ringed plover, it is now a National Nature Reserve. Tufted duck, goosander, waders, black terns, great crested grebe.

Brass rubbing

The following is a short list of churches that have brasses for rubbing. Permission is almost invariably required.
Bedfordshire. Cople, Elstow, Shillington, Wymington.
Buckinghamshire. Drayton, Beauchamp, Eldesborough, Eton College Chapel, Hambleden, Lillingstone Lovell, Stoke Poges, Thornton, Twyford, Upper Winchendon, Waddesdon.
Essex. Aveley, Chrishall, Latton, Little Easton, Little Horkesley, Pebmarsh, Stifford, Wivenhoe.
Hertfordshire. Berkhamsted, North Mimms, St Albans Abbey, St Albans (St Michael's), Sawbridgeworth, Standon, Watford, Watton-at-Stone.
Kent. Chartham, Cobham (18 exceptionally fine brasses), East Sutton, Graveney, Hever, Minster in Sheppey, Northfleet, Saltwood, Upper Hardres, Woodchurch.
Surrey. Beddington, Crowhurst, East Horsley, Stoke d'Abernon.
Sussex. Battle, Cowfold, Etchingham, Fletching, Herstmonceux, Trotton, West Grinstead.

Fossil hunting

Visit the local museum. Its fossil collection usually states where individual fossils have been found. When visiting quarries always seek permission to enter if they look privately owned or worked. Be careful of falls of rock.

Bognor Regis
W. Sussex. On the foreshore at low tide can be found Eocene lamellibranchs, corals, crustaceans, fish bones, etc.

Leighton Buzzard
Beds. Nearby pits and quarries contain ventricles of fossiliferous limestone up to 10 feet in length containing brachiopods, shells, ammonites, etc.

North Downs
Kent and Surrey. The chalk yields echinoids, brachiopods, sponges and ammonites. There are many quarries at the base of the chalk escarpment along the Pilgrims Way (vast and awesome pits at Snodland and Burham). Also search the cliffs between Folkestone and Dover (look in the gault of the famous landslip area of the Warren whilst you are here).

Sevenoaks
Kent. Pits of gault clay at Greatness and at Ford Place near Wrotham contain ammonites, belemites, gasteropods, marine worms and the occasional shark's tooth. Avoid a wet day—it gets sticky!

Swanscombe
Kent. Pleistocene bones and artefacts in nearby gravel pits.

South Downs
Sussex. Chalk pits under the ridge of the South Downs, notably at Arundel, Boxgrove, Burpham, Durrington, Friston, Houghton, Lavant, Lewes, Offham, Singleton.

Walton-on-the-Naze
Essex. The coastal cliffs of Red Crag give sharks' teeth, gastropods, lamellibranchs.

Forests

Ashdown Forest   **E7**
E. Sussex. Part of what was once the huge Roman Wealden forest of Anderida. There are 20 undulating square miles of wild heath, moorland, woodland and rocky outcrops. Iron country with hammer ponds in the valleys.

Burnham Beeches   **C5**
Bucks. 3 miles E of Maidenhead. 600 acres

with huge beech trees, it was once part of a vast forest that extended over the Chiltern Hills.

Epping Forest E4
Essex. 5,600 acres on the fringes of Greater London. A remnant of the vast hunting reserve for Saxon, Norman and Tudor kings, it was bought by the Corporation of the City of London in 1882. A place of sunlit glades, rough heaths and great hornbeam trees, it was much loved by poets like John Clare and Tennyson.

Hills

Box Hill D6
Nr Dorking, Surrey. A picnic spot on the North Downs popular since the reign of Charles II. John Evelyn, the diarist, praised its yews and box trees. It is one of the best viewpoints in Surrey. Many of the trees were cut in the 18thC when boxwood was used for wood engraving blocks.

Chiltern Hills
Bucks. A ridge of chalk that runs across the southern half of Buckinghamshire, with fine views, magnificent beechwoods and hospitable villages. Watch the gliders on Dunstable Downs.

Devil's Dyke D8
Nr Brighton, E. Sussex. A V-shaped cleft in the Downs with long views across the Weald. Legend has it that the devil, in an effort to quell the growth of Christianity, began to dig a trench through which the English Channel would flood the Weald. A woman watching him held up a candle and the devil fled, mistaking it for the rising sun.

Leith Hill D7
Surrey. 4 miles SW of Dorking. A long, high ridge of woodland with magnificent views and a 65-foot-high ragstone tower with brick surrounds. There are exhilarating walks along the top of the ridge.

North Downs
There are steep ridges of heavily wooded chalk facing the South Downs across the rolling landscape of the Weald of Kent, and Sussex. The rivers Wey, Mole, Darent, Medway and Stour cut through them. Their highest section lies between the Medway and Mole, whilst the eastern end is marked by the white cliffs of Dover. Westward they run into the Hog's back.

Seven Sisters F9
Nr Eastbourne, E. Sussex. These seven dramatic chalk cliffs over 500 feet high are the culmination of the South Downs. They are criss-crossed by fine walking tracks.

South Downs
Less wooded than the North Downs, they are cut by the rivers Arun, Adur, Ouse and Cuckmere. Southwest of Petersfield the Hampshire and South Downs meet. Higher and more wooded from there to Arundel, the South Downs end splendidly in the east at the Seven Sisters and Beachy Head.

Meadows & marshes

Essex Flats
South Essex. Once closely forested with oaks in the middle ages, now a large tract of low-lying land sliding muddily into the North Sea beyond marshes and creeks.

Romney Marsh
Kent. S of Ashford. A large flat expanse, now largely drained and used for sheep farming. Traversed by weedy dykes, it is dank and cold in winter, whilst heavy mists often descend on mid-summer evenings. Ideal area for smuggling until early in the 19thC. Sharp views to Rye and Winchelsea.

Runnymede
Surrey. Upstream from where the Colne enters the River Thames is the level meadow of Runnymede. It was here King John sealed the draft of Magna Carta in 1215. The memorial to President John F. Kennedy is on a hill above Runnymede as well as the Commonwealth Air Force Memorial.

Rivers

River Mole
Surrey. The Mole, a typical Surrey stream, rises in the Wealden Ridge near Gatwick Airport, and crosses the clay plain to Dorking. Then, between that town and Leatherhead, it follows the steep-sided Mole Gap through the chalky North Downs, clad in beautiful beechwoods, to join the Thames at Molesey.

River Ouse
Beds. Most of Bedfordshire lies in the basin of the Ouse, which is navigable all the way from Bedford town for 60 miles north to King's Lynn, a seaport on the Wash. A good boating and fishing river, it has been canalized throughout its lower course to protect the fertile fens from winter floods.

River Ouse
Sussex. A typical Sussex river, the Ouse rises on the Wealden Ridge near Haywards Heath, then crosses a flat clay plain to the county town of Lewes. Cutting a deep gap through the chalk ridge of the South Downs, it joins the sea at Newhaven, a leading harbour for cross-Channel ferries.

River Stour
Kent. Starting near Hythe, close to the south coast, the curious Stour winds north through Ashford and Wye, cutting a picturesque gap through the North Downs chalk hills. At the cathedral city of Canterbury it becomes navigable, continuing eastwards through level pastures to Sandwich, an ancient Cinque Port on Kent's eastern shore.

River Thames
The Thames and its tributaries drain the central region of the aptly named London Basin. Its main stream, made navigable by a system of locks and weirs, forms Buckinghamshire's southern boundary, with boating centres at Henley and Marlow in Buckinghamshire, and also at Kingston-on-Thames and Richmond in Surrey. There, becoming tidal, it plunges into metropolitan London, emerging near Tilbury as a great, commercial, tidal river bearing huge cargo ships, tankers and passenger-carrying craft. The Thames' main northern tributaries, which run south from the Chiltern chalk hills across the clay basin, are the Colne which drains western Hertfordshire, including St Albans, and the Lea, which flows through Luton (once Lea-town) and Hertford.

Canals

The Grand Union Canal
This is one of the better-known waterways of the south-east, and forms the busy trunk route from London to the Midlands. The canal begins at a junction with the Thames in Brentford, then undertakes a steady climb through 55 locks to cross the Chilterns escarpment near Tring, where a complicated system of reservoirs, streams and pumping engines exists to defend the 3-mile summit level against the constant loss of water incurred by the passage of boats through locks at either end. From here the canal drops down to the Vale of Aylesbury and the gentle farming landscape of Buckinghamshire. At Wolverton, on the Buckinghamshire/Northamptonshire border, the Grand Union crosses the River Ouse on an iron aqueduct and then begins the climb up to the Northamptonshire Heights. Best places to see the canal: Berkhamsted, with its houseboats and barges, locks and canal pubs; Wolverton, with the aqueduct over the Ouse;

and Marsworth, with its locks, canal junctions, reservoirs, workshops and canal pubs. An excellent and fascinating 9-mile walk would be to start at Tring Station and go down to Marsworth, then down the 16 narrow locks of the Aylesbury Arm to the basin in the town. The station is nearby.

The Royal Military Canal
This is one of the most amazing canals in England. It was in fact built by the British Government in the time of the Napoleonic Wars to form a line of defence against possible invasion and at the same time to form a useful military transport route for the garrisons based on the south coast. The canal starts at Shorncliffe (just west of Folkestone) and extends through Hythe and Rye to the sea near Winchelsea, thus describing a 30-mile arc around the great Romney Marsh. After the Battle of Trafalgar it became clear that the canal would be unlikely to be required for military purposes, but it was maintained just in case. It is now a favourite haunt of anglers and walkers, with boating at Hythe.

The Thames and Medway Canal
This long-defunct waterway runs from Gravesend to Strood, and used to offer traders an attractive alternative to the much longer route down the Thames Estuary and round the Isle of Grain. Principal traffic on the canal was carried in sailing barges, which would drop their masts and be hauled along the canal—often by men. The most interesting feature of the canal was—and is —the great tunnel between Higham and Strood, which carves its way through the ridge dividing the Thames and Medway estuaries. As built, the 4,100-yard tunnel was so long it became a severe bottleneck to barge traffic, which could only be worked through one way at a time. So the centre of the tunnel was excavated from the top, and a lay-by 200 yards long was created. The one tunnel thus became two relatively short tunnels, and the traffic flow was much improved. Later, when the railway from Gravesend to Rochester was built, the canal company was bought out and the two tunnels drained and converted into railway tunnels. Observant passengers on this line can still notice the unusual tunnel entrances and the brief five-second glimpse of daylight separating the tunnels.

The Wey and Arun Junction Canal
The Wey and Arun, which was built early in the 19thC to connect the River Wey near Guildford, Surrey, to the Arun near Pulborough, W. Sussex, used to provide a fascinating waterway route from the Thames to the south coast at Littlehampton, W. Sussex. A branch was also built from the Arun to Chichester Harbour, thus giving an inland route right through from London to Portsmouth. The canal did not thrive, however, and through navigation has been impossible for over 100 years, during which time the locks have become heavily overgrown, the aqueducts have collapsed, and the bridges have mostly been dropped. The canal is not entirely forgotten, for a canal society is now working to restore at least parts of it, but even seasoned canal-spotters have difficulty in tracing the route of the once busy navigation. 1-inch O.S. maps are essential for any exploration of the Wey and Arun Canal. There are plenty of ruined locks, many of them tucked away in woods, as at Dunsfold. And near Pulborough the energetic may even discover an abandoned tunnel.

Archaeological sites

Bignor Villa   C8
Nr. Petworth, W. Sussex. Roman villa built during the early 4thC on the site of an earlier house. It includes an unusually fine series of mosaics, one of them showing cupids in a gladiatorial combat. *Closed winter.*

Chanctonbury Ring   D8
W. Sussex. 1 mile SE of Washington. On the crest of the South Downs, a magical ring of beech trees planted in 1760 around an Iron Age hill fort. Occupied by the Romans in the 3rdC and 4thC, there are the remains of Roman buildings in the middle.

Cissbury Ring   D9
W. Sussex. 1 mile E of Findon. This Iron Age hill fort is an elongated oval defended by a great rampart and external ditch, with a smaller counterscarp bank outside the ditch. It was not used during Roman times, but hastily refortified with a turf bank during the early part of the dark ages. Views to the Isle of Wight and Beachy Head.

Colchester   H3
Essex. Camulodunum was the first Roman city built in Britain under Claudius in AD49–50. Excavations this century have uncovered a Roman street with a courtyard house in Castle Park; a temple, possibly to Mithras, was also found. The museum possesses the largest number of Roman relics gathered from a single site in Britain, and the castle which houses it is built on the foundations of the Roman temple to Claudius. The Roman Balkerne Gate is still visible.

Fishbourne Roman Palace   C9
Salthill Rd, Fishbourne, Chichester, W. Sussex. An outstanding Roman building covering an area of 250,000 square feet, built between AD71 and 80 at the head of the eastern arm of Fishbourne Creek. One wing of the building, with mosaic floors, and much of the Pompeii-like gardens have been conserved. Finds are housed in the museum on site. *Closed winter.*

Lullingstone Villa   F6
Kent. ¼ mile SW of Eynsford. Set on high ground to the west of the River Darent, with chalk ridges rising above it. Excavations have revealed much of this remarkable Roman villa. It has what must be one of the earliest private Christian chapels in Britain. Fine mosaic floor and other decorative features.

Pevensey Castle   G9
Pevensey Bay, E. Sussex. Here the Roman and Norman worlds are juxtaposed. Centuries after the Romans had left, the great walls were still strong enough for the Norman kings to build castles within them. The 12-foot-thick walls, enclosing about 10 acres, were considerably larger than most of the 'Saxon Shore' forts. The solid round-fronted bastions are irregularly spaced, but in such a way as to ensure that the wall between could be covered by cross-fire.

Repell Ditches   F2
Saffron Walden, Essex. A big attraction for archaeologists are the great earthworks to the west of the town in which 200 Saxon skeletons were found. This is the remains of the town of Waledana of the Ancient Britons. Nearby is a circular earth maze, one of the best surviving in England.

Richborough Castle   K6
Kent. Off A257 ½ mile N of Sandwich. Landing place of the Roman legions during the Claudian invasion of AD43. The walls now standing are those of the 'Saxon Shore' fort of the late 3rdC. Inside are defence ditches of an earlier 3rdC fort, and the foundations of a massive monument, built in the late 1stC, from which bronze letters and imported marble have been recovered. With Reculver, of which little is now visible, Richborough guarded the Channel between the Isle of Thanet and the mainland. A site museum houses excavation finds.

Roman Forts of the Saxon Shore
Girdling the coast of south-east Britain from Brancaster in Norfolk to Portchester in Hampshire was a chain of mighty Roman forts. There were at least 10 forts of which 9 survive, at Brancaster, Burgh Castle, Bradwell, Reculver, Richborough, Dover,

Lympne, Pevensey and Portchester. All are near the sea, usually at strategic points guarding the natural gateways of south-eastern Britain. Each could hold a substantial garrison, and adjoined a harbour from which a Roman fleet could operate.

Verulamium D4
St Michael's, St Albans, Herts. One of the finest Roman towns in England with many excellent buildings and sites. The centre was destroyed by Boadicea during the Icenian revolt. There are fascinating remains of the theatre with its colonnaded stage and auditorium, and of the town walls, which are visible. The Verulamium Museum houses a fine collection of Iron Age and Roman material.

Footpaths & ancient ways

North Downs Way
140 miles of footpath across Surrey and Kent which coincides with part of the old Pilgrims' Way, and runs along the escarpment of the North Downs. A long-distance footpath, it begins at Farnham, passing near Guildford, Dorking, Caterham, Wrotham, Chatham, Ashford, Folkestone, Dover, and then turns in a wide loop to Canterbury.
There are fine views southwards along the escarpment, rising to a height of over 700 feet at Netley Heath. The path leads over the cliff tops between Folkestone and Dover, and there is an alternate route around Lydden Spout Ranges to use on shooting days.

Pilgrims' Way
Stretching for 120 miles across Hampshire, Surrey and Kent, the Pilgrims' Way leads from Winchester to Canterbury, the centre of mediaeval pilgrimage, where stood the shrine of St Thomas à Becket. It follows the trackway, once the route of neolithic tribesmen, that ran from the Straits of Dover to Stonehenge and beyond. In places it coincides with the North Downs Way. The Way passes by Alton, Farnham, Guildford, Dorking, Redhill and Charing and along the lower slopes of the escarpment of the North Downs. Much of it is motor road today, especially in Hampshire. In Surrey and Kent, however, there are miles of country lanes bordered by hedgerows. But for the rest the Way leads across fields and skirts woodlands along shaded paths. In Sandy Lane, West Warren, it has become a hollow path rubbed away by centuries of pilgrim feet. In high summer the nettles grow 6 feet high and hawthorn, blackthorn, wild roses and barbed wire can bar the way. There are fine views from the top of Martha's Hill, 1 mile north of Chilworth, and the Way descends from there into the wood north-east of Shere, below Ranmore, emerging on Box Hill above Dorking. Villages along the Pilgrims' Way, like Chilham, still have their feudal aura intact. The best months to walk are April, May and June.

South Downs Way
The country's first long-distance bridleway, and escape route for the asphalt-weary, set aside for walkers, horse-riders and cyclists. It stretches for 80 miles across Sussex from Eastbourne to the Hampshire boundary in the west, following the South Downs with expansive views over the Weald for most of the way. Also good viewpoints at Devil's Dyke, Firle Beacon and Ditchling Beacon. To the south are rolling hills with an occasional glimpse of the sea. Westward the path leads through woodlands of deciduous and mixed forest. Fine views from Rackham and Bignor Hills, Cocking Down and Harting Down.

Regional sport

Bat and Trap
Canterbury, Kent. This game is one of cricket's ancestors and has been played around Canterbury for at least 180 years. It is played on a grass pitch 21 yards long. A batsman has to hit a ball through two posts 13½ feet apart. The ball is bowled underarm at the trap, which is a block of wood with a wooden plank pivoted like a see-saw. The batsman tees the ball up by hitting the trap and then the ball.
There are 46 active teams round Canterbury, playing from mid-April to mid-September. See the game played at the Golden Lion, Broad Oak or round Canterbury at the Rising Sun, Royal Artillery, Ye Olde Beverly, and Brewers Delight.

Cricket
Hampshire may have given birth to the rules of cricket, but nowhere is it played more widely than in Kent, as the number of towns which run cricket festivals bears witness to. Much of England's cricketing strength and following is drawn from south-east England. Kent, Sussex, Surrey and Essex all run first class teams. County grounds are as follows: *Kent County Cricket Club.* St Lawrence Ground, Old Dover St, Canterbury, Kent. Tel 63421.
Essex County Cricket Club. New Writtle St, Chelmsford, Essex. Tel 54533.
Surrey County Cricket Club. The Oval, Kennington, London. Tel 01-735 2424.
Sussex County Cricket Club. Eaton Rd, Hove, E. Sussex. Tel Brighton 732161.

Gliding
Dunstable Downs, Beds. Here you will find, on the steep north-west-facing slopes of the Chiltern Hills, the regular steady thermal lifts required to make an ideal launching ground for gliders. Flights and instruction can be arranged from the club on the Downs.

Motor Racing
Brands Hatch, nr Farningham, Kent. Shares with Silverstone the distinction of staging the British Grand Prix for Formula One racing cars in July, Brands being the venue in even-numbered years. The circuit is in constant weekend use for both car and cycle racing. Embryo Fangios can use the circuit on most Saturday afternoons, and all day on the first Wednesday of every month if they are in possession of an RAC competition licence and a crash helmet. Tuition is also available.

Polo
Cowdray Park, Midhurst, W. Sussex. This game on horseback originated in India and was brought back to England by the British Army, amongst whom it was very popular. The cost of the game these days is astronomical and none but the very wealthy can afford to play. It is, nevertheless, a most attractive spectator sport. Matches are played at weekends April–August.

Racing
Goodwood, W. Sussex. In the magnificent scenery of the South Downs, the 'Glorious Goodwood' meeting starts on the last Tuesday in July and is among the main events in the racing calendar.
Epsom, Surrey. This is the racecourse on the North Downs where the famous Derby and Oaks are run in early June. It is only in comparatively recent times that Parliament has stopped taking the day off on Derby Day. Other meetings in April and August.

Stoolball
Midhurst, W. Sussex. Around Midhurst, the old Sussex game of stoolball is still played. The game goes back to the 15thC and remained popular throughout the country until the 18thC when its place was taken by cricket. The games are similar, with 11 players each side; but in stoolball the ball is bowled underarm, the bat is like a table tennis bat, and the wicket is a stool, one foot square mounted on a stake 4 feet 8 inches from the ground. Summer evenings.

Festivals, events & customs

There are a number of local festivals and events—contact the local Information Centre for details.

Brighton Arts Festival
Brighton, E. Sussex. An early summer festival of music, theatre and the visual arts. *May.*

Chichester Festival Theatre Season
Chichester, W. Sussex. A much acclaimed festival season of plays, presented by a guest director and a company of distinguished actors, and performed in the bright modern Festival Theatre. *May–Sep.*

Dunmow Flitch
Dunmow, Essex. A side of bacon which is awarded to the couple who can vouch that they have not quarrelled for a year and a day nor regretted their marriage. The Flitch ceremony takes place on Whit Monday, every 3 or 4 years.

Glyndebourne Festival Opera
Glyndebourne, E. Sussex. One of the leading opera festivals in the world. An 800-seat opera house built alongside the home of Audrey and John Christie. Formal dress is the ritual, like the picnic supper in the gardens on the edge of the Downs. *May–Aug.*

Haslemere Festival
Haslemere, Surrey. A festival of early music played on 16thC, 17thC and 18thC instruments. Other old instruments can be viewed in the Haslemere Museum. Pay a visit to the workshops. *July.*

Olney Pancake Race
Olney, Bucks. Said to date from 1445. Legend has it that a woman hearing the church bell ran to church still clutching her frying-pan and wearing her apron. The Pancake Bell is still rung to summon competitors and the race starts at the Market Square. It is run over 415 yards, during which time the pancake must be tossed 3 times. At the same time a race is run in Liberal, Kansas, USA. Immediately after the race they phone up to see who has won. 11.45 am Shrove Tuesday.

Stour Music Festival
Wye environs, Kent. Unusual festival held in the heart of Kent. Rarely heard early music is performed in the local parish churches and country houses. Modern painting exhibition usually held in the church. *July.*

Tilford Bach Festival
Tilford, Surrey. The music of Bach and his contemporaries is performed in the parish church of Tilford. *May.*

Special attractions

Audley End House Railway　　　　**F2**
Audley End, Essex. Off the A11, 1 mile W of Saffron Walden. A 10¼-inch gauge miniature railway runs for nearly a mile through the wooded park, crossing twice over the River Tam. There are two steam locomotives and one diesel. *Closed winter.*

Bekonscot Model Village　　　　**C5**
Warwick Rd, Beaconsfield, Bucks. A superb miniature village of half-timbered villas and a few Georgian houses, inhabited by model villagers. The scale is not always consistent but the effect is delightful. There is also a miniature railway, dock, airport, zoo, racecourse and polo ground. Proceeds go to charity.

Bluebell Railway　　　　**E8**
Horsted Keynes, E. Sussex. One of the first standard gauge lines to be taken over by a preservation society. The railway runs to Sheffield Park Station 5 miles away. A very fine cross section of vintage and British Rail Steam Locomotives are operated. Lots of

Edwardian atmosphere with authentic adverts, oil lamps, etc. Beautiful scenery.

Courage Shire Horse Centre　　　　**B5**
Maidenhead Thicket, Maidenhead, Berks. Off A4. Impressive timber stables set around a courtyard with loose boxes and coach house. There is a farrier's shop and a collection of farm carts and implements as well as the hundreds of rosettes and the gleaming harnesses. See the display of cooperage—the art of barrel making, cages of fighting cocks and, of course the shire horses. *Closed winter.*

Hell Fire Caves　　　　**B4**
West Wycombe, Bucks. 2 miles NW of High Wycombe. These caves, cut out of chalk, achieved great notoriety in the 18thC as the headquarters of the 'Hell Fire Club', a depraved aristocratic set whose interest in Satanism terrorised the area.

North Foreland Lighthouse　　　　**K6**
Nr Broadstairs, Kent (1¼ miles N). Open usually in afternoon except Sunday and in fog. Permission from keeper required. Tel Thanet 61869.

The Romney, Hythe and Dymchurch Railway　　　　**J8**
Hythe, Kent. The railway runs 13¼ miles from Hythe to Dungeness Lighthouse. A 15-inch gauge line, it has an impressive collection of steam engines operating on a frequent and regular service during the summer months. Scenically the Romney Marshes may not be to everyone's taste, but the lonely atmosphere so close to civilization is intriguing.

The Shuttleworth Collection　　　　**D2**
Old Warden, Beds. 4 miles W of Biggleswade, 2½ miles off A1. About 50 historic aeroplanes including a Hawker Hurricane and Spitfire of World War II and a World War I Bristol Fighter. Also cars, motor-cycles, fire engines and horse-drawn carriages. Regular flying days during spring and summer.

Regional food & drink

Aylesbury Harvest Pie
Young rabbit stuffed with prunes, baked with bacon and onions and garnished with forcemeat balls.

Biddenden Cakes
Cakes, distributed at Easter, with an impression of Siamese twin girls who, 400 years ago, left land to provide for the poor of this Kent village.

Brown Shrimps
Native to the Kent coast, they are the same natural transparent colour as other shrimps, but turn brown when cooked. Easily caught at low tide at Camber Sands.

Cobnuts
In the autumn, Kent cobnuts, oval nuts wrapped in a green husk, are harvested. A smaller, wild variety can be found in hedgerows.

Dover Sole
Can be bought fresh in most eastern Kentish seaside towns, but a good place to buy this and other excellent fish still kicking is Hastings Fish Market.

Epping Sausage
Skinless sausage of pork and beef suet heavily flavoured with sage and spiced with thyme, marjoram and nutmeg.

Kentish Cider Wine and Barley Wine
Kentish cider (from the vast acreages of apple orchards) is sweet and very strong. Both this and barley wine are obtainable in the Weald of Kent in many inns. Barley Wine is extremely powerful stuff.

Whitstable Oysters
Whitstable has been famous for oysters since Roman times. Today the Royal Whitstable Native Oyster is world-renowned.

London

As well as being Europe's biggest city, London is by far the most varied and fascinating place in the world. Topographically London is a twenty mile shallow basin with the Thames crossing its middle. It is a collection of a thousand villages that somehow got joined together, and although eroded by the spread of anonymous development somehow these village centres remain. The city of London still has a separate identity despite massive rebuilding – only just curbed in time: you can still see St Paul's from the river. London grows and changes daily; it has immense vitality, friendly people, some of the most interesting shops ever and is full of theatres, museums, libraries, odd squares, quiet parks and some unexpected surprises.

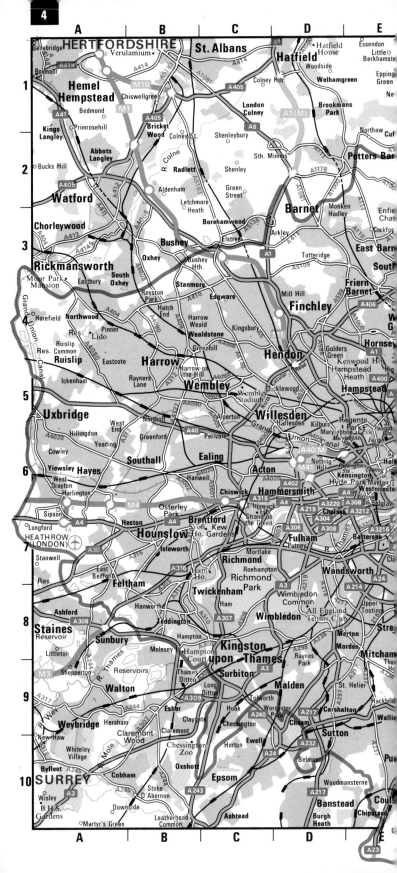

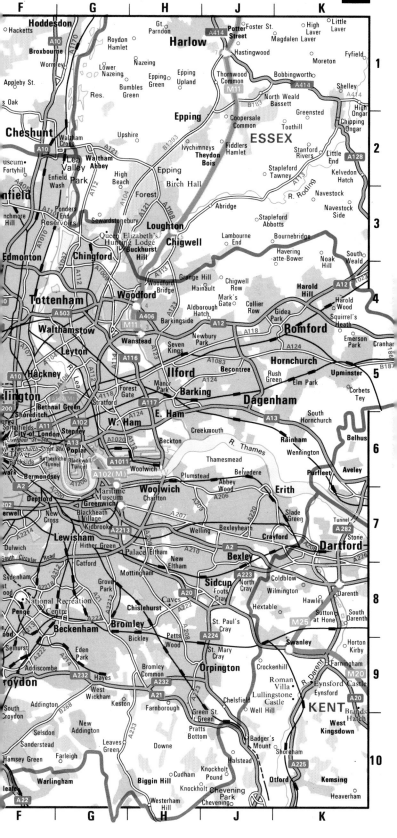

Districts

Bank EC2   F6
The commercial centre of London, this is the home of the Bank of England, the Mansion House, the Stock Exchange and head offices of banks and insurance companies. Just south is Wren's Monument to the Great Fire of 1666.

Bankside SE1   F6
Southwark. The Thames-side walk has the finest views of St Paul's and the City. An area of warehouses, docks, the Anchor pub, and the power station looking like a giant, forbidding fortress.
A plaque marks the site of Shakespeare's original theatre, the Globe. Cardinal's Wharf, a typical narrow cobblestone lane, is where Christopher Wren lived whilst building St Paul's Cathedral.

Belgravia SW1   E6
Handsome Regency squares, crescents, and mews: Eaton Square, Chester Square, Belgrave Square. Designed and built by Thomas Cubitt, 1825 onwards.

Blackheath Village SE3   G7
The Hampstead of the south with a broad common, remnant of a heath once popular with highwaymen, and a cosy row of village shops and houses in the vale. Here golf was introduced to England by James I in 1608.

Chelsea SW3   E6
It's the people not the buildings that attract, though most of the wanderers along the King's Road are probably tourists too. Some lovely Georgian cottages and typical late Victorian houses. Cheyne Walk and Tite Street were the places to live, with neighbours such as Carlyle, Rossetti, Whistler, Turner and Oscar Wilde who gave the place a colourful notoriety with their 'Bohemian' life-style. Georgian houses and some house boats along the waterfront.

Chiswick W4   C6
The Georgian houses beside the river stretch from Kew Bridge to Hammersmith. Originally there were three 18thC mansions with grounds down to the river—Grove House, Sutton Court and Chiswick House. Only the latter remains. Lord Burlington and William Kent who were largely responsible for the elegance of Chiswick are buried in St Nicholas' church. Chiswick Mall is still reminiscent of the wealthy riverside village.

The City EC4   F6
Known as 'the square mile', this was Norman London. It is now the centre of banking, insurance, commerce and international finance. Wren's great St Paul's Cathedral stands on the Ludgate Hill with commercial London spreading out around her. Wander down the alleyways off Carter Lane and you will get a taste of London before the Great Fire. History is about you everywhere, as this is the oldest part of London, there are even Roman remains.

Covent Garden WC2   E6
Originally designed by Inigo Jones as a residential square in 1638; the market buildings were erected in 1831. The smell of flowers, fruit and vegetables has faded from the steps of the Royal Opera House and Drury Lane now that the market has moved to Nine Elms. The area is now packed with fashionable craft shops, restaurants and artists' studios and the lovely old buildings near the Opera House have been turned into a shopping precinct.

Croydon   F9
The town centre is a massive concrete 'metropolis', like a mini Los Angeles. Good facilities for shopping and new office centres. Fairfield Hall is the theatre complex with some excellent productions.

Greenwich SE10   G7
The church which had a vast number of mediaeval relics was completely burnt out during World War II and most were lost as well as the famous 'Tallis Organ' (Thomas

Royal Naval College, Greenwich

Tallis musician, 1510–85, is buried here). In the park the Queen's House, a perfect example of neo-classical architecture by Inigo Jones, houses the National Maritime Museum.
Marked on the path in front of the Old Royal Observatory (founded by Charles II, no longer in use) is the zero meridian from which was calculated Greenwich Mean Time. In 1831 Charles Darwin set off aboard 'The Beagle' on a scientific expedition to South America. The 'Cutty Sark', one of the original tea-clippers, and Sir Francis Chichester's boat 'Gypsy Moth' are in dock near the pier.
Up to the 19thC the only dock system in existence was on the South Bank where the Great Howland dock had been built in 1696 to take the Greenland whalers. Most ships had to dock at the 'legal quays' where all cargo had to be disembarked between dawn and dusk. The India group of docks were opened in 1802 to cope with increased traffic and combat the smuggling which was rife in use as a result of the overcrowding at the legal quays. The royal docks followed from 1855. In 1909 the 3 companies which owned these dock areas privately merged into the Port of London Authority, which then had complete control. Today most of the docks are not in use and will soon be redeveloped.
A complex of superb buildings along the waterfront, formerly known as Greenwich Hospital, house the Royal Naval College. They were designed by Sir Christopher Wren and opened in 1705. The gardens of Greenwich Park were laid out by La Notre, designer of the gardens and park of Versailles.

Hammersmith W6   D6
The riverside Mall stretching from Hammersmith to Chiswick is the place to visit, with its boathouses, pubs and terraces of Georgian houses, including Kelmscott House where William Morris lived and founded his printing press. Hammersmith Bridge, built in 1887, is an ornate and gilded period-piece.

Hampstead Village NW3   E5
Still very much a village of Georgian houses and alleyways. Church Row, Holly Mount and Regency houses on Downshire Hill, including Keats' house, are notable. Hampstead Heath has always been a great attraction with Londoners. Also see the 18thC Spaniards Inn and Kenwood House.

Georgian houses, Hampstead

Highgate N6   E5
A picturesque cluster of Victorian and Georgian houses on top of a hill over-run by traffic. There are many pretty lanes and spacious residential roads. At the foot of Highgate Hill is a memento to Dick Whittington and his cat. See Waterlow Park and Highgate Cemetery.

Kensington W8   D6
Kensington High Street is the main thoroughfare—a busy shopping area. The

more interesting Church Street runs north with its antique shops and stolid stucco buildings. South Kensington centres around Exhibition Road with its massive Victorian museums.

Kew   C7
Elegant 18thC houses around a triangular green. Gainsborough is buried nearby in the churchyard of St Anne's. Tiny houses and pubs along the banks of the Thames at Strand on the Green. Across the green is the entrance to the world-famous Royal Botanic Gardens, better known as Kew Gardens.

Kew Green

Kingston-upon-Thames   C8
An ancient market town and Royal Borough with a gaudy Victorian market hall. Clattern Bridge dates from the 12thC.

Marylebone W1   E6
Nestled between Regent's Park, Oxford Street and Edgware Road, a mainly residential area with many fine 18thC streets and squares. Baker Street is here, home of that gentleman with the deerstalker, ulster and pipe—Sherlock Holmes. But Marylebone High Street is the centre of the once village —a narrow, winding street.

Mayfair W1   E6
An elegant quarter of Georgian and 19thC houses, bow-fronts and boutiques, bounded by Park Lane, Oxford Street, Regent Street and Piccadilly. Savile Row, Bond Street, Burlington Arcade, Berkeley and Grosvenor Squares and Shepherd Market are all here. Hotels and office blocks are encroaching everywhere, but Curzon Street retains some beautiful old houses.

Notting Hill W11   D6
An area of decayed elegance with many stucco buildings and tree-shaded squares. The main attraction is the Portobello Road market—few antiques these days, but much junk.

Richmond   C7
A pleasant almost rural town which has had long associations with royalty. Richmond Palace was a favourite with Elizabeth I. Other famous residents included Joshua Reynolds, first president of the Royal Academy, who had a weekend house here. Leonard and Virginia Woolf lived at Suffield House and set up the Hogarth Press (publishing among other things the early works of T. S. Eliot). The park of 2,400 acres has good herds of deer which Tudor kings once hunted. Private shooting was stopped in 1904. Fine views of the whole area from the main gate at the top of Richmond Hill. Take a trip on the river.

St James's SW1   E6
Once the precinct of the court of Charles II, where he played 'pellmell', and later developed in the 18thC. Famous for its gentlemen's clubs along Pall Mall, shops along Piccadilly and Jermyn and St James's Streets, and a quiet air of aristocratic self-assurance. Visit St James's Palace and stroll in St James's Park.

Soho W1   E6
A notorious and lively place of 18thC streets and undistinguished modern replacements. Old Compton Street is its exotic heart with superb food and wine shops; Wardour Street is the centre of the X-rated film industry; 'Chinatown' is around Gerrard Street; and Carnaby Street is for the purveyors of trendy gear. Strip clubs abound.

Spitalfields E1   F6
The infamous haunt of Jack the Ripper. The fruit and vegetable market remains, for the moment, in the centre of a once thriving area of artisans built up in the 17th & 18thC. Fournier Street has some fine examples of 18thC popular design. Wilkes Street is a haunted row of derelicts beside Hawksmoor's Christ Church, recently rescued from a certain death.

West End W1 & WC2   E6
Piccadilly Circus and Leicester Square are the hub of London night life—with numerous cinemas and theatres along Shaftesbury Avenue, and strip clubs and restaurants spilling over from neighbouring Soho. Frenetic, cosmopolitan and crowded, though once artistic. There are busts of painters and writers in Leicester Square, with Shakespeare in the centre.

Whitehall SW1   E6
A wide thoroughfare used for ceremonial and state processions—with Trafalgar Square at one end and the Houses of Parliament and Westminster Abbey at the other. In between are government offices including the Foreign Office, the Treasury and the Home Office. Also Inigo Jones' Banqueting House and the Cenotaph, memorial to the dead of two World Wars. Leading off Whitehall is Downing Street. The mounted sentries at the Horse Guards are a big tourist attraction.

The Horse Guards

Streets

Bond Street W1   E6
Mayfair's fashionable High Street. Originally laid out in the 1680s it no longer has any architectural distinction but is noted for its art dealers' galleries, fashion and quality shops.

Bow Lane EC4   F6
A huddled curve of Dickensiana full of small shops and cafés, squeezing nimbly past St Mary-le-Bow.

Burlington Arcade W1   E6
Piccadilly. 1819 Regency covered shopping promenade with original shop windows. Still employs a beadle to preserve the gracious atmosphere.

Carnaby Street W1   E6
Neon-lit extravaganza of boutiques, souvenir shops and cafés; now a pedestrian walk.

Cheyne Walk SW3   E6
One of the most famous streets in London. Fronting the river. Turner, Whistler, Thomas Carlyle, George Eliot, Henry James and Rossetti all lived here.

Chiswick Mall W4   C6
Delightful 17th–18thC riverside houses.

Downing Street SW1   E6
A 17thC street, leading off Whitehall, with houses built by Sir George Downing. No. 10 is the official residence of the Prime Minister; No. 11 of the Chancellor of the Exchequer.

Fleet Street EC4   F6
London's 'street of ink'. Has been associated with printing since the days of Caxton. All national and most provincial newspapers have their offices in or near it.

Hammersmith Mall W6   D6
Upper & Lower Mall. Boathouses, riverside pubs and terraces of Georgian houses, including Kelmscott House (1780) where William Morris, artist and leading figure of the 19thC Arts and Crafts movement, lived.

Kensington Palace Gardens W8 **D6**
A street of prosperous town mansions in the grand Italianate style, laid out by Pennethorne in 1843, but continued by other famous architects. No. 8a is by Owen Jones and Decimus Burton; No. 12a by James Murray; Nos. 18–20 by Banks and Barry; No. 13 by C. J. Richardson.

Kings Road SW3 **E6**
Chelsea's enticing hotch-potch, colourful as a rainbow. Expensive boutiques at one end, antiques and junk at the other.

Admiralty Arch

The Malls W1 **E6**
Processional way, from Admiralty Arch to Buckingham Palace, laid out by Sir Aston Webb as a national memorial to Queen Victoria.

Oxford Street W1 **E6**
An exhausting and exasperating mall of department stores and shoe shops amidst the rat race. One of the biggest, busiest, shopping streets in the world.

Pall Mall SW1 **E6**
Early 19thC opulence. This fine street and its surroundings express the confidence and wealth of the London of this period. Pall Mall itself contains two fine buildings by Sir Charles Barry; the Travellers Club, 1829–32 (Italian-Renaissance revival), and his more mature Reform Club 1837–41.

Reform Club *The Athenaeum Club*

Piccadilly W1 **E6**
A straight mile of polished complexities. Of interest—Apsley House; Wren's St James Church; Burlington House, home of the Royal Academy of Art; the Ritz Hotel; view to St James's Palace.

Queen Anne's Gate SW1 **E6**
Quiet, completely preserved 18thC street in its original state. Statue of Queen Anne near No. 13.

Regent Street W1 **E6**
Planned by John Nash in the early 19thC as part of one dashing curve from St James's to Regent's Park. Much altered grandeur with de luxe shops and airline offices.

Royal Opera Arcade **E6**
Between Pall Mall and Charles II St SW1. John Nash 1816, London's earliest arcade. Pure Regency; bow-fronted shops, glass domed vaults and elegant lamps.

St James's Street SW1 **E6**
Contains some of its original 18thC houses and shopfronts. The home of famous clubs, including Boodles (No. 28) 1775 by J. Crunden; Brooks's (No. 60) 1776 by Henry Holland.

Shaftesbury Avenue W1 **E6**
An enticing curve of colour and exotica built in 1880 with a liberal sprinkling of theatres. Named after the Victorian philanthropist, whose memorial is the Eros statue at Piccadilly Circus.

Strand WC2 **E6**
Once a 'strand'—a river-walk, bordered in Stuart times with mansions and gardens. Their names still survive in the streets: Bedford, Buckingham, Villiers.

Woburn Walk WC1 **E6**
Built by Cubitt in 1822 it's an elegant stucco terrace of bow-fronted shops.

Markets

There are so many markets in London that it would be impossible to mention them all here. These are some of the more famous:

Berwick Street **E6**
Soho W1. A bustling street market. Fruit, vegetables and general goods. *Open 8.00–19.00 Mon–Sat.*

Billingsgate **F6**
Lower Thames St EC3. London's fish market has been operating here since Saxon times. Present building 1876. The porters are famous for their strong language and strange leather hats on which they carry fish boxes. *Open from 6.00 daily. Sun—Shellfish only.*

Brixton **E7**
Electric Ave SW9. There's a distinct Caribbean flavour in the market with displays of exotic food, loud reggae music and secondhand clothes. Also general goods. *Open Mon–Sat. EC Wed.*

Camden Lock **E5**
Chalk Farm Rd NW6. On the banks of the Regent's Canal. A market full of antiques, bric-a-brac, junk and craft shops set around a pretty cobbled yard. Good hot food. *Open 8.00–18.00 Sat & Sun.*

Camden Passage **F6**
Islington Green N1. A paved and partly covered area of antique shops, stalls and arcades interspersed with restaurants. A fairly trendy area, therefore expensive. *Open shops 9.00–17.30; stalls 7.00–14.00 Tue, Wed & Sat.*

Club Row **F6**
Sclater St E1. The fish, fur and feather market. People have been selling dogs, cats, mice and other animals here for over 100 years. Further along there are more general stalls; china and household articles. *Open Sun mornings.*

Leadenhall Market **F6**
Gracechurch St EC3. An impressive glass and iron Victorian shopping arcade of 1881. Mainly poultry but also fish and plants. *Open 9.00–17.00 Mon–Fri. Sun—Shellfish only.*

Leather Lane **E6**
Holborn EC1. Very few leather stalls nowadays for a vast range of goods. *Open 11.00–15.00 Mon–Sat.*

Petticoat Lane **F6**
Middlesex St E1. A vast and colourful market which also encompasses the surrounding markets of Brick Lane and Club Row. Sells clothes and anything popular. Very crowded so go early. *Open Sun mornings.*

Portobello Road **D6**
Nr Notting Hill Gate tube. Half the street is full of antiques and junk and the other half fruit, vegetables and boutiques with some very bizarre clothes. *Open Sat only.*

Smithfield **F6**
Charterhouse St EC1. London's wholesale meat market and the largest in the world, covering 10 acres. The painted iron and glass buildings were erected in 1868. Not for the squeamish. *Open from 05.00 Mon–Sat.*

Spitalfields **F6**
Commercial St E1. The market was founded by Charles II in an area once famous for its silk weaving. Wholesale fruit and vegetables in one hall and flowers in another, in all covering 5 acres. *Open from 05.00 Mon–Sat.*

Courts & squares

Ball Court **F6**
Next to 39 Cornhill EC3. Straight out of Dickens. Simpson's Chop House built in 1757.

Bayswater W2 **D6**
Unpretentious Georgian squares and terraces built 1830–60.

Berkeley Square W1   **E6**
The adman's habitat full of grand trees and blandly indifferent buildings. No romantic nightingales left.

Bloomsbury Squares WC1   **E6**
Elegant Georgian houses and squares; Bedford Square, Russell Square, Tavistock Square. Built by Thomas Cubitt mid 19thC.

Cadogan Square SW1   **E6**
A typical 19thC Chelsea square of red-brick houses.

Fitzroy Square W1   **E6**
The south and east sides by Robert Adam 1790-94.

Leicester Square WC2   **E6**
Laid out originally as a Dutch garden in 1720, it's now a leafy and electric foyer to the cinema world. Trees full of starlings.

Trafalgar Square WC2   **E6**
Laid out by Sir Charles Barry, 1829. Nelson's column (granite) by William Railton 1840. Statue by Baily. Bronze lions by Landseer 1868. Fountains by Lutyens 1948. Famous for its pigeons, Xmas tree, New Year festivities and political demonstrations.

Wardrobe Place EC4   **E6**
A tiny 18thC world of gas lamps, plane trees and 18thC brick tucked quietly behind a slice of city backside.

Monument — Duke of York's column — Nelson's Column

Famous people

Thomas Carlyle (1795–1881)   **E6**
24 Cheyne Row SW3. The writer, known as the 'Sage of Chelsea', lived here for 47 years, where he wrote many of his best works. A tall, narrow building stuffed with original furnishings, manuscripts and relics. Cosy and lived in.

Charles Dickens (1812–70)   **E6**
48 Doughty St WC1. 19thC terrace house with relics of Dickens' life and writings. He lived here from 1837 to 1839.

William Hogarth (1697–1764)   **C6**
Hogarth Lane, Great West Rd W4. This 17thC country villa was the home of the master of British caricature from 1749 until his death. He is buried nearby in the churchyard of St Nicholas.

Dr Samuel Johnson (1709–84)   **E6**
17 Gough Square, Fleet St EC4. A simple 17thC brick house where he lived 1748–59, and wrote the 'Dictionary' in the attic. Relics and portraits.

John Keats (1795–1821)   **E5**
Wentworth Place, Keats Grove NW3. The poet lived here during his most prolific period 1818–20. He wrote his 'Ode to a Nightingale' in the garden.

Karl Marx (1818–83)   **E6**
His home at 28 Dean Street is marked by a blue plaque, but the place to see is seat No. G7 in the Reading Room of the British Museum, where he wrote 'Das Kapital'. Devotees also pilgrimage to his grave in Highgate Cemetery.

William Morris (1834–96)   **G4**
Water House, Lloyd Park, Forest Rd E17. The Georgian mansion where Morris spent his boyhood. Now a museum and gallery: textiles, wallpapers and designs by Morris and the pre-Raphaelites.

Florence Nightingale (1820–1910)   **E6**
Lived and died at 10 South St records the blue plaque. Her statue, with wrong type of lamp in hand, stands in Waterloo Pl.

Horace Walpole (1717–97)   **C8**
Strawberry Hill, Waldegrave Rd, Twickenham. The original 'Castle of Otranto'—a Gothic-Rococo fantasy created out of a simple 18thC country villa by Walpole and his friends, the 'Committee of Taste'. Now St Mary's Training College. *Visits by appointment only.*

John Wesley (1703–1791)   **F5**
47 City Rd EC1. Here the founder of Methodism spent the last years of his life. Much of his furniture and relics are here as well as the chapel he founded in 1778.

Cockney   F6

A Cockney is someone born within the sound of Bow Bells.
Rhyming slang was evolved in the East End supposedly by villains in the 1830s, and continues as a living thing. It consists of a repertoire of phrases (often only one word of which is used by the fluent, the other being understood and therefore not needed) rhyming with words which they replace:

believe	Adam and Eve
bird	Richard the 3rd
boots	Daisy Roots
boozer	battle cruiser
car	Lah-di-dah
copper	bottle and stopper
deaf	Mutt 'n' Jeff
dinner	Lilley and Skinner
dole	sausage roll
dope	bar of soap
drunk	elephant's trunk
ear	bottle of beer
eyes	mince pies
fire	Jeremiah
flowers	April showers
get pissed	Brahms and Liszt
hat	tit for tat
head	loaf of bread
house	cat and mouse
knickers	Alan Whickers
lips	apple pips
the missus	cheese and kisses
motor	kipper and bloater
phone	eau de Cologne
piano	Joanna
queer	ginger beer
road	frog and toad
scotch	pimple and blotch
shirt	Dickie Dirt
sky	apple pie
son	currant bun
stairs	apples and pears
steak	Joe Blake
suit	whistle and flute
table	Cain and Abel
tea	Rosy Lea
teeth	Hampstead Heath
thief	tea leaf
time	bird lime
umbrella	Aunt Ella
waiter	hot potato

Cathedrals, abbeys & churches

All Hallows-by-the-Tower   **F6**
Byward St EC3. Foundations date from AD675 audaciously restored by Lord Mottistone after bombing. Fine copper steeple. Crypt museum with Roman pavement.

All Souls Langham Place   **E6**
Langham Place W1. John Nash 1822–24. Corinthian columns with needle spire. Restored after bomb damage.

Brompton Oratory   **D6**
Brompton Rd SW7. Large Italian Renaissance-style church designed by H. Gribble 1884. Fine marbled interior and original statues from the Cathedral of Siena.

Chapel Royal of St John F6
White Tower, Tower of London EC3. The oldest church in London, c1085, original Norman.

Christchurch Spitalfields F6
Commercial St E1. Fine church by Hawksmoor 1723–25. Notable tower and spire, and lofty interior.

Grosvenor Chapel E6
South Audley St W1. 'Colonial'-looking chapel built 1730. Decorations by Comper added in 1912.

Holy Trinity E6
Sloane St SW1. By Sedding in 1890. London's most elaborate church of the 'Arts and Crafts' movement.

The Queen's Chapel, St James's Palace E6
Marlborough Rd SW1. Built by Inigo Jones 1623. Fine restored woodwork and coffered ceiling.

St Andrew-by-the-Wardrobe F6
Queen Victoria St EC4. Fine city church by Wren 1635–95. Restored after bomb damage.

st Andrew by the wardrobe

st Lawrence Jewry

St Andrew Undershaft F6
Leadenhall St EC3. Rebuilt 1532. Altar rails by Tijou, font by Nicholas Stone. Monument to John Stow, London's first historian.

SS Anne & Agnes F6
Gresham St EC2. Wren 1676–87. Attractive church restored after bomb damage.

St Bartholomew-the-Great F6
West Smithfield EC1. Norman choir of Augustinian Priory 1123 with later Lady Chapel: the only pre-Reformation font in the City. Tomb of founder (who also founded St Bartholomew's Hospital) and other fine monuments.

st Mary-le-Strand

St Clement Danes The Strand

st Martin-in-the-Field

St Bride F6
Fleet St EC4. Wren 1670–84. Famous spire 1701–04. Restored after bomb damage. Fine city church.

St Clement Danes E6
Strand WC2. First built for the Danes 9thC. Spire by Gibbs. Rebuilt by Wren 1681. Now the central church of the RAF.

St Clement near Eastcheap F6
Clements Lane, King William St EC4. Wren 1687. Restored by Butterfield 1872, and by Comper 1933. Notable 17thC woodwork and fine organ 1695.

St Cyprian E6
Clarence Gate NW1. Outstanding example of a complete church by Comper in his early style, 1903.

St Ethelburga F6
68–70 Bishopsgate EC2. Tiny church, late 14thC restored by Comper. Fine mural by Hans Feibusch (1693) on East Wall. One of

the City 'Guild churches' whose special concern is with mental and spiritual health.

St George Bloomsbury E6
Bloomsbury Way WC1. Hawksmoor 1731. Statue of George I on top of steeple. Restored in 1870. Six-column Corinthian portico. Classical interior.

St George's Hanover Square E6
Hanover Square W1. Classical church by John James 1721–24. Restored by Blomfield in 1894. Original of 'Last Supper' by Kent.

St George's Southwark F6
Borough High St SE1. A Georgian building with fine ornamental plaster ceiling. 'Little Dorrit's' church. Rebuilt 1734–36 by J. Price.

St Giles Cripplegate F6
Fore St EC2. 14thC church restored 1952 after bombing. Contains Milton's grave. Remains of London Wall in churchyard.

St Helen's Bishopsgate F6
Great St Helen's EC3. The 'Westminster Abbey of the City' built about 1212. Has some fine monuments and brasses.

St James Garlickhythe F6
Garlick Hill EC4. Fine city church by Wren 1687. Well-restored steeple 1713. Good ironwork.

St James's Piccadilly E6
Piccadilly W1. By Sir Christopher Wren 1684. Restored by Sir Albert Richardson in 1954 after serious bomb damage. Reredos, organ casing and font by Grinling Gibbons. Famous 'Father Smith' organ presented by Queen Mary in 1691 and brought from Whitehall Palace.

St Lawrence Jewry F6
Gresham St EC2. Wren 1670–86. Restored in 1957. Replicas of steeple and original Wren ceiling. Official church of City Corporation.

st Stephen walbrook

St Bride Fleet Street

st Magnus the Martyr

St Leonard Shoreditch F6
Between 118 & 119 High St E1. Rebuilt 1736–40 by Dance senior. Fine steeple.

St Luke Chelsea E6
Sydney St SW3. Savage 1824. Sumptuous early-Gothic revival.

St Magnus the Martyr F6
Lower Thames St EC3. Wren, 1671–87. Restored by Lawrence King. One of Wren's finest steeples, 185 feet high, added 1705–06. Baroque interior.

St Margaret Lothbury F6
Lothbury EC2. Wren 1686–93, steeple 1698–1700. Fine fittings, including an open-work screen. Bust of Ann Simpson by Nollekens.

St Margaret's Westminster E6
Parliament Square SW1. Rebuilt 1504–18. Splendid early 16thC east window and an excellent series of stained glass windows by John Piper. The parish church of the House of Commons.

St Martin-in-the-Fields E6
Trafalgar Square WC2. James Gibbs 1726. Famous spire and portico. Fine Venetian east window and white and gold moulded plaster ceiling.

St Mary Abchurch F6
Abchurch Yard EC4. Wren 1681–87. Fine ceiling by William Snow. Reredos by Grinling Gibbons.

St Mary Aldermary   **F6**
Watling St EC4. Late Gothic rebuilt by
Wren. Early 18thC. Fine fan vaulting with
saucer domes.

St Mary-at-Hill   **F6**
Lovat Lane EC3. Wren 1676. Tower 1788.
Box pews and magnificent fittings.

St Marylebone Parish Church   **E6**
Marylebone Rd NW1. Thomas Hardwick
1813–17. Thomas Harris added the chancel
in 1884. Imposing white and gold interior.

St Mary-le-Bow   **F6**
Cheapside EC2. The church of 'Bow Bells'
fame by Wren 1680. Restored by Lawrence
King after bomb damage. Superb steeple.

St Mary-le-Strand   **E6**
Strand WC2. James Gibbs 1714–17. A
perfect small Baroque church in the middle
of the road.

St Mary Woolnoth   **F6**
*Junction of Lombard St & King William St
EC3*. Remarkable 1716–27 Baroque church
by Hawksmoor. Church of England services
on weekdays. Guild church.

St Olave Hart Street   **F6**
8 Hart St EC3. Pre-'fire', Samuel Pepys'
church, 1450. Restored by Glanfield after
bomb damage. Fine vestry and crypt.

St Paul's Cathedral   **F6**
EC4. Wren's greatest work: built 1675–1710,
replacing the previous church destroyed by
the Great Fire.
Superb dome,
porches and
funerary
monuments.
Contains
magnificent stalls by
Grinling Gibbons.
Ironwork by Tijou,
paintings by
Thornhill and
mosaics by Salviati
and Stephens. Crypt
and galleries.

St Paul Covent Garden   **E6**
Covent Garden WC2. Fine 'ecclesiastical
barn' by Inigo Jones. Rebuilt by T.
Hardwick after fire of 1795. Memorials to
actors through the ages. Pleasant gardens at
western (entrance) end.

St Peter-upon-Cornhill   **F6**
Bishopsgate Corner EC2. Very fine church by
Wren 1677–87. Oldest church site in City,
reputedly AD179. Organ (built by Schmidt):
famous for Elizabethan music. Fine carved
screen. 14th and 15thC plays performed at
Christmas.

St Stephen Walbrook   **F6**
Walbrook EC4. Masterpiece by Wren,
1672–79; steeple 1714–17. Dome, with 8
arches, supported by Corinthian pillars, all
beautifully restored. Lord Mayor of
London's Church.

Southwark Cathedral   **F6**
Borough High St SE1. Much restored. Built
by Augustinian Canons 1206. Beautiful early
English choir and retrochoir. Tower built
c1520, nave by Blomfield 1894–97. Contains
work by Comper (altar screen).

The Temple Church   **F6**
Inner Temple Lane EC4. Completely
restored. 12thC round nave and 13thC choir.
Fine recumbent effigies. Reredos by Wren.

Westminster Abbey   **E6**
Broad Sanctuary SW1. (The Collegiate
Church of St Peter in Westminster). Original
church by Edward the Confessor 1065.
Rebuilding commenced by Henry III in
1245 who was largely influenced by the new
French cathedrals. Completed by Henry
Yevele and others 1376–1506 (towers
incomplete and finished by Hawksmoor
1734). Henry VII Chapel added 1503; fine
'Perpendicular' with wonderful fan vaulting.

Westminster Abbey

**Westminster Roman Catholic
Cathedral**   **E6**
Ashley Place SW1. Early Christian Byzantine-
style church by J. F. Bentley, 1903. The
most important Roman Catholic church in
England. Fine marbled interior.

Historic buildings

Abbey Mills Pumping Station   **G5**
Abbey Lane E15. An unusual building of
cupolas and domes built in 1865 to pump
the 83 miles of sewers draining the 100
square miles of the City of London. This
remarkable piece of engineering still survives
intact and perfect.

Albert Memorial   **E6**
Kensington Gardens W8. A vast monument to
the Prince Consort opposite the Royal Albert
Hall. 175 feet high with a bronze statue, and
lavishly ornamented. Sir George Gilbert
Scott 1876.

Apothecaries Hall   **F6**
Blackfriars Lane EC4. Built 1670 with 18thC
renovation. Through the entrance arch is a
charming, quiet churchyard. Inside some
fine panelling and paintings. The
Apothecaries Society, one of the City livery
companies, was founded in 1606.

Bank of England   **F6**
Threadneedle St EC2. Known as the 'Old
Lady of Threadneedle Street', the vaults
hold the nation's gold reserves. Outer walls
are still the original design by Sir John
Soane, architect to the Bank from
1788–1833. Rebuilt by Sir H. Baker
1921–37.

Banqueting House   **E6**
Whitehall W1. Rebuilt
by Inigo Jones, after a
fire in 1619, it was the
first Classical building
in England. The main
room is 110 feet long.
Beautiful Rubens
ceilings 1630.

*Banqueting Hall,
Whitehall*

Burlington House   **E6**
Piccadilly W1. Victorian-Renaissance façade
on one of the great 18thC palaces. Houses
the Royal Academy and various royal
societies.

Carlton House Terrace SW1   **E6**
A magnificent sweep of columns by John
Nash 1827–32, with steps down to the Mall
and to St James's Park.

Chelsea Royal Hospital   **E6**
Chelsea Embankment SW3. A hospital,
founded by Charles II, for old soldiers;
known as Chelsea Pensioners. Fine, austere
building 1682 by Wren. Stables 1814 by Sir
John Soane.

Chiswick House   C6
Burlington Lane W4. Lovely Palladian villa
built in the grand manner by the 3rd Earl of
Burlington 1725–30. Two wings were added
in 1788 by James
Wyatt. Fine
interiors and
gardens by
William Kent.
Some fine
paintings.

Chiswick House

Clarence House   E6
Stable Yard Gate SW1. Mansion by Nash
1825 for the Duke of Clarence. Now the
home of the Queen Mother.

Cleopatra's Needle   E6
Victoria Embankment SW1. A pink granite
obelisk presented to the nation by Egypt in
1819. Carved in 1500BC it was one of a pair
which stood outside the temple of Heliopolis;
its companion is in New York.

Crewe House   E6
15 Curzon St W1. Georgian town house,
1735 by Edward Shepherd who gave his
name to Shepherd's Market nearby. It was
for many years the home of the Marquess of
Crewe.

Fribourg & Treyer   E6
34 Haymarket SW1. Elegant 18thC old shop
front. Unaltered, it has been a tobacconist
since 1720.

Fulham Gasometer   D7
Fulham Gasworks SW6. The oldest gas-
holder in the world; built in 1830 by Winsor
& Mindock. Diameter 100 feet; capacity a
quarter million cubic feet. An extraordinary
piece of early industrial engineering.

Gray's Inn   E6
Holborn WC1. Entrance from passage next to
22 High Holborn. An Inn of Court since the
14thC. The Hall (16thC) and 'buildings'
restored after bomb damage. Gardens were
laid out by Francis Bacon, who lived and
worked here for 50 years. *Hall open by
appointment only.*

Guildhall   F6
Off Gresham St EC2. 15thC with façade by
George Dance 1789 and later restorations by
Sir Giles Gilbert Scott. The Great Hall is
used for ceremonial occasions. Mediaeval
groined vaulting in crypts. Corporation Art
Gallery; the Library contains several signed
Shakespeare folios.

Gunnersbury Park   C6
Acton W3. Regency house of the
Rothschilds. Museum of local history,
including transport. Park.

Hall Place   J7
Bexley, Kent. Nr junction of A2 & A223. A
flint and brick Tudor house with 17thC
extension. Once the home of the rake, Sir
John Dashwood. Splendid topiary in the
shape of the Queen's Beasts. Rose, rock and
herb gardens.

Holland House   D6
Off Kensington High St W8. One wing only
left of this mansion by Thorpe 1607. In
Holland Park (50 acres).

Houses of Parliament

Houses of Parliament   E6
St Margaret St SW1. Also known as the
Palace of Westminster. Victorian-Gothic
building 1840–68 by Sir Charles Barry and
A.W.N. Pugin. Westminster Hall was built
in 1099 as the Great Hall of William Rufus'
new palace: the roof dates from the late
14thC. The clock tower houses the famous
Big Ben, named after its bell.

Inns of Chancery   E6
Before the 18thC a student of law had first
to go through 1 of the 9 Inns of Chancery
then existing.
They have now mostly disappeared. Staple
Inn, High Holborn, remains a fine
Elizabethan building. Others survive only as
names: Barnard's Inn, Clement's Inn,
Clifford's Inn, Furnival's Inn, Lyon's Inn,
New Inn, Strand Inn and Thame's Inn.

Kenwood House (Iveagh Bequest)   E5
Hampstead Lane NW3. Robert Adam house
and interior 1767–69. English 18thC
paintings and furniture. Fine Rembrandt,
Hals and Vermeer. Gardens and wooded
estate of 200 acres. Open air concerts by the
lake on summer evenings.

Lancaster House   E6
Stable Yard, St James's SW1. Early Victorian
London town house. Lavish state apartments
and painted ceilings. Designed by Benjamin
Wyatt, architect of Apsley House.

Lincoln's Inn   E6
Lincoln's Inn WC2. An Inn of Court,
established here in 1422. 17thC New Square,
gardens, barrister chambers and solicitors
offices. A chapel by Inigo Jones (1623) and
the 15thC Old Hall; the Great Hall was
built in 1845. The 'stone buildings' are by
Sir Robert Taylor and were begun in 1774.
Still has Dickensian atmosphere.

Lincoln's Inn Fields   E6
WC2. Seven acres of gardens laid out by
Inigo Jones 1618. Once a famous duelling
ground, now office workers play competition
games. Nos. 12–14 built 1792 by Sir John
Soane, Nos. 57–8 built 1730 by Henry
Joynes, Nos 59 & 60 built 1640 by Inigo
Jones.

Mansion House   F6
Opposite Bank of England EC2. Official
residence of the Lord Mayor. Palladian
building by George Dance 1739. Completed
1752. The main state room is the Egyptian
Hall which is 90 feet long.

Mansion House

Marble Arch   E6
W1. 1825–36 John Nash. Originally the
main gateway to Buckingham Palace. Stands
on the spot where the Tyburn Tree, the
public gallows, once stood.

Marlborough House   E6
Marlborough Gate, Pall Mall SW1. Designed
by Wren 1710, for the victorious Duke of
Marlborough. Contains a painted ceiling by
Genti Peschi which was originally designed
for the Queen's House at Greenwich. The
simple classical-style Queen's Chapel in the
grounds is by Inigo Jones 1626. Wall
paintings by Laguerre depict the Duke's
famous battles.

The Monument   F6
Fish Street Hill EC4. Commemorates the
Great Fire of London of 1666 which started
in a bakery at nearby Pudding Lane. 202
feet high with 311 steps to the balcony at
the top. Designed by Sir Christopher Wren
and built in 1671.

Old Curiosity Shop   E6
13–14 Portsmouth St WC2. Tudor house
built 1567 and now an antique shop. Often
claimed to be the one immortalised by
Dickens in 'The Old Curiosity Shop'.

Old Swan House   E6
17 Chelsea Embankment SW3. Late 19thC
house by R. Norman Shaw.

Osterley Park House   B7
Thornbury Rd, Osterley. Remodelled by
Robert Adam 1761–78 on an already fine
Elizabethan building built round a

courtyard. The magnificent interiors with furniture, mirrors, carpets and tapestry all show the elegance and richness of Adam's genius and is one of his best and most complete works.

Paddington Station D6
Praed St W2. 1850–52. 'Railway-cathedral' engineering at its best by Brunel; the Gothic ornament by Wyatt and Owen Jones; the Renaissance-style hotel by Hardwick.

The Queen's House G7
Romney Rd SE10. Now houses part of the National Maritime Museum. Built by Inigo Jones 1619–35 for the Queen of Denmark.

Queen's House, Greenwich

Royal Courts of Justice E6
Strand WC2. Massive Victorian-Gothic building, with an 80-foot-high great hall as its centrepiece. Best seen from a distance as part of the skyline.

Royal Exchange F6
Corner of Threadneedle St and Cornhill EC3. Built in 1842 by Tite. The third building on this site. Originally founded as a market for merchants and craftsmen in 1564, and destroyed in the Great Fire. The second building was also burnt down in 1838. Ambulatory containing statues and mural painting and courtyard. It is no longer used.

Royal Naval College G7
Greenwich SE10. Once a Royal Naval Hospital and previously the site of the former royal palace for the Tudor sovereigns. A fine and interesting group of classical buildings by Webb 1664, Wren 1692 and Vanbrugh 1728. Chapel by James 'Athenian' Stuart 1789 and Painted Hall by Thornhill.

St Bartholomew's Hospital F6
West Smithfield EC1. London's oldest hospital, founded in 1123. Still on the original site, the gatehouse is 1702 with a statue of Henry VIII above. Just inside is the church of St Bartholomew the Less where Inigo Jones was christened in 1573. The quadrangle, buildings and great hall were designed by James Gibb, 1730–1760.

St Pancras Station E5
Euston Rd NW1. A spectacular and romantic example of Victorian-Gothic revival. 1868 by Sir George Gilbert Scott. Part of the building recently regained its fairy castle-like appearance when it was cleaned.

Syon House B7
Park Rd, Brentford, Middx. The exterior is the original convent building of the 15thC but the interior 1762–69 is wholly and brilliantly by Robert Adam. The imaginative elegance and variety in each room is unsurpassed. Fine furniture and paintings. Garden by Capability Brown. Do not miss Syon Lodge nearby—Crowther's showplace of acres of garden ornaments.

Syon House

The Temple F6
Inner Temple, Crown Office Row EC4. Middle Temple, Middle Temple Lane EC4. Both are Inns of Court. Enter by Wren's gatehouse, 1685, in Middle Temple Lane. An extensive area of courtyards, alleys, gardens and warm brick buildings. Middle Hall 1570. The Temple Church is an early Gothic 'round church' built by the Knights Templar 12th–13thC.

The Tower of London

The Tower of London F6
Tower Hill EC3. A keep, a prison and still a fortress. Famous for the Bloody Tower, Traitors' Gate, the ravens, Crown Jewels and the Yeoman warders or Beefeaters. Norman Chapel of St John. In the Armouries is a collection of arms and armour, based on the arsenal of Henry VIII—the oldest museum in Britain.

Watermen's Hall F6
18 St Mary at Hill EC3. Adam-style front surviving from 1780. Unexpectedly beautiful amid drab surroundings.

York Watergate E6
Watergate Walk, off Villiers St WC2. Built in 1626 by Nicholas Stone as the watergate to York House. It marks the position of the north bank of the Thames before the construction of the Victoria Embankment in 1862. The arms and motto are those of the Villiers family.

Bridges

The River Thames runs right through the middle of London, and therefore means of crossing it have always been of utmost importance. Today there are bridges of all sorts; for the railway, pedestrians and motor cars. Apart from the tubes scuttling under the river by mysterious routes there are also 3 well marked tunnels taking traffic under the Thames. Many of the bridges are lit up at night and look very romantic. One of the prettiest is **Albert Bridge**, a suspension

The Albert Bridge

bridge built in 1873. **Battersea Bridge** was once wooden but was replaced by the present iron bridge in 1890. The present **Chelsea Bridge** is fairly recent, having been rebuilt as a suspension bridge in 1937. Another suspension bridge is **Hammersmith Bridge**, built in 1887. It

Hammersmith Bridge

has a touch of Louis quatorze, with its pavilion topped gilt turrets. **Kew Bridge**, officially called the King Edward VII bridge since the King opened it in 1903, is a fine stone structure with three spans. One of the most famous bridges, **London Bridge**, has had many replacements on this site since Mediaeval times. Up to the early 13thC the bridge was wooden, and then the first stone bridge was built. This was one of the sights of Europe with houses and shops, and even a chapel on the bridge. There were fortified gates at each end, the spikes of which were often adorned with the decapitated heads of traitors. In 1760 the buildings were pulled down, and in 1832 the bridge itself. This was replaced by a granite bridge which in 1971 met a strange fate by being shipped, piece by piece, to the middle of the Arizona desert. The present but functional, London bridge was built in 1973. **Putney Bridge** has long been famous as the starting place of the Oxford and Cambridge Boat Race held at Easter each year since 1829, though the present bridge has only been here since 1884. **Richmond Bridge** is a little

Richmond Bridge

older than the others, having been built in the Classical style in 1777 by James Paine, to replace the earlier horse ferry. One of the main landmarks of London, the picture of which is known to people all over the world, is **Tower Bridge**. Its twin Gothic towers

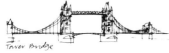
Tower Bridge

standing on stone ramparts, hold the winding gear that opens the arms to allow large ships to pass. These two vast bascules weigh about 1,000 tons each, yet take only a minute and a half to open and have never failed in their duty since the bridge was built. The present **Waterloo Bridge**, designed by Sir Giles Gilbert Scott, dates from 1945. It replaced a bridge completed in 1750—which was a major engineering feat. It had taken 1,600 years for Londoners to get a second bridge across the Thames since the Romans first spanned the river with the original London Bridge.

Palaces

Buckingham Palace   E6
St James's Park SW1. The permanent London palace of the reigning sovereign since Queen Victoria. Originally built 1705 for the Duke of Buckingham; remodelled by Nash 1825; the Classical façade added 1913 by Sir Aston Webb. *Not open to the public.*

Buckingham Palace

Eltham Palace   H7
Off Court Yard, Eltham SE9. 15thC royal palace until Henry VIII. Also remains of earlier royal residences. Great Hall with hammer-beam roof and a very fine 14thC bridge over the moat.

Fulham Palace   D7
Fulham Palace Rd SW6. Official residence of the Bishop of London. 16thC building with riverside park.

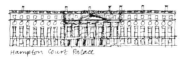
Hampton Court Palace

Hampton Court Palace   B8
Hampton Court. Royal palace built 1514 for Cardinal Wolsey with later additions by Henry VIII and Wren. Sumptuous state rooms painted by Vanbrugh, Verrio and Thornhill. Famous picture gallery of Italian masterpieces. Orangery, mellow courtyards, ornamental ironwork, the 'great vine' and the maze. The formal gardens are probably among the greatest in the world. Exotic plants from 16thC. Tudor tennis court.

Jewel Tower   E6
Old Palace Yard SW1. 14thC fragment of the old Palace of Westminster. Built as a moated treasure house for Edward III, it now houses relics of the old palace.

Kensington Palace

Kensington Palace   D6
Kensington Gardens W8. Simple and charming building acquired by William III in 1689 as a palace. Exterior altered by Wren, interior by William Kent. Queen Victoria and Queen Mary were born here. The warm brick Orangery was built 1704 by Hawksmoor.

Kew Palace   C7
Kew. Small red-brick Dutch-style house, 1631. Souvenirs of George III and a collection of animal and bird pictures. Stands in the Royal Botanic Gardens which were once the Palace grounds.

Lambeth Palace   E6
Lambeth Palace Rd SW1. The London residence of the Archbishops of Canterbury for the past 750 years. Begun in the 13thC the palace has been added to over the centuries. Fine mediaeval crypt and 1660 Great Hall. Portraits 16th-19thC.

Old Palace   F9
Old Palace Rd, Croydon, Surrey. Seat of the Archbishops of Canterbury for 1,000 years. Tudor chapel.

St James's Palace   E6
Pall Mall SW1. Built by Henry VIII with many later additions. Foreign ambassadors are still accredited to the 'Court of St James's', though today the building only comprises 'grace and favour' residences granted by the Sovereign. Ceiling of Chapel Royal by Holbein. *Chapel and courtyards only open to public.*

St James's Palace

Cemeteries

Highgate   E5
Swains Lane N6. Overgrown and sinister, with crumbling vaults and sepulchres, the place where several horror films have been made. The Rosettis are buried here; also George Eliot and Herbert Spencer. The older part is now closed because of vandalism but Karl Marx, the most famous resident, is lying in the newer section, which is still open to the public.

Kensal Green NW10   D5
Old and shady with many familiar names engraved on the 77 acres of tombstones, including Thackeray, Wilkie Collins and Anthony Trollope.

Nunhead Cemetery   F7
Ivydale Rd SE15. Like Highgate plagued by vandals but it's a marvellous haunted place set in a large wooded park with many gloomy family vaults.

St Anne's   E6
Wardour St W1. King Theodore of Corsica was buried here (1756); so was William Hazlitt. A sad place these days, much neglected.

St George's Gardens   E6
Gray's Inn Rd WC1. A small, overgrown graveyard garden, with underground passages and vaults.

St John's   E5
Church Row NW3. The parish church of Hampstead. An overcrowded friendly village

churchyard. Constable is buried in the south-east corner. In the cemetery north of the road are George du Maurier, Sir Herbert Beerbohm Tree and Sir Walter Besant.

St Mary Magdalen RC Church   **C7**
Mortlake SW13. Sir Richard Burton, explorer and linguist, is buried here in a grand Arab tent-shaped tomb with Carrara marble interior. Nothing else equals it.

Museums & galleries

British Museum   **E6**
Great Russell St WC1. One of the largest and greatest museums in the world. Famous collections of Egyptian, Assyrian, Greek and Roman, British, Oriental and Asian antiquities. Egyptian mummies, the colossal Assyrian bulls and lions in the Nimrud gallery, Cambodian and Chinese collections, the Elgin Marbles and the Rosetta Stone. Building 1823–47 by Sir Robert Smirke: the domed reading room roof is by Sidney Smirke.

Commonwealth Institute
230 Kensington High St W8. Resources, way of life and industrial development of the Commonwealth housed in a modern building. Art gallery, library and cinema.

Courtauld Institute Galleries   **E6**
Woburn Square WC1. The Courtauld Collection of French Impressionists (including fine paintings by Cezanne, Van Gogh, Gauguin) and the Lee, Gambier-Parry and Fry collections. Also enamels, ivories, glass and sculpture.

Geological Museum   **D6**
Exhibition Rd SW7. Physical and economic geology and mineralogy of the world; regional geology of Britain. Models, dioramas and a large collection of gems, stones and fossils.

Hayward Gallery   **E6**
Belvedere Rd SE1. Changing exhibitions of major works of art arranged by the Arts Council. Fine modern building and river setting.

Imperial War Museum   **E6**
Lambeth Rd SE1. Very popular national museum of all aspects of war since 1914. Collection of models, weapons, paintings, relics. The building was once Bedlam, the lunatic asylum.

Museum of London   **F6**
150 London Wall EC2. London's new museum. The life and history of London from Roman times to the present day. Antiquities, costume, pictures, coronation robes, the London theatre, toys and games, fire engines. Also 'Orangery' and gardens.

Museum of Mankind   **E6**
Burlington Gdns W1. Exhibitions on various aspects of ethnography. Concentrates on the art and culture of pre-industrial societies. Also permanent exhibition which includes the Benin Bronzes.

National Army Museum   **E6**
Royal Hospital Rd SW3. The story of the Army 1480–1914, its triumphs and disasters, its professional and social life all over the world. Uniforms, pictures, weapons and personal relics.

National Gallery   **E6**
Trafalgar Square WC2. Very fine representative collection of famous pictures. Rich in early Italian (Leonardo da Vinci, Raphael, Botticelli, and Titian). Dutch and Flemish (Rembrandt, Rubens, Frans Hals, Van Dyck). Spanish 15th–18thC (Velasquez and El Greco). British 18th and 19thC (Constable, Turner, Gainsborough and Reynolds). Building 1838 by W. Wilkins.

National Maritime Museum   **G7**
Romney Rd SE10. The finest maritime collection in Britain. Ship models, paintings, navigational instruments, costumes and weapons. Incorporates the Queen's House by Inigo Jones 1616 and the Old Royal Observatory.

National Portrait Gallery   **E6**
2 St Martin's Place WC2. Historical collection of contemporary portraits of famous British men and women from early 9thC to the present day.

Natural History Museum   **D6**
Cromwell Rd SW7. Nearly 4 acres of gallery space house the national collections of zoology, entomology, palaeontology and botany. Particularly notable is the bird gallery, the 90-foot model blue whale and the great dinosaur models. Building 1881 by A. Waterhouse.

Science Museum   **D6**
Exhibition Rd SW7. The history of science and its application to industry. A large collection of very fine engineering models, steam engines, motor cars, aeroplanes and instructive children's gallery. Lots of working models.

Sir John Soane's Museum   **E6**
13 Lincoln's Inn Fields WC2. Soane's personal collection of antiquities, paintings and drawings including Hogarth's 'Election' and the 'Rake's Progress'. Building designed by Soane 1812.

Tate Gallery   **E6**
Millbank SW1. Representative collections of British painting from the 16thC to the present. Blake, Turner, Hogarth, the pre-Raphaelites, Ben Nicholson, Spencer and Francis Bacon; also Picasso, Chagall, Mondrian, Moore, Hepworth, Degas. Building 1897 by Sidney R. J. Smith.

Victoria & Albert Museum   **D6**
Cromwell Rd SW7. A museum of decorative art, comprising vast collections from all categories, countries and ages. Over 10 acres of museum! It includes important collections of paintings, sculpture, graphics and typography, armour and weapons, carpets, ceramics, clocks, costumes, fabrics, furniture, jewellery, metalwork and musical instruments.

Wallace Collection   **E6**
Hertford House, Manchester Square W1. A private collection of outstanding works of art which were bequeathed to the nation by Lady Wallace in 1897. Splendid representation of the French 17th and 18thC also several Rembrandts, a Titian, some Rubens, and paintings by Canaletto and Guardi. French furniture; Sèvres porcelain; Majolica; Limoges enamel; weapons and armour. Fine collection of clocks.

Wellington Museum   **E6**
Apsley House, 149 Piccadilly W1. Known as 'No. 1 London', this was the home of the Duke of Wellington until his death. Full of silver plate, snuff boxes, porcelain, medals and an 11-foot-high nude statue of Napoleon.

Whitechapel Art Gallery   **F5**
80 Whitechapel High St E1. Frequent public exhibitions of great interest. The Whitechapel has successfully introduced new ideas in modern art into London.

Botanical gardens

Avery Hill   **H7**
Bexley Rd SE9. The Winter Garden is a second smaller Kew.
Good collection of tropical and temperate Asian and Australasian plants in glasshouses, including a selection of economic crops.

Royal Botanic Gardens, Kew   **C7**
Kew Rd, Richmond. One of the world's great botanic gardens. Famous for its natural collections, identification of rare plants, economic botany and scientific research. Nearly 300 acres of pure aesthetic pleasure. Arboretum; alpine; water and rhododendron gardens. Magnificent tropical, orchid, palm and Australasian houses. Herbarium contains

Sir Joseph Hooker's famous H.M.S. 'Erebus' and Indian plant collections. The orangery and pagoda were designed by Sir William Chambers (1760), and the glass palm house (1844–48) by Decimus Burton.

Palm House, Kew Gardens

Syon Park   **C7**
Brentford. 55 acres of gardens with beautiful lakeside walk and garden sculpture. The Great Conservatory has free-flying tropical birds, orchids and a collection of live butterflies and moths. Many rare plants, an aquarium, a garden centre and shop.

Zoos & aquaria

The London Zoo Aquarium   **E5**
Zoological Gardens, Regent's Park NW1. Marine and tropical halls; excellently lit and displayed. A well-stocked aquarium of both sea and freshwater fish and amphibians from European and tropical waters. Particularly notable are the fine sea fish, the octopus, stingrays and sharks.

London Zoo   **E5**
Regent's Park, NW1. Founded to collect 'new and curious' animals for scientific study; now one of the largest collections of animals in the world. A.A. Milne came to see *the* Winnie bear. The Royal Family found a home here for exotic four-legged gifts. A veritable Ark. Of interest: world's first reptile and insect houses; Lord Snowdon's walk-through Aviary; 'Moonlight World' of nocturnal animals. First class children's zoo.

Brass rubbing

The following is a short list of places that have brasses for rubbing. Permission is almost invariably required.
London. Bishopsgate (St Helen's); Camberwell (St Giles); City (All Hallows Barking by the Tower; St Dunstan-in-the-West); St James's crypt, Piccadilly; Enfield; Fulham; Harrow; Hillingdon; Wandsworth; Westminster Abbey Cloisters.

Parks

Battersea Park SW11   **E7**
An interesting well-wooded riverside park of 200 acres. Boating lake, deer park, wildfowl collection and children's zoo. Also contains a botanical wild-flower garden. The famous Easter Parade is held here. Athletics, tennis.

Clapham Common SW4   **E7**
A fair example of the broad village greens of London. There are others at Highbury, Wandsworth, Tooting, Streatham and Mitcham, and together they give an illusion of green space, sorely needed around a great shapeless city. They owe their survival as public open spaces to their former use as

grazing grounds for the villagers' cattle, before suburbia swallowed up the last London farms.

Danson Park   **J7**
Bexleyheath, Kent. Water and rock gardens set in a Capability Brown landscape. Also a charming Old English rose garden; aviary; boating lake.

Dulwich Park

Dulwich Park SE21   **F7**
Just east of Dulwich Village, it holds fine trees, landscaped lawns and flower beds and a winding lake. Famous for its rhododendrons and azaleas. A favourite garden of the late Queen Mary. Boating lake and tennis courts.

Greenwich Park SE10   **G7**
A Royal park of 200 acres with pleasant avenues lined with chestnut trees, sloping down to the Thames. Impressive views of the river, the shipping and the 2 classical buildings: the Queen's House by Inigo Jones and the Royal Naval College. Contains also the old Royal Observatory and its pleasant garden. Thirteen acres of wooded deer park, a bird sanctuary and Bronze Age tumuli.

Hampstead Heath NW3   **E5**
High, open and hilly, 800 acres of park and woods. Crowded on Bank Holidays with visitors to the famous fair and the 3 equally famous pubs—The Bull & Bush, The Spaniards and Jack Straw's Castle. Includes Parliament Hill (popular with kite-flyers and tobogganists), Golders Hill (containing a fine 'English' town garden), and Kenwood. Ponds and bandstand, tennis, swimming and model-boat sailing, athletics.

Hampton Court   **B8**
Hampton Court. 1,100 acres of Royal park bounded on 2 sides by the Thames. Hampton is the formal park of the great Tudor palace with ancient courts, superb flower gardens and the famous 'great vine', planted 1768, and maze planted during Queen Anne's reign.

Holland Park W8   **D6**
Behind Kensington High St. 55 acres of calm and secluded lawns and gardens with peacocks. Once the private park of Holland House. 28 acres of woodland contain 3,000 species of trees, full of birds. Dutch garden of 1812 with fine tulips. Rose gardens and orangery. Open-air theatre in summer. Tennis and squash courts.

Hyde Park W1   **E6**
A Royal park since 1536, it was once part of the forest reserved by Henry VIII for hunting wild boar and bulls. It is now a pleasant 340 acres of parkland, walks, Rotten Row with horseriders and the Serpentine—a fine natural lake for fishing, boating and swimming. The famous 'Speakers' Corner' is near Marble Arch.

Kensington Gardens W2   **D6**
A formal and elegant addition to Hyde Park. 275 acres of Royal park containing William III's lovely Kensington Palace, Queen Anne's Orangery, the peaceful 'Sunken Garden' nearby, the Round Pond with its model sailing-boats and the Long Water with

its statue of Peter Pan. On the south is the magnificently Victorian 'Albert Memorial'.

Primrose Hill NW8   **E5**
A minor Royal park of a simple grassy hill 200 feet high giving a fine view over London.

Regent's Park NW1   **E5**
A Royal park of 470 acres, originally part of Henry VIII's great hunting forest in the 16thC. The Prince Regent in 1811 planned to connect the park (and a new palace) via the newly built Regent Street to Carlton House. Although never fully completed the design by John Nash (1812-26) is of great distinction, the park being surrounded by handsome Regency terraces and imposing gateways. Contains also the Zoo, the Regent's Canal, a large boating lake with numerous species of birds and the very fine Queen Mary's rose garden within Nash's Inner Circle. Open-air theatre.

Nash Terrace, Regent's Park

Richmond Park   **C7**
A Royal park of 2,500 acres first enclosed as a hunting ground by Charles I in 1637. Retains all the qualities of a great English feudal estate—a natural open park of spinneys and plantations, bracken and ancient oaks (survivors of the great oak forests of the middle ages) also many red deer and fallow deer. Golf, riding, polo, football, fishing.

St James's Park & Green Park SW1 E6
The oldest Royal park, acquired in 1532 by Henry VIII, laid out in imitation 'Versailles' style by Charles II; finally redesigned in the grand manner for George IV by John Nash in the 1820s. A most attractive park, with fine promenades and walks, and a romantic Chinese-style lake, bridge, and weeping willows. The bird sanctuary on Duck Island has some magnificent pelicans and over twenty species of duck and geese. Good views of Buckingham Palace and the Whitehall skyline.

St James's Park

Shooters Hill SE18   **G7**
Hundreds of acres of woods and open parkland containing Oxleas Woods, Jackwood and Eltham Parks. Castlewood has a folly erected 1784 to Sir William James for his exploits in India.

**Victoria Embankment
Gardens WC2**   **E6**
The joy of the lunchtime office worker on a fine summer day. Banked flowers, a band, shady trees, deckchairs and a crowded open-air cafe.

Wimbledon Common SW19   **D8**
1,100 acres including Putney Heath, comprising wild woodland, open heath and several ponds. Golf courses; 16 miles of horse rides; playing fields; Bronze Age remains; rare British flora. Protected by an act of 1871 as a 'wild area' for perpetuity. Famous, restored, 19thC windmill and traditional nude bathing (men only).

London's river

To every Londoner the 'river' can mean only one thing, the Thames. From Putney upstream to Hampton Court you can explore the Thames's green banks by a footpath that was used, until a century ago, by sturdy horses towing barges. From Putney down to Tower Bridge there are frequent embankments or parks beside public roads, and one bank or the other is usually accessible. Below Tower Bridge, right down to Woolwich, the great river is usually hidden away behind high dock walls, and only exceptionally, as at Greenwich Park, will you get any worth-while view from the land. But the best way to view any great river is from a boat. All through the summer tourist craft sail from Westminster Pier, Charing Cross Pier, and the Tower of London, taking people upstream to Hampton Court, or downstream as far as Greenwich, at a leisurely speed ideal for sightseeing. Following the Thames downstream from Hampton Court Bridge, where there is a large boating centre, you pass first the trees and lawns of Hampton Court Park and then, below Kingston Bridge, reach Teddington Lock. The river flows on north past the green, tree-lined meadows of Ham and Petersham to Richmond, another boating centre. Climb Richmond Hill for its glorious view south-west up the river. Below Richmond's bridges there is a tidal barrage and lock, used only at low tide. Flowing between Syon Park and Kew Gardens the Thames keeps its rural aspect right down to Kew Bridge. Even along the famous Oxford and Cambridge boat-race course from Barnes to Putney—the crews row the other way, upstream—the river makes a rural oasis winding through suburban West London. Now a tamed, urban river, confined between stone embankments and crossed by a dozen bridges, the Thames flows on through the heart of London past the Houses of Parliament on its Westminster banks, and the Tower of London beside the City. Until 1970 ocean-going steamers came daily up the Thames, passing through Tower Bridge to the busy Pool of London below London Bridge. Today only a few small oil tankers, craft carrying coal for power stations, and strings of barges drawn by tugs, use this once active commercial artery. Only the hidden downstream docks harbour larger shipping.

River Trips
Trips, both up and down stream, can be joined from the following points: Charing Cross Pier, Greenwich Pier, Kew, Putney Embankment, Richmond, Tower Pier, Westminster Pier. For further information telephone the London Tourist Board's special River Boat Information Service on (01)-730 4812.

Canals

It is only recently that the canals of the metropolis have ceased to perform their erstwhile function as carriers of goods in and out of London. Nowadays the River Thames carries less freight than ever before, and even the London Docks are handling less and less traffic. The Surrey Docks are now closed down, and the Surrey Canal that served them is closed too.

London's main canal however, the Regent's Canal, is still in good condition, and although trade has virtually finished, it is used by any pleasure boats whose owners can decipher the complicated lock opening hours. However it is more useful as a local amenity for residents in areas with little 'public open space'. To these people the canal is a thing of peace and quiet, a reminder of the past and a fascinating contrast in every way to the humdrum facts of their everyday life. Best places to see the canal are Paddington, where 'Little Venice' entices the towpath walker; Regent's Park, where you can walk along the tree-lined cutting and go right through the Zoo; Camden, where the locks start the 90-foot drop to the river; and Islington, where there is a ½-mile long tunnel and another lock by the great City Road Basin. Here the towpath has been opened up to strollers, and local children learn to row and sail from the youth club based on an old timber barge moored in the Basin. Below here

Lock-gates, Regent's Canal

the towpath is closed, and the canal is still a secret highway. Regent's Canal Dock itself is silent and empty of ships.

Canal Trips
Cruises on the Regent's and Grand Union Canals can be taken from the following points: Blomfield Road W9, Jason's Trip (01)-286 3428; Camden Lock, Chalk Farm Road NW1, Jenny Wren Cruises (01)-485 4433; Delamere Terrace W2, Zoo Water Bus (01)-286 6101; Port-A-Bella Dock, Cnr Ladbroke Grove & Kensal Road W10. (01)-960 5456.

Archaeological sites

All Hallows Barking-by-the-Tower   **F6**
Byward St EC3. The crypt of this church has a Roman mosaic floor, composed of plain red tesserae, dating from the later 2ndC. A gully runs across the pavement, and probably marks the position of a partition wall. The crypt also has a collection of Roman pottery, masonry fragments, and pieces of two Saxon crosses. *Apply to Verger for admission.*

Bank of England   **F6**
Threadneedle St EC2. The Bank of England stands on one of the most archaeologically fertile areas of London, and has produced many Roman finds. One of these, a mosaic floor, has been restored and relaid at the foot of the main staircase, and can be seen by the public during business hours.

City Wall   **F6**
The wall of Roman Londinium was begun AD200, and continued in use, with much rebuilding and addition, through the middle ages. In the north-west corner, the wall incorporated the two outward walls of the Roman fort, which were thickened to bring

them into line (see Cripplegate Fort for sections showing this). Gate-houses were built where roads left the city, and during the later 3rd and 4thC several semi-circular bastions were added at intervals to the face, though most of the surviving bastions are probably mediaeval.
The Wall, with the base of a bastion, can be seen in the Tower of London, behind the ruined Wardrobe Tower. Other stretches with mediaeval rebuilding, can be seen in Wakefield Gardens (opposite the Tower), at 8-10 Cooper's Row, and (with permission from the Postmaster) in the Post Office, St Martin's-le-Grand.

Cripplegate Roman Fort   **F6**
The fort was discovered during post-war excavations, and apparently dates from the early 2ndC. Although built to the standard Roman pattern, it was a barracks for soldiers engaged on the ceremonial and guard-duties connected with a capital city and the presence of an Imperial governor, rather than a defensible military base.
Sections of the stone wall, which originally had a ditch in front and a strong bank behind can be seen in Noble Street and, with later Roman thickening to bring its defences into line with the city wall and some mediaeval rebuilding, in St Alphage Churchyard, and to the south of St Giles Cripplegate. The Noble Street section also has an internal corner tower and an interval turret along the circuit. Part of the West Gate can be seen under London Wall.

Roman Bath-House   **F6**
Lower Thames St. Excavations on this site revealed a late Roman house, and part of the connected bath-suite has been preserved. This includes a wall with an apse, and the tile piers that originally supported the floor and allowed the circulation of hot air underneath.

St Brides   **F6**
Fleet St. The fragmentary remains of a Roman mosaic pavement, composed of red and a few yellow tesserae, can be seen at the east end of the crypt. The building that contained it extended beyond the church, and lay outside the Roman city.

Temple of Mithras   **F6**
Bucklersbury House, Queen Victoria St. The Roman temple dedicated to the Persian god Mithras was the most spectacular of the finds made during excavation of the City bomb-sites after the War. Originally it lay on low ground by the Walbrook, but has now been rebuilt, using the original materials, in front of Temple Court; the Roman earth floor has been replaced with paving. The worship of Mithras was confined to men, and was apparently favoured particularly by merchants and soldiers; the London temple is the only one at present known in Britain that is not associated with a fort. 'Mithraea' are always small, with a central nave and flanking aisles; the focus was a representation of Mithras slaying the Bull, and a sculpture depicting this was found in the late 19thC when the temple was still unknown—it is now housed in the Museum of London. The temple excavations produced the finest group of imported sculptures found in Roman Britain, and a unique decorated silver canister; these finds are now displayed in the Museum of London.

Sport

Sports Council   **D7**
Information Centre, 70 Brompton Road SW3. (01)-589 3411. Answers all kinds of enquiries about sports, clubs and physical recreation. Also produces a calendar of events.

Archery
There are 23 archery clubs in London, each having its own ground. Grounds at Duke of York's headquarters, Crystal Palace, Duke's Meadow, Dulwich and Regent's Park. County of London championships held at

Bowrings Sports Ground, Lee Road, Eltham SE3. *Last Sun in Aug.*

Badminton
All England championship at Wembley in March; also tournaments at Wimbledon, Epsom, Eltham, Crystal Palace, Leyton and Sydenham. All England junior championship held at Wimbledon. *Dec-Jan.*

Boxing
ABA championships held in May. Bouts take place at: Wembley and the Royal Albert Hall. Also at West Ham, Bermondsey, Shoreditch and Walworth town halls. For details of forthcoming bouts consult 'Boxing News'.

Cricket
Many amateur cricket clubs throughout London and first class cricket at Lords and the Oval where test matches are played every year. For latest scores of test matches played in England, phone 154. The season is *Apr-Sept.*

Cycling
Once a predominantly continental sport, now becoming increasingly popular in Britain. The professional, spectacular and incredibly fast 6-day indoor events staged at Wembley are well worth a visit, even for the uninitiated. Details from British Cycling Federation.

Football (Soccer)
By far the most popular British sport from both the playing and spectator's point of view. The English Football League has 92 clubs divided into 4 divisions; then there are Southern and Isthmian League clubs; finally there are hundreds of amateur clubs. Football League matches are played every Saturday and most Bank Holidays at 15.00 with occasional mid-week matches at 19.30. The season lasts from August to April. Occasional international matches at Wembley Stadium, domestic and European knock-out competitions at club grounds. The FA and League Cup finals are held at Wembley but it's impossible to get in unless you already have a ticket.

Greyhound Racing
Win or lose a fortune betting on the 'dogs'. The main stadiums are at Catford, Hackney, Harringay, Walthamstow, Wembley, White City and Wimbledon. See sports press for times.

Lawn Tennis
There are public courts in most London parks but the quality of these varies greatly. There are also plenty of clubs to join. The major event, of course, is Wimbledon fortnight held at the end of June; it is best to apply for tickets 1st October onwards or queue for standing room on the day. There are also various tournaments held in London; those which take place immediately before Wimbledon usually include several top professionals.

Polo
Played April-September at Smith's Lawn, Windsor. Matches most weekends, Bank Holidays and during Ascot Week. Ham House, Richmond Sundays. Richmond Park (nr Roehampton Gate) Tuesday, Thursday and Saturday. Play starts middle or late afternoon.

Rackets & Real Tennis
Real tennis is the original form of tennis and Henry VIII's court at Hampton Court still exists. Nowadays it is rather obscure, as is rackets which is a form of squash but played on a much larger court.

Rowing   D7
Events take place in the summer months, the most notable being the Oxford and Cambridge boat race from Putney to Mortlake in March or April. Other events are the Head of the River event on the Thames; the Schools Head of the River race from Chiswick to Putney; the Sculling Head of the River from Mortlake to Putney; the Wingfield Sculls between Putney and Mortlake. Important regattas are held at Brent (Welsh Harp reservoir, Whit Monday), Chiswick, Hammersmith, Henley, Kingston, Putney (including the Metropolitan regatta) Richmond, Twickenham and Walton.

Rugby Football   C8
The principal association connected with the game of rugby is:
Rugby Football Union, Whitton Rd, Twickenham. The home and headquarters of rugby is at Twickenham and important matches including Internationals are played there.

Show Jumping   C5
The two major events are the Royal International Horse Show at Wembley in July and the Horse of the Year Show at Wembley in October. There are also notable events staged at Windsor, Richmond and Clapham Common.

Stock-car racing
Controlled by the RAC. Noisy, colourful, exciting and slightly dangerous. Contrary to popular opinion, the drivers do actually try to avoid hitting each other (except in 'banger' racing). Events mostly staged Saturday evenings in the summer:
Harringay Stadium   F4
Green Lanes N4. (01) 800 3474.
Wimbledon Stadium   D8
Plough Lane SW17. (01) 946 5361.

Pageants, ceremonies & events

Beating the Bounds   F6
Tower of London EC3. This ceremony dates from the Middle Ages, when there were few maps and it was necessary for an official to point out the extent of each parish. Today, after a service in the chapel of St Peter ad Vincula, the choir boys go round beating the boundary stones with willow rods. *Ascension Day every three years (1981, 1984, etc.)*

Ceremony of the Keys   F6
Tower of London EC3. The Chief Warder of the Yeoman Warders, with an escort of the Brigade of Guards, locks the gates, the Middle Tower and the Byward Tower. One of the oldest military ceremonies in the world. *Every night at 21.40.*

Changing of the Guard   E6
Buckingham Palace SW1. The Guard is usually formed of one of the regiments of Foot Guards. A band leads the New Guard from Chelsea or Wellington Barracks, and after the ceremony in the forecourt, leads the Old Guard back. *Daily at 11.30.*

Blue Coat March   E6
Holborn Viaduct EC1. The boys and girls of Christ's Hospital, wearing 16thC dress, march through the city to St Sepulchre Without Newgate church. *St Matthew's Day, end of September.*

Doggett's Coat & Badge Race   F6
The Thames, London Bridge to Albert Bridge. This annual rowing race of Thames watermen is started by the Fishmonger's Barge Master and was first held in 1715 to mark the ascension to the throne of George I. The winner receives an orange-coloured coat and an arm badge. *Late July.*

Gun Salutes
Mark Royal anniversaries, such as the Queen's ascension on 6th February and her birthday on 21st April. Fired by the King's Troop of the Royal Horse Artillery in Hyde Park and the Honourable Artillery Company at the Tower of London.

Lord Mayor's Procession   F6
The newly-elected Lord Mayor of London is driven in his state coach, accompanied by pikemen, from Guildhall to the Royal Courts of Justice where he takes his oath of office before the Lord Chief Justice. This is the biggest, most colourful, event in the City. *2nd Saturday in November.*

Maundy Money

A custom which started in the Middle Ages when the monarch washed the feet of the poor and gave them alms. Today specially minted silver coins are distributed by the Queen usually to old age pensioners, in London. *Maundy Thursday every third year.*

Oak Apple Day　　　　　　　　　**E6**

Royal Hospital, Chelsea SW3. A parade marking the anniversary of the restoration of Charles II who founded the hospital. The Chelsea Pensioners, in red dress uniform and three-cornered hats, are inspected. *29th May.*

Opening of the Courts　　　　　　**D6**

Westminster Abbey SW1. Judges and leading barristers, in wigs and gowns, walk in procession to the House of Lords after a service in the Abbey. This marks the start of the legal year. *October.*

Swan-upping

Ownership of the swans on the River Thames is shared by the Sovereign and two City Companies, the Dyers and Vintners. A census of swans is taken from London Bridge to Henley when young swans have their beaks nicked to show who owns them. This dates from the Middle Ages when a swan was a great table delicacy. *July.*

Trooping the Colour　　　　　　　**E6**

Horse Guards Parade SW1. Marks the official birthday of HM the Queen and each year the 'colour' or standard of one of the five regiments of Foot Guards is presented to the Queen by being 'trooped' or displayed before her. The Queen is seen riding side-saddle on a horse, whilst massed bands play and troops march. Pageantry at its best. *2nd Sat in June.*

Vintners Roadsweep　　　　　　　**F6**

When their new Grand Master is installed the Vintners Company walk in a procession from Vintners Hall to the church of St James Garlickhythe, led by a wine porter who sweeps the road with a besom. A tradition dating from the reign of Edward III. *July.*

Theatreland

CINEMAS

Since the first picture houses started, opening up a new era in this country, the cinema has proved a boom industry. Even two World Wars and the advent of television have not dislodged it. Today in the centre of London there are more than 50 large cinemas, and a whole host of local ones on the outskirts (though these today are being seriously challenged by Bingo Halls). First-run big releases all over London, whilst premières and long-running box-office 'smashes' run side by side in the West End. Independent cinemas and membership clubs cater for buffs of experimental, foreign or classic films. This means a film to suit any taste can be found simply by looking through the evening paper, Time Out or What's On.

MUSIC & DANCE

Coliseum　　　　　　　　　　　　**E6**

St Martin's Lane WC2. (01) 836 3161. Largest London theatre seating 2,400. Now houses the English National Opera *Aug–May,* and visiting companies during summer.

Covent Garden　　　　　　　　　　**E6**

Royal Opera House, Bow St WC2. (01) 240 1066. World-famous Royal Ballet and Opera companies maintain an international reputation.

The Place　　　　　　　　　　　　**E6**

17 Duke's Rd WC1. (01) 387 0161. Home of the London Contemporary Dance Theatre and the London School of Contemporary Dance, an exciting modern dance company. Immaculate productions with interesting choreograhic ideas.

Purcell Room　　　　　　　　　　　**E6**

South Bank SE1. (01) 928 3191. Chamber music and solo concerts. Generally performances which require more intimate surroundings.

Queen Elizabeth Hall　　　　　　　**E6**

South Bank SE1. (01) 928 3191. Symphony, orchestral and large band concerts. Also special events such as Poetry International take place here.

Royal Albert Hall　　　　　　　　　**E6**

Kensington Gore SW7. (01) 589 8212. Victorian domed hall named after Prince Albert, built 1871. Orchestra, choral, pop concerts and public meetings. Famous for the 'Proms'.

Royal Festival Hall　　　　　　　　**E6**

South Bank SE1. (01) 928 3191. Built in 1951 for the Festival of Britain. Seats 3,000. Orchestral and choral concerts.

Sadler's Wells　　　　　　　　　　**E6**

Rosebery Avenue EC1. (01) 837 1672. Once a spa (the original well discovered by Thomas Sadler is under a trap-door at the back of the stalls). Birthplace of the Royal Ballet company; now used by visiting opera and ballet companies.

THEATRES

London without theatre is unthinkable. English theatre has flourished for 7 centuries—ever since religious drama left the church for the countryside, evolved into Miracle and Mystery plays and sought out its audience from large timber structures on wheels. London's first regular playhouse, aptly named the Theatre, went up on the south bank of the Thames in 1576—almost 14 years before Shakespeare wrote his plays. This theatre later became Shakespeare's immortalised Globe, but sadly no longer exists though a plaque marks the spot. The Drury Lane, where Samuel Pepys caught cold from draughts in 1663, still stands on its original spot. Covent Garden, built in 1732 and the Haymarket, 1705, are national monuments. The number and quality of theatre people and stage-works that have made London's international theatre reputation, has never been equalled. Government subsidies now sustain this tradition, though inflation has recently forced a plethora of sex, farce and formula. Nevertheless, quality still survives at the National Theatre, Royal Shakespeare and a couple of other major companies subsidised by television broadcasts. So whether you prefer classics or fringe, sex or politics, home-grown or imported—it's all here. Comb the evening paper, *Time Out* or *What's On* for details and reviews.

Special attractions

RRS Discovery

HMS 'Belfast'   **F6**
Symons Wharf, Tooley St SE1. Last of the
great British cruisers. A warship
commemorating the age of the gun and
steam propulsion. A Royal Navy museum
with exhibitions, films, etc.

The 'Cutty Sark'   **G6**
King William Walk, Greenwich SE10. Stands
in dry dock. One of the great sailing tea-
clippers, launched in 1869. Museum with an
interesting collection of ship's figureheads.

London Dungeon   **F6**
28–34 Tooley St SE1. A real horror show of
British history. Stationary exhibitions
showing the plague, tortures in the Tower,
sacrifices, martyrs and other grisly things.

London Experience   **E6**
Coventry St, Piccadilly W1. The history and
traditions of London through the ages shown
through unique projection techniques with a
mixture of slides, film and special effects.

Madame Tussaud's   **E6**
Marylebone Rd NW1. The waxworks, which
first settled in London in 1835. Models of
famous people, scenes from history and the
Chamber of Horrors.

Planetarium   **E6**
Marylebone Rd NW1. Projected onto a
domed ceiling are all the glories of the night
sky, with appropriate commentary. Showing
the constellations from both hemispheres and
from outer space. Also 'Laserium' showing
uses of laser beams.

Royal Mews   **E6**
Buckingham Place SW1. Contains the state
coaches, private driving carriages and Royal
sleighs. Also the Windsor Greys and
Cleveland Bay carriage horses that pull
them.

Royal Tournament   **D6**
Earl's Court SW5. Impressive military
spectacle with marching, precision and speed
displays, massed brass bands and gymnastics.

St Katharine's Dock   **F6**
St Katharine's Way E1. Yacht haven and
home of the Thames Maritime Museum.
RRS Discovery, several magnificent Thames
barges, and other craft are here.

Pubs

Most London pubs are 19thC but can be up
to 400 years old. They take on the character
and needs of the locality and are aptly called
'locals'. Of the 7,000 pubs in London we
have selected the following on the basis of
particularly interesting aspects which make
them stand out from the rest. But many
others can be found by the thirsty and
curious.

Anchor   **F6**
Bankside SE1. Tel (01) 407 1577. A minstrel's
gallery and a first edition of Dr Johnson's
Dictionary in the 18thC inn. Five beamed
bars and fine English cooking in the dining
rooms.

Blackfriar   **F6**
174 Queen Victoria St EC4. Tel (01) 236 5650.
Triangular-shaped building in the shadow of
Blackfriars railway bridge. Unique 'Art
Nouveau' interior. Associated with the old
Dominican priory.

Cartoonist   **F6**
76 Shoe Lane EC4. Tel (01) 353 2828.
Victorian and lavishly wallpapered with
cartoons, some famous and all amusing.
Headquarters of Cartoonist Club of Great
Britain.

Cheshire Cheese (Ye Olde)   **F6**
145 Fleet St EC4. Tel (01) 353 6170. Rebuilt
after the Great Fire. Low-ceilinged tavern.
Excellent English food.

Cock Tavern   **F6**
22 Fleet St EC4. Tel (01) 353 8570. Small but
good journalists' tavern with literary
associations. One large dining room. Good
English carvery, steak and kidney puddings
and pies.

Dirty Dick's   **F6**
202–4 Bishopsgate EC2. Tel (01) 283 5888.
Named after Nat Bentley, well known 18thC
miser of the famous ballad. Kept artificially
dirty with cobwebs and stuffed cats in the
vaults.

Grenadier   **E6**
18 Wilton Row SW1. Tel (01) 235 3074.
Mews pub with ceiling covered with wine
labels. Duke of Wellington played cards
here.

Lamb   **E6**
*94 Lamb's Conduit St WC1. Tel (01) 405
5962.* Popular Bloomsbury local with some
intriguing music hall photographs and
Hogarth prints.

Lamb and Flag   **E6**
*33 Rose St, Covent Garden WC2. Tel (01) 836
4108.* Mellow, traditionally preserved pub
with some fascinating curios. Originally
called 'The Bucket of Blood'. Poet Dryden
was nearly killed here.

Mayflower   **F6**
117 Rotherhithe St SE16. Tel (01) 237 4088.
Tudor Thameside inn connected with the
Pilgrim Fathers. Only pub in England
licensed to sell English and American
postage stamps. Good grills.

Nag's Head   **E6**
*10 James St, Covent Garden WC2. Tel (01)
836 4678.* Theatrical pub with Edwardian
interior. Theatre playbills and prints.

Olde Mitre Tavern   **E6**
1 Ely Court EC1. Tel (01) 405 4751. Built in
1546 by the Bishops of Ely for their
servants. Associations with Queen Elizabeth
and Dr Johnson.

Prospect of Whitby   **F6**
57 Wapping Wall E1. Tel (01) 481 1095. 600-
year-old smuggler's haunt next door to
Execution Dock. Terrace overlooking the
Thames. Associations with Pepys.

Running Footman   **E6**
5 Charles St W1. Tel (01) 499 8239. Pub with
the longest name in London: 'I am the Only
Running Footman'.

St Stephen's Tavern   **E6**
10 Bridge St SW1. Tel (01) 930 2541.
Victorian and named after the tower of Big
Ben. An MP's local—there is a division bell
reminding members to go back to Parliament
and vote. Good English cooking.

Salisbury   **E6**
90 St Martin's Lane WC2. Tel (01) 836 5863.
Ornate Victorian pub. Cut-glass mirrors,
illuminated gilt statuettes, sumptuous velvet
seating.

Samuel Pepys   **F6**
*Brooks Wharf, 48 Upper Thames St EC4. Tel
(01) 248 3691.* Warehouse converted in
Jacobean style. A 2-tier terrace overlooks the
river. Constant ticker-tape news from the
wires of UPI and UNS. Restaurant.

Sherlock Holmes   **E6**
*10 Northumberland St WC2. Tel (01) 930
2644.* Perfect replica of Holmes' study at
221b Baker St has been constructed. Whole
pub is saturated with relics of the fictitious
detective.

Spaniards Inn   **E5**
Spaniards Rd NW3. Tel (01) 455 3276.
Popular 16thC tavern opposite the old toll-
house on Hampstead Heath. Associations
with Dick Turpin, Byron, Shelley, Keats
and Reynolds.

Trafalgar Tavern   **G6**
Park Row SE10. Tel (01) 858 2437. An old
waterfront tavern. Try the upstairs bar with
the 18thC man-of-war décor.

Watling (Ye Olde)   **F6**
29 Watling St EC4. Tel (01) 248 6235. Old
oak-beamed tavern rebuilt by Wren after the
Great Fire. Stands on one of the oldest roads
in London.

Regional food

Boiled beef and carrots
This favourite Cockney dish of cured and
boiled beef—either brisket or silverside, is
accompanied by carrots, pease pudding and
dumplings.

Chelsea bun
This yeast-raised sugary currant bun was
originally made to counter the popularity of
the Bath bun in the 18thC.

Eel pie
The eels were traditionally fished from the
Thames between Kingston and Richmond
and the pie gave its name to Eel Pie Island.
Many local recipes exist, the most popular
being of eels, lemon, parsley and shallots.

Jellied eels
One of the delights of London street markets
are the fish stalls where it is possible to buy
prawns, cockles, mussels and the East
Enders' favourite—jellied eels.

Whitebait
This, another traditional Thames fish, was
caught especially near Greenwich. Alas, no
more, but the tradition of eating whitebait at
Greenwich persists.

Restaurants

London has many fine restaurants; we have
chosen some of the best known English
restaurants together with a selection of other
cuisines. 'Nicholson's London Restaurant
Guide' lists over 600 alternatives.
£ inexpensive; ££ medium priced; £££
expensive.

Baron of Beef   F6
Gutter Lane EC2. Tel (01) 606 6961. Vastly
popular City restaurant. Chief interest is in
the roast beef and Yorkshire pudding from
the trolley. *LD. Closed Sat & Sun. £££.*

Bertorelli's   E6
*19 Charlotte St W1. Tel (01) 636 4174. 70–72
Queensway W2. Tel (01) 229 3160.* Busy
straight-forward Italian eating places. Good
food at reasonable prices. *LD. Closed Sun.
££.*

Bloom's   F6
90 Whitechapel High St E1. Tel (01) 247 6001.
Exuberant, kosher restaurant. Handy for
Bethnal Green Market and Whitechapel Art
Gallery. Go early on a Sunday. *LD. Closed
Fri afternoon, Sat & Jewish Hols. £.*

Carrier's   E5
2 Camden Passage N1. Tel (01) 226 5353.
Robert Carrier's famous restaurant.
Individual cooking to high standards. *LD.
Closed Sun. £££. Book.*

English House   E6
3 Milner St SW3. Tel (01) 584 3002. That the
menu consultant is an expert on 18thC
English food is reflected in the imaginative
traditional dishes. *LD. Closed Sun. ££. Book.*

L'Etoile   E6
30 Charlotte St W1. Tel (01) 636 7189.
Typically French in atmosphere and style.
Top-quality food and attentive service. *LD.
Closed Sat & Sun. ££. Book.*

Food for Thought   E6
31 Neal St WC2. Tel (01) 836 0239. Small
and simple serving varied vegetarian dishes.
Compost-grown vegetables, quiches, stews,
bakes and salads. *LD. Closed Sat & Sun. £.*

Le Gavroche   E6
*61–63 Lower Sloane St SW1. Tel (01) 730
2820.* Luxurious and almost faultless 'haut
cuisine'. Excellent pâtisserie, polished
service, magnificent wine list, highly priced.
D. Closed Sun. £££. Book.

Gay Hussar   E6
2 Greek St W1. Tel (01) 437 0973. Robust
Hungarian restaurant. Set lunches good
value. *LD. Closed Sun. ££. Book.*

Hard Rock Café   E6
150 Old Park Lane W1. Tel (01) 629 0382.
Fashionable hamburger joint with non-stop
blaring rock music. Prime meat steaks and
burgers. Expect a long queue. *LD. £.*

Joe Allen   E6
13 Exeter St WC2. Tel (01) 836 0651.
Convivial, noisy, crowded with a picturesque
clientele. Blackboard menu of steaks,
burgers, salads, spare ribs. Cheesecake and
cocktails. *LD. ££. Book.*

Lee Ho Fook   E6
15 Gerrard St W1. Tel (01) 736 9578. A
Chinese restaurant patronised by Chinese.
Eat in cave-like rooms with carved ceiling.
LD. ££.

Luba's Bistro   D6
6 Yeoman's Row SW3. Tel (01) 589 2950.
Individual, down to earth atmosphere. Good
wholesome Russian cooking at low prices.
Borscht, beef Stroganoff, galuptsy. *LD.
Closed Sun. £.*

Manzi's   E6
1–2 Leicester St WC2. Tel (01) 437 4864.
Typical busy provincial Italian fish
restaurant. Wide range of dishes. *LD. Closed
Sun L. ££.*

Overton's   E6
5 St James's St SW1. Tel (01) 839 3774.
Long-established fish restaurant of character.
'Old world' atmosphere in the nicest sense.
LD. Closed Sun. ££. Book.

Peppermint Park   E6
*13–14 Upper St Martin's Lane WC2. Tel (01)
836 5234.* Trendy; predominantly green
décor with splashes of pink. Cocktails,
American food, taped music. *LD. ££. Book.*

Quaglino's   E6
16 Bury St SW1. Tel (01) 930 6767. Luxury,
style and glamour. A mixture of cooking
traditions, nightly cabaret and dancing. *LD.
Closed Sat L & Sun. £££. Book.*

Rules
35 Maiden Lane WC2. Tel (01) 836 5314.
Traditional British food in a splendidly
preserved eating house rich in literary
associations. *LD. Closed Sat & Sun. £££.
Book.*

Scott's   E6
20 Mount St W1. Tel (01) 629 5248. Superbly
executed fish specialities in a restaurant with
an established international reputation. *LD.
Closed Sun L. £££. Book.*

Sheekey's   E6
*28–32 St Martin's Court WC2. Tel (01) 836
4118.* Excellently cooked and served
fish—mostly steamed—with salad and potato.
Crowded. *LD. Closed Sun. ££. Book.*

Simpson's-in-the-Strand   E6
100 Strand WC2. Tel (01) 836 9112. A
famous restaurant with an Edwardian club
atmosphere. The attentive service and the
large carvings from enormous joints of beef
and lamb are its best feature. Only order
English food. Stilton and vintage port by the
glass. *LD. Closed Sun. ££. Book.*

Stone's Chop House   E6
Panton St SW1. Tel (01) 930 0037. Victorian
chop house, rebuilt after the war and given
authentic atmosphere with brass, black
leather seating and Victoriana. Excellent
English cooking, generous helpings. *LD.
Closed Sun. ££.*

La Terrazza   E6
19 Romilly St W1. Tel (01) 734 2504. First of
a famous chain. Remarkable Italian cooking
in a beautifully designed, crowded but
elegant restaurant. *LD. ££. Book.*

White Tower   E6
1 Percy St W1. Tel (01) 636 8141. Elegant;
first class Greek cuisine. Agreeable and
leisurely service. *LD. Closed Sat & Sun. £££.
Book.*

Wiltons   E6
27 Bury St SW1. Tel 01-930 8391.
Traditional British cooking to high standards
in this grand old Victorian building.
Outstanding fish and game dishes. *LD.
Closed Fri D, Sat & Sun. £££. Book.*

Wales

5

Wales is a fiercely independent part of the United Kingdom and there can be no question of its difference. Ringed with great castles, impressive remnants of the days when the Celtic fringe had to be kept under control, Wales offers a feast of scenery. From the valleys and Black Mountains in the south to the glories of Snowdonia in the north, it has so much to offer those who enjoy the outdoors. The coast is varied; there are miles of flat sand and splendid cliffs on the Gower, and at Conway the mountains come so close to the sea that the road takes to a tunnel. Sail from Solva into St Bride's Bay and you are amongst the magnificent Dyfed coastal scenery.

The people are as delightful as their country; talkative and musical with an attractive lilting accent they have preserved their own language and traditions. Sturdy from generations of mining and tough hill farming; they are a great contrast to their more effete English neighbours.

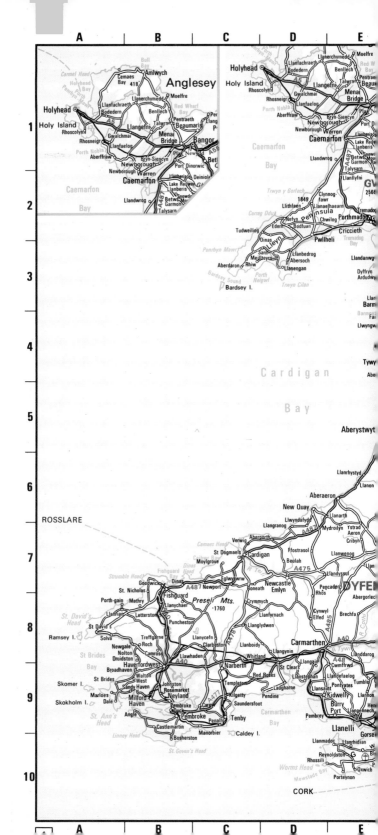

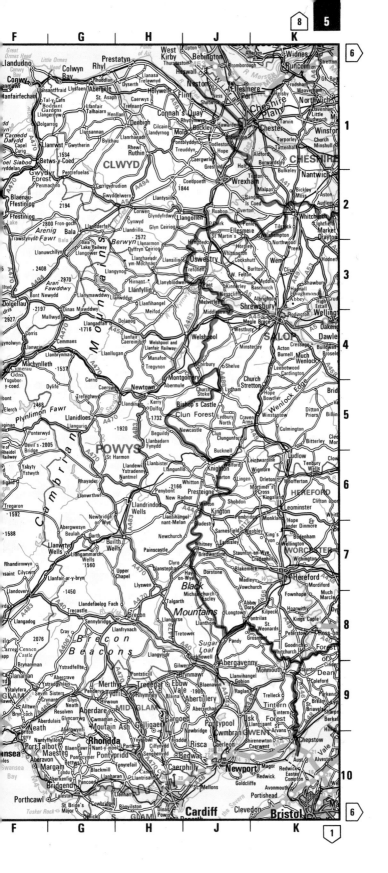

The coast

Aberaeron E6
Dyfed. Pop 1,300. EC Thur. An elegant Regency new town built in the 19thC with comfort, care and spaciousness; the plan is attributed to John Nash. It has a colourful harbour, broad streets and handsome houses, all pastel-washed. There are shingle beaches on either side of the harbour.

Aberavon F10
W. Glamorgan. Pop 31,700. A wilderness of duneland transformed into a monumental pleasure place. There is an Olympic-standard indoor freshwater swimming pool, other sports facilities, a big dipper and scenic railway for the children. Two miles of firm, safe sandy beach.

Aberdaron C3
Gwynedd. Pop 1,200. EC Wed. A remote fishing village of white cottages and a sprightly 6thC church. Y Gegin Fawr, now a café and souvenir shop, was built in the 14thC as a resting place for pilgrims to Bardsey.

Aberdovey E4
Gwynedd. Pop 1,200. EC Wed. A simple and elegant place yet full of real life. A collection of neat colourful shops and houses perch gingerly on a narrow strip of land between the mountains and the sea. Charles Dibdin's 18thC opera 'Liberty Hall' made famous the song 'The Bells of Aberdovey'.
Bathing is safe from the long, sandy, dune-backed beach north of the village.

Aberffraw A2
Gwynedd. Pop 1,400. Spick-and-span cottages and an ancient hump-backed packhorse bridge. It was here the Britons of the west rallied under Maglocunos to halt the Saxon onslaught. On an island in the bay stands the church of St Cwyfan. Founded in the 7thC it was restored in 1893. South of the bridge grassy dunes lead to a quiet sandy beach.

Aberystwyth E5
Dyfed. Pop 10,700. EC Wed. MD Mon. A sober and dignified place strung out along a broad promenade with prim Victorian and Edwardian buildings; it is also a university town with a new arts complex. At the north end is Constitution Hill, the summit of which can be reached on the Cliff Railway. At the opposite end is a grassy hillock crowned with the remains of a 12th and 13thC castle. The beach is of fine gravel, shingle and a little sand.

Amlwch B1
Gwynedd. Pop 3,700. EC Wed. A market town and holiday resort with a busy harbour overlooked by a ruined windmill. In 1768 Amlwch was a small fishing hamlet. With the discovery of huge deposits of copper in the Parys Mountain in the late 18thC it rapidly became a busy and prosperous town; by 1790 it had the largest copper mine in Europe. The boom years ended in the 19thC. Of interest—Llaneilian church, one of the treasures of Anglesey. Small sandy beach at low tide. Excellent bathing and boating.

Angle B9
Dyfed. Pop 300. Consists of a cluster of houses along a quiet village street. At the end is the muddy sand of Angle Bay.

Bangor E1
Gwynedd. Pop 15,200 EC Wed. A busy university town and touring centre by the mouth of the Menai Strait. The monastery was founded in Bangor in AD525. Over the next few centuries a succession of cathedrals was built and destroyed until the present one was begun in 1496. A squat building in a low-lying site, it was restored by Sir Gilbert Scott in 1866–80. Of interest—the Menai Suspension Bridge; the unique Bible Garden; Museum of Welsh Antiquities and Penrhyn Castle at Llandegai nearby. The beach is mainly shingle

Barmouth E3
Gwynedd. Pop 2,100. EC Wed. A collection of ordinary things made special as they cluster uniquely together between a curve of the sea, a hill with a Panorama Walk and the Mawddach Estuary. Barmouth is a twisting narrow place, grey and Victorian, with bay-windowed joviality. Ruskin described the view of Cadair Idris and the Mawddach as 'the finest in Europe'.
An impassive promenade sweeps round to a boat-filled river-mouth harbour. Of interest—Ty Gwyn yn Y Bermo (White House in Barmouth) said to have been built by the Earl of Richmond who later became Henry VII; and the weaver's loft, where traditional Welsh weaves and tapestries are produced. Long sandy beach.

Beaumaris B2
Gwynedd. Pop 2,100. EC Wed. Reached through the shadow between high ground and the sea, it is an irresistible place wrapped round a curve of flat land which juts into Conwy Bay. The curve itself is emphasised by white terraced houses with bay windows. Across the waters are the foothills and mountains of Snowdonia, misty in the distance. Yachts moor in the bay where wooden warships once anchored to deliver supplies to the 13thC castle. Of interest—the 15thC Tudor House in the main street; the old gaol built in 1614. A mainly shingle beach leads to areas of sand at low tide. Bathing is safe on the incoming tide.

Benllech B1
Gwynedd. Pop 2,500. EC Thur. Set on Anglesey's east coast, Benllech is a popular holiday village. Good sailing and walking, plus riding stables, bowling and tennis courts. The beach is long and sandy. It shelves gently and bathing is safe.

Bontddu F3
Gwynedd. Pop 200. EC Wed. An attractive small-scale village, on the northern shore of the pine-clad Mawddach Estuary, directly opposite Cadair Idris.

Broad Haven B8
Dyfed. Pop 300. A popular beach with fine sand flanked by cliffs and rock pools.

Caernarfon E1
Gwynedd. Pop 10,000. EC Thur. MD Sat. A small grey town clustered round a hilltop square. The imposing castle was one of the mightiest of 13thC Europe, and the setting for the investiture of HRH Prince Charles as Prince of Wales in 1969.
Business and tourist centre of Snowdonia, Caernarfon stands on the western end of the Menai Strait where the River Seiont flows into the sea. Of interest—remains of a Roman fort.

Cardiff H10
S. Glamorgan. Pop 300,000. EC Wed. Straddling the River Taff is this lively place full of pubs and bars and spacious streets.

A large seaport and the capital of Wales, Cardiff has a history going back to Roman times. It was a Norman centre of military strength and justice, and during the Civil Wars it was stoutly Royalist. By the middle of the 19thC it was already a prosperous port and has remained implacably Victorian at heart ever since.
Of interest—Llandaff Cathedral, rebuilt after the blitz; St John's Church built in the 15thC; the huge castle; the Edwardian Civic Centre; the National Stadium; St Fagan's Folk Museum; the National Museum of Wales, with its collection of pictures by Welsh artists; the Welsh Industrial and Maritime Museum, appropriately established near the docks; the remains of the Black Friars Priory; the legendary Tiger Bay, a little arid now.

Cardigan C7
Dyfed. Pop 3,800. EC Wed. MD Sat. A vigorous place. Once an important sea-port closed by the silting up of its river. Now it is a bustling market town sitting astride the River Teifi amongst the rich farms and forests of Ceredigion. Of interest—the ancient castle; the remains of a 12thC castle; the abbey ruins; the local market; boat trips up the river.

Ceibwr Bay C7
Dyfed. A shingle cove of utter quietness at the foot of towering cliffs. Grey seals can sometimes be seen.

Cemaes Bay A1
Gwynedd. Pop 800. A handful of whitewashed cottages grouped round narrow streets and a small harbour. The whole place is simple and unadorned. At Wylfa Head across the bay is the nuclear power station. An 8 stage nature trail takes a route around the headland from the power station. The sandy beach is completely covered at high tide.

Clynnog Fawr D2
Gwynedd. Pop 900. Delightfully small-scale, a few whitewashed cottages and the church of St Beuno, founded in the 7thC and a resting place for pilgrims to Bardsey Island. A quiet shingle beach is reached by a pleasant lane.

Colwyn Bay G1
Clwyd. Pop 25,500. EC Wed. Placed in the half-moon curve of the bay. At the turn of the century it was a placid cluster of fishermen's huts. Now it's a busy resort with a lively pier and pleasant promenade. Sandy beach with a sheltered bay good for water sports.

Conwy F1
Gwynedd. Pop 12,200. EC Wed. MD Tue, Sat. An ordinary town in an extraordinary setting—high above a harbour and estuary. Everything here is subservient to the castle. Of interest—Telford's elegant suspension bridge built in 1826; Robert Stephenson's tubular bridge; a house on the quay reputed to be the smallest in Britain; the 14thC church of St Mary; the 12thC abbey; Plas Mawr, the Elizabethan mansion built 1585; Aberconwy House, a mediaeval timber-framed house now used as a museum. Fast currents make the estuary unsafe for bathing. Bathing is safe from Morfa beach 1¼ miles north-west.

Criccieth E2
Gwynedd. Pop 1,600. EC Wed. A family resort dominated by Criccieth Castle, a 13thC stronghold which stands on a grassy headland with incomparable views of Cardigan Bay. Of interest—community hymn-singing which takes place on Sunday evenings in summer at the bottom of Mona Terrace; the church of St Catherine;

Criccieth

Brynawelon, home of Lloyd George. Beach: a curve of shingle and low tide sand.

Dale B9
Dyfed. Pop 300. A sheltered line of colour-washed cottages in a picturesque cubby-hole inside the entrance to Milford Haven. Of interest—Dale Fort, built in the 19thC and now a Field Centre. Surrounded by numerous fine sandy beaches and a good sailing and boating centre.

Druidston B8
Dyfed. A sandy beach backed by sheer cliffs. On-shore winds create ideal conditions for surfing.

Fishguard B7
Dyfed. Pop 4,900. EC Wed. MD Thur. Lower Fishguard is a huddle of old wharfs and cottages round a small harbour, the port for southern Ireland. Perched on top of the tree-covered headland above is Fishguard town. Of interest—the Royal Oak Inn in the square; Tregwynt, 1½ miles south, near St Nicholas, has an interesting old mill producing fine Welsh weaves.

Harlech E3
Gwynedd. Pop 1,300. ED Wed. Like many of the great castle towns in Wales, Harlech is small. Cottage-high grey buildings lie close to the massive stone-built castle. There are sharp views between buildings to an almost table-flat valley. Beyond are the mountains of Snowdonia, misty in the distance. The long sandy beach sweeps north to the mouth of the Glaslyn Estuary where swift currents make bathing dangerous. Of interest—potteries, and a craft village at Maes Artro in nearby Llanbedr; 18-hole Royal St David's golf course.

Holyhead A1
Gwynedd. Pop 10,600. EC Tue. MD Sat. A mixture of sandy bays, industry and bustling port. This is the terminus for Dublin-bound ferries; the harbour is protected by Britain's longest breakwater. Have a look at South Stack's famous lighthouse. Newry Beach, a stretch of clean shingle, runs from the landward end of the breakwater towards Salt Island.

Laugharne D9
Dyfed. Pop 1,000. Pronounced 'Larn' it is one of the most charming small towns in Wales. At the mouth of the River Taf, with the green hills of the Llanstephan Peninsula reflected in the water, Laugharne is a street of Georgian houses, an 18thC town hall, a 12thC castle and a shingle foreshore. Dylan Thomas lived and worked here in the Boathouse (now open to visitors) wedged between the hillside and the river bank along the cliff walk behind the castle. Of interest—the unpretentious grave of Dylan Thomas in the churchyard; Brown's Hotel, the poet's favourite. Not far from a good sandy beach.

Llandanwg E3
Gwynedd. Pop 1,400. A sandy rock-scattered beach. Half-buried in the dunes is a small-scale and derelict church. Parts date from the 6thC. Except on the ebb tide the bathing is safe.

Llandudno F1
Gwynedd. Pop 19,000. EC Wed. A splendid place full of good humour and vitality. This is the resort where Lewis Carroll—the Rev Charles Dodgson—met the little girl who inspired 'Alice in Wonderland'. The pier is something special. Of interest—Professor Codman's Wooden Headed Follies; a funicular ride or cabin lift up the Great Orme's Head. The beach is a gentle arc of

Llandudno

golden sand, limestone headlands at either end, and a line of elegant hotels in the middle.

Llangrannog D7
Dyfed. Pop 200. A colourful village with houses tumbling cheerfully to the beach between a cleft in the high cliffs. Safe bathing and good sea fishing.

Llanstephan D9
Dyfed. Pop 1,000. Backed by harp-shaped hills, it is a maze of narrow lanes on a hilltop. Llanstephan lies on the west side of the estuary of the Towy. Overlooking the estuary is the ruined castle. Of interest—St Anthony's Well; the walk to Scot's Bay. Bathing is safe on the incoming tide.

Manorbier C9
Dyfed. Pop 1,170. EC Sat. An inviting village grouped round an impressive Norman castle which looks out across a broad green valley to the open sea. The beach is sandy with a scattering of shingle.

Mewslade Bay D10
W. Glamorgan. A delightful little bay sheltered by high cliffs. The sandy beach is completely covered at high tide.

Milford Haven B9
Dyfed. Pop 13,700. EC Thur. MD Fri. Designed and built in the late 18thC on steeply sloping ground around a little harbour. Associations with Lord Nelson, who described Milford Haven as the finest harbour in the world. There are magnificent views of the busy waterway. Oil tankers of over 250,000 tons berth at the jetties which reach out into the main stream.

Moelfre B1
Gwynedd. Pop 200. A vigorous, salt-aired fishing village famed for the skill and courage of its lifeboatmen. Almost 900 lives have been saved since the station was founded in 1830. Safe bathing from a shingle beach.

Newgale A8
Dyfed. A lonely sandy beach with curving breakers. Good for surfing.

Newport J10
Dyfed. Pop 1,100. EC Wed. An ancient castled town carved out of the Welsh domains by Martin de Tours in 1093. Of interest—pre-Christian hut circles on Carn Ingli Common. There are two fine beaches— Draeth and Parrog, the town beach with a picturesque quay.

New Quay D6
Dyfed. Pop 700. EC Wed. Steep, twisting narrow streets with everything jammed together in a delightful free-for-all around a sheltered harbour. New Quay was a bustling port and ship-building centre in the early 19thC. The coastal trade was superseded by the railways towards the end of that century. By the 1920s the port had become an attractive holiday centre. The poet Dylan Thomas lived here in the 1940s. East of the harbour is a sandy crescent of sheltered beach 1½ miles long.

New Quay

Pendine D9
Dyfed. Pop 300. 6 miles of flat, firm sand backed by dunes. The beach was used for successful attempts on the world land speed record in the 1920s by Sir Malcolm Campbell and J. G. Parry-Thomas. Wildlife park nearby.

Penmaenmawr F1
Gwynedd. Pop 4,000. EC Wed. A busy little resort backed by the mountains of Snowdonia, and extending down the side of

the hills between the great headlands of Penmaenbach and Penmaenmawr. This was the site of a Stone Age axe factory. Of interest—Puffin Island off the eastern tip of Anglesey.
The long sandy beach is backed by shingle and a railway line. At Penmaenmawr the line is separated from the shore by a broad, traffic-free promenade. Good bathing.

Port Eynon E10
W. Glamorgan. Pop 250. A village full of quiet picturesqueness, with a sandy dune-backed beach flanked by high cliffs.

Porthcawl F10
Mid Glamorgan. Pop 14,100. EC Wed. Developed originally as a 19thC coaling port, Porthcawl is now a teeming giant full of family fun. The 3,000 caravan park is one of the largest in Europe. Sandy beaches with occasional outcrops of rock.

Porthgain A8
Dyfed. Pop 150. A tiny inlet with a snug harbour brim-full of atmosphere. There are several small shingle coves to the east.

Porthmadog E2
Gwynedd. Pop 4,000. EC Wed. Houses of solid 19thC comfort with broad tree-lined streets and a bustling harbour. Conceived in 1807 by William Alexander Madocks on 7,000 acres of reclaimed land. The town became a thriving port with locally built sailing ships carrying slate to many parts of the world. Have a ride on the Ffestiniog Narrow Gauge Railway and visit the M.V. Garlandstone sailing ketch, now a maritime museum, berthed by the 19thC slate wharf. Good bathing at Black Rock Sands, except at the south-eastern end of the beach where there are swift currents; and at Borthygest.

Porthmadoc

Porth Nobla D1
Gwynedd. Miles of golden sand ending beneath a rocky headland.

Porth Penrhyn-Mawr A1
Gwynedd. A quiet shingle beach flanked by low grassy headlands at the end of a country lane.

Portmeirion E2
Gwynedd. Portmeirion is a private village. An elegant anomaly created as a tiny Italianate dream town, begun in 1926 by the Welsh architect, Sir Clough Williams-Ellis. It all started with the 19thC house, now the hotel, at the water's edge. An elegant campanile crowns the hill with 18thC houses round it. Noel Coward wrote his comedy 'Blithe Spirit' in the water house between one Sunday and the next, and it was used as the surrealist setting for the 'Prisoner' TV series.

Prestatyn H1
Clwyd. Pop 15,500. EC Thur. A popular holiday resort. Until the late 19thC it was a lead mining centre. The 700-foot-high hills provide a green partially wooded backdrop. The area known as Central Beach is overlooked by a broad traffic-free promenade flanked by dunes.
Of interest—Dyserth, an old world village with a waterfall at its centre; Edward I's castle of Rhuddlan, 3½ miles west; Bodrhyddan Hall, a 17thC manor house, on the A525.
Three miles of sandy beach. A 300-yd stretch near the western end of the promenade is clearly marked with flags and recommended for swimming.

Rhoscolyn A2
Gwynedd. Pop 300. The epitome of picturesqueness—sand sheltered by rocky headlands and reached by a narrow lane

between high grassy banks. The village is ¼ mile away.

Rhosili D10
W. Glamorgan. Pop 300. An expansive sweep of golden sands reached from a clifftop village. Good surfing and famous as a hang-gliding venue.

Rhyl North G1
Clwyd. Pop 21,700. EC Thur. A magnet for Merseyside and the East Midlands, Rhyl attracts swarms of fun-seekers. Of interest—Royal Floral Hall, complete with children's zoo; the new Sun Centre and monorail; the bathing beauty contests. Long sandy beach.

St David's A8
Dyfed. Pop 1,700. EC Wed. A pint-sized city set on a small stream near the sea. Once of considerable importance it's now a delightful 'has-been'. The cathedral, nestling in a valley, was begun in the late 12thC. Across a brook are the ruins of the Bishop's Palace. Built by Bishop Gower in 1340, it was destroyed by Bishop Barlow in the 15thC. Sheltered sandy beaches at Caerfai and Whitesands Bay.

Sandy Haven B9
Dyfed. Firm sand along the thickly wooded banks of a picturesque creek.

Saundersfoot C9
Dyfed. Pop 2,500. EC Wed. Everything muddled and informal. The little harbour lies in a horseshoe of hills and cliffs. The whole place is flanked by sandy beaches.

Solva A8
Dyfed. Pop 700. A tiny village in a picturesque huddle along Solva Creek, it has become one of the most popular boating centres on St Bride's Bay. Smaus Lighthouse, lying 15 miles offshore, is one of the most isolated in the world. Of interest—a small but fascinating woollen mill at Middle Mill and craft workshops in the village.

Swansea F10
W. Glamorgan. Pop 171,300. EC Thur. MD Fri, Sat. The 'ugly, lovely town' of Dylan Thomas, full of broad, pleasant parks and suburban sobriety. Made a city by Prince Charles following his investiture as Prince of Wales. It's the main shopping centre for south-west Wales. Of interest—the Guildhall's magnificent Brangwyn Hall; the Industrial and Maritime Museum which has a working woollen mill; a superb new leisure centre; Swansea's 16thC fortress; Weobley Castle near Llandimore; 13thC Oystermouth Castle.

Talybont E4
Conwy Valley, Gwynedd. Pop 250. EC Wed. An unself-consciously pretty village of stone-built charm. The beach lies west of the village, ¼mile from the main road.

Tenby C9
Dyfed. Pop 4,700. EC Wed. A richly mediaeval place of close-knit narrow streets round a small harbour in the shelter of Castle Hill. A ruined 14thC stronghold stands on top of the hill. Of interest—the 15thC Tudor merchant's house; St Mary's Church, the largest parish church in Wales; boat trips to Caldey Island; a museum of local history; and the Manor House Leisure Park at nearby St Florence.

Tenby

Tywyn E4
Gwynedd. Pop 4,100. EC Wed. Lies back from the water's edge in the middle of a flat plain. Hills all round except to the west, where it is washed by the sea. Originally settled by the Saxons in 516 it is now a popular holiday resort. Of interest—St Cadfan's Church which houses Cadfan's

Stone, of early Christian origin; the narrow gauge railway of Talyllyn; the ruins of Castell-y-Bere; and the walk to Bird Rock. Three-mile sweep of sand and shingle beach.

Inland towns & villages

Abergavenny J9
Gwent. Pop 9,700. EC Thur. MD Tue, Fri. A big-hearted place with whiffs of elegance. Set in a mountain-ringed valley, Abergavenny is a large market town crammed closely round a long, twisting, narrow high street. This is the gateway to South Wales. The Romans had a fort here; the Normans made it an important stronghold. Of interest—the 19thC Angel Inn; church of St Mary; the great tithe barn of the priory; the castle which houses a museum.

Bala G2
Gwynedd. Pop 1,600. EC Wed. MD Thur. A discreet Victorian town straddling a wide tree-lined street at the eastern end of Bala Lake. It was the home of the Methodist revival in 18thC North Wales. Of interest—Tomen-y-Bala, a grassy mound behind the high street, once the site of a 13thC castle.

Beddgelert E2
Gwynedd. Pop 800. EC Wed. A compact group of stone-built inns and cottages surrounding a diminutive bridge, it's a mountain village set in the spectacular Aberglaslyn Valley. Of interest—the grave of Gelert; not far from the village, Dinas Emrys, an Iron Age and Roman hill fort; Hafod Lwyfog, a typical 17thC Snowdonia farmhouse; potteries; waymarked walks in the Beddgelert Forest.

Beddgelert

Blaenau Ffestiniog F2
Gwynedd. Pop 5,500. EC Thur. Pressed in by dark mountains, the walls of the buildings seem to grow out of the ground, all rugged rock and slate. Fabulous walks and exhilarating views. Of interest—Llechwedd Slate Caverns and Gloddfa Ganol Mountain Centre, both former slate mines, open to visitors; Stwlan dam at Tanygrisiau.

Brecon H8
Powys. Pop 6,300. EC Wed. MD Tues, Fri. A place of extremes in a landscape of hills and valleys. Built at the junction of the Rivers Honddu and Usk, Brecon is a prosperous market town dominated by a 13thC priory church; it's now the cathedral of the diocese of Swansea and Brecon. Look at the Iron Age hill fort to the north on a hill above the town; the remains of the 11thC castle; a partly restored Roman fort 2 miles west of the town; Llangorse lake to the east; the Brecknock Museum in Captain's Walk; the South Wales Borderers' Regimental Museum.

Builth Wells H7
Powys. Pop 1,600. EC Wed. MD Mon. A once prosperous Victorian spa, Builth Wells is now a sedate and sober market town set in broad green meadows and wooded hills. Rebuilt after a devastating fire in 1691 it consists of one long high street running between the 18thC bridge across the River Wye and the mediaeval church. Of interest—the 18thC Pump Room; the old Crown Hotel; the stone-built wool market; the Wyeside Arts Centre.

Builth Wells

Caerphilly H10
S. Glamorgan. Pop 41,500. EC/MD Wed.
Once commanding a tangle of valleys to its
north, the ruined castle totally dominates the
town, which was both a former Roman fort
and a Norman citadel. Its fame now rests on
the fine white crumbly cheese which has
been copied all over the world, but alas is no
longer made in the town.

Carmarthen D8
Dyfed, Pop 13,300. EC Thur. MD Wed, Sat.
An animated old world Welsh town with
bent-backed houses and narrow winding
streets crammed onto a bluff above the River
Towy. The town started life as a Roman
fortress. By the end of the 11thC
Carmarthen was really 2 towns; the Norman
town developed round the castle and the
Welsh town, a ¼-mile to the east, centred on
the Augustinian priory of St John the
Evangelist. The two remained bitterly hostile
until finally fused together. Have a look at
the 13thC church of St Peter; the Guildhall,
built in 1770; the museum now housed in
the former Bishop's Palace at Abergwili; the
Roman amphitheatre on the edge of the
town.

Chepstow K10
Gwent. Pop 8,000. EC Wed. It seems like any
other place at first, until you enter via the
16thC town gate and then everything seems
to happen fast. The town falls rapidly away
before you in a series of twisting streets and
roofscapes. There are views across to wooded
hills, and at the bottom of the town is the
mighty Norman castle. It is an impressive
ruin standing in a shallow cliff on the west
bank of the Wye.
Chepstow was once a busy port before the
railways and bigger ships. It is still a
flourishing market centre. Of interest—the
Norman parish church of St Mary,
extensively restored in 1871; the iron bridge
across the Wye; the 19thC bow-windowed
houses in Bridge Street; the mediaeval
stocks; local museum.

Denbigh H1
Clwyd. Pop 8,400. EC Thur. MD Wed.
Dominated by an impressive 13thC castle,
Denbigh, small-scale and mellow, climbs a
limestone hill. The place is gentle and
ancient. H. M. Stanley, explorer of Africa
and the man who found Dr Livingstone, was
born here. Of interest—the 14thC garrison
chapel; the 16thC town hall; the Hawk and
Buckle Inn with its site of an old cockpit.

Denbigh

Dolgellau F3
Gwynedd. Pop 2,600. EC Wed. MD Fri. A
stone-built market town. It's a knot of
narrow streets and grey-faced houses
hemmed in by foothills and the massive
Cadair Idris mountain. Of interest—the
17thC bridge; Toll House; the 13thC effigy
in the church of St Mary.

Grosmont J8
Gwent. Pop 600. A village on the
England/Wales border standing with its
13thC castle high above the winding River
Monnow, hinting at a mediaeval past of
great importance that the 14thC church
confirms.

Haverfordwest B8
Dyfed. Pop 10,500. EC Thur. MD Tue, Sat.
A tight-packed place built round a 13thC
square-walled fortress on high ground above
the River Western Cleddau. Once an
important port, it is the county town of
south Dyfed, and its main shopping centre.
Of interest—the 13thC church of St Mary
with fine lancet windows; Shire Hall; the
Market House; the old quay along the river;
remains of the 13thC Augustinian priory.
Near to the coast and the quiet creeks of
Milford Haven.

Hay-on-Wye J7
Powys. Pop 1,200. EC Tue. MD Mon, Thur.
A fretted skyline of buildings clambers up a
sharp slope of land to the south of a broad,
shallow part of the Wye. Behind the town to
the south, the Black Mountains add a touch
of thunder to the town's silhouette. A one-
time Roman fort and Norman castle town, it
is now a thriving market and tourist town
and a centre of the book trade, with some
memorable inns. Of interest—Hay Castle,
founded in 1090 but now predominantly
Jacobean in style; 'the world's largest'
secondhand bookshop; the Three Cocks, a
once important coaching stage; the nearby
castle ruins at Clifford, to the north; and
Longtown to the south.

Kidwelly D9
Dyfed. Pop 3,000. A small town full of
mediaeval charm. Kidwelly grew up at the
mouth of the River Gwendraeth Fach in the
days of the Norman invasion of South
Wales. Ruined Kidwelly Castle dominates
the town. A second settlement grew up
across the river, built round the 12thC
Benedictine priory. The 2 townships are
linked by a splendid 14thC bridge. Of
interest—the ruined 14thC gateway near the
castle; the priory church.

Lampeter E7
Dyfed. Pop 2,500. EC Wed. MD alt Tue. A
bustling market town built round a ford of
the River Teifi. In the heart of rich
farmland. Lampeter is famous for the horse
fair held annually in May. St David's
College (now part of the University of
Wales) was founded in 1882 for training
students for holy orders.

Llanddewi Brefi F6
Dyfed. Pop 500. A handful of quiet, austere
houses dominated by an equally stern church
standing on a mound. Serene and dignified
in lonely open landscape. Have a look at the
early Christian memorial stones in the
churchyard.

Llandeilo F8
Dyfed. Pop 2,000. EC Thur. MD Sat. A
modest market town set in a sweep of the
River Towy. As clean as a whistle, Llandeilo
is all shiny-faced houses and well-kept grass
following a Civic Trust scheme. Of
interest—ruins of the 11thC Dinefwr Castle;
Dryslwyn Castle 5 miles west; Carreg
Cennen Castle, built on a limestone hill 3½
miles to the south-east.

Llandrindod Wells H6
Powys. Pop 3,200. EC Wed. A town of
Edwardian spaciousness. Standing on a
700-foot-high plateau overlooking the River
Ithon, it was once the largest and most
popular of Welsh spas. In late Victorian
times it attracted over 80,000 visitors a year.
Of interest—the well preserved Roman fort
of Castell Collen above Llanyre; the Pump
Room; the lake, where boats can be
hired.

**Llanfairpwllgwyngyllgogerychw-
yrndrobwllllantysiliogogogoch**
Gwynedd. A descriptive, enterprising but
extraordinary mouthful. The village's famous
name is a combination of the local names of
Llanfair and Llantysilio. Its meaning is 'St
Mary's by the White Aspen over the
Whirlpool and St Tysilio's by the red cave'.
The railway station is now a café, the
famous nameplate, so often snatched by
jovial students, is now in the Penrhyn Castle
Museum.

Llangollen H2
Clwyd. Pop 3,100. EC Thur. MD Tue. Built
around the singing River Dee with high
ridges of land closing in on both sides. It's a
place of surprises, like a Welsh ballad. The
home of the International Musical
Eisteddfod held annually in early July. Of
interest—the 14thC stone bridge; Plas
Newydd, an 18thC black-and-white timbered
mansion; Llangollen Canal with its Canal
Exhibition Centre; the castle ruins; the
13thC Valle Crucis Abbey.

Llanidloes G5

Powys. Pop 2,300. EC Thur. MD Sat. An historic market town with green hills just beyond, built at the junction of the River Severn with the River Clywedog. Of interest—the 13thC church with a fine hammer-beam roof; the old market hall; the huge Clywedog dam and lake with sailing, fishing and nature trail.

Llantrisant H10

Mid Glamorgan. Pop 2,300. EC Thur. A mediaeval town in the saddle between two hills, dominated by its church and the ruined tower of the castle. This was the home of the eccentric Victorian, Dr William Price who, to the horror of the local inhabitants, cremated his dead son at a time when such a practice was considered barbarous. New development has diluted the brimstone and fire atmosphere. Of interest—an Iron Age hill fort to the east.

Machynlleth F4

Powys. Pop 1,800. EC Thur. MD Wed. A small-scale market town wedged amongst hills, and spread out along a gentle High Street. Note the giant 19thC clock tower. Machynlleth was a former Roman military station. In the early 15thC it was chosen by Owain Glyndwr to be the capital of a Wales freed from the rule of Henry IV. Of interest—the stone-built parliament house in the centre of Maengwyn Street; the 18thC White Lion; a Jacobean house at the upper end of Maengwyn Street; the National Centre for Alternative Technology, near Corris.

Monmouth K9

Gwent. Pop 6,500. EC Thur. MD Fri, alt Mon. Standing at the point where the River Monnow flows into the Wye, it was a strategic stronghold of mediaeval Wales. It held the lower hills between the moorland heart of Wales and the wide fields of the Midlands; it mastered the outfall of the rivers whose upper reaches lead to the central passes between the Severn and the Dovey. Whoever held it could control the whole of South Wales.
This was the site of Roman Blestium, and the 12thC home of Geoffrey of Monmouth. In 1387 Henry V was born in the 11thC castle. Charles Rolls, of Rolls-Royce fame, was born at nearby Hendre (see his statue in Agincourt Square).
Of interest—the mediaeval fortified bridge gateway across the Monnow. It is the only one in Britain, and one of the few remaining in Europe; the 14thC church; the 18thC Shire Hall; Nelson Museum.

Montgomery J4

Powys. Pop 1,000. A lively market town of bow-windowed and cobble-stoned charm, hiding beneath the ruins of a 13thC castle. There are some Elizabethan, Jacobean and Georgian houses. The 14thC church has a fine rood screen. Look at the historic Rhydwhiman Ford.

Newport J10

Gwent. Pop 112,000. EC Thur. MD Fri, Sat. A busy commercial centre. Built on the banks of the River Usk, Newport is a product of the Industrial Revolution. Of interest—the transporter bridge, which carries cars and pedestrians on a moving platform; the castle ruins; the Roman amphitheatre at nearby Caerleon; the museum and art gallery in John Frost Square; the Fourteen Locks Canal Interpretive Centre at High Cross with exhibits on canal history.

New Radnor H6

Powys. Pop 2,000. To the east of Radnor Forest, it was originally an important borough walled-in with a regular pattern of small-scale streets dominated by an 11thC castle. The castle was destroyed first by King John in the 13thC, rebuilt by his son, and destroyed by the Welsh prince Owain Glyndwr in the early 15thC. Only earthworks and part of the town walls remain. Of interest—2½ miles to the east is the hamlet of Old Radnor.

Newtown H5

Powys. Pop 5,400. EC Thur. MD Tue, Sat. A prosperous market town happily ensconced in the Severn Valley. Founded in the late 13thC when the then victorious King of England, Edward I, had a new town built round a small village commanding a ford across the Severn. The birthplace of Robert Owen, factory reformer and founder of the co-operative movement. Of interest—the textile museum in an original hand-loom weaving factory in Commercial Street.

Presteigne J6

Powys. Pop 1,200. EC Thur. A border town deep in the gentle hills and wide valleys between England and Wales. A pleasant and peaceful place with black-and-white half-timbered cottages and houses. Of interest—the church of St Andrew with Saxon and Norman work and a 16thC Flemish tapestry; the Tudor-built Radnorshire Arms; the mediaeval Duke's Arms.

Ruthin H1

Clwyd. Pop 4,300. EC Thur. A pleasant, historic market town and a splendid centre for exploring this part of N. Wales. Of interest—the 13thC Ruthin Castle; the 14thC church; Nantclwyd House in Castle Street, a fine example of a 14thC town house; the 16thC half-timbered Exmewe Hall; the old court and prison, built 1401.

St Asaph H1

Clwyd. Pop 3,100. EC Thur. MD Thur. Dates back to Roman times. A quiet, sensible, hilltop town. The cathedral was remodelled in the 19thC by Gilbert Scott. Of interest—Pont Dafydd, a stone bridge built in 1630; the 15thC St Asaph parish church.

Tintern K9

Gwent. Pop 700. EC Wed. A riverside village in the dramatic Wye valley immortalised by Wordsworth. Of interest—Tintern Abbey; forest and river walks; the old railway station.

Tregaron F6

Dyfed. Pop 4,200. EC Thur. MD alt Tue. Backed by the lovely range of the Cambrian hills, Tregaron is a small town with a simple square—all a little apart from the world. Of interest—the Iron Age hill fort ½-mile to the north-east; the 14thC church tower; the great Tregaron bog to the north.

Tremadog E2

Gwynedd. Pop 1,100. EC Wed. The birthplace of Lawrence of Arabia. Tremadog is set in the deep Glaslyn Valley overshadowed by peaks. A classically planned model town built by Alexander Madocks in the early 19thC. Small-scale but spacious, its grey stone buildings stand formally round the town hall and square.

Usk **J9**
Gwent. Pop 2,000. EC Wed. MD alt Mon.
Built on high ground on the east bank of the
River Usk. There is a modest but broad
square, whilst the ruined castle looks over
broad meadowlands. Eight miles south of the
Usk, at Caerleon, are the remains of a great
Roman legionary fortress, with an impressive
museum.

Wrexham **J2**
Clwyd. Pop 39,000. EC Wed. MD Mon. The
centre of the North Wales coalfield,
Wrexham has one surprising gem, the pit-
shaft-coloured church at St Giles. Listed as
one of the Seven Wonders of Wales, it's a
richly sculptured masterpiece built in 1472.
The wrought-iron gates to the churchyard
are by the Davies Brothers of Bersham. Look
at Pugin's Roman Catholic church in Regent
Street; the 19thC Jacobean market hall; the
Agricultural Museum.

Regional features

Coracles
Shaped like a giant walnut shell, the Welsh
coracle is made of willow and hazel canes
covered with hides. Its design has not
changed since ancient times, and it is still
used for fishing salmon on parts of the Teifi
and Towy rivers.

Eisteddfod
The contests of music and poetry known as
Eisteddfodau have been an outstanding
feature of Welsh life for centuries. One of
the earliest on a national scale was called in
1176 by Lord Rhys, one of the Welsh
princes. He invited all the country's bards to
his castle at Cardigan to compete against
each other. Those of South Wales were
found to excel in music, those of the North
in verse.

The Welsh language
Welsh is a Celtic language related to Breton,
Cornish, Irish and Scots Gaelic and has been
used as a written language since about the
6thC.
Written Welsh is standard, but the phonetic
spoken Welsh varies in accent in different
parts of the country.

aber	—mouth of a river or stream
afon	—river
bach	—small
bryn	—hill
ban	—high place/peak
carreg/ cerrig	—stone/stones
craig	—rock
coed	—wood/trees
dyffryn	—valley
llyn	—lake
traeth	—beach
ynys	—island
bedd	—grave
capel	—chapel
eglwys	—church
plas	—mansion
castell	—castle
dinas	—city/fort
caer	—fort
hafod	—summer residence
hendre	—winter residence
newydd	—new
tŷ	—house
heol fford	—road
llwybr	—path
garth	—enclosure
llan	—saint

Famous people

Owain Glyndwr (c1349–c1415) **H3**
*Sycharth, Clwyd. 2 miles NE of Llangedwyn,
nr Oswestry.* Sycharth was the main
residence of the almost legendary Welsh
hero. The moated mound and bailey castle
have recently been excavated.
After Glyndwr was declared Prince of Wales

he held a parliament at Machynlleth in 1404
in what is now the Owain Glyndwr Institute,
Maengwyn Street. He may have lived in the
Royal House, Penrallt Street. According to
tradition, Glyndwr died and was buried in
Monnington-on-Wye. More romantic is the
fact that he was forced into outlawry some
time after 1408, disappeared, and died in an
unknown hiding place.

David Lloyd George (1863–1945) **E2**
Llanystumdwy, Gwynedd. The Prime
Minister spent his childhood in this lovely
village. He lived with his uncle at Highgate,
on the main Criccieth road, attended the
church school, and died in his home, Ty
Newydd, close by. The Lloyd George
Memorial Museum stands in the grounds of
his estate. *Closed winter.*

Merlin **D8**
Old Oak, Priory St, Carmarthen, Dyfed. King
Arthur's wizard is said to have been born in
Carmarthen. Certainly one of his favourite
haunts was on the winding River Towy. The
gnarled stump of the 'Old Oak' has been
associated with him for centuries. Merlin
prophesied that when the tree fell the town
would perish. They are both still there.

Robert Owen (1771–1858) **H5**
Broad Street, Newtown, Powys. Once the
home of social reformer Robert Owen, it is
now a museum displaying books, pictures,
documents and relics relating to Owen.
Closed winter.

Sir Henry M. Stanley (1841–1904) **H1**
St Asaph, Clwyd. Henry Morton Stanley,
famous explorer who found Dr Livingstone,
spent nine years in the workhouse here
before he set sail for America as a cabin boy.
He was born in a cottage near Denbigh
Castle, where an exhibition relates to his life.

Dylan Thomas (1914–53) **D9**
Boathouse, Laugharne, Dyfed. The poet lived
here for many years and is buried in the
local churchyard. Every year on the 3rd July
the local Thomas Festival presents 'Under
Milk Wood'. *Boathouse open to the public.*

Cathedrals, abbeys & churches

Aberedw Church **H7**
Aberedw, Powys. A 13thC Welsh mountain
church extensively restored in the Tudor
period. There is a fine late 14thC rood
screen. The north porch has a splendid
hammer-beam roof and wooden front.

Bangor Cathedral **E1**
Bangor, Gwynedd. Founded in 548 it was
almost wholly destroyed in the 11thC and
15thC. It was later transformed in the
Decorated style by Sir Gilbert Scott and his
son between 1868 and 1880.

Brecon Cathedral **H8**
Powys. This massive cathedral, originally the
13thC priory church of St John the
Evangelist, stands high above the River
Honddu dominating the narrow streets of
Brecon.

Capel-y-ffin Church **J8**
Capel-y-ffin, Powys. Surrounded by yews the
church is a simple cottage-like building with
a wide porch and a tower in the remote
Gospel Pass in the Black Mountains.

Clynnog Fawr Church **D2**
Clynnog Fawr, Gwynedd. Standing in a
coastal village of whitewashed cottages, this
is the best Gothic church west of Conwy; a
collegiate building with a porch, carved rood
screen, choir stalls and fine timbered roof.
Founded by St Beuno in the early 7thC, it
became a pilgrims' resting place.

Llandaff Cathedral **H10**
Cardiff, S. Glamorgan. A small corner for
quiet contemplation. Lying half hidden in a

hollow the cathedral stands in a village at the end of the creeping suburbs of Cardiff. Begun in 1107, the building is all west-of-England English, particularly the 6 western arches of the nave. The west front was completed in 1220; the elegant Lady Chapel was added in the 13thC. The north-west tower was added by Henry VII's uncle. The cathedral was completely renovated following war damage and its massive arch bears Epstein's figure 'Christ in Majesty'.

Llanengan Church   D3
Llanengan, Gwynedd. A square-towered 15thC miracle dressed in the best of Gothic taste. The fine double nave is crossed by a wonderful rood screen.

Montgomery Church   J4
Montgomery, Powys. The church has a magnificence out of all proportion to the town's size. Built mainly in the 13thC, it has a rood screen of great beauty; seating stalls complete with misericords; a notable Renaissance tomb of Sir Richard Herbert.

St Asaph Cathedral   H1
St Asaph, Clwyd. Perched on a hilltop with the city huddling round, it is the smallest cathedral in Britain. Thoroughly restored by Sir Gilbert Scott in the most sensitive way. It has had a chequered history. Founded in AD 537, it was destroyed by Owain Glyndwr and later burnt by the Roundheads. Setting for the North Wales Music Festival, held every September.

St Asaph Cathedral

St Woolos, Newport

St David's Cathedral   A8
St David's, Dyfed. Set in a shallow vale, the cathedral is the third to stand on this site. Built in the 12thC of purple coloured stone, it has been a place of pilgrimage for centuries.
In 1800 it was heavily restored by John Nash, and by Gilbert Scott in 1862. The nave is an intricate Norman structure. On the choir stalls are some fascinating misericord carvings; delicate fan vaulting above the Holy Trinity chapel. Across a brook are the ruins of Bishop Gower's palace built in 1340.

St David's Cathedral

St David's Church   C9
Caldey Island, Dyfed. A single-minded and rugged monolith as solid as a rock. Built in that twilight Christian period following the Roman exodus, it is a stiff-limbed creation made to withstand the press of gales and time. Short boat trip from Tenby.

St John's, Cardiff   St David's, Caldey Island

St John's Church   H10
Cardiff, S. Glamorgan. A 15thC church in Perpendicular style with an elegant tower built in 1443.

St Woolos Church   J10
Newport, Gwent. Built in the 12thC it has a fine Norman nave. The two outstanding features are the Galilee Chapel and the ponderous square tower.

Wrexham Church   J2
Wrexham, Clwyd. The parish church of Wrexham, nicely sited just off the High Street. It's a lavish 15thC church in the most prosperous of Perpendicular styles. The tower is a splendid pinnacled landmark 135-feet high. In the churchyard is a memorial to the much travelled Elihu Yale, one of the founders of Yale University.

Castles & ruins

Abergavenny Castle   J9
Abergavenny, Gwent. Standing on the wooded hill that dominates the town, it is a melancholy skeleton bereft of self-defence. Built in the 12thC, all that is visible is the gatehouse, the mound, some of the walls, and the foundations of the keep. The castle was captured by Llewelyn in 1215, burned by Owain Glyndwr in 1404, and finally slighted by Fairfax during the Civil War. The 18thC Hunting Lodge in the grounds houses a museum.

Aberystwyth Castle   E5
Aberystwyth, Dyfed. Gaunt remains stand on a steep hill at the end of the promenade. The castle was symmetrical in plan. There was no keep, but it was defended by two lines of walls and a moat. Like the other North Wales castles it could be supplied from the sea. A town was built alongside it as a colony for English settlers.

Beaumaris Castle   B2
Beaumaris, Gwynedd. Guarding the Menai Straits, Beaumaris is the classic example of the concentric plan. The main principle of the design was that any enemy gaining control of the outer curtain would be left at the mercy of the garrison in the inner ward. Begun in 1295, it included a sea-water moat and a dock for shipping protected by the outer defences of the castle.

Beaumaris Castle

Caernarfon Castle   E1
Caernarfon, Gwynedd. Begun in 1285 after Edward I's successful campaign against the Welsh. An uncompromising giant with an aura of the Holy Land. Mirrored in the glassy waters of the River Seiont, it is the most magnificent of the Edwardian Welsh castles. Inside is the Royal Welch Fusiliers Regimental Museum.

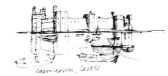

Caernarfon Castle

Caerphilly Castle   H10
Caerphilly, Mid Glamorgan. The castle is one of the largest and finest examples of 14thC military construction from the golden age of castle building in Britain. It was built on the concentric plan by Gilbert, Earl of Gloucester in 1267. There is a rectangular inner ward with a fat drum-tower at each corner and a gatehouse in the centre of each end wall. The outer walls were protected by lakes formed by damming up 2 streams.

Caerphilly Castle

Cardiff Castle   H10
Cardiff, S. Glamorgan. The finest example in Wales of a Norman castle on a mound surrounded by a ditch. Built in 1093 by the Norman war-lord Robert Fitzhamon, it was replaced by a stone keep in the 13thC. In the 15thC the main part of the present castle was built, including the famous octagonal tower. Of interest—the drawing room with a Louis XIII clock, the library, the great hall, the banqueting hall and the Chaucer Room.

Carmarthen Castle   D8
Carmarthen, Dyfed. A gaunt stone ruin standing on a high cliff overlooking the river. Only the gateways and towers remain of what was once an important residence of the princes of South Wales. See also the foundations of a Roman fort.

Carreg Cennen Castle   F8
Nr Llandeilo, Dyfed. Daringly sited on a limestone crag high above a river valley, it's at once austere and yet graceful in decay. Fairly regular in plan, it was built in the 13thC. Between the outer and the inner wards is a strong and elaborate barbican. The passage to the inner ward lay over 3 drawbridges.

Castell Coch   H10
Mid Glamorgan, 6 miles NW of Cardiff. If you were looking for a slightly blood-curdling setting for a Bavarian fairy tale you couldn't go far wrong with this turreted stone dragon. Originally the 13thC home of the princes of Powys, traditional allies of the English, it was rebuilt by William Burges in 1875. The castle was planned in a triangle with round towers at the corners. It guards the mouth of Taffs Well Gorge

Chepstow Castle   K10
Chepstow, Gwent. Built on rising ground on the west bank of the River Wye, in a commanding strategic position, the castle was begun in 1067 by William FitzOsbern. Chepstow is one of the mightiest Norman strongholds in the west. It consists of a series of courtyards following the line of the land. There are a hall keep, round towers and 2 impressive gatehouses at front and rear.

Chepstow Castle

Chirk Castle   J2
Nr Wrexham, Clwyd. 2 miles from Chirk off A5. A 13thC frontier fortress. Rectangular in plan, it has a round tower at each corner. In the central square are relics from the Civil War. The chambers and dining-rooms inside are richly evocative of the castle's history. There is a splendid park with fine ornamental wrought iron gates by the Davies brothers of Bersham. *Closed winter.*

Conwy Castle   F1
Conwy, Gwynedd. Built as a residence as well as a fortress, it is both elegant and formidable with 8 massive drum-towers connected by curtain walls some 15-feet thick. An outstanding example of Edward I's genius for military architecture, it is sited on broad precipitous rock beside the River Conwy. Hiding behind it is the walled town, an excellent touring centre full of interest.

Denbigh Castle   H1
Denbigh, Clwyd. A long, spidery but handsome ruin. The original Welsh castle was a timber castle on top of a mound. During Edward I's successful campaign of 1282 it withstood attack for a period, but after its capture it was replaced by a stone castle built 1282–1322. It has an impressive gatehouse.

Harlech Castle   E3
Harlech, Gwynedd. Begun in 1283, it was built by Edward I on a high rock promontory overlooking what was then an inlet of sea. Overpowering and impressive, it was entered over a moat by a stone arch, and over the drawbridges of an impregnable barbican. Approximately square in plan it has round towers at the 4 corners and a central gatehouse on the east wall.

Harlech Castle

Laugharne Castle   D9
Laugharne, Dyfed. Romantic remains under a mass of ivy. It is a late 13thC stone-built castle standing on the west bank of the River Taf. There was once a strong round keep consisting of 3 storeys, the top storey covered by a pointed dome rising above the battlements.

Llanstephan Castle   D9
Llanstephan, Dyfed. An impressive ruin perched on a headland above this Towy-mouth village. Built in the 12thC it was captured and re-captured by the Welsh and the English. It consisted of an upper ward above the steepest slope, and a lower ward protected by ditches.

Manorbier Castle   C9
Dyfed. 5 miles SSE of Pembroke off A4139. A Norman castle overlooking the sea, privately owned but open to visitors, surrounded by all the features of a mediaeval community: church, ponds, mill, dovecot and orchards. Built in the early 12thC for William de Barri, it has a series of towers linked by high curtain walls and a gatehouse complete with portcullis. *Closed winter.*

Manorbier Castle

Newport Castle   J10
Newport, Gwent. A ruin almost ecclesiastical in appearance. It was built in 1171 along the River Usk as part of the Norman Conquest of the west. Enough of it survived the Border Wars to be remodelled in the 15thC during the Wars of the Roses. Cromwell finally reduced it to ruins. The most impressive part remaining is the central tower.

Ogmore Castle   G10
3 miles SW of Bridgend, Mid Glamorgan. Once the 12thC stronghold of the hated William de Braose, it is now a romantic ruin, with keep and moat, living peaceably by some companionable cottages alongside the River Ewenny.

Oystermouth Castle   E10
Mumbles, W. Glamorgan. Built in 1287 on a hill with wide views, the present ruin is the second castle constructed on the site. It was somewhat irregular in plan, with a gatehouse, an open courtyard and keep, all connected by high curtain walls without towers. On the top floor was the chapel, its piscina and traceried window still preserved.

Pembroke Castle **B9**
Pembroke, Dyfed. An imperious custodian of a rocky ridge above the River Pembroke and surrounding marshes. Begun in the late 11thC it was an important Norman stronghold in South Wales. It was later used as a base for Norman operations in Ireland. Pembroke was the Parliamentarians' first major foothold in South Wales during the Civil War.

Raglan Castle **J9**
Raglan, Gwent. Set between wooded slopes and river valley it is an elegantly aloof giant built in the old Welsh border district of Gwent. The projecting towers in clean, dressed stone are 15thC. The great Yellow Tower of Gwent is a fine example of a self-contained fortified dwelling surrounded by a moat.

Rhuddlan Castle **H1**
Rhuddlan, Clwyd. Now a massive and magnetic ruin, it was begun in 1277 under Edward I. The castle stands at what was the lowest fording place for crossing the River Clwyd and the coastal marshes. Concentrically planned, it had a square inner ward with great round towers and gatehouses at the corners. The ward was protected by curtain walls and wet and dry moats.

Tintern Abbey **J7**
Tintern, Gwent. Once a great Cistercian abbey founded in 1131, it is now an impressive and bare skeleton, elegant and intricate like the winter tracery of trees. Tintern lies in the green fields of a broad valley at the point where the River Wye widens. The nave is all silence and green grass.

Valle Crucis Abbey **J2**
Nr Llantysilio, Clwyd. With hills framed in its glassless windows, it is an attractive ruin in a secluded and sheltered site. Built in the great tradition of the Cistercians, the abbey was founded in 1201. Its choir is said to have rivalled Salisbury.

Unusual buildings

Bangor-is-Coed Bridge **J2**
Bangor-is-Coed, Clwyd. A fine 17thC bridge said to have been designed by Inigo Jones.

City Hall **F10**
Swansea, Glamorgan. Designed by Sir Percy Thomas in 1930 with cathedral precision: an elegant symbol of civic dignity. Inside are murals by Frank Brangwyn.

Conwy Railway Bridge **F1**
Conwy, Gwynedd. Parallel to Telford's bridge, this one was built by Robert Stephenson in 1848. It is of tubular construction in a single span; each of the 2 tubes is 412 feet long.

Conwy Suspension Bridge **F1**
Conwy, Gwynedd. Built over the River Conwy in 1826 by Telford, it is a suspension bridge with iron chains. Telford designed the towers in castellated form to harmonise with the mediaeval castle.

Derry Ormond Tower **E7**
Llangybi, Dyfed. Standing on high ground to the south of Derry Ormond is a circular column with slit windows. It was built in the 19thC.

Holiday cottages **E2**
Porthmadog, Gwynedd. Simple, but richly individualistic housing, jammed informally together along the water's edge. Built on Porthmadog Quay in 1968, the housing was designed by John Phillips.

Menai Suspension Bridge **E1**
Menai Strait. 2¼ miles W of Bangor. It carries the A5 London to Holyhead road and was built when the road was continued to Gwynedd.
Designed by Telford, work on the bridge began in 1820. Although not an original idea it was the largest project of its kind undertaken at that time. The bridge is nearly ½ mile in length and has a central span of 579 feet.

Severn Bridge **K10**
Nr Chepstow, Gwent. Designed by Sir Gilbert Roberts, the bridge was opened in 1966. The gateway to Wales, it is an elegant rainbow of steel soaring over the wide Severn. The whole bridge is over 2 miles in length, and the main bridge is carried on 2 steel towers 445 feet high.

Ty Hyll **F1**
Betws-y-Coed, Gwynedd. A 15thC building named the 'Ugly House' because of its construction: irregular-shaped stones hurriedly heaped together. At the time, any free man could obtain freehold rights on common land if he could build a fireplace and a chimney, starting at dusk by managing to have the chimney smoking by dawn. The rest of the house could then be finished at leisure.

Houses & gardens

Bodnant **F1**
Denbigh, Gwynedd. 4 miles S of Conwy. A superb terraced garden laid out in 1875 by Henry Pochin in the Italian style and developed by the Lords Aberconway. It is one of the finest gardens in the country. The Pin Mill, originally built in Gloucestershire as a pin factory, stands at one end of a long narrow pool surrounded by smooth green lawns edged with herbaceous borders and faced by an open air theatre. *Closed winter.*

Cymerau **F4**
Glandyfi, Dyfed. 5 miles SW of Machynlleth. A garden of medium size set in glorious country with splendid views. There is a large collection of flowering shrubs.

Erdigg J2
Wrexham, Clwyd. Off A483. Fully restored in 1977 after 40 years of decay, the house was built in the late 17thC for the Yorke family. A complete picture of the house in its heyday can be gained from the State rooms and servants' quarters, gardens and outhouses, with the laundry, bakehouses, sawmill and smithy, all in working order.

Gwrych Castle G1
Abergele, Clwyd. A Gothic fantasy designed by C. A. Busby in 1814. The castellated walls and turrets are pure romance.

Gwyllt Gardens E2
Portmeirion, Gwynedd. 2 miles SW of Penrhyndeudraeth. Twenty miles of woodland walks, wild with rhododendrons, azaleas and sub-tropical species surrounding the fairyland setting of Portmeirion, perched above Cardigan Bay with Snowdon in the background.

Hafodty E1
Bettws Garmon in Snowdonia National Park, Gwynedd. Of particular interest are the Nant Mill Waterfalls where the migration of elvers can be seen from June to August, and leaping salmon can be spotted from September to December. There are charming water and rock gardens.

Nanteos F5
Dyfed. 2½ miles SE of Aberystwyth. Set in the shadow of a steeply wooded ridge it is one of the most notable of Georgian manor houses in Wales. Built in 1739, its main block is a sandstone-faced rectangle. Richard Wagner, who visited Nanteos, is said to have composed part of 'Parsifal' here.

Penrhyn Castle E1
Gwynedd. 1¼ miles E of Bangor. A joyous joke like an elaborate Hollywood Valhalla. The castle is splendidly sited on a ridge at the end of the Menai Strait. In the state bedroom is the heavily carved slate bed in which Queen Victoria slept when she visited Penrhyn in 1859.

Plas Newydd E1
Llanfairpwll, Isle of Anglesey, Gwynedd. Built 1800–1810 on the site of an old house. A result of the combined efforts of James Wyatt and Joseph Potter, it is set in civilised parkland against wild views of Snowdonia. Somewhat de-Gothicised in the 1930s, it is basically classic in order and symmetry with a suggestion of romantic fervour.

Powis Castle J4
Welshpool, Powys. An aloof and mediaeval house standing like an abrupt red cliff in the landscape. Renovated in the 18thC by Capability Brown it has all the Italianate whims and fancies of an elaborate wedding cake. The state rooms are full of fine furniture, paintings, murals and relics of Clive of India.
The magnificent terraced gardens were completed in the 18thC at immense cost, dropping down in 4 stages to a lawn. *Closed winter.*

Museums & galleries

Bangor Art Gallery and Museum of Welsh Antiquities E1
Old Canonry, College Road, Bangor, Gwynedd. Collections illustrating the history of North Wales; prehistoric and Roman antiquities, furniture, textiles and clothing.

Glynn Vivian Art Gallery F10
Alexandra Road, Swansea, W. Glamorgan. Exhibits of Swansea porcelain and pottery; a large collection of pictures with many Welsh artists represented; Richard Wilson, Augustus John, Kyffin Williams; bronzes by Epstein and Barbara Hepworth.

Merthyr Tydfil Art Gallery and Museum H9
Cyfarthfa Castle, Merthyr Tydfil, Mid Glamorgan. A Neo-Gothic castle is the setting for this local museum: relics of the iron smelting and coal industries, natural history and antiquities, a replica of a Welsh kitchen, paintings, Swansea and Nantgarw china, coins and medals.

The Narrow Gauge Railway Museum E4
Wharf Station, Tywyn, Gwynedd. Started as a collection devoted to the old Talyllyn Railway which was built in the 1860s, the museum now owns a number of British and foreign built items. Some of the wagons and locomotives are over 100 years old. *Closed winter.*

National Centre for Alternative Technology F4
Llwyngwern Quarry, Machynlleth, Powys. Solar, water, and wind power in action. Organic gardening. Visit an energy conservation house and solar heated houses.

The National Library of Wales E5
Aberystwyth, Dyfed. One of the 6 copyright libraries in Britain. Most of the collection is related to Wales. There is also a magnificent set of over 50 drawings by Thomas Rowlandson.

The National Museum of Wales H10
Cathays Park, Cardiff, S Glamorgan. The essence of Wales and the Welsh amassed under a single roof. Geology, botany, zoology, archaeology, industry and art are all represented. Among the prized possessions are the Dolgellau chalice and paten and the Dynevor plate.

Newport Museum and Art Gallery J10
John Frost Square, Newport, Gwent. Many fine treasures here. Remains from the Romano-British town of Caerwent, a collection of Pontypool and Usk japan-ware, and a superb collection of early English watercolours.

Penrhyn Castle E1
Bangor, Gwynedd. The Norman-style castle built of Mona marble 1827–40, holds a fine collection of over 1,000 dolls from all over the world; also stuffed birds, animals and insects, and a locomotive museum, including rolling stock. *Closed winter.*

Plas Newydd Museum H2
Grapes Hill, Llangollen, Clwyd. A black-and-white 18thC house, once the home of the eccentric blue-stockings, the 'Ladies of Llangollen', and now a museum with some fine oak carvings and stained glass.

The Royal Welch Fusiliers E1
Queen's Tower, Caernarfon Castle, Gwynedd. The museum presents the history of the regiment from its foundation in 1689. On display is the hat ribbon worn by William of Orange, 1690; officer's mitre cap, 1750; campaign medals and portraits.

Welsh Folk Museum H10
St Fagans, nr Cardiff, S Glamorgan. Set in 100 acres of woodland, the museum offers cottages, farms, a woollen mill, chapel, tollgate house, smithy, barn, cockpit, gipsy caravan and furnished Tudor mansion, all beautifully re-erected and preserved. Don't miss the Gallery of National Culture with its collections relating to Welsh life and manners.

Botanical gardens

Duffryn Gardens H10
8 miles SW of Cardiff on A48, S. Glamorgan. Some rare trees and shrubs are included in the 100 acres of gardens. Interesting collection in the greenhouses. Parking for 1,000 cars. *Closed winter.*

Zoos, aquaria & aviaries

Penscynor Wildlife Park F9
Cilfrew, Neath, West Glamorgan. An 11-acre park filled with a glorious bird collection, some mammals and a small aquarium. The Tropical House has free-flying birds, including hummingbirds. The flower gardens have large flight cages filled with multi-coloured feathers, as well as large wading birds, penguins, parakeets and woolly monkeys.

The Welsh Mountain Zoo and Botanic Gardens G1
Flagstaff Gardens, Colwyn Bay, Clwyd. Noted especially for its free-flying birds of prey. Displays are given daily in the summer of hawks, falcons and vultures. There are also bears, monkeys, lions, reptiles, Welsh mountain goats, tropical birds, penguins, flamingoes and an elephant.

Whitson Zoo J10
Whitson, nr Newport, Gwent. A small zoo in the grounds of Whitson Court. There is a fine aquarium with more than 60 varieties of tropical fish; wild-fowl; bears and monkeys.

Nature trails & reserves

Devil's Bridge Nature Trail F5
Dyfed. Start at Hafod Arms Hotel Kiosk. ½ mile. A short but most interesting trail in one of the best areas in Wales for seeing kites.

The Dinas Nature Trail F7
Dyfed. Start clearly signposted from road from Rhandirmwyn NW of Llandovery to the Llyn Brianne Dam. RSPB Information Centre and trail on annexe to Gwenffrwd Reserve. Buzzard, sparrowhawk, raven, redstart, wood warbler and pied flycatcher, with dippers on the River Towy and possibility of kite. Also public footpath to Twm Shon Catti's Cave.

Marloes Sands Nature Trail A9
Dyfed. Start at Marloes Sands Car Park, 13 miles SW of Haverfordwest. 2½ miles, spectacular scenery and good for grey seals. Birds include raven and chough, as well as sea birds offshore. Guide from the West Wales Naturalists' Trust, 4 Victoria Place, Haverfordwest.

Newborough Warren National Nature Reserve B2
Newborough Warren, Gwynedd. Off A4080. The whole area lies to the west, via marked rights of way. Good all-round birdwatching and particularly good for waders at all seasons and wildfowl in winter.

Pembrokeshire Seabird Islands A9
Among the best-known bird areas in Wales and well worth visiting.
Ramsey. Daily crossings (summer months only) from the lifeboat station at St Justinian, 3 miles west of St David's. Permit from boatman. No advance booking necessary. Self-guiding route, leaflet and map from Warden. Ideal for day visits. Breeding birds include Manx shearwater, auks, buzzard, and chough and peregrine are usually present. Noted for grey seals. RSPB Reserve. *Open Apr–Sep.*
Skokholm. Breeding Manx shearwater, storm petrel, guillemot and razorbill. Especially good for seabird watching and for a wide variety of migrants. Further details from West Wales Naturalists' Trust, 4 Victoria Place, Haverfordwest. Accommodation available at the Bird Observatory. *No day visits.*
Skomer. Boat from Martins Haven. Skomer is equally good for migrants, and its breeding birds include Manx shearwater, storm petrel, fulmar, auks, including puffin, chough. Nature trail, but visitors should first contact the West Wales Naturalists' Trust, as above. National Nature Reserve. *Open Apr–Sep.*

Rhosili Nature Trail D10
W. Glamorgan. 15 miles W of Swansea. Start at Rhosili Car Park. 3 miles; guide from Nature Conservancy Council, Gower Countryside Centre, Old School Room, Oxwich. Birds include fulmar, guillemot and razorbill.

South Stack Nature Trail A1
Gwynedd. At W side of Holyhead Island. Guided walk to lighthouse, taking in cliff flora and birds—which include razorbill, guillemot, puffin and kittiwake. Leaflets from the café at South Stack or from Gwynedd Tourist Association centres. *Open mid May–Jul.*

Tregaron Bog Nature Reserve F6
Nr Tregaron, Dyfed. National nature reserve on the headwaters of the River Teifi, near the tiny town of Tregaron. Its impassable expanse of soft peat preserves in half-fossilised form the history of the Welsh flora since the last Ice Age.

Birdwatching

Brecon Beacons H8
Powys. Accessible from minor roads from Brecon, Tal-y-bont and Pontsticill, and from A470 nr Storey Arms. This wild mountain area offering in summer buzzard, red grouse, dipper, ring ouzel, wheatear, pied flycatcher and wood warbler and merlin.

Cemlyn Bay A1
Gwynedd. Nr Tregele on A5025. Owned by the National Trust but readily seen from the track to Trwyn Cemlyn from Plas Cemlyn. Terns are present in the breeding season, while spring and autumn bring migrant waders. Waders and a good selection of wildfowl are present in winter.

Dovey Estuary F4
Dyfed. An extensive estuary which includes a National Nature Reserve, noted for its winter wildfowl (including small numbers of white-fronted geese) and spring and autumn waders.

Gower Peninsula E10
W. Glamorgan. Sand-dunes, saltmarshes, limestone cliffs. Oxwich, Mewslade Bay, and Llanrhidian are among the habitats for waders and kittiwakes, fulmars and stonechats.

Great Ormes Head F1
Gwynedd. N along the coast road from Llandudno. This popular tourist site is very good for breeding seabirds—fulmar, kittiwake, razorbill, guillemot and puffin—and ravens are commonly seen. In addition it can be good for migrant seabirds and other species in autumn.

Milford Haven B9
Dyfed. This is a large tidal complex with perhaps a dozen good birdwatching areas. Particularly good spots are Dale Roads (off Dale, B4327 from Haverfordwest); Hook (A4076 from Haverfordwest, left at Merlin's Bridge and left again after 3 miles); Landshipping Quay (via lanes from Cross Hands, A4075); Cosheston Pill (from Waterloo NE of Pembroke); and Angle Bay (footpath from B4320 at Angle). The area is noted for passage waders and a good variety of winter waders and wildfowl, and in addition St Anne's Head is good for seabirds, raven and chough.

Snowdonia F1
Gwynedd. Among many good areas to explore: Capel Curig (entrance opposite Corwen Hotel) for typical woodland species; the moors west of Bethesda for moorland birds; Cwm Idwal, in the Ogwen Valley, for high ground species. Choughs breed in a few slate quarries and other summer birds likely to be seen include buzzard, red grouse, golden plover, raven, dipper, grey wagtail, wheatear, redstart, ring ouzel and pied flycatcher.

Fossil hunting

Visit the local museum. Its fossil collection usually states where individual fossils have been found. When visiting quarries always seek permission to enter if they look privately owned or worked. Be careful of falls of rock.

Dyfed

Much of the county is made up of Silurian rocks, and Llandoverian graptolites may be found, but are not common throughout. The type-area of the Llandeilo stage of the Ordovician lies in central Carmarthen where flagstones give a shelly fauna including trilobites around Llandeilo; also the Caradocian Mydrim Limestone and Birdshill Limestone near Llandeilo contain trilobites and brachiopods. Similar fossil fauna may be found in the Silurian rocks of the Llandovery stage around Llandovery and other localities in the Towy Valley. The early Palaeozoic

Pembrokeshire coast

Cambrian rocks in the area around St David's and especially Solva Harbour contain a variety of trilobites. Access to the cliffs is difficult in many places. At Abereiddy Bay graptolites are very common in the shales. The coast around Tenby is of carboniferous limestone, as is much of the peninsula south of Milford Haven.

W., Mid & S. Glamorgan

These counties are mainly of carboniferous rock. The lower carboniferous limestone is fossiliferous and can be seen in the cliffs of the Gower Peninsula and in quarries around Bridgend. The upper carboniferous is represented by the coal measures of the valleys where some fossil plants may be found. In the south fossiliferous Rhaetic and Lias are well exposed at Barry, Penarth and Lavernock with many fossil ammonites and bivalves.

North Wales

Not a highly fossiliferous area—many places have thick volcanic ash and lava deposits of Ordovician age, especially around Snowdonia. Much of Gwynedd and the Lleyn is made up of pre-Cambrian rocks. The Cambrian Menevian beds contain many trilobites and may be seen around St Tudwal's Point on the Lleyn Peninsula. The Cambrian forms much of the upland area around Harlech; some of the beds contain fossils. The Ordovician is widespread and contains fossiliferous beds in places; a shelly limestone occurs around Arenig, and in localities around Bala. The Berwyns have many shales and slates which yield graptolites.
Silurian Wenlock shales occur in the Welshpool district with characteristic assemblages of trilobites, brachiopods and bivalves.
Fossiliferous carboniferous limestone forms a high escarpment east of Llangollen, which extends northwards into Clwyd through the Vale of Clwyd. Near Newmarket and Prestatyn are fossil shell-reefs with abundant brachiopods. The coal measures extend under the Triassic sandstone and are mined in Clwyd.

Powys

Mainly Devonian old red sandstone, normally unfossiliferous, but early fishes have been found.
Trilobites, brachiopods and bivalves can be found in the Ordovician Llandeilo beds. They

may be collected in the Builth area, as can a similar assemblage from the Upper Silurian Ludlow beds.

Forests

There are remnants of ancient oak forests in some of the valleys still. They are worth looking out for; very old oaks clinging to steel hillsides and covered with silver grey lichen; of note, Coedydd Dinorwig in the Pardarn Country Park, Llanberis in Snowdonia. They are hundreds of years old and irreplaceable—unfortunately many have been cut down. Much of the wild open and natural countryside of the hills and mountains of Wales is fast changing its character as large areas are drained and planted with quick growing forests of conifers.

Coed-y-Brenin   F3

Gwynedd. North of the little stone town of Dolgellau in Gwynedd the tall woods of Coed-y-Brenin, or Forest of the King, rise on either side of the rushing River Mawddach.

Dyfi Valley and Forests   F5

Travelling eastwards up the broad Dyfi (or Dovey) Estuary, from Aberdyfi (Aberdovey) or Aberystwyth on the coast, you will see a multi-coloured panorama of woodlands of oak and birch, pine and larch, beech, spruce or alder, all the way to Machynlleth.

Gwydyr Forest   F1

In the Conwy Valley, centred on Betws-y-Coed, this forest of pine, larch, spruce, Douglas fir and oak has been created by the Forestry Commission since 1920. Clothing the rugged Snowdonian foothills, it runs far up the Llugwy Valley to Capel Curig, and the Lledr Gorge to Dolwyddelan; outliers rise on bluffs far down the Conwy Valley.

Hills & mountains

The Berwyns   H2

Marching south-west from Clwyd into Gwynedd and Powys, between the valleys of the Dee and the Severn, the Berwyn range forms a wild thinly-peopled ridge of moorlands and sheepwalks. Though 25 miles long, 5 miles wide and 2,700 feet high, they lack distinct peaks.

Black Mountains   F8

Confusingly, South Wales has two ranges both called Black Mountains. Black Mountain is in Dyfed, south of Llandovery, a huge sheepwalk interspersed with scattered hill farms, between the Towy and Tawe valleys. On the Hereford border, between the towns of Brecon, in Powys, and Abergavenny, in Gwent, the eastern Black Mountains rise in wilder seclusion. You can explore deep valleys, with oaks and sprucewoods running far into 2,500 feet hill ranges, where farmers still ride sturdy Welsh ponies as their best means of transport.

Brecon Beacons   H8

Powys. In the south of Powys these sweeping hills, now a National Park, rise to heights around 2,600 feet. A huge, unfenced sheepwalk, they provide grand riding and walking country, with Brecon town as a good centre.

Cadair Idris   F4

The name of this fine mountain means the chair or throne of Idris, a legendary Welsh king. It rises in regal splendour to a height of 2,927 feet, just south of Dolgellau. Glaciers left a deep, rock-bound hidden lake called Llyn Cau, 'lake of the cauldron', on its south flank.

The Cambrian Mountains

Lie between Cadair Idris and the Brecon Beacons—approximately 50 miles long by 10-12 miles wide. This is some of the most remote upland country of southern Wales. There are large tracts with no roads which cross it. It is inhabited by sheep and buzzards and it is always windy and beautiful—except where conifers have been planted to blanket the hills. A popular drive across it is the mountain road from Rhayader to Devils Bridge. The steep (sometimes 1 in 3) and winding narrow road from Tregaron to Abergwesyn is also lovely but getting more filled with cars. These hills are best seen on foot—totally away from it all.

Clwyd Hills   H1
Clwyd. A long spine of hills running north-west parallel to the Dee Estuary and the Vale of Clwyd, and providing wide views over both. The highest point, 1,820 feet, is Moel Fammau, the 'mother mountain', so named from the breast-like shape of its summit.

The Glyders   F1
This precipitous Snowdonian range runs inland from the Gwynedd coast, near Bangor, between the rugged Llanberis and Nant Ffrancon Passes. It is a famous ridge for skilled rock climbers though its highest point, Glyder Fawr at 3,279 feet, can be reached by stiff walking routes.

Moel Siabod   F2
The shapely cone of this isolated, though minor, mountain rises to 2,860 feet, and is constantly in view from most parts of central Snowdonia. An open sheepwalk, snow-capped for much of each winter, Moel Siabod is easily climbed by a ridge-track from either Capel Curig or Dolwyddelan.

Plynlimon   F5
Called in Welsh *Pumlimon,* from its 5 lumpy hilltops, this remote rounded hill range raises its sheep-grazed slopes to 2,466 feet, on the borders of Dyfed and Powys in Mid Wales. From the Eisteddfa Gurig summit on the Llangurig-Aberystwyth main road, A44, you can stroll to its far top, viewing on your way the sources of the Tarenig, Wye, Rheidol, Clywedog and mighty Severn rivers, and half the Welsh hilltops besides.

Preseli Mountains   C8
Dyfed. Inland from the little port of Fishguard, the strange Preseli Mountains stand as an irregular ridge, 1,760 feet high, with heather-clad rocky peaks tinged blue by the prevailing clouds blown off the Irish Sea. They are famous in Britain's archaeological history because the builders of Stonehenge may have quarried great stones here, of peculiar bluish-grey rock, and transported them by land and waterways to the heart of the Wiltshire Downs.

Snowdon   E2
The highest and steepest mountain in England and Wales, 3,560 feet in altitude. Today Snowdon is easily ascended from Llanberis by a broad gently sloping track, and in summer by its unique mountain railway. Away from the well-used paths, the cliffs should be left to skilled rock climbers. Beware of sudden mists, and ice-bound rock surfaces in winter.

The Sugar Loaf   J8
This odd-shaped, aptly-named hill rises to 1,956 feet, north-west of the Gwent town of Abergavenny. There are good views from its summit over Gwent, Powys, Hereford and Worcester.

Valleys

Conwy Valley   F1
Enfolded between the Snowdonian mountains and the Clwyd hills, the level Conwy Valley runs north from Betws-y-Coed's woodlands, past Llanrwst to the river's broad tide-washed estuary at Conwy town.

Severn Valley
Powys. This is in effect the Welsh share of the long valley of the Severn, which completes its course in England.

The South Wales Valleys
The valleys of West Glamorgan, Rhondda, Merthyr, Rhymney and Gwent have always

conjured up an image of smoke-laden industrial activity because of their historical association with coal mining and iron and steel production. Surprisingly this part of Wales is rich in natural beauty, because the industry was largely confined to the narrow valley floors, leaving the hills and moorland above the huddled terraced housing, untouched and peaceful. There is much to explore and enjoy—spectacular views from windy mountainsides, mediaeval castles and wildlife parks, waterfalls and caves. The industrial areas are being transformed, but because of their role during the Industrial Revolution there is a rich heritage of industrial archaeology. This is being preserved, and there are several imaginative museums and former industrial sites, many restored to working order, in and around such well known towns as Tonypandy, Merthyr Tydfil and Abertillery.

Snowdonia National Park   E2
This big conservation region includes a large part of Gwynedd. All the highest Welsh peaks of the Snowdon range come within it, as well as the surprisingly beautiful valleys of the Conwy, Glaslyn, Mawddach and Dyfi rivers, and the great Gwydyr Forest, centred on Betws-y-Coed.

Towy Valley   D8
Rural Wales at its best, the warm and fertile vale of the lower Towy sweeps down past Llandovery south-west to Carmarthen town, legendary seat of that powerful Celtic wizard, Merlin.

Lakes & bogs

Bala Lake   G3
Gwynedd. Llyn Tegid, or Bala Lake, is 4½ miles long and ½ mile wide. Its calm waters, which hold many trout and attract anglers, are surrounded by pastoral farms in a broad vale. A dozen swift hill streams feed it, and the lake discharges its overflow over a barrage to control floods at the start of the great River Dee.

Borth Bog   F5
Dyfed. Called Cors Fochno, meaning 'the mire', this remarkable marsh of rush, sedge, and salt-loving plants lies at sea level, in a triangle of land between the estuary of the River Dovey, the long sandspit where Borth faces the open sea, and the inland foothills of the Plynlimon range. Three miles long by 1 mile wide, Borth Bog is easily reached by the A487 Aberystwyth-Machynlleth road on the east, or the railway on the west. Since nobody can drain it, it remains a nature reserve, the haunt of rare marsh plants, nesting gulls and shelducks.

Clwyd Moors   G2
Clwyd. Between the Conwy Valley and the Vale of Clwyd, crossed by the high road A543 from Denbigh to Pentrefoelas, lies the expanse of wild moorland, strangely called in Welsh Mynydd Hiraethog, or 'mountains of yearning'. Here stands the huge, ugly and highly productive national Forest of Clocaenog, largely comprising spruce trees, and the broad Alwen Reservoir that supplies water to Birkenhead.

Newborough Warren   B2
Gwynedd. At the south-western corner of Anglesey, wind and tide have thrown up a sandbank, called Aber Menai Point, which holds back the tides of the Menai Straits and fresh water flowing seaward from central Gwynedd. The resulting marshland has become the home of seabirds.
Rare plants include the yellow horned poppy and the shiny, blue-flowered sea holly. Now carefully preserved as a National Nature Reserve, the Warren can be viewed from the track towards Llanddwyn Island; car park nearby.

Snowdonian Lakes   F1
Gwynedd. During the Ice Age, great glaciers gouged out deep basins in the mountains of

what is now Snowdonia National Park; these hollows filled with water when the last ice melted.

The loveliest are Llyn Gwynant and Llyn Dinas on the Betws-y-Coed to Beddgelert road, A498. Llyn Ogwen on the Bangor road, and Llyn Padarn on the Caernarfon road, have stonier shores in wilder surroundings, while Llyn Llydaw stands below Snowdon's summit crags.

Trawsfynydd Lake   F3
Gwynedd. The name means 'beyond the mountains'—it is a huge man-made reservoir on the A487 road from Porthmadog to Dolgellau. Set high on bleak moors, it serves as a cooling tank for a nuclear power station, and a source of hydro-electric power.

Tregaron Bog   F6
Dyfed. Known in Welsh as Gors Goch Glan Teifi, or 'red bog of the Vale of Teifi', Tregaron Bog lies on a flat plain, 500 feet above sea level, beside the B4343 by-road north of Tregaron town. Here the River Teifi wanders through an impassable peat bog, 2 miles long by 1 mile across. The bog is called 'red' because of the orange-brown colour of its sedges, marsh grasses, and heather. Now preserved by the Nature Conservancy Council for its unique flora and fauna, and the fact that pollen grains preserved in the peat reveal the history of many thousands of years of vegetation of Mid Wales.

Rivers

River Conwy   F1
Rising high on the Gwynedd moors, this river plunges over the rock-girt Conwy Falls near Betws-y-Coed, and then meanders over a flat flood plain past Llanrwst to Conwy town.

River Dee   G2
The Welsh Dee begins as tributary streams of Llyn Tegid or Bala Lake, 4½ miles long and nearly 1 mile wide, west of the town of Bala. Flowing through a rocky cleft, beside the A5 London-Holyhead road from Corwen, past Llangollen to Ruabon, it winds north over the flat Cheshire Plain to the walled frontier town of Chester.

Gwynedd Rivers   F3
The Mawddach follows a deep forest-clad valley south to Dolgellau, then turns west as a grand tree-lined estuary, broadening towards the sea at Barmouth. Farther south it is matched by the even finer Dyfi (or Dovey) which runs through farmlands to Machynlleth, then follows a broad sandy estuary to Aberdyfi (Aberdovey).

River Severn   K10
The Severn, so-named from the original Welsh Afon Hafren, is Britain's longest river. Rising high on Plynlimon Mountain, it runs for 220 miles to the sea below Gloucester. The upper course past Llanidloes and Newtown in Powys runs through a long narrow forested gorge. 8 miles north-east of Newtown it enters a broad, well farmed valley and winds slowly north-west past Welshpool towards Shrewsbury, beyond the English border.

River Towy   F8
Rising on remote uplands north of Llandovery it winds through a broad vale past Carmarthen town to its wide estuary, where coracle fishermen still net salmon from their quaint cockleshell craft.

River Usk   H8
Powys and eastern Gwent hold the crystal-clear Usk, a salmon river with a perpetually lovely course above and below Brecon, past Abergavenny and Usk town. The river ends at the Newport docks on the Bristol Channel.

River Wye   H7
Rising from a little spring on Plynlimon, the Wye takes a tortuous course of 130 miles south towards the Bristol Channel. The Wye's upper course past Llangurig and Builth Wells to the Hereford border at Hay is exceptionally beautiful. It ends its course in a magnificent limestone gorge between Tintern and Chepstow.

River Wye at Tintern

Rivers Ystwyth and Rheidol   E5
Dyfed holds the twin rivers Ystwyth and Rheidol, each with impressive gorges hidden amid oaks, woods and boggy moors; they unite at the tiny harbour of Aberystwyth.

Canals

The Llangollen Canal
Traverses mountainous country for part of the way, and runs through the lovely wooded Vale of Llangollen. It has one of the best known canal aqueducts in Britain—Telford's Pontcysyllte Aqueduct. Completed in 1805 this tremendous structure carries the canal across the valley of the River Dee in a narrow cast-iron trough supported on 18 brick pillars. It is over 1,000 feet long, and 127 feet high. At the canal wharf on the edge of Llangollen is the Canal Exhibition Centre, which features all the important aspects of the canal era.

The Brecon and Monmouthshire Canal
Really 2 canals, which run through some of the most beautiful scenery in the country.

The Brecon and Abergavenny canal. Since early 1979 this canal has been navigable for its full 33 miles, from Brecon to Pontypool, passing through the spectacular scenery of the Brecon Beacons National Park. It creeps along the sides of mountains, overhung by trees and overlooking the steep slopes of the Usk Valley. There are good boat hire facilities at points along the way, such as the attractive villages of Govilon and Gilwern. There are 6 locks on the canal, most of them grouped at Llangyndr. There is a short tunnel at Ashford, and a 3-arched aqueduct over the Usk at Brynich. At Talybont and elsewhere picturesque bascule-like lift bridges can be seen.
The Monmouthshire canal. With a total of 41 locks, this canal runs from Pontypool to Newport. Fourteen of these locks come together in a series near Rogerstone. Along a pleasant towpath walk is the Fourteen Locks Canal Interpretative Centre, where you can learn about the industrial history of the canals in South Wales.

Archaeological sites

Bryn-Celli-Ddu   B2
Nr Llanfair P.G., Isle of Anglesey, Gwynedd. A well-preserved example of a stone-built circular-chambered cairn of Neolithic date. Unlike earthen barrows, these cairns had stone-built chambers and access passages, and must have been used over a period of time, as family or group graves.

Caer Gybi   A1
Holyhead, Gwynedd. The 4thC fort at Caer Gybi is unique in Roman Britain, a

beachhead fortification for ship landings connected with fleet activity.

Caerleon   **J10**
Nr Newport, Gwent. Roman Isca, 1 of the 3 permanent legionary fortresses of Britain, occupied by the II Augustan Legion. The barrack blocks in the western corner of the fortress are laid out in Prysg Field, long narrow buildings containing small rooms for the men with a verandah running along 1 side, and a larger block at the end with more spacious quarters for a centurion. Remains of interesting amphitheatre.

Caernarfon   **E1**
Gwynedd. Roman Segontium; strategically sited to cover the approaches to Anglesey, the fort at Caernarfon held a squadron of auxiliary soldiers. Approximately two-thirds of the fort is now visible. The site museum houses excavation finds.

Caerwent Roman Site and Walls   **K10**
Caerwent, Gwent. Roman Venta Silurum, the tribal capital of the Silures of south-east Wales. The single-arched north gate is well preserved, and the blocked south gate is also visible, but only fragments of the west and east gates survive.
The foundations of a courtyard house, and of a combined house and shop with a forge, are laid out in Pound Lane. The church porch has 2 inscribed stones.

Carneddau Hengwm   **E3**
Nr Barmouth, Gwynedd. An unusual group of long mounds that have eluded precise interpretation, and whose date is still uncertain. They may belong to a local type of Neolithic chambered long barrow.

Din Lligwy Ancient Village   **B1**
Penrhos Lligwy, Gwynedd. The finest of the enclosed settlement sites characteristic of north-west Wales in the later Roman period, Din Lligwy was occupied during the 4thC. It consists of a polygonal walled enclosure containing rectangular buildings, with 2 circular huts about 22 feet across.

Moel Hiraddug   **H1**
Dyserth, Clwyd. A large Iron Age hill fort with multiple bank and ditch defences, at the eastern end of a hill fort system running along the coast and down the Clwydlan Range. Other large forts can be seen at Foel Fenlli (between Mold and Ruthin), Pen y Cloddiau, and Pen y Corddyn (Penmaenmawr), and smaller ones with a similar complex defensive system at Moel y Gaer (Ruthin), and Parc y Meirch, Dinorben (near Abergele).

Offa's Dyke
Stretching across Clwyd, Shropshire, Powys, Hereford and Worcester and the Gwent-Gloucestershire border, the great bank and ditch earthwork was constructed by Offa, King of Mercia, in the late 8thC. It is not continuous, making use of water obstacles along the course of the middle Severn and the Lower Wye. The northern section is doubled on the eastern side by Wat's Dyke, crossing Clwyd and Shropshire.

St David's Head   **A8**
Nr St David's, Dyfed. Dyfed has a group of Iron Age forts built to defend coastal promontories. The best are those at St David's Head and at Castell Penpleidian, St David's, which have multiple defensive banks; others can be seen at Castell Heinif, St David's Head, and Nab Head, St Bride's, on St Anne's Head.

Tre'r Ceiri   **D2**
Nr Llanaelhaearn, Gwynedd. An Iron Age hill fort with a single defensive bank. Inside are numerous huts, suggesting permanent settlement rather than the usual temporary defensive use of hill forts.

Tinkinswood Burial Chamber   **H10**
St Nicholas, S. Glamorgan. A Neolithic chambered long barrow, constructed of stone, with an access gallery. These cairns were probably intended as tombs for a group or family.

Footpaths & ancient ways

Offa's Dyke Path   **K10**
From Sedbury Cliffs to Prestatyn the path covers the 168-mile length of Wales along the English border. For 60 miles it coincides with the bank and ditch construction built by Offa, King of Mercia, in the 8thC. Starting from the Severn Bridge the path continues beside the banks of the Wye, across the Gwent countryside dotted with tiny villages, to the eastern slopes of the Black Mountains, where the path climbs steeply along the ridge to Hay-on-Wye. Following the dyke from Kington to Knighton the uplands and valleys of the border country give way to the woodlands of Lymore and Leighton Parks, and beyond to the heights of Long Mountain. North beyond Llanymynech there are views of Oswestry and the Shropshire Plain to the east. Across the River Dee the path follows the escarpment of the Clwydian Range leading to Prestatyn and the sea, with broad views of Snowdonia and the hills to the west.

The Pembrokeshire Coast Path   **C9**
The first long distance footpath to be opened in Wales, it runs along the coast for 170 miles from Amroth in the south of Dyfed to St Dogmaels in the north.
The path meanders around bays and coves, and over cliff tops, with dunes, long stretches of beach and wild surf in view. On the Dale Peninsula the islands of Skokholm and Skomer are in sight, where migrants and breeding birds are protected on the nature reserve. Following the broad sweep of St Bride's Bay to St David's Head, the route passes Newgale Sands, with its pebble beach. Not far away is St David's, the birthplace of the patron saint of Wales. On to Strumble Head with its lighthouse and broad views along the coast. North of Fishguard the path climbs eastwards over Dinas Head to the seaside resort of Newport. Round Cemaes Head and St Dogmaels lies just beyond, on the River Teifi.

Regional sport

Canoeing   **F1**
The River Dee at Llangollen is a favourite white water course for canoeists. Competitions are held there mainly in the autumn. There is lake canoeing at Mymbyr Lakes near Capel Curig and Llyn Padarn at Llanberis. The Rivers Usk, Wye and Ithon in the south can provide interesting sport. Canoes can be hired on the beaches at Criccieth and Llanbedrog. Experienced canoeists can enjoy canoe surfing near Abersoch.

Caving   **G9**
In the Vale of Neath below the Craig-y-Llyn moors in W. Glamorgan there are waterfalls and caving holes with miles of underground passages and lakes open to the public.

Climbing and hill walking   **H8**
From the Brecon Beacons in the south, up the rocky spine of the Cambrian Mountains to Snowdonia in the north, Wales offers much to the walker and climber. Pen y Fan at 2,906 feet, the summit of the Brecon Beacons, is a bleak and imposing challenge to the mountaineer; but the empty vastness of Snowdonia is the greatest test of all.
The chief centres in Snowdonia are rock faces at Llanberis Pass and Nant Ffrancon Pass. Plas y Brenin, the National Mountaineering Centre, is at Capel Curig. Mighty Snowdon at 3,560 feet dominates the area, while slightly further south the beautifully named Cadair Idris at 2,927 feet lies waiting for experienced climbers.

Fishing   **F1**
Wales was made for the fisherman, with its

excellent sea angling, game and coarse fishing.

Coarse Fishing. There are perch in Lake Trawsfynydd, bream in the lower River Dee, roach in Bala Lake, and pike in Llangorse Lake in the Brecon Beacons. Sea and coarse fishing can be combined at Bosherston Lakes in Dyfed. Fish for tench in the lakes and, just over the sand dunes, in the sea for good bass, and rock fishing for tope.

Game Fishing. Particularly memorable along the Rivers Usk, Wye and Severn. Further north from the River Towy at Ferryside to the Rivers Llugwy and Dwyryd of Gwynedd, sport is also good. There are plenty of hotels with their own private stretches of water open to residents and non-residents. Most mountain tarns and streams hold small but delicious brown trout.

Sea Fishing. Looking for bait! At Lleiniog, Beaumaris, blow holes betray monster rag; there is crab in the weed at Port Dinorwic, and plentiful brown lug at Conwy Morfa. On the Mid Wales coast you will save yourself a lot of nugatory work by consulting the locals about bait. In the south at Milford Haven there's good lug, but you have to dig for it. Razor fish are plentiful at Kilpaison Angle.

Rugby Union   H10
It's a national sport. On the banks of the River Taff near the centre of Cardiff is The National Stadium, the home and capital of Welsh Rugby. There is nothing more thrilling than when late in the second half, with Wales winning, the crowd breaks out spontaneously into the Welsh national anthem, and even if you aren't Welsh you will find your emotions fully engaged. This excess of emotion and enthusiasm resounds around the valleys of South Wales as the teams from Maesteg, Llanelli and other valleys battle it out on Saturday afternoons. If you get the opportunity, watch one of the valley games.

Surfing   E10
Apart from Cornwall, Wales is the only part of Britain offering all year round surfing. The M4 Motorway and the good main road through to Swansea have made the Gower Peninsula a surfing Mecca for Londoners. One of the best beaches is Langland Bay, which is patrolled by a lifeguard. For holiday makers in the north, Gwynedd offers many good beaches. Try Whistling Sands (Porth Oer), near Aberdaron, on the Lleyn Peninsula.

Festivals, events & customs

There are a number of local festivals and events—contact the local Information Centre for details.

Coracle racing   C7
The coracle is a primitive boat made of animal skins stretched over a light wood framework. It is still used by fishermen on the River Teifi, and at Cilgerran in Dyfed every August there is a traditional race down the river.

International Music Eisteddfod   H2
Llangollen, Clwyd. 10,000 competitors converge on Llangollen every year from all over the world. A special event is the folk dancing and singing. Tremendously popular. *Early Jul.*

Mari Lwyd Mummers   G10
Llangynwyd, Mid Glamorgan. Wales is surprisingly short of folklore traditions. There is of course the great National Eisteddfod, but the Mari Lwyd (Holy Mary) Mummers seem to be one of the few to survive. The mummers appear in fantastic dress, the leader wearing a horse's skull decorated with ribbons. They march round the town singing their traditional songs, stopping at certain houses where they are offered hospitality. The event takes place on the 31st December each year.

National Drama Festival   B2
Llangefni, Gwynedd. Devoted to presenting Welsh plays by Welsh authors in the Welsh language. An interesting experience—even if you can't understand the language. *Early Oct.*

Royal National Eisteddfod
Held alternately in North and South Wales in various centres every year. It is a celebration of Wales and the Welsh language with music, Penillion singing and folk dancing. Special events include the crowning of the Bard ceremony, chairing of the Bard and a day of choral music. The bardic ceremonies are based on Druidic rituals. *Early Aug.*

Special attractions

Narrow Gauge Railways
Railways came early to Wales, the Ffestiniog was opened in 1836 just 11 years after the Stockton and Darlington. Because of the hilly nature of the land most of the early railways were built to a narrow gauge of approximately 2 feet. The quaint steam locomotives with antique coaches running through glorious countryside make them tremendous fun. Wales Tourist Board publishes 'The Great Little Trains of Wales', free from P.O. Box 1, Cardiff CF1 2XN.

The Ffestiniog Railway   E2
Porthmadog, Gwynedd. Tel 2384. The railway runs for 10 miles up the renowned Vale of Ffestiniog to a temporary terminus at Dduallt on the shoulders of Moelwyn Mawr (2,527 feet). Once a small mineral railway, it nevertheless introduced many innovations which were later copied by the bigger standard gauge lines. First in the world to use articulated steam locomotives, still in use today, it pioneered the use of iron-framed coaches. The original pair dating from 1875 are still going strong. The round trip takes about 2 hours.

The Talyllyn Railway   E4
Tywyn, Gwynedd. Tel 71 0472. This was the first railway in Britain to be saved from extinction by volunteers. The line climbs for 6¼ miles up the side slope of the Fathew Valley to Dolgoch, with its 3 magnificent waterfalls in a wooded gorge. The round trip takes about 2 hours, unless you make a day of it and have a picnic lunch there. *Closed winter.*

The Vale of Rheidol Railway   E5
Aberystwyth, Dyfed. Tel Aberystwyth 61 2377. Runs 12 miles up the valley to the famous Devil's Bridge (a trio of bridges over the River Rheidol Falls). The only British Rail steam-operated line now left. The return trip takes 2¼ to 3 hours depending on the time of day. *Closed winter.*

Regional food

Bara Brith and Pice Bach
Two Welsh teatime specialities, currant bread and Welsh cakes (a sort of griddle scone). Traditional Welsh teas can be enjoyed in many Welsh hotels and farmhouses, normally between 15.00 and 17.00.

Cawl
The dish once most commonly served on the farm for dinner during the winter months in South and West Wales. Like Pot-au-Feu, the broth itself was served in bowls, with bread, and the meat and vegetables served as a main course.

Laverbread
A popular delicacy made of edible seaweed. An unattractive treat to the uninitiated! Sold in local markets, often mixed with oatmeal and served fried in butter or bacon fat.

The Midlands

Some people call this region the real England and in many ways it is her true heart. Birmingham forms the hub, England's second city, it embodies much of the industry and thrust that have transformed the Midlands. Full of car factories, hosiery works and all kinds of technology this area is prosperous.

The rebuilt centre of Birmingham has all the faults and merits of the 20th century writ large in reinforced concrete! Coventry's new cathedral is at the centre of a city that has risen out of the ashes of war time and rebuilt itself for the future. But it's not all industry, these great towns are set in some of the most beautiful countryside in England. Birmingham is a good centre for Shakespeare country and the gardens and trim cottages of Warwickshire. To the west are the glorious Welsh Marches, the weeping Malvern Hills (where the young Elgar distilled the essence of England into his music) and the fertile farms and forests of the Vale of Evesham. From busy Derby it is only moments to the Derbyshire Dales and in the east, Leicester's hinterland is the fields of Rutland where fox hunting is still the local passion.

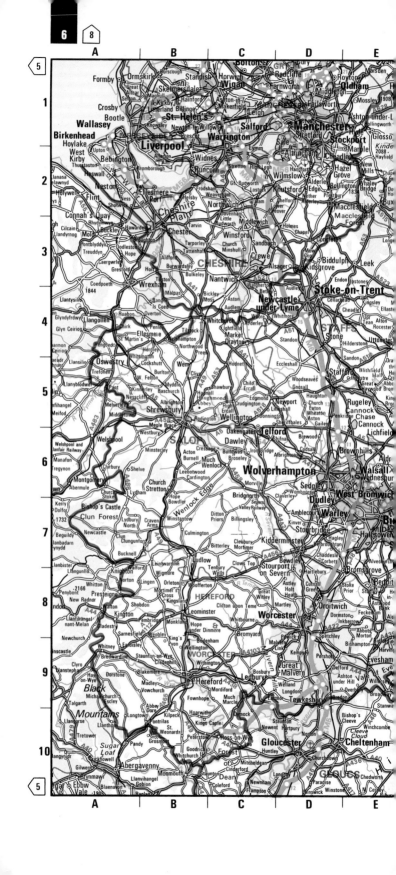

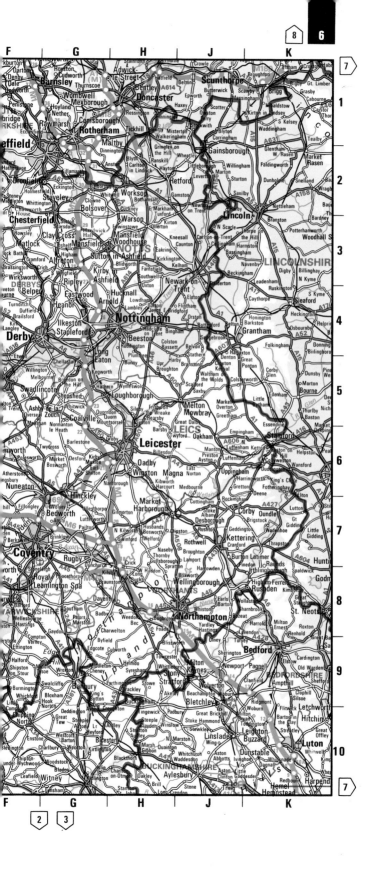

Towns & villages

Abbots Bromley E5
Staffs. Pop 1,500. A lyrical place of inns, old
black-and-white cottages, a church with
14thC arcades, and an ancient butter-cross.
Abbots Bromley is most famous for its
ritualistic Horn Dance, held annually.

Abbots Morton E8
Hereford & Worcs. Pop 100. A village of
black-and-white houses. The 14thC church,
surrounded by oaks and elms, stands on a
hill at one end of the village street.

Abbots Morton, Worcestershire

Acton Burnell B6
Shrops. Pop 300. The village of Acton
Burnell is as English as they come—a blend
of black-and-white cottages and quiet
Georgian houses blandly indifferent to the
changing world about them. Tucked away in
a corner of the village stands the ruin of one
of the oldest fortified houses in England.
Have a look at the 13thC church and the
excavations of parts of Roman Watling Street
and of a Roman bridge.

Alton E4
Staffs. Pop 1,300. A stone-built village of
towers, turrets and spires stretching across
the wooded slopes of the Churnet Valley. All
hills and bends and close knit houses. Of
interest—remains of a Norman castle; grey
stone lock-up in the village centre; Alton
Towers.

Ashbourne F4
Derby. Pop 5,700. EC Wed. MD Thur, Sat.
Gateway to the Peak District, it's a cheerful
market town enveloped in an undulating
eiderdown of green hills and quiet dales.
The church is a 13thC and 14thC
masterpiece, standing in a magnificent
churchyard of yews and cypresses. With a
212-foot-high spire it is called 'The
Cathedral of the Peak'. Of interest—
Elizabethan grammar school founded in
1585; Green Man Hotel where Dr Johnson
and Boswell stayed.

Ashby-de-la-Zouch G5
Leics. Pop 8,900. EC Wed. MD Sat. Not far
from the Leicestershire coal fields, it is a
pleasant, small scale former spa and market
town. Market Street, where a market has
been held since the early 13thC, is a long,
wide and generous space. But the
architectural heart is the parish church and
the 15thC castle ruins grouped together on
the south side of the town. To the north is
the tournament setting of Scott's 'Ivanhoe'.

Bakewell F3
Derby. Pop 4,200. EC Thur. MD Mon. A
market town set in a valley along the banks
of the Wye, and surrounded by low, wooded
hills. It's a place of quiet streets, with
cottages, gardens and gabled roofs,

Bakewell, Derbyshire

dominated by an impressive church with an
octagonal central tower and spire. Of
interest—late 17thC Market Hall; Town
Hall, built 1709; Bath House, built 1697; the
Georgian Rutland Arms Hotel, mentioned in
Jane Austen's 'Pride and Prejudice'; 15thC
arched bridge and packhorse bridge of 1664.

Belton J6
Leics. Pop 300. EC Sat. A delightful hill top
village grouped round the 14thC church. Of
interest—17thC Old Hall; Westbourne
House of the Queen Anne period.

Betley D4
Staffs. Pop 600. A half-hour's pleasure on a
sunny day. Betley is a village of contentment
with a wide street, half-timbered houses, and
a very companionable 13thC church.

Bidford-on-Avon E8
Warwick. Pop 2,500. EC Thur. This large
village has strong Shakespearean associations
and one of the most attractive mediaeval
bridges in the county with marvellous views
of the river. The 16thC Falcon Inn has been
fully restored and has a Falstaffian air.

Birmingham E7
*W. Midlands. Pop 1,000,000. EC Wed. MD
Mon-Sat.* Britain's second largest city, a
place of aspidistras and flyovers it is, in
spirit, a frontier town, trouble-shooting its
way from the Industrial Revolution to the
micro-chip eighties. The Industrial
Revolution caused the whole place to
explode with crafts and trades and it became
one of the greatest industrial cities in the
world. It also managed to produce the best
art galleries outside London, a world-famous
university, repertory theatre and orchestra.
The Bull Ring, a sort of shopping centre of
subways, is an Aladdin's cave that misfired.
Still, they tried.
Of interest—18thC cathedral church of St
Philip with inspired Burne-Jones windows;
red-brick Roman Catholic cathedral in 14thC
Gothic style designed by Pugin; Gas Street
Basin—the junction of two canals.

Blyth H2
Notts. Pop 1,130. EC Wed. An eloquent
village of small scale delights on the River
Ryton. The parish church was developed
from the 11thC priory. In the centre of the
wide High Street is a 12thC stone building
on an elm-shaded island. Once the Hospital
of St John, it's now a school.

Bothamsall H2
Notts. Pop 200. A pastoral picture, neat and
quiet like a long lost watercolour. It is a
small village on the slopes of a valley where
the Meden and Maun flow together to
become the River Idle.
Fine views to Sherwood Forest from the hill
top. West of the village is the earthwork of a
Norman castle.

Bredwardine A9
Hereford & Worcs. Pop 200. A peaceful spot
on the banks of the Wye with a backdrop of
wooded hills. A mellow village with a long,
curiously shaped Norman church.
Of interest—18thC brick bridge; 18thC Red
Lion Inn.

Bridgnorth C6
Shrops. Pop 7,600. EC Thur. MD Mon, Sat.
An important town in the middle ages, it is
spread across the top and at the foot of a
sandstone ridge on the west bank of the
Severn. It is really two towns, High Town
and Low Town, threaded together by flights
of steps and a cliff railway. Of note—the
17thC Town Hall; the church of St Mary
Magdalene, designed by Thomas Telford;
Cann Hall.

Broadway E9
Hereford & Worcs. Pop 2,700. EC Thur. The
epitome of the perfect Cotswold village,
Broadway consists of a long grass-fringed
High Street which climbs a hill at one end.
Notable are Abbot's Grange, from the
14thC; the 12thC church; Fish Inn;
spectacular views to Tewkesbury Abbey,

Worcester Cathedral and Warwick Castle
from Beacon Tower; an 18thC folly.

Burton-upon-Trent F5
Staffs. Pop 50,200. EC Wed. MD Thur, Sat.
The spiritual home of brewing, which
probably began here at Burton Abbey in the
11thC. The modern industry dates from the
18thC. Deep wells in the underlying rock,
containing gypsum, supply the special clear
water. Of interest—18thC St Modwens
church; the statue of Michael Bass, whom
Gladstone created Lord Burton; the Bass
Museum Centre.

Buxton E2
Derby. Pop 20,300. EC Wed. MD Sat. Centre
of the Peak District, Buxton is an 18thC
market town and spa riding a saddle of land
amongst the undulating hills of the
Derbyshire High Peak. Roman watering
place and Pilgrimage centre of the middle
ages, it was here Mary Queen of Scots, as a
prisoner, was treated for rheumatism. The
town centre, built by the fifth Duke of
Devonshire from the mineral springs, was
conceived as a rival to Bath, but did not
really prosper until after the arrival of the
railway.
The town is old and new, Higher and Lower
Buxton. Originally centred around the village
green beyond The Slopes, Higher Buxton is
now a busy market square. In the 19thC the
town centre moved down into the valley
below. This is Lower Buxton, with a
Crescent in the Grand Design tradition,
Pump Room and terraced gardens.
Of note—the Devonshire Royal Hospital;
Solomon's Temple, St Ann's Well and the
recently restored Opera House.

Castleton F2
Derby. Pop 700. EC Wed. Magnificently sited
at the western entrance to Hope Valley this
large village has weathered stone houses
around a green. Rising above are the ruins of
Peveril Castle beneath which a lane leads to
the gaping mouth of Peak Cavern, one of the
finest underground caverns in the area.

Chesterfield G2
*Derby. Pop 70,400. EC Wed. MD Mon, Fri,
Sat.* Standing in the Rother Valley among
blustering hills, its fake Tudor from head to
toe, with the exception of some timid 20thC
buildings and the genuine Tudor bits in the
market place and Shambles. Visit All Saints
Church with its crooked spire 228 feet high.

Cleobury Mortimer C7
Shrops. Pop 1,500. It has a church with a
wooden spire complete with distinct twist, a
main street with pavements at different
levels, and a row of pollarded trees and
terraces of mostly Georgian houses. Look at
the Vicarage and the Manor House, both
early 18thC.

Collyweston K6
Northants. Pop 400. EC Wed. A village of
stone-built houses, climbing up a gentle hill.
The roofs are all of Collyweston tiles, the
tiles still being manufactured in the
traditional way in the village. The Manor is
dated 1696, but there is an Elizabethan
dovecot and the remnants of an older house
to the west of the church.

Coventry F7
*W. Midlands. Pop 335,000. EC Thur. MD
Wed, Fri, Sat.* Devastated during the last
war, the city has been rebuilding ever since.
Despite the odd excesses it's still a pleasant
matter-of-fact kind of place. Originally
developed around a 7thC Anglo-Saxon
convent, it was the 11thC Benedictine abbey
that precipitated the town's early growth. But
few mediaeval buildings remain. The most
important is the church of Holy Trinity.
Have a look at the Merchant Guild's Hall;
and St Mary's Hall, built in 1340, has a
splendid 15thC tapestry. The new cathedral,
approached through the charred ruins of the
old, is a disturbing experience. Also of
interest—Bond's Hospital, built 1506; and
the University of Warwick.

Deene K6
Northants. Pop 100. A discreet limestone
village, tiny and unspoilt, playing hide and
seek among the trees. Have a look at Deene
Park, a beautiful house of pale Weldon
stone.

Derby G4
*Derby. Pop 219,500. EC Wed. MD Tue,
Thur–Sat.* Fought over by Romans, Saxons
and Danes, it was by the 12thC already a
busy trading centre. And by the beginning of
the 18thC England's first successful silk mill
was established here. The Market Place,
once the Grande Place of the Midlands, is
slowly coming alive again. On the south is
the Guildhall, built in 1841. On the west
side are some fine 18thC houses. On the
north side are the fine new Assembly
Rooms, and Irongate leads up to the
cathedral.
Of interest—19thC Westminster Bank
House; 18thC Lloyds Bank; Friar Gate, a
street with some Georgian houses; 18thC St
Mary's Bridge with mediaeval chapel
alongside.

Dudley D7
*W. Midlands. Pop 185,900. EC Wed. MD
Mon–Sat.* An ancient industrial town. It is
called the 'Capital of the Black Country',
with some justification, as it was here in the
17thC that coal was first used for smelting
iron. From the keep of the Norman castle,
the only important ruin of its kind in the
county, the panorama extends over 7
counties.

Eastwood G4
Notts. Pop 11,400. EC Wed. The birthplace
of D. H. Lawrence and the broad canvas of
impressions for his novel 'Sons and Lovers'.
A rural place of indiscriminate optimism
amidst stone buildings and pit-head
machinery in the colliery area.

Edensor F3
Derby. Pop 200. On the threshold of
Chatsworth it is a picturesque assortment of
gables, chimneys, turrets and roofs in a free-
for-all round a green and wayside edged with
lawn. Originally too close to Chatsworth, the
village was moved and the present one
planned and laid out by Joseph Paxton in
1839.

Ellesmere B4
Shrops. Pop 2,400. EC Thur. MD Tue. The
capital of Shropshire's 'Lake District', it is a
small market town set among 9 meres.
Ellesmere is a town of some warmth which
has attractive old streets and houses. The
Town Hall, built in 1833, is three bays wide,
ashlar-faced and originally had an open
ground floor.
Of interest—the timber-framed White Hart;
Fullwood House; St Mary's parish church.

Empingham K6
Leics. Pop 600. A warm sunny sort of place,
even in miserable weather. It's a large,
cinemascope handsome village with a
splendid 13thC church. Overlooks the
equally handsome Rutland Water reservoir.
Of interest—Prebendal House c1700; The
Wilderness.

Evesham E9
*Hereford & Worcs. Pop 14,000. EC Wed. MD
Mon–Fri.* Pleasantly mannered market place
on the right bank of the Avon. Its air of
distinction and charm is set by the tree-lined
walks and lawns along the river. Look at the
15thC Booth Hall, occupied by a bank; the
17thC Dresden House in the High Street;
the ruined Benedictine Abbey founded 714

Evesham, bell tower

Evesham, Booth Hall
Worcestershire

with its Bell Tower; the two splendid parish churches in the same churchyard.

Fotheringhay K6

Northants. Pop 200. A leafy place with a melancholy air. The road crosses the 18thC bridge spanning the River Nene. The 12thC castle where Mary Queen of Scots was beheaded in 1587 is now a mound at the end of a narrow lane. And on a hill opposite, the tower of the church rises in stages like a mediaeval space rocket. On the corners of the first stage are four small turrets and crowning them, in place of a spire, is a superb octagonal lantern.

Fotheringay

Glossop E1

Derby. Pop 25,000. EC Tues. MD Fri, Sat. The largest town in the Peak District, first mentioned in the Domesday Book. Surrounded by the mountains and moors of the High Peak it has, unfortunately, been almost swallowed up by the outward thrust of Manchester's suburbs. Worth seeing, within easy reach, are Mill Hill, Kinder Downfall, Snake Pass, The Nab and Bleaklow.

Hallaton J6

Leics. Pop 400. A rambling and handsome village amid some of the most attractive hill country of east Leicestershire.
Of interest—the village museum; the conical market cross; Old Royal Oak; the church.

Hampton-in-Arden F7

W. Midlands. Pop 1,500. Supposedly the setting for Shakespeare's 'As You Like It', the village is a 16thC world of steep streets and timber-framed houses. The church has a late Norman nave as well as some extremely rare Calvary tiles, dating from the Wars of the Roses.
Of interest—16thC Moat House; 15C packhorse bridge over the River Blythe.

Henley-in-Arden F8

Warwick. Pop 1,500. EC Thur. MD Mon, Wed, Sat. Once the stronghold of Plantagenet power, in the heart of the Forest of Arden. Today a small market town beside the River Alne with a main street of timbered buildings.
Of interest—15thC Guildhall; the White Swan; the Old George, the Blue Bell Inn, and the 15thC church.

Hereford B9

Hereford & Worcs. Pop 46,900. EC Thur. MD Wed. Edged on its south side by the River Wye, Hereford is steeped in history, but it is also the administrative and social centre of the county. The 11thC cathedral has a massive central tower of red sandstone built in 1300. The 14thC Church of All Saints is also of interest. In the centre of the town stands an attractive timber-framed house, Old House built in 1621. Nearby is Booth Hall, now a hotel.
Look in the City Museum and Art Gallery and see the Bronze Age burial.

Hereford

Hoar Cross E5

Staffs. Pop 400. A diminutive, but perky village which has for a church one of the most beautiful ever built in 19thC England.

Hoarwithy B10

Hereford & Worcs. Crossed by a loop in the Wye, it is a pleasant village with an extraordinary Italianate church, built in the 19thC. Much of the detailing is straight out of early Roman basilicas.

Honington F9

Warwick. Pop 200. An agreeable village, built round a green. Visit Honington Hall, built in 1682; timber-framed Magpie House.

Ilam F4

Staffs. Pop 200. Ilam is a model village rebuilt with 19thC sensibility. Set in the Manifold valley, near where the Rivers Manifold and Hamps disappear underground.
Of interest—the 13thC church; Ilam Hall.

Ketton K6

Leics. Pop 1,100. An attractive giant of a village with a 13thC town-sized church. St Mary's has an exquisite spire which looms above the trees and sepia coloured slate roofs of the village.

King's Pyon B8

Hereford & Worcs. Pop 300. A tranquil village scene set in beautiful wooded country. The church stands aloof on a hill overlooking the village. It has a fine Norman doorway in the south; glorious black-and-white 14thC roofs over the nave and over the south transept.
Of interest—the 17thC timber-framed house the Butthouse.

Lambley H4

Notts. Pop 1,000. A handful of houses in a deep sheltered vale with the Lambley Dumble running in between the lot. A nursery rhyme dream.
Have a look at the church, built in 1450 in a sort of club-room Perpendicular.

Lapworth F8

Warwick. Pop 800. A village of scattered houses linked by a feeling of companionship. The church has a small Norman north window.

Laxton H3

Notts. Pop 300. Registered as an ancient monument, the village is famous for preserving the old agricultural system of strip-farming. Saxon in origin, it consists of hedgeless, one-acre, co-operatively farmed fields. Large dignified late 15thC church; village inn.

Leamington Spa F8

Warwick. Pop 45,000. EC Mon, Thur. A fashionable spa in the late 18thC and early 19thC, it is a sedate place of Georgian, Regency and Victorian detachment. The Royal Pump Room was opened in 1814, but was rebuilt in 1925. Queen Victoria granted a 'Royal' prefix to the town name in 1838.
Of interest—The Parade, Lansdowne Crescent and Newbold Terrace; pleasant art gallery and museum.

Ledbury C9

Hereford & Worcs. Pop 3,600. EC Wed. MD Tue. The birthplace of John Masefield, the poet, Ledbury has a long main street with an angled market place dominated by a 17thC timber-framed Market House. An annual fair and festival—once a hiring fair—is held in October.
Of interest—14thC St Katharine's Hospital; 16thC Ledbury Park; cobbled Church Lane; the Feathers Inn; the mostly 14thC church with late Norman zigzag work.

Leek E3

Staffs. Pop 20,000. EC Thur. MD Wed. A settlement long before the Romans came, Leek is a sober-looking place standing at the southern end of some of the most impressive scenery in Staffordshire.
Of interest—remains of a 13thC abbey; the 14thC church; the Red Lion Inn, built 1626.

Leicester H6

Leics. Pop 290,600. MD Wed, Fri, Sat. The county town and commercial centre. An apparent desert of red-brick houses, ugly and featureless, yet at its heart one of England's historic cities. Long before the Romans established their township at Ratae by the River Soar, the Celts were here. And it was

here that the largest Roman bath in England was found beside the Roman Jewry Wall. The Norman church of St Nicholas is close by, whilst St Mary de Castro was the castle church, built 1107. In Guildhall Lane is the Guildhall begun in 1390, one of the most remarkable civic buildings in England.
Of interest—Leicester cathedral; Newarke House (now a museum) built in 1511; Roger Wygston's House with its costume museum.

Leominster   **B8**
Hereford & Worcs. Pop 7,000. EC Thur. MD Fri. Wide Georgian thoroughfares of classical symmetry make an invigorating contrast to the overhung and gabled streets of mediaeval Leominster. Once a wool town, it is set among pasture land, hop gardens and orchards. Of note—the old timber-built Town Hall of 1633 enriched with elaborate carvings; the reddish stone priory of the 12thC; Berrington Hall, built in the 18thC 3 miles north of Leominster by the younger Henry Holland.

Lichfield   **E6**
Staffs. Pop 23,000. EC Wed. MD Mon. From whatever direction you approach Lichfield it is dominated by the three spires of the red sandstone cathedral. Once inside the city, narrow streets huddle closely together in a convivial manner. The cobbled market square is in contrast to the conservatively pleasant cathedral close. Associations with Dr Johnson, James Boswell and David Garrick.

Litchfield Cathedral

Llanyblodwel   **A5**
Shrops. Pop 700. Despite its name it is wholly English in appearance—a fistful of cottages spread-eagled on the hillside above a swift-running river, a stone bridge, a 16thC black-and-white inn and, among the trees, one of the most unusual churches in the country.

Ludlow   **B7**
Shrops. Pop 7,400. EC Thur. MD Mon, Fri, Sat. A town of huddled magnificence which grew in the shadow of a castle and of a large 12thC church. Wealthy from the cloth trade, Ludlow was planned on a hill with a discreet network of streets of varied scale and character. Its centre is delightfully tortuous, the narrow streets breathlessly alive.
Of note—Broad Street; Reader's House; the Rose and Crown; the Feathers Hotel.

Malvern   **D9**
Hereford & Worcs. Pop 30,000. EC Wed. A cheerfully elegant former spa, famed for its pure, clear spring water. Fashionable by the beginning of the 19thC, it was a rival to Buxton, Bath and Cheltenham. A hillside town of largely mid-Victorian buildings, it is dominated by the Norman priory church of SS Mary and Michael.
Collectively called Malvern it has five annexes—Malvern Link, which did not exist before 1846; Malvern Wells, a pleasant residential suburb; Malvern West, Little Malvern, the smallest of the Malverns, with a gem of a church which is all that remains of another great priory founded in 1171, and Great Malvern, all of which climb up the side of the beautiful Malvern Hills.
Look at some of the ambitious buildings in Malvern College; Folly Arms Hotel, built 1810; the former Pump Room in Worcester Road, built 1819–23.

Mansfield   **G3**
Notts. Pop 58,500. EC Wed. MD Thur, Fri, Sat. An ancient market town and now an industrial centre second in importance to Nottingham. In the heart of Robin Hood country and a good place from which to tour Sherwood Forest.
Of interest—the Norman church of St Peter; the Moot Hall of 1752; the museum with its displays of natural history and lustre ware; the old railway viaduct.

Market Bosworth   **G6**
Leics. Pop 1,300. EC Wed. MD Wed. A little town around a market place. Important during the middle ages, it's now a quiet place with some pleasant thatched cottages and a famous Hall. Built in the best Queen Anne manner, it is all red-brick and white stone. Market Bosworth is famous in English history for the battle fought here on the 22nd August 1485: the course of events is illustrated on the battlefield trails, and in the displays at Battlefield Centre.

Market Drayton   **C4**
Shrops. Pop 7,000. EC Thur. MD Wed. A handsome town, famous as the birthplace of Clive of India. Its centre is the High Street, which is more like a market place. From here the main streets fan out with the church appearing only in odd glimpses.
Of interest—the Butter Market of 1824; the Star Hotel, dated 1669; the Crown Hotel; the 16thC grammar school.

Market Harborough   **H7**
Leics. Pop 14,500. EC Wed. MD Tue, Sat. A market town created by Henry II, it is a good-to-be-alive kind of place. The parish church, a mixture of Decorated and Perpendicular, has a magnificent tower and spire which dominates the good-looking market place.
Of interest—the gabled grammar school, built 1613; the Three Swans.

Market Overton   **J5**
Leics. Pop 400. With the remains of Roman earthworks and some remarkable Anglo-Saxon finds, Overton is a place knee deep in historical associations. Set on a high limestone plateau, it had a market as early as 1200. The church is almost wholly in Decorated style. On the village green are the stocks and whipping post. Have a look at Market Overton Hall, an early Georgian building.

The Matlocks   **F3**
Derby. Pop 20,000. EC Thur. MD Tue, Fri. There are 5 Matlocks—Matlock Bath, Matlock Dale, Matlock Bridge, Matlock Town and Matlock Bank. They are a chain of small towns running north and south down the wooded Derwent Valley. A crag, High Tor, rises 350 feet straight from the valley floor by Matlock Dale. Another side of the Dale is shut in by Masson, which rises 1,100 feet above sea level.
Matlock Bath was developed as a comfortable spa round warm springs. With a museum illustrating the history of the local lead-mining industry, show caves and a model village. Matlock Bank is on a steep hill. Its church, built 1884, has stained glass by William Morris and Burne-Jones. Matlock Bridge has a fine 16thC 4-arched bridge and pleasant riverside walks and gardens.
Matlock Town, high above the river, is the oldest of the Matlocks. On the dominating hill top above stand the ruins of Riber Castle, built in the 19thC—and now a rare breeds survival centre.

Melton Mowbray   **J5**
Leics. Pop 20,000. EC Thur. MD Tue, Sat. The hunting metropolis of early 19thC England, it is now a light-hearted and breezy market town on the River Wreake. The church is one of the most impressive in the country, a stately encyclopaedia of Gothic styles. The town has also a fine open air market. Melton Mowbray is also the home of pork-pies, Stilton cheeses and the Quorn Hunt.

Of interest—15thC Anne of Cleves House; Melton Carnegie museum; Ye Olde Pork Pie Shoppe.

Much Wenlock C6
Shrops. Pop 2,500. EC Wed. MD Sat. A small market town with a village-scale High Street, some spacious Georgian brick houses and a delightful 16thC Guildhall. Its most famous attraction is the ruined priory founded as a nunnery in AD680. Have a look at the 15thC house near St Owen's Well which has an archway made of 3 pairs of oak boughs.

Newport D5
Shrops. Pop 7,000. EC Thur. MD Fri, Sat. It's a small market town which is really one long High Street winding its way downhill to the canal. Half way down is a large town church. Have a look at the Guildhall, dated 1615; the Royal Victoria Hotel c1830.

Northampton J8
Northants. Pop 126,500. EC Thur. MD Wed, Sat. A lively county town known for its shoe industry. It was a Saxon town once burned by the Danes. The Normans built a great castle here on the site of the present railway station, and Thomas à Becket was tried there before being exiled to France.
Hooked in an arm of the Nene, Northampton reached the peak of its prosperity in the 13thC and 14thC. A decline set in following the Wars of the Roses. The town revived again during the Civil War, but in 1675 a fire destroyed most of the city. Today it's largely a place of through roads and indifferent buildings, relieved by some fine churches and spacious parks.
Of interest—Market Square, believed to be the largest in England; the Norman parish church of St Peter; the Holy Sepulchre, built in 1100, and one of the few round churches in England; the Italianate Manfield Warehouse.

Nottingham H4
Notts. Pop 295,000. MD Mon–Sat. A city famed for its lace, tobacco and pharmaceutical industries. William the Conqueror built a castle here and, some 600 years later, Charles I raised his standard nearby during the Civil War. The city's character was moulded by the Industrial Revolution. Here Hargreaves and Arkwright first set up a mill to spin cotton, and in 1811 gross overcrowding and poverty brought unrest in the form of the Luddite riots. Modern planning has wrought its worst but, despite failures like Maid Marian Way, the city still has a kick to it. St Mary's is an imposing Perpendicular church. The City Museum and Art Gallery at the Castle has good paintings by Bonington and Sandby; Wollaton Hall is a fine piece of Elizabethan Renaissance; the mediaeval Goose Fair is three days of fun in the first week of October; the Edwardian Theatre Royal has been beautifully restored; and modern architecture has two notches to its credit—the Boots factory and the Nottingham Playhouse. Visit the two ancient inns—the well-known Trip to Jerusalem and the Salvation.

Oundle K7
Northampton. Pop 3,800. EC Wed. MD Thur. A refreshing leafy riverside town with stern stone-built houses divided by inviting alleys and narrow yards. A satisfying place of almshouses, hospitable inns, a famous school and the romantic spire of St Peters.

Overbury E9
Hereford & Worcs. Pop 300. A village that has taken good care of itself. Greatly restored church with Early English chancel and Norman nave. See the gardens at nearby Overbury Court.

Pershore E9
Hereford & Worcs. Pop 5,200. EC Thur. MD Mon, Fri. A remarkably intact Georgian town, set in woodlands. Delightful and prosperous, it is set in the middle of the fruit-growing district with the River Avon to the south of the town. Many of the houses are of brick with stone or stucco dressings, a number with Venetian windows, bow windows, fanlights, pillared porches and flights of steps.
The Benedictines built here what was probably one of the greatest pre-Reformation abbeys in the country. Destroyed at the Dissolution, all that remains is the monastic part of the church.
Look at the Three Tuns Inn; 14thC foot bridge over the Avon; Perrott House.

Rockingham J6
Northants. Pop 100. A leafy place of stone-built houses striding briskly up a steep hill by the River Welland. On a hill is the Elizabethan castle incorporating parts of the former Norman castle. Interesting Jacobean pulpit in the church.

Ross-on-Wye C10
Hereford & Worcs. Pop 6,500. EC Wed. MD Thur, Sat. A gentle jack-in-the-box sort of place, with buildings popping up in unexpected places, on a delightful wooded cliff along a bend in the Wye. It is a modest market town largely developed by one man, John Kyrle, in the late 17thC. The Market Place is dominated by the 17thC Market Hall, a double-gabled businesslike sort of building, like a mediaeval cash register. Fine 14thC church rich in monuments.

Ross-on-Wye

Rugby G7
Warwick. Pop 60,000. EC Wed. MD Sat. A town around a major railway junction. Developed during the latter stages of England's industrialization, it's a smouldering giant in hob-nailed boots. It's best known for Rugby School; founded by Dr Arnold (father of Matthew); rugby football, invented by accident at the school, and Thomas Hughes' 'Tom Brown's Schooldays', inspired by the school.

Shipston-on-Stour F9
Warwick. Pop 2,000. A once prosperous sheep-market town with a wealth of well preserved Georgian houses. Of interest—Horseshoes Inn in Church Street; George Hotel in the High Street.

Shrewsbury B5
Shrops. Pop 57,300. EC Thur. MD Tue (cattle), Wed, Fri, Sat. A mystical place of fine church spires and an abundance of gentility, it is one of the best preserved mediaeval towns in the country, filled with black-and-white buildings. Formerly a Roman town; built, following the departure of the Roman Legions in the 5thC, on rising ground in a loop of the Severn. When the Normans arrived a castle was built, now used as a council chamber and open to the public. Of interest—the Abbey Church of the Holy Cross; the Church of St Mary; Clive House, the 18thC town house of Clive of India; 16thC Old Market House; Shrewsbury School; and Old Malting House in the suburb of Ditherington, built in 1796 and the oldest surviving iron-framed building in the world.

Stafford D5
Staffs. Pop 55,000. EC Wed. MD Tue, Fri, Sat. Built around a ford across the River Sow it has a history going back 1,200 years. It was mentioned in the Domesday Book, and by the middle of the 13thC already had a busy market. The birthplace of Izaak Walton in 1593. Look at the church of St Mary with its unusual octagonal tower; the timbered High House where Charles I and Prince Rupert stayed in 1642 while recruiting; the 17thC Noel Almshouses in Mill Street.

Stoney Middleton   **F2**
Derby. Pop 500. A place of lurking drama as
narrow streets and old houses rise tier on tier
on ledges of rock under steep hanging cliffs.
The church in the village square is
completely octagonal. It was built on to a
squat 15thC tower in 1759.

Stratford-upon-Avon   **F8**
Warwick. Pop 19,500. EC Thur. MD Fri.
The birthplace of Shakespeare on the 23rd
April 1564, it has kept intact the cloth cap
character of a thriving Midland market town.
It was first a Bronze Age settlement and
then a Romano-British village. A monastery
was founded in Anglo-Saxon days, and in
1196 Richard I established it as a market
centre. The buildings are predominantly
Elizabethan and Jacobean, plus a good
Georgian overlay. A natural backcloth to
Shakespeare, it was in 1769 that David
Garrick, the actor, organised the first
Shakespeare celebrations. Of interest—15thC
Clapton Bridge; Anne Hathaway's Cottage;
church of the Holy Trinity; Harvard House;
Royal Shakespeare Theatre; the Canal Wharf
on the Birmingham Canal; Church Street
and Chapel Street.

Sudbury   **F4**
Derby. Pop 8,200. Another of Derbyshire's
model villages. Feudal in concept, it was
built in mellow red-brick around a wayside
green in the rich meadows of the Dove.
Sudbury Hall, begun in 1613, has a fine long
gallery and some exceptional carvings by
Grinling Gibbons as well as a fascinating
Museum of Childhood with a fully furnished
mousehole!

Tenbury Wells   **C8**
*Hereford & Worcs. Pop 2,000. EC Thur. MD
Tue.* A disarming little market town situated
on the banks of the Teme in the midst of
meadows, orchards and hop gardens. In 1839
the Saline Springs were discovered, a pump
room erected, and for a time the town
enjoyed some popularity as a spa.
The square tower of the church is late
Norman. Have a look at the 19thC Royal
Oak and the 17thC Cornwall House.

Tissington   **F3**
Derby. Pop 200. A village ensemble with
triangular green, mellow stone houses, with
the church and Jacobean hall in the
background.

Tissington, Derbyshire

Uppingham   **J6**
Leics. Pop 2,000. EC Thur. MD Fri. An
18thC place of quiet streets and bow-fronted
shops, with a charming market place with
the church porch leading off it. It's a sleepy
town with the great public school taking up
a large part of the south-west corner.
Of interest—Tudor House c1600; the Manor
House; The Hall, built 1612.

Waltham-on-the-Wolds   **J5**
Leics. Pop 700. EC Tue. One of the oldest
inhabited villages in the region with Roman
and Saxon connections. Formerly a market
town in 19thC England, it is a large stone-
built village standing high on the oolitic
limestone. The church is handsome 14thC
with a central tower. Also see the black
smock windmill.

Warwick   **F8**
Warwick. Pop 18,000. EC Thur. MD Sat.
Almost entirely rebuilt following a disastrous
fire in 1694, Warwick stands on rising
ground to the north of the River Avon.

Perched eagle-eyed on a crag above the river
is the mediaeval castle. Another dominant
feature of this county town is the church of
St Mary. Of Norman origin, it has an
impressive 13thC crypt.
Of interest—14thC Lord Leycester's Tudor
House in West Street; 15thC Bridge End in
Brome Place; Doll Museum in an
Elizabethan house; late 14thC bridge.

Whichford   **F9**
Warwick. Pop 200. A serene collection of
stone and thatched-roof houses in a jocular
mood. Nothing too serious here, life's for
having fun, so the buildings seem to say.
Of interest—19thC village pumps; Norman
church with a dog-toothed arch over the
south doorway; remains of a Norman castle.

Wigmore   **B8**
Hereford & Worcs. Pop 300. A large village
with the church at the top of the village
street and half-timbered houses at its feet.
To the west of the church is the mound of
the Norman castle.
Of interest—Wigmore Hall; the remains of
the 12thC Wigmore Abbey.

Wolverhampton   **D6**
*W. Midlands. Pop 269,000. EC Thur. MD
Wed, Sat.* Famous for its iron and brass
foundries. The most outstanding building is
the church of St Peter which has all the
grace of a small cathedral. St John's is almost
a carbon copy of London's St Martin-in-the-
Fields.
Of interest locally—Mosely Old Hall;
Wightwick Manor; Chillington Hall.

Worcester   **D8**
*Hereford & Worcs. Pop 74,000. EC Thur.
MD Mon, Sat.* Repeatedly sacked by
Romans, Danes, Saxons, Welsh and
Roundheads, this ancient cathedral city was
built on both sides of the Severn. The
principal part of the city has grown over the
centuries on the steeper eastern bank, more
to avoid floods than the many marauding
armies. A once fine Tudor town, robbed of
its uniqueness by senseless redevelopments,
but nonetheless rewarding for its leftover
pleasantries. The whole place is dominated
by the cathedral, with its magnificent 14thC
tower. The 18thC Guildhall is one of the
most gracious Queen Anne buildings in the
county. Look at the 16thC King Charles
House, New Street, and the 15thC guest
house of the Franciscan friary in Friar
Street, the Commandery.

Regional features

Battlefields
So many battles were fought across the
Midlands Plain that it has earned the title of
the 'Cockpit of England'. Some of the
famous battles include Evesham (1265),
Northampton (1460), Tewkesbury (1471),
Bosworth (1485) and Worcester (1651). The
Civil War began with a skirmish at Powick
near Worcester, and was settled with
Cromwell's victory at Naseby,
Northamptonshire, in 1645 where a
monument marks the battlefield. In
Warwickshire, two circular memorials mark
the battlefield of Edgehill (1642). The Sealed
Knot society re-enact bygone Civil War
battles wearing uniforms and carrying
weapons modelled on the originals.

Eleanor Crosses
In 1290, Edward I set up 12 crosses to mark
the resting places of the coffin of his wife,
Queen Eleanor of Castile, on its journey
from Harby in Nottinghamshire to its shrine
in Westminster Abbey. Three of these tall,
elaborate monuments survive today—at
Geddington and Hardingstone in
Northamptonshire and Waltham Cross,
Hertfordshire.

The Potteries
Staffs. The five towns of Arnold Bennett's
novels, Tunstall, Burslem, Hanley, Fenton
and Loughton. Amalgamated with Stoke-on-

Trent when the present Stoke-on-Trent came into being. It's a coal-scarred land, made famous by the great names in pottery—Wedgwood, Minton, Spode, and Coalport. The original clay kilns are curious bottle-shaped buildings; the few remaining today are no longer used.

Famous people

Lord Byron (1788–1824)   **H3**
Newstead Abbey, Notts. 4¼ miles S of Mansfield off A60. Ancestral home of the Byrons from 1540, when it was converted into a house. When Lord Byron, the poet, inherited his title the abbey was crumbling away with neglect. For a while he was passionately involved in restoring the place. Stories abound of Byron and his friends, in monks' dresses hired from a masquerade warehouse, imbibing burgundy, claret and champagne from a 'skull-cup'. By 1818 he was forced to sell Newstead to pay his debts. Byron's favourite retriever, Boatswain, is buried close by. The skull-cup is on view.

Sir Edward Elgar (1857–1934)   **D8**
Broadheath, Hereford & Worcs. 2 miles W of Worcester. This trim red-brick cottage is where the composer was born. His father was the organist at St George's Roman Catholic church and also owned a music shop. Elgar himself taught violin before he was able to devote his full time to composition. The cottage is now a museum, with a delightful jumble of Elgar relics to explore: scores, photographs, awards and medals, violin case, bow, desk, golf clubs and chemistry apparatus.

Samuel Johnson (1709–84)   **E6**
Birthplace, Breadmarket St, Lichfield, Staffs. A childhood friend remembered the great Dr Johnson spending his holidays sauntering in the fields around Lichfield, and more engaged in talking to himself than to his companion. He was born above his father's bookshop. The house is now a museum stuffed with relics, pictures, furniture, manuscripts and a fine library.

D. H. Lawrence (1885–1930)   **G4**
Eastwood, Notts. Lawrence was born at 8a Victoria Street, the fourth son of a miner, in this mining community. The surrounding farmland and collieries became the background for his early books, especially 'Sons and Lovers'. The house is now open to the public.

Robin Hood (c1160–c1247)   **H3**
Sherwood Forest, Notts. Some say he never even existed, but doubting Thomases aside, Robin and his Merry Men still haunt the greenwood in Sherwood Forest. In the part of the forest known as Birklands, the Duke's Drive leads to Robin Hood's Larder, the tree where Robin used to hang his venison after a day's hunting in the king's forest. Tradition has it that he married Maid Marian in Edwinstowe church, and he met King Richard in what is now the ruins of King John's Palace, once the royal hunting lodge of Sherwood Forest. Richard actually did stay there on his return from the Crusades. Robin Hood is said to be buried on the edge of Kirklees Park, near Huddersfield, Yorkshire, and a stone cross, and now a headstone, mark the spot. There is a Robin Hood statue and exhibition at Nottingham Castle.

William Shakespeare (1564–1616)   **F8**
Stratford-upon-Avon, Warwick. Shakespeare *is* Stratford. From birth, marriage, to death, there is a sacred spot marked somewhere to commemorate the event. There is the 'birth room' in Henley Street, furnished in the style of the period; King's New School where seven-year-old William learnt his Latin grammar; his wife Anne Hathaway's thatched farmhouse, complete with original furnishings; Hall's Croft, his son-in-law's

home; Mary Arden's House, where his mother was born, and New Place, the largest house in the town, which Shakespeare bought in 1597, and where he died. He is buried in Holy Trinity Church. On the wall on the north side of the chancel is Shakespeare's bust, executed soon after his death, and believed, by the intrepid few, to contain evidence that Shakespeare was really Christopher Marlowe.

Izaak Walton (1593–1683)   **D5**
Halfhead Farm, Shallowford, Staffs. 3¼ miles SW of Stafford. Fisherman and author of 'The Compleat Angler, or the Contemplative Man's Recreation', Walton lived here from time to time during his retirement. The half-timbered cottage is preserved as a memorial to Walton, and there is a small museum. A bust can be seen in St Mary's church, Stafford, inscribed 'Izaak Walton, Piscator'.

Cathedrals, abbeys & churches

All Saints   **J7**
Brixworth, Northants. A large, darkly brooding church built in the 7thC during that strange twilight age when Roman Britain was slowly crumbling. A comparatively sophisticated building utilising bricks and tiles from the many deserted villas around. Numerous Norman and mediaeval additions. The church's 1,300 anniversary was celebrated in 1980 with a festival.

All Saints   **J8**
Earls Barton, Northants. The fortress-like tower of this church is perhaps the most famous Saxon tower in England. Rising in four stages, it's built of packed rubble, plastered and elaborately decorated with the typical Saxon pilaster strips. The corners are in long-and-short work.

Earls Barton,
Northamptonshire

Ashbourne Church   **F4**
St Oswald, Ashbourne, Derby. Called 'the Cathedral of the Peak' it has a magnificent 212-foot-high spire. The earliest part of the church is the long east chancel with lancet windows. The nave arcade and the great windows in the transepts are Decorated. The tower and spire are 14thC.

Ashbourne Church

Cheadle Church   **E4**
Cheadle, Staffs. One of Pugin's masterpieces. Built in 1846 it's a red stone Roman Catholic church full of explosive brilliance, with a 200-foot steeple.

Coventry Cathedral   **F7**
W. Midlands. Designed by Basil Spence, it was completed in 1962. Built on to the north side of

the old bombed cathedral and joined to it by a porch, the great west screen of clear glass enables the old cathedral to be seen from inside the new. Relatively simple exterior, interior enriched with works by Graham Sutherland, John Piper and others.

Coventry Cathedral

Derby Cathedral   G4
Derby. A cathedral since 1927, it was rebuilt by James Gibbs in the 18thC. It contains the elaborate tomb of Bess of Hardwick, a superb wrought-iron screen, the work of Robert Bakewell and has a 178-foot-high pinnacled tower, built during the reign of Henry VIII.

Hereford Cathedral   B9
Hereford, Hereford & Worcs. Begun in 1079 by the Norman Bishop Robert Losinga it has been much altered over the years. It is notable for the superb Norman work in the great pillars of the nave arcade and choir. Famous for the 13thC Mappa Mundi, a map of the world as it was known then; its chained library, the largest in the world, and its repainting, restoring it to its original mediaeval appearance.

Holy Trinity   B5
Meole Brace, Shrops. Built 1867–8, it is a big church with a square tower. However, its chief glory is in its stained glass. Executed 1869–70 it was designed by William Morris and Burne-Jones—perhaps their best work.

Kilpeck Church   B9
Kilpeck, Hereford & Worcs. Architecturally one of the richest and best preserved Norman churches in Britain. The interior consists of a nave, chancel and apse, and a huge Norman font. The south doorway is a magnificent piece of carving, a lovely mixture of ideas and motifs.

Leicester Cathedral   H6
St Martin, Leics. Large and prosperous-looking, it was the parish church until 1927. Although on an ancient site, it has been restored so often that externally it's very Victorian looking. The pier decoration of the interior remains unchanged.

Lichfield Cathedral   E6
Lichfield, Staffs. Built of red sandstone on sloping ground, it was begun in 1190. The nave, transepts, chapter house and west front are Early English. Forming the only triple group of spires in England, the graceful central and western spires are in the Decorated style. The 16thC stained glass in the Lady Chapel is amongst the best in England. Beautiful illuminated manuscripts in the library.

Pershore Abbey   E9
Pershore, Hereford & Worcs. A 7thC abbey standing in a meadow. All that survived the Reformation was the splendid tower, crossing, transepts and presbytery. The south transept has a Norman arcade of intersecting arches. The vaulted roof to the presbytery is the crowning glory of 14thC England.

St Bartholomew   E6
Wednesbury, Staffs. Dating from the 12thC, it's the most aloof and upright of Perpendicular churches in the Midlands.

St Chad's Roman Catholic Cathedral   E7
Birmingham, W. Midlands. Sharp and austere, it was designed by Pugin in 1839 in the full flush of the Gothic revival—the first Roman Catholic Cathedral to be built since the Reformation.

St Chads, Birmingham

St Mary Magdalene   D9
Croome d'Abitot, Hereford & Worcs. An 18thC Gothic fantasy. The architect is unknown. There are some superb monuments inside including a fine tomb by Grinling Gibbons.

St Mary's   E5
Ingestre, Staffs. A miniature masterpiece, built in 1676 to the designs of Sir Christopher Wren. A delicate thing, fragilely balanced like a spring blossom.

St Michael and All Saints   D8
Great Witley, Hereford & Worcs. Self-assured and unshowy it complements Witley Court. A clean, classical concept, it has a central west tower complete with cupola. Faced with ashlar work, it was built in 1735. The interior is worth seeing for its magnificent stained glass and painted and plastered ceilings.

Great Witley Church, Worcestershire

St Peter   B5
Melverley, Shrops. A black and white timber-framed church in a wide meadow above the River Vyrnwy, and one of only two in the county. Probably built in the 15thC, timbered inside as well as out.

St Philip's Cathedral   E7
Birmingham, W. Midlands. Built originally as a new church 1710–15. The architect was Thomas Archer, and he gave the city a fiery piece of warm European baroque. The church became a cathedral in 1905. Burne-Jones windows in the east and west ends.

Dormston Church, Worcestershire   *Southwell Minster, Nottinghamshire*

St Nicholas   E8
Dormston, Hereford & Worcs. Something out of a Bavarian fairy tale. Built in 1450, it has a timber-framed west tower standing on a low stone wall. The roof is steeply pitched.

St Nicholas   H6
Leicester, Leics. It is one of the best-known Anglo-Saxon churches in England, probably dated as early as the 7thC, with some Norman and later work.

St Nicholas   J2
Littleborough, Notts. A miniature masterpiece. A tiny aisleless Norman church with large areas of herring-bone masonry everywhere. It has a nave 24 feet long and a 13-foot chancel.

Shrewsbury Abbey   **B5**
The Holy Cross, Shrewsbury, Shrops. Founded in
1080 there is still some Norman work to be
seen. The squat square tower has a fine
Perpendicular window and there is some 19thC
glass in the chancel.

Southwell Minster   **H3**
Southwell, Notts. A clean, sharp building,
proud and aloof, it dominates and dwarfs the
small town. Work began on the church in
1108. The façade, nave, towers and transept
are Norman, the whole composition robust
and lively. The choir was added in 1234.
The minster is unique in that it retains all
three of its Norman towers, two of them
with their pyramidal roofs, rebuilt to the
original design. The Chapter House's foliage
carvings are world-famous.

Tideswell Church   **F2**
Tideswell, Derby. A 14thC embattled and
pinnacled church, one of the finest in the
county. Built in one period it consists of a
spacious nave with lofty aisles, huge
transepts with giant Decorated windows, and
a long chancel with four big flat-headed
windows. Interesting font, stone screen
behind the high altar, original roof, Victorian
stained glass.

Worcester Cathedral   **D8**
Worcester, Hereford & Worcs. A superb sight,
it sits on level ground on the banks of the
Severn. Although dating back to the late
7thC, the present building was begun in
1084. It has a Norman crypt, transepts, and
a circular chapter house which is the only
one in England. The choir is Early English.
The nave, cloisters and central tower,
Decorated and Perpendicular.

Castles & ruins

Acton Burnell Castle   **B6**
Acton Burnell, Shrops. Almost intact, apart
from its roof. One of the oldest fortified
castles in England. Built for Robert Burnell
between 1284 and 1293. A tall building of
warm red sandstone, with 4 projecting angle
towers. The ground floor was an undercroft,
the main rooms lying above.

Ashby-de-la-Zouch Castle   **G5**
Ashby-de-la-Zouch, Leics. The ruins of a
formidable stronghold. Begun in the 12thC
it was developed extensively by Lord
Hastings from 1473 until his death. During
the Civil War it held out for over a year
against the Commonwealth troops, and in
1648, by order of Parliament, it was
disarmed and demolished.

Bolsover Castle   **G2**
Bolsover, Derby. 6½ miles E of Chesterfield. A
curious affair, built in the 17thC at a time
when fortresses were no longer needed. It is
a fairy-tale castle of consciously romantic
taste, designed to catch the flavour of
yesteryear. It stands on a terrace of land
pontificating over the town below.

Buildwas Abbey   **C6**
Buildwas, Shrops. A Norman abbey in a
meadow beside the Severn. Reckoned to be 1
of the 3 finest ruined abbeys in the country,
it was founded in 1135 by Roger de Clinton,
Bishop of Coventry and Lichfield.

Goodrich Castle   **C10**
Goodrich, Hereford & Worcs. A brooding ruin
standing on a spur above the Wye. Built in
the 12thC and considerably enlarged in the
13thC, it was the last Herefordshire defence
to hold out for Charles I. The walls were
finally breached by a locally made cannon
called Roaring Meg.

Haughmond Abbey   **C5**
Haughmond Abbey, Shrops. Founded 1135, it
was rebuilt 50 years later. After the
Dissolution it passed into private hands and
at times was used as a dwelling house. There
is an impressive grey stone front to the
abbot's lodging with its large bay window.

The 12thC chapter house has a finely carved
Norman doorway.

Kenilworth Castle   **F7**
Kenilworth, Warwick. The grandest fortress
ruin in England. It started as a wooden
fortress in 1122. The keep, still standing,
was built in 1162. Kenilworth was later
developed into a palace by Plantagenet and
finally Tudor monarchs.

Kirby Hall   **J6**
Northants, 4 miles NE of Corby. A
renaissance palace grafted on to an
Elizabethan home. Begun in 1570, the hall
was considerably altered and improved in the
mid-17thC by Inigo Jones. Deserted in the
mid-18thC, it gradually fell into its present
state—a majestic ruin.

Kirby Muxloe Castle   **G6**
Kirby Muxloe, Leics. A magnificent brick
castle begun in 1480, but left incomplete
when Lord Hastings for whom it was built
was beheaded in 1483. It was intended to be
a fortified stronghold complete with moat
and gun posts at a time of near-anarchy in
England. All that remains are the great
gatehouse and the west tower.

Lilleshall Abbey   **C5**
Lilleshall, Shrops. The ruins of a Norman
abbey founded in 1148. Planned with an
aisleless nave crossing 2 transepts, 2 square-
ended chapels and a longer square-ended
chancel.

Ludlow Castle   **B7**
Shrops. Built in the 11thC to repel Welsh
raiders. Norman, Plantagenet and
Lancastrian monarchs extended it. Finally
abandoned in the 18thC. Here the two sons
of Edward IV were sent for 'safe keeping'
before they were murdered in the Tower of
London. The terraced walk round the castle
was laid out by Arthur, elder brother of
Henry VIII, for his fiancée Catherine of
Aragon whom Henry later married.

Shrewsbury Castle   **B5**
Shrops. The Norman castle was completed in
1083. Edward I strengthened and enlarged it
by 1300, but by 1540 it was in ruins. In the
Civil War it was repaired and both sides
held it for a while. Given to the town in
1926, and opened to the public.

Stokesay Castle   **B7**
*Craven Arms, Shrops. 3 miles S of Craven on
A49.* A fortified house built in the late
13thC. It consists of two stone towers linked
by a long, gabled banqueting hall.

Warwick Castle   **F8**
Warwick. A 14thC castle perched on a crag
above the Avon. The outstanding buildings
are Caesar's Tower, the Gatehouse, and
Guy's Tower. Good collection of armour;
paintings by Van Dyck, Velasquez and
Rubens.

Unusual buildings

Bear Steps   **B5**
Fish Street, Shrewsbury, Shrops. A tiny
enclave that time and development have by
passed. This small group of buildings
probably dates from the 15thC and there
have been few changes over the centuries.
The whole group is steeped in the history of
old Shrewsbury.

The Duke's Archway   **H3**
Clipstone, Notts. 5 miles NE of Mansfield.
Otherwise known as the Duke's Folly. It
stands north of the village, built 1842–44
and decorated with the figures of Richard I,
Robin Hood, Little John, Friar Tuck, Allan-
a-dale and Maid Marian.

Iron Bridge   **C6**
Ironbridge, Shrops. A majestic, intricate
construction, like winter foliage, this was the
first iron bridge to be built. It was designed
by Abraham Derby and cast in 1778 at his
foundry in Coalbrookdale. Spanning the
River Severn, it consists of semicircular

arches with a web of connecting members. The major span is 100 feet long.

Leicester University,   **H6**
The Engineering Building
Leicester, Leics. By Stirling and Gowan, it was built between 1959 and 1963 on a small, restricted site. An aggressive building designed with the fun of a folly and the visual strength of 19thC dock buildings.

Longden-upon-Tern Aqueduct   **B6**
Longden-upon-Tern, Shrops. A spectacular and unbelievable piece of reality. It is the first cast-iron aqueduct. Built in 1794 by Thomas Telford to carry the Shropshire Union Canal over the River Tern. It is a long, narrow iron duct on 4 arches.

Triangular Lodge   **J7**
Rushton, Northants. Off A6 2 miles E of Desborough. Built to symbolize the Holy Trinity, everything about it plays on the number 'three'—3 sides and floors, trefoil windows, 3 gables, and a 33-foot inscription containing 33 letters divided into 3 equal sections around the building.

Houses & gardens

Alton Towers   **E4**
Staffs. 4½ miles E of Cheadle off B5032. Begun in 1814 by the Earl of Shrewsbury, this is a garden bordering on the fantastic, with an imitation Stonehenge, several ornate conservatories, colonnading, a decorative canal and statuary. The most memorable feature is the Chinese pagoda crowned with a fountain. All can be viewed by cable car.

Beaumont Hall Botanic Gardens   **H6**
*Stoughton Drive South, Oadby, Leics.*The University of Leicester's 16-acre gardens, comprising several areas of different character. Rock gardens, roses, trees, shrubs and glasshouses.

Belvoir Castle   **J4**
Leics. 7 miles WSW of Grantham off A607. Originally built in the 11thC, rebuilt in the 16thC, again in the 17thC and finally, in the 19thC it was remodelled in the shape of a mediaeval castle. A spectacular and monumental ornament of towers, turrets and crenellations lying on a hill top. Inside are magnificent Gobelin tapestries and paintings by Gainsborough, Reynolds and Poussin. It has one of the finest paintings by Holbein of Henry VIII. Magnificent state rooms. *Closed winter.*

Blithfield Hall   **E5**
Staffs. 4 miles W of Abbots Bromley. Home of the ancestors of the Bagot family since 1086. Built around a central courtyard the house contains some fine Stuart relics and Georgian costumes. There is also a marvellous collection of antique toys and other childhood mementoes. The landscaped grounds have a unique herd of Bagot goats, named after the family, and originally presented to them by Richard II for giving him good hunting.

Burford House gardens   **C8**
Shrops. 1 mile W of Tenbury Wells off A465. A most original selection of plants of decorative form and foliage (yuccas, ornamental grasses, lilies and hellebores) makes this garden interesting. The beautiful River Teme winds its way through the grounds, its water providing both a fountain in a formal pool and a stream garden with a good collection of bog plants. *Closed winter.*

Burghley House   **K6**
Cambs. 1 mile SE of Stamford, Lincs. A great Elizabethan house, begun in 1552 by Sir William Cecil, and built round a central courtyard. From a distance it's a magnificent mongrel of a building with a forest of obelisks and pillared chimneys crowned with miniature castles in the roofscape. The great hall has a double hammer-beam roof incorporating both Gothic and Renaissance elements. Interesting Roman staircase and

fine carved woodwork by Grinling Gibbons. Fine furniture, tapestries and works of art. *Closed winter.*

Chatsworth House   **F3**
Bakewell, Derby. ¼ mile E of Edensor on A623. The seat of the Dukes of Devonshire, set in the Derwent Valley near Bakewell. Begun in 1687, it's more a palace than a house; a complex giant of stone buildings set against a wooded slope. The architects were William Talman, James Paine and Sir Jeffry Wyatville. The magnificent state rooms include works by Tijou, Verrio and Laguerre, and paintings by Rembrandt and Reynolds. The gardens were remodelled by Thomas Archer and Joseph Paxton, with terraced water gardens and lakes. *Closed winter.*

Compton Wynyates   **G9**
Tysoe, Warwick, 10 miles W of Banbury off B4035. An unbelievably fine house lying in a hollow of the hills. It's a brick-built Tudor building with weathered wood and mellow stone. Begun in 1480 on the site of an old Norman house, it's an Alice in Wonderland place with a garden full of sculptured yews. *Limited opening times.*

Coton Manor   **H7**
Guilsborough, Northants. 10 miles N of Northampton. An outstanding old English garden with lakes, waterfalls and rose gardens. The water garden is enhanced by a collection of ornamental waterfowl, cranes and flamingoes. 1662 manor house not open to the public.

Eastnor Castle   **C9**
Hereford & Worcs. 2 miles E of Ledbury on A438. With the Malvern Hills as a backcloth, conifers both rare and exotic dominate the skyline. A *pinus muricata,* the Bishop's pine from California, *pinus montezumae,* a huge Atlas cedar and the *abies venusta* fir generally only seen growing in the Santa Lucia mountains, are all here. There are also noble pines from China, Japan and the Alps. *Closed winter.*

Haddon Hall   **F3**
Derby. 2 miles SE of Bakewell on A6. The home of the Duke of Rutland, it's a grey stone mediaeval manor house occupied and adapted since the 13thC. It has a fine banqueting hall and 110-foot-long gallery. A series of grey stone terraces forms the backbone of the garden. The carved balustrades and flights of steps provide perfect support for clematis, honeysuckle, tree peonies and the superb roses for which Haddon Hall is justly famous. *Closed winter.*

Hanbury Hall   **D8**
Hereford & Worcs. 2½ miles E of Droitwich on B4090. A palatial and complacent 18thC house of red brick with stone dressings and a central cupola. The interior decoration is by Sir James Thornhill. The Long Room has fine plasterwork. *Closed winter.*

Hardwick Hall   **G3**
Derby. 2 miles S of Chesterfield-Mansfield road (A617). More glass than wall, it was built by Smythson for Bess of Hardwick between 1591 and 1597. Distinguished for its symmetry, it's a brilliant Elizabethan house. The High Great Chamber is one of the most beautiful rooms in Europe. The whole is set amidst extensive gardens. *Closed winter.*

Hardwick Hall

Hodnet Hall   **C5**
Shrops. 12 miles NE of Shrewsbury, 5½ miles SW of Market Drayton. 60 acres of woodland valley in which a stream plays the major part, forming a series of lakes linked by cascades and enhanced by bold groups of

astilbe, water iris, the giant-leaved gunnera,strongly scented azaleas, and some magnificent forest trees. *Closed winter.*

Kedleston Hall **F4**
Derby. 4½ miles NW of Derby. Grand design on a grand scale. Begun in 1758 by Matthew Brettingham who designed the north-east pavilion. James Paine replaced him in 1761 and built the great north front—the grand central block linked, in the Palladian manner, to 2 smaller pavilions by curving arcades. Robert Adam then designed the domed south front and the superb interiors. *Closed winter.*

Kedleston Hall, Derbyshire

Lea Rhododendron Gardens **F3**
Derby. 5 miles SE of Matlock off B6024. Set in 3 acres of natural woodland habitat is an extensive collection of specie and hybrid rhododendrons and azaleas. Also heather and alpine gardens. *Open spring.*

Manor House **G5**
Donington-Le-Heath, Leics. 2 miles S of Coalville. One of the most important 13thC manor houses in England. It was built in 1280 and slightly altered in 1600. The Hall is on the upper floor. *Closed winter.*

Melbourne Hall **G5**
Derby. 8 miles S of Derby on A514. Former home of Lord Melbourne and Lady Caroline Lamb. Splendid formal gardens by Wise, laid out in the style of Andre Le Notre, landscape designer to Louis XIV, and largely unaltered today. The exquisite gilded wrought iron pergola 'The Birdcage' made by the 18thC blacksmith Robert Bakewell is strategically sited to form the focal point of one of the many intersecting vistas. There are some good pieces of sculpture including 'Four Seasons' by John Nost, a gift from Queen Anne. *Closed winter.*

Packwood House **F7**
Warwick. 2 miles E of Hockley Heath on A34. A clean piece of domestic Tudor architecture, built by a yeoman in 1560. It has fine groups of chimneys and some beautiful Jacobean panelling. It is famous for the topiary yew garden planted about 1650 representing the Sermon on the Mount—around the Christ are 4 evangelists, 12 apostles, with the multitude in the foreground. There is an old furnace house used to warm the walls where tender fruit trees once grew. Also a charming Carolean formal garden.

Quenby Hall **H6**
Leics. 8 miles E of Leicester. The most important house in the Elizabethan-Jacobean style in the county. It was built 1621-36 in brick with a stone trim, and planned in an H. Interior recently restored and opened to the public.

Ragley Hall **E8**
Nr Alcester, Warwick. 9 miles W of Stratford-on-Avon. Beautiful Palladian house built in 1680 by Robert Hooke. Finest Baroque plasterwork in England in the Great Hall. French furniture, collection of porcelain, paintings. The Capability Brown park contains a children's adventure wood, country trail and maze.

Rockingham Castle **J6**
Northants. Built by William the Conqueror and used as a fortress. Elizabeth I gave it to Edward Watson and it has remained in the same family ever since. The present house is mainly Elizabethan but the Norman gateway and towers survive. Fine collection of furniture and paintings.

Shugborough **E5**
Great Hawood, Staffs. 5½ miles SE of Stafford. Begun in the 1690s, it was extensively developed in the late 18thC. The principal rooms contain a variety of interesting French and English furniture, china, busts, tapestry and paintings. Interesting gardens with classical monuments and a little Chinese house.

Trentham Gardens **D4**
Staffs, 3 miles from Stoke-on-Trent on A34. In 700 acres of parkland, owned by the Countess of Sutherland, a national exhibition of gardening now. The heart of Trentham is the magnificent Italian garden. It also includes a rock and peat-block garden, a flower arranger's garden and special ones for the blind, the W.I. and T.G. Splendid show of spring bulbs.

Weston Park **C6**
Shifnal, Shrops. 12 miles NW of Wolverhampton. A superb early Restoration house built in 1671 by Lady Wilbraham. Contains a treasure-trove of tapestries, furniture and pictures, especially noted for its art collection. The Capability Brown parklands have a nature trail, an architecture trail and woodland picnic areas. Deer and rare breeds of sheep roam the park.

Wightwick Manor **D6**
W. Midlands. 3 miles W of Wolverhampton (A454). A many-gabled Jacobean-style manor, but actually built in 1887. Designed by Edward Oald for Theodore Mandor, industrialist, it was begun in 1887. Fine William Morris wallpapers and materials as well as drawings and paintings by Burne-Jones, Holman Hunt, Madox Brown, Millais and Rossetti. Tiles by de Morgan and stained glass by Kempe. Formal gardens.

Wollaton Hall **H4**
Nottingham, Notts. 2½ miles W of city centre. Built by Robert Smythson for Sir Francis Willoughby 1580-88. One of the most important Elizabethan houses in England, distinguished from all the others by its spectacular all-round symmetry and its raised central hall. On a raised mound in a billiard-smooth deer park; it now houses the Natural History Museum of Nottingham.

Museums & galleries

Abington Museum **J8**
Abington Park, Northampton, Northants. This remodelled mediaeval manor house preserves a reconstructed 18thC street, collections of Chinese and English porcelain and the uniforms, weapons and medals of the Northamptonshire Regiment 1741-1960.

The Avoncroft Museum of Buildings **E8**
Stoke Prior, nr Bromsgrove, Hereford & Worcs. An open-air museum with a good selection of reconstructed old buildings: a 15thC timber-framed merchant's house, a windmill, Iron Age dwellings, a nail and chainmaker's workshops, a thatched barn, and the 14thC Guesten Hall roof. *Closed winter.*

Bass Museum Centre **F5**
Horninglow Street, Burton-upon-Trent, Staffs. Situated in a 1866 joiner's shop the museum shows the history of brewing in the area from the 11thC. Outside there are some fascinating steam engines, including an old locomotive and coach and early delivery vehicles. Trips around the brewery itself can also be arranged but no children under 13.

Birmingham City Museum and Art Gallery **E7**
Congreve St, Birmingham, W. Midlands. Special collections of the Pre-Raphaelites; sculpture by Rodin and Henry Moore. There are also departments of archaeology and natural history with exhibits from Nineveh, Ur, Mexico and Cyprus, collections of British birds and gemstones.

Black Country Museum **D6**
Tipton Road, Dudley, W. Midlands. A little 19thC industrial village is being recreated

here, which will bring to life the old traditional skills—canal crafts and boats; coal fired bakery; chainmaking, complete with typical houses; a chapel; and old transport vehicles. *Closed winter.*

Derby Museum and Art Gallery G4
Strand, Derby. Bonnie Prince Charlie stopped in Derby during the 1745 rebellion and a room in the museum commemorates the occasion. Also collections of Derby porcelain, costumes, archaeology and paintings by Joseph Wright of Derby. Also working scale model of former Midland Railway.

Doll Museum F8
Oken's House, Castle St, Warwick. This Elizabethan house holds a beautiful collection of antique and period dolls, made of china, metal, wax and wood; mechanical and musical. The building itself is a museum piece, having survived the fire which destroyed most of Warwick in 1694.

The Dyson Perrins Museum of Worcester Porcelain D8
The Royal Porcelain Works, Severn St, Worcester, Hereford & Worcs. The finest collection of Old Worcester in the world, on display in this converted Victorian school house; also see china being made and decorated in the factory. *Closed winter.*

Hereford & Worcester County Museum D7
Hartlebury Castle, Hartlebury, nr Kidderminster, Hereford & Worcs. The north wing of the Bishop's Palace houses this museum of Worcester life. There are gypsy caravans, horse-drawn carriages and a cider mill on show. Also costumes, toys, furniture, a forge and wheelwright's shop.

Ironbridge Gorge Museum C5
Telford, Shrops. The place where the Industrial Revolution started in 1709. The site covers 6 square miles through a unique series of industrial monuments: Coalbrookdale Furnace and Museum of Iron, The Severn Warehouse, the Ironbridge, Blists Hill Open Air Museum, Coalport China Works Museum and all the community's houses, machinery, transport and institutes. The museum is a European award winner.

Jewry Wall Museum H6
St Nicholas Circle, Leicester, Leics. Jewry Wall is all that remains of Roman Ratae Coritanorum, and the museum is devoted to Roman relics. Fine mosaic pavements and the remains of 2ndC Roman baths.

Museum of Childhood and Costume E5
Blithfield Hall, nr Rugeley, Blithfield, Staffs. Lovely exhibition of miniature and toy theatres, Victorian dolls' houses, antique dolls and toys, embroidered Georgian costumes, coronation robes and uniforms.

Northampton Central Museum and Art Gallery J8
Guildhall Rd, Northampton, Northants. Queen Victoria's wedding shoes, the ballet shoes of Nijinsky and Fonteyn—and boots for an elephant, are part of the shoe-making collection illustrating Northampton's local industry. Also an old cobbler's shop.

Nottingham Castle H4
City Museum and Art Gallery, Nottingham, Notts. Built on the site of a mediaeval castle, the present castle was a 17thC residence adapted as a museum in 1878. There are special collections of paintings by Bonington and Sandby, lace and embroideries, and also the museum of the Sherwood Foresters Regiment.

The Royal Shakespeare Theatre Picture Gallery F8
Royal Shakespeare Theatre, Stratford-upon-Avon, Warwick. Original costumes and designs from RSC productions, Shakespeare's gloves and a collection of relics of famous actors, including David Garrick

and Ellen Terry, and some fine portraits, from the 'Flower Portrait' of Shakespeare to those of Irving, Kean, Gielgud and Olivier.

Wedgwood Museum D4
Barlaston, Stoke-on-Trent, Staffs. A fine collection of early Wedgwood ware including experimental pieces and original pattern books. Tours round the factory.

Zoos, aquaria & aviaries

Birmingham Nature Centre E7
Cannon Hill Park, Pebble Mill Road, Birmingham. A miniature wildlife park covering 6 acres, with British and European animals and birds. Natural habitats have been established to attract wild birds, butterflies and insects. Also fish ponds, duck ponds, aviaries and beehives.

Dudley Zoo D7
Castle Hill, Dudley, W. Midlands. An open-air zoo of enclosures without bars in a natural setting surrounded by hills and dense woods. The aquarium has been built in the crypt beneath the ruined Dudley Castle chapel. Several rare breeds as well as farmyard animals.

Guilsborough Grange Bird and Pet Park H7
Guilsborough, Northants. Various birds, wildlife and pets in beautiful natural surroundings in the gardens of a country house.

Matlock Bath Aquarium F3
North Parade, Matlock, Derby. In the old bathrooms of the hydro there are now over 40 aquaria of tropical water-creatures, including piranha fish and turtles. In the thermal pool divers can be seen feeding the fish by hand on Sundays.

Riber Castle Fauna Reserve and Wildlife Park F3
Derby. Off B6014 2 miles from Matlock. The reserve has two sections, British and European, and includes deer, otter, game birds, lynx, wild boar and brown bears. Also rare farm animals. *Closed winter.*

Twycross Zoo Park F6
Norton-Juxta-Twycross, nr Atherstone, Leics. A spacious zoo specialising in apes, monkeys, orang-utans, lions, tigers, kangaroos, crocodiles and elephants.

Nature trails & reserves

Brockhampton Woodland Walk C8
Hereford & Worcs. Park opposite Bringsty Post Office, 2 minutes from start, E of Bromyard off A44. Typical oakwood birds, including buzzard, raven and pied flycatcher. Commoner waterfowl on the lake. 1–2 miles. Guide at Post Office or at start.

Cannock Chase Forest Trail E5
Staffs. Start 1½ miles from Ladyhill on by-road S from Rugeley–Penkridge road. Pinewood and heathland birds.

Coombes Valley Nature Reserve E3
Staffs. On Apesford road S of Leek. An RSPB Reserve in a wooded valley with a rocky stream, the Coombes Brook. Breeding birds include sparrowhawk, kingfisher, dipper, wood warbler and pied flycatcher. Access to main area by permit only; details from RSPB, The Lodge, Sandy, Beds. There is also a nature trail, and a public footpath crosses part of the reserve.

Earlswood Nature Reserve E7
Solihull, W. Midlands. A variety of oakwood and lake species. Guide from the Museum and Art Gallery, Congreve Street, Birmingham.

Edale Nature Trail E2
Edale, Derby. Start at the bridge over Grindsbrook Stream. In the Peak National Park, there is a good selection of typical species of a series of habitats—moorland,

stream and mixed woodland. 3 miles. Guide at National Park Information Centre at Edale, Castleton, Burton or Bakewell.

Hawksmoor Nature Reserve   E4
Staffs. 1¼ miles NE of Cheadle. Commoner birds of moorland, forest and newly afforested areas, seen in an interesting gradation of habitats. There are 3 nature trails, and a leaflet for these is available from P.L. Wilson, The Spinney, Greendale, Oakmoor.

Ilam Nature Walk   E3
Staffs. 4½ miles NW of Ashbourne, at Ilam Hall. Good woodland birdwatching in Manifold Valley. 1¼ miles, open mid April–October. Staffordshire Nature Conservation Trust. Leaflet from Ilam tea rooms and caravan site.

Ravenshill Woodland Reserve   D8
Hereford & Worcs. W of Worcester at Alfrick. A varied woodland with nature trail. Assorted warblers and woodcock among its typical birds. Details from Hon Sec, High Wood Alfrick, Worcester.

Birdwatching

Attenborough Gravel-Pits   H4
Attenborough, Notts. 3 miles SW of Nottingham on S side of A453 and railway. Flooded gravel-pits with reedbeds and islands. Grebes, common terns, little ringed plovers, tufted ducks, reed and sedge warblers and water voles. Information centre by car park.

Blithfield Reservoir   E5
Staffs. N of Rugeley on B5013. An extremely good water for winter wildfowl, with particularly large numbers of teal, wigeon, pochard and tufted duck and many grebes, goldeneye and goosander. Wader passage is often very good, both in spring and autumn, and migrant black terns and little gulls are regular.

Clumber Park   H2
Notts. 2½ miles SE of Worksop and within ½ mile of the A1. Clumber Park is accessible from several points and easily explored. Its parkland and woodland holds a rich variety of breeding birds, including nightingale, redstart, nightjar, and hawfinch, and is equally rewarding in winter, when its large lake has a good selection of wildfowl.

Ellesmere and North Shropshire Meres   B5
Shrops. NW of Shrewsbury. These meres are notable for their wildfowl in winter; regular species including wigeon, goldeneye, goosander and cormorant; breeding reed and sedge warblers, great crested grebes on some of them; and autumn migrants, eg waders and black terns.

Eye Brook Reservoir   J6
Leics. Good views from public roads from Caldecote on A6003; turn W to Stoke Dry and the reservoir. A notable area for winter duck, including wigeon, pintail, shoveler, and goosander and, with its 'natural' banks and margins, excellent for a variety of waders in spring and autumn. Black terns are regular on passage, and it is a good place to see kingfishers.

Rutland Water Reservoir   K6
Empingham, Leics. 10 miles E of Oakham off A606. The largest man-made lake in England with over 3,000 acres of water. Two main arms divided by Hambleton Hill. Islands and 'bunds' attract waders, terns and waterfowl. Also sailing, trout fishing, walking and picnic areas. Information centre.

Wyre Forest   D7
Hereford & Worcs. W of Kidderminster. The area can be explored from Buttonoak on B4194. A good variety of woodland birds may be found in this mainly deciduous forest, including redstart, wood warbler, pied flycatcher and tree pipit, while kingfishers live along the Dowles Brook.

Brass rubbing

Brass rubbing
The following is a short list of churches that have brasses for rubbing. Permission is almost invariably required.
Hereford & Worcs. Hereford Cathedral, Fladbury, Kidderminster.
Leicestershire. Castle Donington, Little Casterton, Stockerston, Wanlip.
Northamptonshire. Ashby St Ledgers, Brampton-by-Dingley, Castle Ashby, Charwelton, Cotterstock, Easton Neston, Greens Norton, Higham Ferrers, Lowick, Newton-by-Geddington.
Nottinghamshire. St Mary the Virgin, Lacemarket, Nottingham.
Shropshire. Acton Burnell, Adderley, Edgmond, Harley, Tong.
Staffordshire. Audley, Horton, Norbury, Okeover, Standon.
Warwickshire. Baginton, Merevale, Warwick (St Mary), Wixford.

Fossil hunting

Derbyshire
The best area for fossils is the carboniferous limestone moorland of the Peak District—the Dales to the north of Ashbourne and around Matlock and Bakewell. The limestone hills around Castleton contain coral reefs with abundant fossils.

Hereford and Worcester
Much of the county is of old red sandstone which for the most part is unfossiliferous, but Silurian rocks, shales and limestones with fossils occur around Woolhope and in the Malvern Hills.
The most famous site is Dudley where Upper Silurian limestones crowded with fossils and fossil coral reefs may be seen at the Wren's Nest.

Leicestershire
Although much of Leicestershire is made up of unfossiliferous red Triassic sandstones and the ancient rocks of Charnwood Forest, Rutland and the east of the county are of Lower and Middle Jurassic rocks. The Liassic rocks exposed at Barrow-on-Soar, in addition to normal ammonites, bivalves and gastropods, have in the past yielded many fossil lobsters.

Northamptonshire
The best fossiliferous exposures are in the Middle Jurassic rocks; the Northampton Sands and ironstone have been extensively quarried over large areas around Kettering and Wellingborough. Other Middle Jurassic limestones may be seen in the districts around Irchester and Blisworth, and the highly fossiliferous Cornbrash beds around Thrapston and Islip. The Northampton ironstone can be collected in the large quarries around the steel works of Corby.

Nottinghamshire
There are few fossiliferous areas as much of the county is covered by red Permian and Triassic desert sandstones.

Shropshire
The south of Shropshire is one of the classic geological areas where many of the Lower Palaeozoic beds have many fossils.
The main areas are, for Ordovician rocks: the district around Shelve and Hope in the southwest, around Craven Arms and Church Stretton and to the east of Caer Caradoc Hill; for Silurian rocks the limestone ridges running south from Much Wenlock to Ludlow where the very fossiliferous Wenlock and Aymestry limestones occur, with shale in the valleys containing trilobites and graptolites.

Staffordshire
Permian and Triassic rocks cover much of the county with coal measures beneath. Only in the south fossils may be found in Silurian beds exposed to the north of Great Barr (the

Barr Limestone). Around Leek in the northwest, the carboniferous limestone is fossiliferous.

Warwickshire

The Lower Lias is exposed in clay pits in the district around Rugby and at Wilmcote near Stratford-upon-Avon, and the Middle Lias Marlstone rock bed with its 'nests' of fossil brachiopods caps Edge Hill near Kineton where there are several old quarries.

Valleys and plains

Derbyshire Dales

The Derbyshire Peak District holds a fascinating series of dales, all tending southward. Derwentdale, the longest, runs from the heather moors west of Sheffield past Bamford and Chatsworth to Bakewell, Matlock and Derby. It carries the picturesque trunk road A6 from Rowsley south. Edale, near Hope, isolated in the folds of the hills below Kinder Scout, preserves a hill-farming pattern established in Norse settlement times. The Derbyshire Wye runs south from Buxton through Miller's Dale, a gorge in sheer limestone rocks, and on past Monsal Dale, fringed with its native ashwoods. Through Dovedale the River Dove takes a lonely isolated path deep in the hills, from Longnor, south of Buxton, to Ashbourne.

Hereford Plain

Hereford & Worcs. Most of Hereford forms one great plain, across which all roads lead to the county town and cathedral of Hereford, standing beside the broad River Wye. This is the home of the fat Hereford beef cattle, easily known by their red hides with a white stripe above; bulls are exported all over the world to improve local herds or breeds. Hops are grown here for beer, and small sour apples for strong cider.

Vale of Evesham

Hereford & Worcs. Around the town of Evesham, this vale extends as the most fertile tract in all England. A warm, sunny climate and light soil favour the growth of valuable fruit and vegetable crops, including strawberries and asparagus, and there are thriving orchards of plums and pears, cherries and apples.

Hills & mountains

Kinder Scout

Derby. Highest point of the Peak District, Kinder Scout forms a bleak moorland, 2,000 feet above sea level, covered by 6-foot-deep peat bogs holding roots of prehistoric pine trees. This waste is crossed by the unfenced Snake Pass road, A57, from Sheffield via Glossop to Manchester. Kinder Downfall, where a stream cascades over crags, and gives wide views to the west. The 270-mile-long Pennine Way starts here.

Leicestershire Wolds

Leics. Between Leicester and Grantham these little-known wolds extend as rolling well-farmed pastures, based on their soft-grey Cotswold stone.

Malvern Hills

The steep-sided Malvern Hills raise their grassy slopes like true mountains above the Plain of Hereford and Worcestershire's broad vale. There are wide views over several counties.

Northamptonshire Uplands

In the heart of the Midlands, between Northampton and Rugby, these gentle grassy ridges form the source of many rivers.

North Staffordshire Uplands

Staffs. Off the beaten track, the uplands east of Stafford town, around Cheadle, attract all who appreciate rounded wooded hills, with pastures surrounding old stone-built farmsteads.

Peak District

Derby. Named after the ancient tribe of Peacs who lived here, and remotely from the Norse Pikr, pointed hill, the Peak District comprises all the North Derbyshire uplands. The 'Dark Peak' so named because of the brown gritstone rocks which form high flat moors ending in dramatic cliffs called 'edges'. Elsewhere it is named the 'White Peak' because of the white limestone which provides narrow gorges bounded by sheer cliffs, with underground caverns and huge quarries. As a National Park, the Peak District makes grand walking and touring country, easily explored from centres like Buxton, Bakewell, Matlock and Ashbourne. Visit the Peak Park Information Centre at Edale.

South Shropshire Uplands

Shrops. The hills of south-west Shropshire provide magnificent walking and touring country. Each main ridge has well-wooded flanks, topped by pastures that are often common grazing; all have paths to their summits.

Forests

Arden Forest   F8

From the ancient royal Forest of Arden, in the lowlands of Warwickshire and Herefordshire and Worcestershire, Shakespeare drew his first-hand knowledge of woodland life, revealed in plays such as 'Twelfth Night', 'As You Like It' and 'A Midsummer Night's Dream'.

Cannock Chase   E5

Once a vast hunting ground that covered much of Staffordshire during Norman times. Now an oasis of forest and heath on the doorstep of the Black Country. Miles of lovely walks—and good viewpoints, especially the 600-foot Coppice Hill from which the Clee Hills in Shropshire 30 miles away can be seen. Brockton Coppice in the north west still has some of the original huge oaks. Large herds of fallow deer. Badgers, foxes and lizards. Good birdlife including woodpeckers, buzzards, meadow pipits and nut hatches.

Charnwood Forest   G5

Leics. A broken upland of ancient Pre-Cambrian rock, near the M1 motorway north-west of Leicester, Charnwood lends the Midlands a touch of highland scenery. Well wooded, it survives as fragments of a large mediaeval forest.

Clun Forest   A7

Shrops. This remote hill region lies around the little village called Clun, on the Welsh border in south-west Shropshire. It extends east through the great Mortimer Forest of oaks and conifers towards Ludlow. Many of Clun's hidden winding valleys hold woods of oak, ash, birch and alder, surviving from the ancient forest.

Rockingham Forest   J6

Northants. The forest survives around Rockingham village as a fragment of a widespread mediaeval hunting ground.

Sherwood Forest   H2

Notts. North of Nottingham, between Mansfield and Worksop, the great mediaeval forest of Sherwood (the Shire Wood) still survives as a group of well-timbered estates, three of which are now Country Parks, Sherwood, Rufford and Clumber). These are also called 'The Dukeries' since at one time most were owned by sporting dukes. Here Robin Hood and his band of outlaws hid, traditionally robbing the rich to aid the poor. Great oaks still survive, the best known being the Major Oak, near the Sherwood Forest Visitors' Centre, and others in Clumber Park, a National Trust property.

Rivers

River Avon
Warwick. Rising on the Midland plateau near Coventry, the Warwickshire Avon flows past Warwick Castle and Stratford-upon-Avon, Shakespeare's birthplace. It then runs through the warm, fertile and well cultivated Vale of Evesham to Tewkesbury where it joins the Severn.

River Derwent
Derby. The River Derwent rises on the high Peak District moorlands west of Sheffield and flows through the scenic Derwent Valley Reservoirs, fringed with pine forests, to Bamford. It then follows a lovely wooded and steep-sided valley south through Bakewell and Derby, to join the River Trent near Long Eaton.

River Nene
Northants. The River Nene is a sluggish waterway running north-eastwards from the Midland plateau through Northampton, through the attractive town of Oundle, to Peterborough city. It continues north-east as a slow canalised and navigable stream, almost at sea-level, to join the Wash.

River Severn
Leaving the Welsh border near Welshpool, the River Severn winds east to Shrewsbury, which it almost encircles in a great loop. At Ironbridge it is crossed by the graceful arch of one of the world's earliest metal bridges. Then it turns south east and passes the hill-top town of Bridgnorth, piercing the hills through the steep-sided Severn gorge. Turning south, the River Severn, now a slow, navigable stream, wanders over a broad flood plain to Worcester. It leaves this region at Tewkesbury, flowing south through Gloucestershire to the sea.

River Soar
Leics. Cutting a deep, broad valley northwards through the Midland hills, the River Soar runs through Leicester city and Loughborough to join the Trent at Long Eaton.

River Trent
Starting as a trickle on the bleak Staffordshire moors near Leek, the River Trent runs south west through the bustling pottery town of Stoke-on-Trent, past Stafford and Lichfield, and then north-east through the brewery town of Burton-on-Trent. Skirting Derby, it then runs eastwards through Nottingham, where it becomes navigable. Thence it runs north, almost at sea-level, over a broad flat plain along Nottinghamshire's eastern border, to join the Humber near Goole.

River Wye
Hereford & Worcs. The western part of the county lies wholly in the lovely, well-farmed and well-wooded valley of the River Wye, or Plain of Hereford. This clear, salmon-rich stream flows from Plymlimon in the Welsh hills past Hereford and its cathedral. It leaves the county at Symond's Yat, through the dramatic gorge it has worn through the limestone hills on its way to the Bristol Channel.

Canals

There is a large mileage of navigable canals in this section, for this area includes the whole of the intricate Midlands canal network. These canals were of course all built by individual canal companies, mostly in the late 18thC, and they provided the base for the whole of the industrial prosperity of the Midlands. The Birmingham area in particular is still a maze of waterways, most of them now decaying and forgotten, little used by boaters and undiscovered by walkers. There are plenty of contrasts. There is the winding rural course of the lovely but isolated Chesterfield Canal, the dead straight line of Telford's Shropshire Union Canal striking off from Wolverhampton towards Liverpool, the delightful course of the Grand Union Canal's Leicester section, twisting and turning through the gentle uplands of Leicestershire, and the business-like but daunting passage of the Grand Union main line through endless locks on its way to Birmingham.

Places to see:
Cromford Near Matlock. Trips on a horse-drawn narrow boat at weekends.
Foxton Near Market Harborough, a busy canal junction with a flight of 10 staircase locks and the remains of the ingenious 'inclined plane' that once replaced them.
Harecastle Near Kidsgrove, where 2 of the greatest canal tunnels ever built lie side by side, 3,000 yards long.
Gas Street Basin Birmingham, one of the old-style canal communities, where there is always a collection of traditional narrowboats and their families—right in the heart of Birmingham.
Stourport-on-Severn A canal port with fascinating basins, locks and old warehouses.
Hatton Near Warwick, where the Grand Union Canal climbs a flight of 21 wide locks on its way up to Birmingham. Beside these locks can be seen the remains of the former narrow locks, replaced in the 1930s.
Braunston Near Rugby, a canal village complete with boatyards traditional and modern, canal pubs, a flight of six locks and a mile-long tunnel through the hills of Northamptonshire, though there have been extensive tunnel closures for major repairs.
Stoke Bruerne A canal village with a fine collection of old canal photographs, machinery, signs and paintings.

Archaeological sites

Arbor Low Stone Circle   **F3**
Arbor Low, Middleton, Derby. The Bronze Age 'henge' monument at Arbor Low consists of a circular earth bank with a ditch on the inside, and 2 entrances at opposite ends. A complete stone circle of recumbent stones lies round the inner side of the ditch; as they obstruct the entrances, these may be a later feature. This type of monument apparently had a religious significance; the classic example is Stonehenge.

Bredon Hill   **E9**
Nr Tewkesbury, Hereford & Worcs. Bredon Hill Iron Age hill fort, with its system of multiple bank and ditch defences, commanded a considerable area of surrounding countryside, and is a notable viewpoint. The hill also has an Iron Age cemetery site; finds are contained in a private museum at Overbury Court.

Creswell Crags   **G2**
Notts. Creswell Crags is one of the best preserved of the inhabited cave sites in Britain, and dates from the Upper Palaeolithic (later old Stone Age). Displays at the Visitors Centre explain its significance.

Great Casterton   **K6**
Leics. Great Casterton was one of the smaller towns of Roman Britain but like larger cities, these were provided with wall and ditch defences during the 3rdC.

Leicester   **H6**
Leics. Roman Ratae Coritanorum, the tribal capital of the Coritani. The Jewry Wall, a stretch of walling that formed part of the city baths, is one of the most impressive Roman town monuments surviving in Britain. The foundations of the baths are visible in front of the wall, and are displayed in the grounds of the Jewry Wall Museum which houses other Roman finds.

Letocetum Wall   **E6**
Staffs. 2 miles SW of Lichfield on A5. The Roman town of Letocetum probably originated as a trading settlement around a 1stC fort; later it was able to draw its custom from the nearby junction of the two major

Roman roads, Watling Street, on which it stands, and Ricknield Street. A large building that has been found on the site was probably a *mansio*, an official posting-station where lodgings and a change of horses would be available. The visible remains are those of the town bath building, and include plunge baths, hot rooms raised on tile columns above the heating pipes, and exercise rooms. The site museum houses excavation finds, including brooches and military name-tags.

Melandra Castle   E1
Glossop, Derby. The Roman fort of Melandra is well situated on a hill overlooking the town. Parts of the rampart and ditch defences and foundations of the surrounding wall, including a small internal turret, can still be seen.

Midsummer Hill   D9
Nr Ledbury, Hereford & Worcs. One of the most impressive of the Iron Age hill forts in the county, Midsummer Hill has a system of multiple ditches and banks enclosing a large hilltop area.

Nine Ladies Stone Circle   F3
Stanton Moor, Stanton, Derby. The Nine Ladies belongs to a type of Bronze Age monument peculiar to upland areas of Great Britain, and is characterised by having cremation burials inside the enclosure. It consists of a low bank with upright stones set in it in a circle.

The Wrekin   C6
Nr Wellington, Shrops. The large Iron Age hill fort on top of the Wrekin was probably the defensive centre of the Cornovii; in Roman times they were moved away from their fortified sites, and had their tribal capital at Wroxeter.

Wroxeter Roman City   B6
Wroxeter, Shrops. Roman Viroconium Cornoviorum, the tribal capital of the Cornovii. Like many major Roman towns, Wroxeter was originally a military base, and was occupied by the XIV Gemina legion during the conquest of Wales in the 1stC. The town that developed around the fortress was later made the tribal capital, and grew into a large and wealthy city. The visible remains consist of a magnificent town bath building, arranged in the customary 'Turkish bath' system favoured by the Romans, with exercise halls, hot and cold plunge baths, dry and damp heat rooms, and a large swimming pool. The site museum houses a fine collection of Roman objects.

Footpaths & ancient ways

The Pennine Way
The 250-mile-long Pennine Way from Derbyshire to the borders of Scotland begins at Edale, a lonely Derbyshire village. From here Kinder Scout looms down from the north—a magnificent sight. The first ascent of the Way is over Grindsbrook, deceptively easy-going at first, but it gets tougher as you go, with many streams crossing the route, and some rock-clambering to the 2,000-foot summit. The black peat-bogs stretch beyond for 2 miles. The path then crosses Black Ashop Moor, descending into the valley along the lower Snake Path.
Featherbed Moss is another soggy patch to be tackled, and Bleaklow is a swampy wasteland not to be tackled on a misty day. Crowden will take you to the W. Yorkshire border.
The weather can change quickly here, especially in winter—the latitude is the same as Siberia! Check with the Peak Park Information Centre at Edale before setting out.

The Staffordshire Way
A pathway that crosses the whole county. First section starts at Mow Cop, 2 miles N of Kidsgrove and proceeds to Rocester. The second section starts at Rocester and finally ends at Cannock.

Regional sport

Angling
There are many excellent rivers flowing through the Midlands—the portion of England furthest from the sea. The Derbyshire Peak District rivers and streams such as the Wye, Lightwood, and Derwent have a national reputation among trout fishermen. Indeed the Wye is among the few rivers in the country where rainbow trout breed naturally. The Rutland Water reservoir provides important trout fishing *(Anglian Water Authority).*
The lazy flowing River Trent, and the numerous canals in the Pottery district, provide first class coarse fishing. Most of the fishing is privately owned and carefully controlled. Further information from: *Severn-Trent Water Authority,* Abelson House, Coventry Road, Sheldon, Birmingham. Tel 743 4222.

Cricket
The Midland Counties over the last hundred years have provided a solid base for English cricket, and produced many great players for England. It would be invidious to select a single club, so here are 5 top-ranking county teams:
Derbyshire County Cricket Nottingham Road, Derby. Tel 44849.
Leicestershire County Cricket The County Ground, Grace Road, Leicester. Tel 831880.
Nottinghamshire County Cricket Trentbridge, Nottingham. Tel 861381.
Warwickshire County Cricket The County Ground, Edgbaston, Birmingham. Tel 021-440 3521.
Worcestershire County Cricket The County Ground, New Road, Worcester. Tel 53607.

Football
There are many first class and good professional Association Football teams in the Midlands. At the age of 49, Stanley Matthews made football history when he was in the team that took Stoke City back into the First Division of the Football League in 1963. Other Midland clubs worth watching are the following, who are usually matched against the country's best. Look in the local papers for details: *Aston Villa, Birmingham City, Coventry City, Derby County, Leicester, Nottingham Forest, Notts County, West Bromwich Albion & Wolverhampton Wanderers.*

Gliding
This is a popular sport in Britain, and the Midland skies are fortunate in not being over cluttered with commercial and military air space.
Burton and Derby Gliding Club. Church Broughton, Derby. 12 miles E of Derby on A516. This is a gliding club which also offers cheap tuition under the aegis of the East Midland Region Sports Council, 26 Musters Road, West Bridgford, Nottingham. Also gliding at Great Hucklow, Derbyshire.

Motor Racing
Silverstone, near Towcester (pronounced Toaster), Northamptonshire, shares the distinction with Brands Hatch of staging the British Grand Prix for Formula 1 racing cars in the July of alternate years. Victory in the Grand Prix counts towards the world motor racing championship. Besides the Grand Prix the track is in regular use throughout the year. The circuit has been improved in recent years and is the fastest in Britain. Further information from the Booking Office, Silverstone Circuit, Silverstone, nr Towcester. Tel Silverstone 857271.
There are also 2 tracks in Leicestershire—Donnington Park and Mallory Park.

Festivals, events & customs

There are a number of local festivals and events—contact the local Information Centre for details.

Bottle Kicking and Hare Pie Scramble
Hallaton, Leics. Two unusual customs; in the first the villagers and their neighbours from Horninghold and Medbourne compete to push two casks, or 'bottles', of beer over a stream. Afterwards the casks are opened and the beer is drunk at the conical market cross. In the second the local residents share a large hare pie—originally the rent for a field—traditionally provided by the village rector. *Easter Monday.*

Bromsgrove Festival
Bromsgrove, Worcs. A spring festival with something for everyone. A foreign theme is incorporated each year, and new musical works, drama, and music old and new, including classical and folk.
2 weeks in Apr.

Buxton Festival
Buxton, Derby. An annual programme of music and drama held in the newly restored Opera House. *Jul.*

Dudley Spring Festival
Dudley, W. Midlands. Music, drama and arts, old and new, classical and folk. *Mid May.*

Horn Dance
Abbot's Bromley, Staffs. According to ancient custom the Horn Dance takes place annually in this village of black-and-white half-timbered houses to celebrate traditional hunting rights. In Tudor costume, a hobby-horse rider, jester, 6 men wearing antlers, musicians and others perform in the streets. *Early Sep.*

Ludlow Festival
Ludlow, Shrops. The main event at Ludlow is the performance of one of Shakespeare's plays in the open-air theatre beside the castle walls. There are also concerts and exhibitions. *2 weeks in early Jul.*

Malvern Festival
Great Malvern, Hereford & Worcs. Performances of Elgar's music and Shaw's plays in the main but with fringes of folk music and other drama. *Mid-May–Mid Jun.*

Nottingham Festival and Goose Fair
Nottingham. The festival is held over *two weeks in June* and on the *first Thur, Fri & Sat in Oct* the largest fair in England is held. The fair was granted its charter in 1284 when it was the principal hiring and autumn fair in the Midlands. At its height 20,000 geese used to change hands.

Pershore Festival
Pershore, Hereford & Worcs. Art, drama, folk and classical concerts are performed in the Abbey. *Mid-end Jun.*

Royal Shakespeare Theatre Season
Stratford-upon-Avon, Warwick. The first Shakespeare festival at Stratford was initiated by David Garrick, the 18thC actor-manager. The present theatre was opened in 1932, and from April to December every year Shakespeare's plays are performed by a distinguished cast. Shakespeare's birthday celebrations on the 23rd April are a special event with bands, flag waving and a public luncheon given by the Shakespeare club.

Three Choirs Festival
Founded before 1719 the festival claims to be the oldest continuous music festival in Europe. It is held every year, in succession in the cathedral cities of Worcester, Hereford and Gloucester. *Aug.*

Well Dressing
Derby. A custom peculiar to this county. Probably pagan in origin, but later adapted by Christianity as an act of thanksgiving for plentiful water supplies. Of particular interest is the village of Tissington where, on Ascension Day, 5 wells are dressed with biblical pictures composed of flower petals, leaves and grasses. Well dressing ceremonies at Eyam, Wirksworth, Buxton, Barlow, Youlgreave and many other villages.

Special attractions

Billing Aquadrome   **J8**
Little Billing, Northants. 3 miles from Northampton off A45, 5 miles from M1 Motorway. The Aquadrome is an aquatic fun park set in beautiful countryside. Besides an old working water mill and milling museum, there is a lakeside marina, fishing, slides, and a miniature diesel railway. Space for caravans and campers at reasonable rates. For further details: Tel Northampton 408181.

Blue John Cavern and Mine   **F2**
Derby. ½ mile W of Castleton. Blue John is a translucent variety of the mineral fluorspar which is veined in red, blue, purple and yellow. It is so rare that it is found only here, and ornaments have been made from it since Roman times. Small vases made from Blue John can be bought at the mine and in Castleton. The caves are very beautiful with their coloured stalactites.
Other caves to visit include: Speedwell Cavern, Castleton (by boat); Poole's Cavern, Buxton; Heights of Abraham, Matlock Bath.

Bridgnorth Cliff Railway   **C6**
Bridgnorth, Shrops. The railway track that connects High Town on its sandstone ridge, and Low Town on the banks of the Severn, has a 1 in 1½ gradient. When you get to the top have a look at the Norman castle keep; it leans at 17°—three times the angle of the Leaning Tower of Pisa!

Hilton Valley Miniature Railway   **C6**
Hilton Valley, Shrops. Off A454 9 miles from Wolverhampton, 4 miles from Bridgnorth. A mile of 7¼-inch gauge track runs through attractive scenery among trees and beside a trout stream. In addition to the four steam engines, this line is of interest for its comprehensive signalling system which is unusual on a model railway. *Limited opening times.*

Sarehole Mill   **E7**
Colebank Rd, Hall Green, Birmingham, W. Midlands. Once used for working metal this water mill is now restored and houses a museum on milling.

Stapleford Park   **J5**
Leics. 4 miles E of Melton Mowbray off B676. An extensive and imaginative 10¼-inch gauge miniature railway runs around the park for over a mile and to the Hall. At the Hall you can continue your steam-hauled journey in the Boat Train which connects with two scale drawings of the Shaw Saville liners—Northern Star and Southern Cross. *Closed winter.*

The Tramway Museum   **G3**
Matlock Rd, Crich, Derby. 5 miles SE of Matlock. Created by a band of dedicated tramway enthusiasts it houses a good selection of trams which bring forth tears of pure nostalgia. Take your children for a ride on the mile of track and tell them what you got for a penny ticket when you were young. *Closed winter.*

Regional food

Bakewell Pudding
The original is still made by hand at 'The Old Original Pudding Shop' in the square at Bakewell, to a secret recipe discovered by accident at the Rutland Arms in 1860.

Cheeses
Derby still provides the mild creamy cheese and also the rarer Sage Derby. Buxton or Melton Mowbray are the places to buy your Stilton: it can be made only in the Vale of Belvoir or in Hartington. Other famous cheeses to buy in their towns of origin are Red Leicester and Double Gloucester.

Melton Mowbray Pie
This famous pie can still be bought at Melton Mowbray, freshly made from pork and well seasoned.

East Anglia and the Fens

A character in Noel Coward's play 'Private Lives' once asked 'How was Norfolk ?'. The reply was 'Flat'. This is however, a simplification because this region could more fairly be called boundless. After a drive through East Anglia it is the sky you remember, great rolling expanses of piling clouds that glide across these infinite, fertile acres.

The smoothness of the terrain only helps to emphasise the soaring Suffolk church towers and their dominance over the peaceful landscape. The fens of Cambridgeshire and Lincolnshire, now drained and dyked, remain wide and windswept, but nothing can match the moment when Ely Cathedral comes into view on its watery island like a glorious ship.

Lincolnshire has white stone churches, bulb fields, the stone elegance of Stamford and of course the great cathedral at Lincoln soaring over the roof-tops of the city. There's more to Cambridgeshire than its university city – the countryside has a rare remote quality for somewhere so near London and there are thatch and white-wash villages among the great elms.

Norfolk and Suffolk are arable, calm and full of unexpected villages with magnificent churches. This is Constable country, still full of great trees, flat fields and silent, reflecting pools. In parts of Norfolk you'll find the placid Broads and have that rare experience, the sight of a ship sailing slowly through the fields.

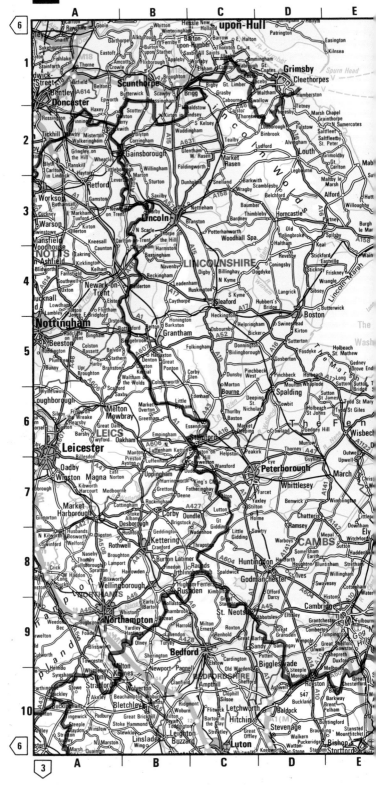

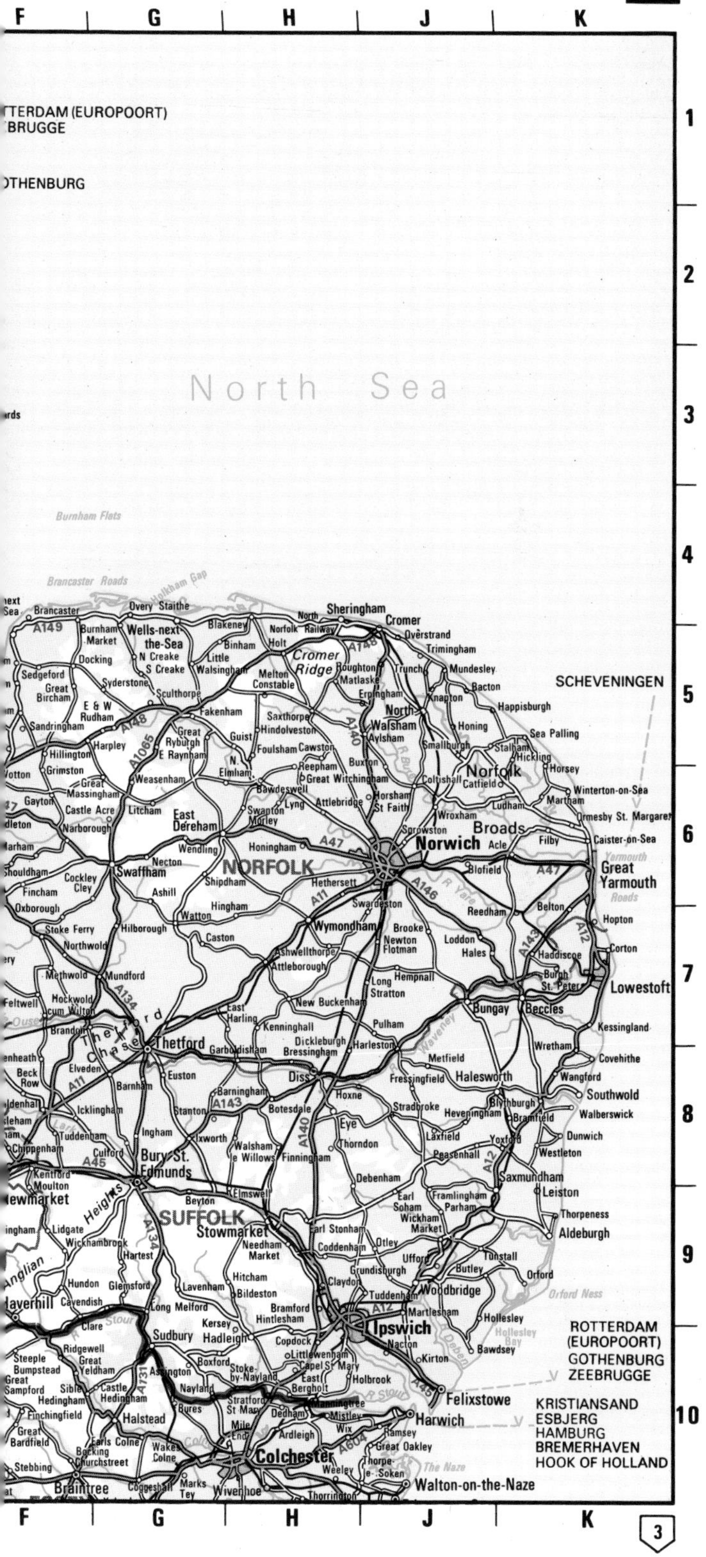
F
G
H
J
K
1
2
3
4
5
6
7
8
9
10
TERDAM (EUROPOORT)
BRUGGE
OTHENBURG
North Sea
Burnham Flats
Brancaster Roads
Holkham Gap
Brancaster
Overy Staithe
Wells-next-the-Sea
Burnham Market
Blakeney
Sheringham
Cromer
Overstrand
Trimingham
Mundesley
Bacton
Happisburgh
Sea Palling
SCHEVENINGEN
Cromer Ridge
Holt
Binham
Little Walsingham
N Creake
S Creake
Docking
Sedgeford
Great Bircham
Syderstone
Sculthorpe
Fakenham
E & W Rudham
Sandringham
Harpley
Great Ryburgh
E Raynham
Guist
Melton Constable
Saxthorpe
Hindolveston
Foulsham
Cawston
Aylsham
North Walsham
Knapton
Honing
Smallburgh
Stalham
Hickling
Horsey
Winterton-on-Sea
Martham
Ormesby St. Margaret
Caister-on-Sea
Great Yarmouth
Yarmouth Roads
Norfolk Broads
Catfield
Ludham
Coltishall
Wroxham
Sprowston
Norwich
Acle
Filby
Blofield
Reedham
Belton
Hopton
Gorton
Lowestoft
Kessingland
Hillington
Grimston
Gayton
Great Massingham
Weasenham
N. Elmham
Reepham
Great Witchingham
Bawdeswell
Lyng
Attlebridge
Horsham St Faith
Buxton
Swanton Morley
Castle Acre
Narborough
Litcham
East Dereham
Wendling
Necton
Honingham
Swaffham
NORFOLK
Shipdham
Hethersett
Cockley Cley
Fincham
Oxborough
Ashill
Watton
Hingham
Swardeston
Wymondham
Brooke
Newton Flotman
Loddon
Hales
Haddiscoe
Burgh St. Peter
Stoke Ferry
Northwold
Hilborough
Caston
Ashwellthorpe
Attleborough
Long Stratton
Hempnall
Methwold
Mundford
Hockwold cum Wilton
Feltwell
New Buckenham
Bungay
Beccles
Brandon
Thetford Chase
Thetford
East Harling
Kenninghall
Garboldisham
Dickleburgh
Bressingham
Pulham
Harleston
Wrentham
Covehithe
Elveden
Beck Row
Euston
Diss
Metfield
Fressingfield
Halesworth
Wangford
Southwold
Walberswick
Barnham
Barningham
Hoxne
Stradbroke
Heveningham
Blythburgh
Bramfield
Dunwich
Icklingham
Stanton
Botesdale
Eye
Laxfield
Yoxford
Westleton
Tuddenham
Ingham
Ixworth
Walsham le Willows
Thorndon
Finningham
Peasenhall
Chippenham
Culford
Bury St. Edmunds
Kentford
Moulton
Newmarket
Debenham
Saxmundham
Leiston
Framlingham
Parham
Earl Soham
Wickham Market
Thorpeness
Aldeburgh
Beyton
Elmswell
SUFFOLK
Stowmarket
Lidgate
Wickhambrook
Hartest
Needham Market
Earl Stonham
Coddenham
Otley
Ufford
Tunstall
Butley
Orford
Orford Ness
Grundisburgh
Claydon
Hitcham
Bildeston
Lavenham
Glemsford
Hundon
Cavendish
Haverhill
Long Melford
Tuddenham
Woodbridge
Martlesham
Hollesley
Hollesley Bay
Bawdsey
Bramford
Hintlesham
Kersey
Hadleigh
Ipswich
Nacton
Clare
Stour
Sudbury
Copdock
Little Wenham
Capel St Mary
Kirton
Deben
ROTTERDAM (EUROPOORT)
GOTHENBURG
ZEEBRUGGE
Steeple Bumpstead
Ridgewell
Great Yeldham
Great Sampford
Sible Hedingham
Castle Hedingham
Assington
Boxford
Stoke-by-Nayland
Nayland
East Bergholt
Holbrook
Felixstowe
KRISTIANSAND
ESBJERG
HAMBURG
BREMERHAVEN
HOOK OF HOLLAND
Finchingfield
Halstead
Bures
Stratford St Mary
Dedham
Manningtree
Mistley
Harwich
Great Bardfield
Earls Colne
Wakes Colne
Mile End
Ardleigh
Wix
Ramsey
Great Oakley
Bocking
Churchstreet
Colchester
Thorpe-le-Soken
The Naze
Stebbing
Weeley
Walton-on-the-Naze
Braintree
Coggeshall
Marks Tey
Wivenhoe
Thorrington
A149
A148
A1065
A47
A11
A140
A146
A143
A12
A134
A45
A131
A604
A133

The coast

Aldeburgh K9
Suffolk. Pop 2,800. EC Wed. An offspring of the prosperous mediaeval fishing village of Slaughden which was swallowed up by the sea. It is a main street of elegant houses behind a shingle beach. Nothing spectacular, but full of character.
A prosperous port in the 16thC and a haven for smugglers, it went into hibernation with the silting up of the estuary waters. Spring came with the leisure boom in the 20thC and with its association with music through Sir Benjamin Britten and the Aldeburgh Festival. Shingle beach.

Bawdsey J10
Suffolk. A huddle of houses behind a steep beach of dark red shingle. A paradise for beachcombers, it's a wild and lonely beach like the edge of the world, protected by a stalwart Martello tower.

Blakeney H4
Norfolk. Pop 700. EC Wed. Red-brick and flint houses climb down a narrow street which leads to the 15thC Guildhall, tucked in a hillside facing the small quay.
Overlooking a creek with sandy banks Blakeney has an aura of sun-swept calm in an ever endless horizon of salt marshes, sand and open sea. One of the most attractive villages in Norfolk, it was a thriving port in the middle ages. So prosperous were the woollen and fishing trades that German and Flemish merchants settled here. Later came the grain trade, but the tides continually carried the spit of land at Blakeney Point farther west so that the channel slowly silted up. Today it is a boating centre and a mecca for birdwatchers.
Lovely 15thC hammer-beam roof in the church nave. Remains of a 13thC Carmelite Friary.

Boston D4
Lincs. Pop 26,000. EC Thur. MD Wed, Sat. By 1204, when King John granted a charter to Boston, its fame as a port was second only to that of London. In the 13thC the North Sea and its Hanseatic League were important. Merchants grew rich in the wool trade with Flanders, and when the tower was added to the 14thC Boston church, they fashioned it in the style of those in Antwerp or Bruges. Known as the 'Stump,' it is a landmark for miles around.
Plagues, floods, and the turning of trade towards America, with the subsequent importance of western ports like Bristol, turned Boston into a depressed area by the 16thC.
In the 15thC Guildhall are the cells where some of the Pilgrim Fathers were imprisoned in 1607. By 1620 they finally landed in New England and founded a colony which they called Boston. Though still a busy commercial centre, it has kept many remnants of its past with buildings from all eras. Reminders of its days as a port are seen in the warehouses along the old quays. Magnificent views from the top of the 'Stump' of ships going down the River Witham to the sea.

Boston Stump

The Burnhams G5
Norfolk. The Domesday Book listed 7 'Burnhams by the Sea' of which 2 have disappeared. The 5 remaining, Burnham Deepdale, Burnham Market, Burnham Norton, Burnham Overy and Burnham Thorpe, are all small and unspoilt. Burnham Deepdale has a church with an early round tower and an exceptionally fine Norman font. The 13thC church at Burnham Overy has an early central tower. Nelson was born in the rectory at Burnham Thorpe; it no longer exists.

Covehithe K8
Suffolk. The nicest place on the Suffolk coast, full of settled silence. A remote hamlet at the end of a narrow lane. Has a 17thC brick church built with a thatch roof and standing within the ruins of a much larger church which was partially dismantled in 1672. Shingle beach.

Cromer J5
Norfolk. Pop 5,300. EC Wed. A fishing village and small port which became a 'railway-age' resort, fashionable and exclusive, in the 19thC. Along the sea front a number of Edwardian hotels back on to narrow streets of fishermen's cottages. The church is an imposing 15thC building with a magnificent west tower, the highest in a county of high church towers. There are miles of sand and swimming is safe except in rough weather. Watch for the crab fishermen bringing in their catch.

Cromer

Dunwich K8
Suffolk. A thriving town in the 12thC, the 'beginning of the end' came in January 1326 when a storm blocked the harbour mouth and demolished 3 churches. Gradually the harbour defences, then the cliffs and the town were destroyed by further storms. By 1677 the sea had reached the market place. Only a few houses and part of an old graveyard remain and the sea is still eating the cliffs away.
Ruins of a Franciscan Priory; a museum of town relics including its charter from King John. Shingle beach.

Felixstowe J10
Suffolk. Pop 18,900. EC Wed. Strung out along a gently curving bay, it's a booming container port where once the Romans built a castle. A priory was founded at the time of the Norman Conquest; King Edward III probably resided here in the 14thC, and Landguard Fort was built in the 17thC. But its real business, leisure, began with the arrival of the railway in 1877. Banks of red shingle with patches of sand at low tide are backed by a traffic-free promenade, neat lawns and flower beds. Good bathing.

Great Yarmouth K6
Norfolk. Pop 50,200. EC Thu. MD Wed, Sat. A long narrow town which was formerly a small fishermen's settlement on a sandbank. In the 14thC the town was enclosed on 3 sides by walls 23 feet high and 7 feet thick. Within the walls houses were packed tightly together in 145 streets known as 'rows'. Mostly damaged during the last war, traces of them can still be seen.
In the prosperous days of the East Anglian wool trade, Yarmouth was busy shipping first wool, and then woven cloth to the Low Countries which lay opposite her to the east. In the 19thC the wool trade moved north, and Yarmouth's shipping declined further when the growth of the railways deprived her of much of her coastal trade.
Running parallel to the harbour is the sea front, with its wide promenades, gardens and streets. Flat sandy beaches; watch for warnings before swimming.
Of interest—the 12thC parish church; the dungeons in the mediaeval Tolhouse; the 16thC Old Merchants House, now a museum; the Church of St George, built 1714.

Happisburgh **J5**
Norfolk. Dominated by the 110-foot-high tower of the 15thC church, it's a village of windy charm which stands on a rounded hillock of meadows set back from the sandy beach. For centuries its fortunes have been bound up with shipwrecks, and the formidable Happisburgh sands, littered with the bones of many ships, are only 7 miles off-shore.
In 1904 there were so many wrecks on the beach that they had to be blown up by Trinity House to clear them away.
The gaily painted red and white lighthouse was built on the low hill south of the village in 1791. Swimming is safe.

Holkham Gap **G4**
Norfolk. The Holkham 'Meals' which line the coast were once sandy islands like Scolt Head. Now they are part of the mainland and are covered with pine trees which provide attractive, sheltered picnic spots. The tide retreats over half a mile. Bathing is safe.

Hunstanton **F5**
Norfolk. The only East Anglian resort that faces west, being comparatively sheltered in the Wash. Long stretches of fine sand backed by striped brown and white cliffs. Victorian town with a large green stretching to the promenade. Popular for boating and safe bathing.

Ipswich **H9**
Suffolk. Pop 122,800. MD Thur, Fri. A dozen miles from the open sea you will find a row of sea-captains' houses and brick and timber houses with private quays. This one-time merchants' town of mediaeval charm is the county town of East Suffolk. At the head of the River Orwell, it's been a busy port for centuries. First developed by the Saxons, it was rapidly expanded by the Normans who realised its potential.
The town was the boyhood home of Cardinal Wolsey. Dickens stayed at the Great White House in Tavern Street, which formed a backdrop to some of the misadventures of Mr Pickwick.
A wealth of things to see: the Ancient House in Butter Market; Christchurch Mansion, a fine Tudor house and now a museum with furniture, fine panelling, model ships and dolls' houses; St Margaret's Church.

King's Lynn **F6**
Norfolk. Pop 30,100. EC Wed. MD Tue (cattle), Sat. Mediaeval streets run down to the quays interspersed with some classical buildings. The rivers flowing through Lincolnshire, Northamptonshire, Huntingdonshire and Cambridgeshire made Lynn the natural gateway to the Continent. Already a busy port in the 14thC, her banks were lined with robust warehouses and her streets with the elegant houses of rich merchants; the 2 fine Guildhalls stand today. As her prosperity was based on the inland waterways, a decline set in with the growth of railways in the 19thC.
The town's heart is Tuesday Market-Place, a large sea-bright space. Ships still unload by numerous staithes and quays and by the famous 17thC Custom House, which is almost perfectly preserved Of interest: the 15thC St George's Guildhall, once a theatre; the 12thC St Margaret's Church with Norman work in the south-west corner; the 17thC Duke's Head.

Customs House, King's Lynn

Lowestoft **K7**
Suffolk. Pop 52,200. EC Thur. MD Fri. The most easterly place in England whose fortunes were made by the discovery of the Dogger Bank and other North Sea fishing grounds in the mid 19thC. The railway brought the rich London markets within easy reach, and put the Thames Estuary fishing ports out of business.
In an enviable position both on the sea coast, (extending round a fine harbour), and on the edge of the Broads, it is a town of salt-aired sincerity. Divided into 2 parts south and north of the piers and harbour.
South of Claremont Pier, which forms the southern arm of the harbour, the beach is sandy and firm and safe for bathing.
Birthplace of Benjamin Britten, son of a local dentist.

Mablethorpe **E2**
Lincs. Pop 6,200. EC Thur. The ideal family holiday resort with mile upon mile of gently sloping golden beaches. The town is protected from the sea by a terraced concrete promenade.
Tree stumps which appear on the sands at spring low tides are all that remain of a village and woodland swept away by the sea in 1289. Clean beach, particularly safe for children.

Overstrand **J5**
Norfolk. Pop 1,000. This quiet village overlooks a sandy beach and the all-encroaching sea. In the year 1398 its church seems to have been washed away, for the lord of the manor gave half an acre for a new churchyard and the next year a patent was granted for the building of the present church of St Martin. Safe swimming.

Overy Staithe **G4**
Norfolk. EC Wed. A pretty village with a harbour and the remains of a quay. One of the most attractive of the North Norfolk ports with a channel which twists between mud and sandbanks. Several footpaths lead across the marshes.

Burnham Overy Staithe

Sheringham **H4**
Norfolk. Pop 4,700. Once a small fishing village with a reputation for lobsters (which it still has), Sheringham became a popular seaside resort with the advent of the railways. Neat and well planned, it lies along the cliff edge with Edwardian hotels and wind bleached houses overlooking the beach where fishing boats are drawn up. Safe swimming.

Skegness **E3**
Lincs. Pop 13,600. EC Thur. Six miles of unblemished beaches, safe for swimming and one of the best planned pleasure parks in Europe. As the old posters used to say, the air is 'bracing'. Skegness grew up in the Railway Age, linked to the industrial towns of the Midlands and providing millions with day excursions. The town itself, with many tree-lined streets, is set back from the sea front. Donkey rides for children between the dunes.

Southwold **K8**
Suffolk. Pop 2,000. EC Wed. MD Mon, Thur. Lying on a green knoll surrounded by marshes and with an aura of Edwardian elegance, this gracious little town was rebuilt around wide greens after a devastating fire in the 17thC. A white lighthouse, topped with a golden weather vane, stands lookout over the rooftops. A battery of cannon, sent to Southwold by Charles I in 1645 for protection against privateers based at Dunkirk, glare out over the grass-topped cliffs above the sandy beach.
Have a look at 'Southwold Jack' the 15thC oak figure of a man at arms who strikes the bell of the church clock. St Edmund is one of the finest Perpendicular churches in England.

There is a small pier with good fishing and concrete terraces with bathing huts along the foot of the cliffs. Swimming from the beach is safe.

Southwold.

Thorpeness   K9
Suffolk. A unique 'created' town, laid out this century by the dramatist and author Glencairn Stuart Ogilvie. Houses were built in a variety of styles, including Tudor, Jacobean and the tarred weather-boarded and mellow-brick styles of East Anglia. The water tower was disguised as a house and called the House in the Clouds. A windmill was brought from Aldingham, and in 1910 a 65-acre lake, 3 feet deep, was dug. The wide shingle beach is safe for bathing.

Walberswick   K8
Suffolk. Pop 500. EC Wed. A once-flourishing port, it has weathered into a quiet village of mellow brick houses. Trapped neatly between the River Blyth and a large area of reed-filled marshes, it offers the best view of Southwold. The shore is sandy, and there are holiday houses on the extensive sand dunes. Safe bathing from an immense beach.

Wells-next-the-Sea   G4
Norfolk. Pop 2,400. EC Thur. MD Wed. A port, delightfully old fashioned. Full of memories like faded photographs, the town consists of a number of narrow streets with flint houses round the church and an attractive green, the Buttlands, with trees and Georgian houses. A street runs down to a little used quay, dominated by a tall granary. Famous for its whelks and sprats. From the western shore of the harbour a narrow lane leads to an attractive beach overlooked by pine trees and small huts. Safe bathing.

Inland towns & villages

The Acres   G6
Norfolk. Pop. 1,300. The most important of the Acres, Castle Acre, is a large village within the outer bailey of the castle. A wide street with rows of cottages runs down to the river. South Acre, 1 mile south across the river, nestles among trees whilst West Acre was once the site of a 12thC Augustinian priory.
Nothing spectacular here, but all 3 villages are full of gentle atmosphere. Of interest— the remains of a Clunaic priory to the west of Castle Acre; the 15thC church of St James; the church of St George, South Acre, and the priory gateway at West Acre.

Aylsham   J5
Norfolk. Pop 2,600. EC Wed. MD Mon. Small graceful town on the River Bure with a handsome marketplace surrounded by neat 18thC houses. To the north is the church of St Michael, a juggle of Decorated and Perpendicular.
Of interest—Black Boy Inn, built in the time of Queen Anne; the Knoll, the Manor House and other fine houses; in the church is a memorial in manicured Gothic to Humphrey Repton, the landscape gardener.

Bury St Edmunds   G8
Suffolk. Pop 25,600. EC Thur. MD Wed, Sat. A cathedral town that grew up round the 7thC Saxon monastery of Beodericsworth. The burial place for a martyred king, it was also the birth place of Magna Carta.
Georgian in appearance and spaciousness, the original plan, conceived by Abbot Baldwin in the 11thC, was Roman in concept. The town plan was later developed on the mediaeval formula of a square for God and a square for man. The former—just outside the Abbey—is known as Angel Hill; the latter is the market place, still the commercial heart of the town.
The remains of the 11thC Abbey Church has Tudor, Georgian and Victorian houses as infilling.
Of interest—Angel Hotel where Mr Pickwick stayed; Moyse's Hall, a rare 12thC house; Cupola House built 1639; the Town Hall, originally designed as a theatre by Robert Adam in the 1770s.

Cambridge   E9
Cambs. Pop 103,700. EC Thur. MD Mon, Sat. At the foot of a hill was a ford across the River Cam, the junction of a network of Roman roads with canals and rivers just before the Fens. Of such great strategic and commercial importance was this ford that successive Roman developments probably included the building of a bridge, hence the city name. Already an important commercial centre by the time Peterhouse College, the first of the university's buildings, was established by Bishop Ely in 1284. Today much of the city's charm is in small streets and passages like St Edwards Passage and Botolph Lane. The collegiate idea came into being in the 13thC to replace the derelict lodgings the students were forced to live in, grouped as they were round the religious and lay teachers whose ideas most appealed to them. The principal accents are set by university and public buildings. Many of the colleges are on the main street which runs between the river and Market Hill. Peaceful green lawns, the Backs, run down from the colleges to the river which is crossed by bridges and shaded by willows.
Best mediaeval houses and cottages in the city (two and three storied timber and plaster houses, many with projecting upper floors) are to be found in Northampton Street and Magdalene Street. Little Rose Inn, a 17thC inn, is probably the last to have extensive stables. Enclosed stone bridge over the River Cam at St Johns and fine hammer-beam roof in the 16thC Hall. See Wren's magnificent library for Trinity College, with carvings by Grinling Gibbons, and Kings College Chapel with its fine 15thC fan-vaulted roof plus Rubens' 'The Adoration of the Magi'. A cornucopia of treasures in the Fitzwilliam Museum.

'The Backs', Cambridge

Castle Rising   F5
Norfolk. Pop 200. An important sea port when King's Lynn was but a marsh, it's now a small pretty village stranded on a beach of grass green country from which the sea receded long ago. There is an impressive Norman castle standing behind Roman earthworks. Approached through a ruined gatehouse, it has a hall-keep with a great stone staircase leading up to a fascinating sequence of rooms, galleries and minor staircases. Granted to the Duke of Norfolk by Henry VIII in 1544.
Interesting 17thC brick almshouse.

Cavendish   G9
Suffolk. Pop 800. A warm assembly of pinkly pleased thatched cottages clusters round a sloping green and elegant 14thC church in a fairy tale setting of countryside. The characters from 'Lord of the Rings', like Bilbo and Frodo, Sam and Tom Bombadil seem more in place here than 20thC man.

Note the 16thC timber-framed farmhouse of Nether Hall; the 19thC Cavendish Hall; the 15thC flushwork panelling and clerestory in the church.

Cavendish

Clare F9
Suffolk. Pop 1,700. EC Wed. MD Mon.
A beautiful little town set in the heart of Constable country. It's full to the brim with half-timbered, tile hung houses, and some discreetly Georgian. Dominated by a magnificent wool church, whilst the 15thC priest's house at the churchyard corner has an exuberant flourish of pargetting as fine as spring blossom.
Of interest—the Swan Inn; an Iron Age fort; Cliftons, with its splendid 17thC chimneys.

Debenham H8
Suffolk. Pop 900. EC Tue. A village of overhanging timbered houses, surrounded by desolate landscape. The first trickles of the River Deben run alongside the gently sloping main street, and rush-weaving is still carried out here. Look at Crow's Hall, built in 1508 and surrounded by a moat. It is the perfect example of an ancestral home. Interesting Galilee porch in the church of St Mary.

Diss H8
Norfolk. Pop 4,500. EC Tue. MD Fri. An invigorating mixture of Tudor, Georgian and Victorian buildings built round a large lake, the Were. A small town of twisting streets with a sloping market square for a heart, dominated by the church at its head. The church, austere like a Lenten hymn, was built right on the street with processional arches either side. John Skelton, Henry VIII's tutor, was rector here in the early 16thC.
Look at the Shambles; the former Dolphin Inn and Greyhound Inn; also mid-19thC Corn Exchange.

Downham Market F6
Norfolk. Pop 4,100. EC Wed. MD Fri. A small congested market town all yellow and brown, brick and carrstone, which stands on a hill at the very edge of the Fens, 12 miles south of King's Lynn on the River Ouse. Rising above is the Perpendicular church, in a big churchyard of yews and weeping ashes reached by a steep lane.
Of interest: Elizabethan-style workhouse, built in 1836, and the Neo-Gothic Clock Tower in cast iron (1878).

East Bergholt H10
Suffolk. Pop 2,000. An unspoilt village full of grand houses and fine trees. Lying along a haphazard ridge above the River Stour, it has some enthusiastic half-timbering dating from the influx of Flemish weavers. The birthplace of John Constable whose parents are buried in the church.
The church of St Mary is remarkable for its unfinished tower, begun in 1525. A 16thC timber-framed cage in the churchyard contains the church bells. Look at Flatford Mill and Willy Lott's cottage.

Edenham C6
Lincs. Pop 400. Graceful cottages built of crisp mellow stone, and a large church, under an umbrella of cedars; the shaft of a mediaeval cross stands in the churchyard. Grimsthorpe Castle commands attention in a palatial park with a magnificent chestnut avenue and herds of fallow and red deer. Look at the collection of Brussels tapestries and paintings by Lawrence, Reynolds and Van Dyck in the castle.

Ely E8
Cambs. Pop 10,000. EC Tue. MD Thur. A small town standing on a bluff above the River Ouse. Dominated by the cathedral, Ely is set in the flatness of the Fen landscape, of which it is the capital. Formerly an island, accessible only by boat or causeways until the Fens were drained in the 17th and 18thC, it was here Hereward the Wake, 'The Last of the English', held out against William the Conqueror. A jumble of niceties, but best of all is Waterside: informal and humble, a street of 18thC cottages opening on to the Ouse. Here was the quay in the middle ages and later.
Worth seeing are the late Norman doorway in the Headmaster's House, King's School; the great south gatehouse—all that remains of the 14thC Abbey; Bishop Alcock's Palace, and the chantry on the north side of Palace Green.

Euston G8
Suffolk. Pop 300. An affable street of half-timbered, thatch and tile-hung, flint and brick houses with a low ridge of downland behind. The church sits within the sleepy grounds of the Elizabethan Hall. The landscape around here was the setting for Robert Bloomfield's 18thC tale of rural life 'The Farmer's Boy'.
High quality carvings inside the church in Grinling Gibbons manner.

Folkingham C5
Lincs. Pop 500. A village of splendid houses round a large square on the edge of the Fens—an 18thC coaching halt which has its original atmosphere intact. Interesting church of St Andrew with an outstanding Perpendicular tower.

Gainsborough B2
Lincs. Pop 17,400. EC Wed. MD Tue, Sat. Busy market town and industrial centre on the east bank of the Trent linked to Nottinghamshire on the opposite bank by a 3-arched 18thC bridge. Canute's father, King Sweyne, was murdered here in 1014 following a series of raids.
St Ogg's, in George Eliot's 'The Mill on the Floss', was modelled on Gainsborough.
There are some interesting 18thC warehouses on the quayside; note also the Old Hall, c1500, one of the largest mediaeval houses in the county.

Grantchester E9
Cambs. Pop 500. Immortalised in the famous poem by Rupert Brooke. The place where he lived and wrote before the First World War, it's almost an integral part of Cambridge life and loved by generations of undergraduates and tutors. A tranquil carefree little village in timber, plaster and thatch. Interesting 15thC Manor Farm and 17thC Old Vicarage.

Grantham B5
Lincs. Pop 27,900. EC Wed. MD Sat. A former coaching town on the road to the North, Grantham, on the River Witham, has many finely preserved houses. Sir Isaac Newton, honoured by a statue, went to the Grammar School. Visit Grantham House with its 14thC hall and the Early English St Wulfram's church with its 16thC 'chained' library and early crypt. A one-time landlord of the mediaeval Angel and Royal inn left a legacy for an annual sermon denouncing drunkenness.

Helpston C6
Cambs. Pop 700. This is a genial stone-built village round a pleasant green. It was here that John Clare, the peasant poet, was born in 1793.
Look at the College House, complete with 2 buttresses, slit window and 4 centred archways; Helpston House with canted bay window, gables and dormers; 12thC Woodhall Manor.

Hemingford Grey D8
Cambs. Pop 1,500. A picture book village of timber, thatch and mellow brick cottages set amongst trees by a curve of the Great Ouse. Little seems to have changed since a violent storm in 1741 nipped off the steeple top of St James' Church. The 12thC moated stone-

built Manor House is claimed to be the oldest inhabited house in England.

Hemingford Grey

Horncastle **D3**
Lincs. Pop 4,000. EC Wed. MD Thur, Sat.
An engaging market town situated at the south west foot of the Wolds on the site of the Roman fort of Banovallum, traces of the Roman walls still being visible. The town buildings are straight-forward Georgian, grouped informally round a sloping market place. Horncastle was once famous for its annual horse-fairs, said to be the largest of their kind in the world.
Have a look at the Fighting Cocks Inn, which still has a cockpit in the yard and the interesting relics, in the church, of the Battle of Winceby fought in 1643 during the Civil War.

Houghton **D8**
Cambs. Pop 3,000. A tranquil riverside village as refreshing as a cold drink on a long summer's day. Pleasant tree shaded walks, picturesque cottages, a brown cobbled church, known as the Slipper Chapel because pilgrims once removed their slippers before entering, and a village green complete with an elaborate Gothick-style cast iron pump.
Have a look at the massive timber watermill built on the River Ouse in the 17thC; also the wall paintings of 1622 in the Three Jolly Butchers Inn.

Huntingdon **D8**
Cambs. Pop 17,200. EC Wed. MD Sat. The twin towns of Huntingdon and Godmanchester, now 1 borough, lie at the intersection of 3 Roman roads. The towns are separated by the 300-acre meadow of Port Holme on one side of a 17thC raised causeway, and West Side Common on the other. They are linked by one of the finest mediaeval bridges in the country.
Invaded by the Danes, Huntingdon then endured the Normans, only to be nearly wiped out by the plague in 1348. It sank into oblivion except for a short period during the Civil War when first Cromwell, and then Charles I, made their headquarters here. Both Cromwell and Samuel Pepys were pupils at the Grammar School, built in 1565, and now the Cromwell Museum.
Of interest—the George Hotel which still has 2 sides of its 17thC courtyard intact, one with an open gallery and external staircase; the Falcon, with oriel windows and massive doors, believed to have been the headquarters of Cromwell.

Kersey **G9**
Suffolk. Famous in the middle ages for cloth. The village is a handful of weavers' cottages and pastel tinted half-timbered houses running downhill to a small stream. Across the ford the street runs uphill again, this time to the 15thC church of St Mary. There are carved reminders of the Black Death in the north aisle.
Priory Farm has the remains of an Augustinian priory founded late 12thC.

Kimbolton **C8**
Cambs. Pop 1,200. EC Wed. A beauty of a place with a hustle of red roofs, a 13thC church and a mediaeval castle where Katherine of Aragon spent her last 4 years. Set in the green valley of the River Kim. Look at the square gatehouse designed by Robert Adam; St Andrew's 14thC tower with a broach spire; the 19thC Moravian church, the only one in the country.

Lavenham **G9**
Suffolk. Pop 1,300. EC Wed. Perfect 15thC half-timbered houses along irregular streets. Its prosperity was founded in the mid-14thC when many Flemish weavers settled here. The 14th and 15thC church of SS Peter and Paul is one of the finest churches in England founded on wool prosperity. Look at the Old Wool Hall, built 1500; the 16thC Swan Hotel and Guildhall. Some particularly fine pargetting work on house façades.

The church at Lavenham

Lincoln **B3**
Lincs. Pop 74,200. EC Wed. MD Fri, Sat.
The city is situated on the site of a former Roman military garrison built in AD48 to command the meeting of 2 great highways, Ermine Street and Fosse Way. In 1068 William the Conqueror built an impregnable castle here.
The historic centre climbs a 200-foot-high limestone hill to the triple-towered cathedral built in the 11thC. The third largest in England, it stares out across the River Witham, a mass of mediaeval buildings at its feet.
Of particular interest is the 12thC Jews House and the 'House of Aaron the Jew'; the Roman Newport Arch; the 16thC gateway with the guildhall above it and the 16thC half-timbered shops on the High Bridge.

High Bridge, Lincoln

Little Gidding **C8**
Cambs. A small church and a huddle of buildings. It was here in 1625 that Nicholas Ferrar, the son of a prosperous merchant family, turned his back on wordly things and founded a religious community. The beliefs and practices of this community inspired the last of T.S. Eliot's 'Four Quartets' called 'Little Gidding'.
Charles I visited the community in search of a hiding place from Cromwell's forces.

Long Melford **G9**
Suffolk. Pop 2,900. EC Thur. Once a mediaeval manufacturing town set in the picturesque valley of the Stour. It has an impressive High Street, long and wide, lined with dignified houses and charming shops. At one end is an 18thC bridge, at the other,

the finest of Suffolk churches set behind the grandest of all village greens.
Look at Melford Hall, the best of early Elizabethan houses; the 15thC stained glass in the church; the old Grammar School and

the half-timbered Bull Inn with its galleried courtyard.

Nayland   G10
Suffolk. Pop 1,200. EC Wed, Sat. A gem in most senses of the word, sitting comfortably alongside the River Stour. Its 15th and 16thC houses congregate in a pleasantly unassuming way, as the best of village buildings do.
Look at White House and Queen's Head Inn; also 15thC Alston Court; Constable's painting behind the altar in the church.

Newmarket   F8
Suffolk. Pop 13,000. EC Wed. MD Tue, Sat. Set magnificently on the splendid open heathland which straddles the road from London to Norwich, it is the centre of the English horse racing world, and the home of more studs than any other town in England. The hunt-loving King James I started it when he built a hunting lodge here after his visit in 1605. Charles II was devoted to racing and the whole court would come during the season.
The High Street is an agreeable amalgam of Georgian and Victorian buildings. Of interest—the Rutland Arms Hotel with a red-brick front; the Georgian Jockey Club; the mediaeval piscina in the 14thC church; Nell Gwynn's cottage.

Norwich   J6
Norfolk. Pop 121,700. EC Thur. MD Sat. The social capital, market and shopping centre for Norfolk and a large part of Suffolk. The Industrial Revolution which gave the coup-de-grâce to its handweavers saw the birth of the city as one of the chief shoe manufacturing towns in the country. The city centre is enclosed on 3 sides by the old city wall, the curve of the River Wensum defining the fourth. Industry is spread out along the river; civic buildings around City Wall; the ecclesiastical area centres on the cathedral with the shopping centre dissecting the lot. Three major landmarks dominate the centre—the cathedral, a masterpiece set in a low-lying hollow of land inside the curve of the river; the Norman castle, set high on a mound; and the City Hall, also set on high ground. The market place, bright with coloured awnings, sits in the saddle of land,

Norwich Market

between the City Hall and the castle. Originally the city was a series of villages, the Normans having developed the old Saxon centre in Tombland. Today its scale is still basically the same—narrow, intimate streets opening on to a series of plains, one of the biggest being St Andrew's Plain.

Peterborough   D7
Cambs. Pop 70,000. MD Wed, Fri, Sat. Crisply businesslike, it is a prosperous city and handsome market town, with the Market Place for its centre, dominated by the 17thC guildhall.
The Barnack stone built cathedral is one of the most complete and impressive Romanesque buildings in England. Its real glory is in the unique west front, created when an ingenious screen wall was placed in front of the old Romanesque façade.
The best Georgian houses are in Priestgate; the Bull Hotel, Westgate, is an interesting 18thC building.

St Ives   D8
Cambs. Pop 8,400. EC Thur. MD Mon, Sat. Originally a village called Slepe on the north bank of the River Ouse, it was renamed in 1050 when a priory was built and dedicated

to St Ivo, a Persian bishop whose remains were found in a nearby field.
St Ives is a leafy sunlit place with refreshing riverside views. It has a narrow 6-arched bridge, built in 1415 with a miniature bridge chapel, one of only 3 of its kind in England. A ruined wall is all that remains of the priory.
Have a look at the Elizabethan manor house by the bridge with fine brick chimneys; the early 13thC double piscina in All Saints. Church.

St Neots   C8
Cambs. Pop 18,000. EC Tue. MD Thur. An ancient riverside market town which owes its origin to a priory founded in the 10thC by Benedictine monks. Its heart is the long and spacious Market Place which backs onto the river.
The beautiful church of St Mary's, one of the largest mediaeval churches in the country, is tucked neatly away from the town centre in a large churchyard.
Look at the interior roof carvings of angels, birds and animals in the church; the 17thC Bridge Hotel and the Cross Keys Hotel.

Spalding   D6
Lincs. Pop 17,000. EC Thur. MD Sat. Busy Fenland centre of farming and horticulture. Warm red-brick and Dutch-style architecture along the River Welland. Of interest—the Bird Museum; Ayscongfee Hall and gardens; the museum of the Spalding Gentleman's Society to which distinguished men of letters and science have belonged since the 18thC; the bulb fields and Flower Festival in spring.

Stamford   C6
Lincs. Pop 14,500. EC Thur. MD Fri, Sat. A quiet, sober town, built from the richly mellow local stone. Once the Danish capital of the Fens, it is one of Europe's finest mediaeval towns. An important wool centre in the 12thC, it had a university and 17 churches of which only 6 remain. All but destroyed during the Wars of the Roses, it became socially desirable in the 18thC due to the proximity of the Great North Road. Of interest—All Saints' Place, the raison d'être of the town; the 17thC Barn Hill House; the ruined 7thC chapel of St Leonard's Priory; the golden choir of the church of St Mary.

Stilton   C7
Cambs. Pop 800. A village on the edge of the Fens with a reputation for cheese it has never produced. It was really a half-way house in the business, for the famous cheeses made in Leicestershire were loaded on to coaches for London and the North at the 17thC Bell Inn.

Stoke-by-Nayland   H10
Suffolk. Pop 700. EC Sat. A village as alive as a breeze in a field of corn, but in its own quietly simple way. Another delicious slice of country fare in a countryside choc-a-bloc with such delights.
On the ridge rising up out of the Stour Valley stands the church, puritanically Perpendicular, and proud of it.
Of interest is Giffords Hall, with an intriguing red-brick gatehouse on the south side; 17thC Thorington Hall; a yeoman farmhouse in Ox's Farm.

Stowmarket   H9
Suffolk. Pop 8,700. EC Tue. MD Thur, Sat. A small market town with a number of light industries. Despite a chequered history dating back to Saxon times few old buildings remain. In a sense it's a place without a memory, but friendly all the same.
It was a prosperous town in the early 19thC when the River Gipping was made navigable to Stowmarket.
Of interest—the half-timbered Vicarage of the 16thC; the Fox Hotel; the Butter Market; Abbot's Hall with its largely open air museum of rural life.

Swaffham   G6
Norfolk. Pop 4,300. EC Thur, MD Sat. A busy but beautiful 18thC market town of

sturdy buildings, built round a huge
triangular market place with an elegant
Palladian market cross. The church is a
magnificent 15thC miracle with fine
hammer-beam roof.
Some good Georgian buildings, including the
School House and the Assembly Room.

Market Cross, Swaffham.

Thetford   G7
Norfolk. Pop 15,700. EC Wed. MD Tue, Sat.
A quiet little market town by a river. In the
Tudor period it was the cathedral city of
East Anglia, with over 20 churches and 4
monasteries. The Dissolution brought a halt
to all this splendour. Built, like so many
mediaeval towns, within the outer defences
of its castle, Thetford has winding streets of
well-proportioned 18thC houses, with an
element of surprise round each corner.
Dormant until an attempt in 1820 to turn it
into a full-blown spa, it then slipped serenely
back into obscurity with the dignity of a
Chelsea pensioner.
See the Old Gaol of 1816; St Mary's
Church; the mediaeval Bell Hotel; the mid-
18thC King's House built on the site of the
hunting lodge of James I, and the remains of
a Clunaic priory.

Wisbech   E6
Cambs. Pop 17,000. EC Wed. MD Sat. A
Georgian market town and river port, at the
centre of the rich agricultural Fenland.
Wisbech prospered in the 18th and 19thC
when river traffic made it an important
trading centre in East Anglia. The chief
glory is its front along the River Nene. At
Wisbech the river forms a bend; on the bend
is a bridge and around this, on either side of
the river, the town has grown. On the south
side, are the castle, church and market place,
and across the bridge on the north side, the
town hall and Corn Exchange. Along either
side of the river are the quays and
warehouses that represented the real business
of the town. Beyond the bridge, where the
vessels did not go, are the elegant houses of
the rich merchants in 2 terraces, South Brink
and North Brink, divided by the river.
Of interest—Peckover House, Flint House
and Nene Quay.

Wymondham   H7
Norfolk, Pop 8,500. EC Wed. MD Fri. A
charming market town, rebuilt in 1615 after
a fire had destroyed most of the town. In the
centre is the market place with its beguiling
market cross, and all around are winding
streets built in the 17th and 18thC. The
most impressive building is the church of SS
Mary and Thomas of Canterbury with 2
towers dominating the town. In its
churchyard, the remains of the abbey
founded in 1107.
Of interest—Carick House, early 18thC with
fine plaster-work internally; Burfield Hall,
another 18thC house on a moated site;
mediaeval Gunvil's Hall with 17th and
18thC additions.

Regional features

Martello Towers
A pair of Martello towers stand guard over
the mouth of the River Deben by
Woodbridge. Another 4 line the shingle
beach between Bawdsey and Shingle Street,
whilst south of Aldeburgh at Slaughden
Quay is the last of the Martello towers at
this end of the coast.

Cambridgeshire Mills
The post-mill at Great Chishill was built in

1819. The fantail turns the mill on a central
post.
Burwell has 2 tower-mills. One was working
until recently but is now derelict; of the
other, bigger one, only the stump survives.
At Swaffham Prior there is another tower-
mill. Built in 1875 it is preserved on a
mound originally made for a post-mill.
Nearby is a derelict smock-mill of the same
date.
At Eye there's an 80-foot-high tower-mill, of
8 stories. It is now power driven, and used
for producing animal foods.

post-mill, Great Chishill

Lincolnshire Mills
At Alford the 5-sail, 6-storey tower-mill, built
in 1837, is still grinding corn. Heckington
Mill is a unique 8-sail tower-mill built in
1830. Burgh le Marsh, 5 miles W of
Skegness, has a 5-sail tower-mill built in
1833. It last worked in 1947 but today it is
still free-wheeling and in a good state of
preservation.

Heckington   Boston

Norfolk Mills
There is a straight-forward tower-mill on the
Yare, and a fine rust red-brick tower-mill
with an elegant cap at Cley-next-the-Sea. Just
south of the village of Mundesley is a smock-
windmill complete with cap and sails.
Eleven miles north of Yarmouth is Horsey
Mill. It was built in 1912 as a drainage mill
on the site of an earlier one.

Cley - next - the Sea

Suffolk Mills
There is an elegant white painted post-mill
on Saxtead Green, dating from the 18thC; it
was rebuilt in 1854.

Norfolk Churches
The Norfolk countryside is dominated by
churches that are isolated elements in a
completely flat and lonely landscape. Some

South Walsham   Bawburgh   Corney   Potter Heigham

of the earliest of them are round, because it
was easier to build a tower of that shape
with the local pebbles. It wasn't until the
13thC that stone from Barnack in
Northamptonshire became more readily
accessible.

Famous people

John Constable (1776–1837)　　**H10**
Flatford Mill, East Bergholt, Suffolk. Born at
East Bergholt, the second son of a
prosperous miller, Constable spent a year
working in his father's water-mill at Flatford
when he was 18 years old, before setting out
for London to try his luck at painting. There
are conflicting accounts of how he spent his
year as a miller. Some say he was most likely
to be found observing nature, sketching in
the fields and copying drawings by Girtin.
This area of Suffolk was immortalised in
some of Constable's best pictures. The mill
is now a field study centre.

Flatford Mill

Oliver Cromwell (1599–1658)　　**D8**
Huntingdon, Cambs. Huntingdon is full of
associations with Cromwell. His family once
owned Hinchingbrooke House, now a
grammar school; the Protector was born in a
house in the High Street (the site is marked
by a plaque), and attended the grammar
school, now the Cromwell Museum. The
record of his birth and baptism is kept in the
church of All Saints in the High Street.

Thomas Gainsborough (1727–88)　　**G10**
Sudbury, Suffolk. His father's original Tudor
house with an added Georgian front, where
the artist was born, is now a museum,
lecture and exhibition centre with attractive
gardens.

Sir Isaac Newton (1642–1727)　　**B5**
*Woolsthorpe Manor, Lincs. 7 miles from
Grantham.* English mathematician and
natural philosopher. He was born at
Woolsthorpe in 1642, educated at the
grammar school in Grantham, and at Trinity
College, Cambridge. When the plague came
to Cambridge he returned to the manor,
1665–66. It was in the garden that he
conceived the notion of gravitation as he
watched an apple fall from a tree. The room
in which Sir Isaac was born is on view.
Closed winter.

Samuel Pepys (1633–1703)　　**D8**
Pepys's House, Brampton, Cambs. The home
of the Pepys family. A 15thC farmhouse
where the diarist was born.

Alfred, Lord Tennyson (1809–92)　　**D3**
Somersby House, Somersby, Lincs. The poet
laureate, Tennyson, was the fourth of 12
children. Born at Somersby, he spent the
first 7 years of his life in this house; it was
then the rectory. 'Ode to Memory', one of
his early descriptive poems, describes the
rural charm of Somersby. There is a
memorial to Tennyson in the church.

Cathedrals, abbeys & churches

Burgh St Peter　　**K7**
Burgh St Peter, Norfolk. A lanky 13th–14thC
building, thatched and with a crisp arch-
braced roof. It has a splendid tower, like a
giant toy—a series of brick squares piled one
on top of another in diminishing size, the
topmost one being of white brick.

Ely Cathedral　　**E8**
Ely, Cambs. Begun in 1080 it has a rather
abstracted and sleepy air. The best views are
seen approaching across the fenland from the
south or east—it's a silhouette standing out
for miles above a flat, uniform and
practically featureless landscape.
It has a majestic Norman nave and transepts
with a timber roof. The choir is remarkable
for its carving. There's a unique central
octagon 70 feet in diameter with rich
wooden vault with octagonal lantern.
Exceptional Lady Chapel and imposing west
front.

Ely

Hales Church　　**J7**
Hales, Norfolk. A 12thC thatched church
with a round tower, arcaded apse and
splendid doorways. Impressive, with a sort of
small child's wide-eyed sincerity.

Hales

Knapton Church　　**J5**
Knapton, Norfolk. It has one of the finest
hammer-beam roofs in East Anglia, retaining
much of its original colour. The 13thC font
has a purbeck marble bowl and a charming
cover of 1704.

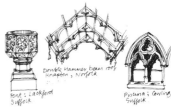

font : Lackford Suffolk

Double Hammer beam roof Knapton, Norfolk

Piscina : Cowling Suffolk

Lincoln Cathedral　　**B3**
Lincoln. Rebuilt 1185–1280 on a steep hill
dominating the town. Resembling
Canterbury in general outline, but very
English in treatment, it has double transepts,
2 western towers, and the highest central
tower in England (271 feet high). The nave,
transepts and choir are early English, the
'Angel Choir' Decorated. The unusual west
front, which is partly Norman, consists of a
screen wall in front of the 2 western towers.

Burgh St. Peter

Lincoln Cathedral

Norwich Cathedral   J6
Norwich, Norfolk. A masterpiece with a spire second only to that of Salisbury. It has a long, narrow Norman nave, built 1096–1145, with aisle-less transepts, and choir with apsidal chapels. The bold central spire,

choir, clerestory, some windows on the south of the nave and the vaulting, are Perpendicular. The remains of the original Bishop's throne are behind the high altar. It has 3 elaborate land-gates and a water-gate on the river at Pulls Ferry. Despite the additions it is, with the exception of Durham, one of the few English cathedrals to retain the appearance and characteristics of a great Anglo-Norman abbey church.

Peterborough Cathedral   D7
Peterborough, Cambs. Built 1117–90 it's a Norman cathedral with the finest interior after Durham. A squat, low lying building, it has a nave with a painted timber roof, probably the oldest in England. The grand western façade is a 158-foot-high Early English portico of 3 gigantic arches. A gable crowns each arch.

St Boltoph   D4
Boston, Lincs. A giant among English parish churches, begun in 1309 with a unified Decorated interior. Externally everything is overpowered by the 'Stump', a lofty tower in the style of Bruges, but more graceful. A landmark for travellers and sailors, with Decorated battlements and Perpendicular panelling around the doorway and on the main buttresses.

St Edmund   K8
Southwold, Suffolk. Impressive—with lofty aisle arcades and clerestories, and a high-pitched hammer-beam roof running the whole length of the nave and choir, it is one of the finest Perpendicular churches in

England. Look at the flushwork on the buttresses and at 'Southwold Jack', an oak figure that strikes the church bell.

St Neots Church   C8
St Neots, Cambs. A 15thC church with an elegant Perpendicular tower. Inside are wonderful interior roof carvings of angels, birds and animals.

SS Peter and Paul   G9
Lavenham, Suffolk. A massive square-buttressed tower of flint, 141 feet high, dwarfs the main body of the church. There is a superb porch with fine carvings and fan-vaulting. Very large windows with some mediaeval glass.

Trunch Church   J5
Trunch, Norfolk. Perpendicular church with a lofty tower. There's a 14thC font with a magnificent canopy. It has 6 slender,

delicately carved pillars supporting 6 flat and crested arches and a vault with a central pendant. The nave has an arch-braced hammer-beam roof with intricately traceried spandrels.

Castles & ruins

Castle Rising   F5
Castle Rising, Norfolk. Built in 1150, the ruined castle stands within spectacular and mighty earthworks rising to 120 feet. The finest stronghold of its time left in the country, only the shell of the keep remains. Queen Isabella, wife of the murdered Edward II, was banished here in 1330.

Lincoln Castle   B3
Castle Square, Lincoln. Built on a Roman site by William the Conqueror in 1068 the castle remains include a complete curtain wall, a Norman shell keep, part of a barbican and the eastern gateway. From 1787–1878 it was used as the county gaol and has a unique prisoner's chapel. Today it is still used as the Courts of Assize.

Tattershall Castle   D3
Lincs. 3½ miles SE of Woodhall Spa. A huge square fortified manor house built about 1440 by Ralph Cromwell, who had become Treasurer of England some years before, on the site of a mediaeval castle. The great 100-foot brick tower of this stronghold still stands and is one of the best examples of a mediaeval brick building in Britain.

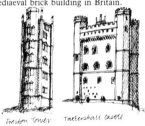

Freston Tower   Tattershall Castle

Thetford Priory   G7
Thetford, Norfolk. One of the most extensive monastic remains in Norfolk, founded by Cluniac monks from Lewes in 1103.
The oldest parts are the church and the west half of the chancel and the transepts, built in 1114. The chancel as well as aisles ended in apses.

Unusual buildings

Cambridge University, Clare College   E9
Cambridge, Cambs. Best seen from the river lawns of King's, it is a beautifully proportioned building in mellowed sandstone topped by balustrades and pierced by handsome windows. Built in 1638, it is more like a palace than a college. This is English Renaissance right out of the top drawer. Also see the Classical bridge and ironwork gates. *The colleges are open to the public on most days during daylight, but there are restrictions in term time.*

Clare College, Cambridge

Cambridge University, Faculty of History   E9
Cambridge, Cambs. By James Stirling, 1964–8. Perhaps the most imaginative and creative of modern English buildings, it's a mammoth glass shed built like a greenhouse. It has an intriguing but elusive scale.

Cambridge University, King's College Chapel   E9
Cambridge, Cambs. Full of fiery enthusiasm,

King's College, Cambridge

the chapel was the only completed mediaeval part of this college, founded 1441. On a magnificent site overlooking the banks of the River Cam this Perpendicular style building was completed in 1515.

Cambridge University, St John's College　　　**E9**
Cambridge, Cambs. An embalmed world of ordered calm. Founded in 1511, it has 3 magnificent red-brick courts and a fine gate-tower, complete with turrets and gilded heraldry. Inside the gate is the early 16thC First Court, with the college dining hall. The doorway at the far side leads to 2 further courts, the first of these being one of the finest in Cambridge, and then out across the river by the 19thC Bridge of Sighs to New Court.

Cambridge University, Trinity College　　　**E9**
Cambridge, Cambs. Founded by Henry VIII in 1546 by amalgamating a number of earlier colleges and adding his own endowments, it is the most spacious college in Cambridge. Its oldest buildings surround the 2-acre Great Court, claimed to be the largest university court in the world.

Cambridge University, Trinity College Library　　　**E9**
Cambridge, Cambs. A relatively sober Classical building begun in 1676 to the design of Sir Christopher Wren. The fourth side to Nevile's Court, the library is on the first floor above a ground floor open to the court through a round-arched arcade. Some fine 17thC wood carvings by Grinling Gibbons.

East Anglia University　　　**J6**
Norwich, Norfolk. Designed by Denys Lasdun to accommodate 3,000 students in a splendid site with a view of the river.

Flatford Mill　　　**H10**
East Bergholt, Suffolk. The mill of John Constable's 'Hay Wain', it was built with the mill house in the 18thC and belonged to his father. Constable himself worked in the mill.

Freston Tower　　　**H10**
Freston, Suffolk. One of the earliest of follies to be found. An elegant red-brick tower built on the banks of the Orwell. 10 foot by 12 in plan, it has 6 small rooms piled one on top of the other with increasingly larger pedimented windows.

The Guildhall　　　**G9**
Lavenham, Suffolk. The first of Lavenham's 3 guildhalls. At one time a prison, workhouse and wool store. Through most of the 17thC it was used as the town hall, but originally it was a hall built in the 1520s for the Guild of Corpus Christi.
Little of the original panelling and carving inside has survived, but the outside remains a good example of the rather ornate style of half-timbered buildings in fashion under Henry VIII.

Guildhall, Lavenham

Jew's House　　　**B3**
Lincoln, Lincs. As wealthy money lenders in 12thC England, Jews could afford to build their own houses. This is a modest stone built house, a symbol both of power and wealth. It was an impregnable little block house, strengthened for protection from the periodic anti-Jewish riots which occurred. Now a restaurant. Jew's Court next door, used as a craft centre, is also of interest

St Ives Bridge　　　**D8**
St Ives, Cambs. A 15thC bridge which crosses the Great Ouse at the market town of St Ives, it has a chapel in its centre bay. One of only 3 mediaeval bridge chapels surviving in England, it was converted into a house in the 19thC.

chapel on the bridge, St. Ives

Triangular Bridge　　　**D6**
Crowland, Lincs. Almost an April Fool's joke—it's a triangular bridge at the meeting of 4 streets in the town. Originally it was built to cross the junction here of 3 streams of the River Welland. Late 14thC.

Yarmouth Pavilion　　　**K6**
Norfolk. Built like an elaborate but eccentric railway station, the Pavilion wiles away the time in an expressive rumba of curves which have danced themselves right out of a '30s musical.

pavilion, Yarmouth.

Houses & gardens

Anglesey Abbey　　　**E9**
Cambs. NE of Cambridge on B1102 in Lode village. Begun by the late Lord Fairhaven in 1926, this 100-acre garden possesses all the grandeur of the 18thC with its superbly placed classical statuary framed by perfectly proportioned hedging and impressive trees. Noted particularly for the great avenues such as Emperor's Walk, flanked by the busts of a dozen Roman emperors, the large porphyry vase and the open temple with Corinthian columns which were created to mark the coronation in 1953. The main emphasis is on sculpture but look at the herbaceous border with its good clumps of *Dictamnus fraxinella* (Burning Bush), the dahlia bed, and the rose garden. The 13thC abbey was once an Augustinian priory and later a Tudor house. It contains marvellous tapestries, paintings and sculptures. *Closed winter.*

Belton House　　　**B5**
Kesteven, Lincs. 2½ miles NE of Grantham on A607. Unusual for Lincolnshire in that it is a garden set upon a limestone escarpment. The park surrounding the attractive 17thC house in the style of Wren contains some magnificent trees and flocks of black sheep and fallow deer.
The formal gardens near the house are worth seeing, as are the extensive rose gardens. Seek out the sundial depicting Father Time and Cupid, the Gothic ruin, the Bellmont Tower of 1750 and, with a cup of tea in mind, try the Orangery with its camellias. The house contains fine furniture, tapestries and old masters.

Blickling Hall　　　**J5**
Aylsham, Norfolk. A fine Jacobean house built for Sir Henry Hobart by Robert Lyminge 1616-28. A symmetrical building of

clean-cut charm, it is built of mellowed rose-red brick with many gables, chimneys, pinnacles and 4 corner turrets with lead caps. There is an elaborate Jacobean plaster-work ceiling in the Long Gallery, and a fine tapestry woven in St Petersburg in 1764 representing Peter the Great at the Battle of Postawa. Lovely formal gardens and crescent-shaped lake. *Closed winter.*

Blickling Hall

Doddington Hall   **B3**
Lincs. 5 miles SW of Lincoln. A fine Elizabethan manor house with a gabled gatehouse and crowned with belvederes and cupolas. Contains Stuart and Georgian furniture, tapestries and china.

Grimsthorpe Castle   **C6**
Edenham, Lincs. The earliest part, a bastion in the south-east corner, dates from the 13thC. The castle was considerably enlarged in 1540, and a north front was added by Sir John Vanbrugh in 1722. In a landscape of rolling grass and corn. The hall, arcaded in 2 tiers, is dramatically inventive. Contains coronation robes, paintings and plate.

Grimsthorpe Castle.

Harlaxton Manor   **B5**
Harlaxton, Lincs. Built in the 1830s. Designed by Anthony Salvin for George Gregory, it's sort of high church Victorian, with massive stone banded piers, rusticated stone niches, angular bay windows and a forest of oriental turrets and pinnacles. It is reached by an undulating drive which drops into a valley before climbing to this great house nestling in the hillside.
It's now the European Campus for the University of Stanford, USA.

Heveningham Hall   **J8**
Heveningham, nr Halesworth, Suffolk. Designed by Sir Robert Taylor and built in 1777, it's a Palladian building with a pillared centre block rising from an arcaded basement with a pedimented wing on either side. James Wyatt decorated the interior of the house, and the grounds were laid out by Capability Brown. Still contains a lot of its original furniture. *Closed winter.*

Heveningham Hall, Suffolk.

Holkham Hall   **G5**
Wells, Norfolk. A Palladian mansion built 1734–59 on reclaimed dunes and salt marshes on the edge of an artificial lake. Designed for Thomas Coke by William Kent, it consists of one central block connected to 4 lower oblong blocks. In a light grey brick the main building has a rusticated basement with small windows and a superb *piano nobile*. The overall length is 340 feet. There are 4 corner towers with pyramid roofs and a great central portico. The interior is as lavish as the exterior is arid. A marble pillared and galleried entrance hall leads to a salon of dark velvet and gold with the Rubens painting of 'The

Return from Egypt' as its dominant theme. With the full measure of 18thC magnificence, the interior was planned to give a long vista of connecting rooms. The grounds of Holkham were laid out by Capability Brown in 1762. *Closed winter.*

Houghton Hall   **G5**
Houghton, Norfolk. Designed for Sir Robert Walpole in the 1730s, it stands in a beautifully landscaped park. A simple statement, visibly expressed, in fine ashlar masonry, it is an oblong of 9 by 5 bays, with a rusticated ground floor, a tall *piano nobile*, a lower second floor, and domed caps at each corner. The architects were Colin Campbell and Thomas Ripley, whilst William Kent handled much of the interior design.
There are rare Mostlake tapestries by Francis Poyntz; elaborate Renaissance jewellery and fine 18thC book bindings.

Ickworth   **G8**
Bury St Edmunds, Suffolk. The eccentric Bishop of Deny with a taste for travel had the idea of building this unusual house to display his fine collection of paintings and sculpture. Begun in 1794 it was completed by his son in 1830. 700 feet long it consists of a large oval rotunda housing a central hall, with 2 curved corridors leading to the main rooms.
Paintings include a Velasquez portrait of a son of Philip IV of Spain, and family portraits by Reynolds, Gainsborough and others.

Kimbolton Castle   **C8**
Kimbolton, Cambs. A mediaeval castle where Katherine of Aragon spent her last 4 years, it was re-modelled in the reign of William and Mary.
In 1707 part of the building collapsed and Vanbrugh was commissioned to rebuild it. It's a building with an inner courtyard, and battlemented mediaeval exterior. Robert Adam added the outer gatehouse and the gateway in 1766. *Closed winter.*

Melton Hall   **H5**
Melton Constable, Norfolk. Standing some distance away from the small village of Melton Constable, the Hall, built 1670, is forlorn and neglected, overlooking a beautiful park and lake. The home of the Astleys, it was built to impress. A place of memories in the sky-filled Norfolk countryside. It has some ceilings with very fine plaster-work. Used as the setting for the film 'The Go-between'.

Moat Hall   **J9**
Parham, Suffolk. This famous moated brick house of the Willoughbys is one of the most romantic sights of Suffolk. It's a small farmhouse with pantiles and Tudor chimney-stacks.

Oxburgh Hall   **F7**
Norfolk. 7 miles SW of Swaffham. A fortified manor house, built in 1482 by Sir Edmund Bedingfield. Built of brick, it sits squarely round a courtyard. The Great Tower, rising 80 feet straight from the edge of the moat, is impressive. A tenacious bulldog of a place with an enormous gatehouse.
Displayed in the rooms are some panels of needle-work embroidered and signed by Mary Queen of Scots. Near the hall is a small chapel by Pugin, 1835. *Closed winter.*

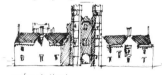

Oxburgh Hall

Sandringham   **F5**
Sandringham, Norfolk. 5 miles NE of King's Lynn. The private residence of 4 generations of monarchs and still lived in by HM the Queen. The main rooms are now open to the public and contain beautiful furniture and

paintings. The saloon has carved wood panelling and a minstrel's gallery. Lovely gardens ablaze with spring flowers and shrubs. Also a museum, nature trail and country park. *Closed winter, part summer.*

Wenham Hall   **H10**
Little Wenham, Suffolk. Best preserved of the 13thC English fortified houses, and the earliest to be built in brick. The lower 5 feet of the walls are of rubble, the rest are of pink and pale yellow brick with stone buttresses. L-shaped in plan, the long side is occupied by a hall, the short side by a chapel. Both are on the first floor above a brick-vaulted undercroft.

Wimpole Hall   **D9**
Wimpole, Cambs. Set in a park betwen 2 Roman roads, it is the most spectacular country mansion of Cambridgeshire. Its architecture is remarkably shy and domestic—a large red brick house of Palladian aspirations in a magnificent setting. Reached by a ceremonial avenue of trees 100 yards wide and 3 miles long. The hall was begun in 1640 with considerable alterations and additions in the early 18thC.

Artificial Ruins, Grounds of Wimpole Hall.

Museums & galleries

Boston Museum   **D4**
The Guildhall, South St, Boston, Lincs. The old Guildhall, 1450, contains a museum of local history and archaeology. Associations with the Pilgrim Fathers who set out from Boston in 1620.

Bridewell Museum   **J6**
Bridewell Alley, Norwich, Norfolk. Once a prison, dating from the 14thC, now a museum of rural crafts and industries. Weaving, leatherwork, fishing and agricultural equipment, clockmaking and a collection of early bicycles and tricycles.

Cambridge and County Folk Museum   **E9**
2–3 Castle St, Cambridge, Cambs. An interesting collection of local bygones dating from mediaeval times and kept in the former White Horse Inn (16thC).

City and County Museum   **B3**
Broadgate, Lincoln. Collections covering the whole of Lincolnshire from prehistoric to mediaeval times. Also natural history and a series of models illustrating the area's engineering industries. Roman collection including carvings and inscriptions.

The Cromwell Museum   **D8**
Market Sq, Huntingdon, Cambs. Once the grammar school where Cromwell and Samuel Pepys were educated, the museum displays a fine collection of Cromwelliana, including the Protector's death mask.

East Anglia Transport Museum   **K7**
Chapel Rd, Carlton Colville, Lowestoft, Suffolk. For the transport fanatic, tram-cars trolleybuses, cars and buses galore, a miniature railway and an operating tramcar service.

Fitzwilliam Museum   **E9**
Trumpington St, Cambridge, Cambs. World-famous collections of Egyptian, Greek and Roman antiquities, coins and medals, mediaeval manuscripts, paintings, drawings, prints, ceramics, glass and armour.

Gershom-Parkington Memorial Clocks and Watches   **G8**
8 Angel Hill, Bury St Edmunds, Suffolk. A small but very special collection of clocks, watches and time pieces from 500BC onwards, kept in humming order in a Queen Anne house.

Museum of East Anglian Life   **H9**
Stowmarket, Suffolk. An open-air museum set in 34 acres. 17thC barn, watermill, 14thC farmhouse and smithy have been re-erected here. Also, a collection of farm implements, wagons and ploughs. *Closed winter.*

Museum of Lincolnshire Life   **B3**
Burton Road, Lincoln. A display showing all aspects of life in Lincolnshire during the last 300 years, including domestic, agricultural and crafts exhibits.

Norwich Castle Museum   **J6**
Norwich, Norfolk. The castle with its Norman keep has been a museum since 1894. An Iron Age hoard of gold and coins from Snettisham is on display. Also Lowestoft porcelain, firearms, a small aquarium.

The Scott Polar Research Institute   **E9**
Lensfield Rd, Cambridge, Cambs. Memorial museum to Scott and his companions. Relics of Arctic and Antarctic expeditions, including some 400 watercolours and sketches by Edward Wilson, and Eskimo art.

Strangers' Hall   **J6**
Charing Cross, Norwich, Norfolk. A merchant's house, once the centre for immigrant weavers, then the assize judge's lodging and now a museum of domestic life. Rooms are furnished in the style of different periods from early Tudor to late Victorian. Cooking equipment, dolls' houses and coach house with the Lord Mayor's coach.

Usher Gallery   **B3**
Lindum Rd, Lincoln, Lincs. Fine collection of watches, miniatures and porcelain; the Peter de Wint collection of oils, watercolours, drawings and portraits; relics and first editions of Alfred, Lord Tennyson.

Wisbech and Fenland Museum   **E6**
Museum Square, Wisbech, Cambs. Fenland and natural history, archaeology and antiquarian collections are all here. 12,000 books and manuscripts, including the original manuscript of Dickens' 'Great Expectations'. *Library by appointment only.*

Botanical gardens

Bressingham Gardens   **H8**
Norfolk, 2¼ miles W of Diss, on A1066. Like a brilliant patchwork quilt thrown upon the flat Norfolk fenland, Bressingham is noted for its enormous collection of herbaceous perennials to which this remarkable garden is almost entirely devoted. In island beds, there are over 5,000 species and varieties grouped in imaginative and colourful settings, many of them acquired by exchanges with botanic gardens both in Britain and abroad. There are interesting beds of alpines and dwarf specimens and also a quantity of water and bog plants. *Closed winter.*

Cambridge University Botanic Garden   **E9**
Cambridge, Cambs. 1 mile from city centre, Trumpington Rd. Although founded in 1761, the recently completed and very large rock garden is of particular interest as is the range of greenhouses with their good plant collections. There are some fine specimen trees and shrubs.

Zoos, aquaria & aviaries

Cromer Zoo   **J5**
Cromer, Norfolk. Set in 5 acres and overlooking the sea, this zoo has a good range of animals which include: lions, leopards, bears, wallabies and monkeys, etc.

Kilverstone Wild Life Park & Falabella Horse Stud   **G7**
Thetford, Norfolk. Falabella horses come from Argentina and include many breeds of

horses, only in miniature. Other Central and South American animals and birds, like jaguars, bison, macaws and flamingos. Set in 50 acres of parkland and garden.

Mablethorpe Animal & Bird Gardens E2
North End, Mablethorpe, Lincs. Set in 2 acres of gardens and dunes there is a walk-through aviary and a butterfly display. Animals and birds include monkeys, parrots, skunks, owls, llamas, seals, donkeys and emus.

Otter Trust J7
Earsham, Suffolk. 2 miles SW of Bungay on A143. There are 4 species of otter here in natural-looking enclosures and 3 lakes with waterfowl. Muntjac deer and riverside walks.

Skegness Natureland Marine Zoo E3
North Parade, The Promenade, Skegness, Lincs. Sea lions, seals and penguins. Tropical, freshwater and marine fish, as well as native east coast fish. Tropical House with snakes and insects, free flying birds and a Floral Palace. Children's corner.

Thorney Wildlife Park E6
Thorney, 7 miles NE of Peterborough, Cambs. Large paddocks of elephants, giraffes, llamas, red kangaroos; cages of lions, tigers, Asiatic black bear and various small mammals. *Closed winter.*

Witchingham Park H6
Great Witchingham, 12 miles NW of Norwich, Norfolk. Collection of European endangered species bred in large natural enclosures in the 40-acre parkland. Deer, wolverines, lynx, ibex, mouflon, bears. Also, one of the largest pheasant collections in the world.

Nature trails & reserves

Blakeney Point Nature Reserve H4
Blakeney, Norfolk. 4 miles NW by boat. A wildfowl breeding ground on a shingle spit with sand dunes. Occasional seals. Boat from Blakeney or Morston.

East Wretham Heath Nature Trail G7
Norfolk, N of Thetford, starting at the Warden's Office, East Wretham. 2 miles. Breckland birds, also those of associated meres and pines. *Closed winter.*

Havergate Island Nature Reserve K9
Suffolk. In River Ore S of Orford. Main avocet breeding ground in England. Good waders on passage and winter wildfowl. Access strictly by permit only from R.S.P.B., The Lodge, Sandy, Beds.

Hickling Broad National Nature Reserve J6
Norfolk. N of Potter Heigham. Outstanding area for waterfowl, reedbed birds, passage terns and waders. Easy access by boat. Viewpoints south from Hickling village (northwest corner) and, from the north, Hill Common. Permits for the reserve area from Norfolk Naturalist's Trust, 4 The Close, Norwich.

Holme Nature Reserve F5
Norfolk. NE of Hunstanton. Wildfowl, waders and migrants. There is also a nature trail. For the Holme Bird Observatory, details from Warden, The Firs, Holme, Hunstanton, Norfolk. *Closed winter.*

Minsmere Nature Reserve K8
Suffolk. On the coast nr Saxmundham, S of Dunwich. Outstanding reserve with breeding bittern, marsh harrier, avocet, tern, bearded tit, red-backed shrike, and over 90 others, plus many and varied migrants. Public hides on the beach are always open, but entry to the reserve is strictly by permit only from R.S.P.B., The Lodge, Sandy, Beds.

Ouse Washes Nature Reserve E7
Norfolk & Cambs. Public access along banks and public hides at Purl's Bridge, Manea, but otherwise limited access. Outstanding area with immense numbers of winter wildfowl, especially widgeon and Bewick's

swan. Breeding birds include garganey, ruff and black-tailed godwit. Details from Wildfowl Trust, Slimbridge, Glos. (Welney northwards); R.S.P.B., The Lodge, Sandy, Beds. (Welney to Welckes Dam); and Cambridge and Isle of Ely National Trust, 1 Brodeside, Cambridge.

Scolt Head Island National Nature Reserve F4
Norfolk. Access by boat from Brancaster Staithe on A149. Autumn and winter waders, winter Brent geese and a very large colony of common and sandwich terns. No restrictions except at the ternery in summer—but contact the Warden at Dial House, Brancaster Staithe, King's Lynn, Norfolk.

Snettisham Nature Reserve F5
Snettisham, Norfolk. Outstanding for Wash waders, some important roosts included, and good for assorted migrants and winter wildfowl, the last on flooded gravel pits. Public access along the beach only, and access restricted at the southern end. Contact the R.S.P.B. Warden at 18 Cockle Road, Snettisham, King's Lynn, Norfolk, or R.S.P.B., The Lodge, Sandy, Beds.

Wicken Fen Nature Trail E8
Cambs, 3 miles W of Soham, A1123 and A142. Wetland and reedbed birds. For full details apply to Warden, Lt Col C. E. Mitchell, Lode Lane, Wicken, Ely.

Birdwatching

Blyth Estuary K8
Suffolk. East of A12 and best seen from just north of Blythburgh and from the footpath starting near the White Hart Inn. Excellent for waders, especially black-tailed godwits in spring, waders on passage and winter wildfowl. Spotted redshanks are regular in winter and autumn.

Breydon Water K6
Norfolk. An exceptionally good area immediately behind Yarmouth. The recommended route is around the southern shore from the railway bridge to Burgh Castle. Brent and grey geese and large numbers of duck and waders occur in winter, plus hen harrier, merlin, short-eared owl, snow bunting and twite, while in spring and autumn the area is noted for a variety of migrant waders. Spoonbills in spring.

Cley and Salthouse H4
Norfolk. Among the most famous bird-watching areas in Britain, the reed marshes, grazing meadows, lagoons and shore are easily accessible from A149 between Cley and Salthouse via roads and the East Bank—but permits are required for entry to the areas off these access routes (Norfolk Naturalists's Trust, 4 The Close, Norwich). Breeding marsh birds include bearded tit and water rail, duck, especially widgeon, in large numbers, snow buntings and shore larks in winter, and an incredible variety of migrants of all kinds in spring and autumn, including many rarities.

Grafham Water C9
Cambs. 2 miles W of A1 at Buckden. A large reservoir much used for sailing and fishing, but nevertheless exceptionally good for winter duck and other water birds, and for migrant waders in autumn. It is accessible from 3 well-signposted public car parks and from the fishermen's car park near Grafham village, from which much of the water area can be seen.

Holbeach D5
Lincs. 8 miles N of Holbeach on A151. This area is best viewed from the sea wall between Fotheringham House and Holbeach St Matthew. While pinkfooted geese and various other wildfowl occur in winter, and short-eared owls are regulars, Holbeach is most interesting for the vast assemblages of waders from the Wash which roost in the area at high tide.

Brass rubbing

The following is a short list of churches that
have brasses for rubbing. Permission is
almost invariably required.
Cambridgeshire. Balsham, Burwell,
Diddington, Ely Cathedral, Fulbourn,
Hildersham, Horseheath, Offord D'Arcy,
Sawtry, Trumpington, Westley Waterless,
Wisbech, Wood Ditton.
Lincolnshire. Barton-upon-Humber (St Mary),
Broughton, Gunby, Irnham, Lincoln Brass
Rubbing Centre, (Chapter House, Lincoln
Cathedral), Linwood, Scrivelsby, Stamford
(All Saints), Tattershall.
Norfolk. Aylsham, Elsing, Hunstanton,
King's Lynn, Methwold, Narborough,
Norwich (St George Colegate, St John
Maddermarket and St Lawrence), Reepham,
Southacre, Upwell.
Suffolk. Acton, Barsham, Burgate, Ipswich
(St Mary Tower), Letheringham, Long
Melford, Mendlesham, Playford, Stoke-by-
Nayland, Yoxford.

Fossil hunting

Visit the local museum. Its fossil collection
usually states where individual fossils have
been found. When visiting quarries always
seek permission to enter if they look
privately owned or worked. Be careful of
falls of rock.

Aldeburgh Suffolk
Pliocene coralline crag with plentiful
lamellibranchs, gastropods, bryozoa, forams
and occasional fossil crabs and sea urchins in
pits at Aldeburgh, Chillesford, Orford and
Sudbourne.

Cromer Norfolk
The coast here is the youngest chalk found
in England. At Trimingham rich cretaceous
fauna and abundant yields of small oyster
fossils. At West Runton mammal remains,
plants, seeds and fruit can be found in the
cliffs. The Pleistone gravels on the coast
around Cromer have yielded many bones of
vertebrates from the Ice Ages.

Ipswich Suffolk
Cretaceous belemnites, sea urchins, corals,
crinoids, etc, are found in exposures at
Bramford Claydon and Sudbury.

Lincolnshire
Good Jurassic fossils in pits at Ancaster,
Appleby, Bracebridge, Castle Bytham,
Denton, Greetwell, Sleaford and Stickney.
Chalk quarries also in the Lincolnshire wolds
e.g. Caistor.

Peterborough Cambs.
The Jurassic clay is exposed in clay pits at
Yaxley and at Warboys south of
Peterborough. Yields abundant pyritized
ammonites, gastropods, lamellibranchs and
brachiopods.

Southwold Suffolk
Easton cliffs north of the town has fossil
shells and the occasional bones of prehistoric
animals. Look out also for semi-precious
stones (cornelian and agates).

Forests

Aldewood
Nr Aldeburgh, Suffolk. The Forestry
Commission's national Aldewood Forest near
the Suffolk coast, draws its name from the
River Alde nearby. Pines from Scotland and
Corsica have been established on former
sandy wastes and now provide shady walks,
with car parks, picnic places, and views over
estuaries towards the sea. Handy centres for
visitors are Woodbridge, Aldeburgh,
Dunwich and Southwold.

Thetford Chase   G7
Norfolk/Suffolk. England's largest lowland
forest, Thetford Chase, has been farmed for
timber since 1920 on 45,000 acres of the old
Breckland, a sandy waste on the borders of
Norfolk and Suffolk, near the towns of
Thetford and Brandon. Pines are the only
trees that thrive and can be used for timber
and 2 kinds are grown, one from Scotland
and the other from Corsica. They yield
thousands of tons of softwood annually.
From the forest centre at Santon Downham,
signposted footpaths lead along the banks of
the Little Ouse, lined with poplars, and on
through shady rides flanked by stately pines
or Douglas firs. Relics of past ages include
the prehistoric Grimes Graves at Brandon,
where Stone Age man quarried flints
underground for tools and weapons. A
Norman castle mound dominates Thetford, a
market town fought over by Danes and
Saxons, and given fresh life today as a
thriving 'new town'. The woods hold red
and roe deer. Rare birds include crossbills
that wrench pine seeds from cones, and the
heath-loving stone curlew which probes
below pebbles for insect food.

Hills

Cromer Ridge
Norfolk. East Anglia's only impressive
upland, this ridge extends along the north
coast of Norfolk from Holt, past Sheringham
and Cromer, to Mundesley. It is a land of
breezy heaths with sandy soils and the
scattered pinewoods of Wensum Forest.
Views to the broad North Sea give a sense of
space. The highest point, 327 feet, is near
East Beckham.

East Anglian Heights
Suffolk. A misleading name for the rolling
countryside of central Suffolk, which is
nowhere more than 420 feet above the sea.
Between Sudbury and Bury St Edmunds.
This watershed between the Wash and the
Thames Estuary does however hold
charming valleys and picturesque villages
well worth exploring.

Gog Magog Hills
Cambs. 4 miles SE Cambridge. Two low
mounds, reaching a height of 234 feet, rising
from the plain. Named after the legendary
Celtic giant-gods who once defended London
against prehistoric invaders. This is a
favourite walk for Cambridge people, who
otherwise never see a hill.

Kesteven Heights
Lincs. An upland ridge in the south of
Lincolnshire, where the soft, fawn grey of
limestone walls lends character to well-
tended fields, prosperous villages and
thriving market towns like Stamford and
Grantham. Good hunting country with many
woodlands, fine mansions and broad views
over lowland plains to north, east and south.

Lincoln Edge
Lincs. From the famous cathedral set on its
spine in the heart of Lincoln city, the
Lincoln Edge runs due north for 25 miles to
Scunthorpe, and also 25 miles south to
Grantham. A limestone ridge, averaging 200
feet above sea level, its course is followed by
a prehistoric trackway that became a Roman
road, and finally a modern highway, A15.
The Edge has few villages or houses; its
slopes form pastures for settlements at its
foot, on either hand. Grand views to the
Wolds on the east, and westwards over the
Trent Valley.

Lincolnshire Wolds
Lincs. These high chalk hills form a long
spine that follows the line of Lincolnshire's
north east coast, about 10 miles inland.
Nowhere steep, they give a sense of
spaciousness, thanks to their wide views over
the coastal marshes towards the grey North
Sea. The main road along the flanks of the
Wolds runs from Skegness, an attractive
seaside resort, through Louth, the principal
market town, to Grimsby, a major fishing
port on the Humber. The Wolds were
settled between the 5th and 10thC, first by

Anglians and later by Danish invaders, and have been farmed intensively ever since. Scattered woods near Wragby, Market Rasen and Caistor, on the sandy eastern fringes. Highest point, 548 feet, is at Normanby-le-Wold, 4 miles south of Caistor.

Meadows & marshes

Blakeney Marshes
Norfolk. On the north coast, beside the villages of Blakeney and Cley-next-the-Sea. This marshland has developed where the little creeks are held back by the shingle spit called Scolt Head (now a National Nature Reserve). Rare salt-marsh flowers grow along the muddy streams and many unusual birds nest and feed, or rest on seasonal migrations.

Broadland Marshes
Norfolk. The slow rivers and open broads of north east Norfolk are bordered by peaty fens of reeds and rushes, with occasional willows and alder trees. These remain haunts of rare waterfowl, including the bittern and the marsh harrier that nest in their midst; several have become nature reserves. They are the strongholds of the coypu, a huge water-rat introduced from South America for its fur, now running, and swimming, wild.

The Fens
A broad region of dead-flat country lying inland from the Wash, including much of southern Lincolnshire, Cambridgeshire, and part of Norfolk. Traversed by the lower courses of 4 great rivers, the River Witham, the River Welland, the River Nene, and the Bedfordshire Ouse, the Fens were subject to seasonal floods and remained trackless marshes through the middle ages. Here Hereward the Wake—or the Watchful—the last Saxon leader to assert independence, defied William the Conqueror around 1070. Only fishermen, wildfowlers and reed-cutters frequented winding streams through alder and willow-tree swamps called 'carrs'.
From the 17thC onwards the Fens have been tamed by immense drainage schemes, planned originally by Dutch engineers. The upland rivers are confined within banks, the sea is kept back by dykes, the fields are drained by networks of ditches, and surface water is pumped uphill into higher carrier waterways.
The black humus-rich carr soil, thus safeguarded, yields exceptionally heavy crops. View this vast treeless farmer's paradise from some hill-top town like March or Ely. Near Shippea 'Hill' 6 miles east of Ely, several square miles are actually below sea level.

The Spillway
Cambs. The Spillway, also called the 'Wash', is a unique watermeadow on the Isle of Ely, midway between the towns of Ely and March. To drain the fens and to cope with the floods of the Bedfordshire Ouse, engineers built 2 parallel drains, the Old Bedford River and the New Bedford River, for 20 miles north east between St Ives and Downham Market. When winter floods exceed their combined capacity, the Spillway carries the surplus. In summer it is grazed by herds of fat bullocks.

Wash Marshes
The shores of the Wash, from Skegness round past Boston and King's Lynn to Hunstanton, a total distance of 50 miles, are bordered by tidal marshes. On their inland side, high dykes protect fertile reclaimed land from flooding. A grim, grey, roadless region, and popular only with fishermen and wildfowlers.

Rivers

River Ouse and River Cam
The Ouse begins half-way across England, near Banbury, and passes Bedford and Huntingdon on its way to King's Lynn, a seaport at the eastern corner of the Wash. The Cam, its main tributary (which rises near Royston), is broad enough to carry the university racing eights at Cambridge and flows on, almost at sea level, past Ely Cathedral to Downham Market. The Ouse drains a large area of west Norfolk and north west Suffolk. A huge boundary drain keeps its eastern floodwaters clear of the Fens.

River Stour
Suffolk. The Stour, a typical Suffolk river, rises on the East Anglian Heights east of Cambridge, and wanders slowly eastwards in a shallow vale, passing a score of farmland villages and the little towns of Clare and Sudbury. Below Nayland its valley broadens out into the fertile Dedham Vale, beloved of Constable who painted its trees, mills, fields, and barges under striking cloud and sunlight. Beyond Manningtree it becomes a broad tidal estuary, forming a harbour for ferry steamers from Denmark and Holland to Harwich port.

River Trent
For most of its lower course the great River Trent forms the boundary between Nottinghamshire and Lincolnshire, flowing between dykes through a level plain won for agriculture by draining the marshes. Newark, Retford and Gainsborough are market towns drawing prosperity from farms in this almost treeless vale. The Isle of Axholme, once isolated by fenland backwaters, is still surrounded by canals, and defended by dykes from the Humber tides to the north.

Rivers Witham, Welland & Nene
The River Witham rises near Grantham, runs north to Lincoln and there, surprisingly, breaks through the Lincoln Edge, to continue south west through the Fens to Boston and the Wash. The Welland comes down from Leicestershire past Stamford and Spalding, crossing the Fens to the western corner of the Wash. The larger Nene begins above Northampton, winds past Peterborough, and crosses the marshlands near Wisbech at the Wash's centre. All cross the dead-flat Fens within high flood-banks, and drainage water is pumped up to them from fields below.

Canals

East Anglia contains none of the familiar 18thC canals linked together as a waterway transport network. So the main 'canal interest' in this area must be the Fenland waterways which are connected to the rest of the canal system via the River Nene and the Grand Union Canal.
There are plenty of river navigations in this part of the world, most of which are still used by commercial seagoing craft. In Norfolk the River Yare still carries small freighters for 28 miles inland from Yarmouth to Norwich, and the Rivers Great Ouse, Welland, Nene and Witham serve the ports of King's Lynn, Wisbech and Boston and then empty into the Wash.

Fossdyke & Witham Navigations The Fossdyke Navigation was built in about AD120 by the Romans, and is the oldest artificial waterway in the country still navigable. It was designed to connect the River Witham with the Trent and Humber. In the 18thC, Acts of Parliament were made to improve the navigation and the Grand Sluice at Boston was built. In the 18th and 19thC further improvements were made and it assumed the wide straight course we see today. Starts at Torksey and ends at Boston.
Watsham & Dilham Canal Now disused but it was part canal, part river navigation.

Archaeological sites

Burgh Castle   H6
Nr Belton, Suffolk. Roman Gariannonum belongs to the series of Saxon Shore forts

constructed by the Romans in the late 3rdC around the south east coast. It is a narrow rectangle in shape, of which 3 walls survive to a height of 15 feet—probably their full height apart from a parapet, since some of the 5 remaining bastions have a floor at this level, with a circular setting to hold a catapult turntable. One gate survives in the long east wall, and a postern in each of the short walls. The masonry, flint facing stones with tile courses, is amongst the finest in Roman Britain.

Caistor St Edmunds   **J6**
Norfolk. The Roman Venta Icenorum was the tribal capital for the Iceni, whose queen, Boudicca (Boadicea), led a revolt against the Romans in AD61, during which London, Colchester, and St Albans were razed. The town walls were probably built in the 3rdC, and are still standing; much of the town plan has been revealed by aerial photography. A major Saxon cemetery lay just outside the town. *Accessible with permission from the farm.*

Devil's Dyke   **F8**
Reaches to Ditton Green across Newmarket Heath, Cambs. Seven miles of linear earthworks with a massive embankment, cutting across the Icknield Way. Post-Roman in date, at least in part, and likely to have been constructed by early Saxon invaders as a defence against the Britons. The Dyke is best seen from the Swaffham Prior–Burwell road, which crosses it at right-angles.

Grimes Graves   **G7**
Nr Weeting, Norfolk. Before the discovery of metals, prehistoric man depended upon hard stone for manufacture of his tools and weapons, and in Britain flint was the best material for shaping fine, and often highly sophisticated, objects. Grimes Graves is the only ancient flint mine accessible to the public; it was in use from the later Neolithic into the early Bronze Age, and supplied implements over a wide area. The mines consist of massive shafts sunk through chalk to the flint layer, with galleries fanning out to follow the deposits, and show as pits on the surface. There is a small display of finds at the site.

Lincoln   **B3**
Lincs. Lindum Colonia, one of the major cities of Roman Britain, originated in AD48 as a timber-built fortress during the Roman conquest. It was occupied successively by the IX Hispana Legion and the II Adiutrix, and tombstones of soldiers of both legions have been found along the roads to the south. As the frontier was advanced northwards, Lincoln was abandoned as a military site and established as a settlement (*colonia*) for veteran soldiers. Later the town expanded southwards, towards the river, and the whole area was enclosed with stone walls, probably during the 2ndC.
Two of the stone gateways survive in remarkably good condition: the Newport Arch in the North Wall, and, in Orchard Street, a gate inserted into the defences in the 4thC which contains much re-used decorative stone. At East Bight is a section of wall and the heavy square foundation for a watertank where an aqueduct entered the city. The foundations of a corner tower, showing successive phases of timber fortress and stone town defences, is visible in Eastgate. Lincoln City and County Museum houses a fine collection of Roman material, including tombstones and pottery from local kilns.

Sutton Hoo   **J9**
Nr Woodbridge, Suffolk. A fine group of Saxon barrows, Sutton Hoo includes the site of the famous ship-burial, which was probably a memorial to an East Anglian king, and is dated by coins to the mid-7thC. The superb treasure, which included a gilt-decorated helmet and objects of gold, silver, and enamel, is now in the British Museum; replicas of the finest pieces are in Ipswich Museum. *Site not accessible, but visible from the public footpath.*

Footpaths & ancient ways

Icknield Way
A prehistoric trackway once stretching from the Wash to the Channel. The best sections of the way are west of Cambridge, but there are still a few traces of green way in East Anglia worth exploring.
Near Lackford by the River Lark there is a rough trackway for 3¾ miles through King's Forest to Weatherhill Heath, where it becomes the boundary of Elveden Park. Just 2 miles short of Thetford all trace is lost but there are signs of a causeway leading over arable land, from Weatherhill Heath to Croxted Park.

Peddars Way
This is a prehistoric trackway running from what is now the High Street, Ixworth in Suffolk to the site of the Roman fort at Brancaster, which once guarded the entrance to the Wash. Castle Acre is the only village of any size that it touches.
The Romans improved the road, and for many miles it is a straight track across the countryside south of Brancaster. Parts of the Peddars Way are still green way, and there is much evidence of prehistoric occupation to intrigue the rambling Sherlock Holmes.

Via Devana
Built by the Romans, from Godmanchester to Cambridge, the Via Devana is a main road today. From Cambridge it becomes a trackway climbing over the Gogmagog Hills, across Wandlebury Camp, passing no villages and entering Suffolk at Withersfield, near Haverhill, where it disappears without trace.

Regional sport

Association Football
Norwich City, a professional team, now in the First Division of the football league. Nicknamed the 'Canaries', the team has its ground at Carrow Road, Norwich, Norfolk. Tel Norwich 23612.
The other top team of the area is Ipswich (also in the First Division), who are usually a good match for any team in the country. The ground is at Portman Road, Ipswich. Tel 57107.

Fishing
The main coarse fishing rivers are the Rivers Bure, Waveney, Welland, Witham and Yare. They are particularly noted for their rudd and bream, but good carp, dace, pike, perch, roach, tench and gudgeon abound. On many of the Broads rudd will provide good sport on fly, though a long line must be cast. One of the chief joys of this area is the number of cosy country pubs from which a day's angling can be enjoyed.
Acle, Norfolk. Fishing on the River Bure at Acle is free to River Authority licence holders.
Boston, Lincs. Exceptionally good fishing on the River Witham. With few exceptions RD rod licence sufficient.
Homersfield, Suffolk. On the River Waveney. Licences for fishing can be obtained from the landlord of the Black Swan Hotel.
Suffolk and Norfolk River Authority, Yare House, Thorpe Road, Norwich, Norfolk.
Lincolnshire River Authority, 50 Wide Bargate, Boston, Lincs.

Flat Racing
Newmarket, Suffolk. A fine race course and the headquarters of horse racing in Britain since the 17thC. The home of the Jockey Club and the National Stud, it originally owed its pre-eminence to the interest shown by King James I (1603-25). Fixture cards can be obtained from the Jockey Club Office, High Street, Newmarket, Suffolk.

Motor Racing

There is a large motor racing circuit at Snetterton, Norfolk. This is one of the country's top 15 circuits featuring a varied programme of important racing car and motor cycling events. More important events are regularly televised. Also at Cadwell Park, near Louth, Lincolnshire.

Sailing

The Norfolk and Suffolk Broads, large lakes interconnected by winding, slow moving rivers, support many sailing clubs. If membership in a club is being contemplated it is worth choosing carefully. Many areas are densely shielded by trees giving flukey light winds. Oulton Broad at Lowestoft is a fine, large open lake on which a wide variety of dinghies and powerboats race.
The Waveney and Oulton Broad Yacht Club offers temporary membership for a month. The regatta is held in August. For details write to: the Hon. Secretary, H. D. Hannant, 29 The Avenue, Lowestoft, Suffolk.
Also at *Brayford Pool, Lincoln.*

For further information on other yacht clubs in the area write to Nigel Hacking, Secretary of the *Royal Yachting Association,* 5 Buckingham Gate, London SW1.

Festivals, events & customs

There are a number of local festivals and events—contact the local information centre for details.

Aldeburgh Festival of the Arts

The Maltings, Snape and at the Jubilee Hall, Aldeburgh, Suffolk. A small, intimate and world famous festival associated with Benjamin Britten. Traditionally first performances of new works are given, but early music is much in demand. Concerts too, in the local parish churches. *Jun.*

Cambridge Festival

Cambridge, Cambs. Festival of music, representing the arts in both city and university. Events are held in the colleges, the Guildhall and Ely Cathedral. *Late Jul.*

King's Lynn Fair   F6

King's Lynn, Norfolk. Not a permanent fair, but included because of its antiquity. It has been held on the 14th February, Valentine's Day, since the early 11thC. Only the Plague in 1666 and the 2 world wars temporarily stopped its appearance. It lasts for 6 days, and is one of the earliest fairs of the year, with a ceremonial opening by the mayor who, with his party, has the privilege of being first to ride on the roundabouts.

King's Lynn Festival

King's Lynn, Norfolk. Events centre around the 15thC Guildhall. The Westminster Abbey Choir, the Hallé Orchestra and many famous soloists have performed here over the years. Music is the main attraction, but there are also exhibitions, historic films and talks. The annual flower show coincides with the first Sunday of the festival. *Late Jul.*

Spalding Flower Parade   D6

Spalding, Lincs. Millions of flower heads make up the fantastic floats which comprise this parade. It travels for 4½ miles through the streets of the town. *Mid-May.*

Special attractions

Bressingham
Live Steam Museum   H8

Bressingham Hall, Norfolk. On the side of A1066, 4 miles W of Diss. There are 5 miles of rides on narrow gauge and miniature railways, 50 steam engines and a roundabout with its own organ. This is probably the best private collection of steam and railroad locomotives in the country. For all those who find the combination of smoke and steam irresistible.

Cushing's Steam Engine &
Organ Museum   H5

Thursford, Norfolk. 5 miles SE of Fakenham. A colourful and musical collection of steam relics, and they all work. Gleaming paintwork and shining metal. All sorts of farm engines and wagons, steam rollers and static engines. A Mighty Wurlitzer theatre organ, beautiful and colourful dance organ and showman's organs, and a gondola switchback ride.

Great Yarmouth Funfair   K6

Great Yarmouth, Norfolk. The town possesses a large varied funfair, and the biggest of big dippers in Britain. For those with the nerves and stomach repeat rides are free. The fair is situated conveniently by the beach with good parking.

Norfolk Lavender   F5

Caley Mill, Heacham, Norfolk. N of King's Lynn off A149. 100 acres of lavender make a breathtaking sight in summer. Harvesting takes place early-July to mid-August and you can see the oil distillation process, and maybe take a plant home with you.

North Norfolk Railway Co   H4

Sheringham Station, Sheringham, Norfolk. An ideal visit for a wet summer's day as the exhibition is housed under cover. Working steam train trips on some days.

Regional food

Cambridge Sausage
A pork sausage flavoured with sage.

Cromer Crabs
Caught along the Norfolk coast, together with lobsters, have a very fine flavour.

Felixstowe Tart
A shortbread tart filled with jam and topped with meringue.

Frumenty Suffolk Style
Made of new crushed wheat, soaked in milk and water overnight, and then boiled with honey and cinnamon. The Frumenty is traditional home cooking, eaten during the 12 days of Christmas and a little put outside for the fairies. Ely Frumenty is similar to Suffolk Frumenty but distinctly laced with rum.

Lincolnshire Plum Bread
A rich, dark, fruit cake with a touch of brandy.

Lincolnshire Potatoes
The flat Lincolnshire fenlands are perfect for growing and producing the famous Lincolnshire potato. The seed potatoes are still much in demand all over the country.

Mustard
Norfolk is famous for the growing, milling and blending of mustard, particularly in the Norwich area.

Norfolk Apple Dumpling
This is a popular farmhouse dish. A whole apple is stuffed with jam or sugar, covered in a flaky pastry cover, baked and sprinkled with castor sugar.

Norfolk Turkeys
Norfolk is noted for turkey breeding. Around Christmas time it's a particularly busy place.

Sprats and Whelks
Come from the north-west saltings of Norfolk especially from Wells-next-the-Sea.

Suffolk Cheese
A very hard cheese, and as the saying goes "hunger will break stone walls and anything except a Suffolk cheese".

Yarmouth Bloaters
Bloaters are becoming increasingly rare: uncleaned herrings are salted and smoked to give a distinctly gamey flavour.

Northern Cities, Moors and Dales

It was the Industrial Revolution that transformed this part of Britain, but it is not all 'dark satanic mills'. The best of the towns are rich and industrious and they have cleared up the worst excesses of industrial squalor. Some towns like Manchester and Bradford have been a little too eager to sweep away their past and you'd better go quickly to see the remaining Victorian splendours. This region is full of splendid towns and tough scenery; the Yorkshire Moors have a remote beauty that is rare in Britain. Lancashire can claim two of Europe's greatest cities: Manchester and Liverpool and both are vitally alive not just with football fans but music and glorious Victorian architecture.

York itself, from Roman times an important centre, is almost a perfect walled city at the heart of a region full of great houses and warm villages. The people of the industrial north are friendly and warmhearted with a rich sense of humour, the Beatles, Prime Ministers and comedians have come from here and when you come 'up north' you will find you are welcome.

A B C D E

1

Point of Ayre
Ifenheads
Eastgate Stanhope Wolsingham Tow Law Durham
Brandon
gate Frosterley Crook Willi
Bride Spennymoo
Jurby Andreas
Ballaugh Sulby Ramsey **DURHAM** Bishop Auckland
Kirk Michael 1860 Maughold Head Newbiggin St. Helen Auckland Escomb Shi
Ramsey Bay Teesdale Eggleston Woodland West Al
Snaefell Clay Head Fell Romaldkirk Staindrop Heighingto
Peel 2034 Barnard Castle Winston Gainford
Patrick rough **Stainmore** R Greta Caldwell Darlingt
Glenmaye St. John's **Isle of Man** oulby Barningham Ravensworth
Dalby 1585 Foxdale Crosby Onchan Winton Kirkby Stephen Richmond Scotch C
St Marks Nateby Ravensworth Marrick
adda Head Colby **Douglas** ebay Ravenstonedale Marrick Richmond
Port Erin Ballasalla Derbyhaven Catterick
Cregneish Port Castletown Thwaite Muker Reeth Camp
St Mary 2220 Feetham Castle Redmire Leyburn Brompton
Lowgill Hardrow Reeth Bolton W Witton Middleham Healey

3
Oxenholme Sedbergh Askrigg **Wensleydale** Wensle Jervaulx Ab
on in Furness Crosthwaite Natland Dent Hawes Bainbridge Aysgarth Carlton E Witton
Colton Lakeside Haverthwaite Middleton Aysgarth Horsehouse
verbeck Greenodd Railway Heversham 2419 **Langstrothdale** W Witton
ergate Lindal Bouth Milnthorpe Barbon Kirkby Lonsdale **Chase** Buckden 2302 Horsehouse Healey
Iverston Cartmel Grange-over- Burton Melling in Lonsdale **Ingleborough** Horton in Litton Middlesmoor Kirby
Bardsea Flookburgh Sands Burton Ribblesdale Kettlewell Great Ramsgill Malzeard
4 Carnforth Hornby Ingleton Clapham Austwick Arncliffe **Whernside** Conistone Studley Ro
Aldingham Morecambe Bolton-le-Sands Wray Bentham Grassington Pateley Sum
Bay Hest Bank Claughton Stainforth Threshfield Hebden Bridge Bride
Heysham **Morecambe** Caton Giggleswick Settle Linton Burnsall Appletreewick Blubberhouses
Lancaster Long Kirkby Airton Hebden
Glasson 1531 Clougha Pike Preston Malham Rylstone Thwaite Fews
5 1836 Marshaw **Forest** Wigglesworth Hellifield Skipton
Fleetwood Cockerham Dolphinholme **of Bowland** Slaidburn Newton Gargrave Askwith
Pilling Calda Fell Gisburn Thornton- Carleton Addingham Ilkley
Winmarleigh **LANCASHIRE** Barnoldswick in-Craven Silsden Airedale Otley
veleys Preesall Chipping Waddington Chatburn Pendle Earby Cowling Aire Guiseley Ye
Thornton Hambleton Eccleston Clitheroe Hill Foulridge Haworth Keighley Bingley
n-le-Fylde Inglewhite Longridge Gt. Mitton Whalley Colne Trawden Haworth& Worth Shipley
6 **Blackpool** Woodplumpton Grimsargh Ribchester Barrowford Oxenhope Valley Railway **Bradford**
Kirkham Goosnargh Harwood Clayton Padiham Brierfield Hebden Queensbury Pud
Lytham Wrea Green Clayton Risnton le-Moors Nelson Bridge **Halifax** Batt
St. Annes Leyland **Preston** **Blackburn** Accrington **Burnley** Sowerby Bridge Elland Dews
Penwortham Oswaldtwistle Forest of Todmorden Mirfield
Hesketh Bank Farington Darwen Haslingden **Rossendale** Bacup Littleborough Ripponden Hud
7 **Southport** Banks Tarleton Croston Chorley Rawtenstall Walsden Golca Slaithwaite Hudd
Ainsdale Rufford Adlington Edgworth Ramsbottom Rochdale Milnrow Marsden Meltham Kirk
by Parbold Tottington Bury GR Denshaw Holmf
Formb Burscough **Bolton** Radcliffe Roy ton **Oldham** Mossley 1908 Denton Holmfirth
Ormskirk Standish Horwich Farnworth Middleton Ashton-under-Lyne Blacklow S
Great Skelmersdale **Wigan** Leigh **Manchester** Mollingworth 2060 YOF
8 Crosby Altcar Maghull Kirkby Ashton-in- Failsworth **Stockport** Glossop Kinder Scout Sh
Bootle **Wallasey** Knowsley Newton-le-Willows Makerfield **Salford** Stretford Marple 2088 Edale
St. Helens Prescot **Warrington** Sale Cheadle Hayfield New
Liverpool Widnes Lymm Altrincham Mills Whaley Chapel-en- Hope
Bebington Allerton Runcorn Stretton High Legh Handforth Hazel Bridge le-Frith Peak Bradwel
ston Bromborough Frodsham Weaverham Lostock Wilmslow Grove Bollington Dove Forest
9 Ellesmere Port Helsby Northwich Alderley Prestbury 1834 Holes Tideswell
uay Neston Tarvin Davenham Chelford Nether Buxton
Shotwick **Cheshire** Little Middlewich Holmes **Macclesfield** Taddington
Buckley Hawarden Chester **Plain** Budworth Winsford **Macclesfield** Bakewell
Hope Dodleston Tarporley Church Sandbach Chapel **Forest** Longnor Youlgreave
10 aergwrle Gresford Aldford Minshull Crewe Congleton Hartington Parwich
Holt Burwardsley Alsager **Biddulph** Leek Ash
Wrexham Bulkeley Nantwich **Kidsgrove** Endon Stanlow Tissingto
peoth Malpas Bickley Betley Audley Cellarhead Kingsley Mayfield Ashb
Bangor Coed Aston Audlem **Newcastle-** **Stoke-on-Trent** Cheadle Ellastone
Ruabon Overton Moss Moore Whitmore **under-Lyme** Upr

A B C D E

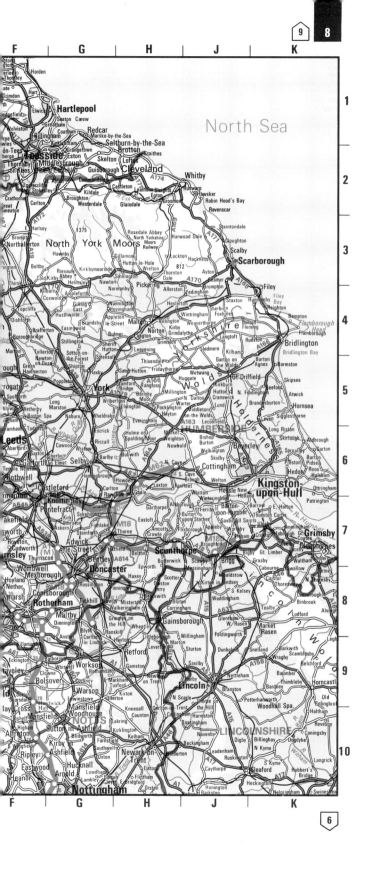

The coast

Blackpool   A6
Lancs. Pop 151,300. EC Wed. It was in 1887
when the Morning Post wrote 'Blackpool has
discovered the lost art of entertaining . . .
and offers more fun for less money than
anywhere else!' It's still true today but on a
much bigger scale. It is Britain's largest
resort and the holiday season covers almost
half the year; the political parties hold
conferences there.
Everything is larger than life. The Prom is 7
miles long, the tower is the nearest thing in
England to the Eiffel Tower, the
illuminations are legendary and there are 3
piers. If it rains or the frantic pace of the
Golden Mile gets too much for you there are
nearly 20 theatres and top flight summer
shows, including an epic ice show.
Two things remain unique to Blackpool, the
first English monorail and the first electric
tramway in the world. The beaches are
sandy, patrolled by lifeguards and there are 4
swimming pools.

Blackpool

Bootle   A8
Mersey. Pop 74,200. Solid Mersey dockland
softened a little by 2 indoor sea water
pools—come to Bootle to see what a
development area looks like. Masses of
decanted offices from London including the
National Giro Centre and some 20 acres of
new buildings. Sad that so much growth and
development gives no indication at all of
human imagination at work.

Bridlington   K4
*Humber. Pop 26,700. EC Thur. MD Wed,
Sat.* Sheltered by Flamborough Head from
the worst of the north-east gales, Bridlington
is a popular beach resort with 2 long
stretches of level sand. The railway arrived
in 1842 and changed the character of the
town, originally planned for the rich families
who built their elegant villas on the sea
front. Piers, a harbour and every sort of
holiday amusement are added attractions. A
good place for fishing and sailing.
Bridlington is the model for Hardascliffe in
Winifred Holtby's powerful Yorkshire novel
'South Riding'.

Cleethorpes   K7
Humber. Pop 35,800. EC Thur. A hundred
years ago it was a little fishing village. Now
a large seaside town with a short season
attracting over a million visitors a year, it's a
place you can read between the lines or take
straight—a joke for some and paradise for
others.
It has a huge open air swimming pool, a zoo
and a 1,200-foot-long pier. The sport of sand
yachting is now establishing itself in the
resort.
Good views of shipping on the Humber
from the busy promenade. Three miles of
sandy beach, safe for swimming.

Filey   K4
N. York. Pop 5,300. EC Wed. A place for
quiet family holidays with a lot of old-world
charm. The 6 miles of sandy beaches are safe
for swimming and sheltered enough for those
who just want to play about with bucket and
spade. Good donkey rides.

Flamborough Head   K4
Humber. The great headland is surrounded
by coves and rock pools that can be explored
at low tide. The ideal spot for scrambling
among the rocks or investigating the
seaweed-filled pools. Swimming is very
dangerous. Danes Dykes, an Iron Age fort, is
a paradise for bird watchers.

The 85-foot-high lighthouse on the headland
is an important warning light for North Sea
shipping; you can visit it during the
afternoons.

Fleetwood   A5
Lancs. Pop 30,000. EC Wed. MD Mon, Fri.
A rich young entrepreneur, Peter Hesketh
Fleetwood, engaged the distinguished
architect Decimus Burton to build a new
town at Fleetwood in 1837. He achieved a
great deal on the barren site and strict rules,
even fines for not having thatched roofs
covered with slate, made Fleetwood the
beginnings of an elegant town.
Alas, the cash ran out and the completion of
the railway over Shap made the proposed
Glasgow-Fleetwood-London link
unnecessary—so Fleetwood stands as an
incomplete dream. It has gradually developed
as one of Britain's chief fishing ports. Wide
sandy beaches.

Formby   A7
Mersey. Pop 23,500. The Mersey's
Lancashire shore is now mostly dockland but
Formby still has an unspoilt beach. Long
stretches of high grassy dunes are an
excellent vantage point to watch the Mersey
shipping. Bathing is not safe.

Goxhill Haven   K6
Humber. Pop 1,200. Reached from a
farmyard, it's a wild and lonely part of the
Humber. A piece of muddy foreshore, with
the cranes and the roofs of Hull visible on
the opposite bank as well as spectacular
views of river craft.

Grimsby   K7
*Humber. Pop 95,700. EC Thur. MD Tue, Fri,
Sat.* An old world fishing port, with a new
town centre, but full of salty vigour; its
name synonymous with trawlers and fishing.
Little ships from North Sea ports sail into
Grimsby, one of the oldest chartered towns
in England. The Fish Dock, with nearly a
mile of quays, is the largest fish market in
the world, though its activity has diminished
since the 'Cod War'. Sandy beaches towards
Cleethorpes.

Hornsea   K8
Humber. Pop 7,000. EC Wed. Although this
is a seaside resort and a very intimate and
pleasant one, the main reason for a visit is
the inland freshwater lake or the Hornsea
Pottery.
Hornsea Mere is the result of some glacial
action in the distant past. Over 2 miles long,
it is the home of water birds and large
gatherings of swans. Take a rowing boat out
for a watery wander among the reeds. The
beach is sandy and there are amusements.

Hoylake   West A8
Mersey. Pop 32,200. EC Wed. This is a well
tended rather swish little town, the opposite
of Blackpool or New Brighton. Rather than
disturb the retired residents you had better
tiptoe across the bowling greens to the
spacious sandy beach. Good golf links.

Hull   K6
*Humber. Pop 282,900. EC Mon, Thur. MD
Tue, Fri, Sat.* Don't be put off by the
industrial nature of this town, it is Britain's
major deep-water fishing port and a visit to
the fish dock when the trawlers come in
from Iceland and beyond is fascinating,
though there are not so many since the 'Cod
War'. The docks extend for many miles
along the Humber and there are some recent
additions—oil tanker jetties and modern car
ferries.
In the town itself there is a range of
museums from William Wilberforce's
birthplace to the Transport Museum. The
university is worth a visit for its imaginative
new Gulbenkian Theatre. Nearest beach on
river shore near Kilnsea.
The largest single-span suspension bridge in
the world is being built to link Hull to
Grimsby.

Liverpool   A8
Mersey. Pop 574,600. EC Wed. The city of
Liverpool is large, prosperous and in many

Birkenhead, Liverpool

ways outrageous. It has more of everything:
more docks than anywhere in England; more
cathedrals than most cities, and both of them
modern; more successful football teams; it's
produced more pop stars and comedians than
anyone cares to count.
Liverpool grew very fast during the late 19th
and early 20thC as Atlantic trade prospered
and the wide Mersey accommodated more
and more ships. There are nearly 40 miles of
quay and a glance at only one dock, Albert
Dock, is enough to show the quality of this
early industrial architecture.
The town centre has an amazing series of
Victorian civic buildings of a certain
grandeur; St George's Hall is at the heart of
this group. On the waterfront 3 commercial
buildings are typical of the the city's style
and wealth—the Cunard building, the Royal
Liver Friendly Society building, and the
head offices of the Mersey Docks and
Harbour Board.
Worth visiting for contrasts in style are the 2
cathedrals, one (Anglican) designed in the
Gothic style in 1901, is the largest religious
building in the country. The Roman
Catholic cathedral is a white concrete,
circular structure opened in 1967, with good
stained glass by John Piper. The university
and the Walker Art Gallery are both worth
visiting. Sea and estuary too dangerous for
swimming—go to Crosby for sandy beach.

Lytham St Anne's   A6
Lancs. Pop 42,100. EC Wed. A quiet merger
brought 2 genteel resorts together in 1922,
and despite the overpowering influence of
nearby Blackpool they form a leafy retreat
from seaside razmataz. Beaches sandy,
backed by dunes, becoming muddy towards
the River Ribble. Watch for sand yacht
racing in the summer.

Morecambe   A4
Lancs. Pop 41,900. EC Wed. MD Tue, Thur.
A bustling, busy holiday town where the
shrimps are the best to be found—try them
in a screw of newspaper from the stalls on
the seafront. There are new attractions every
year; they include performing dolphins and
extensive illuminations
The beaches are muddy with some shingle in
the northern part, but sandy as you approach
Heysham.

Morecambe Bay   A4
Lancs. At low tide there are 150 square miles
of sand exposed in the bay, and they vanish
with amazing rapidity as the sea comes in.
Walkers trying to cross the bay should take
great care and watch for red flags and listen
for sirens that warn of the fast incoming
tide. In the 19thC carriages hurtled across the
sands to take travellers on the quickest route
to the Lakes—sometimes they ended up
taking a very long journey indeed. The
possibility of a barrage across the bay is
under discussion.

Robin Hood's Bay   J2
N. York. Pop 200. EC Wed. Yorkshire's most
picturesque fishing village. A jocular mob of
buildings tumbles round a tight maze of
steep streets. The bay itself is a curve of
rocky cliffs that overlook a foreshore
scattered with large boulders.
Rocky beaches.

Robin Hood's Bay

Scarborough   J3
N. York. Pop 44,400. EC Wed. MD Thur.
Exhilarating and elegant. The discovery of
medicinal springs in 1620 started the town
off as a spa to be visited by people of
fashion, and the invention of the bathing
machine added the attraction of sea water to
'the cure'. The natural beauty of
Scarborough's 2 great bays has ensured the
town's continuing success as a resort.
Jammed between the 2 is the ruined castle,
standing on an imposing headland.
Of interest—The Crescent (1832) which puts
Scarborough on a par with Bath and
Edinburgh; the Mere, a sheltered lake.
Beaches are sandy in both bays, and there
are 2 good heated outdoor pools.

Southport   A7
*Mersey. Pop 86,000. EC Tue, Sat. MD Mon,
Tue, Wed, Thur a.m., Fri & Sat.* A genteel,
Victorian town with no slums and lots of
churches. Now a busy holiday spot because
of its enormous sandy beaches; there is no
shortage of things to do. The marine lake by
the river has dinghy racing. There is golf,
archery, trampolines, sailing, and a long pier
with its own railway.

Staithes   H2
N. York. A tough little village that hasn't
changed much since the days when Captain
Cook explored it as a boy. There are steep
streets with abrupt changes of level on the
precipitous site. Swimming is safe only from
a few sheltered sandy patches among the
rocks when the tide is in. Two miles W, you
will find England's highest cliffs, 700-foot
Boulby Cliff.

Wallasey/New Brighton   A8
Mersey. Pop 94,500. EC Wed. A brash and
busy seaside town on the Wirral peninsula
that has always attracted day visitors from
the surrounding industrial areas. Lots of
'Kiss-me-Quick' hats and candy floss and all
that goes with it. The beach is sandy with
patches of mud and shingle; swim only
where the beach is patrolled by lifeguards.

Whitby   J2
N. York. Pop 12,700. EC Wed. MD Sat. One
of the best towns on the east coast. This is
the spot where Captain Cook started his
sailing life in coal ships.
Climb up from the busy harbour and nearly
200 steps later you will be at St Mary's
church, one of the most fascinating churches
in the country. The ruined abbey on the hill
was the scene of the great Synod of Whitby
in AD664.
Sandy bathing beaches to the west of the
harbour.

Withernsea   K6
*Humber. Pop 6,000. EC Tue. MD Thur, Sat,
Sun.* Very small, quiet and simple,
Withernsea is a family spot with 2 miles of
clean, sandy beaches. The atmosphere is
totally unsophisticated, yet you will get a
friendly welcome, and, if the sun shines, a
good day on the beach with the children.
There is a lighthouse and a well equipped
caravan park. There really are bonny baby
contests here during August.

Isle of Man

*Reached by regular ferries from Liverpool,
Heysham, Ardrossan, Belfast and Dublin; and
flights from London, Liverpool, Manchester
and most airports in the British Isles.* The
island is a dependency of the British Crown,
and is not part of the United Kingdom, the
Lord of Man being Her Majesty the Queen.
It has its own parliament, the Tynwald,
founded by the Vikings, which celebrated its
millennium in 1979. The House of Keys
(lower house) meets twice a week. It also has
its own radio station, Manx money, a special
breed of cat with extra long back legs and no
tail, and a breed of sheep, Laoghtan, which
have 4 or sometimes 6 horns. The scenery is
a rich mixture of moors and mountains, lush

meadows and deep forest. Palm trees and
fuchsia abound. The coast is mostly sandy
beaches interspersed with cliffs. Unless you
love motorbikes avoid the first week in June
during the roaring TT races on the 38-mile
mountain road circuit in the north.

Castletown. *Pop 2,800. EC Thur.* The one
time capital of the island, dominated by
Castle Rushen which is built on the site of a
Viking fort. The castle displays all the arms
of the Lords of Man in the main halls, and a
clock with only one hand given by Queen
Elizabeth I. Good harbour and large sandy
beaches on the bay towards Langness
Peninsula.

The Castle, Castletown

Derbyhaven. Site of the first Derby horse
race as long ago as 1627. Now a place to
visit for the beach of fine sand; some rocks
and lots of seaweed.

Douglas. *Pop 20,000.* Capital of the island;
the long promenade curves along the edge of
Douglas Bay where the beaches are wide and
sandy. Horse trams, steam trains and the
quaint Manx Electric Railway are some of
the unusual forms of transport that survive
here. There are also horsedrawn coaches and
the mountain railway.
A lively resort with good beaches and plenty
of entertainment. The great indoor leisure
centre, Summerland, offers all-weather, all-
day entertainment for all the family.

Dhoon Glen. A magical spot. Leave the car
at the Manx Electric Railway station and
wander down the narrow path through the
trees to a rocky cove. A lovely mixture of
trees, sea, beach and wild flowers. Also a
waterfall.

Glen Maye. A thickly wooded glen on the
west side of the island; the stream rushes
over a beautiful waterfall, through woods to
the sea. A small sandy beach amongst the
rocks.

Jurby. On the island's rather weird northern
plains—the cliffs here overlook miles of sand
and shingle. Towards the Point of Ayre the
cliffs turn into sand dunes. Don't miss the
dazzling whitewashed church.

Laxey. *Pop 1,200.* A busy visitors' spot with
a tiny harbour. Here the Snaefell Mountain
Railway line starts, and you can see the
largest water wheel in the world, now over
100 years old. Sailing, sand and shingle
beaches.

Peel. *Pop 3,300. EC Thur. MD Wed.* A
fishing port that is rightly famous for its
juicy kippers. Harbour and beach are
overtopped by castle and cathedral. Lots of
sandy beaches. In summer the Vikings return
to an annual festival.

Port Erin. *Pop 2,400 EC Thur.* At the end
of the steam railway from Douglas. This
resort is renowned for its fine bay with
sandy beaches. Boat trips to the bird
sanctuary on the Calf of Man; ideal
conditions for underwater swimming.

Port St Mary. *Pop 1,500. EC Thur.* The
rather gaunt row of Victorian guest houses
belies the cheeriness of this sailing resort.
The beaches are sheltered and sandy and
there is a spectacular footpath to the
Chasms, a series of romantic ravines. Sailing,
swimming and golf.

Ramsey. *Pop 5,400. EC Wed. MD Mon.*
Lies sheltered at the foot of the North
Barrule mountain; the town clings around
the harbour. Beaches either side of the
harbour are sand and shingle. The north is
the sunniest and least windy part of the
island.

Inland towns & villages

Appletreewick   **D5**
N. York. Pop 200. Lives up to its delightful
name. Full of gabled 16thC cottages that
were once proud houses called High Hall,
Low Hall, etc. Thoughtful 16thC builders
provided pigeon holes over the windows.
The tiny church was originally 2 cottages.

Aysgarth   **D3**
N. York. Pop 200. In the centre of some of
the loveliest country in Yorkshire. Stand on
the single-span Elizabethan bridge and watch
the foaming River Ure plunge over 3
cataracts. Of interest—St Andrew's church,
with good Victorian glass.

Beverley   **J6**
*Humber. Pop 17,100. EC Thur. MD Tue,
Wed.* An elegant market town that has kept a
15thC gateway and several fine Georgian
houses. But you really come here for the
minster which is one of the finest Gothic
churches in Europe. Another church, St
Mary's, built around 1520 is overshadowed
by the minster but should be seen.

Blackburn   **B6**
*Lancs. Pop 142,000. EC Thur. MD Wed, Fri,
Sat.* A hilly mill town—the kind of place
where you can see or sense the surrounding
country from the centre of the town. Full of
impressive mills, plain chapels and even a
little cathedral converted from the parish
church. The art gallery holds unexpected
pleasures; apart from good English
watercolours there are more than a thousand
rare Japanese prints. Look out for the
excellent and informative Lewis Textile
Museum.

Bolton   **C7**
*Gt Manchester. Pop 261,000. EC Wed. MD
Tue, Thur, Sat.* The distant moors and
outlying stone cottages serve to redeem the
otherwise industrial features of this
Lancastrian city. Close historical connections
with the textile trade. Arkwright worked as a
barber here and Samuel Crompton, the
inventor of the spinning mule, spent his
childhood at Hall-i'-th'-Wood, an attractive
early Tudor half-timbered house on Tonge
Moor, restored by Lord Leverhulme at the
beginning of this century.

Bradford   **E6**
*W. York. Pop 293,800. EC Wed. MD Mon,
Tue, Thur, Fri & Sat.* Solid Victorian
prosperity created this town. It was
developed by local builders and architects in
a fairly undisciplined mixture of styles.
There is a vigorous Gothic town hall and a
Venetian Wool Exchange with the interior a
forest of polished pink granite columns.
Look for St Clement's in Barkerend Road, a
19thC church with a rare chancel roof by
William Morris. Try and find the miniature
Albert Memorial in Lister Park, and the
monument to material wealth, Waterhouse's
gabled red brick Prudential Assurance block.
The city is a treasure trove of Victoriana—go
soon before it's too late.

Chester   **A9**
Cheshire. Pop 117,200. MD Tue, Thur. An
important centre on the River Dee for more
than 2,000 years; there are lots of remains of
Roman Deva to be seen in the Grosvenor
Museum. The partly Roman and mediaeval
walls still encircle the area of the fortified
mediaeval town. The Rows is a unique and
famous feature of the city—a 2-tier system of

Chester

shopping built in the striking black-and-white timbering that belongs to this region. The Bridge Street Rows have been effectively extended by a well designed modern 2-level system. Visit also the 12thC church of St Mary-on-the-Hill, the excellent zoo, and the riverside promenade—the Groves.

Coxwold G4
N. York. Pop 200. A beautiful 'North Riding' village. Particularly interesting is Shandy Hall, a humble brick house where Laurence Sterne lived and wrote 'Tristram Shandy' in 1769. One mile south is Newburgh Priory whose former owners rode to battle in the Light Brigade at Balaclava, and where it is said Cromwell's body is buried in a bricked-up vault.

Great Ayton J8
N. York. Pop 4,700. EC Wed. On the tiny River Leven. Was once the home of Capt. James Cook, the explorer and navigator. A monument to him stands on the moor above the village on the spot where his cottage stood. It was taken down stone by stone and rebuilt in Australia.

Halifax D6
W. York. Pop 88,600. EC Thur. MD Fri (cattle). A much under-rated town in a spectacular position on the River Calder. Hills rise on all sides, most of them so steep that moorland often looks into the windows of the houses. Roads, bridges and deep cuttings are mixed up with mills and tiny houses. Look at Barry's town hall; the 1779 Piece Hall—a large open cloth market; and the old farms and manors that were incorporated into the city when it expanded so feverishly in the 19thC. See the folk museum at Shibden Hall.

Wainhouse's Tower, Halifax

Harrogate F5
N. York. Pop 64,600 EC Wed. Sulphur and iron springs made this town into a successful spa. It still has the air of a restful recuperative sort of place. Full of fine gardens, particularly the Valley Gardens and the Harlow Car Trial Gardens. The English passion for municipal gardening reaches its height in Harrogate. The happily haphazard scattering of spa and bath buildings among the buxom blooms is enough to effect a cure before you've tasted the waters.

Haworth D6
W. York. EC Tue. A village full of gruff character. The steep main street is still cobbled and it's not impossible to imagine the Brontës' arrival up the hill at the Parsonage. The house is now run by The Brontë Society and the rooms where Charlotte and Emily wrote are arranged as they were then.
The village is surrounded by the Pennine Moors of 'Wuthering Heights' and some stiff climbs are possible to the houses and farms mentioned in the Brontë novels. A visit to the plain Georgian Parsonage set in the sombre beauty of the Pennines is a memorable experience.

Helmsley J9
N. York. Pop 1,300. EC Wed. MD Fri. An attractive market town and a good centre for outdoor pursuits; from here you can catch trout, ride horses or ponies, or just walk through the splendid scenery of the Hambleton Hills. Two miles N.W. are the impressive ruins of Rievaulx Abbey.

Huddersfield E7
W. York. Pop 131,000. EC Wed. MD Mon. Growing fast from its original river valley position has meant that the town now clambers all over the hills, and it is an impressive sight among the smoky mills.

Now worth seeing not just for its industrial grandeur but also for its 19thC churches (one, St John, by William Butterfield) and flat non-conformist chapels; also the fine Victorian railway station.

Hutton-le-Hole H3
N. York. Pop 200. A moorland village with a stream that runs through the centre; a kind of rugged Cotswold scene. The grass verges and village green are kept closely cropped by sheep that roam freely. Do visit the Ryedale Folk Museum.

Knaresborough F5
N. York. Pop 12,500. EC Thur. MD Mon, Wed. Apart from possessing a most picturesque river gorge, the atmosphere of this town is designed to delight visitors. The terraces, rocky crags, caves and the celebrated Dropping Well are all fascinating to see. In the caves are suspended a varied selection of encrusted objects 'petrified' by the calcium-based water. Close by is Mother Shipton's Cave, the reputed birthplace of that famed priestess whose prophecies have now become history.

Knutsford C9
Cheshire. Pop 16,000. EC Wed. MD Fri, Sat. The olde-worlde charm of 19thC Knutsford inspired Mrs Gaskell to immortalise this town as 'Cranford'. Her tomb can be seen behind the Unitarian Chapel. The Royal George with its minstrel gallery is one of several buildings mentioned by her that still stand today. Nearby the 2,000 acres surrounding Tatton Park, the former seat of the Egerton family, is surely elegant economy run wild.

Lancaster A5
Lancs. Pop 50,600. EC Wed. MD Mon, Tue, Thur, Fri & Sat. A town you remember for its castle, its associations with John of Gaunt and the 18thC Custom House and Georgian merchant houses. It has a good silhouette of castle towers and the church of St Mary seen across the River Lune. Once a flourishing port that lost trade as the silt moved up the river; in 1787 Glasson Dock took over most of the trade.
Now Lancaster has all the attractions of a comfortable, busy county town and the new university has helped to add some life.

Ashton Memorial, Lancaster

Leeds F6
W. York. Pop 500,200. EC Wed, MD Tue, Fri, Sat. Very big and prosperous, Leeds was the national meeting point for the roads, railways and canals of the Industrial Revolution. Its massive columned Town Hall with the 8-foot-high clock tower is the high point of the city's Victorian splendour—based on coal, heavy industry and Yorkshire 'grit'.
Today there is a traffic-free centre for easy shopping, an art gallery full of European masters, nearby Temple Newsam, set in lovely grounds, houses superb English paintings, and in the City Museum there's a detailed working model of a coal mine. For cricket enthusiasts a visit to Headingley is essential, and theatregoers should try the Leeds Playhouse.

Macclesfield D9
Cheshire. Pop 44,200. EC Wed. MD Tue, Fri & Sat. This mediaeval town, once famous as

the centre of the silk industry, is now chiefly concerned with the modern textile industry, although several early mill buildings survive today. Two notable churches—the 13thC St Michael's and 18thC Christchurch.
Look out for the remains of 3 mediaeval crosses in the pleasant West Park. Enjoy the charm of ancient Gawsworth Hall, once the home of Mary Fitton, thought to be the Dark Lady of Shakespeare's sonnets.

Malham, N. York

Malham   **C4**
N. York. Pop 100. A tiny village at the head of the River Aire, it is an agricultural community (mostly cattle and sheep) and dates back to before the 7th and 8thC. The village was once held by the 2 monasteries Fountains Abbey and Bolton Priory.
The Pennine Way passes through here and there is a good Youth Hostel. Charles Kingsley is believed to have planned his book 'The Water Babies' while on a visit to Malham Tarn House, and the fantastic Gordale Scar to the east of the village inspired the poet William Blake. The limestone above Malham Cove has been wrought by rain into sculptured shapes like Henry Moore's work.

Malpas   **A10**
Cheshire. Pop 1,300. A small peaceful town set against a back-cloth of the Welsh mountains and the Wrekin. The parish Perpendicular church of St Oswald contains the Brereton family chapel amidst elaborate woodwork and good plasterwork.

Manchester   **C8**
Gt Manchester. Pop 530,500. EC Wed. MD Mon, Wed & Sat. Centre of the cotton industry and from the middle ages an important weaving centre. The arrival of the canals in the late 18thC brought raw cotton right into the city and spinning, weaving and the Industrial Revolution had arrived. Manchester grew and grew, helped by cheap labour and the ingenuity of inventors who improved the spinning and weaving processes. Its prosperity is reflected in its great Victorian buildings both commercial and public—particularly the Gothic revival Town Hall by Alfred Waterhouse. With the opening of the Ship Canal in 1894 Manchester became a port. The city has a great public library, several good museums and galleries and a large university. Much of the central area, Piccadilly, has been rebuilt since the 1950s. A great city, well worth a visit.

Town Hall, Manchester

Nantwich   **B10**
Cheshire. Pop 11,700. EC Wed. MD Thur AM, Sat. This attractive, friendly town was for many centuries a salt mining town ('wich' meaning salt town). Situated on the

River Weaver, it houses several fine buildings worth seeing including the 14thC church of St Mary and Churche's Mansion, an outstanding example of half-timbered architecture. Good shopping centre.

Nether Alderley   **C9**
Cheshire. Pop 600. This village near Macclesfield was the birthplace of Dean Stanley. The picturesque mediaeval church of St Mary contains striking monuments and the family pew. The machinery at the old water mill, east of the church, has been restored by the National Trust.

Pateley Bridge   **E4**
N. York. EC Thur. MD Sat. Known as the capital of Upper Nidderdale, a Dale region that has a stern, rugged grandeur. The mixture of thickly wooded slopes, rock-strewn glens and gorges make this exhilarating territory to explore on foot. Once you've visited the fortnightly sheep and cattle fair in this little town take the road into Wharfedale. It climbs one of the longest and steepest hills in the county to the bleak, windy village of Greenhow, the highest village in England.

Pontefract   **F7**
N. York. Pop 31,300. EC Thur. MD Sat. There's not much left of the castle here but it has witnessed some stirring events: not just the Civil War sieges in the 1640s, but the tragic death of King Richard II. Now the castle guards the museum where the money manufactured during the Royalist occupation is on view. The peculiar art of liquorice growing is still practised in Pontefract; it dates back to the 13thC. Flat lozenges of juicy liquorice, Pontefract cakes, are still made here. A most unusual hermitage (monk's or hermit's cell) can be seen in Southgate; it dates back to 1368 and had the rare feature of an underground stream.

Prestbury Village   **D9**
Cheshire. Pop 2,200. One of Cheshire's oldest and prettiest villages, Prestbury on the River Bollin is now a popular stop for tourists. The Priest's House and the bright murals in the 18thC church of St Peter and separate 12thC chapel are particularly worth visiting.

Preston   **B6**
Lancs. Pop 132,000. EC Thur. MD Mon, Wed, Fri, Sat. This is cotton mills country. Arkwright was born here in 1732 and the first cotton mill started in 1777. A fast growing population meant that Preston didn't expand in a leisurely, beautiful way but it has benefited from the enlightened patronage of rich mill owners.
The Harris Library and Museum in Market Place is a spectacular Victorian classical pile full of good intentions. A good walk is a wander around the Fishergate area; plain, pleasing streets of brick houses with rich doorways. Visit Lancastrian Brigade Museum for good regimental relics.

Richmond   **E2**
N. York. Pop 7,200. EC Wed. MD Sat. This is the one after which all the other Richmonds are named. A beautiful town with a busy cobbled market place and fascinating buildings, including the castle which overlooks the town and surrounding countryside. Do not fail to see the theatre built in 1788 and completely restored in 1962—it is one of the oldest theatres still in use.
There is a strong masculine profile to Richmond, and it is still the garrison town for Catterick Camp, and regimental headquarters of the famous Green Howards.

Ripon   **F4**
N. York. Pop 12,600. EC Wed. MD Thur. The earliest records of this town date back to 886 when Alfred the Great granted its charter. Make a point of being in the ancient square around 21.00 when a strangely-clad figure executes the time-honoured tradition of 'Setting the Watch'—a horn is blown, which in mediaeval times used to signify that

the Wakeman had taken charge of the city's security for the night.

Runcorn   B8
Cheshire. Pop 54,400. EC Wed. MD Tue, Thur, Sat. One of the more recent new towns built around the older small settlement. Tightly planned around an express bus transport system, it is worth a visit to see how well a new community can function. There are some very pleasing housing areas and the enormous indoor town centre is an extremely pleasant place to shop in or stroll around.

Sheffield   F8
S. York. Pop 511,800. EC Thur. MD Mon, Tues, Wed, Fri & Sat. The centre of this prosperous town is largely new, no longer grimy, and now famous for its clean air. Still the centre of steel manufacture and justly renowned for good cutlery and plate. Look out for the vast new terraces of Park Hill to the east of the centre, a giant concrete vision of the future—already built! The university has interesting new buildings and you can shop in traffic-free centres. Of great interest is the new Crucible Theatre with its thrust stage and experimental productions.

Thirsk   F3
N. York. Pop 2,900. EC Wed. MD Mon. It was in this busy market town with its ancient cross that Thomas Lord was born in 1755. He went on to found the cricket ground, Lord's, in London.
The town was once an important posting station on the stage coach routes; nowadays visited for the panoramic views of the Vale of York, and for an excellent race course. Growing in importance as a gliding centre.

Thorton Dale   H3
N. York. Pop 1,200. EC Wed. Largely unscathed by the effects of being known as 'the prettiest village in Yorkshire'; all its scenic charms remain. Good centre for riding over the dales.

York   G5
N. York. Pop 104,500. EC Mon, Wed. MD Tues–Sat (cattle Mon, Thur). The city is where the North, East and West Ridings met and it is the pride of Yorkshire. York still looks almost totally mediaeval, encircled by giant grey stone walls and dominated by the majestic Minster which was consecrated in

York.

1472. Inside those soaring walls is some of the most amazing mediaeval coloured glass in the world. The whole structure of the Minster has been restored and cleaned.
A wander on the city walls is an essential start to a visit to York, and then into the Shambles, a cluster of narrow streets full of houses that lean across the road to greet one another—these are the kind of streets where you can shake hands with the neighbour opposite. Visit the Castle Museum, where cobbled streets and reconstructed buildings represent scenes from Tudor to Edwardian times; the elegant Treasurer's House, and the National Railway Museum with a wonderful collection of old locomotives.

Regional features

Brass bands
The textile workers and colliery hands still let off steam in the traditional way. Famous works' bands compete regularly and reach dizzy heights of brassy musical splendour.

Choral singing
If you have never heard the 'Messiah' by Handel sung by the Huddersfield Choral Society, you haven't experienced true choral singing. No one else can make the hallelujahs ring out in the same way; Handel would have loved it.

Dialect
In Yorkshire and Lancashire dialects remain closer to their Anglo-Saxon roots than in many other areas. It's a refreshing and important regional difference that must be maintained.

'Magpie' houses
Cheshire. Timber beams—originally not black, but brown—and whitewashed plaster are typical of the Cheshire region—these houses are the model for all the by-pass Tudor that has spread all over the world. Among the finest are Moreton Old Hall, Woodford Old Hall, Adlington Hall and numerous cottages in East Cheshire.

Manx cats
Legend says the original cat was a cross between cat and hare, probably because of its rather long back legs. The tail-less Manx cat is peculiar to the Isle of Man and has been there for about 300 years.

Pot holes
There are hundreds of holes and caves under the Pennines and exploration can be a dangerous game. Gaping Gill is the largest and is big enough to take the whole of York Minster.

Famous people

Sir Richard Arkwright (1732–92)   **C7**
Bolton, Gt Manchester. The water-frame dubbed the 'Devil's bagpipes' by suspicious neighbours, was invented by Arkwright, who began his career as a successful barber and went on to revolutionise textile manufacture. The machine is on view at the local Textile Machinery Museum.

The Brontës   **D6**
Brontë Parsonage Museum, Haworth, W. York. Rev. Patrick Brontë brought his family to the parsonage in 1820. It was here that Charlotte, Emily and Anne wrote their novels and Branwell immortalised the neighbouring Black Bull Hotel.
The surrounding bleak moorlands of 'West Riding' are alive with Brontë associations: a 4-mile hike will take you to the site of 'Wuthering Heights' on Far Withens. Wycoller Hall, now a ruin, was probably the model for Ferndean Manor in 'Jane Eyre'. This stark Georgian parsonage now a museum, has a fine collection of Brontë manuscripts and relics.

Samuel Crompton (1753–1827)   **C7**
Bolton Hall-i'-th-Wood, Gt Manchester. 300 yards N of Crompton Way By-pass. This half-timbered manor house is where Crompton lived and invented the spinning mule which combined the principles of Arkwright's water-frame and Hargreave's jenny. The house is now a museum with 16thC furnishings and Crompton relics.

James Hargreaves (d. 1778)   **B6**
Blackburn, Lancs. The inventor of the spinning-jenny was a Blackburn carpenter and weaver. His house and machinery were destroyed by a reactionary mob of spinners, so Hargreaves moved to Nottingham. Visit the local Lewis Textile Museum and see the jenny in action.

Laurence Sterne (1713–68)   **G4**
Shandy Hall, Coxwold, N. York. Sterne wrote part of 'Tristram Shandy' and 'A Sentimental Journey' here. The 15thC hall was renamed in his honour, and is now a museum. Sterne is buried in the churchyard nearby. *Closed winter.*

William Wilberforce (1759–1833)   **J6**
Wilberforce House, 25 High St, Hull, Humber. Slave emancipator Wilberforce was born here, in this lovely Elizabethan mansion. The house is now a historical museum with Wilberforce relics and a collection relating to the abolition of the slave trade.

Cathedrals, abbeys & churches

All Hallows   **A8**
Allerton, nr Liverpool, Mersey. A late Victorian sandstone church with a range of Burne-Jones windows that must be seen. The glass is of vividly coloured tracery designs made by William Morris.

All Saints   **H6**
Holme-upon-Spalding Moor, Humber. The battlemented 15thC tower on a hill in the Wolds acts as a landmark for miles around. The outside of the church is a mixture of all types of stones, indicating the complexity of the region's geology. The interior is delightfully unspoilt: a mixture of all the centuries from the 15th to the present.

Beverley Minster   **J6**
Beverley, Humber. A magnificent Saxon church of cathedral size with Gothic restorations dating from the 13thC to 15thC. It contains work from all periods—from the 14thC altar screen and Percy tomb to Hawksmoor's great west door.

Beverley Minster

Bradford Cathedral   **E6**
Bradford, W. York. A large parish church dating chiefly from the 15thC is now the cathedral. Dedicated to St Peter, it has been greatly enlarged since the completion in 1965 of Sir Edward Maufe's extensions.

Chester Cathedral   **A9**
Chester, Cheshire. Originally a monastery founded by an Earl of Chester in 1093, it became a cathedral during the reign of Henry VIII. It is a red sandstone building tucked into a corner of the city and still retains a fascinating range of monastic buildings. The cloister, chapter house, the infirmary, refectory and parlour are massive, albeit restored.
Inside the cathedral the choir is the highspot. Largely built in 1300 it contains remarkably carved stalls made around 1380. Each stall has a fine misericord illustrating fables and incidents from mediaeval bestiaries.

Liverpool Cathedral (Anglican)   **A8**
Liverpool, Mersey. This massive building stands on a marvellous site that dominates the river and the city. The architect was chosen by competition and Giles Gilbert Scott was only 21 when his design was selected. The cathedral was started in 1904 and work is still going on, red sandstone being used in a completely traditional way. The 600-foot-long nave is now complete. Liverpool must be the last of the great Gothic revival cathedrals. It is impressive and right for the city.

Liverpool Cathedral by Gilbert Scott

Liverpool Cathedral (R.C.)   **A8**
Liverpool, Mersey. Dedicated to Christ the King, the circular building towers up to a spiky crown and at night the top part of the tower glows with brilliantly-lit coloured glass. Again the building was the result of a competition held in 1959 when the original giant designs of Lutyens had to be abandoned. Sir Frederick Gibberd's design was chosen, and it is now the newest cathedral in the British Isles. The central altar is lit by the dramatic lantern of John Piper's stained glass. Full of modern art, the cathedral is in great contrast to the Anglican one—clearly you have to visit them both.

Cathedral of Christ the King, Liverpool (1962)

Manchester Cathedral   **C8**
Manchester, Gt Manchester. The 15thC collegiate church of St Mary became a cathedral in 1848. It's a good Perpendicular building with modern additions. Lovely ornate porch. The choir stalls are amongst the finest in the country: early 16thC with exquisitely carved canopies and crests, and charming carved animals and flowers.

Ripon Cathedral   **F4**
Ripon, N. York. One of the oldest Christian shrines in Britain—the crypt is said to have been built in AD672 by St Wilfrid. It is topped by a splendid Gothic nave of 1502 and an Early English west front. The towers were once crowned by wooden spires.

St Anne   **A6**
Woodplumpton, Lancs. The long, low, warm coloured stone building is topped by a fish weather-vane. Three low aisles lead to the screen across the amazing width of the church.

St Helen   **A8**
Sefton, nr Liverpool, Mersey. A late Perpendicular church that is worth seeing for the excellent woodcarving and monuments. The tombs of the Molyneux family are a great mediaeval series; look for the effigy in chain mail that has been there since 1296. Good brasses.

St Mary the Virgin   **E4**
Studley Royal, N. York. A mid-Victorian dream church, standing in a lovely deer park—it was designed by W. Burges 1871-78. Full of rich colour, mosaic floors and stained glass. In a dome over the altar, choirs of Angels sing a Te Deum. Well worth a visit.

St Michael   **A9**
Shotwick, Cheshire. A strong tower dominates this very peaceful hamlet. Inside the church has twin naves and a rare 3-decker pulpit. Two lovely 14thC glass windows.

St Oswald   **C9**
Lower Peover, Cheshire. Go down a cobbled lane and you come to the inn, church and schoolroom. Behind the massive stone tower is a good example of a timber church. Inside all is dark oak, box pews and whitewash. Superb.

St Patrick   **K7**
Patrington, Humber. A 14thC church is often known as 'The Queen of Holderness' because it is the size of a small cathedral and is dominated by a central spire. The church is a consistent example of the Decorated style.

St Peter's   **J7**
Barton-upon-Humber, Humber. A fine 10thC church with a Saxon tower and text book nave to the west of it. Interesting 14thC glass in the east window.

St Peter's   **C10**
Congleton, Cheshire. A 1742 town church; inside the plain walls is a handsome galleried

interior complete with box pews. Good
18thC glass and candelabra.

Sheffield Cathedral F8
Sheffield, S. York. Formerly the parish
church of SS Peter and Paul, the present
building represents a virtual reconstruction
of the Perpendicular church. Much of the
work is modern and not particularly
distinguished. Some good Tudor monuments
in the Shrewsbury Chapel.

Wakefield Cathedral F7
Wakefield, W. York. All Saints parish church
became the cathedral early this century. It is
large and plain and dates largely from the
14thC. The east end is modern and the
church is especially worth seeing for the fine
range of Jacobean fittings.

York Minster G5
N. York. The cathedral church of St Peter is
one of the largest English cathedrals. The
present building is hard to grasp as one large
building because it is so surrounded by tiny
houses. In the north transept adjoining the
Chapter House are the famous 'Five Sisters',
5 tall lancet windows of mediaeval stained
glass. Over the crossing is the largest central
tower in England, massive and simple. In
contrast the west front with its 2 pinnacled
towers is richly decorative. Inside the
Minster, the highest and broadest nave in
England is in fact somewhat dull. The great
glory of York is the glass. The steady
development of English glass painting can be
traced here through 3 centuries. The earliest
13thC are the pale 'grisaille' of the 'Five
Sisters' and the slightly later glass in the
Chapter House is similar.
In the aisles and nave are 14thC windows,
but the triumph is the amazing coloured sea

York Minster, York

of glass that fills the east end. It was
completed by John Thornton of Coventry in
1405 and is one of Europe's finest windows,
with 117 yard-square panels telling the
Biblical story from the creation to the
Apocalypse.

Castles & ruins

Conisborough Castle G8
S. York. 5 miles SW of Doncaster. The
magnificent 95-foot-high white keep, perched
on a steep valleyside, is the oldest surviving
circular keep in England. It was built in
1180–1190, and was the setting for Sir
Walter Scott's 'Ivanhoe'.

Fountains Abbey E4
N. York. 2 miles SW of Ripon. A moving and
beautiful sight. The ruins of Fountains
Abbey show that this was one of the
mightiest monastic institutions in Europe.
Founded in 1132 by the Cistercians, many of
the outstanding features remain including
the long range of western buildings
impressively vaulted in 22 double bays.
During the 18thC the ruins were landscaped
with pools, waterfalls and lakes when they
were incorporated into the Studley Royal
estate.

Fountains Abbey, N. York

Lancaster Castle A5
Lancaster, Lancs. Dates from 1102 when the
Norman motte-and-bailey replaced the Saxon
fortifications on the hill overlooking the
River Lune. King John added a surrounding
wall with round towers and a great gateway.
John of Gaunt (son of Edward III) added
towers and feasting rooms and donated many
damp dungeons. Now used as a law court
there is little chance of prisoners leaping
over the 78-foot-high walls. *Closed winter.*

Lancaster Castle, Lancs

Richmond Castle E2
Richmond, N. York. A huge, almost square
keep built by the Normans to dominate
Swaledale. Long walls of 11thC masonry run
for 150 yards along the riverside. Visit the
barbican, Robin Hood's Tower and St
Nicholas's Chapel.

Rievaulx Abbey

Rievaulx Abbey G3
N. Yorks. 2½ miles NW of Helmsley. Must be
seen first from the Rievaulx Terraces, part of
an 18thC landscaped park. The Cistercians
founded the monastery on the banks of the
River Rye in 1131. The Early English choir
and presbytery have good stone ribbed
vaults, arcading and moulded capitals. The
140-foot-square cloister is surprisingly
complete.

Scarborough Castle J3
Scarborough, N. York. This is the castle that
Edward II gave to his favourite, Piers
Gaveston. Situated on a headland it surveys
a narrow neck of land that links it to the
mainland. Today it remains a mass of 13thC
walls and dykes—it looks pretty frightening,
even the Germans had a go at it from the sea
in 1914.

Scarborough Castle, N. York

Skipton Castle   D5
N. Yorks. Perched on a rock, the castle towers above the town. Built in the 13thC, it is unique in being still fully roofed, though it was repaired after being besieged for 3 years in the Civil War. See the huge kitchen, the 50-foot-long banqueting hall and the dungeons.

Unusual buildings

Abbeydale Industrial Hamlet   F9
Abbeydale, S. York. ½ mile SW of Sheffield. A complete picture of industrial life, from workers' cottages to a 200-year-old steel and scythe works where the manufacture of a steel-edge tool can be traced from the raw material to the finished product. There is also a grinding wheel and a 1584 water-driven Shepherd Wheel—a cutler's grinding wheel.

The Ashton Memorial   A5
Lancaster, Lancs. England's own Taj Mahal, built in 1909 to commemorate the life of a local merchant peer. A vast Portland stone edifice that is crowned by a high dome, you have to climb an elaborate staircase to reach it from Williamson Park.

The Druid's Temple   E4
Nr Masham, N. York. William D. Danby wanted to express his mystical leanings when he set about building a copy of Stonehenge (smaller and not to scale) on the moors, in the 1820s. It is a very spooky spot and should be visited in the dark when the luminous lichens glow.

Port Sunlight   A8
Cheshire. Built in the early 20thC as a model town for the employees of Lever Brothers, soap manufacturers. Almost every known style of European architecture has been plundered to inspire the domestic and public buildings; the result is a fascinating *fin-de-siècle* village that is unique. The amazing variety of houses sits in a green setting—a curious mixture of sylvan vista and practical allotments. The whole place is dominated by the ever present soap works and the air of benevolent capitalism.

Quarry Bank Mill   C8
Styal, nr Wilmslow, Cheshire. A well preserved cotton mill, designed in the simple Georgian Vernacular tradition in 1784. The mill is surrounded by a complete village of small cottages, all situated in lovely woodland.

Railway Viaduct   C8
Stockport, Cheshire. A solid brick viaduct built about 1850. The railway threads its way between riverside warehouses and crosses the river on giant piers. The setting of the great structure is typical of the Industrial Revolution that created this cotton town in the 19thC.

Sisters Folly   A7
Ormskirk, Lancs. In the 14thC 2 rich sisters agreed to build a church for the town, but they couldn't agree about giving it a spire or a tower. So they compromised and now the church has both. This must be the country's first folly.

Houses & gardens

Arley Hall Gardens   C9
Arley, Cheshire. 19 miles S of Warrington off M6. A patchwork quilt of a garden with lots of interest. The flag garden was made on the site of an old rubbish tip; the herb garden ornament came from Piccadilly Circus and the fish garden has stones engraved with epitaphs to a favourite horse. There is a marvellous avenue of clipped holm-oaks.

Bramham Park   F6
Boston Spa, W. York. 5 miles S of Wetherby. A friendly, lived-in stately home built for Lord Bingley, Lord Chamberlain to Queen Anne, in 1698 and still occupied by his descendants. Good pictures by Reynolds and Kneller. The park is delightfully laid out with great beech hedges, and vistas leading to temples or obelisks. *Closed winter.*

Burnby Hall Gardens   H5
Pocklington, Humber. 13 miles E of York. The place to see water-lilies. Over 50 different species in 2 lakes that started their life as trout ponds. Fascinating collection of hunting and fishing trophies from around the world.

Burton Agnes Hall   J5
Burton Agnes, nr Bridlington, Humber. A comfortable, unspoilt Elizabethan (1598–1610) country house full of carved and panelled rooms. Inside a collection of paintings includes some unexpected French impressionists. *Closed winter.*

Burton Agnes House

Burton Constable Hall   K6
Nr Hull, Humber. ½ mile N of Sproatley. Elizabethan red brick with stone trimmings. The house has very fine 18thC interiors. Good contents including rare mediaeval vestments in the chapel and don't miss the room decorated with murals of the Alice in Wonderland story. Standard stately home attractions—model railway, zoo, aviaries and traction engine rallies. *Closed winter.*

Castle Howard   J10
N. York. 6 miles W of Malton. A quite stupendous house, it is the most stately of them all. Designed by the wilful architectural genius Sir John Vanbrugh in 1699, the great façade is dominated by a superb dome. Beneath this is the great hall, one of the grandest rooms in England. Don't miss the grounds with the sublime temples and the circular mausoleum by Hawksmoor. Superb paintings and costume gallery. *Closed winter.*

Castle Howard

Harewood House   F5
Leeds, W. York. At Harewood village 5 miles from A1 at Wetherby. One of the finest of Yorkshire's great houses and the home of Lord Harewood, it was designed by John Carr and Robert Adam. The interior is a series of exquisitely decorated rooms by Adam with fine plasterwork and painted ceilings. Much of the furniture and carved window swages are by Chippendale. There is a large collection of Sèvres china and a solid line of family portraits. The park is mostly Capability Brown's work; a recent addition is the Harewood Bird Garden and butterfly collection. *Closed winter.*

Harewood House, W. York

Little Moreton Hall   **C10**
Congleton, Cheshire. One of the finest
examples of 16thC black-and-white half-
timbered houses in the country, looking so
much like a film set that you can't help but
wonder if it's a fake. But it is the real thing.
The timber frame is the structure and it has
been carved at the gable ends. It is built
around a courtyard. *Closed winter.*

Little Moreton Hall

Lyme Hall   **D8**
Stockport, Cheshire. Off A6 S of Stockport.
A 1,000 acres of moor and parkland with free
roaming red deer. Lovely gardens with a
wild dell and Italian garden bright with
flowers. The Hall, built 1346, has a secret
panel behind a portrait of the Black Prince.

Newby Hall   **F4**
N. York. 3 miles SE of Ripon. An elegant
17thC mansion later redesigned and
extended by Robert Adam. The gardens lead
down to a beautiful river and you can
wander about freely among the old-fashioned
roses or the enchanting sunken parterre
garden of misty blues and greys. Don't miss
the Gobelin tapestries or the classical statues.
Closed winter.

Newby Hall, Yorkshire

Ravenshurst   **B7**
Bolton, Gt. Manchester. Off A58 W of Bolton.
A beautiful collection of all types of roses,
with water gardens, terraces and pergolas.
Also a lovely sunken garden. Full of interest
all year round.

Speke Hall   **A8**
Nr Liverpool, Mersey. A long, low, gabled,
black-and-white timbered house which dates
from Tudor days. The rooms are beautifully
panelled and carved and full of attractive
furniture. It is a refreshing place to visit,
only 7 miles from busy Liverpool.

Studley Royal   **E4**
N. York. 4 miles SW of Ripon. A supremely
elegant garden of sweeping lawns, grand
vistas and huge expanses of water.
Throughout are well-placed Classical
ornamental buildings. The romantic ruins of

the great Cistercian monastery of Fountains
Abbey add to the haunting, mysterious
quality of this park.

Tatton Park   **C9**
Cheshire. 3½ *miles N of Knutsford on Ashley
Rd.* Fifty-four acres of woodland and
ornamental gardens planned by Humphrey
Repton, with a surprising variety of styles
and periods dwelling together in apparent
harmony. The fernery of 1856, with its
jungle atmosphere and giant New Zealand
tree ferns, is in contrast to the very English
serenity of the mile-long lake, its calm
ruffled only by the many waterfowl. There is
a 1,000-acre deer park and many specimen
trees and shrubs. Perhaps the most delightful
part is the Japanese garden, complete with
Shinto temple upon a tiny island, and
approached by an attractive bridge. There
are authentic Japanese plants, stone lanterns
and rock work. *Closed winter.*

Tatton Park, Cheshire

Victoria Park   **A7**
Southport, Mersey. Although not strictly a
garden, it is noteworthy for the outstanding
collection of hardy perennials which
flourish in a half-mile roadside stretch of
herbaceous border on the edge of the park in
Rotten Row. At its best in August.

Museums & galleries

Abbey House Museum   **E6**
Kirkstall, Leeds, W. York. Once the
gatehouse of Kirkstall Abbey, and now a folk
museum. Among the many exhibits are
costumed dolls, musical instruments and 3
'streets' of houses, shops and cottages that
once stood in the Leeds area.

The Ashworth Museum   **C7**
Turton Tower, Chapletown Rd, Turton, Lancs.
A fine collection of weapons including
blunderbuss, rapiers and flintlocks. Also
brasses and the Timberbottom skulls. *Closed
winter.*

Bankfield Museum and Art Gallery D6
Haley Hill, Halifax, W. York. A
comprehensive collection of costume, fabric
and textile machinery. Local history,
archaeology and natural history. Also the
Duke of Wellington's Regimental Museum.

Batley Art Gallery   **E6**
Market Place, Batley, W. York.
Contemporary paintings and drawings
including the works of L. S. Lowry, Francis
Bacon and Graham Sutherland.

**Blackburn Museum and
Art Gallery**   **B6**
Library St, Blackburn, Lancs. Coins, English
watercolours, mediaeval manuscripts and
over 1,200 Japanese prints. There are also
primitive weapons and African tribal
costumes.

**Bradford City Art Gallery
and Museum**   **E6**
Cartwright Hall, Bradford, W. York.
Collections relating to West Riding include
natural history, Roman coins, and electric
tramcars once operating in the streets of
Bradford. Also some fine paintings by
Vasari, Gainsborough, Reynolds, Corot,
Sickert and Sargent.

City of Liverpool Museums   **A8**
William Brown St, Liverpool, Mersey. Many
fine treasures are gathered here. Greek,
Roman and Egyptian antiquities, Anglo-
Saxon jewellery, armour, Liverpool pottery,
African masks and figures and horsedrawn
and steam road vehicles. There is also an
aquarium and planetarium.

Grosvenor Museum   A9
Grosvenor St, Chester, Cheshire.
Archaeological exhibits come from the
Roman legionary fortress of Deva. Many
inscriptions and sculptured stones,
instruments of torture, mediaeval pottery and
Anglo-Saxon coins.

Grove Rural Life Museum   B1
Andreas Rd, Ramsey, IOM. Victorian house
with garden and outbuildings. Attractive
period rooms, household displays, costumes
and toys, agricultural gear, vehicles and a
horse-drawn threshing mill.

Manx Village Folk Museum   A2
Cregneash, IOM. A typical Manx village with
thatched houses including a furnished
crofter-fisherman's cottage, weaver's shed,
smithy and joiner's shop. *Closed winter.*

Manx Museum, Douglas, IOM

Nautical Museum   A2
Bridge St, Castletown, IOM. Housed in a
200-year-old boat-house, there are models of
deep sea vessels, local fishing boats and a
reconstructed sailmaker's workshop. Star
attraction is the 'Peggy' a schooner-rigged
armed yacht. *Closed winter.*

Pilkington Glass Museum   A8
Prescot Rd, St Helens, Mersey. Glass-making
through the ages is illustrated here. An
exquisite collection including an ancient
Egyptian god-figure.

Royal Pump Room Museum   F5
Harrogate, N. York. Opposite Valley Gardens.
Local history, Yorkshire china, toys,
costumes and Victoriana are housed in the
Pump Room. The old sulphur well is here
too, with an exhibition of the history of the
springs.

Ryedale Folk Museum   H3
Hutton-le-Hole, N. York. Set in one of the
prettiest villages in the North York Moors
National Park. Illustrating life in an
agricultural community over the past 400
years. Many tools, appliances, furniture, an
Elizabethan glass kiln and a blacksmith's
shop.

Sheffield City Museum   F8
Weston Park, Sheffield, S. York. The world's
largest collection of cutlery appropriately
resides here. Some date from the stone age.
Also Old Sheffield Plate.

Temple Newsam House   F6
Temple Newsam, W. York. A magnificent
treasure house full of English paintings and
silver; the birthplace of Lord Darnley.
During the reign of Elizabeth I it was a
centre of English and Scottish intrigue. Now
owned by Leeds Corporation and well
maintained.

**Tonge Moor Textile
Machinery Museum**   C7
Tonge Moor Rd, Bolton, Gt. Manchester. A
superb collection of textile machinery
including Crompton's mule, Hargreave's
jenny and Arkwright's water frame.

Town Docks Museum   J6
Queen Victoria Sq, Hull, Humber. Shipping
and the fisheries of Hull are represented
here. A good display of 'Whales and
Whaling' shows Hull's importance in the

days when Britain took thousands of whales
from the sea around Greenland. *Closed
winter.*

Wakefield City Art Gallery   F7
Wentworth Terrace, Wakefield, W. York. A
fine collection of 20thC art including works
by Henry Moore, Barbara Hepworth, Sicker,
Sutherland and Alan Davie.

**West Park Museum
and Art Gallery**   D9
Prestbury Rd, Macclesfield, Cheshire. Egyptian
antiquities, Victorian paintings and a stuffed
giant panda.

**Whitby Literary and Philosophical
Society Museum**   J2
Pannett Park, Whitby, N. York. A fine
collection of fossils and flint weapons, relics
of Roman occupation, and trappings of
Captain Cook who sailed to Tahiti from
Whitby. *Closed winter.*

Whitworth Art Gallery   C8
Oxford Rd, Manchester, Gt Manchester. Fine
collections of watercolours, prints and
textiles. Turner and the Pre-Raphaelites are
well represented. Coptic and Peruvian
cloths, Spanish and Italian embroideries.

York Castle Museum   G5
Tower St, N. York. One of the most
important folk museums in the country.
Kirkgate, with its cobbled street of original
Victorian shop fronts, lamp-posts, cabs and
stage coach is fantastic, and very popular.
Also the Edwardian Half Moon Court with a
gaslit pub and a gipsy caravan.

Botanical gardens

Churchtown Botanic Garden   A7
Mersey. N of Southport. Of greatest interest
here is the Victorian fernery with a good
collection grown amidst moss, water and
rock. Outside is a pretty rose garden and a
colourful display of carpet bedding with
summer annuals.

Harlow Car   E5
*N. York. 1½ miles from Harrogate on Otley
Rd.* The Wisley of the north, being the show
gardens and trials area of the Northern
Horticultural Society. Formed in 1948 to
illustrate the type of gardening and planting
that could be possible in the colder, more
difficult northern climate.
Apart from a splendid heather garden, there
are some fine specimen azaleas and
rhododendrons in a woodland setting which
follow the drifts of daffodils and narcissi
which have now naturalised. There are good
herbaceous plants, interesting trial beds and
greenhouses, a water garden and a splendid
rose garden. Plants can be purchased.

**Liverpool University
Botanic Gardens**   A9
Ness, Wirral, Cheshire. The gardens were
started by Arthur Kilpin Bulley at the turn
of the century. The heather garden is said to
be one of the best in Britain. Also rose
gardens with demonstration beds tracing the
development of the rose from the Chinese to
the present hybrids.

Zoos, aquaria & aviaries

Bridgemere Wildlife Park   B10
Nantwich, Cheshire. This 30-acre park was
one of the first of its kind in this part of the
country, with over 90 different species of
European animals and birds. Rare deer,
foxes, otters, puma, wolves, wildcats and
birds of prey.

Chester Zoo   A9
Upton-by-Chester, Cheshire. Outsized
describes this excellent zoo: 333 acres of
land, a 30-foot waterfall in the Tropical
House which houses 200 free-flying birds of
85 species. Also apes, crocodiles and
nocturnal animals. Probably second only to
London Zoo in size and variety. To see it
all, take a conducted tour on a canal

waterbus. Look for the rare pigmy hippo, mountain gorilla, and both black and white rhinos. Beautiful plants and gardens too.

Curraghs Wildlife Park **A1**
Isle of Man. 1 mile E of Ballaugh Bridge.
This is a bird and botanical sanctuary within a designated nature reserve and wildlife park. Many birds to be seen in the walk-through aviary and wading birds' aviary. Also sea lions, deer, pumas and penguins and a Noah's Ark for the children. *Closed winter.*

Flamingo Park **H4**
Kirby Misperton, Malton, N. York. Super-progressive zoo and walk-through safari park exhibiting over 1,100 animals in natural surroundings. The spacious 360 acres contain performing dolphins and a jungle cruise, sea lions and crocodiles. Also a tropical house and children's farm, a wild west city and fun fair.

Harewood Bird Garden **F6**
Harewood House, Leeds, W. York. This bird garden offers flamingoes wandering by the lake, penguins seen underwater through a glass-sided pool, and a tropical house with birds at liberty. Included are snowy owls, macaws and humming birds. An added attraction is Harewood House, designed by Adam with a park laid out by Capability Brown.

Knowsley Safari Park **A8**
Knowsley, Mersey. 3 miles NE of Liverpool. A wide variety of animals in natural surroundings on 450 acres, including tigers, cheetahs, elephants and white rhino. There is a dolphin show, pets corner and amusements for the children.

Manx Cattery **B2**
Nobles Park, Douglas, IOM. Breeding house owned by Douglas Corporation for preserving the Manx Cat strain. Cats exported throughout the world.

Marineland Oceanarium and Aquarium **A4**
Morecambe, Lancs. Guaranteed professional performances from the sea lions, dolphins, seals, penguins and chimpanzees who dive, toot and drink tea to order. In the aquarium see the origin of your turtle soup (green turtle), your tortoiseshell comb (hawksbill turtle) and the fish for your chips (marine life from Morecambe Bay).

Port Erin Aquarium **A2**
Port Erin, IOM. Local fishes and invertebrates at the Marine Biological Station (a teaching and research department of the University of Liverpool). *Closed winter.*

'Winged World' **A4**
Morecambe & Heysham, Lancs. Nr Heysham Head Entertainment Centre. The tropics transplanted in Britain. See scarlet ibis, spoonbills, toucans, fruit pigeons, many flying free in this conservatory-aviary landscaped with banana palms. In the children's zoo prosaic lambs rub shoulders with white-eared marmosets bred in 'Winged World'. Don't miss the flying fruit bats.

Nature trails & reserves

Eaves Wood Nature Trail **A4**
Silverdale, Lancs. N of Lancaster. Start from Woodland Hotel or Waterslack. 1¼ miles. Natural and managed woodland, with interesting flora on limestone pavement. Guide from National Trust, 27 Springbank, Silverdale; Waterslack Farm; local post office; National Trust and Lake District National Park Information Centres.

Leighton Moss Nature Reserve **A4**
Leighton Moss, Lancs. Nr Silverdale, reached via Yealands from A6 N of Carnforth. A large reedbed with open water. Details from RSPB, The Lodge, Sandy, Beds.

Malham Tarn Nature Trail **C4**
Field Centre, Malham Moor, Settle, N. York. 1½ miles. A gentle walk looking at birds, trees, geology and pleasant views of the Tarn. Leaflet available from the Field Centre.

Ravenscar Geology Trail **J2**
Nr Scarborough, N. York. Start from road junction nr Raven Hall Hotel. 4 miles. Impressive cliff scenery and of considerable geological interest. Noted for fossils. Guide available at local shops and cafés.

Rivelin Nature Trail **E8**
Rails Rd, Western Sheffield, S. York. 2 miles. A scenic walk in the valley of the River Rivelin. The dams which once provided water power for the cutlery forges have been restored and the area has now reverted to its natural state. Leaflet available from Rivelin Post Office or Sheffield Recreation Dept, Meersbrook Park, Sheffield.

Slurring Rock Nature Trail **D6**
Hardcastle Crags, Hebden Bridge, Halifax, W. York. 1 mile. A scenic area of woodland and valley clearings with abundant birdlife, small mammals and flora. Leaflet available from the starting point at The Lodge.

Spurn Peninsula Nature Reserve **K7**
6 miles S of Withernsea, Humber. Off B1445 Easington to Kilnsea road. 3½ miles. 757 acres of land and foreshore with sand and shingle. Plenty of bird life all year round. Starting point from Warren Cottage. Further details from Yorkshire Naturalists' Trust, 20 Castlegate, York, N. York.

Tatton Park Nature Trail **C9**
Cheshire. From Knutsford via A50 and A5034. Start within the Park. 1½ miles. Birds of mixed woodland and a mere which is well known for winter wildfowl, breeding great crested grebes and black tern on passage. Further details from County Hall, Chester, or Manager, Tatton Park, Knutsford.

Birdwatching

Bempton Cliffs **K4**
Humber. Turn left in Flamborough to Bempton village; a small road leads to the cliffs. While much of the area is an RSPB reserve, access is unrestricted along the clifftop public footpath. Huge numbers of seabirds breed in a spectacular colony, with tens of thousands of kittiwakes and a large population of guillemots and razorbills. Puffins, fulmars and herring gulls are also present, and the small gannet colony (the only one on the mainland of Britain) is a particularly noteworthy feature. Permits are not required.

Dee Estuary **West A9**
Hilbre, Cheshire. An estuary noted for very large numbers of passage and winter waders, a variety of other winter birds and numerous winter wildfowl. The best area is around West Kirby and Hilbre, with the islands of Hilbre, Little Hilbre and Little Eye; the Marine Lake at West Kirby is also worth a look.
The islands are accessible on foot from West Kirby, which you should leave at least 3 hours before high tide, the best route being from Little Eye north to the main island. Permits are required for the main island from Hoylake UDC, Hoylake, Wirral, Cheshire.

Derwent Floods **H6**
Derwent Valley, Humber. 6 miles NE of Selby via A19 N from Selby. Turn onto A163 to Bubwith 1 mile past Barlby. Work N from Bubwith and left onto B1228. This and other minor roads in the area cover the best spots. Visit in February and March when the floods bring duck, often in spectacular numbers. It is regularly used by a sizeable flock of Bewick's swans.

Flamborough **K4**
Humber. N from Bridlington via B1255 and B1259. Has breeding kittiwakes and is a very good vantage point for seeing passing seabirds—including spring and autumn migrants.

Morecambe Bay   **A4**
*Lancs. The best viewing areas are from
Heysham to Morecambe and Hest Bank, most
of which is beside A5105.* This immense intertidal area holds the largest concentrations of
winter passage waders in Britain, and the
numbers of oyster-catchers, knot and dunlin,
for example, are often spectacular. Also quite
good for wildfowl, notably sea duck and
sawbills. There are good shore walks at
Lower Heysham (minor roads from
Heysham) and Hest Bank (cross the railway
north of the station).

Southport   **A7**
Mersey. A very good area, easily accessible
from the town itself, for waders and winter
wildfowl. The Southport Marine Lake is
good for sea duck; Hesketh Park Lake has
various roosting duck. The whole shore is
good for waders—the pier is one place to
look at. Several thousand pink-footed geese
roost out on the sands and feed at nearby
Martin Mere and the mosses between
Southport and Scarisbrick, and Lydiate and
Hightown.

Brass rubbing

The following is a short list of churches that
have brasses for rubbing. Permission is
almost invariably required.
Cheshire. Wilmslow, Macclesfield.
Gt Manchester, Mersey & Lancs. Childwall,
Manchester Cathedral, Ormskirk, Sefton,
Winwick.
N. York, Humber. Allerton Mauleverer,
Brandesburton, Cottingham, Cowthorpe,
Harpham, Ripley, Topcliffe, Wensley, York
Minster.

Fossil hunting

Visit the local museum. Its fossil collection
usually states where individual fossils have
been found. When visiting quarries always
seek permission to enter if they look
privately owned or worked. Be careful of
falls of rock.

Cheshire
But for a small area of lower lias on the
Shropshire border, Cheshire is almost
entirely made of Triassic sandstones and
marls laid down in desert conditions. Almost
completely unfossiliferous but for rare
fossilised reptile footprints and bones found
in large-scale quarrying operations. In
addition much of the area is covered by
glacial drift in which it is sometimes possible
to find small shells of recent aspect.

Lancashire
Lancashire proper is mainly carboniferous
with a strip of unfossiliferous Triassic
sandstone in the west. The eastern uplands—
Bowland Fells and the west side of the
Pennines—are largely millstone grit with few
fossils, but for the carboniferous limestone
hills around Clitheroe and Ribblesdale which
contain many fossils: corals, bryozoans,
brachiopods, algal reefs, bivalves and
gastropods. The lower land to the west
around Manchester is of coal measures
poorly exposed and with few fossils. Plant
remains and rare shells may turn up in coal
workings and tips.

N. York
Main collecting areas are in the Jurassic
rocks which are best exposed in the cliffs of
the coast: the Liassic rocks are famous for
fossils in the line of cliffs and the foreshore
from Redcar in the north to Whitby and
Robin Hood's Bay in the south; upper
Jurassic beds may be seen around
Scarborough and inland around Hackness.
The middle lias in the escarpment to the
south of Guisborough were formerly worked
for iron ore and the tips and old workings
contain iron-stained fossils. Upper Jurassic
corallian beds may be collected in scattered
small exposures in the west of the Vale of
Pickering to the west of Malton.

Scarborough and Whitby Museums have
collections of local fossils.

Humberside
The area is largely made up of Cretaceous
and Jurassic rocks. The chalk forms the
upland areas, the Wolds, where small
quarries are scattered around, and reaches
the sea in the cliffs around Flamborough
Head to the north. A ridge of chalk runs
south to the Humber with some large
quarries towards the southern end, and
middle and upper Jurassic limestones are
exposed in places to the west of it as in
South Cave, with ammonites, belemnites,
sea-urchins, occasionally fish and reptiles,
bivalves and gastropods.

W. York
Largely carboniferous rocks—in the west the
Dales of lower carboniferous limestones, in
the east the upper carboniferous coal
measures of the Yorkshire coalfield. It is a
feature of carboniferous limestone that it
forms areas of thin soil cover, so that
exposures of the rock are numerous. The
best known areas are around Malham and
Ingleton and the valleys of Wharfedale,
Wensleydale and Swaledale.
South from this area the Pennines consist of
the upper carboniferous millstone grit series
which though largely unfossiliferous does
contain a few goniatites and bivalve shells.
The coal measures form a belt of strata
running from Leeds south to Sheffield and a
few fossils, eg plants, may be found. Lower
Palaeozoic rocks with a few fossils (trilobites
and graptolites) are found in the Howgill
Fells on the Lancashire border and small
areas around Ingleton.

Forests

Macclesfield Forest   **D9**
Cheshire. Though little remains wooded
today, Cheshire's eastern hill country around
the silk-weaving town of Macclesfield was
formerly a royal forest and hunting ground.
A profusion of grassy hills rises steeply from
rippling streams—the Dean, the Bollin and
the Dane—that wander west to the Cheshire
plain, past attractive black-and-white half-
timbered farmhouses. Good walking country.
If you motor expect fierce gradients on
narrow, winding by-roads.

Forest of Rossendale   **C6**
Lancs. This, with the neighbouring Forest of
Trawden, comprises the hill country of east
Lancashire, north of Manchester. Once a
mediaeval hunting ground, it saw the growth
of the Lancashire textile industry using first
wool, then cotton, from a cottage industry
based on local sheep with water power, to a
coal-based technology with world-wide export
trade. Breezy moorlands still separate
bustling manufacturing towns like Bury,
Burnley and Blackburn.

Trough of Bowland   **B5**
Lancs. The Trough or Forest of Bowland
holds the course of the River Hodder, a
tributary of the Ribble, which winds down
past Clitheroe towards Preston. Surrounded
by high falls, the Trough holds stone-built
farmsteads in tree-clad folds of green
pastures. Its restful, harmonious scenery
merits a leisurely tour. Whalley, near
Blackburn, has an old church and abbey
ruins, for Bowland was once a Cistercian
sheep-walk.

Hills & mountains

Calder Fell and Clougha Pike   **B5**
Lancs. On either side of Wyersdale, source of
the River Wyre, these bold hills stand out
above Lancashire's northern coastal plain,
just south of the county town of Lancaster.
Inland their closely-grazed sheep walks rise
to Ward's Stone (1,856 feet) and Sykes' Fell
(1,707 feet), high points of the Bowland hill
range. 'Pike', from Norse *pikr*, means a
pointed hill; 'fell' is Norse for mountain.

Langstrothdale Chase   C4

N. York. A wilderness of high fells amid the headwaters of the west-flowing Rivers Lune and Ribble, and several Yorkshire Dale streams, Langstrothdale once formed a mediaeval chase or hunting territory. Roads are few, but the hills and dales, largely open pastures, can be explored from the tiny stone-built towns of Sedbergh, Hawes, Askrigg and Leyburn on the north, Pateley Bridge, Grassington and Settle to the south, and Ingleton on the west. The highest hills, all around 2,300 feet high, are Great Shunner Fell, Ingleborough, Pen y Ghent, Buckden Pike and Great Whernside.

Pendle Hill   C6

Lancs. Lancashire's central hill, Pendle, raises its odd, wedge-shaped form to a height of 1,851 feet above the Ribble Valley, between Clitheroe and Burnley. The name embodies the old Celtic word of *pen* for headland or hilltop. Its broad slopes, often hidden in mists, formed the mediaeval forest of Pendle, wild country indeed until the industrial towns of Nelson and Colne grew up on the south-east. To the west and north all is unspoilt farmland rising to high, far fells.

Rivington Pike   B7

Lancs. Above the village of Rivington, midway between Bolton and Chorley, the Pike rises to 1,498 feet as a western outlier of the Pennines, with views over the whole South Lancashire plain. Rivington reservoirs at its foot send water gathered from the high Belmont moorlands to Liverpool.

Moors & dales

Cheshire Plain

Cheshire. Most of Cheshire forms a broad plain, a few hundred feet above sea level, with a clay soil over sandstone. It is all well farmed, with year-round green pastures and a pond in every field. Little rivers meander through wooded clefts, and good roads make exploration easy.

The Fylde

Lancs. This flat coastal plain between the Rivers Lune at Lancaster and Ribble at Preston is well farmed with dairy cattle, pigs and poultry, though otherwise featureless. The Fylde coast is now a 15-mile-long promenade from Blackpool to the Fleetwood fishing harbour, but its broad sandy beach, washed every tide, survives and it's usually sunny. The main river, the River Wyre, flows from Wyersdale near Garstang to Fleetwood.

North York Moors   G2

N. York. This splendid National Park in N. Yorkshire extends over 600 square miles from a rugged cliff-bound coastline between Middlesborough and Scarborough towards Northallerton and Thirsk in the Vale of York. The central and northern moors are broad expanses of heather, over 1,200 feet above sea level. They rise on their north-western border to the steep-sided Cleveland Hills, whose western slopes carry extensive forests of pine and larch.

Vale of York

Running through the heart of Yorkshire, from Darlington on the Tees in the north to Doncaster on the Don in the south, the Vale of York forms a level plain with a warm sunny climate, ideal for prosperous farming. The walled city of York, with its tall Minster towers, rises in the centre, and at intervals good roads run through prosperous market towns like Selby, Wetherby, Ripon, and Thirsk, each with its bridge across a river, and a historic church.

Yorkshire Dales and Pennine Moors

All the west of Yorkshire, along the high Pennine Chain, is dales country. The rural regions north of the industrial part of W. Yorkshire, from Skipton and Ilkley north to County Durham, comprise the Yorkshire

Dales National Park. A typical dale is bounded at its head, and down both sides, by fells or moorlands, around 2,000 feet above sea level. These open, unfenced treeless areas of heather and many species of grasses are grazed by neighbouring farmers, who hold ancient rights to pasture sheep, cattle and ponies 'in common'. The sheltered dale bottom holds a string of pastures and meadows, bounded by stout dry-stone walls, with stone-built barns and farmsteads at regular intervals, and grey stone villages, each with its church, set a few miles apart. A tree-lined river flowing over occasional waterfalls courses down the dale, giving it its name, and is followed by a winding by-road. Until recently every steading housed an independent farmer, possibly a descendant of Scandinavian settlers who gave this region its wealth of harsh-sounding Norse place names. Today, with fewer men needed for the land, many houses have become holiday or retirement homes for wealthy people from northern industrial cities. But the peaceful Dales scenery is safeguarded, preserving magnificent country for leisurely wanderings by car or afoot.

Outstanding northern dales include Swaledale, Wensleydale, Nidderdale and Wharfedale.

Yorkshire Wolds

Humber. In the old East Riding of Yorkshire, between the busy commercial port of Hull and the seaside resort of Scarborough, the Wolds rise as a broad whale-back of chalk, 40 miles long, 10 miles across and from 400 to 800 feet high. This is all well farmed pastoral country. The underlying chalk is dramatically exposed in the sheer cliffs of Flamborough Head.

Swaledale, N. York

Rivers

River Derwent

N. York. The Yorkshire Derwent rises high on the North Yorkshire Moors north of Scarborough, within sight of the North Sea. Leaving the hills through a lovely wooded valley near Hackness, it turns inland to wind through the level Vale of Pickering to York.

Rivers Lune and Ribble

Lancs. In north-west Lancashire the River Lune gives its name to the city of Lancaster, the Lune *castra* or Roman fort, and hence to the whole county. It rises high on breezy uplands, and flows south to this small industrial seaport.

The River Ribble, beginning farther east, takes a parallel course south past the beautiful, though nowadays little-wooded, ancient forest—or Trough—of Bowland, through Clitheroe to Preston. Below this big industrial town and minor port it broadens into a wide, muddy estuary.

River Mersey

The Mersey, from the Norse *myr sjo*, or marshy lake, draws its name from its broad, muddy, tidal estuary between Liverpool and Widnes (the wide *ness* or headland). It is fed by several small Pennine rivers, including the Goyt, the Etherow, the Tame and the Irwell, each with an industrialised valley. Near Warrington it is canalised as part of the Manchester Ship Canal. At Liverpool it is crossed by ferry boats and tunnels. Dangerous sandbanks fringe its final seaward outlet. Most of Cheshire is drained by small Mersey tributaries, notably the River Weaver, winding over its pleasing plain.

Rivers Ouse and Humber

Several of Yorkshire's major rivers converge and unite at or near the cathedral city and county town of York to become the Ouse, a broad, winding navigable river. It has carried in turn the ships of Anglian and Danish settlers and the war-galleys of invading Norsemen. Below Goole the River Ouse broadens out into the broad tidal estuary called the Humber, flowing east past the port of Hull to the North Sea at Spurn Head.

Yorkshire Dales Rivers

N. York. From the 2,000-foot-high Pennine Chain, which forms a classical water-parting, the Yorkshire Dales rivers run eastwards towards the North Sea. Every major river rises on high, misty, rain-soaked and peaty moorland, and after a rapid descent, often over waterfalls, through picturesque, well-farmed uplands used for stock-raising, takes a winding course over a lowland flood plain. Reservoirs are frequent in the uplands, to meet the region's immense water demands for industry and domestic use. From north to south the succession of Dales rivers run: the Swale and Ure from Wensleydale; the Nidd from Nidderdale and the Wharfe, all coming within the Yorkshire Dales National Park. Then in the industrialised south of the county you will find the Aire, the Calder and Don.

Canals

The canals and navigable rivers in this area range from the wide and heavily used industrial waterways of South Yorkshire to the beautiful meandering course of tiny rural canals like the upper Peak Forest Canal and the Trent and Mersey Canal. The geography of all these waterways is of course much affected by the Pennine Hills, the great ridge that runs north to south all the way from Scotland to Derbyshire. The Pennines have effectively divided Lancashire from Yorkshire since the Ice Age, and it was only when 3 canals—the Rochdale Canal, the Leeds and Liverpool Canal, and the Huddersfield Narrow Canal—were built to cross these great hills that effective communication and trade was opened up between the 2 regions.

The Aire and Calder Navigation

This waterway, which runs from Leeds to Goole, with branches to Selby and Wakefield, is of interest as the only really busy trading canal in this country. It is based on the River Aire, which has been at least partly navigable for many centuries. The countryside it passes through shows considerable signs of long-established mining activities, and is nowadays mostly unattractive. But the navigation is fascinating for the coal barges, oil tankers and miscellaneous trading craft that plough constantly up and down. Much of the traffic is coal from the collieries of South Yorkshire to Goole for onward shipment in large sea-going freighters—often in trains of little compartment boats hauled by a tug. At Goole the compartment boats are lifted right out of the water by tall gantries and turned upside down, spilling their cargo into the holds of the waiting ships. This unusual but efficient technique was evolved at the beginning of this century, and has been very much the basis of the Aire and Calder's continued prosperity to this day. Things to see: Goole Docks; the big locks at Ferrybridge, Castleford and Pollington; and the interesting waterway 'crossroads' at Castleford. There is also a shipbuilding yard at Knottingley.

The Leeds and Liverpool Canal

This is the only one of the 3 trans-Pennine canals that is still open to navigation, and it is very handsome indeed. On the Lancashire side, it leaves the outskirts of Liverpool and enters the little valley of the River Douglas. The Five Rise Locks at Bingley raise the water level 60 feet, an impressive feature, which in the 18thC was considered to be one of the world's leading engineering achievements. From here onwards it assumes an industrial guise, passing through many manufacturing towns of east Lancashire before reaching a long tunnel on the summit level. Some very fine scenery leads into Yorkshire, where the canal enters the valley of the River Aire. The upper part of Airedale is rural and of great scenic interest (the Yorkshire Dales are nearby) but at Keighley the industrial towns begin, and lead inevitably to the vast manufacturing conurbation of Leeds.

Archaeological sites

Aldborough Roman Town   **F4**
N. York. 1 mile SE of Boroughbridge. Site of the Roman town of Isurium Brigantum, it was laid out on a conventional grid plan with a central public forum. Has 2 of the finest surviving mosaic pavements in Britain. Museum with a good collection of relics.

Blackstone Edge   **D7**
5 miles W of Ripponden, W. Yorks. The finest example of a paved Roman road in Britain. The surface is made up of small blocks with occasional transverse ribs. The road lies in a deep cutting through the peat, and in parts the natural rock has been used for the road surface.

Bleasdale Circle   **B5**
Nr Garstang, Lancs. A Bronze Age 'henge' monument consisting of a stone circle constructed around a burial site. Excavation has shown that the whole monument was surrounded by a timber palisade. *Accessible with permission from the farm.*

Castle Hill   **E7**
Almondbury, nr Huddersfield, W. York. One of the major hill forts of the Brigantes, the Iron Age people of the Pennines area, with multiple earth bank and ditch defences. Its ancient name was Camulodunum, 'Fortress of Camulos', after a Celtic war-god. Its fine strategic position led to later use as the site of a mediaeval castle, and a Victorian tower now stands on the hill.

Chester   **A9**
Cheshire. Roman Deva, one of the 3 fortresses that were occupied virtually throughout the Roman period. The permanent garrison was the XX Valeria Victrix legion, whose symbol of a boar can be seen stamped on tiles in the Grosvenor Museum. The mediaeval city walls were built on the line of the fortress walls, and Roman work survives on the north side, and on part of the east side near the cathedral; the south-east corner tower foundations can be seen in Newgate. The amphitheatre, which was probably used as a parade-ground as well as for games, is now open to the public, and the nearby Hypogeum is laid out as a garden with Roman pillars. The Grosvenor Museum has models of Roman Chester and a collection of Roman objects, including carved stones, stamped water-pipes, and lead ingots from the Flintshire mines.

Danes' Graves   **J5**
Nr Driffield, Humber. Humberside is the richest area for burial mounds of known Iron Age date, and the group at Danes' Graves contains a large number of small barrows. Some of the excavated burials have produced dismantled chariots buried in the grave.

The Devil's Arrows   **F4**
Boroughbridge, N. York. An important group of 3 standing stones, probably dating from the Bronze Age. The gritstone shafts are set up in line, and the deep vertical ribbing is due to weathering of the millstone grit.

Isle of Man   A2

From the 8th to the 13thC most of Britain suffered to some degree from the Viking invasions, and the Isle of Man was one of the areas completely taken over and settled. Vowlan Fort is typical of the small promontory forts of this date, with a strong landward defence of earth bank and ditch; there is just room inside for one of the characteristic Viking 'longhouses'. It may belong to the initial raiding period, as it guards a landing-place and commands wide views of the sea. The Braaid probably represents a more permanent settlement site, and contains large round and long buildings. Tynwald Hill was the assembly place for the Tynwald, the Manx parliament, during the Viking period.

Ribchester   B6

Lancs. Roman Bremetennacum, a fort site occupied by a squadron of Sarmatian cavalry from the area of modern Romania. The foundations of 2 granaries are visible, with small internal columns to raise the floor level and so prevent rodents from reaching the grain. The porch of the White Bull is supported on 2 Roman columns, and various pieces of Roman stonework can be seen re-used in the church walls. Ribchester Museum contains Roman finds.

Scamridge Dykes   J3

On moorland between Pickering and Scarborough, N. York. The finest of the complex series of boundary banks, probably of Iron Age date, characteristic of the Yorkshire Wolds and the North York Moors. Built to prevent the wandering or theft of livestock.

Scarborough Signal Station   J3

Scarborough, N. York. The best preserved of the series of Roman signal stations built along the Yorkshire coast in the 4thC. Their function was to provide a look-out for raiders.

Thornborough Circles   E4

Nr Ripon, N. York. A major Bronze Age 'henge' monument consisting of 3 concentric earthen circles, approximately 550 feet across overall. It has 2 opposed entrances, and a ditch on each side of the earthwork. An earlier feature is the 'cursus', a pair of parallel banks with external ditches of which little now remains. As commonly occurs with henge monuments several burial mounds were constructed nearby.

York   G5

N. York. The Roman fortress of Eboracum was established in AD71; it became one of the leading cities of the Roman Empire and the capital of Lower Britain. Like Chester, most of the fortress is buried under the mediaeval city, but the 'multangular' tower at the west corner, with the foundation of its interior walls, and a section of wall beside it, are basically Roman and can be seen in the museum gardens. There was also a large civilian town south-west of the fortress. Hadrian used it as a base for his campaigns northwards and the emperors Septimius Severus and Constantine both stayed there. The Yorkshire Museum, Museum St, York, has a large collection of Roman material including inscriptions, a sculptured head of Constantine, and objects carved from Yorkshire jet.

Footpaths & ancient ways

The Cleveland Way   G3

Opened in 1969 the Cleveland Way stretches from the cross in the square at Helmsley across the top of the North York Moors with spectacular views of the Vale of York, round to meet the coast at Saltburn, then on south down the coast through Whitby to Filey. It is contained wholly within the North York Moors National Park and most of the coast path runs along some of the most outstanding coastal scenery. It is one of the waymarked long-distance footpaths and there is accommodation along the route.

Lyke Wake Walk   G3

This is a 40-mile-long moorland walk across the North Yorkshire Moors from Scarth Wood Moor, near Osmotherley, to Wyke Point at Ravenscar. Start from Scarth Wood Moor and continue to Scarth Nick where the scarp stares down over the Cleveland Plain. From here to the sea the Walk is across miles of bog and heather, over Coalmire to Botton Head, the highest point of the North Yorkshire Moors, to Shunner Howe, with sweeping views almost to the sea. From Hamer continue to Simon Howe where the bogs are murky and difficult to cross, and on to Ravenscar and Wyke Point, a short distance beyond.

The Pennine Way   C4

A strenuous high-level path through predominantly wild country from Derbyshire to the Scottish border, the Pennine Way winds along the backbone of England. At Crowden the route enters Cheshire, then leads north-west to Wessenden Head Moor, past the reservoirs, across White Moss and Black Moss, and beyond to where the Roman road climbs over Blackstone Edge and on to Broadhead Drain, the eastern side of Edge End Moor, Heptonstall Moor, Keighley Moor, Cowling, Lotheradale and Thornton. At Thornton stop by Market Street and see the house where the Brontës were born.

The track across Fountains Fell was once used by packhorses carrying coal. Pen-y-ghent, famous for its purple mountain saxifrage in April, and Ingleborough are in the heart of pot-holing country. Descending Dodd Fell towards Hawes there are magnificent views across the smooth, green dales of Wensleydale.

The Wolds Way   K4

The northern stretch of the Way begins at Filey Brigg on the N.Yorkshire coast, and continues to Thixendale.

Leave the steep cliff on Filey Brigg, and take the road to Muston village via cinder track and hedgerow. On from Fordon to Ganton, with the Vale of Pickering and the glowering Wold escarpment in view, and on to Settrington, the loveliest village along the route.

Wharram Percy is the most famous of the 'lost villages', abandoned around 1500 and has been excavated for several years. Just beyond, Raisthrope is another deserted site, and ½ mile away is Thixendale.

The southern half of the Way starts at Thixendale, and the surrounding area has some of the broadest views along the Way, with Garrowby Hill rising to 807 feet, the highest point of the Wolds.

Regional sport

Cricket and cricketers

It is in Lancashire and Yorkshire that the cricket battles become serious, and the Wars of the Roses live again on the turf.
Yorkshire County Cricket Club. Headingley Cricket Ground, St Michael's Lane, Leeds. Tel 52865.
Lancashire County Cricket Club. Old Trafford Ground, Manchester. Tel 061-872 0261.

Fell walking   D4

The Yorkshire Dales offer some of the best opportunities in the country for fell-walking as there is an excellent network of footpaths and bridleways. This is a tough occupation calling for boots and strong legs; full details from any National Park Information Centre.

Football

The crowded lengths of Merseyside have become a northern football capital over the years. The best known team in the area, or perhaps even in Britain, is Manchester United, though Liverpool have now taken over to become the country's top team.
Everton Football Club. Goodison Park, Liverpool. Tel 051-521 2020
Liverpool Football Club. Anfield Rd,

Liverpool. Tel 051-263 2361
Manchester City Football Club. Maine Rd,
Moss Side, Manchester. Tel 061-226 1191/2
Manchester United Football Club. Old
Trafford, Manchester. Tel 061-872 7771.

Pigeon racing
Competitive racing of pigeons is a
widespread sport, but particularly so in the
industrial areas of Northern England. Many
races are in excess of 400 miles and starting
points on the Continent, such as for the
classic Avranche Race, are by no means
uncommon.

Pot holing
Also known as 'caving'—lots of opportunities
in Yorkshire and Lancashire for
underground ramblings. As long as the rules
are followed accidents can be avoided.
Strictly for those with subterranean tastes
and under experienced guidance.

Rugby League
There are 2 varieties of rugby played in
Britain, Rugby Union and Rugby League.
Rugby League is a game developed from
Rugby Union, which used to be played by
the clubs in the Northern Rugby League.
There are only 13 men to a team, as opposed
to 15 in Rugby Union. The game is confined
principally to Yorkshire and Lancashire
where many of the smaller industrial towns
have their own teams.

Festivals & events

There are a number of local festivals and
events—contact the local Information Centre
for details.

Bathing Beauty Contests
These famous contests, where a possible
Miss World could be spotted, are held
throughout the summer at the large resorts
of Blackpool, Morecambe and Fleetwood.

Bolton Festival of Music   C7
Bolton, Lancs. The festival lures many
visitors to this industrial area. The orchestras
and soloists are the best in the country. The
biennial festival is devoted to individual
composers such as Mozart and Brahms. *Mid
Sept.*

Chester Festival   A9
Chester, Cheshire. The main event in this
major arts festival every 3 years is the
Chester Mystery Plays. Written by a local
monk in 1375, they are now presented in the
very latest theatrical genre. *Late June.*

Harrogate International Festival   F5
Harrogate, N. York. A mixed arts festival;
presenting the world's foremost artists,
orchestral and choral concerts, celebrity and
chamber recitals, drama, literary events and
the visual arts. Exhibitions and children's
entertainments. *Early Aug.*

**York Mystery Plays and
Festival of the Arts**   G5
York. Every third year the 14thC York cycle
of 48 miracle plays is faithfully re-created by
200 York citizens. Staged dramatically in the
ruins of St Mary's Abbey or on wagons
around the city in mediaeval style, the plays
cover the whole Bible story, from Creation
to the Last Judgment. The arts festival is
another major attraction with some excellent
performers.

Special attractions

Blackpool Tower   A6
Blackpool, Lancs. Britain's answer to Mr
Eiffel's little steel confection in Paris. Believe
it or not there is a zoo on the top floor
housing a lion, tiger, bear, dingo and hyena.
At the bottom is an aquarium which houses
amongst other things a red-tail shark. The
tower is by the sea front; look up and you
can't miss it.

Jodrell Bank Telescope   C9
Jodrell Bank, nr Knutsford, Cheshire. One of
the largest radio telescopes in the world. A
great dish 250 feet in diameter supported by
5 lesser elliptic paraboloids—it tracked the
first sputnik. They look like massive abstract
sculptures. The Concourse Building has an
exhibition, demonstrations and a model radio
telescope for visitors to operate.

**North York Moors
Railway**   H3
*Pickering, N. Yorks. 7 miles SW of Whitby
off A169.* At Goathland Station is an
interesting collection of locomotives and
coaches from the steam age. The
preservation society have purchased the 6
miles of ex-BR track from Grosmont to
Pickering and are running trains. *Closed
winter.*

National Railway Museum   G5
Leeman Rd, York. No one could pass up the
opportunity of seeing such a superb
collection of steam locomotives, rolling stock
and smaller relics of the railways' heyday.
North-eastern England was the cradle of the
railways and here you can see a complete
panorama of British railway history.

Stump Cross Caverns   D4
*N. Yorks. Between Pateley Bridge &
Grassington on B6265.* The best place in the
country to see stalactites and stalagmites, but
here you will have to like your caves floodlit
in technicolour. The mystery of these caves
has gone but they are easier to visit than
most potholes—you won't need a torch.

The White Horse   G4
Kilburn, N. Yorks. A giant horse cut into the
turf of the Hambleton Hills, it is really big;
over 300 feet long. You can see it clearly
from a distance of 20 miles and 20 people
can picnic quite comfortably on the grass
eye.

Regional food

Cakes
Eccles and Chorley cakes are the best
known of this region—both being a spicy
currant mixture enclosed in pastry. Fig or
fag pie and simnel cake are traditional
Mothering Sunday offerings. Parkin is made
for 5th November.

Cheese
Lancashire is a crumbly white cheese. When
young it has a mild and creamy flavour
which lends itself to toasting. Most of the
cheese is consumed locally and is popular as
part of a ploughman's lunch.
Wensleydale is produced in the Dales of
Yorkshire. This white cheese has a unique
lingering flavour and is sweet and velvety in
texture. Blue cheese is available but much
rarer.
Cheshire the oldest of English cheeses is
made in 3 colours—red, white and blue—the
latter happening rarely and purely by
accident.

Isle of Man
The island is noted for its scallops, queenies
and lobster—scallops are known as 'tanrogan'
locally. The Manx kipper is traditionally
smoked, and it is illegal to dye them as they
often are elsewhere.

Lancashire hot pot
This traditional dish comes from Burnley
and was devised when oysters were plentiful.
Oysters also feature in Scouse—the Liverpool
version of their lamb, potato, onion and
kidney stew. Pickled red cabbage and spice
vinegar are the accompaniments.

Yorkshire pudding
Surely one of Britain's best known dishes,
which is traditionally eaten with roast beef.
The pudding should be light and well risen
and in Yorkshire it is often served before the
meat with a little gravy—to help make the
meat go further!

Northumbria and the Lakes

The Lake District and England's most northerly counties are two contrasting regions both hilly, the lakes have a green mellowness while Northumbria is high and remote. Cumbria takes in the last northern thrust of the Pennines that leads to the fells and pikes of the Lakes. The coast on the west alternates between the wild and the industrial from coal mining under the sea to the cool power of Britain's first atomic plant at Calder Hall. Wordsworth and the lakeland poets have said almost all that can be said about the green glories of the Lake District. The neighbouring large towns have tapped the almost inexhaustible water supply and the weekend invasion of small boats and water skiers means you have to travel a bit further off the beaten track to find the peace that delighted the poets.

County Durham still has a grey, gaunt, silent quality best seen in the high fells of Weardale and Upper Teesdale where blue gentians can be found in remote hollows. You cannot fail to be impressed by the rugged splendours of the east coast and along the silver spine of Hadrian's Wall you may yet hear the clang of the Roman centurions patrolling the farthest reaches of their civilisation.

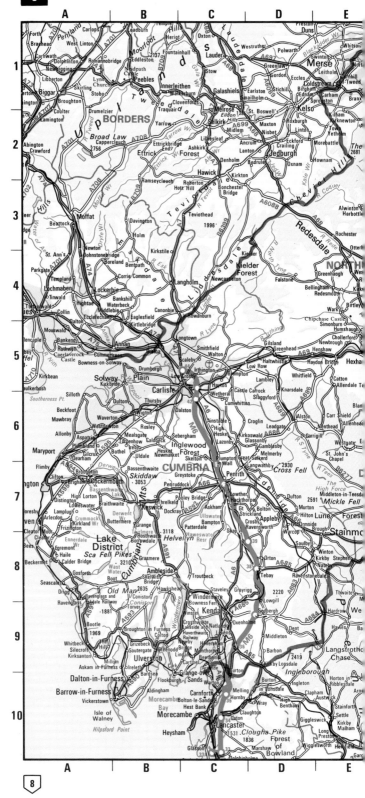

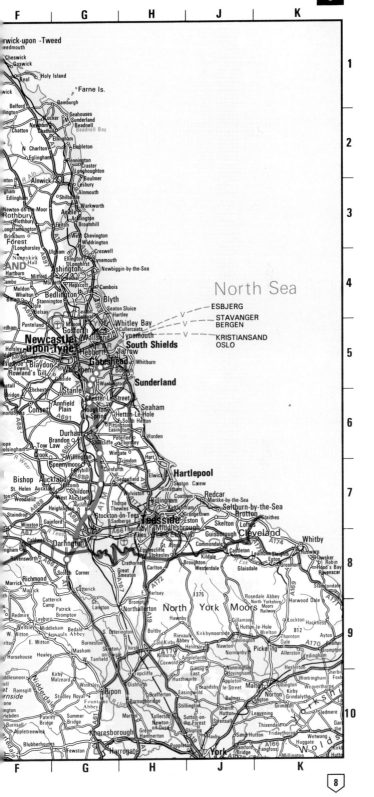

North Sea

ESBJERG
STAVANGER
BERGEN
KRISTIANSAND
OSLO

The coast

Alnmouth **G3**
Northumberland. Pop 700. EC Wed. A
boisterous undulation of red-roofed houses
beside the estuary of the River Aln. The
port for Alnwick in the 12thC, later an
important grain-port and now a centre for
yachting. Has one of the oldest golf courses
in England.
A quiet resort with a good sandy beach.

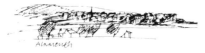
Alnmouth

Bamburgh **G1**
Northumberland. Pop 400. A popular and
unspoilt resort. It has a very fine 13thC
church, but the town is dominated by the
massive fortress of Bamburgh Castle, once
the seat of the kings of Northumbria. Many
films have been made using the fortress and
the sandy beach. A museum commemorates
Grace Darling, the heroine who rescued the
survivors of a shipwreck.

Berwick-upon-Tweed **F1**
*Northumberland. Pop 11,600. EC Thur. MD
Wed, Sat.* The northernmost town in
England, crouching behind an encircling
town wall. Once an important Elizabethan
port, and now a busy market centre, it was
for centuries a bone of contention along the
Scottish-English border. Of interest—the
18thC town hall; the remarkable town
defences; the 18thC barracks; the castle; the
3 bridges; quay walls. Sandy beach.

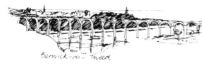
Berwick-on-Tweed

Craster **G2**
Northumberland. Pop 500. A diminutive
village set in a tiny fishing harbour. A poetic
memorial, built by the Craster family in
1906 for a brother who died in far-off Tibet.
Of interest—Craster Towers; the gaunt ruins
of Dunstanburgh Castle. Sandy beach.

Cullercoats **H5**
Northumberland. A small village between
Whitley Bay and Tynemouth it still manages
to retain an air of independence. It is a
huddle of houses spread-eagled on a cliff top.
Of interest—18thC church of St George,
built with 13thC fervour. Fine sandy beach.

Drigg **A8**
Cumbria. Pop 600. Unruly houses lead to
high dunes which curve down to a broad
sandy beach. Of interest—the late Georgian
Carlton Hall; the church of St Peter. Sandy
beach.

Grange-over-Sands **B10**
Cumbria. Pop 3,600. EC Thur. A sweeping
vista of sand and sea and right across the bay
to Morecambe, 9 miles south. Known as the
Torquay of the North because of its warm
spring temperatures which makes it a
popular place at that time of the year. Of
interest—Holker Hall; Cartmel Priory and
gatehouse 5 miles north-west.

Hartlepool **H7**
Cleveland. Pop 96,900. EC Wed. Complete
with charters from King John, Elizabeth I
and Victoria. The 13thC parish church
stands on the site of St Hilda's 7thC abbey.
An important sea port. The modern town
has remains of 13thC walls. To the south are
long sandy beaches.

Holy Island (Lindisfarne) **F1**
Northumberland. Pop 200. A lyrical place. It
was the cradle of Christianity in England
during that twilit period following the

Roman exodus. There is a small village, a
16thC castle built on a knoll, the ruins of
the 11thC priory, and a farm or two.
Swimming is safe.

Holy Island

Jarrow **H5**
Tyne & Wear. Pop 29,000. Part of the
teeming industrial Tyneside, it was the scene
of intense poverty and the starting place of
the famous Hunger March in 1933 following
the closing of the shipyards. Of interest—St
Paul's church and the remains of the
monastery in which the Venerable Bede
spent his life in the 8thC; Jarrow Hall.

Maryport **A6**
Cumbria. Pop 11,600. EC Wed. Once a busy
port until the docks silted up, it is now a
quiet holiday resort full of narrow streets.
The Romans built a fort here. Of
interest—the Roman altars and relics in the
local museum; the Maryport Maritime
Museum. Good sandy beaches.

Millom **B9**
Cumbria. Pop 7,100. EC Wed. Tucked into a
corner of the Duddon Estuary is this bright
and animated little stone-built town
silhouetted by Black Combe mountain. Of
interest—the 14thC castle; the late Norman
church of the Holy Trinity; the Folk
Museum. A good centre for fell walking.
Marshy shore and low tide mud flats.
Superb sands nearby.

Newbiggin-by-the-Sea **G4**
Northumberland. Pop 10,700. EC Wed.
Huddled in a horseshoe of sand is an
indiscriminate cluster of cottages. A stone
breakwater provides harbour for a handful of
brightly coloured fishing boats. Look at the
13thC church of St Bartholomew. White
sandy beach; good swimming.

Ravenglass **A8**
Cumbria. Pop 300. EC Sat. An endearing
fishing village of cottages wedged between
shingle foreshore and a steep wooded ridge
of land behind. Of interest—the Eskdale
Miniature Railway; the 4-acre Roman fort;
and nearby Muncaster Castle.

Redcar **J7**
Cleveland. Pop 39,000. EC Wed. Not a very
beautiful town to look at but the place to go
for sand and sea. There are 3 miles of sandy
beaches and good facilities for children to
the east of the town. The neighbouring
towns of Coatham to the north and Marske
and Saltburn to the south have turned this
stretch of coast into a playground for the
workers of Teesside. Beaches are sandy,
patrolled by lifeguards, and safe for
swimming. Mackerel fishing, and fresh crab
and lobster for sale on Redcar's beaches.

St Bees **A8**
Cumbria. Pop 1,200. EC Wed. Now
developing as a resort the village grew up
round a 7thC priory and a Norman abbey of
the 12thC. The public school of St Bees was
founded in 1587. A broad shingle bank
reinforces the sandy beach. Superb headland
walks.

Seahouses **G2**
Northumberland. Pop 2,000. A tiny
unchanged harbour in a small fishing village,
but also a lively resort with modern
amenities. Good fishing, and sailing at
Beadnell 1½ miles south. Boats make regular

trips to the Farne Islands, famous with birdwatchers, but seal also breed here. Marvellous beach to the north of the village with miles of National Trust sand dunes.

Seascale   **A8**
Cumbria. Pop 2,000. Pleasant and uncommercialised place along a gentle sea shore. Of interest—St Cuthbert's church built in 1890; 18thC Seascale Hall; Windscale and Calder Hall atomic stations. Sandy beaches.

Silecroft   **A9**
Cumbria. An ordinary village leads to a spectacular stretch of sandy beach, open-ended to the sky.

Silloth   **A6**
Cumbria. Pop 2,700. EC Tue. Broad, practical streets of simple yet dignified terraced houses make up this mid-Victorian holiday resort.
Separated from the sea by an expansive green and a wave of pine trees. There are exhilarating views to the Scottish coastline. Pleasant sandy beach, but watch the tide!

South Shields   **H5**
Tyne & Wear. Pop 96,900. EC Wed. MD Mon, Sat. A popular seaside resort and busy port stranded at the southern shore of the Tyne Estuary. It was here that the world's first lifeboat service began. Of interest—Arbeia Roman fort and museum at the north end of Baring Street; the museum with the prototype model of the first lifeboat designed in 1790 by William Wouldhave.
Mile-long pier sheltering a sandy beach. Safe bathing.

Sunderland   **H5**
Tyne & Wear. Pop 214,800. Having wisely chosen to throw in its lot with Cromwell during the Civil War, Sunderland then benefited from a judicious takeover of the coal trade from Royalist Newcastle. Able to trace its origins back to the 7thC, the town has also been a busy shipbuilding centre since the 14thC. Of interest—the stuffed walrus in the museum, said to have inspired Lewis Carroll's 'The Walrus and the Carpenter'; the football team; the modern civic centre.
Wide beaches with safe bathing.

Tynemouth   **H5**
Tyne & Wear. Pop 67,000. EC Wed. At its best a bright and bracing place terracing the cliff tops to the north of the river mouth. This was the fashionable part in the early 19thC when Tynemouth was a popular watering place. Of interest—ruins of the 11thC priory; the 14thC castle ruins; the terrace houses in Dawson Square, Bath Terrace and Allendale Place. Magnificent sea front, particularly Long Sands.

Tynemouth Priory

Warkworth   **G3**
Northumberland. Pop 1,200. EC Thur. Dominated by its 12thC castle, an alive little town above a loop of the Coquet. Of interest—the 14thC fortified bridge complete with tower; the 18thC Bridge End House; the Norman church of St Laurence. Sandy beach 1 mile away.

Whitehaven   **A7**
Cumbria. Pop 26,700. EC Wed. MD Thur, Sat. A conspicuous and charming place of agreeable streets running down to a busy

harbour. Inspired by Christopher Wren's plans for rebuilding London after the Great Fire. Its port rivalled Liverpool and Bristol in the 18thC. Of interest—St James's church built 1752–53; the 17thC Town Hall; the old quay of 1687; the 18thC Whitehaven Hospital.

Whitley Bay   **H5**
Tyne & Wear. Pop 37,800. EC Wed. MD Tue, Thur, Sat. A busy and bracing place. The most popular seaside resort for Tyneside with lots of seaside attractions. Sandy beaches provide safe bathing.

Workington   **A7**
Cumbria. Pop 28,400. EC Thur. MD Wed, Sat. An industrial town that is still growing, on the site of what was once an important Roman town and fort. Workington is a town that prospered on the exploitation of coal. Of interest—the delightful Portland Square; St John, Washington Street; 14thC Workington Hall. A mud and sand beach.

Inland towns & villages

Alnwick   **G3**
Northumberland. Pop 7,100. EC Wed. MD Sat. An undulating market town full of poker-faced buildings and narrow mediaeval streets, hidden in the shadow of an enormous 12thC castle. Of particular interest is the Hotspur Gate (1450); 15thC church of St Michael; the Lion Bridge, built in 1773 by John Adam; the 18thC town hall.

Alston   **D6**
Cumbria. Pop 2,100. The highest market town in England. A friendly place which slides down a steep cobbled hill. From Market Place you can see the bleak heads of the Pennine hills peeping above the rooftops. Alston was an important mining town until the early 19thC. Look at the 19thC town hall; 18thC Friends' Meeting House; Clarghyll Hall.

Ambleside   **C8**
Cumbria. Pop 2,600. EC Thur. MD Wed. Now the centre of the Lake District, and always full of walkers, this grey-slated little town has a literary pedigree as long as your arm with its memories of the Wordsworths, the Coleridges, Ruskin and others. Of interest—the church of St Mary (1850–54); the curious Bridge House; 19thC Rothay Holme. Boating on nearby Lake Windermere.

Bridge House, Ambleside

Appleby-in-Westmorland   **D7**
Cumbria. Pop 2,000. EC Thur. MD Sat. This grey-stone place is divided by the broad River Eden. The main street has a touch of Georgian gentility. Look at the 12thC castle; the church of St Lawrence; the 16thC moot hall. Appleby Fair in June is the meeting place of gipsies from all over Britain.

Bampton   **C7**
Cumbria. Pop 400. EC Sat. A gentle rustic village, quietly meditating in open landscape. Pleasant Georgian church.

Barnard Castle   **F7**
Durham. Pop 5,400. EC Thur. MD Wed. A market town ideally situated for exploring Teesdale and the rugged west Durham moors. High on the banks, still guarding a crossing point of the River Tees, stands the ruined castle. Of interest—the market cross; the marvellous Bowes Museum; Egglestone Abbey.

Barrow-in-Furness   **B10**
Cumbria. Pop 64,000. EC Thur. MD Wed, Fri, Sat. An uncompromising place as hard as nails, famous as an industrial and shipbuilding town. It was here that the monks of Furness Abbey smelted iron with wood in the early 13thC.
The present town developed in the mid 19thC when the local iron field was first exploited. Of interest—the 19thC church of St James; the town hall; Abbey House built 1913-14 by Lutyens; Furness Abbey.

Bellingham   **E4**
Northumberland. Pop 1,200. A small-scale market town which once had an iron industry. 13thC church has an interesting vaulted nave.

Belsay   **F4**
Northumberland. Pop 500. One of those imperious gestures by which a whole village was bodily uprooted from in front of the drawing room windows of Belsay Hall and neatly rebuilt in a less intrusive part of an estate. This one happened in the 1830s, and the result was an attractive arcade of sandstone shops in the Italianate style. Of interest—the 19thC Belsay Hall; also the ruins of 14thC Belsay Castle.

Blanchland, Northumberland

Blanchland   **F6**
Northumberland. Pop 200. EC Tue. A gentle, dignified and unspoilt village in a narrow leafy valley of the Derwent with wild moorland above. Look at Blanchland Abbey, founded in 1165.

Bolton   **D7**
Cumbria. Pop 300. A ruddy-faced village, standing on the west bank of the River Eden. The north and south doorways of the church of All Saints are Norman. Look at the ruins of Bewlay Castle.

Bothal   **G4**
Northumberland. A leafy, sleepy hamlet with an interesting 14thC miniature castle of the tower house type. The little 13thC church has an unusual triple bell tower.

Bowness-on-Windermere   **C8**
Cumbria. Pop 3,500. EC Thur. A wistful place with an aura of Victorian England's heyday. Italianate villas and barge-boarded and gabled boarding houses are built out across the waters of Windermere. Of interest—Belle Isle; 19thC Storrs Hall; Broadleys, Voysey's masterpiece built in 1898; the marvellous stained glass in St Martin's church.

Brampton   **C5**
Cumbria. Pop 4,000. EC Thur. MD Wed. A handsome sandstone town which stands round a hearty market place. Of interest—19thC church of St Martin with fine stained glass designed by Morris and Burne-Jones; the Roman quarry 2 miles SW still bears the inscriptions scratched by their workmen; Sands House Curio Museum; Talkin Tarn Country Park.

Branxton   **E1**
Northumberland. A short footpath by Branxton Church leads to the simple monument to the 25,000 Scottish and English soldiers who died on Flodden Field a few hundred yards south of the village in September 1513. The spot marks where James IV was slain during the bloody battle after the Scottish Army crossed the Tweed.

Brough   **E8**
Cumbria. Pop 500. EC Thur. An ancient market town with the remains of a castle standing on the site of a Roman fort. There are lovely wooded walks, though beware of Army firing ranges. Of interest—the mediaeval church; the annual horse fair.

Buttermere   **B6**
Cumbria. Pop 255. Set at the north end of Lake Buttermere in a beautiful valley. There is a tiny 1841 church and walks through lovely woodland and bracken to several beauty spots. An ideal centre for exploring the Lake District National Park, in particular the Cumbrian mountains and valleys.

Bywell   **F5**
Northumberland. An enchanting village, on the edge of the coalfields, in a secluded bend of the Tyne. Every sign of a once lively town has gone. All that remains are 2 magnificent parish churches, a fortified manor house and a mediaeval cross. Bywell Castle is a particularly well preserved tower house of the 15thC.

Carlisle   **C5**
Cumbria. Pop 71,500. EC Thur. MD Wed, Sat. A lively commercial and industrial centre as well as the foremost agricultural centre of the north of England. Since Roman times, Carlisle has been a key defence and trading centre standing near the western end of Hadrian's Wall. Warred over by the Picts, sacked by the Vikings, and conquered by the Normans it then became a perpetual bottleneck for the border wars between England and Scotland. The small sandstone cathedral was begun in 1130. Of interest—the castle founded in 1092; the 15thC Tithe Barn; the Citadel built by Sir Robert Smirke in 1807; the 18thC town hall.

Carlisle, Assize Courts

Cockermouth   **A7**
Cumbria. Pop 6,400. EC Thur. MD Mon. A sharply etched market town with an optimistic air. Mary Queen of Scots held court here; Fletcher Christian, leader of the mutiny on the Bounty, and Wordsworth were sons of the town. Of interest—the 12thC ruined castle; church of All Saints; Wordsworth House which is now a museum.

Coniston   **B8**
Cumbria. Pop 1,100. EC Thur. The climbing centre for Coniston Fells. A weather-beaten village which combines a mining history past with a tourist industry present.

Corbridge   **F5**
Northumberland. Pop 2,900. EC Thur. A Tyneside town full of sombre stone-built houses. It was here Ethelred, King of Northumbria, was slain in AD796 and King Ragnal the Dane defeated the English and

Scots in AD918. Visit the Roman camp of Corstopitum; the Saxon church of St Andrew and the National Tractor and Farm Museum at Newton.

Corbridge

Crosby Ravensworth   **D7**
Cumbria. Pop 500. Wrapped in antiquity it sits surrounded by the fells. St Lawrence church, enveloped in splendid trees, is invigorating. Nearby is the site of a large Iron Age Settlement.

Darlington   **G7**
Durham. Pop 85,900. EC Wed. MD Mon. An energetic little town which grew from a humble Anglo-Saxon settlement, via a lively market and textile town to become the birthplace of the railway. The locomotive engineering shops were closed in 1966. St Cuthbert's with its needle-sharp spire is a fine Early English church.

Durham   **G6**
Durham. Pop 29,500. EC Wed. MD Sat. Dominated by its cathedral, monastery and castle, the old city struggles over a rocky peninsula wrapped in a loop of the Wear. Founded in AD875, the present cathedral was begun in 1093. Of interest—Durham University; some 18thC corners in South Street and Old Elvet Street; the Gulbenkian Museum of Oriental Art; the Durham Light Infantry Museum; the 13thC monastic ruins of Finchale Priory 2 miles to the north-east.

Edmondbyers   **F6**
Durham. Pop 200. Crisp as an icicle, the village stands high in the moors. Have a look at the 12thC church; also the giant reservoir built on the River Derwent.

Elsdon   **E4**
Northumberland. Pop 200. A solitary moorland village, once the Norman capital of Redesdale. A handful of mainly 18thC houses squashed round a large triangular green. The 14thC church of St Cuthbert has an interesting bell-cote. Look at the remains of the 11thC motte-and-bailey castle; the stone circles on Catcleugh Hill; the 14thC tower house to the north of the church.

Elsdon, vicar's pele   Pele tower Corbridge

Etal   **E1**
Northumberland. An enchanting piece of village vernacular with a sprinkling of stone and white-washed houses with the occasional thatched roofing. Of interest—the ruins of Etal Castle; the 19thC church of St Mary; the 18thC Etal Manor.

Gainford   **G7**
Durham. Pop 1,100. An unfussy place full of warmth and tranquillity. A mainly stone-built village crowded round a large green and down tight-knit streets. The accent is predominantly Georgian. Of interest—the 13thC church with fine Jacobean font cover

Gateshead   **G5**
Tyne & Wear. Pop 91,200. EC Wed. A severely practical place in a businessman's world, linked to Newcastle-upon-Tyne by 6 bridges. A fire in 1854 destroyed most of its past. Here Daniel Defoe is said to have written 'Robinson Crusoe'.

Gilsland   **D5**
Northumberland. EC Wed. When the chalybeate springs were discovered in the 19thC this gentle little village flourished briefly as a spa. It was here Sir Walter Scott met his wife. Have a look at the ambitious Spa Hotel, built 1865; the ruins of Triermain Castle, built in the 14thC and nearby sections of Hadrian's Wall.

Grasmere   **B8**
Cumbria. Pop 1,000. EC Thur. A surprising place, full of atmosphere jammed between towering crags and broad lake. To the south is a handful of houses, Town End. Here, in Dove Cottage, Wordsworth and his sister lived. Home of the Grasmere Sports every August.

Guisborough   **J7**
Cleveland. Pop 14,900. EC Wed. MD Thur, Sat. A discreet town beneath the Cleveland Hills. The long main street is tree-lined and full of unpretentious small houses. Of interest—the dovecot, a rare monastic survivor in the priory ruins; the gargantuan chestnut tree in the priory gardens and the grounds of Guisborough Hall.

Haydon Bridge   **E5**
Northumberland. A gruff stone-built village straddling the broad South Tyne. Standing alone on a hillside to the north is the old church where the mediaeval village lay. Of interest—the 14thC Langley Castle; the ruined 17thC tower of Staward Pele; the 18thC church.

Haydon Bridge

Heighington   **G7**
Durham. Pop 2,400. A handful of houses, perched on a 450-foot escarpment, in an endearing tangle round a spacious green. St Michael's is a fine Norman church.

Hesket Newmarket   **B6**
Cumbria. A fine village with a handsome wide high street complete with a rambling green and some elegant 18thC houses. Of interest—17thC Hesket Hall.

Hesket Newmarket

Heversham   **C9**
Cumbria. Pop 700. A village with a lively atmosphere spread-eagled on a hill top. The church of St Peter has a delightfully pompous Victorian tower built in the Early English style. Look at the 14thC Heversham Hall; early 19thC Plum Tree Hall.

Hexham   **E5**
Northumberland. Pop 9,800. EC Thur. MD Tue. A romantic market town spread over a hillside. It's been a tempestuous place ravaged by the Danes and pillaged half a dozen times by the Scots. The abbey, founded in AD673, made Hexham important. Have a look at the colonnaded 18thC market building; the Moot Hall, built in 1415; the 9-arched bridge built in 1785. A centre for the dales.

Kendal   **C9**
Cumbria. Pop 21,700. EC Thur. MD Wed, Sat. A grey-faced and breezy town riding a ridge of high ground along a curve in the River Kent. The largest town in the county, Kendal was an important weaving centre in the middle ages. Of interest—the prosperous Perpendicular church of Holy Trinity; the 19thC Friends Meeting House; the

earthworks of the 12thC castle; Abbot Hall, built in 1759; Little Holme built by Voysey in 1908. Good centre for Lake District walks.

Keswick B7
Cumbria. Pop 5,200. EC Wed. MD Sat. Within a short distance of Derwentwater, a poetically allusive place of twisting narrow streets. The main street has an unexpected fillip—an early 19thC town hall astride an island site.
Charles Lamb came here for holidays whilst Coleridge lived at Greta Hall. Of interest—the Royal Oak Hotel; the 3 islands on Derwentwater; Salvin's church of St John Evangelist built in 1838; the local museum.

Kirkby Lonsdale D9
Cumbria. Pop 1,500. EC Wed. MD Thur. Dark grey buildings jammed round a market square. As you wander through the town you catch glimpses of the fells. Hidden behind Market Street is the church of St Mary the Virgin with some rich Norman trappings. Of interest—the motte-and-bailey castle; the mid 19thC Market House; 16thC Abbots Hall.

Kirkby Stephen E8
Cumbria. Pop 1,600. EC Thur. MD Mon. A sprightly old market town nestling down amongst the moors. Of interest—the church of St Stephen with an elegant Perpendicular west tower; 16thC Wharton Hall.

Kirkoswald C6
Cumbria. Pop 800. EC Wed. A pretty village built of red sandstone beside the River Eden. A 2-mile walk along the wooded river banks, known as Nunnery Walks, takes you past some spectacular waterfalls. Of interest—the 13thC moated castle; the 15thC church with its Victorian tower standing 200 yards away; the College, seat of the Featherstonehaugh family since 1613.

Kirkwhelpington F4
Northumberland. Pop 200. Well heeled stone cottages stand around a 13thC churchyard in a rolling sea of farmland.

Lowther Village and New Town C7
Cumbria. Lowther village, a miniature 18thC masterpiece, consists of 2 well-mannered closes of properly proportioned houses. Not far away is Lowther New Town full of hipped-roof rusticity. Built in the late 17thC as a replacement to the old village. Of interest—the decorative remains of Lowther Castle, rebuilt by Smirke in 1806; Hackthorpe Hall, a fine Jacobean house.

Middlesbrough D7
Cleveland. Pop 157,000. EC Wed. MD Sat. Built on the River Tees in 1829 as a port for the Durham coalfields. Today it is a busy modern commercial centre, but a good place from which to tour the Cleveland hills and Durham dales. Of interest—the Captain Cook Birthplace Museum; the Dorman Museum of the natural and social history of the area; Ormesby Hall.

Morpeth G4
Northumberland. Pop 14,100. EC Thur. MD Wed. A dog-eared place with only modest signs of antiquity, and yet it's as old as the hills. Trapped in a U-bend of the River Wansbeck it has an unassuming market place; the town hall rebuilt in 1870, but originally designed by Sir John Vanbrugh in 1714; a 15thC clock tower; the ruins of a 12thC Cistercian monastery, Newminster Abbey; the 14thC church of St Mary.

Newcastle upon Tyne G5
Tyne & Wear. Pop 212,400. EC Wed. MD Tue, Thur, Sat. Dreary streets and drab houses break out into a flourishing hotch-potch of culture and comfort at the centre of one of Britain's most important cities. A dignified and exuberant place. Of interest—the church of All Saints, built in 1786; the cathedral; the 17thC guildhall; Central Station; High Level Bridge, built in 1849 by Robert Stephenson; the university; the Theatre Royal; the castle keep, one of the best preserved in England; the National Bagpipe Museum

Norham E1
Northumberland. Pop 600. One of the largest villages in the county. Eagle-eyed above it all stands the great keep of the 12thC castle on high rocks overshadowing the River Tweed.

Orton D8
Cumbria. Pop 600. A place full of earthy honesty. Have a look at Orton Hall, built in 1604; the 13thC church of All Saints.

Patterdale C7
Cumbria. Pop 700. EC Tue (winter only). A tranquil little village hemmed in by Ullswater and heady mountain peaks. Look at Patterdale Hall; the prehistoric settlement south of Brothers Water; take a steamer trip on the lake.

Penrith C7
Cumbria. Pop 11,300. EC Wed. MD Tue. An historic town. Occupied by the Celts in 500BC, and later by the Romans who built a road through it. The castle is a compact square. Of interest—the Mitre Hotel, 1669, and the Crown Hotel, 1794; the castle; the 3-acre Roman fort 5 miles along the Penrith-Carlisle road; the Wetheriggs 19thC pottery.

Peterlee H6
Durham. Pop 21,800. EC Wed. A distinctive but self-conscious new town built to accommodate 30,000 people.

Rosthwaite B7
Cumbria. EC Wed. A sprinkling of houses amongst peaks and fells. Everything sharp, bright and crisp. See the 2000-ton Bowder Stone balancing on an edge where it came to rest after falling from a crag.

Rothbury F3
Northumberland. Pop 1,800. EC Wed. An attractively situated hillside market town in the heart of Coquetdale and in the shadow of wooded hills. Of interest—Whitton, a 14thC tower house; Norman Shaw's mansion, Cragside, built in 1870, and gardens.

Rothbury

Sedgefield G7
Durham. Pop 5,300. Half asleep round a comfortable green is this pleasant small-scale market town. The 13thC church has an alert and sharp-faced nave, 17thC brasses and an 18thC organ.

Simonburn E5
Northumberland. Pop 200. Whitewashed cottages gather about a square green. Of interest—the 13thC ruined castle; the rebuilt 13thC church.

Stamfordham F5
Northumberland. Pop 1,200. A lean and lanky village green trapped by rows of 18thC houses. Of interest—the little market building; the 13thC church.

Stanhope F6
Durham. Pop 5,100. 700 feet up, with the fells all around, Stanhope is a handsome little Weardale town memorable for its lime

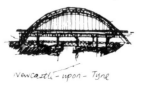

Newcastle-upon-Tyne

trees. There is a mediaeval church with the fossilised stump of a 250-million-year-old tree in the churchyard; some 18thC houses and a castle built in 1798.

Tebay   **D8**
Cumbria. Pop 700. A railway village of apparent rock-faced indifference until you get to know it. Look at the church of St James, built by the sweat of railway workers and the money of their companies in 1880. Not far away is the site of a motte-and-bailey castle, and the magnificent Lune Gorge.

Temple Sowerby   **D7**
Cumbria. Pop 300. EC Thur. Discreetly, this small scale village awakens your every sense to the pleasanter things in life. Of interest—the church of St James; Temple Sowerby Manor; Acorn Bank garden.

Troutbeck   **C8**
Cumbria. EC Thur. A handful of houses thrown casually along a spectacular and wild valley. There is some fine stained glass by Burne-Jones and Morris in Jesus Chapel; Townend is a fine yeoman farmhouse built in 1626.

Wark-on-Tyne   **E4**
Northumberland. Pop 700. EC Thur. An invigorating village round a central green on the edge of the Border Forest Park. Visit the early 19thC church of St Michael.

Washington   **G5**
Tyne & Wear. Pop 47,000. EC Wed. Once a village where the ancestors of George Washington, the American president, lived. It is now part of a growing new town. For a view of the surrounding coalfields take a trip to the top of Penshaw Hill, 2 miles south-east. Of interest—Washington Old Hall, 17thC home of the Washington family and restored with American funds; the waterfowl park; Washington 'F' Pit, where the pit-head workings of a closed down mine are preserved.

Whittingham   **F3**
Northumberland. Pop 400. This demure little place straddles the River Aln. Of interest—Callaly Castle; Eslington Hall; Whittingham Tower.

Windermere   **C8**
Cumbria. Pop 8,000. EC Thur. Formerly a small lakeside village, it was popular during the railway age, and has been a holiday centre ever since. Of interest—the 19thC church of St Mary; the splendid Gothic priory; 17thC Rayrigg Hall, Belle Isle, the only inhabited island on the lake, with a Georgian house and formal garden; Fell Foot Country Park.

Wooler   **F2**
Northumberland. Pop 2,000. EC Thur. On the edge of the Cheviot Hills it was frequently raided during the middle ages; now mainly a 19thC market town clambering eagerly up a hillside to its church tower.

Regional features

Early Christian Relics
This area is the cradle of Christianity in Britain, from where saints, monks and scholars set out to convert the whole of the country. Relics of their churches and monasteries can be seen, a lot of which date from the 7thC. From Lindisfarne Priory to the Heavenfield Cross at Chollerford; St Paul's, Jarrow; Corbridge Church; St Hilda's, Hartlepool and many others. There is a Christian Heritage trail that can be followed; details from the Tourist Board.

Fortified houses and churches
Perpetual raids from marauding Scots created problems for those outside the castle walls. From the 13th to the 16thC many houses and churches were fortified. Church towers often provided refuge with access to an upper floor being by ladder only. Marks on the door pillars of Elsdon Church,

Northumberland, are said to have been made by parishioners sharpening their swords when called from prayer to battle.
The most distinctive feature of the area is the tower house. Called pele-towers, after the old French *Pel*, meaning stake, they consisted of a barricaded ground floor for cattle; people took refuge on the first floor. The floor itself was vaulted as a precaution against fire. Living quarters were later added to many of the towers. Good examples at Corbridge, Doddington, Aydon Castle, Cresswell, Dacre and Preston Tower, Chathill.

Famous people

Dr Thomas Arnold (1795–1842)   **C8**
Foxhowe, Ambleside, Cumbria. The renowned headmaster of Rugby spent his summers at Foxhowe with his family.

Thomas Bewick (1753–1828)   **F5**
Cherryburn House, Ovingham, Northumberland. Noted for his illustrations to 'Gay's Fables', 'Select Fables', and the famous 'British Birds' this superb wood engraver was born at Cherryburn, and is buried in the churchyard at Ovingham.

Lancelot 'Capability' Brown (1715–83)   **F4**
Kirkharle, Northumberland. The landscape gardener and architect was born in Kirkharle. His debut as a landscape gardener was at Kirkharle Park, which is now a farm. Many of the country's finest houses are set in parks and gardens which he designed.

James Cook (1728–79)   **H7**
Stewarts Park, Marton, Middlesbrough, Cleveland. The Captain Cook Birthplace Museum built to commemorate the great circumnavigator who was born in Marton. He spent his childhood in Great Ayton where he attended the local village school. A granite obelisk now marks the spot on nearby Easby Moor where his cottage once stood—since transported to Melbourne, Australia.

Grace Darling (1815–42)   **G1**
Bamburgh, Northumberland. A museum of memorabilia of the family and the actual coble (local fishing boat) in which the heroine with her father, William, the Farne Lighthouse keeper, rescued the survivors of the 'Forfarshire' in 1838.

The Lake poets   **B7**
Grasmere and Keswick, Cumbria. Wordsworth's arrival at Dove Cottage attracted other poets to the Lake District. Coleridge and his family settled at Great Hall, Keswick, in 1800. Robert Southey arrived in 1803 (he and his family are buried in the churchyard in Keswick), and Hartley Coleridge came later and is now buried in the same churchyard.

Harriet Martineau (1802–76)   **C8**
The Knoll, Clappersgate, Ambleside, Cumbria. The much loved literary lioness built The Knoll, where she spent the last 30 years of her life. She entertained many of the leading literary figures of her day, and among those who visited Ambleside were Charlotte Brontë, Emerson, George Eliot and Wordsworth.

John Peel (1777–1803)   **B6**
Park End Cottage, Caldbeck, Cumbria. The immortal huntsman of the famous song, written by his friend John Woodcock Graves, was born and died here. His headstone in the churchyard depicts a whip and hunting horn.

Beatrix Potter (1866–1943)   **C8**
Hill Top, Near Sawrey, Cumbria. Beatrix Potter lived in this 17thC house. While she was busy creating her Peter Rabbit books a parade of small animals inhabited the house, from mice to rabbits and pigs. When she married and went to live on a neighbouring

farm her writing virtually ceased. *Closed winter.*

John Ruskin (1819–1900) **B8**
Brantwood, Coniston, Cumbria. Ruskin lived here from 1871 until his death. The house is now owned by the Council for Nature, and relics and paintings are on show. A fine collection of related manuscripts, drawings and photographs at the Ruskin Museum near the church. *Closed winter except by appointment.*

George Stephenson (1781–1848) **F5**
Wylam, nr Newcastle upon Tyne, Northumberland. A small stone built 1750 cottage was the birthplace of the pioneer of steam locomotion and the first passenger train.

Sir Hugh Walpole (1884–1941) **B7**
Brackenburn, Keswick, Cumbria. The New Zealand writer lived here for many years. The surrounding country was the background for many of his novels, particularly the well known 'Herries' series. He is buried in the churchyard of St John's in Keswick.

William Wordsworth (1770–1850) **B8**
Dove Cottage, Town End, Grasmere, Cumbria. Most of the poet laureate's life was centred round the Lake District. He was born in Cockermouth and grew up there and in Hawkshead and Penrith.
In 1799 he moved to Dove Cottage with his sister Dorothy. His most productive years were spent here, with Dorothy and Coleridge as constant companions, and in 1802 with his wife Mary Hutchinson. He is buried in the churchyard.

Cathedrals, abbeys & churches

All Saints **G5**
Newcastle upon Tyne, Tyne & Wear. Proud and expressive, like a trumpet voluntary. Built by David Stephenson in 1786, it towers above the quayside. Some extravagant woodwork inside.

Brinkburn Priory **F3**
Brinkburn, Northumberland. The Augustinian priory was founded about 1135 in a secluded loop of the River Coquet, and was a roofless ruin until restored in 1858. A cavern of a building, it is one of the most dignified and elegant Gothic churches in Northumberland.

Carlisle Cathedral, Cumbria

Carlisle Cathedral **C5**
Carlisle, Cumbria. Originally part of an Augustinian abbey, it became a cathedral in 1133. Only 2 bays of the Norman nave are left. Have a look at the magnificent 14thC east end.

Durham Cathedral **G6**
Durham. Begun in 1093 this is the most impressively situated of all the English

Durham Cathedral, Durham

cathedrals as it soars above the wooded cliffs of the River Wear. The Norman nave is the most spectacular in Europe.

Gibside Chapel **G5**
Gibside, Tyne & Wear. Standing in grounds of Gibside House, which were landscaped by Capability Brown, is this late 18thC chapel dressed in the most impeccable of Classical garments.

Hexham Abbey **E5**
Hexham, Northumberland. Extremes jammed up against each other in the most unpredictable of ways—brilliant in one part, dull in another. Founded in AD673, the building today consists of a patchwork of early 13thC and late 19thC pieces with a fine Saxon crypt.

Over Denton Church **D5**
Cumbria, 3 miles W of Greenhead. This small church is believed to have been built with stones from Hadrian's Wall and the chancel is probably a rebuilt Roman arch. The design is Norman, with Saxon details.

Pittington Church **G6**
Pittington, Durham. An alert and sensitive church. Originally Anglo-Saxon, it has a fine 12thC north arcade, composed of 6 round arches with bold zigzag carving and wall paintings. Pleasant Norman font.

St Andrew's **G7**
Bishop Auckland, Durham. A late 13thC church with a west tower and a 2-storey south porch. Inside there is a fragment of a carved Saxon cross of about AD800, and a 14thC cross-legged knight carved from oak.

St Andrew's **F4**
Bolam, Northumberland. A mildly mannered church with a late Saxon tower, tall and unbuttressed. Predominantly Norman interior.

St Andrew's **H5**
Roker, Nr Sunderland, Tyne & Wear. Built in 1907 by S. Prior it is a massive church with a Gothic tower above the chancel. Inside there are Arts & Crafts Movement fittings: a William Morris carpet; a Burne-Jones tapestry behind the altar; tablets by Eric Gill; and altar cross by Ernest Gimson.

SS Andrew and Peter **F5**
Bywell, Northumberland. Two unlikely miracles—St Andrew's, called the White Church because it belonged to the White Canons of Blanchland, has a fabulous Saxon Tower; St Peter's, called the Black Church because it belonged to the Benedictine monks of Durham, is pleasantly 13thC with some invigorating 11thC features.

St James **D7**
Ormside, nr Appleby-in-Westmorland, Cumbria. Overlooking Roman Fell, this Norman church is situated on a hill beside the River Eden. Its strong west tower was fortified as a defence against marauding Scots. It was here that the Ormside Cup, a Saxon piece of gold and enamel, was excavated, which is now in York. Inside there is a 400-year-old chancel roof.

St James   **A7**
Whitehaven, Cumbria. Built 1752–53 it
stands on a hill. Nothing special outside, but
it has a glowing Georgian interior, as
magnificent as anything in the county.

St John's   **F2**
Edlingham, Northumberland. A fierce little
church with half a mind to swap roles with
some fortified castle. The Norman porch has
a tunnel vault.

St John the Evangelist   **G7**
Escomb, Durham. An Anglo-Saxon church as
sharp as the north wind. Probably built in
the 7thC, it's the most complete example of
its kind. Have a look at the striking round-
headed chancel arch; the pre-Norman carved
stone cross behind the altar.

church, Escomb

St Laurence   **G3**
Warkworth, Northumberland. An imposing
and forceful monolith. A fairly complete
Norman church unique in Northumberland.
St Laurence has one of the few vaulted
chancels of 12thC England.

St Martin's   **C5**
Brampton, Cumbria. The only church by
Philip Webb. Built 1874–78 it's a jittery and
jumpy masterpiece, like a nervous prima
donna. A strange and imaginative building,
with vibrant stained glass by William Morris
and Burne-Jones.

Brampton church

St Mary's   **F7**
Staindrop, Durham. Of Anglo-Saxon descent.
The west tower, aisles and arcades are
Norman. In the 14thC the south aisle and
porch were added. The only pre-Reformation
screen in the country is here.

SS Mary and Bega   **A8**
St Bees, Cumbria. Originally part of a 12thC
Benedictine priory, an expressive and
memorable building. The doorway is an
exotic Norman masterpiece complete with
figure work and zigzag ornamentation.

St Michael's   **B6**
Torpenhow, Cumbria. Unpretentious but
beautifully proportioned church built in
1170. The interior is warm and friendly. Bell
cote and battlements are 17thC.

St Nicholas Cathedral   **G5**
Newcastle upon Tyne, Tyne & Wear. Outside
it's an affable 14thC and 15thC parish

church made a cathedral in 1882. The
joyous and distinguished 'crown spire' was
built in 1435. The interior is something
special—alert and sensitive.

Castles & ruins

Alnwick Castle   **G3**
Alnwick, Northumberland. A Border castle
which began life as a wooden motte-and-
bailey. In 1157 a stone shell-keep was built.
The Percys purchased the castle in 1309,
and by the middle of the 14thC had
assumed its present form.
Considerably restored in the late 18thC and
early 19thC. The barbican is the best in the
country. Many splendidly furnished rooms
and a magnificent grand staircase. *Closed
winter.*

Bamburgh Castle   **G1**
Bamburgh, Northumberland. A lion of a
castle, standing confidently on its own on a
precipitous outcrop of the Whin Sill. An
enormous spectacle over ¼ mile long and
covering 8¼ acres. It consists of a 12thC keep
and 3 baileys. The first castle to fall to
gunfire it was derelict throughout much of
the 18thC. It was drastically restored in the
late 19thC by the engineer, Lord Armstrong.
Closed winter.

Barnard Castle   **F7**
Barnard Castle, Durham. A violent and
agitated skeleton glowering down from a cliff
above the Tees. Built in 1150. Of
interest—the circular keep, the 14thC Round
Tower, said to have inspired Sir Walter
Scott when he was writing 'Rokeby'.

Bowes Castle   **F8**
Bowes, Durham. On A66 to Brough. A
massive keep, built for Henry II in 1171.
Made of sandstone including some re-used
Roman materials, it was meant to guard the
Yorkshire approach to Stainmore Pass over
the Pennines.

Brough Castle   **E7**
Brough, Cumbria. A majestic ruin, begun in
the late 11thC, on the site of a Roman fort,
it is perched in a dominant position above a
steep bank of the Swindale Beck.

Brougham Castle   **C7**
Penrith, Cumbria. Begun in the 12thC, it's
an impressive and explosive giant. Built on
the banks of the River Eamont, the castle is
largely late 13thC. Of interest—outer and
inner gatehouses; the keep. Nearby are St
Wilfrid's chapel and St Ninian's church.

Calder Abbey   **A8**
Calder Bridge, Cumbria. Founded in 1135 by
William de Meschines for the order of
Savigny, all that remains are the ruins of the
cloister, the nave and church aisles. Part of
the monastic buildings are tucked inside a
late Georgian house.

Carlisle Castle   **C5**
Carlisle, Cumbria. Standing on the highest
point along the Eden it guarded the west
end of the border in case of a Scottish attack.
The existing keep was built in the 12thC. Of
interest—Tile Tower; Queen Mary's Tower;
the museum.

Castle Corby   **C6**
Wetheral, Cumbria. Incorporating an ancient
pele tower and priory gatehouse the castle is
perched above the River Eden. The castle
was destroyed during the Civil War.
Surrounded by gardens, including
rhododendrons in fine woodlands, fish traps,
caves and a summer house.

Dunstanburgh Castle   **G2**
Northumberland. 2 miles E of Embleton. A
forlorn skeleton clutching the coastal cliffs. It
was a great 14thC fortress. Below was the
harbour, now blocked, which once sheltered
Henry VIII's navy.

Dunstanburgh Castle

Norham Castle

Egglestone Abbey F7
Durham, 1¼ miles SE of Barnard Castle.
Situated close to the River Tees, the abbey
was built for the Premonstratensian canons
in 1196. Now just a very romantic ruin set
in woods and water. Turner painted the
ruins. A place to visit by moonlight.

Egglestone Abbey, Durham

Finchale Priory G6
Durham. 4 miles N of Durham. Trapped in a
bend of the River Wear are the wistful ruins
of this priory. A stone chapel was built in
the 12thC on the site of a hut where St
Godric lived as a hermit. This was later
extensively enlarged by Durham Priory in
the 14thC.

Lanercost Priory C5
Brampton, Cumbria. A tranquil ruin tucked
into a secluded corner along the River
Irthing. The priory was founded in 1166 by
Robert de Vallibus for the Augustinian
canons. The church is exceptionally well
preserved.

Lindisfarne Castle F1
Holy Island, Northumberland. A tiny 16thC
fort built to defend the harbour, which never
saw action. Converted into a private house
by Sir Edward Lutyens in 1903.

Lindisfarne Priory F1
Holy Island, Northumberland. Founded by
the Benedictines in the 11thC it's a weather-
beaten dark red ruin. Much of the original
detailing was copied from Durham
Cathedral. Have a look in the museum.

Middleham Castle F9
Leyburn, N. York. On A6108 to Ripon. Built
to guard the road from Richmond to
Skipton, it is a rectangular Norman keep of
1170, and one of the largest in England: 105
by 78 feet. Ruins of the chapel and
gatehouse also remain.

Naworth Castle D5
Cumbria, NE of Brampton. Restored by
Salvin after a disastrous fire in 1844, it is
wrapped round a central courtyard. Built on
an impressive site it was begun in 1335.
Extensive alterations and additions were
made in the 16thC. Of interest—the great
hall; Lord William Howard's Tower; fine
tapestries. *Private.*

Norham Castle E1
Norham, Northumberland. Planted
menacingly on high rocks above the River
Tweed are the remains of a once powerful
border stronghold. It was built in 1160 by
Bishop Pudsey of Durham.

Shap Abbey D7
Shap, Cumbria. Founded in the late 12thC.
A wistful skeleton buried in a valley of the
River Lowther. Very little remains except
memories. Nearby are the Shap Standing
Stones, the principal of which is the
Goggleby Stone.

Sizergh Castle C9
Cumbria. 3 miles S of Kendal on A6. Since
1239 owned by the Strickland family. A
14thC pele-tower, perhaps one of the most
memorable houses of its type in the area.
There is a wealth of early Elizabethan
woodwork and some fine chimney pieces.
Beautiful gardens and lakes. *Irregular
opening. Summer only.*

Warkworth Castle G3
Warkworth, Northumberland. A domineering
bully sneering at all and sundry from the top
of a high hill. Building was begun in the
12thC, and the great keep was added in the
late 14thC. It was the setting for
Shakespeares' Henry IV.

Warkworth Castle

Unusual buildings

Calder Hall and Windscale A8
Calder Bridge, Cumbria. Calder Hall, which
was opened in 1956, was the first full-scale
nuclear power station in the world. It
consists of 2 giant cooling towers and 3
reactor buildings built like elephantine car
batteries. Windscale, opened in 1951, is now
a nuclear research centre.

The Devil's Bridge D9
Kirkby Lonsdale, Cumbria. Spanning the
River Lune, an elegant stone bridge built
with 3 acrobatically round arches. Probably
13thC.

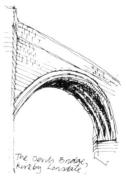

The Devils Bridge, Kirkby Lonsdale.

Dunelm House, Durham University G6
Durham. Seen at its best across the River
Wear. An alert and cheeky building skipping

along the edges of a sloping bank. Designed
by Architects Co-Partnership in 1964, it is
the university staff house and student club.
The elegant and slender footbridge is by Ove
Arup.

Penshaw Monument　　　　　　　**G5**
Penshaw, Tyne & Wear. A Doric temple
shivering in the northern light. Built in 1844
as a memorial to John George Lambton, first
Earl of Durham and first High
Commissioner to Canada. This roofless
edifice would be more at home in Paestum
than on Penshaw Hill.

Raby Castle Folly　　　　　　　　**F7**
Staindrop, Durham. Standing on a hill
behind the castle, about 25 feet high with a
long castellated façade with pairs of tapering
stone towers on either side of an arch.
Gothic windows have been painted on the
brick between the towers. The whole thing's
ludicrous but jolly.

Sharp's Folly　　　　　　　　　　**F3**
Whitton, Northumberland. Used as an
observatory and prospect tower it's a plain
round tower, 30 feet high. Built in 1720 and
designed to relieve unemployment among
stone masons in Archdeacon Thomas Sharp's
parish.

Town Hall　　　　　　　　　　　**F1**
Berwick-upon-Tweed, Northumberland. Built
1754-60 this Wagnerian town hall stands
bold as brass in the most prominent part of
the main square, Marygate, with a portico of
Tuscan columns up a high flight of stairs.
The top floor was once the town gaol. Above
is a socking great belfry.

Berwick-on-Tweed

Twizel Bridge　　　　　　　　　　**E1**
Twizel Bridge, Northumberland. A graceful,
beautifully shaped 15thC stone bridge slung
in a single 90-foot span across the wooded
glen of the River Till.

Twizell Bridge

Houses & gardens

Acorn Bank　　　　　　　　　　**D7**
Temple Sowerby, Cumbria. Set against a red
sandstone house, the herb garden is of
special interest here. There is also a
delightful walled herbaceous garden and lots
of bulbs in spring. *Closed winter.*

Askham Hall　　　　　　　　　　**C7**
Lowther, Cumbria. A 14thC tower-house
with Elizabethan wings spread round an
oblong courtyard. Fine 17thC staircase.

Askham Hall

Belsay Hall　　　　　　　　　　**F4**
Belsay, Northumberland. A lovely
honey-coloured stone house built 1810-17.
Created by the owner, Sir Charles Monck,
following studies undertaken during his
honeymoon in Athens. Raised on a podium
like a Greek temple the front façade is
punctuated by giant Doric columns; the
others by Doric pilasters. *Private.*

Belsay

Callaly Castle and Gardens　　　　**F3**
*Whittingham, Northumberland. 10 miles W of
Alnwick.* Originally built in the 13thC, much
of today's building is 17thC with Georgian
and Victorian additions. There is a fine
saloon with 18thC plasterwork; interesting
pictures and furniture. *Open Sat, Sun &
B.hols summer.*

Chillingham Castle Park　　　　　**F2**
*Alnwick, Northumberland. 6½ miles SE of
Wooler.* 300 acres of parkland surround a
mediaeval castle. In 1220 the park was
walled in, and a herd of wild white cattle
were trapped inside. Today, still living wild,
they are the country's only direct surviving
herd, saved from outbreaks of disease by
their isolation and self-sufficient save for
winter hay feeding. *Park and gardens open to
the public. Closed winter.*

Chillingham Castle

Cragside　　　　　　　　　　　**F3**
Rothbury, Northumberland. A heady and
romantic Wagnerian giant set against a
theatrical back-drop. In real life the mansion
is a turreted and bay-windowed Tudor myth
created by Norman Shaw for the first Lord
Armstrong in 1870. Some lush William
Morris glass in the library. *Closed winter.*

Cragside

Chipchase Castle　　　　　　　　**E4**
Chipchase, Northumberland. One of those
tricks that nature is usually best at. A large
mid-14thC tower crossed with a Jacobean
mansion and Georgian additions – and hey
presto, an elegant rough house. *Private.*

Chipchase Castle

Dalemain   **C7**
*Pooley Bridge, Cumbria. 5 miles SW of
Penrith.* A house of mixed history, being part
mediaeval, part Elizabethan and part early
Georgian. Surrounded by fine gardens, a
countryside park and picnic areas. Home of
the Cumberland and Westmorland
Yeomanry Museum.

Holker Hall   **C9**
Grange-over-Sands, Cumbria. W off B5278. A
Victorian park which should be seen when
the rhododendrons and azaleas are in bloom.
There are many flowering trees, and deer
wander freely. The 17thC house has some
fine woodcarvings and period furniture. Also
the Lakeland Motor Museum.

Hutton-in-the-Forest   **C6**
Cumbria. E of Skelton. Originally a 14thC
pele-tower. The exuberant bits of Jacobean
and Baroque were added with some panache
during the 17thC. Later additions date from
the 19thC.

Levens Hall   **C9**
Levens, Cumbria. A richly evocative
Elizabethan house consisting of pele-tower
and an attached hall. Of interest—the grand
staircase; plasterwork ceiling in the drawing
room.
The topiary garden is one of England's most
famous. Laid out in 1689 by Beaumont,
there are fantastic forms cut in yew and box
including 'Maids of Honour', 'Coach and
Horses', as well as birds and other shapes.
Closed winter.

**Lake District Horticultural
Society's Garden**   **C8**
Holehird, Cumbria. 2 miles S of Troutbeck. A
marvellous collection of ornamental
flowering shrubs and trees and alpine and
heather gardens.

Lingholm Gardens   **B7**
Keswick, Cumbria. SW off A66. Right on the
shore of Derwentwater it is the perfect place
for autumn walking. Beatrix Potter wrote
'Squirrel Nutkin' here. Lots of interesting
shrubs in a forest setting. A good place for a
picnic.

Lowther Castle   **C7**
Lowther, Cumbria. A gaunt shell of a once
spectacular stately home. Begun in 1806; the
architect was Smirke, fresh from Greece and
Italy. The castle stands in a 3,000-acre park.
Closed winter.

Lowther Castle

Middleton Hall   **D9**
Middleton, Cumbria. An unobtrusive manor
house built round a courtyard in the 15thC.
A Roman milestone, erected near the Hall,
marks the distance of 53 miles from Carlisle.

Moresby Hall   **A7**
*Moresby, Cumbria. 2 miles NNE of
Whitehaven.* An elaborately rusticated
building all dark and brooding. Built
1690–1700.

Muncaster Castle   **A8**
Ravenglass, Cumbria. An elaborate and
sumptuous building standing in magnificent
landscape. Completely reconstructed by
Anthony Salvin in 1862, the original castle
was built in the 13thC. Splendid collection
of furniture; some beautiful chimney pieces.
A lush 300-acre garden, with fine views over
the River Esk valley, and bird garden. *Closed
winter.*

Raby Castle Gardens   **F7**
Staindrop, Durham. NW of Darlington. A
10-acre sheltered garden famous for sweet

peas. There are also large walled formal
gardens, majestic trees, clipped yews and a
good collection of fruit trees. Herds of deer
wander at will through the 270-acre park.
House closed to the public. *Gardens closed
winter.*

Rydal Mount   **C8**
Ambleside, Cumbria. Wordsworth's home for
over 37 years, the very interesting garden
with its 2 long terraces was designed by the
great man himself. Many unusual trees and
shrubs. See also Dora's Field (1½ miles
north-west of Ambleside), 1½ acres of
daffodils planted by the poet for his
daughter.

Seaton Delaval Hall   **G4**
*Northumberland. ¼ mile from coast at Seaton
Sluice.* Begun in 1720 it is one of the best of
Sir John Vanbrugh's great houses, damaged
by fire in 1822 and restored. A haunting and
magnificent place of sombre grey stone. A
square symmetrical Palladian plan with a
touch of Piranesi creeping in at dusty
corners. *Closed winter.*

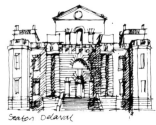
Seaton Delaval

Wallington Hall   **F4**
*Cambo, Northumberland. 12 miles W of
Morpeth on B6342.* A late 17thC mansion
built in a lush park. In 1855, on the advice
of Ruskin, a breath of fresh air crept in. The
courtyard was roofed in and given an
Italianate arcade. For the mural paintings he
suggested William Bell Scott, a follower of
the Pre-Raphaelites. The whole effect is
stimulating.
The gardens, ½ mile away from the house,
were laid out by Capability Brown in 1766.
The conservatory has a superb collection of
fuchsias. *Closed winter.*

Washington Old Hall   **G5**
Washington, Durham. The home of George
Washington's ancestors, it's an early 17thC
manor house, incorporating parts of an
earlier mediaeval house. An awkward rather
cottagey sort of place built on a grand scale.

Museums & galleries

Abbot Hall Museum   **C9**
Kendal, Cumbria. Lakeland life and industry
are represented here. Costume, printing,
weaving and local industries.

Berwick-upon-Tweed Museum   **F1**
and Art Gallery
*Marygate, Berwick-upon-Tweed,
Northumberland.* Paintings presented to the
gallery by Sir William Burrell include Degas'
'Russian Dancer'. Also a 16thC wall-painting
and small collections of silver, bronze, brass
and ceramics. *Closed winter.*

The Bowes Museum   **F7**
Barnard Castle, Durham. A magnificent
collection of Spanish paintings including
some by El Greco and Goya; period settings
of English and French furniture of the 17th
and 18thC; porcelain, glass, jewellery and
metalwork.

Carlisle Museum   **C5**
and Art Gallery
Tullie House, Castle St, Carlisle, Cumbria.
This handsome Jacobean mansion contains
the city's art gallery, library and museum
with Roman finds from Hadrian's Wall. Pre-

Raphaelite paintings, sculptured stones, a bird display and porcelain. *Closed winter.*

The Clayton Collection E5
The Chesters, nr Chollerford, Northumberland. Finds from Hadrian's Wall including sculpture, coins, pottery, Roman inscriptions, weapons and tools.

Darlington Museum G7
Tubwell Row, Darlington, Durham. Early railway material and models (the Stockton and Darlington Railway was the first locomotive passenger line). Also local history and machinery.

Fitz Park Museum B7
and Art Gallery
Station Rd, Keswick, Cumbria. Original manuscripts of Wordsworth, Walpole and Southey, who is buried in nearby Crosthwaite Church. *Closed winter.*

Gulbenkian Museum G6
of Oriental Art
Elvet Hill, Durham University, Durham. A beautiful collection of Chinese carved jade, pottery, porcelain, ivories and textiles, Tibetan art, Indian sculpture and Japanese and Egyptian antiquities.

Hancock Museum G5
University of Newcastle upon Tyne, Barras Bridge, Newcastle upon Tyne, Tyne & Wear. Stuffed animals and birds and ethnological specimens—some probably brought back by Captain Cook from Africa and the South Sea Islands. Egyptian mummy cases, fossils and a freshwater fish aquarium.

Laing Art Gallery and Museum G5
Higham Place, Newcastle upon Tyne, Tyne & Wear. British paintings and watercolours from the 17thC to the present. Also Greek and Egyptian antiquities, costumes and textiles.

Monkwearmouth Station Museum G5
Monkwearmouth, nr Sunderland, Tyne & Wear. Inside the imposing Classical façade the old booking office has been turned into an exhibition of land transportation.

Newcastle upon Tyne Museum G5
of Science and Engineering
Exhibition Park, Great North Rd, Newcastle upon Tyne, Tyne & Wear. Mining and engineering of the north-east are represented here. Also shipbuilding; and there's George Stephenson's locomotive built for Killingworth Colliery in 1830, and the first turbine-powered boat.

Preston Hall Museum H7
Preston Park, Eaglescliffe, Stockton-on-Tees, Cleveland. Victorian social history including antiquities and industrial equipment. The Spence arms and armour collection and archaeology and natural history, toys and local pottery.

South Shields Roman Fort H5
and Museums
Baring St, South Shields, Tyne & Wear. Memorial stones, the South Shields Roman sword, stamped roof tiles, lead seals and enamels.

Windermere Steamboat Museum C8
Windermere, Cumbria. A collection of mostly Victorian and Edwardian steamboats from 1850 to 1911. Also a 1780 sailing boat, early speed boats and an 1898 motor boat.

Wordsworth Museum B8
Grasmere, Cumbria. Wordsworth manuscripts and first editions are preserved here, near Dove Cottage where the poet once lived.

Zoos, aquaria & aviaries

Lambton Pleasure Park G5
Chester-le-Street, Durham. 2 miles E off A183. A drive-through safari park with lions, zebras, camels, rhinos and bison. There are also smaller animals and birds to look at, as

well as a garden centre, picnic area, children's play area and the usual amenities.

Lowther Wildlife Park C7
Hackthorpe, Penrith, Cumbria. Animals and birds live free in the 130 acres of the Earl of Lonsdale's estate. Of interest—Old English longhorns and Highland cattle, the Lowther herd of red deer, fallow and sika. Also sheep, monkeys, and waterfowl on a 5-acre lake. *Closed winter.*

Nature trails & reserves

Farne Islands Nature Reserve G1
Northumberland. One of Britain's outstanding bird 'meccas', famous for many breeding birds and access is by boat from Seahouses. There is an excellent nature trail on Inner Farne.

Friars Crag Nature Trail B7
Cumbria. Start at the car park, Friars Crag, Keswick. 1¼ miles. Lake edge and woodland birds and plants at Keswick-on-Derwentwater. Historical interest and superb scenery. Guide and information from the National Park Information Centre in Keswick.

Lindisfarne National F1
Nature Reserve
Northumberland. This magnificent coastal reserve includes Holy Island, and much of the adjacent coast, particularly Goswick Sands, Fenham Flats, Skate Road, and Budle Bay. The whole area is notable for migrants in season, and Holy Island for bird and marine flora-watching.
Holy Island is accessible from Beal (off A1) and the Causeway at low tide, while roads off the A1 to Fenham and Fenham Lowmoor lead to Fenham Flats. Skate Road is reached from the A1 via Elwick and Ross, and Budle Bay from the A1 via Warren Mill.

Ravenglass Nature Reserve A8
Cumbria. Ravenglass and Drigg Dunes are best known for birds and particularly for the largest British breeding colony of black-headed gulls, shore and dune wild life and vegetation. Much of the estuary can be seen from A595 at Ravenglass. Visits to the reserve are by permit only—details from Cumbria County Council, The Courts, Carlisle.

Tarn Hows Nature Trail B8
Nr Hawkshead, Cumbria. Reached via Hawkshead-Coniston Rd (B5285). 1¼ miles. Mixed woodlands with good botanical interest and outstanding scenery. Guide from all National Trust and National Park Information Centres.

Walney Nature Reserve B10
Walney, Cumbria. Access by bridge from Barrow-in-Furness. Large numbers of birds and shore vegetation of special interest. Details from 82 Plymouth St, Walney Island, Barrow-in-Furness. *By permit only.*

Birdwatching

Bamburgh/Seahouses G1
Northumberland. Accessible from B1340. For Bamburgh, leave A1 S of Belford on B1342 or B1341. This stretch of coast with the Farnes offshore is excellent for sea duck, divers and grebes in winter, for a variety of passage migrants in autumn and for seabirds during the breeding season. Birdwatching can be very worthwhile, especially from Islestone (Stag Rocks).

Cresswell Ponds G3
Northumberland. 1 mile N of Cresswell. Noted for a wide variety of migrants in season, including waders of many kinds, while the foreshore is also a good wader haunt. Sea duck are good offshore in winter. The ponds are on private land but can be seen well from the road, as can the sea and the shore.

Cumbrian Coast

Colonies of birds dwell in their hundreds of thousands along this coast. From the Solway Firth with species like the rare snow goose, and flocks of greylag geese; to Drigg Dunes and Ravenglass where the largest breeding colony of black-headed gulls in Europe is found; down to Walney Island; the whole area is a paradise for birdwatchers. Also see St Bees below.

The Lake District   C8

The fells around Scafell, Borrowdale, the Grasmere area and Easedale can all be recommended. A long walk away from the roads produces the best results.
Breeding birds include buzzard, peregrine, common sandpiper, ring ouzel, redstart, wood warbler, pied flycatcher, dipper and raven—and the lucky observer may glimpse the area's latest addition, the golden eagle.

Marsden Rocks   H5

Durham. S from South Shields on A183. A footpath leads along the cliff top to this interesting area. 'Sea watching' can be good in autumn and winter, while in summer Marsden Rock itself, a huge offshore stack, has breeding fulmars, cormorants, shags and kittiwakes.

St Bees Head   A7

Cumbria. Footpath after leaving Sandwith, right off B5345 1½ miles S of Whitehaven. An important seabird colony is situated here, with breeding fulmar, guillemot, black guillemot, razorbill and puffin, as well as nesting ravens. A public footpath along the cliff tops allows good views of the birds and in due course details of an RSPB reserve on the Head will be available.

Teesmouth   H7

Durham. In spite of being virtually surrounded by industry of all kinds, and the proximity of a very large urban complex, Teesmouth is famous for its birds. The 'marshes' north of the Tees, parts of which are visible from the Seaton Carew road and its offshoots, contain many pools and fleets, often good for wildfowl and waders, while Greatham Creek (crossed by the Seaton Carew road) is also worth a look. Seal Sands are being rapidly reclaimed, but are still noted for waders and duck. Sea watching from South Gare breakwater can often be very rewarding.
For the visitor this is a difficult area, especially as access arrangements may change frequently. Prior enquiries are therefore recommended. Contact the Secretary, Teesmouth Bird Club.

Brass rubbing

The following is a short list of churches that have brasses for rubbing. Permission is almost invariably required.
Cumbria. Carlisle Cathedral, Edenhall, Great Musgrave.
Durham. Auckland (St Andrew), Sedgefield.
Tyne & Wear, Newcastle upon Tyne.

Fossil hunting

Visit the local museum. Its fossil collection usually states where individual fossils have been found. When visiting quarries always seek permission to enter if they look privately owned or worked. Be careful of falls of rock.

Cumbria

In the Lake District the rocks are mainly Silurian—shales, mudstones and some coarser rocks—with fossils in places. The best areas are around Kentmere where the Stockdale and Skelgill shales contain graptolites and the Brathay flags contain a shelly fauna of trilobites and brachiopods. Most of the east of the county is of carboniferous limestones containing corals, bryozoans, brachiopods, crinoids, algal reefs etc., to be seen in the areas around Tebay, Ravenstonedale, Kirkby Stephen and the escarpment to the east of Appleby to the Yorkshire border at Stainmore.
The Ordovician Skiddaw slates, which occur in a broad band in the north of the Lake District, especially around Skiddaw Mountain, have a few fossils—mainly graptolites—but these are not common. The Coniston Limestone Group with shelly fossils—brachiopods and trilobites—of Upper Ordovician age crops out on the hills near Millom.
Around Whitehaven on the coast tip-heaps from mining may give a few fossils such as plants. The carboniferous limestone, containing corals, algal reefs and brachiopods, is exposed in 2 main outcrops: around the northern and eastern edges of the Lake District massif—from Cockermouth round to the west of Penrith on the western side of the Vale of Eden; to the east of the Eden forming part of Alston Block of the Pennines. Exposures are common everywhere especially on the escarpment on the east side of the Eden Valley, at Melmerby Fell, Renwick Fell and around Alston itself.

Durham

The coal measures outcrop in the west has been extensively mined for coal, with few fossils but rare plants and thin bands containing small shells. Many of the mines were on the magnesian limestone area, extracting the coal beneath, so tip-heaps of waste material of coal measures may be found there.
Around Barnard Castle and Brough the carboniferous limestones crop out with plenty of fossils—corals, crinoids and brachiopods.

Northumberland

Except for a patch of Devonian (old red sandstone) lavas with sands and no fossils, in the Cheviot Hills, Northumberland is mostly carboniferous. The east, and most of the coast consists of coal measures with fossils occurring rarely. The coast is all coal measures plus fell sandstone and limestone between the mouths of the Tyne and the Aln. Further west and north is the millstone grit series and the limestones of the carboniferous which may be seen in the valley of the River Tyne and in Redesdale, Tweeddale and Berwick-upon-Tweed with the normal coral-algal reefs brachiopods, crinoids and bivalves fauna to be found as well as their locally-developed coal beds.

Forests

Border Forest Park   D3

Northumberland. The largest man-made forest in Europe it covers 200 square miles and extends over the whole of upper Tynedale from the Roman Wall to Scotland. There is an 11-mile forest drive, nature trails and walks. The information centre is at Kielder.

Grizedale Forest   B9

Cumbria. In the Furness region of Cumbria, between Coniston Water and Windermere, the national forest of Grizedale has been established over 12 square miles of wild fell-sides. It is centred on Satterthwaite, where pastures and oak-woods lie by a stone-built village. There is a Visitors Centre at Hawkshead with wildlife and forestry exhibitions, theatre, forest trails, picnic sites and information.

Lune Forest   E7

Durham. Named after the minor River Lune, a tributary of the River Tees, this wild mediaeval hunting territory lies between Middleton-in-Teesdale and Brough. Rugged Mickle Fell, a limestone, crag-girt ridge in the heart of trackless moorland, is the highest point, at 2,591 feet. Best viewed from the B6277 Middleton to Alston road.

Mountains, moors & plains

The Cheviots   E2
Form a 50-mile-long high-level sheep pasturage between the Northumbrian plain and Scotland's Tweed Valley.
The heights are totally natural with vast areas of moorland and deep bog. The Pennine Way follows the boundary between Scotland and England along the crest. Magnificent views.

The Lake District's mountains
900 square miles of some of the wildest, highest and most attractive mountains in Great Britain. Make sure you buy locally the little guide books by A. Wainwright, a local writer who put into them a whole lifetime of love and accurate observation—they are not only the best for hill walking but a joy to look through. There are 3 principal groups of mountains. North of Keswick are the Skiddaw Slates which include Skiddaw itself and the Saddleback. The central massif consists of the Borrowdale Slates, rugged high peaks that provide the most dramatic climbing. This includes the famous Great Gable, Scafell Pike, the Langdale Pikes, and Helvellyn with a host of smaller mountains between 2,000–3,000 feet in height. Around Windermere Lake and Coniston Water are the Bannisdale Slates, rounded wooded hills below 1,000 feet and lovely country it is. All the major mountains above are around 3,000 feet with Scafell the highest at 3,210 feet. This area is totally unspoilt and forms the most marvellous walking and climbing country. There are many paths and established routes through cols or to the tops of mountains. Never walk alone high up and acquire some elementary knowledge at least of survival as the weather can change to mist or snow without warning. Even in early spring near-Arctic conditions can exist above 2,000 feet with blinding blizzards and sub-zero temperatures. However in bright weather nothing can equal the beauty of this unspoilt region. Visit the Lake District National Park Centre at Brockhole, nr Windermere.

Northumberland's coastal plain   G3
For 80 miles from the industrial city of Newcastle upon Tyne to the border stronghold of Berwick-upon-Tweed, the coast of Northumberland holds a level plain of pastoral farms. Castles at Bamburgh on the sea-cliffs and at the market towns of Alnwick and Morpeth show how this fertile country was defended during its troubled past.

The Pennines
The northern part of the Pennine range has 2 formidable peaks: Mickle Fell (2,591 feet) and Cross Fell (2,930 feet) the highest point of the Pennines—a wild boggy summit but with fine views to the Lake District. The rest of the range is high fells and moors and superb walking country.

Solway Plain   C5
From the castle and cathedral of Carlisle you look out over a spacious plain stretching down to the broad Solway Firth. Across this level, well-farmed expanse 5 great rivers wind their way to the tide-washed sandbanks of the estuary.

Rivers & lakes

Kielder Reservoir   D4
Northumberland. This lake, which is now filling, will be the largest man-made lake in Europe. There will be nature reserves, and facilities for water sports, fishing, camping, etc.

The Lakes
Most of the valleys of the Lake District, which fan out like the spokes of a wheel from Scafell and Great Gable, are delightful, cradling clear streams and splendid lakes. The whole area is still working farmland as well as being within the Lake District National Park, and this adds to its charm. Notable lakes are 10½-miles-long Windermere and lovely Rydal Water, Grasmere, Haweswater, Ullswater, Thirlmere, serene Derwentwater with its islands, Bassenthwaite, quiet Buttermere, Ennerdale and the awesome Wastwater, deep and black. In addition there are a total of 463 mountain tarns.

The River Tees   F7
The River Tees starts as a moorland stream in a National Nature Reserve, then tumbles over magnificent High Force waterfall. From its beautiful dale around Barnard Castle it flows through Darlington and the modern industrial complex of Teesside and Middlesbrough.

The River Tyne   G5
The North Tyne starts at Deadwater on the Scottish border, and flows through forests and hill farms to Hexham, where it meets the South Tyne from the Cumberland Fells. At Newcastle upon Tyne the combined stream becomes a busy, industrial river lined by shipyards and wharves to Tynemouth on the coast. Impressive bridges cross it at Newcastle, with a tunnel lower down.

The River Wear   G6
Starting on high bleak moorlands, the River Wear flows down a lovely dale to Durham, encircling the castle and cathedral in a great loop.

Archaeological sites

Castlerigg Stone Circle   B7
Cumbria. 2 miles E of Keswick. Also known as Keswick Carles this great stone circle dates from Neolithic times. There are 38 stones standing, making an oval 100 feet in diameter, with a rectangle of a further 10 stones on the south east side of the circle.

Hadrian's Wall   D5
Bowness-on-Solway, Cumbria to Wallsend-on-Tyne, Northumberland. The great Roman frontier work of Hadrian's Wall was originally built during 2ndC, after a visit by the Emperor Hadrian to Britain. The Hadrian's Wall system is composed of several types of defensive works, of which the Wall itself is only one part.
The Ditch. To the north the Wall was defended by a ditch some 27 feet wide, which was separated from it by an open strip, a *berm*, 20 feet wide.
The Wall. Originally built partly of turf, it was later reconstructed in stone throughout its length.
The best preserved sections are in the centre, particularly at Walltown Crags and Sewingshields.
The Vallum. To the south of the Wall was a second ditch, 20 feet wide and crossed by causeways to the forts and milecastles. A good example of a causeway can be seen at Benwell.
The Military Way—The Stanegate. Between the Wall and the Vallum ran a road linking the various stations, used primarily for supplies and couriers.
Milecastles. Small forts built every mile along the length of the Wall. Well-preserved milecastles can be seen at Winshields, Poltross Burn, Harrow's Scar, and Cawfields.
Watchtowers. Two were built between each pair of milecastles. Good examples are at Denton Hall, Brunton, Piper Sike, Leahill, and Banks East.
Forts. 17 forts were placed at strategic points along the Wall. The size varies from under 2 acres for a force of 500 infantry to almost 9½ acres for a cavalry force of 1,000. The best preserved are at Chesters (which includes a

bath-house), Housesteads, Chesterholm, Great Chesters and Birdoswald.

Hadrian's Wall, Northumberland

Supply Bases. In addition to the defensive works, large supply depots had to be constructed to maintain the garrisons. Corbridge was originally a fort south of the Wall, but was later converted into a depot, with massive granaries and workshops. South Shields also held granaries, and was probably the fleet base at which goods were unloaded. Some sites have a museum, and there are collections at the Tullie House Museum, Carlisle, and the Museum of Antiquities, Newcastle upon Tyne. The Newcastle Museum also has a fine series of models of the Wall, and a reconstruction of the Carrawburgh Mithraeum.

Hardknott Castle   **A8**
Eskdale, Cumbria. Mediobogdum, one of the most spectacularly sited Roman forts in Britain. The granaries, headquarters building, commandant's house, and much of the defensive wall are preserved, and a simple bath-house can be seen outside. Uphill from the fort an area was flattened to form a parade-ground.

Long Meg and Her Daughters   **D6**
Long Meg, Cumbria. A large Bronze Age stone circle, over 50 feet in diameter. Like henge monuments, these circles probably had religious and burial significance.

Old Bewick   **F2**
Northumberland. 2 miles E of Wooperton. A promontory hill-fort protected by a steep scarp-slope, ramparts and a single bank and ditch. The ramparts have stonework facing over a clay core. The western section has circular huts, whilst the eastern section was used to protect their animals. Close to the fort are several decorated stones.

Yeavering Bell   **E2**
Northumberland. An impressive Iron Age hill fort with single bank defences. Shallow depressions on the interior show the situations of circular huts. Excavations at the foot of the hill revealed the timber halls of a royal residence belonging to the Saxon king Edwin of Northumbria, but these are not now visible on the surface.

Footpaths & ancient ways

The Pennine Way   **D6**
From Wensleydale, north across Durham, Cumbria and Northumberland, the Pennines and the Cheviots, the Way comes to an end at Kirk Yetholm, on the Scottish border. From Great Shunner Fell, rising to 2,340 feet, the Way descends into Thwaite. Tan Hill boasts the highest licensed inn in England at 1,730 feet. Cross Stainmore Gap to Teesdale, past the magnificent waterfall at High Force, crashing down from a 72-foot-high cliff. Climb again to Cross Fell (2,930 feet), the highest point in the Pennines; below is Alston, the highest market town in England. North of Hadrian's Wall are the moors and Forestry Commission plantations near Redesdale, and at Chew Green, the Roman camps. Descend Halterburn Valley, and the end of the Way is in sight at Kirk Yetholm.

The Wear Valley Way   **E6**
Durham. A new long-distance Way opened in August 1979. It is 46 miles long and designed to be undertaken in 24 hours or in 9-mile sections for the less ambitious. Start at the wheel of the old lead mine in Killhope off the A689, and pass through the village of Cowshill, across Race head, which at 1,918 feet is the highest point on the walk, to the lead miners' dam at Rookhope. Follow the old railway line (closed since 1923) to Weatherhill Engine and past Millstone Riggs Quarries, then up to Pikestone Fell. Past the old mine shafts (beware!) and into Hamsterley Forest. From here the Way passes through Bedburn and Old and New Hall to Witton Castle and Park. After the village of Escomb the next stop is Bishop Auckland from where the path crosses the River Wear by the Newton Cap Bridge and passes the old Mill House to the finish at Jubilee Bridge, Willington.

Regional sport

Angling
Northern England with its miles of coastline to the east and west, its deeply incised interior, and abundance of lakes gives the angler a wide choice of fishing areas and catches. On the east coast there are salmon and trout in the River Coquet at Warkworth, Felton, Rothbury, and Acklington, and there is coarse fishing on the Rivers Wansbeck and Blyth. Other rivers to fish are the Tees, the North and South Tynes, and the famous River Tweed providing the finest salmon fishing in England.
In the west the Cumbrian lakes offer superb coarse fishing. There is also excellent sea fishing along the coast, enhanced by its remoteness from major industrial outpourings.
Much of the Northumberland coastline offers superb sea fishing from boat or beach.

Climbing
Nearly all the valleys of the Lake District provide good rock climbing, but Great Langdale and Wasdale are the principal centres. From Wasdale rises England's highest mountain, Scafell Pike (3,210 feet); at Langdale is the famous Grimmer Crag with climbs all rated more than 'very difficult'. Because of the extensive use made of the rocks in this region many of the important foot and toe holds are becoming more polished each year, and boots with tough (vibram) soles which give a good grip, are necessary.

Fell racing   **B8**
Normally the race is started from an arena and the runners race to the top of the nearest hill and back.
The honour of winning these races is highly prized by the shepherds and young farm lads who have the physique and stamina for this testing sport. Fell running can be seen at Ambleside, Patterdale, Beetham, Grasmere, and other places in Lakeland.
A more arduous adaptation is the marathon fell race: to conquer as many peaks over 2,000 feet as possible in 24 hours.

Sheepdog trials
Take place all over the Lake District during the summer, with the most important events in August and September. The dogs, responding to whistle signals, have to collect the sheep, herd them together, coax them past obstacles, and finally drive them into a narrow pen. A marvellous display of obedience, intelligence and stealth.

Hound trailing   **B8**
The circuits are some 8 to 10 miles in length. A trail is laid by 2 men who set out from the furthest point on the course and take 2 different routes to the start point, by dragging along the ground a large old sock impregnated with aniseed and other delectable canine olfactory stimulants. A bit like foxhunting without the foxes. There are fixtures throughout the summer, but the biggest events take place at Coniston,

Torver, Ulverston, Cartmel, Rusland, and Armathwaite. Dates vary, so look out for placards.

Wrestling C8
Cumbria. One of the traditional sports of north-west England. The wrestlers stand facing each other with their hands locked across their opponent's back. The aim is to throw your opponent to the ground. During the summer wrestling can be seen at Ambleside, Patterdale, Beetham, Grasmere and other places. Look out for placards, as dates vary from year to year.

Special attractions

Hunday Museum F5
National Farm & Tractor Museum, West Side, Newton, Northumberland. 3 miles E of Corbridge off A69. A unique collection of tractors and farm equipment. There is a fine line-up of stationary engines and a beautiful fire engine. A 1920 narrow gauge railway and a small animal park are planned for the future.

Lake Side and Haverthwaite Railway C8
Ambleside, Cumbria. Join one of the lakeland steamers at Ambleside for a trip from the northern extremity of Lake Windermere to Lake Side at the southern end. At Lake Side disembark and join the railway for a 7-mile return journey by steam-hauled train through magnificent countryside. For information Tel Newby Bridge 594.

North of England Open Air Museum G6
Beamish, Durham. Off A693 from Stanley 3 miles from A1M. Beamish Hall and its surrounding 200 acres was designed to show the social and industrial history of the region. The site has a railway station, an electric tramway, a colliery with workings, miners' and farmworkers' cottages and an old farm. There is also a collection of early vehicles and machinery, including old locomotives.

The Ravenglass and Eskdale Railway A8
Ravenglass, Cumbria. Starts adjacent to the British Rail station. This is probably the most scenic narrow gauge railway in the country. It climbs from the ancient port of Ravenglass up 2 beautiful valleys.

Ryhope Engines Museum H6
Ryhope, nr Sunderland, Tyne & Wear. This is possibly the finest single industrial monument in north-east England, and is a distinctive example of the industrial architecture of mid-Victorian times. The huge engines are now in full running order again. *Closed winter.*

Watermills
There are several well restored water-driven corn mills in working order. *Eskdale Mill* in Cumbria dates from the 16thC, whilst the *Little Salkeld Watermill* dates from the 18thC. The *Heron Corn Mill,* Milnthorpe, Cumbria takes advantage of an unusual natural weir and the *Heatherslaw Mill* at Ford, Cornhill-on-Tweed, Northumberland, lies on the west bank of the River Till. All have museums showing the history of the mills and exhibitions featuring the milling techniques and agriculture.

Festivals, events & customs

There are a number of local festivals and events—contact the local Information Centre for details.

Allendale Baal E5
Allendale Town, Hexham, Northumberland. The men of the town in costumes carry tubs of blazing tar in procession to a midnight bonfire to welcome in the New Year. The ceremony dates back to pagan times. *31st Dec.*

Blessing of the Nets E1
Norham, Tweedmouth, Berwick-upon-Tweed, Northumberland. An ancient ceremony to bring luck and prosperity to the fishing fleet at the start of the salmon-fishing season. *14th Feb.*

Durham Festivals G6
Durham. The city seems to enjoy itself throughout the year; starting in *June* with the Regatta; in *July* there is the Durham Miners' Gala; in *August* the City Carnival; and in *October* Durham Castle hosts the modern Music Festival.

Gipsy Fair & Gathering D7
Appleby-in-Westmorland, Cumbria. A huge gathering of gipsies where horses are bought and sold. *2nd Wed in June.* The town also hosts the Sulky Trotting races for horses and carriages *on Spring B.hol, and Mon & Tues before the Gipsy Fair.*

Hexham Abbey Festival E5
Hexham, Northumberland. Hexham's abbey, an artistic haven in the middle ages, inspired this modern festival to promote the arts. Many of the concerts, poetry readings and exhibitions are held within its walls; very popular are the unaccompanied motets by candlelight. *Late Sep.*

The Lake District Festival C8
Cumbria. This festival provides a rare opportunity for the Lake District to hear artists of international standing. Concerts are given in the parish churches of Ambleside, Windermere, in Kendal Town Hall and at Cartmel Priory; opera is performed in the 16thC Levens Hall and Wordsworth poetry readings in Grasmere church. *May–Jun.*

Shrovetide Football Match G3
Alnwick, Northumberland. This football match is held between the parishes of St Michael and St Paul. The rules vary somewhat from those of the FA: the ball is piped onto the field, there can be as many as 150 people per side and the goals are a quarter of a mile apart. *Shrove Tues.*

Walking or Riding the Boundaries G4
These customs date back to the days before maps when it was necessary to point out the extent of the parishes. In Morpeth the boundary is ridden in *April.* In Newbiggin-by-the-Sea the bounds are walked in *May.*

Regional food & drink

Cumberland sausage
An expensive pork and herb sausage which is mostly meat. Local butchers have their own recipes.

Fish G2
Salmon are caught from the River Leven and Solway Firth in the west and the River Tweed and River Coquet in the east. Local fish include char from Lake Windermere and Flookburgh flooks, flat fish which are driven into the nets—this process marks the dorsal side with 3-inch diamonds. Fine kippers are prepared at Craster, a delightful Northumbrian seaside village. Lobsters and crabs are a fine delicacy of this part of the coast.

Northumbrian beer
This was one of the first areas in Britain to brew beer. 'Newcastle Brown' is said by beer connoisseurs to be the strongest beer produced in quantity in this country.

Singin' Hinny
This traditional Northumberland rich currant scone is baked on a griddle and sings whilst it cooks. Hinny is a local term of endearment.